Attention and Orienting:
Sensory and Motivational Processes

Attention and Orienting: Sensory and Motivational Processes

Edited by

Peter J. Lang

Robert F. Simons

Marie T. Balaban

LEA LAWRENCE ERLBAUM ASSOCIATES, PUBLISHERS
1997 Mahwah, New Jersey   London

QP 405 .A85 1997

Attention and orienting

Lawrence Erlbaum Associates, Inc., Publishers
10 Industrial Avenue
Mahwah, New Jersey 07430

Library of Congress Cataloging-in-Publication-Data

Attention and orienting : sensory and motivational processes
/ edited by Peter J. Lang, Robert F. Simons, Marie Balaban.
     p. cm.
  Includes bibliographic references and index.
  ISBN 0-8058-2089-2 (cloth : alk. paper)
  1. Graham, Frances K. (Frances Keesler), 1918– . 2.
Attention—Congresses. 3. Motivation (psychol-
ogy)—Congresses. 4. Psychophysiology—Congresses. I.
Lang, Peter J. II. Simons, Robert F. III. Balaban, Marie T.
  QP405.A85 1997
  153.7'33–dc20   96-32753
                                    CIP

Printed in the United States of America
10 9 8 7 6 5 4 3 2 1

Contents

Preface   ix
Rachel K. Clifton and Phyllis W. Berman

Acknowledgments   xv

List of Contributors   xvii

Introduction   xix
Peter J. Lang, Robert F. Simons, Marie T. Balaban

I Current Investigations of the Classical Theory of Orienting and Defense

1   Orienting and Defense Reflexes: Vector Coding the   1
Cardiac Response
E. N. Sokolov and John T. Cacioppo

2   Orienting, Habituation, and Information Processing: 23
The Effects of Omission, the Role of Expectancy,
and the Problem of Dishabituation
David A. T. Siddle and Ottmar V. Lipp

II Biological and Evolutionary Foundations of Orienting, Startle, and Defense: Motivational and Emotional Factors That Modulate Attention

3 Origins of Orienting and Defensive Responses: An   41
   Evolutionary Perspective
   Byron A. Campell, Gwendolyn Wood, Thomas McBride

4 The Neurophysiological Basis of Acoustic Startle   69
   Modulation: Research on Fear Motivation
   and Sensory Gating
   Michael Davis

5 Motivated Attention: Affect, Activation, and Action   97
   Peter J. Lang, Margaret M. Bradley, Bruce N. Cuthbert

6 Differentiating Orienting, Startle, and Defense   137
   Responses: The Role of Affect and Its Implications for
   Psychopathology
   Edwin Cook III and Graham Turpin

7 As Fast as the Blink of an Eye: Evolutionary Preparedness 165
   for Preattentive Processing of Threat
   Arne Öhman

III Startle Reflex and Electro-Cortical Studies of Attention and Stimulus Gating

8 Attentional Factors in the Elicitation and Modification   185
   of the Startle Reaction
   Howard S. Hoffman

9 The More or Less Startling Effects of Weak Prestimulation— 205
   Revisited: Prepulse Modulation of Multicomponent
   Blink Reflexes
   Steven A. Hackley and A. J. W. Boelhouwer

10 A Tale of Two Reflexes: An ERP Analysis of Prepulse   229
Inhibition and Orienting
Robert F. Simons and William M. Perlstein

11 Cognitive, Clinical, and Neurophysiological Implications   257
of Startle Modification
Michael E. Dawson, Anne M. Schell, Neal R. Swerdlow,
Diane L. Filion

12 Gating in Readiness   281
C. H. M. Brunia

13 Magnetoencephalography in Studies of Attention   307
Risto Näätänen, Risto J. Ilmoniemi, Kimmo Alho

IV Studies of Attention, Affect, and Action
in Child Development

14 Functions of Orienting in Early Infancy   327
Michael I. Posner, Mary K. Rothbart, Lisa Thomas-Thrapp

15 Attention Across Time in Infant Development   347
W. Keith Berg and John Richards

16 Attention, Emotion, and Reactivity in Infancy and   369
Early Childhood
Marie T. Balaban, Nancy Snidman, Jerome Kagan

17 Activity, Attention, and Developmental Transitions   393
in Infancy
Joseph J. Campos, Rosanne Kermoian,
David Witherington, Hongtu Chen, Qi Dong

Afterword: Pre-Attentive Processing and Passive and   417
Active Attention
Frances K. Graham

Author Index   453

Subject Index   469

Frances Keesler Graham

"Great Thoughts Come From the Heart"

Preface

"Les grandes pensées viennent du coeur"
Number 127, Vauvenargués *Maximes* (1746)

On October 5–6, 1994, a special conference was held in honor of Frances Keesler Graham prior to the annual meeting of the Society for Psychophysiological Research in Atlanta, Georgia. On this joyous occasion scientists from many disciplines and many countries gathered to pay tribute to Fran's outstanding contributions to science throughout a career that has already spanned more than 5 decades. In each of those decades Fran produced truly significant research that is still recognized as seminal and creative. Several characteristics of her work stand out: breadth of subject matter, meticulous and ingenious methodology, sophisticated theory construction, and a continuous flow of work throughout her career. Her style has been to concentrate on one area for a number of years, making substantial contributions in that area before moving on to a new research topic. As a result she has achieved a well-deserved reputation for excellence in several fields such as pediatrics, child psychology, and psychophysiology. Classic papers that are still cited today emerged from each phase of her career. While this volume attests to the exciting developments of recent years, this preface serves to remind readers of Fran's earlier accomplishments, as well as personal characteristics that contributed to her outstanding success as a researcher, colleague, and mentor.

When she was 19, Frances Keesler arrived at Yale University, a bastion of male supremacy in those days. At her first interview with the chair of the department, he welcomed her as the holder of a Mary E. Ives Fellowship, saying that they were very happy to have her as a new graduate student, but warned that her long range prospects were poor. As a petite, attractive, young woman, she did not fit his image of a serious scientist. He cautioned her that she might be unable to find a job after graduation. But he had little idea of the intellect and determination of the young graduate student before him. While at Yale she worked with Don Marquis and Clark Hull on her dissertation, and trained in developmental psychology with Pat Sears and Dorothy Marquis.

In 1941 Fran married David Graham. Together, following Fran's graduation in 1942, they moved to St. Louis where Dave continued his medical education and Fran sought a position that would allow her to pursue a research career. Most of her first 15 years were spent at Washington University Medical School, with a short period at Barnard College. Three children were born during these years: Norma and Andrew during World War II, when Dave was in service and sent overseas, and Mary, born a few years later. At first Fran was only able to put together two clinical half-time appointments. During these early years Fran and Barbara Kendall constructed the Memory-for-Designs Test, still used today with adults with suspected organicity. Over time, by small increments and with unavoidable interruptions, Fran shaped a position that would allow her to begin a project on the effects of anoxia on newborn infants with start-up money from Washington University's Department of Pediatrics. It was at this point that Fran set the pattern for her long research career by applying for her first grant from the National Institutes of Health, supporting her research and paying her own salary with grant funds.

The anoxia project was a complex and beautifully designed study that has served as a model for many prospective studies of high risk infants since that time. New methods of measuring anoxia were developed, using analysis of blood oxygenation, direct observation in the delivery room, and weighted variables in the infant's perinatal history. Fran also developed a scale for assessing newborn behavior, from which a modified version called the Graham-Rosenblith Scale was later derived. This research was published in a series of articles in the *Journal of Pediatrics* in 1956–1957 and in two *Psychological Monographs* in 1956. Fran's methods of sampling and scaling newborn behavior laid the foundation for the Brazelton scale, which came almost 2 decades later. Inspired by Fran's research, the large-scale Collaborative Project involving 14 institutions around the nation was launched by the National Institute of Neurological Diseases and Blindness in the 1960s. Fran helped plan this massive project and was a consultant for many years. The study of high risk infants and sequelae of unfavorable perinatal conditions are now well-researched, but Fran's work prefigured this field by 25 years.

When Fran and Dave moved to the University of Wisconsin in 1957, Fran had two grants. The anoxia grant remained at Washington University under Fran's continuing direction. She worked with Claire Ernhart, who remained at Washington University, traveling to and from Madison. Fran brought a new grant on the validation of tests for brain injury in preschool children with her to Wisconsin. During the next few years, much of Fran's work concerned the effects on childhood development of brain injury that was experienced either in the neonatal period or beyond. The work was published in a series of articles, including three *Psychological Monographs* in 1962 and 1963. Prior to this time it was assumed that young children with perinatal injury would perform particularly poorly on perceptual and perceptual-motor tests, a pattern commonly found in individuals who suffered central nervous system injury as adults. Fran's work demonstrated the critical importance of the individual's age at the time of injury. Preschool children who had been anoxic at birth showed greater decrement from the norm in performance on conceptual tasks than on perceptual-motor tasks.

Fran also collaborated with Harry Waisman and Phyllis Berman in a longitudinal study of the effects of phenylketonuria, a rare inborn error of metabolism, on children's neurological status and intellectual development. Waisman was using a new dietary treatment in an attempt to circumvent the disastrous effects of the inability to metabolize phenylalanine on the developing central nervous system. It was possible to test some children before they began treatment at various ages, and with wide variations in intelligence. All siblings who were unaffected by this recessive disorder were followed as controls. Although the sample was small, it was possible to disentangle the effects of the age at which children were first treated and number of years of treatment on children's intellectual development. This work was critical in establishing that diet treatment should begin as early as possible if mental retardation is to be lessened or avoided.

In the 1960s Fran began a new phase in her career. She had been collaborating with David Graham on studies of the linkage between specific attitudes and various psychosomatic disorders. In the course of this work she had mastered psychophysiological techniques and had set up a lab for recording heart rate, respiration, skin temperature, and other measures. The appearance of E. N. Sokolov's book, *Perception and the Conditioned Reflex*, translated into English in 1963, instigated her thinking in a new direction. Also in 1963, Rachel Keen (later Clifton) came as a postdoctoral fellow to work with her, specifically to learn how psychophysiological responses might be used with infants to assess their reactions to stimulation. Inspired by Sokolov's theory of the orienting reflex, Fran combined her growing expertise in psychophysiology with her deep knowledge of infant behavior to produce an outstanding series of studies on infant attention and orienting. Together with Clifton, she published a *Psychological Bulletin* review article in 1966 that integrated Sokolov's theory with the Laceys' hypothesis that heart rate decrease accompanied and enhanced attention to stimulation, whereas heart rate acceleration reduced sensory intake. Although heart rate change had been used to reflect subjects' reaction to stimulation prior to 1966, the trickle turned to a torrent of research using heart rate after the appearance of the 1966 paper. The importance of Graham and Clifton's analysis lay in the significance it gave to the direction of heart rate change in psychological terms. The value of an easily recorded response that could reveal covert processes was immediately recognized by researchers studying animal, adult, and infant attentional processes. By 1978 the field's enthusiasm for heart rate as an index of orienting and defense responses had propelled the 1966 article to the status of a Citation Classic, as designated by *Current Contents*.

For over a decade Fran and her students crafted a careful series of studies that explored theoretical questions of habituation and orienting. She delineated the components of the orienting response and their maturation during early human development, noting the implications for noncortical and cortical maturation. As in her previous work with clinical populations, her sophisticated methodology and theorizing set the standards for the field. The study of the orienting response continues to be a lively and exciting research area, as many chapters in this book indicate.

In the 1970s Fran turned to the startle blink paradigm in a continuing exploration of different levels of central processing. As with heart rate change, this methodology can be used with nonverbal, nonhuman, and even sleeping subjects. Her first report of this research startled her audience; the occasion was her 1975 Presidential address to the Society for Psychophysiological Research. Most people expected a summary of the previous decade's distinguished work on heart rate and orienting; instead they got a description of an exciting new paradigm for investigating attentional processing and brain-behavior relations across the lifespan. Fran was not wrong about the importance of this paradigm. Although she did not invent the startle reflex modulation paradigm, she recognized its significance and utility for studying neuronal mechanisms. From this beginning 20 years ago, the use of the startle blink has spread to many labs and other continents. The content of this volume attests to Fran's intuition and vision about what is critical science. In recent years following her move in 1986 to Delaware, Fran began and is continuing studies of evoked responses in attention and sensory-perceptual gating.

Fran's accomplishments have been recognized through honors bestowed from every professional society to which she belongs. Her numerous awards include the award for Distinguished Contributions to Psychophysiology from the Society for Psychophysiological Research; the G. Stanley Hall Medal from The Division on Developmental Psychology (Division 7) of the American Psychological Association; the award for Distinguished Scientific Contributions from the American Psychological Association; the Distinguished Scientific Contribution Award from the Society for Research in Child Development; the American Psychological Foundation Gold Medal Award for Life Achievement in Psychological Science; and she was named a William James Fellow by the American Psychological Society. She was elected to the National Academy of Sciences in 1988. She has been President of the Society for Psychophysiological Research, the Society for Research in Child Development, and the Physiological and Comparative Psychology Division (Division 6) of the American Psychological Association. She held a Research Scientist Award that paid her salary from the National Institute of Mental Health continuously between 1964 and 1989. Institutions with which she has been associated have also recognized her. The University of Wisconsin awarded her a Hilldale Professorship during her tenure and, in 1996, an honorary Doctor of Science degree; the Pennsylvania State University gave her its Distinguished Alumna Award in 1983; the University of Delaware named her to a Distinguished Faculty Lectureship in 1989; and Yale University gave her its Wilbur L. Cross Medal in 1992.

We cannot close without attempting to convey some idea of what it is like to work with Fran. The pleasure that Fran finds in her work is obvious and infectious; students and colleagues alike cannot help but be affected by her excitement in sharing ideas. Conversations with her challenge the intellect. Her rapid-fire questioning keeps one on the alert. She is the best of mentors through her own excellent example and her explicit admonitions about adherence to the highest standards of data collection, analysis, and exposition. For the women in her lab she has also served as an extraordinary role model. In the early days of her career there were few women who combined marriage and family with a successful, demanding career. Fran always kept her eye on the essentials: family, research, students, and the wider psychological community. During the period when she chose to leave the lab each day to spend the lunch hour with her youngest child, she also assumed leadership roles in professional organizations. We would like to close with a quotation from Fran's contribution to the book, *Models of Achievement: Reflections of Eminent Women in Psychology*. Speaking to the issue of coping strategies she says, "I do think one conscious attitude was an advantage: having a clear idea of my priorities. Family and research [note that she said "research," not "career"] came first, and anything else could be sacrificed, if necessary, including paid work . . . Knowing what you want and what losses you can accept makes it easier to negotiate and refuse options . . . my main operating principle was, and is, that I find research the most exciting activity imaginable." Despite her many outstanding accomplishments, Fran Graham was not granted tenure until 22 years after she received her doctorate. Nevertheless, she went on to become a member of the National Academy of Sciences. We think her priorities have always been in the right place.

—Rachel Keen Clifton and Phyllis Waldman Berman
July 25, 1995

Acknowledgments

The idea for this book arose at a conference honoring Frances Keesler Graham in Atlanta, October, 1994. The organizing committee for that conference included Bruno Anthony, Marie Balaban, Keith Berg, and Lois Putnam. They were responsible for arranging the participation of speakers, most of whom are the contributors to this volume. The conference was held just prior to the 34th meeting of the Society for Psychophysiological Research (SPR). Financial support for the conference was provided by grants from SPR, the American Psychological Society (APS), the University of Delaware, and the NIMH Center for the Study of Emotion and Attention (CSEA: P50-MH52384) at the University of Florida. Lauren Butler of APS helped with conference arrangements in Atlanta. Financial management was provided by the CSEA through the University of Florida Foundation.

We would like to acknowledge the help of the LEA editorial staff including Teresa Horton, Kathleen Dolan, Judy Amsel, and Marcy Pruiksma. Marie Balaban's editorial work was supported in part by NIMH grant RO3-MH5113. The CSEA provided continued clerical support, bore much of the costs of communication between editors, LEA, and the authors, and covered travel expenses for the editorial meeting. We appreciate particularly the yeoman work (i.e., "great and laborious services") of Sarah Hayden, Research Coordinator at CSEA, who maintained contact with the authors and publisher, insisted or cajoled when needed, compiled manuscripts from disk, assisted in copyediting, and coordinated the final author and subject indexing. Finally, we wish to thank Frances Keesler Graham who inspired this book and whose continued attention to the project assured the very best efforts of authors and editors.

Peter J. Lang
Robert F. Simons
Marie T. Balaban

List of Contributors

Kimmo Alho   University of Helsinki

Marie T. Balaban   Johns Hopkins University

W. Keith Berg   University of Florida

Phyllis Waldman Berman   National Institute of Child Development

A. J. W. Boelhouwer   Tilburg University

Margaret M. Bradley   University of Florida

C. H. M. Brunia   Tilburg University

John T. Cacioppo   Ohio State University

Byron A. Campell   Princeton University

Joseph J. Campos   University of California at Berkeley

Hongtu Chen   University of California at Berkeley

Rachel K. Clifton   University of Massachusetts, Amherst

Edwin Cook III   University of Alabama at Birmingham

Bruce N. Cuthbert   University of Florida

Michael Davis   Ribicoff Research Facilities of the Connecticut Mental Health Center, Yale University School of Medicine

Michael E. Dawson   University of Southern California

Qi Dong   Beijing Normal University

Diane L. Filion   Kansas University Medical Center

Frances K. Graham   University of Delaware

Steven A. Hackley   University of Missouri–Colombia

Howard S. Hoffman   Bryn Mawr College

Risto J. Ilmoniemi   Helsinki University Central Hospital

Jerome Kagan   Harvard University

Rosanne Kermoian   University of California at Berkeley

Peter J. Lang   University of Florida

Ottmar V. Lipp   University of Queensland

Thomas McBride   Princeton University

Risto Näätänen   University of Helsinki

Arne Öhman   Karolinska Institute, Stockholm

William Perlstein   University of Delaware

Michael I. Posner   University of Oregon

John Richards   University of South Carolina

Mary K. Rothbart   University of Oregon

Anne M. Schell   Occidental College

David A. T. Siddle   University of Queensland

Robert F. Simons   University of Delaware

Nancy Snidman   Harvard University

Evgeny Sokolov   Lomonasov, Moscow State University

Neal R. Swerdlow   University of California, San Diego

Lisa Thomas-Thrapp   University of Oregon

Graham Turpin   University of Sheffield

David Witherington   University of California at Berkeley

Gwendolyn Wood   Princeton University

Introduction

Peter J. Lang
Robert F. Simons
Marie T. Balaban

Orienting is the gateway to attention. In Pavlov's first description of the concept (1927), he emphasized overt behaviors that facilitated sensory input and, thus, permitted the higher (cortical) processing of stimuli. As the idea of orienting was subsequently developed by Sokolov (1963), Graham and Clifton (1966), and others, the focus shifted from the behavioral to the cognitive *mechanisms* of attentional engagement and their explication in terms of covert physiological responses.

The founding theory emphasized the organism's reactions to novelty—how novelty captures attention and how reactions change when the novel becomes routine. Sokolov postulated a neuronal model of the stimulus environment in memory, and a comparator circuit, such that attention is captured by any stimulus input that fails to match (i.e., is different from) the currently active representation. Repeated stimulation generates a new model of the now familiar stimulus. Presuming the input has no motivational significance, there is then a progressive reduction in attention and in the physiological responses that are associated with orienting.

Orienting also occurs to non-novel events that are meaningful. Through associative learning, stimuli can become signal cues and the habituation process itself is then inhibited. That is, these signal stimuli prompt physiological reactions similar to those occasioned by new input.

A current computer search under the heading "orienting" quickly uncovers a vast bibliography of titles. The concept and associated ideas have had a profound influence in research on attention and the research has, in turn, enriched the theory. Pavlov also specified a second, stimulus reactive process—the defense reflex—and it too has undergone new development in psychophysiological research and thought. Defense responding is specific to stimulus changes that are at a nociceptive level of intensity. These strong stimuli prompt sympathetic activation and command reactions that persist despite repetition. The reflex is conceived, however, to have a protective function. Unlike orienting, defense does not always facilitate attention, but may actually limit stimulus engagement. In its active form the defense reflex is "expressed by behavior directed to the removal of or escape from the destructive agent" (Sokolov, p.14).

All the work presented in this volume has been significantly influenced by these conceptions. Orienting is commonly held to be the first step in stimulus information processing, and the explication of attentional mechanisms is primarily in terms of central and peripheral physiological events. Sokolov's (1963) original analysis of orienting emphasized vascular changes recorded from the dermal surface: Thus, orienting was associated with vasodilation of the temporal blood supply, and defense with vasoconstriction. Graham (1966), influenced by Lacey (1959), emphasized heart rate change—deceleratory in orienting and acceleratory in defense.

As this volume shows, current students of attentional processes are now equipped with a greatly expanded armamentarium of psychophysiological tools: (1) Cardiovascular measurement continues to be an important measure in attentional studies, with many new insights into both its biological function and cognitive significance. Other peripheral measures—electrodermal activity, somatic reflexes—also continue to provide valuable data. (2) In recent years, stimulated again by Graham's (1979) research, considerate attention has been directed at study of the startle reflex. In some experiments the startle stimulus is used as a probe in assessing attentional allocation to a foreground event. Other research has focused on how preceding inputs effect processing of the startle stimulus itself. (3) In this decade of the brain, researchers are increasingly concerned with specifying the specific cortical and subcortical structures that mediate attention. This work involves, on the one hand, pharmacologic and surgical explorations of brain pathways in animal subjects, and on the other, bioelectric and biomagnetic studies of attentional processing in intact human subjects.

Content and Organization

The study of attention is a central topic in contemporary cognitive psychology. As such, it has been the main occupation of a host of investigators, exploring its many aspects, using diverse methods and experimental paradigms, and guided by a variety of theories. This volume focuses on two aspects of attention that appear to be fundamental: First, it addresses the specific sensory mechanisms involved in the primary processing of environmental input. These are the mechanisms that elucidate stimulus selection, anticipation, and that might control rate of input, e.g., mechanisms that "protect" processing of a prior stimulus in the rapid segue to a new sensory event. Second, the volume assesses the effects of motivational factors in stimulus selection and processing. That is, how is attention modulated by the organism's drive state or evoked emotion? Are there basic differences in attentional responses to appetitive and aversive cue stimuli?

The book is organized into four parts: The initial section is made up of two chapters that present current developments in the classical theory of orienting and defense. The first chapter is co-authored by Evgeny Sokolov, whose 1963 book defined these conceptions for the field of psychology. In the present work he joins with John Cacioppo (the current editor of *Psychophysiology*) to provide a contemporary view, modeling the unique cardiovascular patterns of parasympathetic and sympathetic control that are occasioned in orienting and defense. The second chapter, by David Siddle and Ottmar Lipp, focuses on three central issues in orienting—the problem of stimulus omission, the role of expectancy, and the robustness of the dishabituation phenomenon—analyzing their effects on the autonomically mediated skin conductance response.

The second part of the book is composed of five chapters that consider the role of motivational factors—and evoked emotion—in orienting and more sustained attentional processing. These chapters emphasize evolutionary interpretations of orienting and defense and the significance of attention's neural substrate. Byron Campbell, Gwendolyn Wood, and Thomas McBride wrote chapter 3, a new exploration of the evolutionary origins of orienting and defense. They consider, for example, the similarity of cardiovascular change in the "diving reflex" and in "fear bradycardia," the stage in phylogenetic history when orienting appears, and the significance for these phenomena of structural changes in the autonomic nervous system. The fourth chapter, by Michael Davis, describes his fundamental work with animal subjects that has helped define the neural circuits and neural transmitters in the brain that mediate startle modulation in fear and sensory gating. In chapter 5, Peter Lang, Margaret Bradley, and Bruce Cuthbert use current work on picture perception to develop a motivational analysis of attentional processing. They consider a variety of autonomic, cortical, and somatic measures, with emphasis on the motivational priming of the startle reflex. Edwin Cook III and Graham Turpin present a current analysis of cardiac rate responses in orienting and defense, as they are modulated by task and emotional content, in chapter 6. The final chapter in Part II, chapter 7, is by Arne Öhman who describes new findings on the pre-attentive processing of fear stimuli. This work emphasizes that species survival depends on rapid processing of aversive cues, which occurs even when stimuli are masked, blocking higher cortical analysis.

Part III presents research on central sensory mechanisms of attention. Several of these chapters focus on the startle prepulse paradigm: In this procedure, inhibition of the reflex is obtained when a startle stimulus is immediately preceded by some other input event. The phenomenon is seen as an afferent mechanism that reduces startle impact and "protects" processing of the prepulse. This part begins with a chapter by Howard Hoffman, a pioneer of the startle paradigm in animal research, who reports recent experiments with human subjects assessing startle modulation under conditions of delayed auditory feedback. Steven Hackley and Jan Boelhouwer (chap. 9) focus on modality specific action components of the reflex response, and note an important difference in the startle blink response when visual startles are produced by abrupt change in illumination and when they are generated by a threat-movement directed at the eye. Robert Simons and William Perlstein (chap. 10) examine cortical evoked potentials in the context of both prepulse inhibition and orienting. Michael Dawson, Anne Schell, Neal Swerdlow, and Diane Filion (chap. 11) review our current understanding of the prepulse neural circuit, and analyze the implications of prepulse methodology for understanding schizophrenia. Kees Brunia (chap. 12) addresses the sensory gating phenomenon in the context of motor readiness, and Part III concludes with the latest research of Risto Näätänen, Risto Ilmoniemi, and Kimmo Alho, who use the magnetoencephalogram to plumb cortical processing in selective attention.

A stimulating chapter by Michael Posner, Mary Rothbart, and Lisa Thomas-Thrapp begins the fourth, developmental part of the book. These authors trace the beginnings of orienting in early infancy. This chapter covers a range of research topics that are of general relevance to the study of attention, illuminating both developmental questions and issues raised by studies of adult populations. Keith Berg and John Richards examine the problem of anticipatory processing—how we come to apprehend both the present stimulus and the possible, in chapter 15. Chapter 16, by Marie Balaban, Nancy Snidman, and Jerome Kagan, examines attentional modulation mediated by affect, temperament, and stress. Joseph Campos, Rosanne Kermonian, David Witherington, Hongtu Chen, and Qi Dong focus on developmental transitions, considering early fears of heights, the ontogeny of object permanence, and the way children come to use the referential gestures of others to direct their own attentional processing in chapter 17.

The reader is fortunate to have at the end of the book an integrative review of these chapters written by Frances K. Graham, a major researcher and theorist in the field of attention for more than 3 decades. She contributes an Afterword to the present volume that organizes and integrates the findings of the preceding parts in terms of preattentive processing, the arousal systems of orienting and defense, and selective attention.

I

Current Investigations
of the Classical Theory
# of Orienting and Defense

Orienting and Defense Reflexes: Vector Coding the Cardiac Response

E. N. Sokolov
Lomonasov, Moscow State University

John T. Cacioppo
The Ohio State University

The notion of an orienting or "what-is-it" response (OR) emerged from Pavlov's (1927) studies of classical conditioning in dogs. Pavlov observed that a dog's conditioned response to a stimulus would fail to appear if some unexpected event occurred:

> It is the reflex [OR] which brings about the immediate response in men and animals to the slightest changes in the world around them, so that they immediately orientate their appropriate receptor organ in accordance with the perceptible quality in the agent bringing about the change, making a full investigation of it. The biological significance of this reflex is obvious. (p. 12)

Pavlov contrasted the OR with the defense response (DR), which he characterized as a "reflex of self-defense" with postural shifts and orientation of receptor organs away from rather than toward the stimulus.

The conceptions of the OR and DR, and methods for studying the OR and DR, have changed dramatically since Pavlov's seminal observations. We begin with a brief history of theory and research on the OR and DR, including the role psychophysiological measures generally, and phasic cardiac responses in particular, have played in studies of the OR and DR. We then survey recent theory and research on the autonomic substrates of autonomic (e.g., cardiac) responses and the utility of focusing on autonomic substrates rather than manifest visceral responses for advancing our understanding of the biological substrates and behavioral significance of OR and DR. In view of theoretical developments, specific indices of sympathetic and parasympathetic control may provide a more detailed probing of the autonomic components of the OR and DR. Therefore, we conclude with representative research from eastern and western laboratories on noninvasive methods for estimating the autonomic origins of visceral responses.

CHANGING CONCEPTIONS OF THE ORIENTING AND DEFENSE RESPONSE

The OR and DR were initially conceptualized as having common and context-specific adjustments and were often treated as artifacts to be avoided in studies of classical conditioning. In *Perception and the Conditioned Reflex* (Sokolov, 1963), both conceptions were changed. The OR and DR were reformulated as biobehavioral phenomena that subserved perception and learning (e.g., by amplifying or reducing the effects of stimulation), evidenced many common features across evocative contexts, and could be quantified by psychophysiological measures. For instance, a distinction was made between the physiological adjustments that generalized across evocative stimuli and more stimulus-specific associated adaptational reflexes. In contrast to the adaptational responses, the autonomic components or signatures of both the OR and DR were posited to (a) be independent of stimulus quality, and (b) act directly on sense receptors and indirectly by feedback to central mechanisms to control receptor sensitivity. The OR and DR were further differentiated as follows: (a) an OR is elicited by stimuli of low or moderate intensity, whereas the DR is elicited by stimuli of high intensity; (b) an OR is marked by reciprocal peripheral vasoconstriction and cephalic vasodilation, whereas the DR is associated with peripheral and cephalic vasoconstriction; (c) an OR has the same autonomic signature to the onset and offset of a stimulus because both represent changes in stimulation, whereas the autonomic response to stimulus onset is larger than to stimulus offset in the DR; and (d) the OR habituates rapidly to stimulus repetition, whereas the DR is either intensified or diminished much more slowly by stimulus repetition.

The intention was to provide a coherent and testable theory of the OR as an information regulator or filter. Thus, when an organism is exposed to a stimulus, this stimulus is represented in the central nervous system as a neuronal model. Subsequent stimuli are compared to this neuronal model. Discrepancies between these stimuli and the neuronal model result in physiological and behavioral changes that amplify perception of the stimulus (as well as updating the neuronal model), whereas matches between a stimulus and the neuronal model diminish the perception of the stimulus. In this way, attention to changes or novelty is fostered and an organism's limited attentional resources are freed through habituation from the demands of constants in the continually unfolding transaction between the organism and the environment. The DR, in contrast, denotes threatening, noxious, or intense stimulation and is characterized as a biobehavioral response that served a protective function. Thus, the DR served a complementary role, fostering retreat from the provocative stimulus and a blunting of sensation to further reduce stimulation of the senses.

ORIENTING AND CARDIAC RESPONSES

Paralleling these developments, John and Beatrice Lacey (Lacey, 1959; Lacey, Kagan, Lacey, & Moss, 1963) also proposed that autonomic feedback to central neural structures amplifies or reduces the effects of environmental inputs. Specifically, the Laceys proposed that cardiac deceleration during psychological tasks was not only associated with attentional processes but could foster sensory intake, whereas cardiac acceleration was associated with and fostered sensory rejection. Among the evidence reviewed in support of this hypothesis were neurophysiological studies demonstrating that heart rate (HR) and blood pressure increases could decrease cortical excitation and increase sensory thresholds via baroreceptors in the carotid sinus and aortic arch. As Graham and Clifton (1966) noted, the notion that heart rate deceleration might mark increased sensory intake appeared to conflict with the suggestion (Sokolov, 1963) that increased sympathetic activity has a facilitating effect on sensory input through its excitatory effects on cortical activation. Graham and Clifton further noted, however, that the conflict was likely more apparent than real, as Sokolov had not dealt in depth with heart rate differences, and the Laceys had not examined tasks that were really comparable to those used to study the OR or DR.

In what has proven to be one of the most influential deductions in psychophysiology, Graham and Clifton (1966) reasoned that if the Laceys were correct in their inferences from neurophysiological evidence, heart rate deceleration should be able to predict changes in the kind of simple situations usually used to study the OR. More specifically, they wrote:

> In inferring that similar cardiac responses should occur with the OR and during relatively prolonged attention to complex stimuli, it is not assumed that attention and orienting are identical processes. However, HR changes are presumed from Lacey's hypothesis to be especially relevant to the fea-

ture that both processes have in common and that both Sokolov and the Laceys have emphasized—the feature of enhancing sensitivity to environmental inputs. (p. 306)

As predicted by Graham and Clifton (1966), the phasic HR response to stimuli has proven to be a more reliable and discriminating index of ORs and DRs in the Western literature than cephalic or peripheral vasomotor changes, with the OR associated with phasic bradycardic responses and the DR associated with tachycardia (Graham, 1979, 1984; Turpin, 1986). Graham (1979, 1984) also specified the physical parameters of the stimuli that elicit the OR and DR: the OR was characterized as more likely to be elicited by novel stimuli of low to moderate intensity with slow rise-times, and the DR was characterized as preferentially elicited by intense or aversive stimuli. Graham (1979, 1984) also noted that both DRs and startle responses are associated with cardiac acceleration but proposed that startle responses are preferentially elicited by stimuli with fast rise-times, are associated with shorter latency tachycardic responses, and habituate more quickly than DRs.

The concepts of OR and DR, and their autonomic signatures, are among the most heavily investigated topics in psychophysiology. Cardiac responses are complexly determined autonomic responses that can be influenced by basal conditions and various "adaptational reflexes" (e.g., stimulus significance, motivational and somatic factors), however. Although the OR may promote bradycardia, skin conductance responding, peripheral vasoconstriction, and cephalic vasodilation and the DR may promote slow habituating tachycardia, skin conductance activity, and both peripheral and cephalic vasoconstriction (Sokolov, 1963), other influences may obfuscate these autonomic outcomes. For instance, cephalic vasomotor responses to orienting stimuli have not been particularly replicable across eastern and western laboratories. It is conceivable, however, that methodological differences in eastern and western laboratories, through their effects on basal conditions or adaptational reflexes, altered the form of the cephalic vasomotor response that was observed to orienting stimuli. For instance, recent studies using PET and MRI have shown a novelty-dependent increase in rCBF in humans (Tulving, Markowitsch, Kapur, Habib, & Houle, 1994), whereas pain stimulation was associated with a partial reduction in rCBF (Coghill et al., 1994; Gulyas, Roland, Heywood, Popplewell, & Cowey, 1994). Alternatively, questions could be raised about the generality of the autonomic markers of the OR and DR and the utility of the concepts of OR and DR (e.g., see Saiers, Richardson, & Campbell, 1990; Turpin, 1986). Such questions have helped stimulate new theoretical analyses of the OR and DR, a topic to which we turn next.

THE AUTONOMIC ORIGINS OF THE CARDIAC RESPONSES PROMOTED BY OR AND DR

Traditionally, the cardiac responses to environmental stimuli and challenges were thought to be determined by reciprocal central control of the sympathetic and parasympathetic nervous system, with increasing activity of one branch associated with decreasing activity of the other. It is now clear, however, that the cardiac responses to stimuli can be controlled centrally by reciprocal, uncoupled, or nonreciprocal (e.g., coactivational) changes in sympathetic and parasympathetic activation (see reviews by Berntson, Cacioppo, & Quigley, 1991, 1994; Berntson, Boysen, & Cacioppo, 1991). Recent evidence further suggests that cardiac responses to stimuli that appear at a nomethetic level to reflect the reciprocal actions of the sympathetic and parasympathetic branches of the autonomic nervous system mask consistent and profound individual differences in the mode of autonomic control (Berntson, Cacioppo, Binkley, et al., 1994; Cacioppo, Uchino, & Berntson, 1994; see review by Cacioppo, 1994). Given the antagonistic effects of the sympathetic and parasympathetic branches on, for instance, the chronotropic response of the heart, a tachycardic response to a stimulus may reflect uncoupled sympathetic activation, reciprocal sympathetic activation and vagal withdrawal, uncoupled vagal withdrawal, or even coactivation of the sympathetic and parasympathetic branches in which the effects of increases in the former exceed those of changes in the latter. Measures of heart rate responses per se, therefore, may not provide an accurate reflection of the underlying autonomic response.

Vector Coding

The study of perception (color vision), targeting responses (eye and head movements), and instrumental conditioning (in fish, rabbits, and monkeys) has suggested vector code in neuronal networks as a basic principle of information processing (Sokolov, 1994, 1995; Sokolov & Vaitkyavicus, 1989). The mapping of behavioral–physiological relationships (e.g., autonomic components of the OR and DR) and our understanding of the adaptive significance and mechanism underlying these relationships, may also be advanced by using vector coding to distinguish among similarly manifesting cardiac responses that differ in their autonomic determinants. In the case of the heart, this can be done by replacing the conceptualization of heart rate responses as a unidimensional (e.g., sympathetic activation) vector with a bivariate autonomic plane. Berntson, Cacioppo, and Quigley (1991, 1993a) recently outlined such a bivariate autonomic space and reviewed the evidence consistent with the notion that HR reactivity can derive from multiple modes of autonomic control including but not limited to the reciprocal mode of cardiac control. The model entails a bivariate

vector space bounded by sympathetic and parasympathetic axes and reflecting all possible combinations of activities of the two autonomic divisions (see Fig. 1.1). Any baseline HR in this autonomic plane is specified by
its cartesian coordinates along the autonomic axes, and phasic autonomic
responses are characterized by movements within this autonomic plane.

The functional state of a visceral organ (e.g., the heart) for any location
in autonomic space is represented along a third axis as specified by the
following general equation (Berntson, Cacioppo, & Quigley, 1991):

$$fij = b + cs^*si + cp^*pj + Iij + e \qquad (1)$$

where fij is the functional state of the target organ for any i (sympathetic)
and j (parasympathetic) input or locus in autonomic space, b is the
intrinsic heart period in the absence of autonomic inputs, si and pj are
the independent activities of the sympathetic (i) and parasympathetic (j)
innervations at point ij, and cs and cp are coupling coefficients that reflect
the relative impact of sympathetic and parasympathetic activities on the
visceral organ (e.g., heart period),[1] Iij reflects potential interactions among
the ANS divisions, and e is the error term.[2]

Equation 1 makes it possible to characterize the functional state of the
heart for any locus on the bivariate autonomic plane by describing an
overlying effector (i.e., cardiac response) surface, yielding a three-dimensional depiction of autonomic space. The mean values for each of the

---

[1]C_s and C_p can be conceptualized as the dynamic ranges of the sympathetic and
parasympathetic autonomic branches, respectively. In the case of the heart, for instance, c_s
$= HP_s$ (max) $- \beta$ and $c_p = HP_p$ (max) $- \beta$, where HP_s (max) is the heart period at isolated
maximal sympathetic activation and HP_p (max) is the heart period at isolated maximal
parasympathetic activation.

[2]Equation 1 can be conceptualized in various ways. For instance, assuming $I_{ij} = 0$ and e
$= 0$, factoring out the intrinsic heart period (i.e., the background period of the pacemaker
of the simus node) in Equation 1 results in:

$$f_{ij} = \beta(1 + c_s/\beta^*s_i + c_p/\beta \, {}^*p_j) \qquad (2)$$

where f_{ij} = heart period under stimulation ij, c_s/β = sympathetic synaptic weight on the
pacemaker cells, and $c_p/\beta \, {}^*pj$ = parasympathetic synaptic weight on the pacemaker cells.
C_s/β and C_p/β can be conceptualized as the components of synaptic weights of a weight
vector C. Similarly, Si and Pj can be conceptualized as components of an excitation vector,
E. $c_s/\beta^*s_i + c_p/\beta \, {}^*p_j$ = inner product of the weight vector C and the excitation vector E, that
is, (E, C). Thus, Equation 2 can be rewritten as follows:

$$f_{ij} = \beta(1 + [E, C]) \qquad (3)$$

The heart period is equal to the background pacemaker period β multiplied by background
activation of the pacemaker plus the inner product of the excitation vector E and weight
vector C.

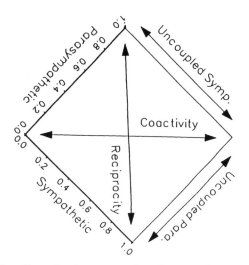

FIG. 1.1. Two-dimensional representation of autonomic space. Axes are expressed in proportional units of activation of the sympathetic and parasympathetic branches. The arrow extending from the left to the right axes intersections depicts the diagonal of reciprocity. The arrow extending from the back to the front axes intersections represents the diagonal of coactivity. The arrows along the axes depict uncoupled changes in the single autonomic nervous system divisions. These arrows, and vectors parallel to them, illustrate the major modes of autonomic control. From Berntson, Cacioppo, and Quigley (1993a). Reprinted wih permission.

parameters in Equation 1 have been determined for humans (Berntson et al., 1993a) and for rats (Berntson, Cacioppo, Quigley, & Fabro, 1994). Berntson et al. (1993a) found considerable individual differences in the intrinsic heart period in humans, as well as phasic nonautonomic contributions to heart period (e.g., temperature, exercise). However, the cardiac effector surface reflecting neurally determined changes in heart period in humans is depicted in Fig. 1.2 where, on average, cs = −230 ms and cp = 1,713 ms (Berntson et al., 1993a).

An important feature of the effector surface depicted in Fig. 1.2 is that the same heart rate response can occur for very different reasons. A deceleratory heart rate response may occur due to vagal activation, sympathetic withdrawal, or various combinations of the two. Thus, a given heart period may be ambiguous with regard to its autonomic origins. This is depicted as isoeffector contour (dotted) lines in Fig. 1.2. These contours illustrate the multiple loci on the bivariate vector plane that yield equivalent cardiac responses. The many-to-one mapping from the autonomic plane to the effector surface underscores the indeterminism when inferring changes in autonomic activities or behavioral processes based solely on changes in cardiac response (Cacioppo & Tassinary, 1990).

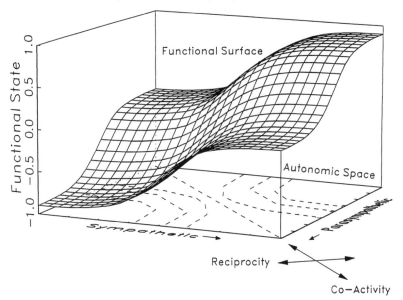

FIG. 1.2. Two-dimensional autonomic plane and its associated functional
surface. The functional surface represents the operational state of the target
organ, expressed in relative units, as derived from Equation 1 with
weighting coefficients = + 1.0. The axes dimensions are in decile units of
functional activation. Dotted lines represent isofunctional contour lines
projected on the autonomic plane, illustrating loci within the autonomic
plane that have equivalent functional outputs. The arrows indicate the
directional vectors associated with the modes of autonomic control. From
Berntson, Cacioppo, and Quigley (1991). Reprinted with permission.

Autonomic Origins of the OR and DR as Revealed
by Autonomic Blockade

Because identical cardiac responses may arise from different autonomic
loci, Berntson et al. (1993a; Berntson, Boysen, & Cacioppo, 1991) suggested
that information beyond the description of the cardiac response may
contribute to the differentiation of the OR and DR. Quigley and Berntson
(1990), for instance, presented brief nonsignal acoustic tones of two intensities (60 vs. 80 dB, SPL) to evoke bradycardia and tachycardia, respectively,
in rats (see Fig. 1.3). The administration of the postganglionic parasympathetic antagonist, scopolamine methyl nitrate, and the sympathetic b1
antagonist, atenolol, further revealed the autonomic origins of these cardiac
responses. The tachycardic response to the high-intensity stimulus, which
would appear to reflect a DR, was attributable primarily to sympathetic

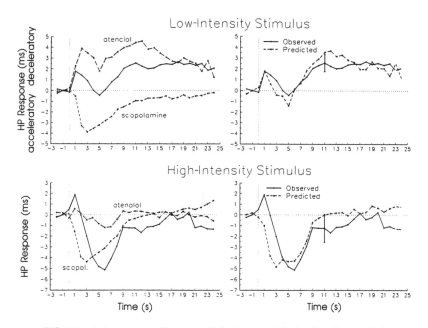

FIG. 1.3. Autonomic cardiac control during postinfusion baseline period as revealed by autonomic blockades. Left panel: Mean heart rate under saline, atropine sulfate, metoprolol, and double blockade. Middle panel: Mean respiratory sinus arrhythmia under saline, atropine sulfate, metoprolol, and double blockade. Right panel: Mean pre-ejection period under saline, atropine sulfate, metoprolol, and double blockade. The terms, s and p at the top of each panel represent quantitative estimates of the sympathetic and parasympathetic contributions, respectively, to the corresponding cardiac index. The term, eblk, represents an estimate of the range of error in the quantitative estimates based on autonomic blockades. Quantitative estimates with dissimilar superscripts differ at $p < .05$. From Cacioppo (1994). Reprinted with the permission of Cambridge University Press.

activation, as it was diminished dramatically by atenolol and affected only minimally by scopolamine. Conversely, the bradycardic response to the low-intensity stimulus, which would appear to reflect an OR, reflected both strong vagal activation and a less potent sympathetic activation to the stimulus. That is, vagal blockade by scopolamine not only eliminated the deceleratory cardiac response to the stimulus but unmasked a significant acceleratory response to the stimulus, and sympathetic blockade enhanced substantially the bradycardic response to the low-intensity stimulus (see Fig. 1.3). These observations are consistent with the coactivation of the parasympathetic and sympathetic branches controlling the heart in the OR. The vector approach in the autonomic space model differentiates the OR and DR by their specific trajectories on the functional surface overlying the autonomic plane.

Although the manifest cardiac responses in Quigley and Berntson (1990) may have been sufficient to differentiate the OR and DR to low- and high-intensity tones, respectively, a recognition of the multiple determinants of autonomic responses and the multiple modes of autonomic control underlying these responses may increase the power and specificity of cardiac measures of OR and DR (Berntson et al., 1993a). For instance, Richardson, Siegel, and Campbell (1988) found that the transfer of rats to an unfamiliar testing environment inhibited the cardiac component of the OR to a pulsating tone. Saiers et al. (1990) replicated these findings in preweanling rats and observed similar results following electric shock. Because the stimulus change (pulsating tone) was the same across contexts, the authors interpreted their results as inconsistent with contemporary conceptualizations of the OR. As Quigley and Berntson (1990) suggested, however, the cardiac component of the OR appears to be characterized by coactivation of the vagal and sympathetic branches—a neural substrate that, with small changes in activation of either branch, can mask consistent effector responses (Berntson, Boysen, & Cacioppo, 1991). Moreover, novel or challenging environments may be especially likely to promote coactivation of the sympathetic and parasympathetic divisions to foster directional flexibility in effector outcomes. As Berntson et al. (1993a) noted:

> The attenuated cardiac orienting responses reported by Richardson et al. (1988) and Saiers et al. (1990) could reflect greater conjoint parasympathetic and sympathetic activation (i.e., coactivation), rather than an attenuation of the vagal response associated with the OR (Quigley & Berntson, 1990). Examination of the second x second HR changes in the Saiers et al. study (their Fig. 6) supports this interpretation. The sympathetic system is known to have a longer latency than vagal influences on the heart. . . . In the Saiers et al. study, the experimental manipulations (shock or context change) did not alter the heart rate response during the first second after the stimulus, rather experimental curves progressively diverged from the control condition over the subsequent 2 to 3 sec. This is consistent with a concurrent (longer latency) sympathetic activation, which would obscure the vagal response. Autonomic co-activation is also consistent with the absence of baseline increases in heart rate in the Saiers et al. study, even after repeated shocks. (p. 195)

The vector representation of the OR and DR in terms of sympathetic and parasympathetic components may also elucidate the vascular differences in cephalic and peripheral response, with the DR associated with general sympathetic vasoconstriction and the coactivation of sympathetic and parasympathetic influences elicited by OR producing peripheral vasoconstriction but more variable cephalic vasomotor manifestations across eastern and western laboratories.

NONINVASIVE INDICES OF AUTONOMIC SUBSTRATES

In view of these considerations, specific indices of sympathetic and parasympathetic control may provide a more detailed probing of the autonomic components of OR and DR. For instance, the cardiac OR to a novel stimulus and to an adaptively meaningful stimulus may share common features but the attentional, cognitive, and behavioral dispositions toward these classes of stimuli may differ. Independent measures of the relative activities of the sympathetic and parasympathetic divisions may improve the resolution of the autonomic measures and help illuminate the common and context-specific autonomic components of the OR and DR. Research on these issues from western and Moscow laboratories is described in this section.

One approach that sometimes serves as a standard against which other approaches are measured involves the use of pharmacological blockades. Although not without problems, autonomic blockades provide information about the contributions of each of the autonomic divisions to responses from specific effector organs (for a detailed discussion of the underlying logic, see Berntson, Cacioppo, & Quigley, 1994). Autonomic blockades may be especially appropriate when the autonomic components of punctate responses are of interest because they allow moment-by-moment estimation of the neural determinants of visceral responses.

Noninvasive indices of sympathetic and parasympathetic contributions to effector responses may also be helpful, particularly when the autonomic components of the OR or DR are extended in time (e.g., Saiers et al., 1990). For instance, two of the more promising noninvasive measures of the autonomic control of the heart currently available are the cardiac pre-ejection period and respiratory sinus arrhythmia. The pre-ejection period is a systolic time interval representing the period of time commencing with the onset of ventricular depolarization (ECG Q-wave) and ending with the opening of the semilunar valves. The greater the sympathetic activation of the myocardium and the greater the myocardial contractility, the shorter the pre-ejection period as long as the effects of preload and afterload are controlled or are held constant (Binkley & Boudoulas, 1986). A shortening of the pre-ejection period accompanies increases in HR that derive from adrenergic cardiostimulation but not from vagal blockade or atrial pacing (e.g., Harris, Schoenfeld, & Weissler, 1967). Studies further suggest that HR per se does not influence the pre-ejection period unless changes in HR are associated with inotropic changes, or are accompanied by changes in preload or afterload (Lewis, Leighton, Forester, & Weissler, 1974).

Respiratory sinus arrhythmia refers to the high-frequency (e.g., 0.12–0.40 Hz in adults) component of the oscillations of heart period produced by respiratory processes. For instance, the inspiratory and expiratory phases of the respiratory cycle are associated with HR acceleration and HR deceleration, respectively. The magnitude and changes in respiratory sinus arrhythmia appear to vary as a function of vagal control of the heart as long as significant variations in respiratory activity are controlled or accounted for (Berntson, Cacioppo, & Quigley, 1993a; Grossman, Karemaker, & Wieling, 1991).

Accurate measurement of the pre-ejection period and respiratory sinus arrhythmia requires analyses of a series (e.g., 60 secs) of heartbeats. This requirement has limited the usefulness of these noninvasive measures in most studies of OR and DR in humans. However, orienting and defense reflexes have been studied in animals using, for instance, pulsating tones over sufficiently long periods (e.g., see Saiers et al., 1990) that noninvasive indices become feasible.

In a study of the psychometric properties of pre-ejection period and respiratory sinus arrhythmia, cardiovascular and respiratory measures were made during a 2-min standing baseline and a 2-min sitting baseline (Cacioppo, Berntson, et al., 1994). After baseline testing, subjects were given 4 min to prepare and 4 to 5 min to present a public speech. Approximately half (2 min) of the speech was delivered while seated, and approximately half (2 min) of the speech was delivered while standing. (The postural manipulation allowed examination of the reliabilities of respiratory sinus arrhythmia and pre-ejection period reactivity at two different levels of the autonomic activation of the heart.) After speaking for 2 min, the recordings were paused surreptitiously, and subjects were instructed to change posture and to continue their speech. Subjects assumed the alternate posture (standing or sitting) and continued speaking. The recordings were surreptitiously initiated 30 sec later and continued for another 2 min, at which point recordings were stopped and subjects were instructed that they had done well and could stop.

Nomethetic analyses indicated that the HR responses to the speech task were the result of the reciprocal activation of the sympathetic and parasympathetic branches: The speech stressor led to an elevation in HR, a reduction in respiratory sinus arrhythmia (depicting vagal cardiac withdrawal), and a shortening of pre-ejection period (indicating sympathetic cardiac activation). Idiographic analyses of these data, however, revealed considerable individual differences, with an exaggerated HR response to the stressor arising from various modes of control, ranging from strong parasympathetic withdrawal to reciprocal increases in sympathetic, and decreases in parasympathetic, activation to large increases in sympathetic activation. Among the high HR reactors, for instance, were three subgroups: individuals who showed primarily vagal cardiac withdrawal, individuals who showed primarily sympathetic cardiac activation, and individuals who showed both vagal cardiac withdrawal and sympathetic cardiac activation.

Psychometric Properties

Analyses of the measurement properties of the baseline, task, and reactivity (simple and residualized change) measures of HR, pre-ejection period, and respiratory sinus arrhythmia were also conducted. The internal consistency of each of these indices was examined by calculating Cronbach alphas across baseline and task periods within each posture, and again after aggregating across postures. The Cronbach alphas for the entire sample of 67 projects ranged from .79 to .91, with aggregation modestly improving the Cronbach alpha for each index ($ps < .001$).

If individuals are to be classified not only in terms of their HR reactivity but also in terms of vagal and sympathetic cardiac reactivity, then ideally HR reactivity, respiratory sinus arrhythmia reactivity, and pre-ejection period reactivity should yield consistent classifications of individuals in terms of their level of reactivity. To examine this question, rank orderings of subjects were constructed in terms of their HR, respiratory sinus arrhythmia, and pre-ejection period reactivity in the sitting posture, and corresponding rank orderings were constructed in terms of their reactivity on each measure in the standing posture. The Spearman correlation for each measure was then computed to determine the stability of the rank orderings across posture—that is, at two different levels of tonic autonomic control of the heart. These analyses were then repeated using residualized change scores. In every instance, the Spearman coefficient was statistically significant at the $p < .01$ level despite differences in basal autonomic tonus across posture. Furthermore, the reliability statistics for classifying individuals in terms of stress-induced respiratory sinus arrhythmia reactivity and in terms of pre-ejection period reactivity were comparable to those for HR reactivity ($ps < .01$).

Next, basal HR, task HR, and HR reactivity (calculated as a simple change score and as a residualized change score) during sitting were correlated with the corresponding index during standing to determine test–retest reliabilities, and comparable analyses were performed for the indices based on respiratory sinus arrhythmia and on pre-ejection period. Results revealed that these test–retest correlations ranged from .53 to .82 ($ps < .01$). The finding that HR, respiratory sinus arrhythmia, and pre-ejection period reactivity indices during sitting were highly predictive of the corresponding reactivity measures during standing, although limited to the present paradigm (cf. Sloan et al.), is encouraging from the viewpoint of measuring the autonomic substrates of cardiac response.

The interrelationships among the reactivity measures were also consistent with the use of respiratory sinus arrhythmia and pre-ejection period reactivity as noninvasive indices of the vagal and sympathetic determinants, respectively, of cardiac responses. First, the correlations between stress-induced changes in respiratory sinus arrhythmia and in

HR were all negative, reflecting the negative chronotropic effects of vagal input to the heart. That is, individuals who displayed stress-induced increases in respiratory sinus arrhythmia also were likely to show small increases in HR, whereas individuals who showed stress-induced decreases in respiratory sinus arrhythmia (reflecting vagal withdrawal) also displayed large increases in HR. Furthermore, the median correlation among these measures was statistically significant (median $r = -.53$, $p < .01$). Second, the correlations among stress-induced changes in pre-ejection period and in HR were uniformly large and negative, consistent with the notion that stress-induced sympathetic cardiac activation shortens pre-ejection period and elevates HR. The median correlation among these measures was also statistically significant (median $r = -.54$, $p < .01$). Finally, the correlations between the respiratory sinus arrhythmia and pre-ejection period reactivity measures revealed that these indices did not consistently covary across individuals, and the median correlation among these measures was not significant (median $r = .29$, ns). The results of this study, therefore, were consistent with the notion that stress-induced changes in respiratory sinus arrhythmia and in pre-ejection period can vary independently, and that each may predict unique autonomic determinants of cardiac response.

Autonomic Blockade Analyses of Respiratory Sinus Arrhythmia and Pre-Ejection Period

The use of respiratory sinus arrhythmia and pre-ejection period to index stress-induced changes in the autonomic control of the heart is not without problems or controversy, and alternative indices (e.g., rate-corrected pre-ejection period, low-frequency heart period variability) have been proposed in the psychophysiological and cardiologic literatures. The cardiac rhythm spectrum, for instance, typically contains three main peaks. The high-frequency peak (around 0.25 Hz) is related to respiratory sinus arrhythmia representing parasympathetic input to the heart. The low-frequency peak (around 0.10 Hz) is influenced primarily by vascular rhythmicity and, therefore, has been thought to reflect sympathetic input to the heart. Finally, metabolic (humoral) influences have a greater impact on the very low-frequency peak (around 0.01 Hz) than on the low- or high-frequency peaks. Spectral analysis provides one means of decomposing the heart period time series into frequency components, making it possible to quantify the high, low, and very low frequency amplitudes. However, whether these amplitudes reflect vagal, sympathetic, and humoral control of the heart, respectively, or whether statistical procedures can be developed to improve these indices remains an important area for future research. For instance, Cacioppo, Berntson, et al. (1994) reported a a single and double autonomic blockade study to evaluate various putative measures of autonomic control of the heart, including pre-ejection period and low-frequency HR variability as indices of sympathetic control of the heart, and respiratory sinus arrhythmia as an index of parasympathetic control of the heart. Although autonomic blockades can help illuminate the underlying autonomic origins of cardiac indices, systematic biases in estimates of the contributions of the autonomic branches can arise from both methodological and physiological factors (e.g., due to interactions among the autonomic branches at the level of the organ; indirect or reflexive alterations in the unblocked branch; nonselective actions of the blocker agents). Consequently, autonomic estimates that were based on data from single and double blockade conditions were developed to quantify systematic biases as well as the neural contributions of each autonomic division (Berntson, Cacioppo, & Quigley, 1994).

Subjects were tested under three drug conditions (saline, atropine sulfate, metoprolol) on three consecutive days, with drug condition counterbalanced across subjects and days. Cardiovascular and respiratory measures were obtained prior to and following infusion of either saline (Saline Condition), atropine sulfate (Atropine Condition), or metoprolol (Metoprolol Condition). Subjects who qualified for participation in the study were tested under all three drug conditions, and the order of drug administration was counterbalanced across subjects. Following venipuncture at each session, subjects rested quietly for 30 min to allow adaptation to the laboratory, and initial baseline recordings were made during the final 3 min of this adaptation period. Intravenous infusion of saline, metoprolol (14 mg), or atropine sulfate (2 mg) followed (using a double-blind procedure), and subjects sat quietly for 15 min. Recordings were taken during the final 3 min of this postinfusion baseline and in response to an orthostatic stressor (3 min standing, 3 min sitting, order counterbalanced). Afterward, subjects were exposed to 3 min reaction time, mental arithmetic, and speech stressors, with a resting 3 min baseline preceding each stressor, and the order of stressors counterbalanced across days and subjects. At the end of the metoprolol session, atropine sulfate was infused and responses were monitored during the postinfusion (i.e., double blockade) baseline and during orthostatic stressor (Berntson, Cacioppo, Binkley, Uchino, Quigley, & Fieldstone, 1994; Cacioppo, Berntson, Binkley, et al., 1994).

Analyses revealed that drug condition was unrelated to the cardiovascular measures at preinfusion baseline, as would be expected given the counterbalancing and double-blind procedures that were used. As illustrated in the left panel of Fig. 1.4, HR during the postinfusion baseline varied significantly as a function of autonomic blockade, with mean HR under saline about 72 beats per minute (bpm), under atropine about 119

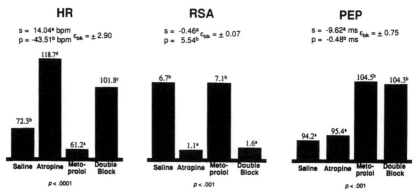

FIG. 1.4. Mean cardiac response of rats to a nonsignal acoustic stimulus of low intensity (60 dB) and high intensity (80 dB). Left panels illustrate the heart period responses in the unblocked condition (solid lines) and after sympathetic (atenolol, 5 mg/kg) or parasympathetic (scopolamine methyl nitrate, 0.1 mg/kg) blockade. Right panels illustrate the observed response in the unblocked condition and the predicted responses based on the independent responses of the autonomic branches under selective blockades. Error bars depict illustrative standard errors for the unblocked response. Data from Quigley and Berntson (1990). Figure from Berntson, Cacioppo, Quigley, and Fabro (1994). Reprinted with the permission of Cambridge University Press.

bpm, under metoprolol about 61 bpm, and under double blockade 101 bpm (ps < .01). Quantitative analyses indicated that sympathetic contributions to basal HR averaged 14 bpm and parasympathetic contributions to basal HR averaged –43.5 bpm (Cacioppo, Berntson, Binkley, et al., 1994).

Analyses of the blockade data further revealed that pre-ejection period reflected sympathetic but not vagal influences on the heart, and respiratory sinus arrhythmia (high-frequency cardiac variability) reflected vagal and only nominal sympathetic influences on the heart. Quantitative analyses of the postinfusion baseline data, for instance, indicated that sympathetic contributions to respiratory sinus arrhythmia averaged less than 0.5 log units, whereas parasympathetic contributions averaged over 5.5 log units. The quantitative analyses revealed the opposite to hold for pre-ejection period: sympathetic contributions averaged –9.6 ms, whereas parasympathetic contributions averaged –.05 ms and fell within the range of error bias (see Fig. 1.4, middle and right panels, respectively). Importantly, analyses of low-frequency cardiac variability revealed the measure to be affected by vagal as well as sympathetic contributions, with the magnitude of the former exceeding that of the latter under resting conditions. Analyses of the cardiac responses to the orthostatic stressor under single and double autonomic blockade replicated these results. Although the blockade results for high- and low-frequency components of the cardiac rhythm spectrum are consistent with the frequency characteristics of the vagal and sympathetic cardiac synapses (Berntson, Cacioppo, & Quigley, 1993b), they point to the need for additional research and, possibly, the development of more complex analytical methods before the measure of low-frequency HR variability can serve satisfactorily as a specific marker of sympathetic control of the heart.

Heart Rate Variability Spectral Peaks as Measures of Underlying Mechanisms

Although analyses of both high- and low-frequency HR variability by Cacioppo, Berntson, Binkley, et al. (1994) suggested that there were parasympathetic contributions to both frequencies, these components of HR variability reflect different aspects of the vagal and sympathetic control of the heart. As noted, the very low-frequency peak reflects a combination of metabolic influences (e.g., humoral, temperature, baroreceptor); the low-frequency peak reflects vascular influences; and the high-frequency peak, respiratory influences. Analyses of the contributions by an autonomic branch (e.g., parasympathetic) to each of these peaks indicate that they may not be highly correlated and that the magnitude of the correlation may vary across conditions (e.g., baseline, stress). Thus, the "amount" of vagal control of the heart may vary depending on which spectral peak or bandwidth is quantified. This points to limitations in using noninvasive measures such as respiratory sinus arrhythmia to gauge the vagal control of the heart. More interestingly, it raises another potentially fruitful approach to investigating the neural mechanisms underlying the OR and DR: The amplitude of each of the three spectral peaks in heart rhythm variability, which conceivably reflect separable mechanistic influences, can be used to decompose and map the cardiac response in a three-dimensional space. The orthogonal axis representing high-, medium-, and low-frequency bands suggest an independence of three generators operating in parallel and constituting a three-dimensional vector in the frequency domain (Danilova, 1995; Sokolov, 1995).

To illustrate, HR variability was measured in the Moscow laboratory in 90 (45 low-anxious and 45 high-anxious) subjects under conditions of rest and mental arithmetic. Spectral analyses confirmed that high-, in contrast to low-, anxious subjects were characterized by depressed spectral components in HR variability (see Fig. 1.5). Next, a 10×10 correlation matrix of respective frequency bands was constructed for each condition (rest, mental arithmetic). Factor analyses revealed three orthogonal factors

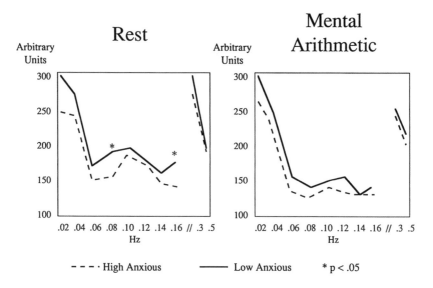

FIG. 1.5. The heart rhythm spectrum in high-anxious (HA) and low-anxious (LA) subjects during rest (top panel) and mental arithmetic (bottom panel). The high- and low-frequency heart rhythms were higher in low-than high-anxious subjects during rest, and were higher generally during rest than during the stressor. Adapted from Danilova (1995). Reprinted with permission.

corresponding to what might be labeled respiratory, vascular, and metabolic oscillators. The same three factors were found during rest as during mental arithmetic.

Using these three factors as a coordinate system, the cardiac responses of high-anxious and low-anxious subjects can be depicted in a three-dimensional space and projected on three planes for the resting condition. Analyses of the configuration of these peaks revealed that the high- and low-anxious groups differed dramatically in terms of the underlying organization of their baseline HR variability. The HR variability of low-anxious subjects was not only greater than that characterizing high-anxious subjects, but this difference appeared to derive from metabolic, vascular, and respiratory influences. Similar analyses were performed on HR variability during mental arithmetic, revealing substantial vagal withdrawal and depressed high-frequency variability (i.e., respiratory sinus arrhythmia) in both groups. Thus, differences between the low- and high-anxious subjects in the underlying organization of HR variability during mental arithmetic were evident primarily in the low (vascular) and very low (metabolic) frequency components. If one assumes that anxious subjects are characterized by a chronic defensive disposition, these data suggest that the highly (in contrast to mildly) anxious subjects show depressed levels of heart period variability during baseline similar to those observed during a psychological stressor (mental arithmetic) in low- and high-anxious subjects.

The fact that both sympathetic and vagal activation can influence very low and low frequency components makes it difficult to use these components to separate the contributions of each autonomic branch to cardiac responses. Furthermore, the vagal contribution to cardiac control, as reflected in high-frequency heart rhythms in the study of high-anxious and low-anxious subjects, was not correlated with, or was inconsistently correlated with, the vagal contribution as indexed in low or very low frequency heart rhythms. This result casts doubt on the validity of estimates of sympathetic influences that "correct" for the vagal influences in the low-frequency HR variability using estimates of vagal activation from high-frequency heart rhythms. It may be possible and illuminating, however, to relate the frequency peaks in the heart rhythm spectra to metabolic, vascular, and respiratory mechanisms, and in so doing to examine the OR and DR in terms of the contributions of each of these mechanisms to cardiac responses. Given the particular tasks the low- and high-anxious subjects performed, extrapolation of these particular data to the OR and DR is tenuous. However, the approach illustrated in this study may shed new light on the biobehavioral significance of the OR and DR reflexes. Because these measures require a time series of heartbeats, these noninvasive measures may be especially suited to tasks designed to study attention such as those developed by Lacey et al. (1963) and to relatively long orienting or defense stimuli such as those developed by Campbell and colleagues (Richardson et al., 1988; Saiers et al., 1990).

SUMMARY

Perception and the Conditioned Reflex (Sokolov, 1963) opened a fertile area of psychophysiological theory and research on the OR and DR. Graham (1979, 1984; Graham & Clifton, 1966) expanded this area by focusing on the cardiac components of the OR and DR. In the 30 years since Graham first drew attention to the cardiac response as a tool for probing these reflexes, empirical anomalies have appeared that have led some to question the utility of the concepts of OR and DR. One possible resolution is to examine the autonomic origins of the cardiac components of the OR and DR rather than focusing exclusively on the cardiac response per se. At present, autonomic blockades provide the clearest means of determining these autonomic substrates, but specific and sensitive noninvasive indices of vagal and sympathetic influences on the cardiac components of the OR and DR would represent important advances. Such measures would allow an unambiguous specification of autonomic response and would likely contribute to meaningful investigations of behavioral-psychophysiological relationships (Berntson et al., 1993a). Another possibility is to map cardiac components of the OR and DR in terms of their physiological (humoral, vascular, respiratory) determinants. Although representing quite different approaches, both are based on the notion that our understanding of biobehavioral organization and control, as represented in the OR and DR, may be advanced by quantifying the neurophysiological origins of these responses. Finally, the bivariate approach to the study of OR and DR is based on the principle of a vector code operating within sympathetic–parasympathetic inputs, a principle that can be extended to frequency-specific independent generators contributing to heart rate variability.

ACKNOWLEDGMENTS

This chapter is based on the address presented at the Symposium devoted to Francis K. Graham, Atlanta, 1994. The authors wish to thank N. N. Danilova, S. G. Korshunova, Gary G. Berntson, Wendi L. Gardner, Peter J. Lang, and Francis K. Graham for their helpful comments on an earlier version of this paper.

REFERENCES

Berntson, G. G., Boysen, S. T., & Cacioppo, J. T. (1991). Cardiac orienting and defensive responses: Potential origins in autonomic space. In B. A. Campbell (Ed.), *Attention and information processing in infants and adults* (pp. 163–200). Hillsdale, NJ: Lawrence Erlbaum Associates.

Berntson, G. G., Cacioppo, J. T., Binkley, P. F., Uchino, B. N., Quigley, K. S., & Fieldstone, A. (1994). Autonomic cardiac control: III. Psychological stress and cardiac response in autonomic space as revealed by autonomic blockades. *Psychophysiology, 31*, 599–608.

Berntson, G. G., Cacioppo, J. T., & Quigley, K. S. (1991). Autonomic determinism: The modes of autonomic control, the doctrine of autonomic space, and the laws of autonomic constraint. *Psychological Review, 98*, 459–487.

Berntson, G. G., Cacioppo, J. T., & Quigley, K. S. (1993a). Cardiac psychophysiology and autonomic space in humans: Empirical perspectives and conceptual implications. *Psychological Bulletin, 114*, 296–322.

Berntson, G. G., Cacioppo, J. T., & Quigley, K. S. (1993b). Respiratory sinus arrhythmia: Autonomic origins, physiological mechanisms, and psychophysiological implications. *Psychophysiology, 30*, 183–196.

Berntson, G. G., Cacioppo, J. T., & Quigley, K. S. (1994). Autonomic cardiac control: I. Estimation and validation from pharmacological blockades. *Psychophysiology, 31*, 572–585.

Berntson, G. G., Cacioppo, J. T., Quigley, K. S., & Fabro, V. T. (1994). Autonomic space and psychophysiological response. *Psychophysiology, 31*, 44–61.

Binkley, P. F., & Boudoulas, H. (1986). Measurement of myocardial inotropy. In C. V. Leier (Ed.), *Cardiotonic drugs: A clinical survey* (pp. 5–48). New York: Marcel Dekker.

Cacioppo, J. T. (1994). Social neuroscience: Autonomic, neuroendocrine, and immune response to stress. *Psychophysiology, 31*, 113–128.

Cacioppo, J. T., Berntson, G. G., Binkley, P. F., Quigley, K. S., Uchino, B. N., & Fieldstone, A. (1994). Autonomic cardiac control: II. Basal response, noninvasive indices, and autonomic space as revealed by autonomic blockades. *Psychophysiology, 31*, 586–598.

Cacioppo, J. T., & Tassinary, L. G. (1990). Inferring psychological significance from physiological signals. *American Psychologist, 45*, 16–28.

Cacioppo, J. T., Uchino, B. N., & Berntson, G. G. (1994). Individual differences in the autonomic origins of heart rate reactivity: The psychometrics of respiratory sinus arrhythmia and pre-ejection period. *Psychophysiology, 31*, 412–419.

Coghill, R. C., Talbot, J. D., Evans, A., Meyer, E., Gjedde, A., Bushnell, H. C., & Duncan, G. H. (1994). Distributed processing of pain and vibration by the human brain. *Journal of Neuroscience, 14*, 4095–4108.

Danilova, N. N. (1995). Serdechnyi ritm I informatsionnaya nagruzka [Heart rhythm and informational load]. *Vestn. Mosk. U-ta, Seria 14, Psikhologiya, 4*, 14–27.

Graham, F. K. (1979). Distinguishing among orienting, defensive, and startle reflexes. In H. D. Kimmel, E. H. van Olst, & J. F. Orlebeke (Eds.), *The orienting reflex in humans* (pp. 137–167). Hillsdale, NJ: Lawrence Erlbaum Associates.

Graham, F. K. (1984). An affair of the heart. In M. G. H. Coles, J. R. Jennings, & J. A. Stern (Eds.), *Psychophysiological perspectives: Festschrift for Beatrice and John Lacey* (pp. 171–187). New York: Van Nostrand Reinhold.

Graham, F. K., & Clifton, R. K. (1966). Heart-rate change as a component of the orienting response. *Psychological Bulletin, 65*, 305–320.

Grossman, P., Karemaker, J. K., & Wieling, W. (1991). Prediction of tonic parasympathetic cardiac control using respiratory sinus arrhythmia: The need for respiratory control. *Psychophysiology, 28*, 201–216.

Gulyas, B., Roland, P. E., Heywood, C., Popplewell, D. A., & Cowey, A. (1994). Visual form discrimination from luminance or disparity cues: Functional anatomy by PET. *Neuro-Report, 5*, 2367–2371.

Harris, W. S., Schoenfeld, C. D., & Weissler, A. M. (1967). Effects of adrenergic receptor activation and blockade on the systolic pre-ejection period, heart rate and arterial pressure in man. *Journal of Clinical Investigation, 46*, 1704–1714.

Lacey, J. I. (1959). Psychophysiological approaches to the evaluation of psychotherapeutic process and outcome. In E. A. Rubinstein & M. B. Parloff (Eds.), *Research in psychotherapy* (pp. 160–208). Washington, DC: American Psychological Association.

Lacey, J. I., Kagan, J., Lacey, B., & Moss, H. A. (1963). The visceral level: Situational determinants and behavioral correlates of autonomic response patterns. In P. H. Knapp (Ed.), *Expression of the emotions in man* (pp. 161–196). New York: International Universities Press.

Lewis, R. P., Leighton, R. F., Forester, W. F., & Weissler, A. M. (1974). Systolic time intervals. In A. M. Weissler (Ed.), *Non-invasive cardiology* (pp. 301–368). New York: Grune & Stratton.

Pavlov, I. P. (1927). *Conditioned reflexes.* New York: Oxford University Press.

Quigley, K. S., & Berntson, G. G. (1990). Autonomic origins of cardiac responses to nonsignal stimuli in the rat. *Behavioral Neuroscience, 104*, 751–762.

Richardson, R., Siegel, M. A., & Campbell, B. A. (1988). Unfamiliar environments impair information processing as measured by behavioral and cardiac orienting responses to auditory stimuli in preweaning and adult rats. *Developmental Psychobiology, 21*, 613–633.

Saiers, J. A., Richardson, R., & Campbell, B. A. (1990). Disruption and recovery of the orienting response following shock or context change in preweaning rats. *Psychophysiology, 27*, 45–56.

Sloan, R. P., Shapiro, P. A., Bagiella, E., Fishkin, P. E., Gorman, J. M., & Myers, M. M. (1995). Consistency of heart rate and sympathovagal reactivity across different autonomic contexts. *Psychophysiology, 32.*

Sokolov, E. N. (1963). *Perception and the conditioned reflex.* Oxford: Pergamon.

Sokolov, E. N. (1994). Vector coding in neuronal nets: Color vision. In K. H. Pribram (Ed.), *Origins: Brain and self-organization* (pp. 463–475). Hillsdale, NJ: Lawrence Erlbaum Associates.

Sokolov, E. N. (1995). Printsip vektornogo kodirovaniya v psikhofiziologii [Principle of vector coding in psychophysiology]. Vestn. Mosk. U-ta, Seria 14, *Psikhologiya, 4,* 3–13.

Sokolov, E. N., & Vaitkyavicus, G. G. (1989). *Neirointellect: Ot neirona k neirokomputeru* [Neurointelligence: From neuron to neurocomputer]. Moscow: Nauka.

Tulving, E., Markowitsch, H. J., Kapur, S., Habib, R., & Houle, S. (1994). Novelty encoding networks in the human brain: Positron emission tomography data. *NeuroReport, 5,* 2525–2528.

Turpin, G. (1986). Effects of stimulus intensity on autonomic responding: The problem of differentiating orienting and defense reflexes. *Psychophysiology, 23,* 1–14.

2

Orienting, Habituation, and Information Processing: The Effects of Omission, the Role of Expectancy, and the Problem of Dishabituation

David A. T. Siddle
Ottmar V. Lipp
University of Queensland

Orienting and habituation have been important topics of investigation for over two decades. Initial interest following Sokolov's (1960, 1963) early publications stemmed from the fact that the sensitivity of orienting to stimulus change seemed to carry implications for how sensory information was coded and processed. Orienting and habituation have now come to occupy a central position in the work of many behavioral scientists and neuroscientists for at least three reasons. First, orienting seems to be related to attentional processes, especially those processes that underlie passive attention to input (Graham & Hackley, 1991; Pavlov, 1927). This means that orienting can be used to study attention itself and to study attentional dysfunction in clinical or subclinical groups (e.g., Bernstein, 1992; Dawson, Nuechterlein, Schell, Gitlin, & Ventura, 1994). Second, habituation is an important aspect of behavioral plasticity (Groves & Thompson, 1970), and third, orienting and habituation can be observed across a wide range of vertebrate and invertebrate species and in a variety of response systems (see Campbell, Wood, & McBride, chapter 3, this volume). For these reasons, orienting and habituation have been subjected to intensive investigation, not only in their own right, but also in connection with theory development in areas such as cognitive development (Graham, Anthony, & Zeigler, 1983), associative learning (Pearce & Hall, 1980, 1992; Wagner, 1978), information processing (Öhman, 1979; Siddle & Spinks, 1992), psychopathology and emotion (Bernstein, 1992; Öhman,

1992), personality (O'Gorman, 1977), and the neuronal mechanisms of behavior (Carew, 1984).

One of the features that characterizes research on orienting and habituation, and that permeates the use of orienting and habituation as explanatory concepts in other domains, is a debate about the type of theory that best accounts for the empirical phenomena. As Siddle (1991) noted, theories of habituation can be divided broadly into comparator (or two-stage) theories and noncomparator (or one-stage) theories. Comparator theories are exemplified by Sokolov's (1963) original formulation, in which it was proposed that iterated stimulation leads to the formation of a "neuronal model" and that orienting on each trial depends on a comparison between sensory input and that predicted by the neuronal model (see also Sokolov & Cacioppo, chapter 1, this volume). Thus, Sokolov's approach emphasized the extrapolatory properties of both the conceptual and real nervous systems. Noncomparator theories (Groves & Thompson, 1970), on the other hand, propose that a decline in response amplitude as a function of stimulus repetition is due to a change in the elements that intervene between stimulus input and response output. The change may be characterized as a hypothetical habituation process or may be described in physiological terms, depending on the type of theory proposed. Response to stimulus change is said to vary inversely as a function of the extent to which the elements stimulated by the habituation training stimulus and the change stimulus overlap; that is, response recovery to change is said to be an example of incomplete generalization of habituation. Dishabituation is explained not by a disruption of the habituation process itself but by a superimposed process of sensitization.

An important analysis in the development of the debate about the advantages and disadvantages of comparator and noncomparator theories of habituation was offered by Graham (1973). Graham's chapter examined critically the effects of a number of variables on habituation and the sensitivity of the orienting response to stimulus change. The results of that critical analysis were then used to examine the adequacy of comparator and noncomparator theories. In addition, Graham (1973) highlighted a number of issues that were considered crucial in theory development.

This chapter takes up three of the issues raised by Graham in 1973 and examines them in the light of evidence that has been accumulated since then. All three issues are of crucial theoretical importance, and their examination provides a perspective on more recent theory development. The three issues to be discussed are the effects of stimulus omission, the role of expectancy in habituation, and the phenomenon of dishabituation. The dependent variables employed in much of the work to be reviewed were skin conductance response magnitude, reaction time to a secondary task probe stimulus, and a continuous measure of stimulus expectancy.

THE EFFECTS OF STIMULUS OMISSION

The development of Sokolov's (1963) model of orienting and habituation was based in large measure on his observations of the sensitivity of orienting, following habituation training, to stimulus change. This phenomenon is known as *response recovery*. As noted by several authors, however, response recovery to many types of change (e.g., tone pitch, stimulus intensity, and stimulus modality) can be accounted for equally well by comparator and noncomparator theories (Gray, 1975; Stephenson & Siddle, 1983). That is, recovery can be attributed either to a discrepancy between stimulation and the neuronal model (Sokolov, 1963) or to incomplete generalization of habituation (Thompson, Berry, Rinaldi, & Berger, 1979). Nevertheless, there is general agreement that a demonstration of orienting to the absence of an event poses problems for noncomparator theories (Gray, 1975; O'Gorman, 1973; Siddle, Stephenson, & Spinks, 1983). As Sokolov (1963) noted, responding to the absence of a stimulus implies that there has been a comparison between anticipated and actual stimulation.

Some data indicate that omission of a regularly presented single stimulus can lead to increased orienting. However, the effects appear to be quite fragile in that only 40% to 45% of subjects display the phenomenon in the electrodermal system (O'Gorman, 1989; Siddle & Heron, 1975). Moreover, there has been little success in delineating the conditions under which the effect occurs most strongly. For example, electrodermal responses to omission are not influenced by stimulus intensity, interstimulus interval, or amount of pre-omission training (Siddle & Heron, 1975). In addition, electrodermal omission responding is no more robust when the habituation stimulus is given signal value, and EEG omission responses (alpha blocking) are not affected by directing subjects' attention to the stimulus either by instruction or by the requirement for a motor response (O'Gorman, 1989).

Recovery to omission of the second of a pair of sequentially presented stimuli, however, appears to be a much more robust effect. The procedure used in this laboratory involves presentation of paired stimuli (S1 and S2) such that the onset of S2 coincides with the offset of S1. S1 and S2 have usually been tone, light, or vibrotactile stimuli of moderate intensity and have been 4 sec in duration so that the measurement of skin conductance responses to each of the events has been possible. A number of experiments (e.g., Siddle, 1985; Siddle, Booth, & Packer, 1987; Siddle & Packer, 1987) have demonstrated that after a number of training trials (usually 15), omission of S2 on Trial 16 produces skin conductance responses that are larger than those that occur in a no-omission control condition. For example, Siddle (1985) presented a control group with 17 tone–light or light–tone pairings. The pattern of stimulation was the same

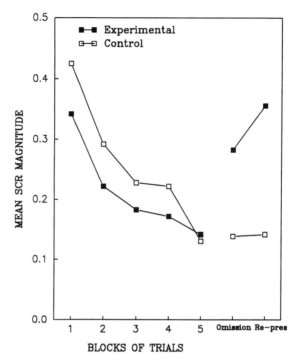

FIG. 2.1. Mean SCR magnitude to S2 across 5 blocks of training trials, to omission of S2, and to S2 re-presentation. From Siddle (1985). Copyright © 1985 by The American Psychological Association. Adapted with permission.

for the experimental group except that S2 was omitted on Trial 16. Figure 2.1 shows that response magnitude to S2 declined across blocks of training trials, but that recovery occurred to the absence of S2 on Trial 16.

An even stronger phenomenon emerges, however, when the effects of omission on responding on the following trial are examined. All our studies of omission effects have included a re-presentation trial that involves a further S1–S2 pairing. The data from the Siddle (1985) experiment (see Fig. 2.1) show that omission of S2 on Trial 16 produced increased responding when S2 was re-presented following S1 on Trial 17, that is, S2 omission produced dishabituation. In addition, some data from this laboratory indicate that S2 omission is just as effective in producing dishabituation as is the replacement of S2 by a novel event (Siddle & Hirschhorn, 1986) or its miscuing by a stimulus it has not previously followed (Siddle, 1985). Finally, the recovery and dishabituation effects produced by S2 omission are attenuated by exposure to S1 prior to pairing (Siddle et al., 1987).

In addition to the psychophysiological effects, stimulus omission results in a reallocation of processing resources as measured by reaction time to a secondary task probe. The rationale for the experimental methodology is that the operation of a limited-capacity processing mechanism can be assessed by monitoring performance on a simultaneously presented secondary task (Kerr, 1973). A deterioration in performance on the secondary task is said to reflect the degree to which the primary task requires processing resources. Following Dawson, Schell, Beers, and Kelly's (1982) demonstration that omission of an unconditioned stimulus resulted in slowed secondary task reaction time, we asked whether S2 omission and its subsequent re-presentation also resulted in a slowing of reaction time.

Our experiments have involved presentation of probe stimuli during some S1 events, some S2 events, and during some of the intertrial intervals. Subjects are instructed to attend to the S1 and S2 events, but to respond as quickly as possible by operating a hand-held microswitch whenever the probe stimulus is presented. Practice at the reaction time task is provided prior to habituation training. Siddle and Packer (1987) presented a control group with 32 S1–S2 pairings. The experimental group also received 32 trials, but S2 was omitted on four of them. Two of the omission trials contained a secondary task probe presented at either 300 or 1,300 ms into the omission interval. Similarly, two of the four re-presentation trials contained a probe at either 300 or 1,300 ms following stimulus onset. The probe was a white noise stimulus of 70 dB and 500 ms duration.

The electrodermal data from unprobed omission and re-presentation trials are shown in Fig. 2.2 (left panel). Responses were larger in the experimental condition than in the control on both omission and re-

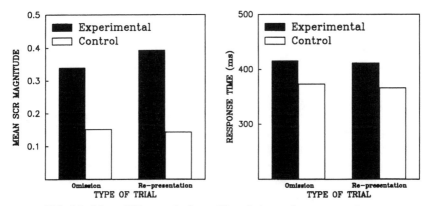

FIG. 2.2. Mean SCR magnitude to S2 omission and re-presentation on unprobed trials in the experimental group and on corresponding trials in the control group (left panel). The right panel shows mean reaction time to secondary task probes presented during S2 omission and S2 re-presentation in the experimental group and on corresponding trials in the control group. From Siddle and Packer (1987). Copyright © 1987 by The Society for Psychophysiological Research. Adapted with permission.

presentation trials. The reaction time data, collapsed across probe position, indicate that reaction time was slower during the omission of S2 and during its re-presentation on the following trial than in the control condition that did not involve omission. Thus, omission of a regularly presented stimulus and re-presentation of that stimulus seem to be events that command processing resources.

The omission-produced dishabituation might be explained in a number of ways. For example, dual-process theory might argue that omission of S2 introduces a longer-than-usual interstimulus interval and that increased responding to S2 on the re-presentation trial is, therefore, an example of spontaneous recovery. This explanation has been ruled out by a control condition that involved a longer-than-usual interval between appropriate S1–S2 trials (Siddle, 1985). A second explanation might be fashioned in terms of sensitization. Thus, it could be argued that S2 omission produces sensitization which, in turn, results in increased responding to S2 on the re-presentation trial. If this were the case, however, increased responding to S1 might also be expected. This has not been found in S2 omission studies.

In summary, we have good evidence that following a number of S1–S2 pairings, omission of S2 results not only in electrodermal orienting responses at the time of omission, but also produces increased responding to S2 when it is re-presented following S1 on the next trial. In addition, there is evidence that, to the extent that performance on a secondary task provides a measure of resource allocation, omission of S2 and its re-presentation are events that command processing resources. An important question to be addressed concerns why an S1–S2 pairing procedure results in more robust omission effects than does omission of a single, regularly presented stimulus. This issue is addressed in the next section, where we consider the processes that might be important in any account of these data.

THE ROLE OF EXPECTANCY

As already noted, Sokolov's (1963) analysis of orienting and habituation emphasized what he called the extrapolatory properties of the nervous system, particularly in connection with an explanation of missing stimulus effects. That is, a comparison was said to occur between incoming stimulation and that predicted in a neuronal model. Graham (1973) also placed considerable store on an expectancy process. Her arguments were based on apparent effects seen in data reported by Furedy (1969) and by Houck and Mefferd (1969) that involved the effects of intermodality change. We examine the effects of intermodality change later in this chapter, but let us first examine how the concept of expectancy might be used to account for the effects of stimulus omission.

One approach (Siddle, 1991) utilizes current theorizing from associative learning (e.g., Wagner, 1978). It can be argued that during S1–S2 pairings, S1 comes to prime a representation of S2 in a short-term memory store. That is, S1 becomes a good predictor of S2. Omission of S2 thus constitutes a surprising event that is elaborately processed. Because the omission of S2 weakens the predictive relationship between S1 and S2, the re-presentation of S2 on the next trial is itself a surprising event that is elaborately processed and that results in augmented orienting.

What evidence is there for such an expectancy process? We have routinely measured subjects' expectation of S2 following S1 by requiring them to operate a pointer mounted on a dial labeled *certain S2 not about to occur* at one extreme, through *uncertain* to *certain S2 about to occur* at the other. Pointer position is measured on one channel of the polygraph with a range of +20 to –20 mm, and expectancy has usually been measured 500 ms prior to S2 onset. Data taken from a study by Siddle et al. (1987) reveal that as S1–S2 trials are repeated, expectancy of S2 in the presence of S1 grows in an orderly fashion (Fig. 2.3, left panel). We also know that exposure to S1 alone prior to S1–S2 pairings retards the development of S2 expectancy in the presence of S1, that is, produces latent inhibition (Siddle et al., 1987). The expectancy analysis of the effects of S2 omission implies that the omission of S2 changes the associative strength between S1 and S2 so that S1 primes S2 less effectively on the re-presentation trial. Data from the same study that illustrate this issue are shown in Fig. 2.3 (right panel) in which S2 expectancy is plotted for both preomission and postomission trials. Clearly, omission of S2 results in a significant decrease

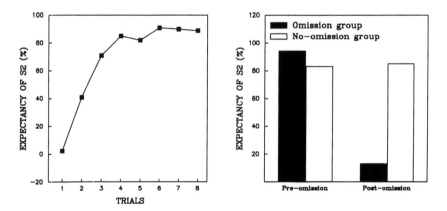

FIG. 2.3. Mean expectancy of S2 in the presence of S1 (left panel) and mean expectancy of S2 in the presence of S1 on preomission and postomission trials in omission and no-omission groups (right panel). From Siddle, Booth, and Packer (1987). Copyright © 1987 by Experimental Psychology Society. Adapted with permission.

in S2 expectancy on the following trial. Thus, the data seem to indicate the importance of an expectancy processes as discussed by Graham (1973).

The notion of expectancy or priming can be used to explain why S2 omission in an S1–S2 pairing procedure produces more robust omission effects than does omission of a regularly presented single stimulus. It is possible that a stimulus must be primed or pre-represented in short-term memory (Öhman, 1979; Wagner, 1978) before its omission can be detected by the information processing system. In the S1–S2 pairing procedure, S1 serves as an explicit retrieval cue for the occurrence of S2. In the case of a single stimulus, on the other hand, it is presumably only the passage of time during the constant interstimulus interval that can serve as a retrieval cue, and it may well be that time is not a particularly effective cue. Evidence for this possibility comes from human temporal conditioning studies where even with a relatively intense unconditioned stimulus, temporal conditioning has been difficult to demonstrate (Harley, 1973). One difficulty with this line of argument is that omission effects should become stronger in the single stimulus procedure when interstimulus interval is reduced. However, Siddle and Heron (1975) were not able to demonstrate this effect using intertrial intervals of 12 and 21 sec.

Notwithstanding these difficulties, there is another set of data derived from experiments on the effects of intermodality change that seems to be consistent with the proposition that changes in expectancy are an important part of the habituation process. As already mentioned, Graham (1973) based her discussion of the role of expectancy on only a small group of findings that seemed to indicate that an intermodality change introduced following habituation training produced larger autonomic responses than did the first trial of the habituation series. A series of studies in our laboratory has verified this effect and explored the phenomenon further. These studies have used simple tone, light, and vibrotactile stimuli, and the intermodality change trial for experimental groups has been preceded by a habituation training series. The nature of the training and test stimuli has been counterbalanced within groups.

The basic effects on skin conductance responses and on secondary task probe reaction time are demonstrated in an experiment reported by Siddle and Jordan (1993). The control group received 25 presentations of the habituation training stimulus, whereas the experimental group received 24 training trials followed by an intermodality change (test) trial. The nature of the training and test stimuli (tone and vibrotactile) was counterbalanced within group. The secondary task probe was a visual stimulus that was presented during some of the habituation trials, some of the intertrial intervals, and on Trial 25. Within-stimulus probes occurred 300 ms after stimulus onset. Mean electrodermal response magnitude on Trial 1 of the habituation series and on the test trial are shown in Fig. 2.4 (left

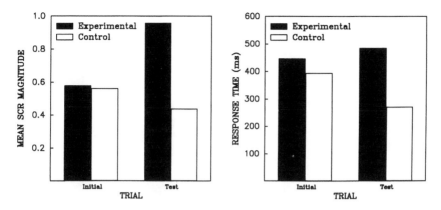

FIG. 2.4. Mean SCR magnitude (left panel) and mean probe response time (right panel) from the first habituation trial and the intermodality change trial in experimental group and from corresponding trials in the control group. From Siddle and Jordan (1993). Copyright © 1993 by The Society for Psychophysiological Research. Adapted with permission.

panel). Not only was response magnitude larger in the experimental group than in the control, but responding in the experimental group was larger on the test trial than on the first trial of habituation training. In parallel with the electrodermal findings, intermodality change also produced a slowing of reaction time to probe stimuli presented 300 ms after stimulus onset (Fig. 2.4, right panel). Moreover, reaction time on the test trial was slower in the experimental than in the control group. However, it was not slower in the experimental group during the test trial than during the first trial of the habituation series.

Although the finding that skin conductance responses were larger on the test trial than on the first trial of the habituation series seems to be of particular theoretical importance, the results were obtained only under conditions in which subjects performed a secondary motor task. Thus, a second experiment crossed the change/no-change manipulation with a secondary task/no-task manipulation. Again, auditory and vibrotactile stimuli were used as habituation and test stimuli and a visual stimulus was used as the probe. The electrodermal results for the task (left panel) and no-task (right panel) conditions are shown in Fig. 2.5. Clearly, test trial responses were larger in the experimental than in the control group, and larger on the test trial than on the first trial of the habituation series. These findings held for both task and no-task conditions.

The reaction time data from the task condition are shown in Fig. 2.6. Reaction time was slower in the experimental than in the control group on the test trial, and within the experimental group, reaction time was slower on the test trial than on the first trial of the habituation series.

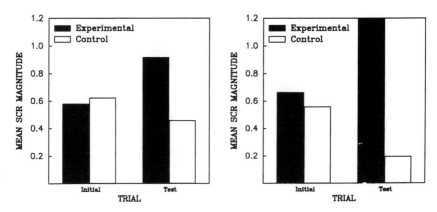

FIG. 2.5. Mean SCR magnitude on the first habituation trial and on the intermodality change trial for experimental and control groups in secondary task (left panel) and no secondary task conditions. From Siddle and Jordan (1993). Copyright © 1993 by The Society for Psychophysiological Research. Adapted with permission.

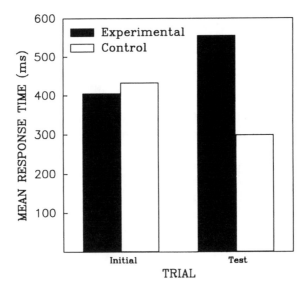

FIG. 2.6. Mean response time from the first habituation trial and from the test trial in the secondary task condition. From Siddle and Jordan (1993). Copyright © 1993 by The Society for Psychophysiological Research. Adapted with permission.

Subsequent research has shown that the effects of an intermodality change can be attenuated by a reduction in the amount of prechange habituation training (Siddle, Lipp, & Dall, 1996) and by exposure, prior to habituation training, to either the test stimulus or to a stimulus change that involves an experimentally irrelevant stimulus (Siddle, Lipp, & Dall, 1994). An approach that ascribes a key role to an expectancy process predicts that the effects of intermodality change will be larger after a relatively large number of training trials than after relatively few. Figure 2.7 shows data from a study in which one condition involved an intermodality change whereas another did not. Within each of these groups, some subjects received 6 training trials prior to change whereas the others received 24. It is clear that within the change condition, responses were larger on the test trial than on the first training trial in the 24-trial condition, but not in the 6-trial condition. The results are consistent with the supposition that expectancy of stimulus input increases as a function of the amount of training.

Taken together, the results seem to be consistent with the view that an expectancy process develops during the course of habituation training,

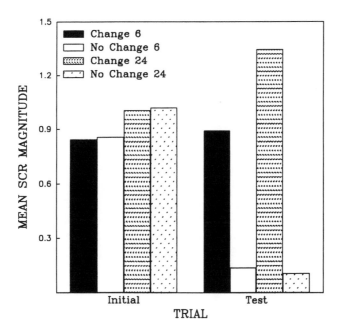

FIG. 2.7. Mean SCR magnitude elicited on the first trial of the habituation series and on the intermodality change trial in experimental groups and on corresponding trials in a no-change control group. From Siddle, Lipp, and Dall (1996). Copyright © 1996 by Elsevier Science B.V. Adapted with permission.

and that violation of the expectancy produces autonomic orienting and a reallocation of processing resources. The data appear to pose problems for noncomparator theories of habituation that predict, at best, that responding on an intermodality change trial will be as large as on the first trial of a habituation series. One curious feature of the data, however, concerns the effects of intermodality change on dishabituation—that is, on responding to the habituation training stimulus on the trial following change. This issue is considered in the next section.

THE PHENOMENON OF DISHABITUATION

The term *dishabituation* is used here to describe an empirical phenomenon and not as a theoretical term. Nevertheless, comparator and noncomparator theories differ sharply in the manner in which they account for dishabituation. Comparator theories of habituation hold that the phenomenon reflects a disruption of the underlying habituation process—literally dishabituation. Noncomparator theories, on the other hand, propose that dishabituation results from a separate, superimposed process of sensitization (Groves & Thompson, 1970). According to comparator theories, any change that results in recovery of orienting after habituation training should also lead to dishabituation. In her 1973 chapter, Graham discussed the then available evidence and concluded tentatively that a number of change manipulations produced dishabituation. Data acquired since then, however, have not always supported Graham's (1973) conclusion.

Relevant data were reviewed by Siddle, Stephenson, and Spinks (1983), who noted some instances of dishabituation. For example, it is clear that dishabituation can be produced by the interpolation into a habituation series of an intense stimulus (Groves & Thompson, 1970), and there is evidence that under some conditions, interpolation of a less intense stimulus results in dishabituation (Magliero, Gatchel, & Lojewski, 1981; Rust, 1976). However, a number of studies have not been able to demonstrate dishabituation (see Siddle et al., 1983), and even intermodality change seems to be relatively ineffective.

Consider for example, the results from one of our intermodality change experiments in which the training stimulus was re-presented following the intermodality change trial. The change trial occurred after 24 habituation training trials. Figure 2.8 shows magnitude of the skin conductance response on the first and last habituation training trials, on the intermodality change trial, and on the re-presentation trial. Although responding on the re-presentation trial was larger in the experimental group than in the control, the difference was not statistically reliable; that is, there was no dishabituation effect.

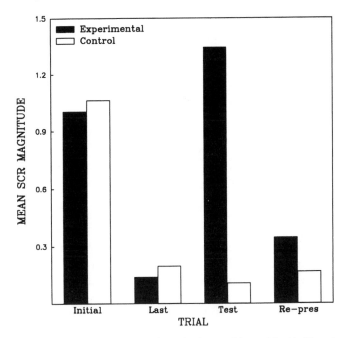

FIG. 2.8. Mean SCR magnitude from the first and last trial of habituation training, the intermodality change trial, and the re-presentation trial in the experimental group and from corresponding trials in a no-change control group.

Dishabituation appears to represent a difficulty for both the comparator and noncomparator theories that have been proposed. It seems to be produced most strongly by two manipulations—presentation of a relatively strong stimulus or omission of an expected event. Dishabituation produced by the interpolation of an intense stimulus can, in principle, be explained in terms of a comparator system and an extrapolatory process. In view of the fact that intense stimuli produce sensitization, however, the phenomenon also lends itself to an account in terms of dual-process theory. Omission-produced dishabituation on the other hand, seems more conducive, for reasons we have already outlined, to a comparator account.

Several factors should be considered when the pattern of dishabituation results is examined. First, theories of orienting and habituation are curiously silent on the question of the time course of the processes that are said to underlie the phenomena. For example, comparator theories assume that the neuronal model or the events represented in a short-term memory store are altered by presentation of a change stimulus. However, the theories do not specify the duration for which the model will be altered for particular kinds of stimulus change. Such information may be important in understanding not only the conditions under which dishabituation occurs, but also the processes said to underlie it. If it is assumed that the modification in a neuronal model that is brought about by a change stimulus displays a decay function, it might reasonably be predicted that dishabituation will be more likely to occur when interstimulus intervals are relatively short than when they are relatively long. It is interesting to note that in many of the studies that have not obtained dishabituation, the original training stimulus has been presented following some kind of stimulus change, but maintaining the same interstimulus interval that was used throughout the experiment. In contrast, at least some of the studies that have reported reliable dishabituation (see Groves & Thompson, 1970) interpolated a novel or intense stimulus into the interstimulus interval between Trial n and Trial $n + 1$ and measured dishabituation on Trial $n + 1$. That is, the interpolated event embodied not only stimulus change, but also a change in interstimulus interval.

A second important factor in comparing the dishabituation produced by stimulus omission and by modality change is that the data are derived from fundamentally different procedures. The robust omission-produced dishabituation has been demonstrated in situations in which paired presentations of events have been used. We have already seen that omission effects themselves are stronger with paired than with single events, and it seems reasonable to assume that temporal cuing is stronger in the former than in the latter. Thus, a thorough evaluation of dishabituation and its implications for comparator theories requires an examination of the phenomenon with a paired stimulus procedure.[1] Specifically, does a change in S2 modality in an S1–S2 procedure produce dishabituation? One of the conditions employed by Siddle and Hirschhorn (1986) involved the replacement of S2 by a novel event, S4, which for some subjects was from a modality different from that of S2. This condition resulted in stimulus-specific dishabituation to S2 on the re-presentation trial. Thus, the data suggest that intermodality change with an S1–S2 procedure may well result in dishabituation, although it is clear that more systematic work is required.

CONCLUSION

This chapter has reviewed a considerable body of research that is relevant to three issues that are important in the development of theories of orienting and habituation: the effects of stimulus omission, the role of expectancy, and the robustness of the dishabituation phenomenon. The

---

[1]We are indebted to Francis K. Graham for valuable suggestions and discussion on this point.

importance of these issues was noted by Graham in 1973, and none of the theoretical or empirical developments during the past 20 years have diminished that importance.

The centrality of omission effects in distinguishing between comparator and noncomparator theories is widely acknowledged, and there is now good evidence that with a paired stimulus procedure at least, omission of the second element not only produces recovery of responding at the time of omission, but also produces quite robust dishabituation. Similarly, the importance placed by Graham (1973) on the effects of intermodality change has been justified by subsequent data that indicate clearly that the magnitude of electrodermal responses elicited by intermodality change can, under appropriate conditions, exceed the magnitude of responses elicited on the first trial of habituation training. These data can be interpreted to indicate the importance of an expectancy process in the development of habituation. There is a pleasing symmetry in the use of an expectancy construct to explain not only omission effects, but also the effects of intermodality change.

One difficulty, however, concerns interpretation of the omission effects produced in the paired stimulus procedure. Our interpretation assumes that S1 and S2 are encoded as discrete events and that subjects learn that S1 predicts S2. Mackintosh (1987), on the other hand, proposed a configural account of the data in which it is argued that because the traces of S1 have always been accompanied (and perhaps modified) by S2, their occurrence alone may constitute a novel stimulus that would be expected to elicit a response. Put simply, S1 alone after a number of S1–S2 pairings is a different stimulus from S1 when it is presented prior to S2. This kind of explanation does not require a comparator type of theory. In reply, it can be argued that if S1 and S2 are encoded as a unique configuration, omission of S2 should lead to dishabituation of responses to S1. This has not usually been found, and the stimulus specificity of the dishabituation observed with the paired stimulus procedure is more consistent with the view that S1 and S2 are encoded as discrete events.

We have argued that extant data on the phenomenon of dishabituation pose problems for both comparator and noncomparator theories. Dishabituation produced by stimulus omission poses difficulties for noncomparator theories, whereas the failure to observe dishabituation following an intermodality change manipulation is an embarrassment for comparator theories. However, the effects of modality change on dishabituation have not been studied with the paired stimulus procedure that has been used to demonstrate omission-produced dishabituation, and this is required before firm conclusions can be reached. Moreover, the time course of the processes assumed by comparator theories to underlie dishabituation needs to be specified, and one approach is to examine the effects of interstimulus interval on the dishabituation produced by a variety of change manipulations.

Finally, our concern here has been to consider the merits of comparator and noncomparator theories in the light of evidence adduced to address three issues of importance that were emphasized by Graham (1973). Although use has been made of Wagner's (1978) emphasis on the importance of memorial processing in habituation, it is clear that some of Wagner's theory is not supported by data. These particular issues have been discussed elsewhere (Mackintosh, 1987; Siddle, 1991; Siddle, Bond, & Packer, 1988) and do not bear reiteration. However, it is clear that the context specificity of habituation that is demanded by Wagner's account has not been demonstrated. One of the strengths of the theory is its purported ability to distinguish between short- and long-term habituation at the level of process. If contextual mediation of long-term habituation cannot be demonstrated, one of the major parts of the theory must be discarded. On the other hand, rejection of even large parts of priming theory does not mean that some key constructs cannot be useful or that a comparator approach to habituation must be discarded. The effects of stimulus omission and the data on the role of expectancy are consistent in pointing to the need for a comparator theory of orienting and habituation. Further examination of this approach will benefit from a more thorough study of dishabituation and the processes that underlie it.

ACKNOWLEDGMENT

The research reported in this chapter was supported by Grant A79030226 from the Australian Research Council.

REFERENCES

Bernstein, A. S. (1992). The orienting response as an index of attentional dysfunction in schizophrenia. In B. A. Campbell, H. Hayne, & R. Richardson (Eds.), *Attention and information processing in infants and adults: Perspectives from human and animal research* (pp. 297–323). Hillsdale, NJ: Lawrence Erlbaum Associates.

Carew, T. J. (1984). An introduction to cellular processes used in the analysis of habituation and sensitization in aplysia. In H. V. S. Peeke & L. Petrinovich (Eds.), *Habituation, sensitization, and behavior* (pp. 205–249). New York: Academic Press.

Dawson, M. E., Nuechterlein, K. H., Schell, A. M., Gitlin, M., & Ventura, J. (1994). Autonomic abnormalities in schizophrenia. *Archives of General Psychiatry, 51*, 813–824.

Dawson, M. E., Schell, A. M., Beers, J. R., & Kelly, A. (1982). Allocation of cognitive processing capacity during human autonomic classical conditioning. *Journal of Experimental Psychology: General, 11*, 273–295.

Furedy, J. J. (1969). Electrodermal and plethysmographic OR components: Repetition of and change from UCS-CS trials with surrogate UCS. *Canadian Journal of Psychology, 23,* 127–135.

Graham, F. K. (1973). Habituation and dishabituation of responses innervated by the autonomic nervous system. In H. V. S. Peeke & M. J. Herz (Eds.), *Habituation: Vol. 1. Behavioral studies* (pp. 163–218). New York: Academic Press.

Graham, F. K., Anthony, B. J., & Zeigler, B. L. (1983). The orienting response and developmental processes. In D. Siddle (Ed.), *Orienting and habituation: Perspectives in human research* (pp. 371–430). Chichester, UK: Wiley.

Graham, F. K., & Hackley, S. A. (1991). Passive and active attention to input. In J. R. Jennings & M. G. H. Coles (Eds.), *Psychophysiology of human information processing: An integration of central and autonomic nervous system approaches* (pp. 251–356). New York: Wiley.

Gray, J. A. (1975). *Elements of a two-process theory of learning.* London: Academic Press.

Groves, P. M., & Thompson, R. F. (1970). Habituation: A dual-process theory. *Psychological Review, 77,* 419–450.

Harley, J. P. (1973). Temporal conditioning as a function of instructions and intertrial interval. *Journal of Experimental Psychology, 100,* 178–184.

Houck, R. L., & Mefferd, R. B., Jr. (1969). Generalization of GSR habituation to mild intramodal stimuli. *Psychophysiology, 6,* 202–206.

Kerr, B. (1973). Processing demands during mental operations. *Memory and Cognition, 1,* 401–412.

Mackintosh, N. J. (1987). Neurobiology, psychology and habituation. *Behaviour Research and Therapy, 25,* 81–97.

Magliero, A., Gatchel, R. J., & Lojewski, D. (1981). Skin conductance responses to stimulus "energy" decreases following habituation. *Psychophysiology, 18,* 549–558.

O'Gorman, J. G. (1973). Change in stimulus conditions and the orienting response. *Psychophysiology, 10,* 465–470.

O'Gorman, J. G. (1977). Individual differences in habituation of human physiological responses: A review of theory, method, and findings in the study of personality correlates in nonclinical populations. *Biological Psychology, 5,* 257–318.

O'Gorman, J. G. (1989). Much ado about nothing: Attempts to demonstrate the orienting response to complete omission of a stimulus. In N. W. Bond & D. A. T. Siddle (Eds.), *Psychology: Issues and applications* (pp. 163–173). Amsterdam: Elsevier.

Öhman, A. (1979). The orienting response, attention, and learning: An information-processing perspective. In H. D. Kimmel, E. H. van Olst, & J. F. Orlebeke (Eds.), *The orienting reflex in humans* (pp. 443–471). Hillsdale, NJ: Lawrence Erlbaum Associates.

Öhman, A. (1992). Orienting and attention: Preferred preattentive processing of potentially phobic stimuli. In B. A. Campbell, H. Hayne, & R. Richardson (Eds.), *Attention and information processing in infants and adults: Perspectives from human and animal research* (pp. 263–295). Hillsdale, NJ: Lawrence Erlbaum Associates.

Pavlov, I. P. (1927). *Conditioned reflexes.* Oxford, UK: Oxford University Press.

Pearce, J. M., & Hall, G. (1980). A model of Pavlovian learning: Variations in the effectiveness of conditioned but not of unconditioned stimuli. *Psychological Review, 87,* 532–552.

Pearce, J. M., & Hall, G. (1992). Stimulus significance, conditionability, and the orienting response in rats. In B. A. Campbell, H. Hayne, & R. Richardson (Eds.), *Attention and information processing in infants and adults: Perspectives from human and animal research* (pp. 137–160). Hillsdale, NJ: Lawrence Erlbaum Associates.

Rust, J. (1976). Generalization and dishabituation of the orienting response to a stimulus of lower intensity. *Physiological Psychology, 4,* 99–101.

Siddle, D. A. T. (1985). Effects of stimulus omission and stimulus change on dishabituation of the skin conductance response. *Journal of Experimental Psychology: Learning, Memory, and Cognition, 11,* 206–216.

Siddle, D. A. T. (1991). Orienting, habituation, and resource allocation: An associative analysis. *Psychophysiology, 28,* 245–259.

Siddle, D. A. T., Bond, N. W., & Packer, J. S. (1988). Comparator theories of habituation: A comment on Mackintosh's analysis. *Biological Psychology, 27,* 59–63.

Siddle, D. A. T., Booth, M. L., & Packer, J. S. (1987). Effects of stimulus preexposure on omission responding and omission-produced dishabituation of the human electrodermal response. *Quarterly Journal of Experimental Psychology, 39B,* 339–363.

Siddle, D. A. T., & Heron, P. A. (1975). Stimulus omission and recovery of the electrodermal and digital vasoconstrictive components of the orienting response. *Biological Psychology, 3,* 277–293.

Siddle, D. A. T., & Hirschhorn, T. (1986). Effects of stimulus omission and stimulus novelty on dishabituation of the skin conductance response. *Psychophysiology, 23,* 309–314.

Siddle, D. A. T., & Jordan, J. (1993). Effects of intermodality change on electrodermal orienting and on the allocation of processing resources. *Psychophysiology, 30,* 429–435.

Siddle, D. A. T., Lipp, O. V., & Dall, P. J. (1994). Effects of stimulus preexposure and intermodality change on electrodermal orienting. *Psychophysiology, 31,* 421–426.

Siddle, D. A. T., Lipp, O. V., & Dall, P. J. (1996). Effects of intermodality change and number of training trials on electrodermal orienting and on the allocation of processing resources. *Biological Psychology, 43,* 57–67.

Siddle, D. A. T., & Packer, J. S. (1987). Stimulus omission and dishabituation of the electrodermal orienting response: The allocation of processing resources. *Psychophysiology, 24,* 181–190.

Siddle, D. A. T., & Spinks, J. A. (1992). Orienting, habituation, and the allocation of processing resources. In B. A. Campbell, H. Hayne, & R. Richardson (Eds.), *Attention and information processing in infants and adults: Perspectives from human and animal research* (pp. 227–262). Hillsdale, NJ: Lawrence Erlbaum Associates.

Siddle, D. A. T., Stephenson, D., & Spinks, J. A. (1983). Elicitation and habituation of the orienting response. In D. Siddle (Ed.), *Orienting and habituation: Perspectives in human research* (pp. 109–182). Chichester, UK: Wiley.

Sokolov, E. N. (1960). Neuronal models and the orienting reflex. In M. A. B. Brazier (Ed.), *The central nervous system and behavior* (pp. 187–276). New York: Josiah Macy, Jr. Foundation.

Sokolov, E. N. (1963). *Perception and the conditioned reflex.* Oxford, UK: Pergamon.

Stephenson, D., & Siddle, D. (1983). Theories of habituation. In D. Siddle (Ed.), *Orienting and habituation: Perspectives in human research* (pp. 183–236). Chichester, UK: Wiley.

Thompson, R. F., Berry, S. D., Rinaldi, P. C., & Berger, T. W. (1979). Habituation and the orienting reflex: The dual-process theory revisited. In H. D. Kimmel, E. H. van Olst, & J. F. Orlebeke (Eds.), *The orienting reflex in humans* (pp. 21–60). Hillsdale, NJ: Lawrence Erlbaum Associates.

Wagner, A. R. (1978). Expectancies and the priming of STM. In S. H. Hulse, H. Fowler, & W. K. Honig (Eds.), *Cognitive processes in animal behavior* (pp. 177–209). Hillsdale, NJ: Lawrence Erlbaum Associates.

II

Biological and Evolutionary Foundations of Orienting, Startle, and Defense: Motivational and Emotional Factors That Modulate Attention

Origins of Orienting and Defensive Responses: An Evolutionary Perspective

Byron A. Campbell
Gwendolyn Wood
Thomas McBride
Princeton University

How did the autonomic nervous system evolve into the role it now plays in human emotions, attention, and information processing? When and in what form did the autonomic nervous system begin to play a role in orienting and defensive behaviors? These are important but unanswered questions in contemporary psychophysiology. From an evolutionary point of view, it seems likely that these responses emerged within the context of predation and predator avoidance, and that their occurrence increased the probabilities of survival and eventual reproductive success. Early in evolution the "what is it?" response observed by Pavlov (1927) was almost certainly not an expression of idle curiosity. Instead, the question must have been: "Is it danger?" or "Is it food?" Autonomic orienting responses to neutral stimuli, to the extent that they represent a separate entity, probably emerged later in evolution than autonomic responses to life-threatening or life-sustaining stimuli.

Comparative physiologists have long been fascinated with the evolution of the autonomic nervous system, and a great deal is now known about its structure and function in primitive cephalopods, fish, amphibians, reptiles, birds, and mammals (Burnstock, 1969; Evans, 1993; Nilsson, 1983; Nilsson & Holmgren, 1993b). In contrast to the extensive fossil record detailing the evolutionary ancestry of the physical characteristics of contemporary living organisms, there is little in the way of fossil evidence documenting the evolution of the autonomic nervous system. Soft tissues are rarely subject to fossilization, and the skulls and vertebral columns that are available reveal little about the evolution of the autonomic nervous system. Because of this, our understanding of the evolutionary origins of the autonomic nervous system is based almost exclusively on research on representative living species from different vertebrate classes. Fortunately, fossil records suggest that a number of existing species are remarkably unchanged anatomically from their ancient ancestral forms. The reader should be warned, however, that the research efforts by comparative physiologists have focused on only a minute fraction of existing species. Moreover, detailed knowledge of autonomic nerve function is based on a limited number of mammals, often chosen for their accessibility and ease of use, rather than their uniqueness of autonomic function. Research on nonmammalian vertebrates is even more limited, and there are many obvious gaps in species comparisons.

Much can be learned, nonetheless, about the evolutionary origins of contemporary traits through comparative analysis. Looking at the behavior and morphology of existing animals, this chapter considers several issues important to the evolutionary origins of orienting and defense. The initial section briefly reviews the evolution of the autonomic nervous system in an attempt to infer when it first became capable of responding to sensory stimuli. Next is a comparison of the autonomic reactions of two reptilian species and the laboratory rat to a range of environmental stimuli intended to elicit orienting and defensive responses. This is followed by a discussion of fear bradycardia, its possible evolutionary antecedents, and its autonomic origins. Next is a discussion of the possible interrelationship between fear bradycardia and orienting response bradycardia, and the final section attempts to distinguish between the two phenomena.

EVOLUTION OF THE AUTONOMIC NERVOUS SYSTEM

To fully appreciate the evolution of the autonomic nervous system, it is helpful to have available a schematic representation of vertebrate evolution. Figure 3.1 portrays the evolution of the major vertebrate groupings with particular emphasis on those that are relevant to evolution of the autonomic nervous system. The figure is taken from Nilsson's *Autonomic Nerve Function in Vertebrates* (1983). It is important to note that the evolutionary trajectory from the nonvertebrate cephalochordates does not progress linearly through the various classes of fish, amphibians, and reptiles to mammals. For example, the most highly evolved fish, the teleosts, are members of the Actinopterygii, a subclass of Osteichthyes in an evolutionary path that does not lead to amphibians. Amphibians, reptiles, and mammals evolved from a different subclass, the Sarcopterygii.

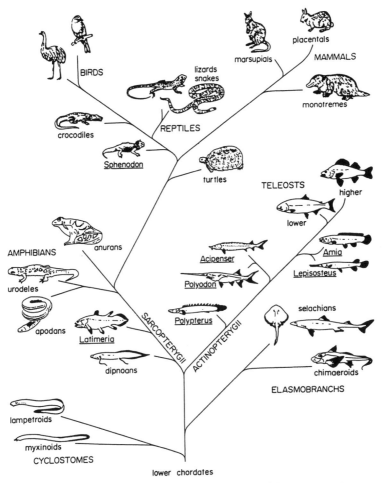

FIG. 3.1.   Summary of the relationships among some of the major vertebrate groups: cyclostomes, elasmobranchs, dipnoans, teleosts, amphibians, reptiles, birds, and mammals. Also included are some of the interesting smaller vertebrate groups. From Nilsson (1983). Copyright © 1983 by Springer Verlag. Reprinted with permission.

Figure 3.2 is presented as a complement to Fig. 3.1 to summarize the major steps in the evolution of autonomic control of the heart. This simplified representation was adapted from a number of different sources including Nilsson and Holmgren (1993b), Morris and Nilsson (1994), and Burnstock (1969) to facilitate discussion of the major differences in autonomic innervation of the heart that occur in living vertebrate species ranging from primitive cyclostome fishes to modern mammals. It shows that there is no extrinsic neural control of the heart in myxinoid fish, the

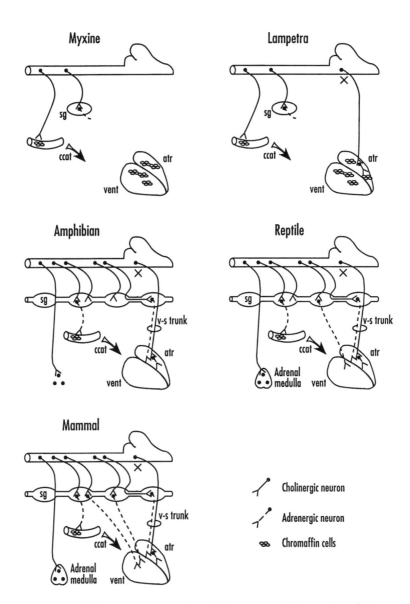

FIG. 3.2. Schematic representation of the patterns of innervation of the heart of two cyclostome subclasses (*Myxine* and *Lampetra*), amphibians, reptiles, and mammals. The abbreviations are as follows: sg, sympathetic ganglia; ccat, circulating catecholamines; atr, atrium; vent, ventricle; v-s trunk, vago-sympathetic trunk.

first subclass of cyclostomes to evolve. There are, however, substantial quantities of catecholamines (adrenalin and noradrenaline) in specialized chromaffin-like cells located both in the circulatory system and on the walls of the heart. Neural control of the heart is first seen in the cyclostome subclass, lampetra, via cholinergic fibers in the vagus that terminate on postganglionic cells located in a pacemaker region, but the innervation is nicotinic and excitatory rather than muscarinic and inhibitory as it is in all other vertebrates (Falck, Mecklenburg, Myhrberg, & Persson, 1966; Lukomskaya & Michelson, 1972). In dipnoans (not shown in Fig. 3.2), the oldest living form of Sarcopterygii, both vagal and direct cholinergic stimulation of the heart produce decreases in heart rate (Nilsson & Holmgren, 1993a). Sympathetic neural control of the heart is absent in dipnoans as in the cyclostomes, but there is a large store of catecholamines in the myocardium.

The amphibian heart is innervated by vagal parasympathetic fibers and by fibers from sympathetic ganglia that join the vagi near the head to form a vago-sympathetic trunk. The parasympathetic fibers terminate primarily in a pacemaker region associated with the atrium. Some sympathetic fibers terminate in the pacemaker region, but their terminals are much more widely dispersed throughout both the atrial and ventricular myocardium. The cholinergic vagal fibers are negatively chronotropic and the sympathetic fibers are positively chronotropic. Innervation of the reptilian heart is remarkably similar to that of the amphibians, except that some sympathetic fibers run directly from spinal ganglia to the heart. The general pattern of innervation of the mammalian heart is remarkably similar to that of the reptilian heart. The vagal cholinergic fibers terminate primarily in the sino-atrial (pacemaker) region, and the postganglionic cholinergic fibers are restricted primarily to the atrium. More sympathetic fibers reach the heart through direct accelerator nerves from an increasing number of sympathetic ganglion cites, and the sympathetic fibers terminate in locations throughout both the ventricle and atrium including the sinoatrial node. Again, parasympathetic stimulation is negatively chronotropic and sympathetic stimulation of the heart positively chronotropic.

Another component of the sympathetic nervous system, the adrenal glands, consisting of a cortex and a distinct medullary region containing chromaffin cells, is present only in reptiles, birds, and mammals. Amphibians have high concentrations of chromaffin cells on the kidney, but there is no adrenal cortex or medulla. Both the adrenal medullary cells and the dispersed chromaffin cells on the amphibian kidney are innervated by preganglionic fibers originating in spinal sympathetic ganglia.

To recapitulate, neural control of the heart appears to have evolved sequentially, with parasympathetic innervation of the heart emerging considerably earlier than sympathetic innervation. Even lampreys, one of the most primitive families of fish still living, have cholinergic preganglionic neurons located in the central nervous system (CNS) with vagal axons leading to postganglionic cholinergic neurons located on the heart. In contrast, centrally controlled, sympathetic postganglionic cells with efferent processes terminating on the heart are first seen in amphibian species, millions of years later in evolutionary time.

Evolution of Vagal Preganglionic Neural Control of the Heart

Given the surprising similarities between autonomic innervation of the heart in amphibians, reptiles, and mammals, and the enormous differences in behavioral capacities and flexibilities among those vertebrate classes, it is possible that there may be pronounced differences in central neural control of the heart. Because the focus of this chapter is primarily on vagally mediated bradycardias in response to neutral and threatening (fearful) stimuli, this review focuses exclusively on the evolution of vagal preganglionic neurons.

In all vertebrates, except the primitive myxinoid fish in which the heart is not innervated, two separate groups of vagal preganglionic neurons are found in adjacent clusters in the brainstem. Even in the lamprey, separate rostral and caudal preganglionic vagal nuclei have been identified (Niewenhuys, 1972). In the later evolving dogfish, a cartilaginous elasmobranch fish, the estimates are that roughly 90% of the vagal motoneurons are located in a brainstem nucleus homologous to the dorsal motor nucleus of the vagus (DMNX), and that the remaining vagal motoneurons are located in a small cluster ventral and lateral to the DMNX, presumably an analogue of the nucleus ambiguus (NA; Taylor, 1992). The relative sizes of these two nuclei, however, do not necessarily reflect the proportion of neurons innervating the heart. Taylor (1994) estimated that the neurons in the ventral lateral nucleus supply about 45% of the efferent axons running to the cardiac branch of the vagus.

In the amphibian Xenopus laevis, two relatively distinct cell groups representing the DMNX and NA have been identified (Nikundlwe & Niewenhuys, 1983; Taylor, 1994) with the DMNX being considerably larger. According to Taylor (1994), the proportion of vagal neurons innervating the heart in Xenopus laevis from those two structures (DMNX and NA) is approximately 2 to 1, respectively. However, there have been very few studies comparing the DMNX and NA in different amphibians, and the generality of this pattern of neural innervation is far from established.

The picture in reptiles is similar. Neuronal groupings that reflect the DMNX and NA have been described in turtles, tortoises, lizards, and crocodiles. In the terrapin (Trionynx sinensis) between 36% and 50% of the vagal motor neurons are estimated to lie in the nucleus ambiguus (Leong, Tay, & Wong, 1984), but in the agamid lizard, *Uromastyx microlepis* (a species that emerged considerably later in evolution) only 20% of the vagal motoneurons lie outside the DMNX (Taylor, 1994). Strangely, in pigeons, a representative avian species in a vertebrate class that is typically viewed as having evolved directly from reptiles, vagal innervation of the heart arises entirely from the DMNX (Schwaber & Cohen, 1978a, 1978b).

In mammals, as in reptiles, there is a great deal of variability between species in terms of the percentage of vagal preganglionic neurons located in the DMNX and NA, respectively. Taylor (1994), in reviewing the mammalian literature, found estimates of the percentage of vagal preganglionic neurons occurring in the NA that ranged from about a third in minks and ferrets to a majority in the pig (Ranson, Butler, & Taylor, 1993). In the cat, a more widely studied species, Taylor (1994) estimated that 78% of the cardiac and 68% of the pulmonary vagal neurons originate in the nucleus ambiguus (Bennett, Kidd, Latif, & MacWilliam, 1981; Jordan, Spyer, Withington-Wray, & Wood, 1985). This compares with 45% of cardiac vagal neurons located ventrolaterally in the dogfish (an elasmobranch) and about 30% in *Xenopus laevis*. This variability in the relative size of the DMNX and NA within and between vertebrate classes suggests that species-specific environmental challenges were more influential than their order of appearance during the course of evolution in determining the central origins of cardiac innervation.

Evolution of Cardiac Vagal Tone

The heart in most vertebrates typically operates under a degree of continuous, vagally mediated parasympathetic inhibition, a state commonly referred to as *vagal tone*. Changes in cardiac vagal tone are utilized by almost all vertebrate species to compensate for changes in environmental factors such as temperature and oxygen availability. High levels of vagal tone, for example, are responsible for the extremely low heart rates of antarctic fish (Axelsson, Davison, Forster, & Farrell, 1992). Further, the presence of vagal tone has been documented in two of the most primitive groups of fish, the elasmobranchs and dipnoans (Nilsson & Holmgren, 1993a; Taylor, 1994).

Cardiac vagal tone also varies widely in amphibians and reptiles, and it is similarly influenced by ambient air or water temperature. Taylor (1994) recently reported that atropine increased heart rate from 6 to 12 BPM at 5°C and from 12 to 70 BPM at 25°C in an amphibian (*Xenopus laevus*). Propranolol reduced the increase somewhat, particularly at higher temperatures, indicating the presence of coexisting sympathetic tone.

Similarly, administration of atropine increased the heart rate of a snake, the puff adder (*Bitis arietans*), from 44 to 56 BPM, and propranolol reduced heart rate from 44 to 21 BPM. To recapitulate, vagal tone, a reflection of systematic variations in the degree of tonic parasympathetic stimulation of the pacemaker region of the heart, appears to have emerged very early in vertebrate evolution and to play a crucial role in regulating oxygenation and nutrient distribution throughout the organism. The early emergence of vagal responsivity to environmental challenges suggests that it may also have been capable of responding to other challenges, such as predation and predator avoidance.

EVOLUTIONARY ORIGINS OF AUTONOMIC
RESPONSES TO NEUTRAL STIMULI

From this review of the evolution of neural control of the heart, it should be clear that all living vertebrates except for one primitive class of fish, the cyclostomes, are capable of vagally mediated bradycardia via cholinergic stimulation of the heart. From a psychophysiologist's point of view it would be exciting to discover that enhanced attention and information-processing capabilities, resulting from centrally induced bradycardia, accompanied the early evolution of vagal control of the heart.

In mammals the cardiac component of the orienting response, bradycardia, can be elicited by an extremely broad range of novel sensory stimuli. Dimly flashing lights, weak pulsating tones, and unfamiliar odors all elicit substantial decreases in heart rate that habituate rapidly with repeated stimulation. For example, auditory stimuli of low to moderate intensity of all types—from pure tones to pulsating white noise—typically produce substantial decreases in heart rate in human infants and adults (e.g., Graham, Anthony, & Ziegler, 1983), infant and adult rats (Hayne, Richardson, & Campbell, 1992; Siegel, Sananes, Gaddy, & Campbell, 1987), rabbits (Kapp, Frysinger, Gallagher, & Haselton, 1979), and many other mammals. The magnitude and duration of these decreases varies as a function of stimulus properties such as duration, complexity, and intensity (Graham, 1979; Hayne et. al., 1992). Similar cardiac responses are elicited by visual stimuli (Haroutunian & Campbell, 1981; Siegel et al., 1987), and olfactory stimuli (Hayne, Richardson, & Campbell, 1991). All of these stimulus-induced bradycardias exhibit rapid habituation. In both rats and humans, for example, the cardiac response to most novel stimuli typically habituates within 5 to 15 trials depending on stimulus characteristics such as intensity, complexity, duration, and frequency of stimulus presentation (e.g., Graham, 1973; Haroutunian & Campbell, 1981).

Moreover, these stimulus-induced deceleratory responses are produced almost exclusively by vagal inhibition of the heart. Both vagotomy and cholinergic receptor blockade eliminate the cardiac component of the orienting response without affecting the behavioral orienting responses to those stimuli (e.g., Haroutunian & Campbell, 1981). Although the adaptive value of these vagally driven bradycardias is not fully established, one possibility is that the resulting redistribution of blood flow accompanying activation of the parasympathetic nervous system may facilitate central processing of incoming sensory information (e.g., Graham & Clifton, 1966; Lacey & Lacey, 1958).

Given that vagal control of the heart evolved considerably earlier than the sympathetic branch of the autonomic nervous system, one might expect that vagally mediated cardiac orienting responses would be fully functional in amphibians and reptiles. Although there have been numerous studies on the cardiac and behavioral responses of amphibians and reptiles to various prey and predator stimuli (e.g., Laming & Austin, 1981; Smith, Allison, & Crowder, 1974), there has been relatively little research on the autonomic responses of amphibians and reptiles to neutral sensory stimuli.

Because of the apparent lack of research on cardiac responses to neutral stimuli in amphibians and reptiles, we conducted the following experiment as an initial attempt to analyze the cardiac and behavioral responses of Sudan plated lizards, *Gerrhosaurus major*, to a representative sample of novel (unfamiliar) neutral stimuli that have been shown to consistently elicit both behavioral and heart rate orienting responses in the Sprague-Dawley rat. In addition, we compared the cardiac responses of the lizards and rats to olfactory stimuli emanating from both a prey species and a predator species, and to an intense acoustic startle stimulus.

Sudan plated lizards, *Gerrhosaurus major*, were selected for this research because they adapt well to a laboratory environment and handling, are large enough to contain implanted biotelemetry devices, and are known to respond behaviorally to olfactory stimuli (Cooper, 1992). In addition, they are primarily carnivorous and are readily available from herpetological supply houses.

The experiment compared the behavioral and cardiac responses of eight Sprague-Dawley rats and eight Sudan plated lizards to two neutral stimuli, one potential predator stimulus, one appetitive (prey) stimulus, and an acoustic startle stimulus using the same apparatus and procedures for both species. We are aware, of course, that neutrality, aversiveness, and appetitiveness are concepts that cannot be precisely defined, because what may appear to be neutral or nonsignificant to one species may contain elements that are "significant" to another species. The neutral stimuli selected were an 80-dB pulsating white noise and the odor of amyl acetate. Cricket odor, a favorite prey species, was presented as an appetitive stimulus and the odor of fox urine as a potential predator stimulus. In addition, a 130-dB acoustic startle pulse was presented as an "interrupt" stimulus (Graham, 1992). The five stimuli were presented in the same order to both species. Each stimulus was presented 10 times at 90-sec interstimulus intervals following an adaptation period, during the course of a single session. The pulsating noise, amyl acetate, fox urine, and startle stimuli were presented on successive days, and the cricket odor 7 to 10 days following the startle stimulus. The apparatus and basic procedures used have been described previously (e.g., Hunt, Richardson, & Campbell, 1994; Richardson, Wang, & Campbell, 1995).

The results of this experiment, which are remarkably consistent within species and surprisingly different between species, are shown in Fig. 3.3.

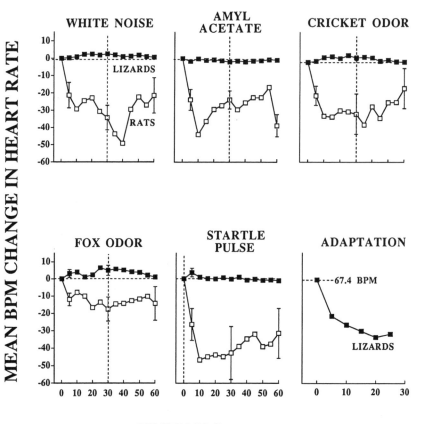

FIG. 3.3. Cardiac responses of Sudan plated lizards and Sprague-Dawley rats to five different sensory stimuli. The vertical dotted lines denote stimulus offset; stimulus onset occurred at time 0. The lower right panel depicts the heart rate of the Sudan plated lizards during adaptation to the test environment.

The lower right panel of Fig. 3.3 depicts heart rate of the lizards during adaptation to the test chamber, and shows that it reached a relatively stable baseline within 25 minutes. This indicates that the lizards had recovered from the stress of handling and habituated to the test environment prior to the first stimulus presentation. Heart rate during adaptation to the test chamber is not shown for the rats because it has been thoroughly documented in previous research (e.g., Saiers, Richardson, & Campbell, 1990).

The remaining five panels of Fig. 3.3 show the cardiac responses of the rats and Sudan plated lizards to white noise, amyl acetate, cricket odor, fox odor, and a startle pulse. All of the stimuli elicited substantial bradycardia in the Sprague-Dawley rats during the first few trials. The rats' cardiac responses to those stimuli typically habituated rapidly during the 10 stimulus presentations. Despite nearly complete habituation to the auditory stimulus on Day 1, the next stimulus, amyl acetate, presented on Day 2, produced an equivalent or larger cardiac deceleration. This pattern of habituation and reappearance of the orienting response on the following day to a different stimulus occurred to each of the five different stimuli.

In contrast, the Sudan plated lizards showed no discernible cardiac response to any of the sensory stimuli, not even to the cricket odor (a familiar food), the acoustic startle stimulus, or fox urine. These results were so surprising to us that we decided to replicate this experiment using a different lizard species before speculating on their significance. The green iguana (*Iguana iguana*) was selected for this purpose because it is a species known to be autonomically responsive to threatening stimuli (Belkin, 1963; see the following section for a description of reptilian autonomic reactivity). Four naive green iguanas were given the same sequence of stimulus presentations already described. The results were identical to those shown in Fig. 3.3; none of the stimuli produced any detectable change in heart rate. Even though the number of iguanas tested was small, the results strongly confirmed our initial observations on the Sudan plated lizard.

The failure of either lizard species to respond to any of these stimuli was quite unexpected for several reasons. First, it has been fully documented that reptilian species can show both tachycardia and bradycardia to some types of predator stimuli (e.g., Smith, Allison & Crowder, 1974). Second, fox urine elicited a substantial number of tongue-flicks in the lizards suggesting that they detected the stimulus, but the tongue-flicks were not accompanied by or followed by either bradycardia or tachycardia. Third, the sensory systems of the Sudan plated lizard are almost certainly capable of responding to the stimuli presented. For example, audiograms based on cochlear microphonics show that they are responsive to acoustic stimuli between 10 and 10,000 Hz with a peak sensitivity between 100 and 2,000 Hz (Wever, 1978). The complete and total absence of cardiac responses to two neutral stimuli and the prey, predator, and acoustic startle stimuli suggests that reptilian species may not show the autonomic orienting responses to either neutral or salient sensory stimuli that are characteristic of mammals.

There are a number of possible reasons for the failure of the two reptilian species to show any type of autonomic responsivity to the broad range of stimuli presented. They include the following:

1. Reptiles respond autonomically only to salient species-specific stimuli and that other stimuli, even though they activate sense organs and the central nervous system, do not elicit autonomic responses.

2. Autonomic responding to environmental stimuli is context specific for each species. The test apparatus used in this research is quite similar to the home environment of the laboratory rat but vastly different from that of the Sudan plated lizard and the green iguana. Even though both the rats and lizards habituated to the test environment as measured by the decline in heart rate of both species to a stable, species-specific baseline, it may be that reptilian species react only when the environmental context permits a relevant species-specific behavioral response.

3. Reptiles in general are less responsive to environmental stimuli unless they pose a direct threat or the immediate prospect of successful predation. For comparative psychophysiologists the striking differences between the two reptilian species and the laboratory rat raise a number of fascinating and important questions for future research.

EVOLUTIONARY ORIGINS OF AUTONOMIC
RESPONSES TO THREATENING STIMULI

In an attempt to better understand how autonomic responsivity to sensory stimuli evolved, this section explores the changes in heart rate elicited by predators and other threatening stimuli. In his analysis of defensive responses Cannon (1932) emphasized the sympathetic components of the "fight or flight" response and relegated the role of the parasympathetic nervous system to the regulation of "vegetative" bodily activities. Contemporary comparative physiologists, however, have shown that the parasympathetic system often plays an equally important role in the autonomic responses of prey to predators.

Smith and De Carvalho (1985) described sympathetic and parasympathetic defensive responses as follows:

> Vertebrates threatened by a predator or another threatening stimulus have a variety of behavioral and physiological responses available. Aggressive

behavior may erupt, or they may flee for cover, thus showing the classic fight or flight response. Sympathetic activity dominates such reactions with marked increases in metabolism, ventilation and heart rate. Alternatively, many animals respond passively and freeze, submerge themselves underwater, or retreat into a burrow when threatened. Here, parasympathetic activity dominates, and decreases are seen in metabolism, ventilation, heart rate, and body temperature. (p. 236)

The remainder of this chapter concentrates primarily on the parasympathetic responses elicited by predators and other danger stimuli for two reasons. First, it is an overlooked aspect of defensive responding among psychophysiologists, and second, it is possible that predator-evoked parasympathetic fear responses are evolutionary antecedents to the autonomic components of the orienting response.

The Discovery of Fear Bradycardia

For about as long as psychophysiologists have been concerned with autonomic orienting and defensive responses (Graham & Clifton, 1966; Sokolov, 1963), comparative physiologists have been fascinated by what they have termed "fear" or "fright" bradycardia. The phenomenon of fear bradycardia in response to threat or perceived threat was first observed in the late 1960s (Belkin, 1968; Gaunt & Gans, 1969), and it is one of the most dramatic autonomic phenomena known to comparative psychophysiologists. Instead of responding to danger with sympathetic activation in preparation for "fight or flight," a remarkable number of animals representing a wide variety of species and different vertebrate classes respond to fear stimuli with profound bradycardia. In one of the first experimental papers to clearly document this phenomenon, Smith (Smith, Allison, & Crowder, 1974) recorded the heart rate of a free ranging alligator in its natural habitat during spontaneous and threat-induced dives. When undisturbed the animal spent most of its time quietly submerged, surfacing every 5 to 7 minutes to breathe. Basal heart rates ranged from 25 to 35 BPM, and no changes in heart rate were observed during either diving or surfacing. At the approach of a canoe, however, the submerged alligator remained quiescent, but its heart rate decreased dramatically from approximately 30 BPM to only 2 to 5 BPM. The cardiac response to the approaching canoe is reproduced in the upper left panel of Fig. 3.4. This dramatic decrease in heart rate was described by Smith et al. (1974) as an example of fear bradycardia.

The phenomenon of fear bradycardia, however, had actually been identified a few years earlier by investigators studying the diving reflex in a variety of amphibians, reptiles, birds, and mammals. One of the most prominent components of the dive reflex observed in laboratory experi-

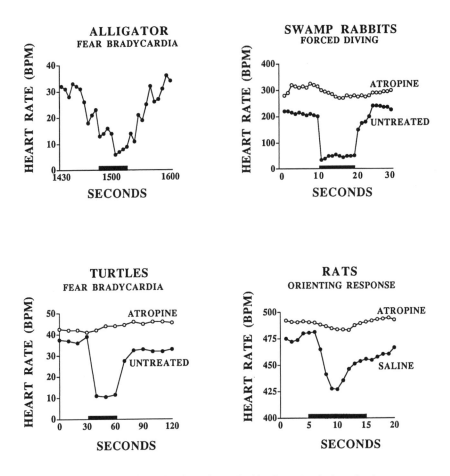

FIG. 3.4. Examples of bradycardia evoked by fear stimuli, forced submergence, and a neutral olfactory stimulus. The effects of atropine on three of the stimulus-induced bradycardias are also shown. The solid line on the abscissa denotes the time period during which the stimulus was present. Upper left panel adapted from Smith, Allison, and Crowder (1974). Copyright © 1974 by ASIH. Adapted with permission. Upper right panel adapted from Smith and Tobey (1983). Copyright © 1983 by University of Chicago Press. Adapted with permission. Lower left panel is adapted from Smith and De Carvalho (1985). Copyright © 1985 by University of Chicago Press. Adapted with permission. Lower right panel adapted from Hunt, Hess, and Campbell (1994). The figure includes pre- and poststimulus data not published in the original paper. Adapted with permission.

ments was a profound and long-lasting bradycardia (see Butler & Jones, 1982, for a comprehensive review). The first known observation of diving bradycardia was based on an experiment conducted in 1870 by Bert (cited in Butler & Jones, 1982, p. 221) in which he forcibly held a duck's head underwater and measured heart rate by feeling the pulsations of the heart through the breast. Submersion produced a sustained decrease in heart rate that persisted until the head was lifted and breathing resumed. Until the late 1960s investigators studying the diving reflex assumed that forced diving procedures such as those employed by Bert produced the same pattern of cardiovascular and metabolic changes as those induced by voluntary dives in the animal's natural habitat. This view was convincingly contradicted by two papers published in the late 1960s. Gaunt and Gans (1969) reported that diving bradycardia in *Caiman crocodilis* was minimal or nonexistent during voluntary undisturbed dives, but increased dramatically when the dive was triggered by the entry of a human investigator into the laboratory room. They concluded that what had been viewed solely as diving bradycardia on the basis of laboratory experiments utilizing forced immersion was strongly influenced by psychogenic (fear) factors. This conclusion was supported by Belkin (1968), writing at about the same time, who also concluded, on the basis of similar observations, that "bradycardia supported by threat is far more pronounced than is that associated with ordinary diving" (p. 775).

These observations should not obscure the fact that bradycardia is one of the "normal" adaptive autonomic responses used by many diving vertebrates to maximize oxygen conservation. This is particularly true of the many amphibian and chelonian species that spend much of their time underwater. During submergence their heart rates are often exceedingly low. In fact, many investigators view the heart rate during submergence in some species as the normal or baseline heart rate, and the heart rate while surfaced as "ventilation tachycardia" (Belkin, 1964). Similarly, bradycardia during submergence is common in animals, such as the Weddell seal, that engage in prolonged voluntary dives.

Once discovered, fear bradycardia was found to occur in a great many vertebrate species that are purely terrestrial. Free ranging woodchucks, *Marmota monax*, for example, responded to threat in two ways. If approached in the open, tachycardia and flight was the response; if threatened near or in their burrows, the response was bradycardia. The largest deceleratory response was elicited by a dog digging at the entrance to the burrow (Smith & Woodruff, 1980). Comparable autonomic responses have been observed in other mammals including Eastern cottontail rabbits (Smith & Worth, 1980), squirrels (Smith & Johnson, 1983), deer fawns (Espmark & Langvatin, 1979; Jacobsen, 1979) and desert rodents (Hofer, 1970). Similarly, in terrestrial birds fear bradycardia is particularly pronounced in nesting species using concealment as a predator-avoidance strategy during incubation. Gabrielsen, Blix, and Ursin (1985) reported that the heart rate of arctic willow ptarmigan hens decreased by approximately 43% at the sight of an approaching human and various simulated predator-approach noises; however, when the experimenter reached a "critical" distance, the cardiac response shifted to tachycardia, followed shortly thereafter by flight.

AUTONOMIC ORIGINS OF FORCED DIVING BRADYCARDIA, DIVING BRADYCARDIA, FEAR BRADYCARDIA, AND ORIENTING RESPONSE BRADYCARDIA

Autonomic Control of Forced Diving Bradycardia

Relatively soon after the initial discovery of forced diving bradycardia in the duck other early investigators found that bilateral vagotomy eliminated the decrease in heart rate produced by forcibly holding the duck's head underwater (e.g., Huxley, 1913; Lombroso, 1913). Subsequent research, all using forced submergence procedures, confirmed and expanded those findings. Parasympathetic blockade, using either atropine or vagotomy, was shown to either eliminate or greatly reduce forced diving bradycardia in ducks (Butler & Jones, 1968), amphibians (Lillo, 1979), harbor seals (Harrison & Tomlinson, 1960), turtles (Santos, Laitano, & Genofre, 1990), water snakes (Murdaugh & Jackson, 1962), and many other species. An example of the effects of atropine on forced diving bradycardia is shown in the upper right panel of Fig. 3.4. In this experiment, atropine-treated and untreated swamp rabbits, a species that dives voluntarily to obtain nutrients, were forcibly submerged. As can be seen, atropine increased baseline heart rate slightly and completely eliminated the forced diving bradycardia. One of the more surprising aspects of this research was the failure to find evidence of coactivation of the sympathetic nervous system. In numerous studies, neither vagotomy nor atropine revealed the increase in heart rate that would be expected if the procedures used to forcibly submerge the animals produced an increase in sympathetic activity that was masked by more intense parasympathetic activity in untreated animals (Berntson, Cacioppo, & Quigley, 1991). This observation is hard to reconcile with the fact that amphibians (e.g., Laming & Austin, 1981), reptiles (e.g., Smith et al., 1974), and mammals frequently show profound tachycardia rather than bradycardia when threatened by an approaching predator. The apparently consistent absence of coactivation of the sympathetic and parasympathetic nervous systems during forced diving is something that comparative psychophysiologists should investigate further.

Autonomic Control of Voluntary Diving Bradycardia

In nearly every species studied that shows bradycardia during voluntary diving, parasympathetic blockade either prevented or markedly reduced the bradycardia. In the turtle, for example, atropine completely prevented the decrease in heart rate that normally accompanies submergence (Belkin, 1964). In addition, the bradycardia developed extremely rapidly after submergence, often within one beat, suggesting strong, rapidly acting vagal inhibition of the heart. Other studies have shown that vagotomy and cardiac cholinergic receptor blockade produce similar effects on voluntary diving bradycardia in other vertebrates, including amphibians and mammals (e.g., Drummond & Jones, 1979; Lillo, 1979; Smith & Tobey, 1983).

Autonomic Control of Fear Bradycardia

Numerous studies have shown that fear bradycardia is primarily the result of vagally mediated, parasympathetic inhibition of the heart. Smith and De Carvalho (1985), for example, found that the decrease in heart rate produced by touching the shell of an ornate box turtle was completely blocked by prior injection of atropine. Injection of atropine raised resting heart rate slightly (less than 10%) and completely eliminated the fear bradycardia. Hand contact did not produce an increase in heart rate in the atropine-treated group, suggesting that the vagally mediated bradycardia was not masking a co-occurring increase in sympathetic stimulation of the heart. These results are shown in the lower left panel of Fig. 3.4.

Autonomic Control of Orienting Response Bradycardia

The autonomic origins of orienting response bradycardia have been under intensive theoretical and experimental analysis for a number of years (see Berntson et al., 1991; Sokolov & Cacioppo, chapter 1, this volume), and there is no need to reiterate those findings in detail in this chapter. Suffice it to say that orienting response bradycardia to neutral stimuli is mediated primarily by vagal cholinergic stimulation of the heart that is occasionally accompanied by simultaneous coactivation of the sympathetic nervous system. An example of the effects of atropine on orienting response bradycardia is shown in the lower right panel of Fig. 3.4. Note that the decrease in heart rate elicited by a neutral olfactory stimulus is proportionately much smaller than that elicited by threatening stimuli in the other panels.

To summarize, the autonomic mechanisms underlying forced diving, voluntary diving, and fear bradycardia appear to be indistinguishable from those mediating orienting response bradycardia. In all instances, the bradycardia is produced primarily by centrally driven, vagal stimulation of the heart, occasionally accompanied by sympathetic activation or withdrawal.

EVOLUTIONARY ORIGINS OF FEAR BRADYCARDIA AND ORIENTING RESPONSE BRADYCARDIA

Fear Bradycardia

One of the unanswered questions in comparative psychophysiology concerns the evolutionary origins of fear bradycardia and its relationship to diving bradycardia. One possibility, presented initially by Belkin (1968), is that diving bradycardia evolved from fear bradycardia. He noted that fear bradycardia associated with threat is typically much larger than that associated with voluntary diving, and that it occurs in a large number of both diving and nondiving species including lizards, turtles, nestling birds, and hares. From these observations he concluded that the bradycardia associated with threat "may have been the primitive cardiovascular adaptation from which the more specialized defenses against asphyxia associated with diving have evolved" (p. 775). The underlying assumptions were: (a) that fear bradycardia reduced blood oxygen utilization, (b) that this autonomic response permitted longer periods of submergence to avoid predators, and (c) that the underlying mechanisms mediating this ability generalized to voluntary diving.

The contrasting possibility is that fear bradycardia may have evolved from diving bradycardia. Amphibians, which may or may not show fear bradycardia (existing research on this question is ambiguous), emerged from completely aquatic ancestors and brought with them many of the cardiorespiratory mechanisms that enabled prolonged submergence, including fully developed vagal control of the heart. Bradycardia during voluntary diving is the normal response, and there appear to be no major differences between voluntary diving and threat-induced diving in amphibians (Lillo, 1979). This suggests that no specialized autonomic adaptations were necessary to make diving and prolonged submergence an effective predator-avoidance strategy in amphibians.

In contrast, as described earlier, many aquatic reptilian species show either minimal or no bradycardia during spontaneous dives, but during threat-induced dives they exhibit profound bradycardia that permits them to stay submerged longer. In a recently published laboratory study, Wright, Grigg, and Franklin (1992) reported that voluntary dives in juvenile crocodiles (*crocodylus porosus*) averaged only 3 minutes accompanied by a 14% reduction in heart rate, whereas "disturbance"-induced dives lasted nearly 20 minutes accompanied by a 65% decrease in heart rate. In an even more extreme version of this phenomenon, some herbivorous terrestrial iguanas dive to escape predators and often stay submerged for more than 4 hours (Belkin, 1963; Courtice, 1978; Moberly, 1968) during which time heart rates decrease from baseline levels of 30 to 40 BPM to as low as 5 BPM. Spontaneous dives in this species, when they are not initiated by a predator, are much shorter, and there is little or no bradycardia (Belkin, 1963). It is also interesting to note that prolonged fear-induced dives typically produce a shift from aerobic to anaerobic metabolism that depletes the animal's energy reserves. Recovery takes a substantial period of time that varies among species; the iguana, for example, will not dive in response to another threatening stimulus for several hours (Moberly, 1968). During nonthreatened diving, however, there is no shift from aerobic to anaerobic metabolism in most species.

These and similar findings raise the possibility that bradycardia may have evolved initially as an adaptation to enable prolonged submersion, and that this adaptation then became the basis for threat-induced diving bradycardia. Further, it is possible that fear-evoked bradycardia in diving species generalized to nondiving terrestrial species. To the extent that bradycardia is an adaptive autonomic response to threat in terrestrial mammals, it is reasonable to assume that it would be preserved. It is also possible that threat-induced diving is accompanied by relative quiescence while submerged to avoid detection by potential predators, and that this behavioral pattern, of quiescence (freezing) accompanied by bradycardia, persisted through reptilian and mammalian evolution in those species where it continued to serve as an effective antipredator strategy. Evolution, however, does not necessarily follow logical pathways, and it is also possible that fear bradycardia evolved independently numerous times in different vertebrate groups as a successful antipredator strategy. For example, whenever behavioral immobility becomes an adaptive response, a decrease in heart rate might facilitate quiescence, especially when accompanied by a decrease in respiration rate or respiratory volume.

Orienting Response Bradycardia

Unlike the plausible evolutionary interrelationships between diving bradycardia and fear bradycardia previously described, there does not appear to be any comparable interconnection between fear bradycardia and orienting response bradycardia. If fear-induced decreases in heart rate, in addition to making the animal capable of remaining motionless longer and less detectable, also facilitated tracking a predator and judging its intentions (Burger & Gochfeld, 1990; Gabrielsen, Blix, & Ursin, 1985), it would seem logical to postulate that those species would also display orienting response bradycardia to novel, neutral stimuli.

Support for this argument is mixed, however. Neither amphibians (based on preliminary research in our laboratory), reptiles (this chapter), nor avians (e.g., Cohen & Goff, 1978) have been shown to display orienting response bradycardia to novel, neutral stimuli even though threatening stimuli elicit fear bradycardia in those vertebrate classes. For example, wild nesting ptarmigan hens (a species that shows pronounced fear bradycardia to threat) showed large (65%) increases in heart rate to distant neutral stimuli that included calls from redwing thrushes, curlews, redshanks, and gulls. Behavioral orienting responses consisting of head-raising and eye-opening accompanied the acceleratory cardiac responses (Gabrielsen et al., 1985). To summarize, to date there is little evidence that any nonmammalian vertebrate species shows bradycardia to novel, neutral stimuli, suggesting that autonomic orienting responses first appeared somewhere in the course of mammalian evolution. Whether mammalian orienting responses are in any way linked to either diving bradycardia or fear bradycardia awaits further research and analysis.

DISTINGUISHING BETWEEN ORIENTING RESPONSE BRADYCARDIA AND FEAR BRADYCARDIA

Distinguishing between fear bradycardia and orienting response brady-cardia is a particularly challenging task because both are characterized by stimulus-induced decreases in heart rate mediated by an increase in parasympathetic stimulation of the heart. In one case the eliciting stimulus is presumed to be neutral, and in the other it is presumed to be threatening. Unfortunately, there is no a priori way of determining with any certainty which stimuli are neutral and which are threatening, particularly in animals. There are, however, at least four possible criteria for distinguishing between orienting response bradycardia and fear bradycardia. As the reader will note, many of these characteristics are strikingly similar to those used to distinguish orienting responses from defensive responses, except that the direction of the cardiac response is deceleratory rather than acceleratory (e.g., Graham, 1979). The potential distinguishing characteristics are:

1. Fear bradycardia is typically much larger than orienting response bradycardia.
2. Fear bradycardia habituates slowly, if at all, whereas orienting response bradycardia habituates rapidly.
3. Fear bradycardia is directly proportional to intensity of the threatening stimulus, whereas orienting response bradycardia is typically maximal at low to moderate stimulus intensities.

4. Fear bradycardia should occur primarily in species and in settings where concealment or behavioral immobility is an adaptive predator avoidance strategy; orienting response bradycardia should be relatively independent of context.

The first distinguishing characteristic is based on an informal survey of representative experiments in which the stated objective was to study either fear bradycardia or orienting response bradycardia. Although the survey was neither systematic nor all-inclusive, the differences were so striking that further analysis seemed unnecessary. The results of this survey are summarized in Table 3.1. In general, we attempted to identify those studies in which maximal bradycardia occurred for each type of autonomic response. The data presented in this table clearly demonstrate that fear bradycardias are typically much larger than orienting response bradycardias.

The second distinguishing characteristic is based more on inference than on extensive research. To our knowledge, no investigator has systematically attempted to study habituation of fear bradycardia to threatening stimuli or potential predators. Although habituation of fear brady-

TABLE 3.1
Comparison of Orienting Response Bradycardia and Fear Bradycardia

Fear Bradycardia			
Investigator	*Species*	*Predator*	*% Bradycardia*
Smith et al. (1974)	Alligator	Human	90%
Gaunt & Gans (1969)	Crocodile	Human	80%
Rosenmann & Morrison (1974)	Deer mouse	Moving shadow	60%
Smith & De Carvalho (1985)	Turtle	Human	68%
Smith & Woodruff (1980)	Woodchuck	Dog	37%
Causby & Smith (1981)	Swamp rabbit	Human	33%
Adams, Baccelli, Mancia, & Zanchetti (1971)	Cat aggressor	Cat	25%
Espmark & Langvatin (1979)	Red deer calf	Human	85%
Gabrielsen, Blix, & Ursin (1985)	Ptarmigan hen	Human	43%
Orienting Response Bradycardia			
Gentile, Jarrel, Teich, McCabe, & Schneiderman (1986)	Rabbits	90 dB tone	10%
Graham et al. (1970)	Human infants	75 dB tone	12%
Graham et al. (1970)	Human adults	75 dB tone	3%
Richardson, Hess, & Campbell (1994)	Adult rats	80 dB tone	7%
Richardson et al. (1994)	Infant rats	80 dB tone	16%
Weisbard & Graham (1971)	Monkey	70 dB tone	8%

cardia may occur in the animal's natural habitat if the eliciting stimulus is not followed by attack or approach, it is almost certain to be a slow process. In contrast, mammals habituate rapidly to "neutral" stimuli that elicit orienting response bradycardia in the laboratory. Presumably this also occurs to neutral stimuli such as the rustling of leaves in natural environments, because continued behavioral and autonomic responding to those stimuli would interfere with other essential activities.

The third characteristic is illustrated by the rapid decrease in heart rate that occurs in Svalbard ptarmigan hens as a potential predator (a human experimenter) comes closer and becomes an increasingly threatening stimulus. Similarly, the sight of an approaching human hand produces a smaller decrease in heart rate in the ornate box turtle than actually touching the shell (Smith & De Carvalho, 1985). In contrast, minimal to moderately intense stimuli typically produce maximal bradycardias in both laboratory animals and human subjects (e.g., Graham, 1979). Lower intensities are not detectable and higher intensities tend to produce the tachycardia characteristic of defensive responding.

The fourth characteristic difference is another that has not been investigated systematically in the laboratory. It is clear from the previously described existing field and laboratory research that fear bradycardia is maximal when shelter is available, either in the form of a burrow or a concealed nesting area, or when an effective species-specific predator-defense response is concealment rather than flight. In contrast, it seems logical to assume that both frequency of occurrence and magnitude of orienting responses would be at least partially independent of those factors. To recapitulate, there are a number of quantitative and qualitative differences between orienting response bradycardia and fear bradycardia, but whether these differences reflect categorical differences or simply differences in the intensity of the evoking stimulus remain to be determined.

SUMMARY AND CONCLUSIONS

The intent of this chapter was to provide psychophysiologists with a framework within which to consider the evolutionary origins of orienting and defensive responses. The introductory sections described the evolution of the autonomic nervous system with the intent of determining when it became capable of responding to environmental stimuli with orienting and defensive responses. This review revealed that vagal innervation of the heart emerged very early in vertebrate evolution, and that, with few exceptions, the structure, neural organization, and function of the vagus has remained remarkably unchanged since its first appearance. The conclusion reached was that all living vertebrates, except those in a primitive class of fish, the cyclostomes, are capable of rapid, vagally mediated decreases in heart rate in response to salient sensory stimuli and physiological challenges. In contrast, sympathetic neural control of the heart did not emerge in mammalian ancestry until the amphibians evolved, and fully developed adrenal glands are seen only in reptiles and later evolving species.

The next section of the chapter described a series of experiments comparing the autonomic responses of two reptilian species, Sudan plated lizards and green iguanas, with those of the laboratory rat to a series of auditory and olfactory stimuli. The stimuli were selected with the intent of eliciting orienting, appetitive, and defensive responses in these animals. Much to our surprise, neither reptilian species displayed a change in heart rate to any of the stimuli, whereas the rat, in contrast, showed profound bradycardia to all of the stimuli. This led to a review of the literature on the evolution of vagally mediated responses to environmental stimuli, with a strong emphasis on the autonomic reactions to fear-eliciting stimuli.

Threatening stimuli, such as the approach of a predator, can elicit either the classic fight or flight response accompanied by sympathetic activation, or they can elicit what the comparative physiologists have termed *fear bradycardia*. In response to threat, many animals become immobile, flee into a burrow, or dive underwater to avoid detection. These behaviors are accompanied by intense parasympathetic activity that can result in decreases in heart rate of over 90% in some species. Further analysis suggested that fear bradycardia might have evolved from diving bradycardia, a vagally mediated response to minimize oxygen utilization and prolong submergence. The possible evolutionary origins of orienting response bradycardia were then discussed, but no firm conclusions were reached. What is strikingly clear, however, is that both fear bradycardia and orienting response bradycardia can be elicited by sensory stimuli that differ only in terms of their significance to the animal. Moreover, both types of bradycardias are mediated by parasympathetic stimulation of the heart, and both can be prevented through prior treatment with a cholinergic receptor blocker such as atropine. These similarities raise a number of questions about their common origins, whether they differ only in intensity, or whether they are truly different phenomena. The chapter concluded by attempting to identify a number of characteristics that might be used to distinguish between orienting response bradycardia and fear bradycardia.

ACKNOWLEDGMENT

Preparation of this chapter and the research reported was supported by National Institutes of Mental Health Grants MH01562 and MH49496.

REFERENCES

Adams, D. B., Baccelli, G., Mancia, G., & Zanchetti, A. (1971). Relation of cardiovascular changes in fighting to emotion and exercise. *Journal of Physiology, 212,* 321–335.

Axelsson, M., Davison, W., Forster, M. E., & Farrell, A. P. (1992). Cardiovascular responses of the red-blooded antarctic fishes *Pagothenia veraccchi* and *P. borchgrevinki. Journal of Experimental Biology, 167,* 179–201.

Belkin, D. A. (1963). Diving bradycardia in the iguana. *Physiologist, 6,* 136.

Belkin, D. A. (1964). Variations in heart rate during voluntary diving in the turtle *Pseudemys concinna. Copeia, 2,* 321–330.

Belkin, D. A. (1968). Bradycardia in response to threat. *American Zoologist, 8,* 775.

Bennett, J. A., Kidd, C., Latif, A. B., & MacWilliam, P. N. (1981). A horseradish peroxidase study of vagal motoneurons with axons in cardiac pulmonary branches of the cat and dog. *Quarterly Journal of Experimental Physiology, 66,* 145–154.

Berntson, G. G., Cacioppo, J. T., & Quigley, K. S. (1991). Autonomic determinism: The modes of autonomic control, the doctrine of autonomic space, and the laws of autonomic constraint. *Psychological Review, 98,* 459–487.

Burger, J., & Gochfeld, M. (1990). Risk discrimination of direct versus tangential approach by basking black iguanas (*Ctenosaura similis*): Variation as a function of human exposure. *Journal of Comparative Psychology, 104,* 388–394.

Burnstock, G. (1969). Evolution of the autonomic innervation of visceral and cardiovascular systems in vertebrates. *Pharmacological Reviews, 21,* 247–324.

Butler, P. J., & Jones, D. R. (1968). Onset of and recovery from diving bradycardia in ducks. *Journal of Physiology, 196,* 255–272.

Butler, P. J., & Jones, D. R. (1982). The comparative physiology of diving in vertebrates. *Advances in Comparative Physiology and Biochemistry, 8,* 179–364.

Cannon, W. B. (1932). *The wisdom of the body.* New York: Norton.

Causby, L. A., & Smith E. N. (1981). Control of fear bradycardia in the swamp rabbit, *Sylvilagus aquaticus. Comparative Biochemistry and Physiology, 69,* 367–370.

Cohen, D. H., & Goff, D. M. (1978). Conditioned heart-rate change in the pigeon: Analysis and prediction of acquisition patterns. *Physiological Psychology, 6,* 127–141.

Cooper, W. E. (1992). Prey odor discrimination and poststrike elevation in tongue flicking by a cordylid lizard, *Gerrhosaurus nigrolineetus, Copeia,* 146–154.

Courtice, G. (1978). *Some aspects of respiration and its control in the Eastern water dragon* Physignathus lesueurii *(Gray).* Unpublished doctoral dissertation, University of Sydney, Australia.

Drummond, P. C., & Jones, D. R. (1979). The initiation and maintenance of bradycardia in a diving mammal, the muskrat (*Ondatra zibethica*). *Journal of Physiology, 290,* 253–271.

Espmark, Y., & Langvatin, R. (1979). Cardiac responses in alarmed red deer calves. *Behavioural Processes, 4,* 179–186.

Evans, D. H. (1993). *The physiology of fishes.* Boca Raton, FL: CRC Press.

Falck, B., Mecklenburg, C. V., Myhrberg, H., & Persson, H. (1966). Studies on adrenergic and cholinergic receptors in the isolated hearts of *Lampetra fluviarillis (Cyclostomata)* and *Pleuronectes platessa (Teleostei). Acta Physiologica Scandinavica, 68,* 64–71.

Gabrielsen, G. W., Blix, A. S., & Ursin, H. (1985). Orienting and freezing responses in incubating ptarmigan hens. *Physiology & Behavior, 34,* 925–934.

Gaunt, A. S., & Gans, C. (1969). Diving bradycardia and withdrawal bradycardia in Caiman crocodilus. *Nature, 223,* 207–208.

Gentile, C. G., Jarrel, T. W., Teich, A., McCabe, P. M., & Schneiderman, N. (1986). The role of amygdaloid central nucleus in the retention of differential Pavlovian conditioning of bradycardia in rabbits. *Behavioral Brain Research, 20,* 263–273.

Graham, F. K. (1992). Attention: The heartbeat, the blink, and the brain. In B. A. Campbell, H. Hayne, & R. Richardson (Eds.), *Attention and information processing in infants and adults: Perspectives from human and animal research.* Hillsdale, NJ: Lawrence Erlbaum Associates.

Graham, F. K. (1973). Habituation and dishabituation of responses innervated by the autonomic nervous system. In H. V. S. Peeke & M. J. Herz (Eds.), *Habituation* (pp. 165–218). New York: Academic Press.

Graham, F. K. (1979). Distinguishing among orienting, defense, and startle reflexes. In H. D. Kimmel, E. H. van Olst, & J. F. Orlebeke (Eds.), *The orienting reflex in humans.* Hillsdale, NJ: Lawrence Erlbaum Associates.

Graham, F. K., Anthony, B. J., & Zeigler, B. L. (1983). The orienting response and developmental processes. In D. Siddle (Ed.), *Orienting and habituation: Perspectives in human research* (pp. 371–430). New York: Wiley.

Graham, F. K., Berg, K. M., Berg, W. K., Jackson, J., Hatton, H., & Kantowitz, S. (1970). Cardiac orienting response as a function of age. *Psychonomic Science, 19,* 363–365.

Graham, F. K., & Clifton, R. K. (1966). Heart-rate change as a component of the orienting response. *Psychological Bulletin, 65,* 305–320.

Haroutunian, V., & Campbell, B. A. (1981). Development and habituation of the heart rate orienting response to auditory and visual stimuli in the rat. *Journal of Comparative & Physiological Psychology, 95,* 166–174.

Harrison, R. J., & Tomlinson, J. D. W. (1960). Normal and experimental diving in the common seal (*Phoca ritulina*). *Mammalia, 24,* 386–399.

Hayne, H., Richardson, R., & Campbell, B. A. (1991). Developmental constraints on the expression of behavioral and heart-rate orienting responses: I. The role of cardiosomatic coupling. *Developmental Psychobiology, 24,* 1–18.

Hayne, H., Richardson, R., & Campbell, B. A. (1992). Developmental changes in the duration of attention to unfamiliar stimuli in the rat. *Psychophysiology, 29,* 283–293.

Hofer, M. A. (1970). Cardiac and respiratory function during sudden prolonged immobility in wild rodents. *Psychosomatic Medicine, 32,* 633–647.

Hunt, P. S., Hess, M. F., & Campbell, B. A. (1994). Autonomic mediation of unconditioned and conditioned heart rate responses in the 16-day-old rat. *Psychobiology, 22,* 209–218.

Hunt, P. S., Richardson, R., & Campbell, B. A. (1994). Delayed development of fear-potentiated startle in rats. *Behavioral Neuroscience, 108,* 69–80.

Huxley, F. M. (1913). On the reflex nature of apnea in the diving duck: I. The reflex nature of submersion apnea. *Quarterly Journal of Experimental Physiology, 6,* 183–196.

Jacobsen, N. K. (1979). Alarm bradycardia in the white-tailed deer fawns. *Journal of Mammalogy, 60,* 343–349.

Jordan, D., Spyer, K. M., Withington-Wray, D. J., & Wood, L. M. (1985). Histochemical and electrophysiological identification of cardiac and pulmonary vagal preganglionic neurons in the cat. *Journal of Physiology, 372,* 87.

Kapp, B. S., Frysinger, R. C., Gallagher, M., & Haselton, J. R. (1979). Amygdala central nucleus lesions: Effect on heart rate conditioning in the rabbit. *Physiology and Behavior, 23,* 1109–1117.

Lacey, J. I., & Lacey, B. C. (1958). The relationship of resting autonomic activity to motor impulsivity. In *The brain and human behavior: Proceedings of the Association for Research in Nervous and Mental Disease* (pp. 144–209). Baltimore: Williams & Wilkins.

Laming, P. R., & Austin, M. (1981). Cardiac responses of the anurans *Bufo bufo* and *Rana pipiens* during behavioral arousal and fright. *Comparative Biochemistry & Physiology, 68A,* 515–518.

Leong, S. K., Tay, S. W., & Wong, W. C. (1984). The localization of vagal neurons of the terrapin (*Trionyx sinensis*) as revealed by the retrograde horseradish peroxidase method. *Journal of the Autonomic Nervous System, 11,* 373–382.

Lillo, R. S. (1979). Autonomic cardiovascular control during submergence and emergence in bullfrogs. *American Journal of Physiology, 237,* R210.

Lombruso, U. (1913). The reflex inhibition of the heart during reflex respiratory inhibition in various animals. *Zoological Biology, 61,* 517–538.

Lukomskaya, N. J., & Michelson, M. J. (1972). Pharmacology of the isolated heart of the lamprey, *Lampreta fluviatilis. Comparative General Pharmacology, 3,* 213.

Moberly, W. R. (1968). The metabolic responses of the common iguana (*Iguana iguana*) to walking and diving. *Comparative Biochemistry & Physiology, 27,* 21–32.

Morris, J. L., & Nilsson, S. (1994). The circulatory system. In S. Nilsson & S. Holmgren (Eds.), *Comparative physiology and evolution of the autonomic nervous system* (pp. 193–246). London: Harwood.

Murdaugh, H. V., & Jackson, J. E. (1962). Heart rate and blood lactic acid concentration during experimental diving of water snakes. *American Journal of Physiology, 202,* 1163–1165.

Niewenhuys, R. (1972). Topological analysis of the brainstem of the lamprey *Lapetra fluviatilis. Journal of Comparative Neurology, 145,* 165–177.

Nikundlwe, A. M., & Niewenhuys, R. (1983). The cell masses in the brainstem of South African clawed frog *Xenopus lacvis*: A topographical analysis. *Journal of Comparative Neurology, 213,* 199–219.

Nilsson, S. (1983). *Autonomic nerve function in the vertebrates.* New York: Springer-Verlag.

Nilsson, S., & Holmgren, S. (1993a). Autonomic nerve functions. In D. H. Evans (Ed.), *The physiology of fishes.* Boca Raton, FL: CRC Press.

Nilsson, S., & Holmgren, S. (1993b). *Comparative physiology and evolution of the autonomic nervous system.* Chur, Switzerland: Harwood Academic Publishers.

Pavlov, I. P. (1927). *Conditioned reflexes.* Oxford, England: Oxford University Press.

Ranson, R. N., Butler, P. J., & Taylor, E. W. (1993). The central localization of the vagus nerve in the ferret (*Mustela putorius furo*) and the mink (*Mustela vison*). *Journal of the Autonomic Nervous System, 43,* 123–138.

Richardson, R., Hess, M., & Campbell, B. A. (1994). The orienting response to brief auditory stimuli in preweanling and adult rats. *Developmental Psychobiology, 27*(2), 93–100.

Richardson, R., Wang, P., & Campbell, B. A. (1995). Developmental and pharmacological analysis of the cardiac response to an acoustic startle stimulus. *Psychophysiology, 33,* 31–41.

Rosenmann M., & Morrison, P. (1974). Physiological characteristics of the alarm reaction in the deer mouse, *Peromyscus maniculatus bairdii. Physiological Zoology, 47,* 230–241.

Saiers, J. A., Richardson, R., & Campbell, B. A. (1990). Disruption and recovery of the orienting response following shock or context change in preweanling rats. *Psychophysiology, 27,* 45–56.

Santos, E. A., Laitano, S. Y., & Genofre, G. C. (1990). Diving physiology of *chrysemys dorbignyi* Dum & Bibr., 1835 (*Reptilia chelonia*). *Comparative Biochemistry & Physiology, 95A,* 229–236.

Schwaber, J. S., & Cohen, D. H. (1978a). Electrophysiological and electron microscopic analysis of the vagus nerve of the pigeon, with particular reference to the cardiac innervation. *Brain Research, 147,* 65–78.

Schwaber, J. S., & Cohen, D. H. (1978b). Field potential and single unit analyses of the avian dorsal motor nucleus of the vagus and criteria for identifying vagal cardiac cells of origin. *Brain Research, 147,* 79–90.

Siegel, M. A., Sananes, C. A., Gaddy, J. R., & Campbell, B. A. (1987). Dissociation of heart rate and somatomotor orienting responses to novel stimuli in preweanling rats. *Psychobiology, 15,* 122–127.

Smith, E. N., Allison, R. D., & Crowder, W. E. (1974). Bradycardia in a free-ranging American alligator. *Copeia, 3,* 770–772.

Smith, E. N., & De Carvalho, M. C. (1985). Heart rate response to threat and diving in the ornate box turtle, *Terepene ornata. Physiological Zoology, 58*(2), 236–241.

Smith, E. N., & Johnson, C. (1983). Fear bradycardia in the eastern fox squirrel, *Sciurus niger*, and eastern grey squirrel, *S. carolinesis*. *Comparative Biochemistry and Physiology, 78A*, 409–411.

Smith, E. N., & Tobey, E. W. (1983). Heart rate response to forced and voluntary diving in swamp rabbits, *Sylvilagus aquatorus*. *Physiological Zoology, 56*, 632–638.

Smith, E. N., & Woodruff, R. A. (1980). Fear bradycardia in free-ranging woodchucks, *Marmota monax*. *Journal of Mammalogy, 61*, 750–753.

Smith, E. N., & Worth, D. J. (1980). Atropine effect on fear bradycardia of the Eastern cottontail rabbit. In C. M. Amlaner & D. W. MacDonald (Eds.), *A handbook on biotelemetry and radio tracking* (pp. 549–555). New York: Pergamon.

Sokolov, E. N. (1963). *Perception and the conditioned reflex.* New York: Macmillan.

Taylor, E. W. (1992). Nervous control of the heart and cardiorespiratory interactions. In W. S. Hoar, D. J. Randall, & A. P. Farrell (Eds.), *Fish physiology* (Vol. 12, pp. 343–387). New York: Academic Press.

Taylor, E. W. (1994). The evolution of efferent vagal control of the heart in vertebrates. *Cardioscience, 5*, 173–182.

Weisbard, C., & Graham, F. K. (1971). Heart rate change as a component of the orienting response in monkeys. *Journal of Comparative and Physiological Psychology, 76*, 74–83.

Wever, E. G. (1978). *The reptile ear.* Princeton, NJ: Princeton University Press.

Wright, J. C., Grigg, G. C., & Franklin, C. E. (1992). Redistribution of air with the lungs may potentiate "fright" bradycardia in submerged crocodiles (*Crocodylus porosus*). *Comparative Biochemistry & Physiology, 102A*, 33–36.

4

The Neurophysiological Basis of Acoustic Startle Modulation: Research on Fear Motivation and Sensory Gating

Michael Davis
Ribicoff Research Facilities of the Connecticut Mental Health Center
Yale University School of Medicine

The power of the startle reflex (Landis & Hunt, 1939) as a tool to study complex processes such as attention and motivation was first highlighted by Graham (1975). Graham's work, the work of Hoffman and Ison (1980) on startle in rats, and the work of Brown, Kalish, and Farber (1951) on the modification of startle by fear have motivated the work in our laboratory that has, over the past 20 years, attempted to: (a) determine the neural pathway involved in startle itself and (b) determine the neural pathways and cellular processes involved in startle modulation by higher order processes such as attention and fear. It is our progress toward these aims that I review in this chapter.

THE PRIMARY ACOUSTIC STARTLE PATHWAY

Because the acoustic startle reflex has such a short latency (e.g., 8 msec measured electromyographically in the hindleg), it must be mediated by a simple neural pathway. In 1982, our laboratory proposed that acoustic startle was mediated by four synapses, three in the brainstem (the ventral cochlear nucleus; an area just medial and ventral to the ventral nucleus of the lateral lemniscus; and the nucleus reticularis pontis caudalis) and one synapse onto motoneurons in the spinal cord (Davis, Gendelman, Tischler, & Gendelman, 1982). Electrolytic lesions of these nuclei eliminated acoustic startle, and single pulse electrical stimulation of these nuclei elicited startlelike responses with a progressively shorter latency

69

as the electrode was moved farther down the startle pathway. Further-more, local infusion of excitatory amino acid antagonists, such as DL-2-amino-5-phosphonopentanoic acid (AP5) into the area just medial and ventral to the ventral nucleus of the lateral lemniscus, markedly decreased acoustic startle amplitude (Spiera & Davis, 1988).

New Evidence Concerning the Role of the Area Around the Ventral Nucleus of the Lateral Lemniscus in Acoustic Startle

Because electrolytic lesions of the area just medial and ventral to the ventral nucleus of the lateral lemniscus eliminated the acoustic startle reflex, we concluded that this area must be part of a primary acoustic startle pathway (Davis et al., 1982). When we did the initial work on this project, techniques were not yet available to selectively destroy cells versus cells plus fibers passing through the area of the lesion. By using newly developed tech-niques that allowed selective destruction of cell bodies without a concomi-tant loss of fibers of passage, we began to doubt whether a synapse, obligatory for the startle reflex, actually occurs at this level of the brainstem. First, although very discrete N-methyl-D-aspartate (NMDA)-induced le-sions of cell bodies in the nucleus reticularis pontis caudalis completely eliminated startle, NMDA-induced lesions of the ventral nucleus of the lateral lemniscus or the area just ventral and medial to it did not, provided the lesion did not extend to the nucleus reticularis pontis caudalis (Lee, Lopez, Meloni, & Davis, 1996). Second, local infusion of the NMDA antagonist AP5 into the nucleus reticularis pontis caudalis reduced startle by 80–90% (Miserendino & Davis, 1993), at doses $\frac{1}{60}$ of those that depressed startle after infusion into the area of the ventral lateral lemniscus (Spiera & Davis, 1988). Moreover, comparably low doses of the non-NMDA antago-nist 6-cyano-7-nitroquinoxaline-2,3-dione (CNQX) also depressed startle after local infusion into the nucleus reticularis pontis caudalis (Miserendino & Davis, 1993), but had no effect when infused into the area of the ventral lateral lemniscus, even using much higher doses. Hence, we believe that the depressant effects produced by excitatory amino acid antagonists infused into the area of the ventral lateral lemniscus (Spiera & Davis, 1988) resulted from spread to the nearby nucleus reticularis pontis caudalis (about 1 mm caudal).

A Direct Projection From Cochlear Root Neurons to the Nucleus Reticularis Pontis Caudalis

These new data questioned the importance of the area around the ventral nucleus of the lateral lemniscus in mediating the acoustic startle reflex, even though this area is known to receive direct auditory input. On the other hand, all the data still pointed to the critical importance of the nucleus reticularis pontis caudalis in the acoustic startle reflex. However, until very recently, it has been unclear how auditory information gets to this traditionally nonauditory part of the brainstem. Many years ago, Harrison and Warr (1962) described a small group (about 20 on each side) of very large cells (35 μm in diameter) embedded in the cochlear nerve in rodents, later termed *cochlear root neurons* by Merchan, Collia, Lopez, and Saldana (1988). More recent studies, summarized in Lopez, Merchan, Bajo, and Saldana (1993), have shown that these neurons receive direct input from the spiral ganglion cells in the cochlea, making them the first acoustic neurons in the central nervous system. These neurons send exceedingly thick axons (sometimes as wide as 7 μm) through the trapezoid body, at the very base of the brain, directly to an area just medial and ventral to the lateral lemniscus and continue on up to the deep layers of the superior colliculus. However, they give off thick axon collaterals that terminate directly in the nucleus reticularis pontis caudalis (Lingenhohl & Friauf, 1994; Lopez et al., 1993) exactly at the level known to be critical for the acoustic startle reflex (Cassella & Davis, 1986; Davis et al., 1982; Gokin & Karpukhina, 1985; Groves, Wilson, & Boyle, 1974; Hammond, 1973; Koch, Lingenhohl, & Pilz, 1992; Lee et al., 1996; Leitner, Powers, & Hoffman, 1980; Lingenhohl & Friauf, 1992, 1994; Rossignol, 1973; Szabo & Hazafi, 1965; Wu, Suzuki, & Siegel, 1988) onto cells that then project to motoneurons in the spinal cord (Lingenhohl & Friauf, 1994).

Effects of Kainate Acid-Induced Lesions of Cochlear Root Neurons on Acoustic Startle

To test the role of cochlear root neurons in the acoustic startle reflex, we first matched rats into groups having equivalent baseline startle levels, and several days later infused kainate acid directly into the auditory nerve at the level of the cochlear root neurons (Lee et al., 1996). This was done in collaboration with Dr. Dolores Lopez, an auditory anatomist specializing in the cochlear root neurons. The surgery involved a complex, angular approach in which a glass pipette (50 μm tip diameter) was angled stereotaxically to go through the cerebellum, ventral cochlear nucleus, and into the auditory nerve. Five days later the animals were again tested for acoustic startle, measuring both whole body and pinna reflexes, as well as their general orientation to auditory stimuli. They were then given special perfusions and the brains prepared for immunohistological visualization of the cochlear root neurons and their projections, using calbindin-sensitive antibodies.

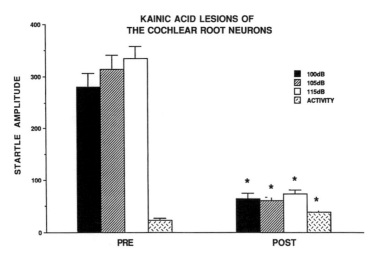

FIG. 4.1. Mean amplitude startle response elicited by either a 100-, 105-, or 110-dB noise burst before and 2 weeks after kainate acid-induced lesions of the cochlear root neurons. Activity represents output of the accelerometers during the same 200-msec period of time used to sample startle in the absence of a startle-eliciting stimulus.

Bilateral lesions of the cochlear root neurons essentially eliminate acoustic startle in rats (Fig. 4.1). Thus far there has been an excellent correlation between the number of root neurons destroyed and the decrease in startle (Lee et al., 1996). In animals with only unilateral cochlear root neuron damage, there was a preferential loss of the ipsilateral pinna reflex, and a partial decrease in whole body startle. In animals with bilateral damage to the cochlear root neurons, there was a marked decrease in whole body startle and the pinna reflex on both sides. Although damage to the auditory root, where the cochlear root neurons reside, has not been fully ruled out, other tests indicated that these animals could clearly orient to auditory stimuli (e.g., suppression of licking) and had normal compound action potentials recorded from the cochlear nucleus (Lee et al., 1996).

Hence, we now believe that the acoustic startle pathway may be simpler than we had originally thought, consisting of only three synapses onto (a) cochlear root neurons, (b) neurons in the nucleus reticularis pontis caudalis, and (c) motoneurons in the facial motor nucleus (pinna reflex) or spinal cord (whole body startle—Fig. 4.2). Electrolytic lesions of the area around the ventral nucleus of the lateral lemniscus may have eliminated startle by destroying the axon collaterals that project heavily to the nucleus reticularis pontis caudalis and by retrograde degeneration of cochlear root neurons caused by severing axons passing through this area en route to more rostral areas (Lee et al., 1996).

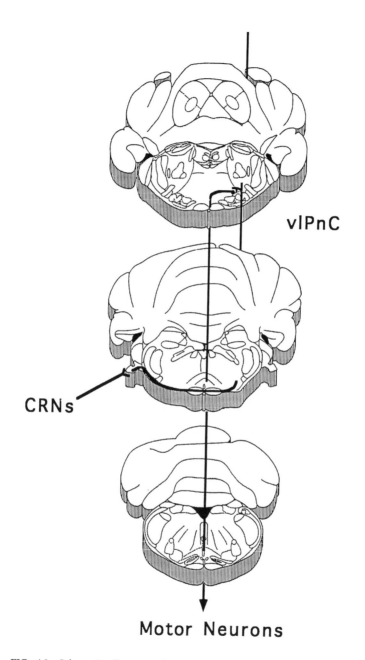

vlPnC

CRNs

Motor Neurons

FIG. 4.2. Schematic diagram of the nuclei and pathways believed to mediate the acoustic startle reflex. vlPnc = Ventral Lateral Nucleus Reticularis Portis Caudalis; CRNs = Cochlear Root Neurons.

TRANSMITTERS OF THE PRIMARY ACOUSTIC STARTLE PATHWAY

Auditory Nerve to Cochlear Root Neuron Synapse

At the present time we do not have any direct data on the identity of the neurotransmitter that may mediate startle at this level. Preliminary experiments suggest it may be glutamate acting on non-NMDA receptors because local infusion of the non-NMDA antagonist CNQX in the vicinity of the root neurons depressed startle, whereas local infusion of the NMDA antagonist AP5 did not (Miserendino & Davis, 1993). Furthermore, attempts to destroy the cochlear root neurons with NMDA were unsuccessful, suggesting a lack of NMDA receptors on these neurons. However, further work is clearly required to test the role of excitatory amino acids on startle at the level of the cochlear root neurons. This will probably require placement of tiny cannulas using the angular approach previously described, and will be technically very difficult because of potential mechanical destruction of these cells and/or the auditory nerve.

Cochlear Root Neuron to Reticulospinal Neuron Synapse

Glutamate acting on both NMDA and non-NMDA receptors may well be the neurotransmitter that mediates startle at the level of the nucleus reticularis pontis caudalis. Figures 4.3 and 4.4 show that local infusion in

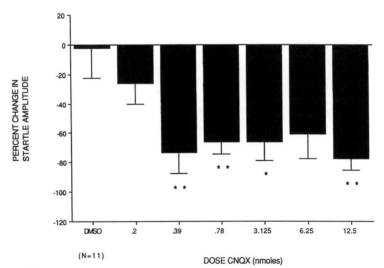

FIG. 4.3. Percentage change in startle amplitude, relative to a preinfusion baseline, as a function of the dose of the non-NMDA receptor antagonist CNQX infused locally into the nucleus reticularis pontis caudalis. * or ** indicates a significant decrease in startle ($p < .05$; $p < .01$, respectively).

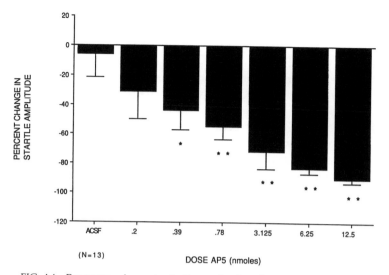

FIG. 4.4. Percentage change in startle amplitude, relative to a preinfusion baseline, as a function of the dose of the NMDA receptor antagonist AP5 infused locally into the nucleus reticularis pontis caudalis. * or ** indicates a significant decrease in startle ($p < .05$; $p < .01$, respectively).

rats chronically implanted with bilateral cannulas aimed at the nucleus reticularis pontis caudalis of either CNQX or AP5 significantly reduced startle amplitude by as much as 70% to 80% (Miserendino & Davis, 1993). The dose range over which AP5 and CNQX attenuated startle indicated that the nucleus reticularis pontis caudalis is extremely sensitive to these compounds. Such sensitivity suggests that small changes in neurotransmitter activity in this area may have a profound effect on the expression of the acoustic startle reflex. For example, NMDA receptor activation may desensitize rapidly and not fully recover for as long as 90 sec (cf. Zorumski & Thio, 1992), a time period comparable to the decrease in startle produced by an immediately prior startle elicitation (e.g., Davis, 1970). Hence, treatments that modulate NMDA transmission—glycine (Thomson, 1989); polyamines (Williams, Romano, Dickter, & Molinoff, 1991)—or treatments that decrease glutamate receptor desensitization (cf. Zorumski & Thio, 1992) might alter the rate of short-term habituation of the startle reflex, especially when applied directly into the nucleus reticularis pontis caudalis.

If excitatory amino acids actually mediated startle at the nucleus reticularis pontis caudalis, it might be expected that high doses of CNQX or AP5 would completely eliminate startle, but this was not the case. However, our cannulas were ventrally placed in the part of the nucleus reticularis pontis caudalis that mediates movement of the hindlimbs. More rostral parts of the nucleus reticularis pontis caudalis and oralis control movements in the neck and forelimbs (Peterson, 1979). Hence, the 20% to 30% of startle remaining may have resulted from the relative ineffectiveness of the drugs at these other sites. Further studies using electromyographic recordings in the hindlegs will be necessary to evaluate this possibility.

Although excitatory amino acid synaptic transmission in the vertebrate nervous system seems to be mediated primarily by activation of non-NMDA receptors (cf. Collingridge & Lester, 1989; Mayer & Westbrook, 1987) activation of NMDA receptors may contribute importantly to synaptic responses as well, especially under conditions that favor removal of the Mg++-dependent blockade of NMDA receptor-gated ion channels. In general, activation of NMDA receptors tends to lead to synaptic enhancement. The present data indicate, therefore, that activation of NMDA receptors may play an important modulatory, rather than a mediational, role on startle at the level of the nucleus reticularis pontis caudalis. This effect might be due to direct actions on these reticular neurons.

Alternatively, activation of NMDA receptors might affect presynaptic processes that normally serve to elevate startle. For example, activation of NMDA receptors might affect presynaptic release of glutamate from root neuron terminals projecting to neurons in the nucleus reticularis pontis caudalis. In the hippocampus (Connick & Stone, 1988; Crowder, Croucher, Bradford, & Collins, 1987; Martin, Bustos, Bowe, Bray, & Nadler, 1991) or striatum (Bustos et al., 1992; Young & Bradford, 1991), glutamate and aspartate enhance their own release by activating NMDA autoreceptors. Another way in which AP5 could depress startle at the level of the nucleus reticularis pontis caudalis would be by blocking the release of neurotransmitters that tonically increase reticular cell excitability. For example, NMDA antagonists can block the excitatory effects of glutamate on the release of norepinephrine in the hippocampus (Jones, Snell, & Johnson, 1987; Schmidt & Taylor, 1988) or dopamine or acetylcholine in the nucleus accumbens (Jones et al., 1987), perhaps by blocking NMDA release-facilitating receptors on presynaptic terminals (Pittaluga & Raiteri, 1990).

Reticulospinal Neurons to Motor Neuron Synapse

Infusion into the subarachnoid space of the spinal cord to allow drugs to diffuse in the vicinity of motoneurons (intrathecal infusion) of the non-NMDA antagonist CNQX or the NMDA antagonist AP5 each reduced the amplitude of the whole body startle reflex in a dose-dependent manner (Boulis, Kehne, Miserendino, & Davis, 1990). Over the dose ranges employed, both drugs were roughly equipotent in depressing whole body startle but neither drug completely eliminated startle after intrathecal infusion into the lumbar spinal cord. Furthermore, combined infusion of

AP5 and CNQX did not totally eliminate whole body startle. As mentioned earlier, whole body startle, as measured in our test cages, represents a complex integral of neck, forepaw, and hindpaw movements, with only the hindpaw movements being dependent on activation of motoneurons in the lumbar spinal cord. Thus, intrathecal administration of hydrophillic compounds such as AP5 or CNQX would not be expected to totally eliminate whole body startle because they would affect the hindlimb components but not the forepaw or neck components.

The most striking finding, therefore, was that when EMG activity in the hindlimbs was used to define startle, intrathecal administration of a combination of AP5 and CNQX completely eliminated all EMG components of the startle response, consistent with the hypothesis that excitatory amino acids actually mediate startle at the spinal level (Fig. 4.5). Moreover, when the EMG components of the startle reflex were separated into early or late components, CNQX preferentially eliminated the early components (mean latency = 8.29 msec) whereas AP5 preferentially eliminated the later components (mean latency = 14.57 msec or longer).

The fact that startle appears to involve both non-NMDA and NMDA receptors at the spinal level can be interpreted in a number of ways. The simplest possibility would be that glutamate is released from reticulo-spinal tract terminals that form monosynaptic connections onto motoneurons expressing both NMDA and non-NMDA receptors. The short-latency EMG components would then reflect activation of non-NMDA receptors, whereas the longer latency EMG components would reflect

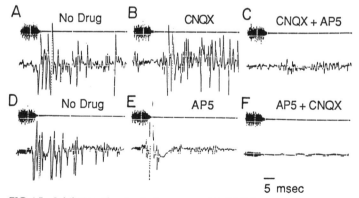

FIG. 4.5. Inhibition of early electromyographic (EMG) component of startle by CNQX and the late EMG component of startle by AP5: Animal 1: (a) EMG recording prior to intrathecal infusion of CNQX (126 nmoles). (b) Early EMG component inhibited after CNQX infusion. (c) Late EMG components inhibited following addition of AP5 (126 nmoles). Animal 2: (d) EMG recording prior to intrathecal infusion of AP5. (e) Late EMG component inhibited after AP5 infusion. (f) Early EMG components inhibited following addition of CNQX.

activation of NMDA receptors (Dale & Grillner, 1986). A second possibility would be that reticulospinal neurons make both monosynaptic connections and polysynaptic connections via interneurons onto spinal motoneurons (Peterson, 1979). The short-latency EMG components would then reflect the monosynaptic connections onto non-NMDA receptors, whereas the longer latency EMG components would reflect polysynaptic connections involving NMDA receptors. A third possibility is that the short-latency EMG components of startle reflect activation of non-NMDA receptors by the short-latency startle pathway described previously, whereas the later components would reflect activity in other brainstem structures, which then eventually activate NMDA receptors on spinal motoneurons. This idea could be tested by direct stimulation of reticulospinal neurons in conjunction with intrathecal infusion of excitatory amino acid antagonists.

In summary, the excitatory amino acid glutamate may well mediate startle at each of the three central synapses along the acoustic startle pathway. NMDA and non-NMDA receptors appear to be involved at both the spinal cord and nucleus reticularis pontis caudalis. Processes involved in the release of glutamate, as well as changes in the sensitivity of glutamate receptors, would be expected to affect startle and startle modulation.

POSSIBLE MODULATION OF PREPULSE INHIBITION IN RATS BY ATTENTION

Habituation of Auditory Prepulse Inhibition

Since Graham's (1975) seminal paper, there has been continued interest in the use of prepulse inhibition (a reduction in the amplitude of the startle response when the strong startle-eliciting stimulus is preceded shortly by a weaker stimulus, or "prepulse") as a bridge between human and infrahuman attentional processes. Recently, a great deal of interest has centered on the use of this phenomenon for its potential as an animal model of attentional dysfunctions in certain human psychopathologies, most notably, schizophrenia (Dawson, Schell, Swerdlow, & Filion, chapter 11, this volume).

Logically, there are at least two possibilities as to the relationship between prepulse inhibition and the attentional process that may be dysfunctional in schizophrenia. One possibility is that prepulse inhibition is a direct measure of the system that gates sensory input. A second possibility is that prepulse inhibition is modulated by the same attentional process that may be impaired in schizophrenia, but is not itself a direct measure of the actual mechanism that accounts for sensory gating. In this latter case, a loss of prepulse inhibition would be yet another marker of a loss of attention.

By definition, there should be no selection of sensory information for further processing prior to the operation of an attentional filter (Deutch & Deutch, 1964). Therefore, if prepulse inhibition is a measure of the sensory gating mechanism itself, it should not habituate as a result of repetition of the prepulse. However, if prepulse inhibition is a marker of attention, then it might habituate with prepulse repetition.

To test this, we designed an experiment to assess whether prepulse inhibition, measured in rats, might habituate under conditions that minimized (a) the potential impact of dishabituation caused by loud startle test stimuli, and (b) changes in baseline startle amplitude over the course of testing for prepulse inhibition (Gewirtz & Davis, 1995). To do this, a relatively small number of startle stimuli, presented at regular intervals, were interspersed among a much larger number of prepulse-alone stimuli. In addition, the startle stimulus was repeatedly presented at the same interstimulus interval prior to any prepulse exposure, in order to establish a steady baseline of the startle response. Finally, we employed an auditory prepulse that was 71.5 dB over an ambient background noise level of 69 dB (i.e., a 2.5 dB signal-to-noise ratio). Subjects received 2 days of training in each of two conditions. In both conditions, prepulse inhibition was always tested with an auditory prepulse stimulus. However, whereas in one condition (Experimental), subjects received repeated, intervening presentations of the same, auditory prepulse, in the other condition (Control), the intervening presentations were of a different stimulus (a visual prepulse), which was not used to test prepulse inhibition. The two conditions were identical in all other respects. Figure 4.6 (top panel) shows that repetitive exposure to the auditory prepulse (i.e., the same stimulus used to produce prepulse inhibition) resulted in a substantial decrease in the magnitude of prepulse inhibition over the course of a session, whereas repetitive exposure to a visual prepulse did not (Fig. 4.6, bottom panel). These observations were confirmed by a mixed-model analysis of variance (ANOVA) performed on prepulse inhibition scores. There was a significant decrease in prepulse inhibition across the session, $F(1, 18) = 21.2$, $p < .001$, with a reliable interaction between treatment and the number of prior presentations of the prepulse, $F(10, 180) = 2.2$, $p < .02$. Hence, the present study shows that when the prepulse is close to sensory threshold, prepulse inhibition does undergo habituation. This suggests, at least with respect to a very weak prepulse, that prepulse inhibition may better be thought of as a marker for the operation of an attentional process, rather than as a direct measure of the mechanism itself by which sensory input is gated.

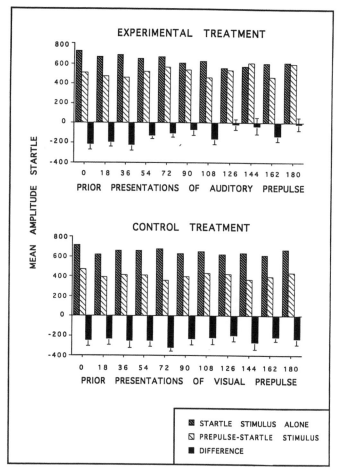

FIG. 4.6. Mean amplitude startle on pulse alone and prepulse trials and the difference between the two trial types (prepulse inhibition ± SEM) to an auditory prepulse 2.5 dB above background noise, measured intermittently over the course of repetitive exposure to the auditory prepulse alone (Experimental Condition), or to a visual prepulse (Control Condition).

Effects of Prior Footshock Stress on Prepulse Inhibition

In rats the amplitude of the startle reflex can be increased by prior presentation of a brief series of footshocks. For example, we elicited startle once every 30 sec for 20-min periods before and after presentation of 10 0.6 mA shocks, one shock every second, and found startle to substantially increase for a long period of time after footshocks had been presented (Davis, 1989). Because lesions of the central nucleus of the amygdala completely blocked this effect (Hitchcock, Sananes, & Davis, 1989), it was suggested that the facilitation of startle by prior footshock resulted from activation of the amygdala, which is known to increase startle when stimulated electrically (Rosen & Davis, 1988).

Accumulating data now suggest that activation of the central nucleus of the amygdala may serve to increase attention (Gallagher, Graham, & Holland, 1990; Kapp, Whalen, Supple, & Pascoe, 1992). If footshock serves to activate the central nucleus of the amygdala with a resultant increase in attention, and prepulse inhibition in rats is increased by attention, then prior presentation of footshock should increase the magnitude of prepulse inhibition. Furthermore, if dopamine agonists such as apomorphine disrupt prepulse inhibition by disrupting attention to the prepulse, then prior presentation of footshock might normalize prepulse inhibition after administration of apomorphine.

To test this, four groups of 15 rats were used. On Day 1, two groups were injected with apomorphine (0.8 mg/kg subcutaneously) and the other two groups with its vehicle, distilled water. They were then placed into startle test boxes and 5 min later one apomorphine-injected group and one water-injected group were presented with 10 0.6 mA footshocks, at a rate of one shock per second. The other two groups were treated identically but not presented with footshocks. Thirty seconds later all groups were presented with the first of 50 startle stimuli at 30-sec intervals, 10 startle stimuli alone (pulse alone trials), and 10 100 msec after either 70-, 75-, 80-, or 85-dB 20-msec noise bursts (prepulse trials). The various trial types were presented in an irregular order with the restriction that each of the five trial types had to occur once within every block of five trials.

Figure 4.7 shows the results. Overall startle levels were generally higher after apomorphine and, on the pulse alone trials, after footshock. Prepulse presentation decreased startle, with greater suppression associated with higher prepulse intensities. Most striking was the fact that prior presentation of footshock increased the magnitude of prepulse inhibition in both the water and apomorphine conditions. These conclusions were supported by an overall ANOVA using drug (water vs. apomorphine) and trial type (pulse alone, 70-, 75-, 80-, or 85-dB prepulse trials) as within-subjects factors and shock versus no shock as a between-subjects factor. The ANOVA showed an overall effect of drug, $F(1, 58) = 65.41$, $p < .001$, and an overall effect of trial type, $F(4, 232) = 153.26$, $p < .001$, but no overall effect of shock, $F(1, 58) = .20$, $p > .10$. Most important, however, was the significant shock by trial type interaction, $F(4, 232) = 4.52$, $p < .002$, reflecting the general increase in prepulse inhibition following footshock. This increase in prepulse inhibition was observed in both the water and apomorphine conditions, and there was no significant drug by shock by test trial interaction.

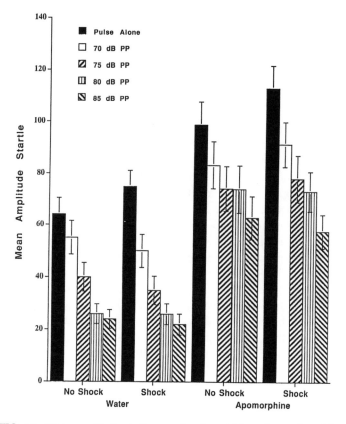

FIG. 4.7. Mean amplitude startle on pulse alone trials and prepulse trials, using either 70-, 75-, 80-, or 85-dB prepulses, following injection of either water or 0.8 mg/kg subcutaneous apomorphine measured 5 min after presentation of 10 0.5 mA footshocks or no footshocks.

Taken together, these data are consistent with the idea that footshock increases prepulse inhibition, perhaps via activation of the amygdala with a consequent increase in attention. Further studies looking at the effects of amygdala lesions on this footshock-induced increase in prepulse inhibition could be used to test this idea.

MODULATION OF STARTLE BY CONDITIONED FEAR

Brown et al. (1951) demonstrated that the amplitude of the acoustic startle reflex in the rat can be augmented by presenting the eliciting auditory startle stimulus in the presence of a cue (e.g., a light) that has previously

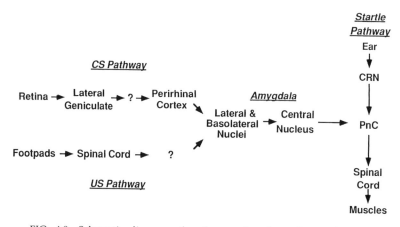

FIG. 4.8. Schematic diagram of pathways thought to be involved in fear-potentiated startle using a visual conditioned stimulus. CRN = cochlear root neurons; RPC = nucleus reticularis pontis caudalis; CS = conditioned stimulus; US = unconditioned stimulus.

been paired with a shock. This phenomenon has been termed the *fear-potentiated startle effect* and has been replicated using either an auditory or visual conditioned stimulus and when startle has been elicited by either a loud sound or an airpuff (cf. Davis, 1986).

With potentiated startle, fear is expressed through some neural circuit that is activated by the fear-eliciting stimulus and ultimately impinges on the startle circuit. Figure 4.8 shows a schematic summary diagram of the neural pathways that we believe are required for fear-potentiated startle in rats using a visual conditioned stimulus. These pathways involve convergence of the conditioned stimulus and the unconditioned shock stimulus at the lateral and basolateral amygdala nuclei, which then project to the central nucleus of the amygdala, which then projects directly to the nucleus reticularis pontis caudalis. Data supporting the involvement of these pathways are summarized in the following.

Effects of Amygdala Lesions on Fear-Potentiated Startle

Electrolytic or chemical lesions of the central nucleus of the amygdala block the expression of fear-potentiated startle using either a visual (Hitchcock & Davis, 1986) or auditory conditioned stimulus (Campeau & Davis, 1995; Hitchcock & Davis, 1987). Chemical lesions of the lateral and basolateral nuclei, which receive sensory input and project to the central nucleus of the amygdala, caused a complete blockade of fear-potentiated startle using a visual (Sananes & Davis, 1992) or auditory conditioned stimulus (Campeau & Davis, 1995). The central nucleus of the amygdala projects directly to the nucleus reticularis pontis caudalis (Rosen, Hitchcock, Sananes, Miserendino, & Davis, 1991) and lesions at several points along this pathway blocked the expression of fear-potentiated startle (Hitchcock & Davis, 1991). Both conditioned fear and sensitization of startle by footshocks appear to ultimately modulate startle at the level of the nucleus reticularis pontis caudalis (Berg & Davis, 1985; Boulis & Davis, 1989; Krase, Koch, & Schnitzler, 1994). However, recent data now suggest that a synapse between the amygdala and central gray may be required for both fear-potentiated startle and shock sensitization because fiber sparing chemical lesions of the central gray have been reported to block both phenomena (Fendt, Koch, & Schnitzler, 1994; Yeomans & Frankland, 1994).

The Role of Excitatory Amino Acid Receptors in the Amygdala in Fear-Potentiated Startle

Because several studies had snown that NMDA antagonists block long-term potentiation (LTP) both in vitro and in vivo, as well as perhaps learning, based on several behavioral tasks, we wondered whether local infusion of the NMDA antagonist AP5 into the amygdala would block the acquisition of fear-potentiated startle. In fact, AP5 caused a dose-dependent blockade of fear-potentiated startle using either a visual (Miserendino, Sananes, Melia, & Davis, 1990) or an auditory conditioned stimulus (Campeau, Miserendino, & Davis, 1992). Control experiments indicated that this effect did not seem to result from a decrease in sensitivity to footshock, neurotoxic damage to the amygdala, or a decrease in visual processing. Moreover, pretest infusion of AP5 in rats previously trained in the absence of the drug did not block the expression of fear-potentiated startle using either a visual (Miserendino et al., 1990) or an auditory (Campeau et al., 1992) conditioned stimulus, whereas pretest infusion of the alpha-amino-3-hydroxy-5-methyl-4-isoxazole propionic acid (AMPA) receptor antagonist CNQX did block the expression of fear-potentiated startle in a dose-dependent manner (Kim, Campeau, Falls, & Davis, 1993). This suggests that the conditioned stimulus ultimately releases glutamate in the amygdala, which activates AMPA receptors for the expression of conditioned fear. Moreover, this finding makes it more difficult to ascribe the fear acquisition deficit observed with AP5 to nonspecific antagonism of AMPA receptors, because AP5, unlike CNQX, did not block the expression of fear-potentiated startle. However, because AP5 can block synaptic transmission in the amygdala (Li, Phillips, & LeDoux, 1993), it is still possible that it prevented conditioning by blocking the footshock from activating amygdaloid neurons. However, we have found that local infusion of AP5 into the amygdala blocked the acquisition of second-order conditioning, which does not involve shock (Falls & Davis, 1992). This finding is especially interesting given that AP5 does not block the expression of potentiated startle using either a visual or auditory stimulus.

The Possible Role of Cyclic AMP at the Level of the Nucleus Reticularis Pontis Caudalis in Startle Modulation

At the present time, a detailed anatomical description of the connections between the amygdala and/or central gray and neurons in the nucleus reticularis pontis caudalis is not yet available, so that it is not clear how activation of the amygdala facilitates the acoustic startle reflex. Recently, we have found that infusion into the nucleus reticularis pontis caudalis of the cAMP analogue 8-bromo cAMP, the phosphodiesterase inhibitor rolipram, or the water-soluble adenylate cyclase activator forskolin-DHA each increased acoustic startle amplitude. These effects probably resulted from intracellular actions because cAMP itself, which does not readily penetrate lipid membranes, had no effect. Moreover, the effects seemed somewhat specific because the precursor of cAMP, ATP, or 8-bromo cGMP, also failed to alter startle at doses where 8 bromo-cAMP did (de Lima & Davis, 1994). Because cAMP can increase the release of glutamate (Dolphin & Archer, 1983), it could increase startle by amplifying the amount of glutamate released, triggered by the startle-eliciting stimulus. Alternatively, cAMP in the nucleus reticularis pontis caudalis might lead to an increase in postsynaptic excitability of reticulospinal neurons. With either mechanism, release of transmitters positively coupled to cAMP into the nucleus reticularis pontis caudalis would be expected to increase acoustic startle. Recent evidence indicates that the neuropeptide, substance P, increases the responsiveness of reticulospinal neurons to acoustic stimuli (Krase et al., 1994). Moreover, local infusion into the nucleus reticularis pontis caudalis of a substance P antagonist completely blocked the normal sensitizing effect of footshock on startle (Krase et al., 1994), which has previously been deduced ultimately to modulate transmission at the level of the nucleus reticularis pontis caudalis (Boulis & Davis, 1989). Because substance P is positively coupled to cAMP in some brain areas (Mitsuhashi et al., 1992), it is possible that it acts in the nucleus reticularis pontis caudalis via activation of cAMP.

Another possibility is that the direct projections from the central nucleus of the amygdala to the nucleus reticularis pontis caudalis contain corticotropin releasing hormone (CRH). In fact, exploratory studies show that local infusion of CRH into the nucleus reticularis pontis caudalis can rapidly increase startle in sites where 8-bromo cAMP was also found to be effective (Birnbaum, Lidow, & Davis, 1995). Currently we are testing whether local infusion of CRH antagonists or cAMP antagonists into the nucleus reticularis pontis caudalis will block the excitatory effects of amygdala stimulation, conditioned fear, or prior shock on the acoustic startle reflex.

The Role of the Perirhinal Cortex in Potentiated Startle

Complete removal of all primary and secondary visual cortices does not block the expression of fear-potentiated startle using a visual conditioned stimulus (Falls & Davis, 1994; Rosen et al., 1992). In contrast, relatively small electrolytic lesions of the perirhinal cortex completely blocked the expression of fear-potentiated startle, provided the lesion included an area of perirhinal cortex just dorsal and ventral to the rhinal sulcus (Rosen et al., 1992). Similar results have been found using an auditory conditioned stimulus and with fiber sparing lesions of the perirhinal cortex using neurotoxic doses of NMDA (Campeau & Davis, 1995) or electrolytic lesions using the experimental context as the CS and freezing as the measure of fear (Corodimas & LeDoux, 1995). All of these lesions have been made following training. Consistent with other work (Romanski & LeDoux, 1992), lesions of the perirhinal cortex made prior to fear conditioning did not block fear-potentiated startle using either a visual or auditory conditioned stimulus. In addition, in rats lesioned after training, fear-potentiated startle to either modality could be restored with further retraining. Hence, subcortical pathways clearly are sufficient to mediate conditioned fear once the perirhinal cortex is removed. Because the perirhinal cortex sends heavy projections to the lateral and basolateral amygdaloid nuclei, we believe that the perirhinal cortex may be an important link in relaying sensory information to the amygdala.

Relearning Potentiated Startle After Lesions of the Amygdala

Although the amygdala plays a crucial role in both the acquisition and expression of fear-potentiated startle, there are examples in the literature where some effects of amygdala lesions on aversively motivated conditioning depend on the degree of learning achieved before surgery (cf. Kim & Davis, 1993). Because our animals typically receive only 10 to 20 training trials prior to amygdala lesions, it is possible that more extensive training would prevent or attenuate the effects of amygdala lesions on the expression of fear-potentiated startle. To test this we gave rats extensive overtraining by presenting two light–shock pairings for 30 consecutive days followed by either sham or electrolytic lesions of the amygdala aimed at the central nucleus (Kim & Davis, 1993). All animals were tested 5 to 6 days later, and then retrained for 7 more days. The results showed that even in highly overtrained animals, lesions of the amygdala still totally blocked the expression of fear-potentiated startle, providing strong evidence that overtraining does not overcome the ability of amygdala lesions to block the expression of fear-potentiated startle, unlike findings from active avoidance tasks.

Most surprisingly, however, these lesioned rats quickly reacquired fear-potentiated startle when retrained. This unexpected result suggests that an intact central nucleus of the amygdala is not necessary for reacquisition of potentiated startle, or for its expression following reacquisition, because histological analysis indicated that the central nucleus was completely destroyed in five of the six lesioned rats. However, when the lesions were made before training, none of the animals showed any evidence of learning. Although the lesion did decrease shock reactivity, the lesioned rats still never learned even when the shock intensity was increased in the lesioned rats to equate the level of shock reactivity in the two groups.

Despite the seemingly critical role of the central nucleus in the expression of fear-potentiated startle, the fact that these same lesions did not prevent reacquisition indicates the presence of a secondary brain system that can compensate for the central nucleus under certain circumstances. However, this secondary brain system cannot compensate for the central nucleus in all cases because central nucleus lesions still prevented initial acquisition of potentiated startle. It would appear that the central nucleus either induces some sort of functional change in this secondary brain system during initial training or plays a permissive role so that this secondary system, alone, can support fear-potentiated startle produced by retraining when the central nucleus is subsequently removed. At the present time, we have no direct information on the identity of a secondary brain structure that could compensate for the central nucleus of the amygdala. Preliminary data show that reacquisition is not observed in rats with lesions of the caudal division of the ventral amygdalofugal pathway.

INHIBITION OF FEAR

Clinically, the inability of some people to inhibit fear and anxiety adequately ranks as one of the major problems in psychiatry. Hence, it would be important to develop methods to begin to identify brain systems involved in the inhibition of fear.

The Role of NMDA Receptors in the Amygdala During the Acquisition of Experimental Extinction

We have found that local infusion of the NMDA antagonist, AP5, into the basolateral nucleus of the amygdala blocked the development of experimental extinction, the decrease in potentiated startle that normally occurs when the conditioned stimulus is presented without the shock (Falls, Miserendino, & Davis, 1992). A great deal of behavioral data indicate that extinction does not erase the original memory, but instead involves the learning of a new association that competes with or inhibits the original memory. The fact that AP5 infused into the amygdala blocked the development of extinction provides the first evidence that an NMDA-dependent process in or close to the amygdala is important for experimental extinction.

Development of a Procedure to Produce Conditioned Inhibition Using Fear-Potentiated Startle

Extinction is closely related to the phenomenon of conditioned inhibition (cf. Bouton, 1991). In the typical conditioned inhibition procedure, one stimulus, denoted as A, when presented alone predicts shock. When A is presented in compound with another stimulus, X (the conditioned inhibitor), shock is not delivered. The result of this procedure is that A comes to elicit a fear reaction when presented alone but not when it is accompanied by the conditioned inhibitor X. Extinction may be analogous to conditioned inhibition where the experimental context serves the same function as X in that it predicts the absence of shock (cf. Bouton & Bolles, 1985; Bouton & King, 1983, 1986). The conditioned inhibition procedure, however, offers advantages over the extinction procedure because in this paradigm, the reduction of fear is under the control of an explicit CS, rather than under the control of less specifiable contextual cues. Moreover, fear reduction is assessed at the same time as fear production, allowing one to disentangle the inhibition of fear from a more global disruption in fear performance or stimulus processing.

Because of the advantages of the conditioned inhibition procedure, we have devised a procedure for obtaining conditioned inhibition of fear-potentiated startle (Falls & Davis, 1995). Rats underwent 2 days of training in which one stimulus, A, was repeatedly paired with footshock (denoted as A+). Following this, the rats underwent either 2, 3, 5, or 10 additional days of training in which a compound, denoted as XA, was not paired with shock (denoted as XA–). A+ training was continued during this second phase. Conditioned inhibition was assessed by measuring the amplitude of the startle reflex alone, in the presence of A, or when A was presented in compound with X.

The results showed substantial fear to A as evidenced by greater startle amplitude in the presence of A than in its absence. The magnitude of the conditioned fear effect grew as a function of the number of training days that employed both XA– and A+ trials. However, the rats showed significantly less fear-potentiated startle to A when it was presented in compound with X, and the magnitude of this difference was also directly related to the number of training days that employed XA− and A+ trials. This suggests that X had acquired the ability to inhibit the fear produced by A. This inhibitory effect of X was dependent on the rats having been given explicit nonreinforced presentations of the XA compound, because, in a control experiment, rats given X alone trials in the second phase of training did not show inhibition of fear-potentiated startle to A presented with X in testing, ruling out external inhibition (Pavlov, 1927). Moreover, the lack of potentiated startle on XA trials cannot be readily attributed to a configural discrimination (i.e., A vs. XA) because in a subsequent experiment, the inhibitory effect of X transferred to another fear-eliciting stimulus, B, such that fear-potentiated startle to XB, which never had been nonreinforced before, was less than that to B alone. Taken together, these results suggest that X in a A+/XA− procedure acquires the ability to inhibit fear-potentiated startle.

Is the Amygdala Necessary for the Expression of Conditioned Inhibition?

The most parsimonious way to explain inhibition of fear would be to assume that the conditioned inhibitor acts by inhibiting activation of the amygdala normally produced by the conditioned fear stimulus (e.g., at the level of the central nucleus). Such a mechanism would account for transfer of conditioned inhibition both across different conditioned stimuli as well as across different fear responses (Rescorla, 1977). Because fear-potentiated startle can be reacquired following amygdala lesions, we asked whether such lesions would block the expression of conditioned inhibition established before the lesion (Falls & Davis, 1995).

Rats were trained in our usual conditioned inhibition procedure, already described. They then were given extensive lesions of the central nucleus of the amygdala and 10 days later retrained with additional A+ training. No further conditioned inhibition training (i.e., XA−) was given after the lesion. Two days later they were tested for potentiated startle in the presence or absence of the conditioned inhibitor. The results (Fig. 4.9) showed that prior to the lesion, startle was larger in the presence of A than XA, demonstrating conditioned inhibition. Lesions of the amygdala completely blocked fear-potentiated startle in the presence of A or XA. Retraining led to reacquisition to A. However, once conditioned fear to A was reacquired, conditioned inhibition was also evident, even though no retraining to XA− was given following surgery. These data indicate that the conditioned inhibitory stimulus X must exert its inhibitory effect on structures other than those destroyed by the lesion, and that inhibition of these other structures must have developed during original learning.

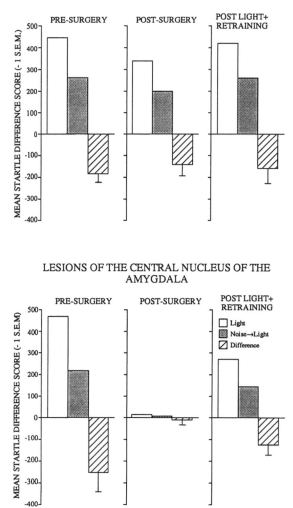

FIG. 4.9. Mean level of fear-potentiated startle to a CS alone or a CS in compound with a conditioned inhibitor and the difference between these two trial types, which reflects the amount of conditioned inhibition before surgery, after surgery, and after light+ retraining in sham operated rats (upper panel) or rats with bilateral lesions of the central nucleus of the amygdala. Note that only A+ training occurred following surgery with no further XA− training (see text).

We believe this is an especially informative experiment, because it suggests that, contrary to expectation, conditioned inhibition must not be expressed exclusively at the central nucleus of the amygdala and perhaps not at any level of the amygdala. In fact, this may be consistent with the phenomenon of superconditioning (Rescorla, 1971), in which conditioning is enhanced to a novel stimulus when it is presented in compound with a conditioned inhibitor and the compound is reinforced with shock. If the conditioned inhibitor decreased activity throughout the amygdala, this would be expected to retard rather than to improve conditioning. Moreover, conditioned inhibition of conditioned analgesia also is not blocked by lesions of the amygdala (Watkins, Wiertelak, Mooney-Heiberger, Grahn, & Maier, 1992). Instead, conditioned inhibition seems to be expressed at the ultimate target area, in this case the spinal cord (Wiertelak, Maier, & Watkins, 1992). Currently we are testing the role of other brain areas in both the generation and expression of conditioned inhibition.

SUMMARY

Our laboratory has used the acoustic startle reflex in the rat as a measure of how attention might alter prepulse inhibition and how conditioned fear alters the startle reflex itself. A major emphasis has been an attempt to delineate the neural pathways involved in startle itself, as well as the neural pathways involved in modulation of startle by conditioned and unconditioned fear. We now believe that the acoustic startle pathway consists of cochlear root neurons that project directly to the nucleus reticularis pontis caudalis, which then projects directly to the spinal cord. Neural transmission at the first synapse may be mediated by glutamate acting on non-NMDA receptors, whereas glutamate acting on both NMDA and non-NMDA receptors seems to be involved at the other two synapses. In addition, the second messenger cAMP appears to be importantly involved in startle modulation.

Prepulse inhibition of the startle reflex in the rat may be subject to attentional effects because prepulse inhibition can display habituation when the intensity of the auditory prepulse is close to background noise, and because prior administration of footshock deepens prepulse inhibition, perhaps by virtue of an increase in attention secondary to activation of the amygdala.

The fear-potentiated startle paradigm has proven to be a sensitive test to measure fear in rats. This test measures conditioned fear by an increase in the amplitude of the acoustic startle reflex in the presence of a cue previously paired with a shock. Using a variety of techniques, we have concluded that a visual stimulus paired with a shock can increase the acoustic startle reflex via ultimately activating the perirhinal cortex which projects to the central nucleus of the amygdala via the lateral and basolateral amygdala nuclei. Activation of the amygdala is necessary and sufficient to facilitate startle via a direct connection between the central nucleus of the amygdala and the nucleus reticularis pontis caudalis or perhaps via an intervening synapse in the central gray.

Although the central nucleus of the amygdala is critical for the expression of fear-potentiated startle, animals given extensive overtraining followed by total removal of the central nucleus of the amygdala can be retrained to show fear-potentiated startle. This indicates the presence of a secondary brain system that can compensate for the central nucleus under certain circumstances.

More recently we have developed a reliable paradigm to produce conditioned inhibition of fear-potentiated startle to begin to explore what parts of the brain are involved in the inhibition of fear, a problem of considerable clinical relevance.

ACKNOWLEDGMENTS

This research was supported by National Institute of Mental Health Grants MH-25642 and MH-47840, Research Scientist Development Award MH-00004, a grant from the Air Force Office of Scientific Research, and the State of Connecticut. I thank Jonathan Gewirtz, Eddie Meloni, and Margaret Bradley for their helpful comments on the manuscript.

REFERENCES

Berg, W. K., & Davis, M. (1985). Associative learning modifies startle reflexes at the lateral lemniscus. *Behavioral Neuroscience, 99*, 191–199.

Birnbaum, S. G., Lidow, M. S., & Davis, M. (1995). Effects of corticotropin releasing hormone on the acoustic startle response. *Society for Neuroscience Abstracts, 21*, 1697.

Boulis, N., & Davis, M. (1989). Footshock-induced sensitization of electrically elicited startle reflexes. *Behavioral Neuroscience, 103*, 504–508.

Boulis, N. M., Kehne, J. H., Miserendino, M. J. D., & Davis, M. (1990). Differential blockade of early and late components of acoustic startle following intrathecal infusion of 6-cyano-7-nitroquinoxaline-2,3-dione (CNQX) or D,L-2-amino-5-phosphonovaleric acid (AP-5). *Brain Research, 520*, 240–246.

Bouton, M. E. (1991). A contextual analysis of fear extinction. In P. R. Martin (Ed.), *Handbook of behavior therapy and psychological science: An integrative approach* (pp. 435–453). New York: Pergamon.

Bouton, M. E., & Bolles, R. C. (1985). *Context, event-memories, and extinction*. Hillsdale, NJ: Lawrence Erlbaum Associates.

Bouton, M. E., & King, D. A. (1983). Contextual control of conditioned fear: Tests for the associative value of the context. *Journal of Experimental Psychology: Animal Behavior Processes, 9,* 248–256.

Bouton, M. E., & King, D. A. (1986). Effect of context with mixed histories of reinforcement and nonreinforcement. *Journal of Experimental Psychology: Animal Behavior Processes, 12,* 4–15.

Brown, J. S., Kalish, H. I., & Farber, I. E. (1951). Conditional fear as revealed by magnitude of startle response to an auditory stimulus. *Journal of Experimental Psychology, 41,* 317–328.

Bustos, G., Abarca, J., Forray, M. I., Gysling, K., Bradberry, C. W., & Roth, R. H. (1992). Regulation of excitatory amino acid release by N-methyl-D-aspartate receptors in rat striatum: In vivo microdialysis studies. *Brain Research, 585,* 105–115.

Campeau, S., & Davis, M. (1995). Involvement of the central nucleus and basolateral complex of the amygdala in fear conditioning measured with fear-potentiated startle in rats trained concurrently with auditory and visual conditioned stimuli. *Journal of Neuroscience, 15,* 2301–2311.

Campeau, S., Miserendino, M. J. D., & Davis, M. (1992). Intra-amygdala infusion of the N-methyl-D-Aspartate receptor antagonist AP5 blocks acquisition but not expression of fear-potentiated startle to an auditory conditioned stimulus. *Behavioral Neuroscience, 106,* 569–574.

Cassella, J. V., & Davis, M. (1986). Neural structures mediating acoustic and tactile startle reflexes and the acoustically-elicited pinna response in rats: Electrolytic and ibotenic acid studies. *Society for Neuroscience Abstracts, 12,* 1273.

Collingridge, G. L., & Lester, A. J. (1989). Excitatory amino acid receptors in the vertebrate central nervous system. *Pharmacological Reviews, 40,* 143–210.

Connick, J. H., & Stone, T. W. (1988). Excitatory amino acid antagonists and endogeneous aspartate and glutamate release from rat hippocampal slices. *British Journal of Pharmacology, 93,* 867–868.

Corodimas, K., & LeDoux, J. E. (1995). Disruptive effects of posttraining perirhinal cortex lesions on conditioned fear: Contributions of contextual cues. *Behavioral Neuroscience, 109,* 613–619.

Crowder, J. M., Croucher, M. J., Bradford, H. F., & Collins, J. F. (1987). Excitatory amino acid receptors and depolarization-induced Ca2+ influx into hippocampal slices. *Journal of Neurochemistry, 48,* 1917–1924.

Dale, N., & Grillner, S. (1986). Dual-component synaptic potentials in the lamprey mediated by excitatory amino acid receptors. *Journal of Neuroscience, 6,* 2653–2661.

Davis, M. (1970). Effects of interstimulus length and variability on habituation of the acoustic startle reflex in the rat. *Journal of Comparative and Physiological Psychology, 72,* 177–192.

Davis, M. (1986). Pharmacological and anatomical analysis of fear conditioning using the fear-potentiated startle paradigm. *Behavioral Neuroscience, 100,* 814–824.

Davis, M. (1989). Sensitization of the acoustic startle reflex by footshock. *Behavioral Neuroscience, 103,* 495–503.

Davis, M., Gendelman, D. S., Tischler, M. D., & Gendelman, P. M. (1982). A primary acoustic startle circuit: Lesion and stimulation studies. *Journal of Neuroscience, 6,* 791–805.

de Lima, T. C. M., & Davis, M. (1994). Involvement of cyclic AMP in the acoustic startle response at the level of the nucleus reticularis pontis caudalis. *Society for Neuroscience Abstracts, 20,* 1763.

Deutch, J. A., & Deutch, D. (1964). Attention: Some theoretical considerations. *Psychological Review, 70,* 80–90.

Dolphin, A. C., & Archer, E. R. (1983). An adenosine agonist inhibits and a cyclic AMP analogue enhances the release of glutamate but not GABA from slices of rat dentate gyrus. *Neuroscience Letters, 43,* 49–54.

Falls, W. A., & Davis, M. (1992). [Blockade of second-order fear conditioning by infusion of an NMDA antagonist into the amygdala]. Unpublished data.

Falls, W. F., & Davis, M. (1994). Visual cortex ablations do not prevent extinction of fear-potentiated startle using a visual conditioned stimulus. *Behavioral and Neural Biology, 60,* 259–270.

Falls, W. A., & Davis, M. (1995). Lesions of the central nucleus of the amygdala block conditioned excitation, but not conditioned inhibition of fear as measured with the fear-potentiated startle effect. *Behavioral Neuroscience, 109,* 379–387.

Falls, W. A., Miserendino, M. J. D., & Davis, M. (1992). Extinction of fear-potentiated startle: Blockade by infusion of an NMDA antagonist into the amygdala. *Journal of Neuroscience, 12,* 854–863.

Fendt, M., Koch, M., & Schnitzler, H.-U. (1994). Lesions of the central grey block sensitization and fear potentiation of the acoustic startle response in rats. *Society for Neuroscience Abstracts, 20,* 1954.

Gallagher, M., Graham, P. W., & Holland, P. C. (1990). The amygdala central nucleus and appetitive Pavlovian conditioning: Lesions impair one class of conditioned behavior. *Journal of Neuroscience, 10,* 1906–1911.

Gewirtz, J. C., & Davis, M. (1995). Habituation of prepulse inhibition of the startle reflex using an auditory prepulse close to background noise. *Behavioral Neuroscience, 109,* 388–395.

Gokin, A. P., & Karpukhina, M. V. (1985). A study of reticular structures in cat brain involved in startle reflexes to somatic stimuli of different modalities. *Neurophysiology (USSR), 17,* 380–390.

Graham, F. (1975). The more or less startling effects of weak prestimulus. *Psychophysiology, 12,* 238–248.

Groves, P. M., Wilson, C. J., & Boyle, R. D. (1974). Brain stem pathways, cortical modulation and habituation of the acoustic startle response. *Behavioral Biology, 10,* 391–418.

Hammond, G. R. (1973). Lesions of pontine and medullary reticular formation and prestimulus inhibition of the acoustic startle in rats. *Physiology and Behavior, 10,* 239–243.

Harrison, J. M., & Warr, W. B. (1962). A study of the cochlear nucleus and ascending auditory pathways of the medulla. *Journal of Comparative Neurology, 119,* 341–379.

Hitchcock, J. M., & Davis, M. (1986). Lesions of the amygdala, but not of the cerebellum or red nucleus, block conditioned fear as measured with the potentiated startle paradigm. *Behavioral Neuroscience, 100,* 11–22.

Hitchcock, J. M., & Davis, M. (1987). Fear-potentiated startle using an auditory conditioned stimulus: Effect of lesions of the amygdala. *Physiology and Behavior, 39,* 403–408.

Hitchcock, J. M., & Davis, M. (1991). The efferent pathway of the amygdala involved in conditioned fear as measured with the fear-potentiated startle paradigm. *Behavioral Neuroscience, 105,* 826–842.

Hitchcock, J. M., Sananes, C. B., & Davis, M. (1989). Sensitization of the startle reflex by footshock: Blockade by lesions of the central nucleus of the amygdala or its efferent pathway to the brainstem. *Behavioral Neuroscience, 103,* 509–518.

Hoffman, H. S., & Ison, J. R. (1980). Reflex modification in the domain of startle. I. Some empirical findings and their implications for how the nervous system processes sensory input. *Psychological Review, 87,* 175–189.

Jones, S. M., Snell, L. D., & Johnson, K. M. (1987). Inhibition by phenycyclidine of excitatory amino acid-stimulated release of neurotransmitter in the nucleus accumbens. *Neuropharmacology, 26,* 173–179.

Kapp, B. S., Whalen, P. J., Supple, W. F., & Pascoe, J. P. (1992). Amygdaloid contributions to conditioned arousal and sensory information processing. In J. P. Aggleton (Ed.), *The amygdala: Neurobiological aspects of emotion, memory, and mental dysfunction* (pp. 229–254). New York: Wiley-Liss.

Kim, M., Campeau, S., Falls, W. A., & Davis, M. (1993). Infusion of the non-NMDA receptor antagonist CNQX into the amygdala blocks the expression of fear-potentiated startle. *Behavioral and Neural Biology, 59*, 5–8.

Kim, M., & Davis, M. (1993). Electrolytic lesions of the amygdala block acquisition and expression of fear-potentiated startle even with extensive training, but do not prevent re-acquisition. *Behavioral Neuroscience, 107*, 580–595.

Koch, M., Lingenhohl, K., & Pilz, P. K. D. (1992). Loss of the acoustic startle response following neurotoxic lesions of the caudal pontine reticular formation: Possible role of giant neurons. *Neuroscience, 49*, 617–625.

Krase, W., Koch, M., & Schnitzler, H. U. (1994). Substance P is involved in the sensitization of the acoustic startle response by footshock in rats. *Behavioral Brain Research, 63*, 81–88.

Landis, C., & Hunt, W. (1939). *The startle paradigm.* New York: Farrar & Rinehart.

Lee, Y., Lopez, D. E., Meloni, E. G., & Davis, M. (1996). A primary acoustic startle pathway: Obligatory role of cochlear root neurons and the nucleus reticularis pontis caudalis. *Journal of Neuroscience, 16*, 3777–3789.

Leitner, D. S., Powers, A. S., & Hoffman, H. S. (1980). The neural substrate of the startle response. *Physiology and Behavior, 25*, 291–297.

Li, X. F., Phillips, R. G., & LeDoux, J. E. (1993). NMDA receptors are involved in synaptic transmission in thalamo-amygdala pathways. *Society for Neuroscience Abstracts, 19*, 1228.

Lingenhohl, K., & Friauf, E. (1992). Giant neurons in the caudal pontine reticular formation receive short latency acoustic input: An intracellular recording and HRP study in the rat. *Journal of Comparative Neurology, 325*, 473–492.

Lingenhohl, K., & Friauf, E. (1994). Giant neurons in the rat reticular formation: A sensorimotor interface in the elementary acoustic startle circuit? *Journal of Neuroscience, 14*, 1176–1194.

Lopez, D. E., Merchan, M. A., Bajo, V. M., & Saldana, E. (1993). The cochlear root neurons in the rat, mouse and gerbil. In M. A. Merchan (Ed.), *The mammalian cochlear nuclei: Organization and function* (pp. 291–301). New York: Plenum.

Martin, D., Bustos, G. A., Bowe, M. A., Bray, S. D., & Nadler, J. V. (1991). Autoreceptor regulation of glutamate and aspartate release from slices of the hippocampal CA1 area. *Journal of Neurochemistry, 56*, 1647–1655.

Mayer, M. L., & Westbrook, G. L. (1987). The physiology of excitatory amino acids in the vertebrate central nervous system. *Progress in Neurobiology, 28*, 197–276.

Merchan, M. A., Collia, F., Lopez, D. E., & Saldana, E. (1988). Morphology of cochlear root neurons in the rat. *Journal of Neurocytology, 17*, 711–725.

Miserendino, M. J. D., & Davis, M. (1993). NMDA and non-NMDA antagonists infused into the nucleus reticularis pontis caudalis depress the acoustic startle reflex. *Brain Research, 623*, 215–222.

Miserendino, M. J. D., Sananes, C. B., Melia, K. R., & Davis, M. (1990). Blocking of acquisition but not expression of conditioned fear-potentiated startle by NMDA antagonists in the amygdala. *Nature, 345*, 716–718.

Mitsuhashi, M., Osashi, Y., Shichijo, S., Christian, C., Sudduth-Klinger, J., Harrowe, G., & Payan, D. G. (1992). Multiple intracellular signaling pathways of the neuropeptide substance P receptor. *Journal of Neuroscience Research, 32*, 437–443.

Pavlov, I. P. (1927). *Conditioned reflexes.* Oxford, UK: Oxford University Press.

Peterson, B. W. (1979). Reticulospinal projection to spinal motor nuclei. *Annual Review of Physiology, 41*, 127–140.

Pittaluga, A., & Raiteri, M. (1990). Release-enhancing glycine-dependent presynaptic NMDA receptors exist on noradrenergic terminals of hippocampus. *European Journal of Pharmacology, 191*, 231–234.

Rescorla, R. A. (1971). Variation in the effectiveness of reinforcement and nonreinforcement following prior inhibitory conditioning. *Learning and Motivation, 2*, 113–123.

Romanski, L. M., & LeDoux, J. E. (1992). Bilateral destruction of neocortical and perirhinal projection targets of the acoustic thalamus does not disrupt auditory fear conditioning. *Neuroscience Letters, 142,* 228–232.

Rosen, J. B., & Davis, M. (1988). Enhancement of acoustic startle by electrical stimulation of the amygdala. *Behavioral Neuroscience, 102,* 195–202.

Rosen, J. B., Hitchcock, J. M., Miserendino, M. J. D., Falls, W. A., Campeau, S., & Davis, M. (1992). Lesions of the perirhinal cortex but not of the frontal, medial prefrontal, visual, or insular cortex block fear-potentiated startle using a visual conditioned stimulus. *Journal of Neuroscience, 12,* 4624–4633.

Rosen, J. B., Hitchcock, J. M., Sananes, C. B., Miserendino, M. J. D., & Davis, M. (1991). A direct projection from the central nucleus of the amygdala to the acoustic startle pathway: Anterograde and retrograde tracing studies. *Behavioral Neuroscience, 105,* 817–825.

Rossignol, S. (1973). *Auditory influence on motor systems.* Montreal: McGill University.

Sananes, C. B., & Davis, M. (1992). N-methyl-D-aspartate lesions of the lateral and basolateral nuclei of the amygdala block fear-potentiated startle and shock sensitization of startle. *Behavioral Neuroscience, 106,* 72–80.

Schmidt, C. J., & Taylor, V. L. (1988). Release of [3H] norepinephrine from rat hippocampal slices by N-methyl-D-asparate: Comparison of the inhibitory effects of MG2+ and MK-801. *European Journal of Pharmacology, 156,* 111–120.

Spiera, R. F., & Davis, M. (1988). Excitatory amino acid antagonists depress acoustic startle after infusion into the ventral nucleus of the lateral lemniscus or paralemniscal zone. *Brain Research, 445,* 130–136.

Szabo, I., & Hazafi, K. (1965). Elicitability of the acoustic startle reaction after brain stem lesions. *Acta Physiology Academy Sciences Hungary, 27,* 155–165.

Thomson, A. M. (1989). Glycine modulation of the NMDA receptor/channel complex. *Trends in Neuroscience, 12,* 349–352.

Watkins, L. R., Wiertelak, E. P., Mooney-Heiberger, K., Grahn, R., & Maier, S. F. (1992). Endogenous anti-analgesia: Effects of amygdala, dorsal raphe and spinal lesions. *Society for Neuroscience Abstracts, 18,* 1025.

Wiertelak, E. P., Maier, S. F., & Watkins, L. R. (1992). Cholecystokinin antianalgesia: Safety cues abolish morphine analgesia. *Science, 256,* 830–833.

Williams, K., Romano, C., Dickter, M. A., & Molinoff, P. B. (1991). Modulation of the NMDA receptor by polyamines. *Life Science, 48,* 469–498.

Wu, M. F., Suzuki, S. S., & Siegel, J. M. (1988). Anatomical distribution and response patterns of reticular neurons in relation to acoustic startle. *Brain Research, 457,* 399–406.

Yeomans, J. S., & Frankland, P. W. (1994). Synapses in rostrolateral midbrain mediate 'fear' potentiation of acoustic startle and electrically evoked startle. *Society for Neuroscience Abstracts, 20,* 1753.

Young, A. M. J., & Bradford, H. F. (1991). N-methyl-D-aspartate releases excitatory amino acids in rat corpus striatum in vivo. *Journal of Neurochemistry, 56,* 1677–1683.

Zorumski, C. F., & Thio, L. L. (1992). Properties of vertebrate glutamate receptors: Calcium mobilization and desensitization. *Progress in Neurobiology, 39,* 295–336.

Motivated Attention: Affect, Activation, and Action

Peter J. Lang
Margaret M. Bradley
Bruce N. Cuthbert
University of Florida, Gainesville

In the human psychology laboratory, attention is commonly treated as a rational, conscious, cognitive activity. The focus of attention is often defined by instructions, or alternatively, by varying "expectancies" for innocuous stimuli (pure tones, words and syllables, geometric objects) to create "oddballs." Although this approach has clearly illuminated many aspects of selective information processing, it neglects a primary feature of what might be called *natural selective attention*: In the competitive world of species survival, attention is determined primarily by motivation.

In natural environments, selective responding to one type of stimulus rather than another is dictated by the organism's pre-existing drive state—hunger, sexual needs, threat of harm. Similarly, attention is more likely to be sustained by stimuli that have motivational significance, compared to routine, affectively neutral events. Furthermore, motivated attention in humans, as in animals, reflects an evolutionary inheritance. To the extent that primary reinforcement systems (with their associated pleasant and aversive affects) are engaged, the phenomenon of attention in humans involves response patterns and supporting neural pathways that are, in broad outline, consistent with those of many less complex organisms. Finally, the manner in which relevant cues are processed by the brain—the direction and vigor of the responses they generate—probably feeds back to modulate both attentional set (or disposition to respond) and the way in which new inputs are perceived and remembered.

Human attention is therefore viewed here as information processing that involves procedures of selection and evaluation of motivationally relevant input, similar to that occurring in an animal as it forages in a field, encounters others, pursues prey or sexual partners, and tries to avoid predators and comparable dangers. This conception of attention is the focus of much current biopsychological and neurophysiological research with infrahuman subjects—a literature that importantly informs the current presentation. It is also clearly related to the biobehavioral context in which Pavlov (1927) originally proposed the concepts of orienting and defense, concepts that later became the pillars of Sokolov's (1963) and Graham's (1979) more general theories of human attention.

Starting with this orientation, we present an analysis of motivated attention in the context of recent research on human picture viewing. Looking at pictures is a ubiquitous human activity: Through exposure to magazines, films, and television, image processing may occupy as much as 10% to 50% of the waking life of children and adults (e.g., Reeves & Hawkins, 1986). Whereas some hold that we see these pictures through an implicit framework of aesthetic rules unique to our species (e.g., Berlyne, 1971; Bullough, 1912), there is much evidence that other highly evolved animals also "like to watch": In the wild, nonhuman primates are often observed to stop activities and passively observe natural events or the social interactions of others (Sapolsky, 1995); in the laboratory, they recognize photographs (Boysen & Berntson, 1989) and appear to respond to television images (Swartz & Rosenblum, 1980) "as if" they were the things depicted. In general, when many stimulus properties match, media and reality merge.

The diverse picture images investigated here evoke a broad range of emotional reactions, varying in intensity, and involving both pleasant and unpleasant affect. It is proposed that the motivational states elicited by these affective cues (and the reflexive, somatic, cortical, and autonomic substrates of their perception) are fundamentally similar to those occurring when organisms stop, look, and listen, sifting through the environmental buzz for cues of danger, social meaning, and incentives to appetite.

The development of this theme begins with a consideration of how human beings perceive a wide range of picture stimuli. We present data indicating that many picture contents evoke strong affective responses, and that these responses are organized along dimensions of emotional valence and arousal. Subsequently, a theoretical approach to motivation is elucidated that postulates two drive systems, appetitive and aversive, that modulate attention and perception. The neurophysiology of these systems is briefly explored, as revealed by animal models, elucidating the different structures and pathways that mediate specific somatic and autonomic responses to motivational cues. Parallel patterns of responses (cardiovascular, sudomotor, myogenic, and cortical) are obtained in the context of human picture viewing, and motivational priming is described and illustrated by studies of startle reflex modulation. The chapter concludes by discussing how these studies of emotional perception add importantly to the classical views of orienting and defense, and usefully enhance our current understanding of human attentional processes.

EMOTION'S MOTIVES

It is generally conceded that pictures can evoke emotions. People surround themselves with images to feel calm or happy, to become excited, fervent, and to inspire. Pictures that capture attention appear capable of making people feel angry, sexually aroused, or afraid. It is said that the film *Psycho* (in which a young woman is murdered in the shower) altered the bathing habits of a generation of female film viewers, including even the star of the film, Janet Leigh (Sanz & Feeny, 1995). In an art gallery in Germany, a painting by Peter Paul Rubens has been repeatedly attacked by a mental patient, thrown into frenzy by the sight of it. Many politicians and advocate groups, some social scientists, and polls of the general public (Kolbert, 1995) all maintain that media depictions of sex and violence are so affectively compelling as to significantly influence the morals and aggressive inclination of our entire society.

Emotions as Action Dispositions

Whereas the evidence for widespread cultural effects is only modest, evolutionary analysis does suggest that the origin of emotional perception lies in the action that the image implies. Emotions, particularly those that James (1894) called the "coarse" affects, seem to be about doing something. They are associated with highly motivated behaviors that are important to the organism's survival (escape, attack, sexual consummation, etc.). In human beings, however, the defining acts, more often than not, never actually occur: The insults of a boss may upset us, but we withhold the angry blow. The picture frightens, but we do not leave our seat.

Emotions often seem to occur, specifically, when actions are delayed or inhibited. Hebb (1949) proposed, for example, that emotion results when novel circumstances prevent completion of cued behavior. Emotions are frequently described as occurring in a behavioral hiatus, as states first "experienced," then reported on and evaluated (see Frijda, 1986, on "feelings"). Thus, affects are more often *dispositions* to action, than they are the acts themselves: Emotional cues can prompt states of heightened, highly focused attention—behaviorally static, but reflecting central activation and preparation for action.

Natural language discriminates among a great variety of emotional states (from *a*morous to zippy). It is our view that this surfeit of affects has evolved from simpler action tendencies. The behavior of very primitive organisms can be wholly characterized by two responses—a direct approach to appetitive stimuli and withdrawal from nociceptive stimuli (see Schneirla, 1959). This modest behavioral repertoire cannot, of course, implement the many subgoals of human beings nor effectively deal with the perceptually rich, complex environment in which we live. Elaborate instrumental acts, behavioral delay, and response inhibition have evolved, complicating the path of simple bidirectional goal-related behavior. Thus, emotional behaviors in man are more adaptive, creative, and less predictable than those of less evolved species. A person's escape from an aversive stimulus may be achieved as well by attack or compliance as by flight, and circumspection often rewards an appetite that a direct approach could not satisfy (Lang, 1995).

Many Emotions; Two Motives

Although emotional expression can be highly varied, many theorists nonetheless view its motivational basis as retaining the simpler, two-factor organization. Konorski (1967) advocated a biphasic model that he founded on a typology of unconditioned reflexes: Exteroceptive reflexes were seen to fall into two classes, *preservative* (e.g., ingestion, copulation, nurture of progeny) and *protective* (e.g., withdrawal from or rejection of noxious agents), based on their biological, motivational role. Differentiating his views from Hess (1957), Konorski stressed that activation or arousal modulated both preservative and protective reactions. These reactions were considered to be the behavioral foundation of affects and expressed emotions. Dickinson and Dearing (1979) developed Konorski's dichotomy into two opponent motivational systems, *aversive* and *attractive*, each activated by a different, but equally wide range of unconditioned stimuli. These systems were held to have "reciprocal inhibitory connections" (p. 5) that modulate learned behavior and responses to new, unconditioned input.

   The view that affects might be organized by overarching motivational factors has also been suggested by researchers studying the emotion reports of human beings, beginning with Wundt (1896). Thus, work on natural language categories (Ortony, Clore, & Collins, 1988; Shaver, Schwartz, Kirson, & O'Connor, 1987) suggests that people's knowledge about emotions is hierarchically organized, and that the superordinate division is between positivity (pleasant states: love, joy) and negativity (unpleasant states: anger, sadness, fear). Osgood and his associates (e.g., Osgood, Suci, & Tannenbaum, 1957), using the semantic differential, earlier showed that emotional descriptors were primarily distributed along a bipolar dimension of affective valance, ranging from attraction and pleasure to aversion and displeasure. A dimension of activation—from calm to aroused—also accounted for substantial variance. Similar conclusions have been drawn by other investigators of verbal reports (e.g., Mehrabian & Russell, 1974; Russell, 1980; Tellegen, 1985) and of facial expression (Schlosberg, 1952).

Tactics and Strategy

The present view integrates several lines of theory development. Although it is clear that the *contextual tactics* of approach and avoidance have become more varied in man, nevertheless, the *strategic frame* of appetite and aversion remains fundamentally relevant. It is proposed that two motive systems exist in the brain—appetitive and aversive/defensive—accounting for the primacy of the valence dimension in affective expression. These two systems are associated with widespread cortical, autonomic, and behavioral activity. *Arousal is not viewed here as having a separate substrate*, but rather, as representing activation (metabolic and neural) of either the appetitive or aversive system, or the coactivation of both systems (see also Cacioppo & Bernston, 1994). Although the tactical demands of context may variously shape affective expression, all emotions are organized around a motivational base. In this sense, we consider valence and arousal to be the strategic dimensions of the emotion world.

Emotions are products of a Darwinian development, and can be characterized as motivationally tuned states of readiness. In human beings, the presumed indices of these affects include responses in three reactive systems: (a) expressive and evaluative language; (b) physiologic changes mediated by the somatic and autonomic systems; (c) behavioral sequelae, such as patterns of avoidance or performance deficits. This is the database of emotion, and a theory of emotion must cope with its breadth and diversity. The task is complicated by the fact that the correlations among emotion indices, within and between systems, are often quite modest (e.g., Lang, 1968; Mandler, Mandler, Kremen, & Sholiton, 1961) and the patterns of response often vary within subjects and across different contexts of stimulation (Lacey, 1958; Lacey & Lacey, 1970). Much of the "noise" in emotion analysis, however, comes from the varying behavioral demands of the context in which affect is evoked. As we discuss next, picture viewing is an attractive method for evoking emotion in the laboratory, precisely because this context naturally controls the processing task within and between individuals.

LOOKING AT PICTURES

In picture viewing (as when an animal scans a field for signs), local action is constrained. The individual is passive and motor interference is reduced. A specific input event is both the implicit and explicit focus of current activity, and all subjects have a common processing task. Thus, the physiological and overt responses observed are primarily those supporting perception and those that index the motivational strategy dictated by the stimulus. Importantly, the picture stimuli can also be easily controlled: Exposure timing and physical intensity can be carefully calibrated, and exact reproduction within and between experiments and laboratories can be assured.

One major aim of our research effort is to develop a set of photographs that can be used to select calibrated emotional stimuli for experimental use, as well as to provide a measurement standard—analogous to those used in physical metrics—to help promote scientific replication in research on emotional perception. Currently there are over 500 pictures in the International Affective Picture System (IAPS; Center for the Study of Emotion and Attention, 1995). In our initial standardization process, a large group of subjects rate their emotional experience of each picture on scales of affective valence and arousal, using the Self-Assessment Manikin (SAM; Lang, 1980). The SAM instrument is pictographic in form, largely culture-free, and can be rapidly administered (see Fig. 5.1). SAM assessments of pleasure and arousal correlate .9 and above with affective judgments of these pictures using Mehrabian and Russell's (1974) verbal semantic differential scale (Bradley & Lang, 1994).

A representative sample of IAPS pictures, distributed in the two-dimensional affective space formed by covarying pleasure and arousal ratings, is presented in Fig. 5.1. The locations of typical picture contents are shown, based on ratings from the initial standardization studies. To help orient the reader, the locations of various emotional words in this affective space are noted, which are also defined by SAM ratings obtained using our standardization procedure. The overall boomerang-shaped distribution of the picture mass appears to have two arms that extend from a common calm, nonaffective base toward either a high-arousal pleasant or high-arousal unpleasant location. This organization is completely consistent with an underlying bimotivational structure: Two systems of appetitive and aversive motivation vary along a dimension of arousal. Despite considerable effort to fill gaps in this affective space (e.g., in the unpleasant-low arousal quadrant) and force a circumplex model, this pattern has remained relatively stable over several years of picture collection and research, and is similar for acoustic (Bradley, Zack, & Lang, 1994) and verbal, as well as pictorial, stimuli.

Picture Processing: Physiology and Behavior

In the experiments described here, picture stimuli were presented either as photographic slides, or, when digitized, as displays on a computer monitor. Physiological responses and overt behaviors in this emotional perception

International Affective Picture System (IAPS)

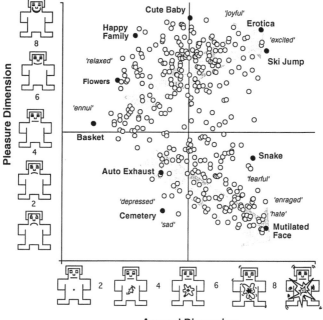

FIG. 5.1. Pictures are organized in a two-dimensional affective space, defined by the judged dimensions of valence and arousal. Specific contents are indicated for the pictures denoted by filled circles. Standardization samples of approximately 100 individuals used the Self-Assessment Manikin (SAM; Lang, 1980) to make these judgments. In its paper-and-pencil version, SAM is a 9-point scale, with valence and arousal represented graphically by changes in a cartoon figure (see x, y axes above). SAM correlated highly with the semantic differential estimate of these same dimensions (Bradley & Lang, 1994). SAM ratings of various emotion words are located in the same space (see words in italics).

task (relatively limited by the passive task context) are modulated in roughly parallel ways across widely varied picture contents. As Fig. 5.2 illustrates, physiological systems covary significantly with pleasure or arousal, as defined by evaluative judgments (see Greenwald, Cook, & Lang, 1988; Lang, Greenwald, Bradley, & Hamm, 1993). For a representative sample of IAPS pictures, facial muscle activity during viewing correlates strongly with subjects' valence ratings, ranked from the most to the least unpleasant for each subject. Heart rate shows a more modest relationship with valence: Pleasant stimuli evoke modest average responses that are not greatly different from neutral pictures; however, unpleasant pictures generally prompt marked deceleration during viewing. In general, a triphasic

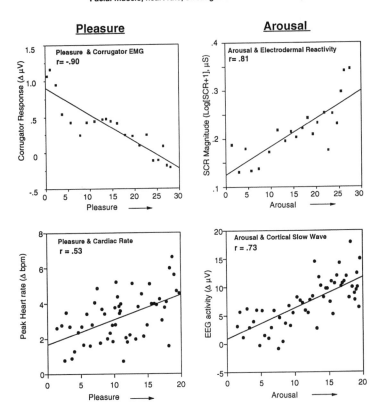

A Dimensional Analysis of EXPRESSIVE PHYSIOLOGY:
Facial muscle, heart rate, sweat gland and cortical activity

FIG. 5.2. The covariation of affective valence judgments for individual picture stimuli and corrugator muscle potentials (EMG) during viewing is shown in the upper left panel of the figure; the covariance of valence judgments and peak heart rate are shown in the lower left panel. The covariation of arousal judgments and skin conductance (electrodermal) responses during viewing is shown in the upper right panel of the figure; the covariance of arousal judgments and cortical slow voltage changes appears in the lower right panel. For each of these four analyses, affect judgments were rank ordered for each individual; the graphs show the mean response for pictures at successive ranks across subjects. The correlation statistics are based on N = 21 pictures for corrugator and skin (Lang et al., 1993) and on N = 54 pictures for heart rate and cortical slow wave (Cuthbert et al., 1996).

heart rate waveform is present when viewing all pictures. Skin conductance activity does not directly vary with picture pleasantness, but instead covaries positively with judged arousal, increasing monotonically regardless of picture valence. The slow cortical response evoked directly by the picture stimuli also demonstrates an arousal pattern. Both pleasant and unpleasant arousing pictures prompt a marked positive-going slow wave (Cuthbert, Schupp, Bradley, Birbaumer, & Lang, 1996). As can be seen in Fig. 5.3, this positivity is sustained for the entire viewing period, whereas the slow-wave response to neutral pictures is distinctly more negative.

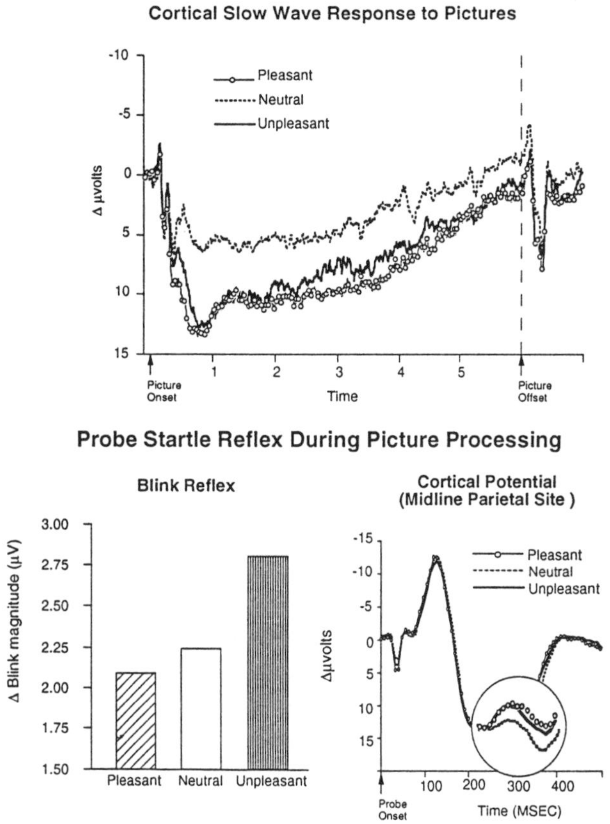

Cortical Slow Wave Response to Pictures

Probe Startle Reflex During Picture Processing

FIG. 5.3. The figure shows the psychophysiological responses of normal subjects during affective picture viewing: Cortical slow wave responses from centerline parietal electrodes are shown for pictures judged to be pleasant, unpleasant, and neutral (upper panel). The lower left panel shows blink reflex responses recorded from the orbicularis occuli muscle. These reflexes were evoked by brief acoustic probes presented during viewing of the three picture types. The lower right panel shows the cortical event related potentials (ERP) evoked by these same probes. The data are from Cuthbert et al. (1996) and Schupp et al. (in press).

Behaviors elicited in the context of emotional picture perception also covary with motivational parameters. When first exposed to a new picture, reaction time responses to probes are significantly slower for emotionally arousing, compared to calm, pictures (Bradley, Cuthbert, & Lang, 1996b; Bradley, Greenwald, Petry, & Lang, 1992). These data suggest that new activating images, and perhaps particularly unpleasant percepts, may use more attentional resources at encoding. Choice viewing behavior, as illustrated in Fig. 5.4, also covaries with arousal. When normal subjects are placed in a free-viewing context, unpleasant pictures are viewed as long as pleasant pictures. As might then be inferred from the popularity of "slasher" movies, or the habitual slowing of traffic at a roadside accident, normal subjects allocate more processing time to arousing, intense images, regardless of valence. This relationship does not occur if pictures evoke very high levels of distress. As Fig. 5.4 (upper panel) illustrates, when phobics view pictures of their own phobic objects, a palpable reduction in viewing time is found, consistent with their general avoidant behavior pattern (see Hamm, Cuthbert, Globisch, & Vaitl, in press).

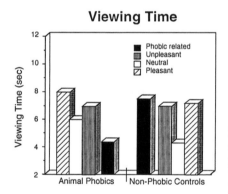

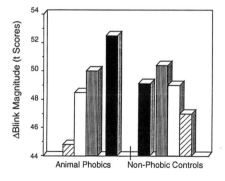

FIG. 5.4. Normal subjects and subjects with snake and/or spider phobias viewed four types of pictures: pictures from the IAPS rated pleasant, neutral, and unpleasant, and pictures of snakes and spiders. Subjects first looked at each of these stimuli for a six second period, during which acoustic startle probes were presented and eyeblinks and other physiological responses were recorded. Subjects subsequently went through the slides again at their own pace, and time of view was recorded. Viewing times for each picture type are presented in the upper panel for both groups. Blink magnitudes by slide type are presented in the lower panel. From Hamm et al. (in press).

As the fear data imply, relationships between specific measures can vary widely for individuals, and to some extent between particular groups. Gender effects are clear. For example, pleasantness ratings covary more closely with facial muscle activity in females than in males; on the other hand, skin conductance changes are more closely correlated with arousal ratings in males than in females (Greenwald et al., 1989; Lang et al., 1993). Overall, however, the motivational variables predominate in organizing the picture perception data. Thus, a factor analysis of various self-report, physiological, and behavioral measures resulted in a strong two-factor solution, with pleasantness ratings, heart rate, and facial muscles loading on a first, valence factor and arousal and interest ratings, viewing time, skin conductance, and cortical slow-wave all loading highly on a second, arousal factor. The cross-loadings for all measures (see Table 5.1) are very low. Affects are built around motivational determinants.

THE BRAIN'S AVERSIVE/DEFENSIVE SYSTEM

As proposed at the outset, the structural foundation of these valence and arousal effects is in the brain's appetitive and aversive motive systems.

TABLE 5.1
Factor Analyses of Measures of Emotional Picture Processing

Measure	Factor 1 (Valence)	Factor 2 (Arousal)
Sorted Loadings of Dependent Measures on Principal Components: Lang, Greenwald, Bradley, and Hamm (1993):		
Valence ratings	.86	−.00
Corrugator	−.85	.19
Heart rate	.79	−.14
Zygomatic	.58	.29
Arousal ratings	.15	.83
Interest	.45	.77
Viewing time	−.27	.76
Skin conductance	−.37	.74
Sorted Loadings of Dependent Measures on Principal Components: Schupp, Cuthbert, Bradley, Birbaumer, and Lang (in press):		
Valence ratings	.89	.07
Corrugator	−.83	−.10
Heart rate	.73	−.02
Arousal ratings	−.11	.89
Cortical slow wave	−.06	−.79
Skin conductance	.19	.77

These systems consist of neurophysiological circuits in the brain, largely subcortical, that are directly activated by primary reinforcement.

What we know about these motivational pathways comes primarily from the research of neuroscientists with animal subjects. Much of this work has focused on the defensive system, as activated in the rat by implicitly nociceptive events (e.g., electric shock) and fear-conditioned stimuli (previously innocuous lights and tones). Using neurosurgical, pharmacological, and electrophysiological tools, the chain of probable neural activation has been traced, starting from the input end in the sensory system—proceeding through the necessary connecting structures, defining the links least prodigal in synaptic connections—to the autonomic and motor effectors. An outline of this conditioned fear circuit, summarizing much of this recent work, is presented in Fig. 5.5.

Input from the environment normally passes from the sense organs to the sensory cortex, although very simple sensory information (e.g., lights or tones) may require only thalamic processing (e.g., see the cortical lesioning studies of DiCara, Braun, & Papas, 1970). From the sensory specific nuclei of the thalamus, the circuit proceeds to the amygdala—first to its lateral and then to its central nucleus (LeDoux, 1990). The bilateral amygdala, located within the temporal lobes of the brain, has long been known as a critical structure in the mediation of emotional expression (see the edited volume by Aggleton, 1992). That is, both stimulation and ablation of this site have reliably altered a variety of affective/motivational behaviors (from fight to flight) in both animals and man (e.g., Aggleton & Mishkin, 1986; Everitt & Robbins, 1992; Ursin, Jellestad, & Cabrera, 1981). Furthermore, some evidence suggests that the amygdala may have greater relevance for negative affect and aversion-driven behavior than appetitive behaviors, particularly that controlled by secondary reinforcers (Cahill & McGaugh, 1990).

Efferent to the central amygdala, the aversion circuit branches, with each path apparently governing separate response outputs. Lesioning studies show that different somatic responses such as "freezing," active fight/flight, and autonomically driven changes in heart rate and increases in blood pressure are mediated through different neural centers: The autonomic response is dependent on an intact pathway through lateral hypothalamus (LeDoux, 1990), and the somatic components require an intact midbrain (periaqueductal) central gray area (Fig. 5.5). Furthermore, the ventral central gray is the fear "freezing" path, whereas the dorsal gray is a critical part of the fight/flight action circuit (see the data and discussion of Fanselow, DeCola, De Oca, & Landeira-Fernandez, 1995, and the papers edited by Depaulis & Bandler, 1991).

These subcortical circuits do not generate fixed behavior patterns. Rather, they are part of a plastic, general motivational system with control

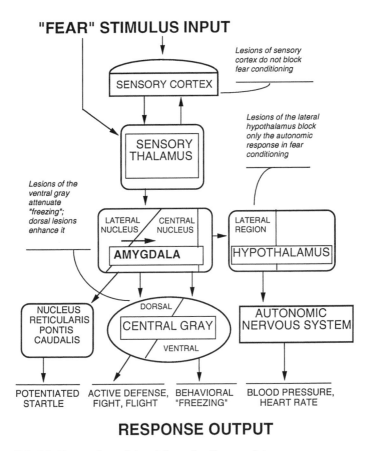

"FEAR" STIMULUS INPUT

Lesions of sensory cortex do not block fear conditioning

Lesions of the lateral hypothalamus block only the autonomic response in fear conditioning

Lesions of the ventral gray attenuate "freezing"; dorsal lesions enhance it

SENSORY CORTEX

SENSORY THALAMUS

LATERAL NUCLEUS / CENTRAL NUCLEUS

AMYGDALA

LATERAL REGION

HYPOTHALAMUS

NUCLEUS RETICULARIS PONTIS CAUDALIS

DORSAL

CENTRAL GRAY

VENTRAL

AUTONOMIC NERVOUS SYSTEM

POTENTIATED STARTLE | ACTIVE DEFENSE, FIGHT, FLIGHT | BEHAVIORAL "FREEZING" | BLOOD PRESSURE, HEART RATE

RESPONSE OUTPUT

FIG. 5.5. Fear and conditioned fear stimuli proceed from sense receptor systems to the sensory cortex and/or sensory thalamus (see LeDoux, 1990). The lateral nucleus of the amygdala receives input signals from the thalamus, transmitting them to the amygdala's central nucleus. There are three important connections efferent to the amygdala: (a) A projection from the central amygdala to the lateral hypothalamic area that mediates the autonomic emotional response; (b) Projections to the midbrain central gray region that mediate coping behaviors (see Fanselow et al., 1995); (c) A direct projection to the nucleus reticularis pontis caudalis that modulates the startle circuit (see Davis, 1989, and Davis, chapter 4, this volume, for details).

paths that vary with previous learning and tactical context. For example, Iwata and LeDoux (1988) noted that heart rate and blood pressure decrease in response to a conditioned tone (previously accompanied by shock) when animals are physically restrained; on the other hand, these same autonomic responses increase when the conditioned signal is presented to freely behaving animals.

Overall, the neurophysiological findings suggest that the amygdala is a general mediator of defensive behaviors, that is, a key site in a general aversive motivational system. Structures downstream from the amygdala are implicated in the different forms of defense. Whereas context dictates that these autonomic and somatic patterns have great variety, they can be functionally organized into two general classes:

1. Defensive action (i.e., contextual variations in fight/flight that are more or less direct responses to nociception or imminent attack).
2. Defensive immobility (i.e., "freezing" and hypervigilance in which the organism is passive but "primed" to respond to aversive stimulation).

MOTIVATIONAL PRIMING

Scientists and laymen agree that the emotions loom large in life. They have, of course, significance as states-in-themselves, with their own surgent response patterns. In addition, they are held to play an important modulatory role on other behaviors—coloring, inhibiting, or energizing thought, perception, and action, often in contexts that are physically and semantically remote from the apparent source of the controlling affect. It is proposed here that this ubiquitous spread of affection across the behavioral repertoire is motivationally mediated.

As we have described thus far, emotions reflect the engagement of neural structures and pathways in either the appetitive or aversive motivation systems. During the period when subcortical circuitry is active, a modulatory effect is presumed to affect the brain's processing operations. Specifically, associations, representations, and action programs that are linked to the engaged motivational system are primed. Priming results in a higher probability that these representations will be accessed (with a concomitant greater potential output strength) than other information, and conversely, that mental events and programs linked to the nonengaged system have a reduced probability and strength of activation. Thus, in the case of an aversively motivated organism (i.e., the affective state is unpleasant), responses to other aversive cues are primed, and at the same time, responses to appetitive cues may be reduced or absent. As an example, findings that suggest that negative or positive affective moods occasion same valence physiological responses, verbal associations, or memories might be construed to be a result of such motivational priming (e.g., Blaney, 1986; Bower, 1981; Bradley et al., 1996b).

The most primitive and fundamental motivational priming is at the level of unconditioned exteroceptive reflexes. It will be recalled that reflexes can be sorted (Konorski, 1967) according to the primary reinforcement properties of their unconditioned stimuli, either appetitive or aversive, and the consummatory or defensive function of the reflex itself. In the priming view, responses to unconditioned stimuli are modulated according to two factors: (a) the classification of the reflex (appetitive or defensive), and (b) the affective valence of the individual's ongoing emotional state. Thus, an independently evoked defensive reflex will be augmented when the organism is already reacting to an aversive foreground stimulus (i.e., is in an unpleasant state); this same reflex will be reduced in amplitude when the organism is processing an appetitive foreground. Finally, both these priming effects—potentiation and diminution of responding—are expected to be enhanced as a function of the level of affective drive or activation.

Startle Potentiation

Evidence for priming of the startle reflex is found in both animal and human studies. In most mammals, an abrupt sensory event will prompt a chained series of rapid flexor movements that cascade throughout the body (Landis & Hunt, 1939). This startle response appears to be a primitive defensive reflex that serves a protective function, avoiding organ injury (as in the eyeblink), and acting as a behavioral interrupt (Graham, 1979), clearing processors to deal with possible threat. According to the motivational priming hypothesis, the defensive startle reflex should be of significantly greater amplitude (and faster) when the aversive motivational system is active, as in a fear state. This was first examined systematically by Brown, Kalish, and Farber (1951), who compared reflex responses to startle probes (shots from a toy pistol) presented to male rats during neutral or shock conditioned stimuli at extinction. Results conformed to expectation: Animals did indeed react more forcefully—as measured by a stabilimeter in the floor of the cage—when the startle stimuli were presented during fear-conditioned signals (see also, Ross, 1961; Spence & Runquist, 1958).

The Rat Brain's Fear-Startle Circuit. Davis and his associates (chapter 4, this volume; also Davis, 1989; Davis, Hitchcock, & Rosen, 1987) and others (Fendt, Koch, & Schnitzler, 1994a) have since gathered considerable evidence that the brain structure mediating fear-conditioned startle potentiation is, at least in the rat, the same aversive system previously described. As Davis (chapter 4, this volume) has shown, following stimulation of the ear by an abrupt noise, the afferent path of the startle reflex proceeds from the cochlear nucleus to the reticular formation; from there efferent connections pass through spinal neurons to the reflex effectors. This is the basic obligatory circuit, directly driven by the parameters of the input stimulus (e.g., stimulus intensity, frequency, steepness of the onset ramp).

Startle potentiation through learned fear implies that a secondary circuit modulates this primary reflex pathway. There is now overwhelming evidence that the amygdala, the key structure in aversively motivated behavior, is a critical part of this modulatory circuit (see Fig. 5.5): It has been shown that, first, there are direct, monosynaptic projections from the amygdala to the key reticular site (i.e., to the structure in the basic circuit on which modulation of the reflex depends); second, electrical stimulation of the amygdala (below the level for kindling) directly enhances startle reflex amplitude; and finally and most important, lesions of the amygdala abolish fear-conditioned startle potentiation.

Human Conditioning and the Blink Response. In studies with human beings, rapid eye closure is one of the most reliable components of the behavioral cascade that constitutes the startle reflex. The latency (occurring within 30–50 msec of stimulus onset) and magnitude of the blink can be measured by monitoring the orbicularis oculi muscle, using electrodes placed just beneath the lower lid (see Fig. 5.6). The acoustic stimulus used to evoke the blink is relatively modest—typically a 50-msec burst of white noise at around 95 dB that, although prompting a clear blink response, rarely interferes with ongoing foreground tasks. Several studies have confirmed reliable potentiation of the blink response in humans following simple shock exposure or as a function of learned associations that parallel the modulatory patterns obtained with rats (Greenwald, Bradley, Cuthbert, & Lang, 1996; Hamm, Greenwald, Bradley, & Lang, 1993). In brief, the blink muscle response to a startle probe is *generally* larger after subjects experience electric shock or when simply anticipating shock (Grillon, Ameli, Woods, & Merikangas, 1991), and *selectively* larger to startle probes presented during exposure to a shock-conditioned stimulus than to probes presented during exposure to an unshocked control stimulus. These results, coupled with clinical neurological evidence linking the amygdala to aversive emotion (Aggleton, 1992) encourage the hypothesis that similar neural pathways might be responsible for potentiation effects in both rats and human beings.

Probing Emotional Perception

In testing the hypothesis that affective state modulates the reflexive startle response, pictures from the IAPS (Center for the Study of Emotion and Attention, 1995) are used, selected on the basis of normative affective ratings (Lang, Bradley, & Cuthbert, 1995). They are organized in many of these experiments into three affective classes—unpleasant (e.g., poisonous snakes, aimed guns, pictures of violent death), pleasant (e.g., happy babies, appetizing food, erotica), and neutral (e.g., umbrellas, hair dryer, and other common household objects).

As mentioned earlier, picture viewing is an observational, intake task in which, like a "freezing" rat or an attentive predator, subjects are generally

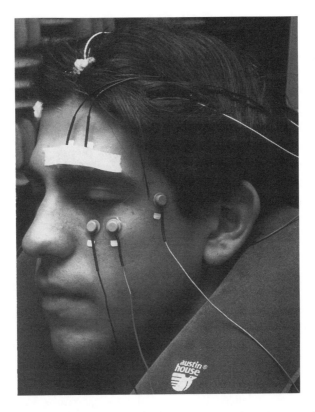

FIG. 5.6. Blink magnitude is determined by measuring the action potentials of the orbicularis oculi muscle. This muscle surrounds the eye and its innervation produces eye closure. To record the blink, electrodes are placed on the skin surface, over the muscle just below the eye. Corrugator muscle and frontal cortical electrode placements are also shown.

immobile, with sensory processors engaged. When startle probes are administered in this context, results have consistently conformed to the motivational priming hypothesis: As Fig. 5.3 (left panel) illustrates, a significant monotonic trend is reliably observed over judged picture valence, with the largest startle blink responses occurring during unpleasant content and the smallest during pleasant pictures (e.g., Lang, Bradley, & Cuthbert, 1990; Vrana, Spence, & Lang, 1988).

These emotional–perceptual effects seem ubiquitous. Balaban (1995) found affective picture modulation of startle probe responses in 5-month-old infants. Jansen and Frijda (1994), using evocative video film clips, and Hamm, Stark, and Vaitl (1990), using IAPS pictures, have obtained the affect-startle effect in European subjects. Interestingly, emotional modulation of the reflex does not seem to depend on novelty. It persists even with repeated presentation of the same picture stimuli. That is, although there is an overall diminution of the startle reflex over blocks of trials with the same pictures, affective potentiation and inhibition remain to the last trial block (Bradley, Lang, & Cuthbert, 1993; Hamm, Globisch, Weilke, & Wietlacke, 1993). Similarly, affective modulation persists when the same set of pictures is viewed in separate experimental sessions (Bradley, Gianaros, & Lang, 1995).

Intensity and Modality. Probe studies of picture perception have generally employed binaural startle stimuli in the range on 90 to 100 dB; however, lower intensities (sufficient to reliably evoke startle) also produce affective startle modulation (Cuthbert, Bradley, & Lang, 1996). Furthermore, significant affective modulation has been shown with monaural acoustic probes. In the monaural case, emotional pictures appear to be differentiated most reliably by probes presented to the left (presumably conferring an advantage in right brain processing) compared to the right ear (Bradley, Cuthbert, & Lang, 1991, 1996a).

Affective modulation of startle is observed for picture stimuli regardless of whether the startle probe is visual, acoustic, or tactile (e.g., Bradley, Cuthbert, & Lang, 1990; Hawk, Cook, Russell, & Dillon, 1994), suggesting that modality-specific processes are not primary in these modulatory effects. Furthermore, affective modulation is not confined to visual percepts: When the foreground stimuli consist of short, 6-sec sound clips of various affective events (e.g., sounds of love-making, babies crying, bombs bursting), and the startle probe is a visual light flash, the same affect-reflex effect is obtained, suggesting that its mediation is broadly motivational and thus consistent across affective foregrounds of differing stimulus modality (Bradley et al., 1994).

Arousal and Reflex Modulation. Consistent with the motivational priming hypothesis, modulatory effects on the startle reflex appear to increase with greater activation in each motive system. That is, probe startle *potentiation* is largest for *unpleasant* pictures that are rated most arousing, whereas conversely, the most arousing *pleasant* pictures prompt the greatest probe startle *inhibition* (Cuthbert, Bradley, & Lang, 1996). And, for individuals reporting high levels of fearfulness, startle potentiation during aversive picture processing is augmented (Cook, Davis, Hawk, Spence, & Gautier, 1992; Hamm et al., in press). On the other hand, stimuli judged to be very low in activation fail to show either systematic valence-driven inhibition or potentiation. Perhaps for this reason, startle modulation does not seem to covary with the dimensions defined by Tellegen's Positive and Negative Affect Scale (PANAS; Watson, Clark, & Tellegen, 1988), which involves a 90° rotation of the affective space depicted in Fig. 5.1 (see McManis & Lang, 1992).

It appears, furthermore, that for some individuals only the activating property of picture stimuli (irrespective of valence) modulates the startle probe response. Incarcerated psychopaths, for example, show the same reflex inhibition (relative to neutral pictures) to both arousing pleasant *and* arousing unpleasant picture stimuli (Patrick, 1994; Patrick, Bradley, & Lang, 1993). This finding—dramatically different from what is seen in the normal population—could mean that this pathological group has a deficit in the aversive motivational system. The finding is also consistent with the view that probe reflex inhibition reflects attentional engagement (Graham, 1992).

The pattern seen in psychopaths (i.e., probe response inhibition to an arousing foreground), occurs reliably under certain circumstances in normal subjects. When a leading pulse immediately precedes a startle evoking stimulus, blinks are generally reduced in magnitude (see Graham, 1975; see Part III, this volume: Dawson, Schell, Swerdlow, & Filion; Hackley & Boelhouwer; Simons & Perlstein). This same inhibitory effect is obtained in the picture paradigm for probes presented shortly after picture onset (less than 500 msec). When pictures serve as lead stimuli, however, the degree of inhibition is content selective (Bradley, Cuthbert, & Lang, 1993). Thus, as can be seen in Fig. 5.7, greater prepulse inhibition is obtained for arousing stimuli, either appetitive or aversive, compared to pictures that are judged low in arousal. With temporally later probes—beyond this early,

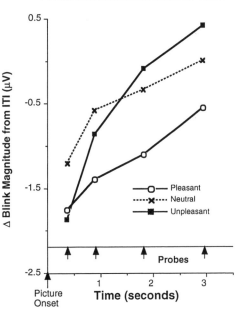

FIG. 5.7. Startle probes were presented at various times following the onset of three IAPS picture types—pleasant, neutral, and unpleasant. Each picture was only probed once. For temporally early probes, picture onset acts as a prepulse stimulus, and blink inhibition was anticipated (see Part III, this volume, on prepulse effects and analyses). Blink magnitudes in response to startle probes are shown as they varied over time and picture type, illustrating significantly greater prepulse inhibition with an emotional picture than for a neutral picture prepulse (data from Bradley, Cuthbert, & Lang, 1993).

prepulse region—the usual valence modulation is observed (i.e., relative potentiation during unpleasant stimuli; inhibition for pleasant stimuli). This result suggests, on the one hand, that affective dispositions take time to develop; on the other hand, it indicates that some motivationally relevant information is, indeed, processed in an eyeblink.

Using a different paradigm, Öhman (see chapter 7, this volume) provides evidence for a similarly early, "preattentive" processing of "prepared" danger cues (e.g., angry faces or threatening animals). The startle data already described suggest that this special, rapid processing of arousing input may be a general phenomenon that occurs for appetitive as well as aversive cue stimuli.

Not surprisingly, other results indicate that the brain separately codes stimulus arousal (independent of its motivational source) even during the later stages of picture processing. Acoustic startle probes evoke cortical potentials, as well as blink reflexes. Unlike the reflex, these brain potentials vary more with the arousal than the pleasantness of picture foregrounds (Schupp, Cuthbert, Bradley, Birbaumer, & Lang, in press). As can be seen in Fig. 5.3 (right lower panel), the P3 component of the probe-evoked cortical potential, compared to neutral pictures, is significantly smaller when either pleasant or unpleasant pictures are being viewed.

Emotionally evocative pictures are consistently rated as more interesting and more complex than neutral, low-arousal images (Bradley, Greenwald, & Hamm, 1993; Lang et al., 1990). Thus, these P3 effects may reflect a variation in attentional engagement that covaries with judged affective arousal. Similar P3 reductions when secondary probe stimuli are presented during a variety of foreground tasks have been noted by other investigators (Polich, 1989; Roth, Dorato, & Kopell, 1984; Sirevaag, Kramer, Coles, & Donchin, 1989). Assuming a limited capacity model of attention, and given a major allocation of resources to more compelling foregrounds, the smaller P3s indicate a reduced available capacity for the probe.

Startle and Appetitive Drive

We earlier discussed the known circuitry of the brain's aversive/defensive system and how it appears to mediate potentiation of the startle response. Unfortunately, no similarly elegant model can yet be summoned from the animal literature to explain the *reduction* in probe startle amplitude observed during exposure to pleasant/appetitive stimuli.

Generalized Drive. Early studies of appetitive motivation and the startle probe with animal subjects were intended to examine Hull's (1943) hypothesis of generalized drive (D). "Big D" was conceived to be unimodal and not implicitly directional. Therefore, both aversive and appetitive subdrives were hypothesized to have the same potentiating effect on an incidental reflex, and furthermore, to summate to produce a larger response when both states were simultaneously activated. Some research appeared to support the Hullian hypothesis. For example, Merryman (1952, described in Brown, 1961) observed increasing startle potentiation in fear conditioned animals as the number of hours of food deprivation increased.

On the other hand, several studies that manipulated only hunger drive, and presented startle probes during exposure to food cues, found no potentiation effect (Trapold, 1962). Other investigators, given the Hullian zeitgeist, were surprised to find a reduction in startle magnitude in the context of appetitive stimuli, relative to the findings for control animals or conditions (Ison & Krauter, 1975). These latter results are, of course, consistent with the contemporary hypothesis of a priming mismatch, predicting that appetitive stimuli would prompt inhibition of a defense (startle) reflex.

An experiment by Wagner (1963) highlighted a variable that, if uncontrolled, could account for the earlier, inconsistent findings. Wagner observed that when deprived animals (24 hours) were exposed to food cues, *but no longer rewarded with consummation*, startle was markedly potentiated. That is, potentiation occurred under conditions of "frustrative nonreward"—an unpleasant state that in the priming view should enhance defensive startle. A similar affect of food deprivation has recently been observed in human subjects (Drobes, Hillman, Bradley, Cuthbert, & Lang, 1995): As can be seen in Fig. 5.8, non-food-deprived subjects show the typical startle inhibition to pictures of appetizing food, as for other pleasant pictures. When food is withheld for a significant period, however, human subjects begin to show relative startle potentiation, consistent with the idea that this produces an unpleasant state of "frustrative nonreward."

Schmid, Koch, and Schnitzler (1995), using animal subjects, recently demonstrated that when this "frustrative" element is absent, appetitive cues reliably prompt startle inhibition in rodents. In their paradigm, food was first paired with a light cue that, when subsequently presented alone, resulted in diminished probe startle reflexes. This paradigm provides an animal model that parallels appetitive startle inhibition in humans. Koch and his colleagues are currently exploring the neurophysiology of this effect, using methods similar to those employed in studies of the aversion circuit. Preliminary results indicate that the appetitive stimulus–probe inhibition effect is lost with lesioning of the dopamine receptors in the nucleus accumbens. Other experiments suggest that amygdala lesions do not interfere with appetitive inhibition (M. Koch, personal communication, November 13, 1995). It will be exciting to see if the neural structures and pathways involved in appetitive startle inhibition are the same as or

Probe Startle Reflex

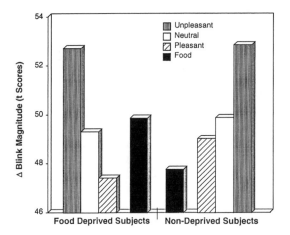

FIG. 5.8. Nondeprived subjects and subjects that were food deprived for 6 hours viewed pleasant, neutral, and unpleasant pictures from the IAPS, and a selection of pictures of appetizing food. Startle probes were presented during viewing. Blink magnitudes to the probes, for each of the four picture types, are shown for both groups. From Drobes et al. (1995).

different from those implicated in simple attention and sensory gating (Swerdlow, Caine, Braff, & Geyer, 1992; see Dawson et al., chapter 11, this volume).

ATTENTION AND MOTIVATION

A great many researchers (Graham, Hoffman, Dawson, all this volume) hold that startle inhibition indexes attentive or preattentive sensory processing. The supporting data are derived from two main experimental paradigms: First, startle probe reflex magnitudes are diminished when attention is directed to a modality or task different from the startle probe (suggesting attentional resources are expended on a center of interest and less are available to the probe); second, a diminished reflex is observed when the startle probe is immediately preceded by a prepulse. Startle inhibition is sometimes attributed to a partial "gating out" of the probe stimulus to "protect" sensory processing of the prepulse.

The motivational hypothesis presented here seems to be an alternative interpretation; that is, the defensive startle reflex is reduced because it is inconsistent with an ongoing appetitive drive state that may inhibit transmission in relevant neural pathways or generate opponent responses. As we have come to better understand the probe startle response, however, the motivational and attentional views seem less clearly at odds, and appear more like different perspectives on a common phenomenon.

Why Pay Attention?

In cognitive studies of human beings it is usual to manipulate attention through instructions. We tell the participant to attend to x and not y, or to respond quickly when z appears. Cooperative subjects are preselected, and the experimenter gives little thought to what environmental events generally motivate an attentional set. In animal research, on the other hand, the motivational conditions significantly determine the phenomenon. That is, the animal reacts to cues because they are intrinsically nociceptive or appetitive, or because they have been associated with such stimuli in the past. It is proposed here that when emotion is evoked in human subjects, motivational state is similarly a central consideration. Attention is automatically directed to cues that have motivational significance, and many of the same CNS, somatic, and autonomic covariates of attention appear across species.

Watching for Prey, While Looking Out for Predators and Other Disasters

Mammals orient automatically to new stimulus events. This attentive disposition involves postural adjustments, sense organ modulation, and autonomic changes that may facilitate stimulus analysis. As described previously, much of the neural circuitry mediating responses to motivationally pertinent events is specific and well understood in rodents. Thus, the initial response of a rat to the appearance of a cat is to "freeze"—immobile, eyes fixed on the predator (Blanchard & Blanchard, 1977). This freezing behavior is mediated through the ventral central gray, subsequent to activation of the amygdala. A similar immobility, which may involve the same neural mechanism, is also found in predators when a potential prey first appears in their field of view.

Novel stimuli of all types (appetitive and aversive) also engage the autonomic nervous system, producing, for example, pupilary, pilomotor, and sudomotor responses. Cardiovascular responses, as we have seen (e.g., Graham & Clifton, 1966; Sokolov, 1963, chapter 1, this volume), are given special emphasis in studies of orienting. Heart rate slows to any new or signal stimulus. Animals respond to threatening stimuli, in particular, with very dramatic bradycardia (see Campbell, chapter 3, this volume). Lacey and Lacey (1970) have long held that cardiovascular reactions of this type feed back centrally, modulating brain activity to facilitate perception.

It is in this context, during attentive observation, that startle probe modulation is observed in perception. The picture paradigm requires this attentional set of human participants. Probe responses are, however, clearly directional. Thus, in the case of a pleasant-appetitive cue, the reflex response to an irrelevant, mildly nociceptive input (an abrupt noise) is inhibited. It could be argued that this disposition has functional, evolutionary origins, as with the surveillant pause of a stalking predator: The lioness crouches immobile, eyes directed at the distant herd of gazelle. While a high drive state primes appetitive reflexes (as a spring forward with movement of the herd), only the strongest nociceptive stimulus (not the simple bite of a fly) disrupts her attentive set. A reduced startle reflex is consistent both with an overall disposition of immobile observation and an allocation of attentional resources to prey observation.

Conversely, from the perspective of the prey, cues signaling a potential threat engage the aversive/defense system (see Masterson & Crawford, 1982). In this case, the animal is broadly alerted to possible nociceptive input, "like a cocked pistol," with all defensive reflexes primed. Thus, the mildly aversive acoustic startle probe invokes a supraordinary, potentiated reflex response. As we have seen, this same reaction occurs when humans look at unpleasant pictures.

Attention and Action

Obrist (1981) emphasized repeatedly that a reduction in muscle activity—immobility—is one of the most reliable features of an attentive posture. In animal research, reliable startle potentiation is only seen in the overtly passive, vigilant animal—startle potentiation does not occur during activity (e.g., after the trigger has been pulled and the animal fights or is in headlong flight). Rather, startle potentiation is highly correlated with "freezing" behavior in the rat. Thus, for example, footshocks presented in an unfamiliar environment result in both "freezing" (Blanchard, Fukunaga, & Blanchard, 1976) and potentiated startle (Davis, 1989). Passive "freezing" (Fanselow et al., 1995), and perhaps potentiated startle as well (Fendt, Koch, & Schnitzler, 1994b), are disrupted by lesions in the ventral periaqueductal gray. Interestingly, when the grosser defense responses (fight/flight) are engaged they appear to activate the dorsal path (Fanselow et al., 1995) and interfere with the expected increase in potentiated startle. In fact, lesions of the dorsal central gray can restore potentiated startle in some circumstances (D. Walker & M. Davis, personal communication, March, 1995).

If "freezing" is construed to be an aversively motivated preparatory set, startle stimuli seem to act as releasers that, when sufficiently intense, interrupt attentive processing and initiate an action sequence. From a behavioral perspective, the startle response appears to be defensive (and like other defense reactions, it is accompanied by cardiac acceleration; e.g., see Graham, 1979; Cook & Turpin, chapter 6, this volume). From a neurophysiological viewpoint, startle stimuli could be seen as switching the efferent path from the ventral to the dorso-lateral central gray. For probe stimuli that elicit but a blink, the sensory hiatus is momentary. If the startling stimulus is sufficiently aversive or is part of, or simultaneous with, a motivationally relevant event (e.g., the sudden appearance of a predator), the reflex can lend speed and force to appropriate defensive action.

Probing Nonviewing Foreground Tasks

Consistent with the previous analysis, several recent studies of human subjects have failed to obtain startle potentiation in anxious or stressed subjects who, instead of simply watching for cues, were actively preparing for or were already involved in stressful situations. Chapman and Blumenthal (1994), for example, observed diminished rather than potentiated blink reflexes when probes were presented to anxious subjects who were expecting or were participating in a social encounter; similarly, Hoffman (chapter 8, this volume) observed diminished blinks in subjects actively engaged in a stressful dichotic listening task.

The action/perception distinction also appears to be relevant for memorial experience. That is, when subjects are asked to sustain the image of a just-observed arousing picture stimulus, affective modulation of probe stimuli (potentiation and inhibition) is observed, as for the pictures themselves (Schupp et al., in press). However, when subjects are instructed to imagine highly arousing events *in which they are active participants*, the startle probe response is augmented for both arousing pleasant and unpleasant images, relative to neutral images (Bradley, Cuthbert, & Lang, 1991, 1995; Miller, Levenston, Geddings, & Patrick, 1994; Witvliet & Vrana, 1995). That is, activation of either motive system—not just the aversive—prompts potentiation.

ORIENTING AND DEFENSE

Studies of emotional perception show that both appetitive and aversive motive systems strongly modulate the orienting response. The pattern of modulation can be very different, however, depending on the specific measure of orienting that is assessed, the motive system that is active, and the intensity of that activation. These phenomenon are illustrated in Fig. 5.9 with data from a recent experiment (Cuthbert et al., in press). Skin conductance responses to picture stimuli are shown, along with blink reflex

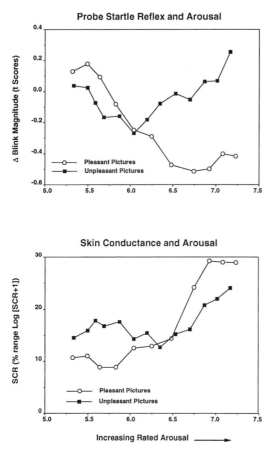

FIG. 5.9. The upper panel illustrates the mean blink magnitudes prompted by startle probes presented during increasingly arousing picture stimuli. The pictures were ranked according to IAPS normative arousal ratings, separately for pleasant and unpleasant stimuli. From 38 to 47 subjects contributed to each data point, with the *N* varying because of rejected trials and the fact that subjects were not startled during all pictures. For clarity, the data were smoothed prior to graphing with a 5-point moving average (Rafferty & Norling, 1989).

Mean skin conductance responses during picture viewing are presented in the lower panel, organized as above by normative arousal ratings. All data are from Cuthbert, Bradley, and Lang (1996).

responses to late interval startle probes. Picture stimuli are distributed on the abscissa on a continuum of increasing, judged arousal. Smoothed curves for pleasant and aversive stimuli are presented separately. Only data above the midpoint of the arousal scale are illustrated, as below this level, evidence of a systematic group response to pictures is meager.

Indexing greater activity in the sympathetic chain, skin conductance increases progressively with judged stimulus arousal, similarly for both pleasant and aversive pictures. A similar pattern has recently been observed for slow potentials from the brain; that is, the cortex shows greater positive activity during more arousing stimuli, irrespective of valence (Cuthbert et al., 1995), consistent with a hypothesis of greater attentional processing for broadly significant stimuli.

The probe reflex, on the other hand, shows a motive-specific pattern. For pleasant pictures, the reflex decreases progressively in magnitude with increasing picture arousal. An initial reduction in blink magnitude is also suggested for aversive pictures, with somewhat greater inhibition as arousal begins to increase. Somewhat farther along the scale, however, the response direction is abruptly reversed. Startle magnitude begins to increase, peaking for pictures judged unpleasant and highest in arousal level.

In many ways, this change in the direction of the reflex response, associated with increasing arousal of unpleasant pictures, recalls Sokolov's (1963) description of how orienting changes to consistent defense, after a period of oscillation between the two responses—with increasing intensity of physical stimulation. It also reminds one of Miller's (1959) classic conflict theory (Miller, 1948, 1951; for a recent assessment, see Cacioppo & Berntson, 1994): In their analysis, a goal that has been the site of both punishment and reward is assumed. Approach and withdrawal motivation contribute to an overall increase in arousal with increasing proximity to the goal. The gradient of avoidance motivation is, however, intrinsically steeper than that of approach (see Fig. 5.10).

Modeling the picture-startle data from this perspective—and considering that aversive pictures are consistently judged to be more "interesting" as well as more unpleasant than neutral pictures—we might anticipate that probes would be increasingly inhibited up to the point of

Approach and Avoidance Gradients

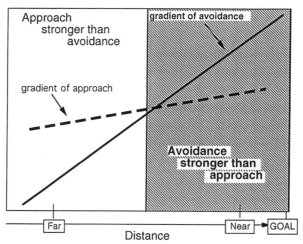

FIG. 5.10. "Simple graphic representation of an approach–avoidance conflict. The tendency to approach is the stronger of the two tendencies far from the goal, whereas the tendency to avoid is the stronger of the two near to the goal. Therefore, when far from the goal, the subject should tend to approach part way and then stop. In short, he should tend to remain in the region where the two gradients intersect" (p. 206). Figure adapted from Miller (1959).

gradient intersection (Miller noted that animals were normally stopped, immobile in this region). The abrupt change to increasing potentiation reflects the subsequent dominance of avoidance motivation, as stimuli become more unpleasant and threatening.

Heart Rate and Stimulus Arousal

For pleasant, neutral, and low-arousal unpleasant pictures the heart rate waveforms during picture viewing are classically triphasic, characterized by a brief initial deceleration, a small subsequent rate increase, and a modest secondary slowing (e.g., Bradley, Lang, & Cuthbert, 1993, p. 975; Lang, Bradley, Drobes, & Cuthbert, 1995). This pattern is not unlike that found for simple novel or target stimuli or for easily recognized tones in a varying stimulus series (Lang & Hnatiow, 1962; Simons & Lang, 1976). The average of this activity over the viewing interval tends to be below baseline, supporting the hypothesized role of heart rate slowing as a general index of attention (Graham & Clifton, 1966).

Sustained cardiac deceleration throughout the picture period (similar in magnitude to the short decelerations to brief, complex novel stimuli, reported by Simons & Perlstein, chapter 10, this volume), however, is reliably observed only when subjects watch pictures with aversive content. This phenomenon is illustrated in Fig. 5.11: Mean heart rate changes, during viewing of increasingly arousing pleasant and unpleasant pictures, are summarized. Unpleasant pictures prompt slower heart rates throughout. Furthermore, this deceleration increases progressively as unpleasant pictures are judged more arousing. This phenomenon resembles the "fear bradycardia" widely observed in animals (see Campbell, chapter 3, this volume).

The augmented bradycardia is clearly vagal. It is, however, accompanied by increased activity in the sympathetic chain (indicated by the simultaneous augmentation of the conductance response). This is consistent with findings showing that the heart is dually innervated during orienting (Berntson, Cacioppo, Quigley, & Fabro, 1994; Sokolov & Cacioppo, chapter 1, this volume). Arousal results in increasing stimulation from both sides of the ANS, but with the parasympathetic system clearly dominant.

Interestingly, bradycardia does not characterize the response of phobic subjects to pictures of the phobic object (see the lower panel, Fig. 5.11, from Hamm et al., 1995; see also Klorman & Ryan, 1980; Klorman, Weissberg, & Wiesenfeld, 1977; Cook & Turpin, chapter 6, this volume). When these very high fear subjects view pictures of the phobic object, the sympathetic system dominates. Phobic subjects also show larger startle responses, and rate their arousal to be much higher than the maximum ratings of average subjects. Also unlike average subjects, they quickly

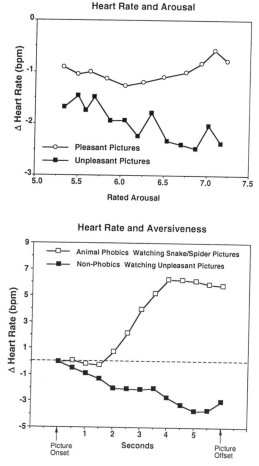

FIG. 5.11. The upper panel shows mean heart rate responses during the viewing of picture stimuli judged to be increasingly arousing. The pictures were ranked according to normative arousal ratings (SAM), separately for pleasant and unpleasant stimuli, and the data averaged by stimulus rank (from Cuthbert et al., 1996).

The lower panel shows the average heart rate waveform for nonphobics viewing unpleasant pictures from the IAPS for a 6-sec exposure, and the waveform recorded for animal phobic subjects viewing pictures of their phobic objects (snakes and spiders). Waveforms (not shown) for phobics viewing the same IAPS unpleasant pictures, and for nonphobics viewing pictures of snakes and spiders, were deceleratory, and similar to the one shown for nonphobics (from Hamm et al., in press).

terminate "looking" in a free-viewing situation (see Fig. 5.3). Overall, the response of phobics fits most descriptions of the defense reflex.

It is clear that different measures change in very different ways over the arousal dimension. That is, instead of a single orienting response, giving way at some point to defense, and reflected in a wholly parallel way by all measures, we instead observe a cascade of different response events, changing in different ways and at different levels, as activation increases. It is also apparent that orienting is not a response confined to neutral or pleasant stimuli, or if considered to be synonymous with attentive processing, something that occurs only briefly at stimulus onset. As was long ago noted by Lacey (1958), even very unpleasant events can evoke a physiology consistent with sustained attention. Aversive stimulus contents are not automatically "rejected;" rather, attention is allocated to processing them in detail, particularly when they first appear. On the other hand, strong aversive motivation is clearly a major factor in initiating defense.

Rethinking the Defense Reflex

Several psychobiological theorists have given thought to how defensive behavior might be staged as organisms confront an environment of myriad potential dangers. We have already alluded to the work of Masterson and Crawford (1982), who proposed a two-stage model of defensive behavior—a preparatory defense reaction in which the organism is vigilant and mobilizes for threat, and a subsequent "alarm reaction," as fight or flight responses are triggered. Fanselow (1994), building on an earlier analysis of Timberlake's (1993), proposed a somewhat more detailed sequence that he related to the neurophysiology of the subcortex's periaqueductal area of central gray. Considered in the context of a prey confronted by a predator, he described three stages:

1. *Pre-encounter*, in which target specific defense behavior is not yet engaged and appetitive motivation may be simultaneously present. Presumably, this is the realm of transient detection responses (TDR; Graham, 1992), determined by modest differences in the arousal value of stimuli, readily habituated, and not valence relevant.
2. *Post-encounter*: For Fanselow (1994), motor responses at this stage include "freezing"—mediated by ventral gray. This is also the stage of focused attention (conceivably conscious appraisal in man, Öhman, Esteves, Flykt, & Soares, 1993), associative learning, sustained cardiac deceleration, defensive nonopiate analgesia, and potentiated startle.
3. *Circa-strike*, the final stage, involves active defense and is mediated by the dorso-lateral gray in the rat. Like Masterson and Crawford's "alarm" stage, it involves active fight or flight, cardiac rate acceleration, and a shift of blood to the gross muscles—processes that prompt the motor system and thus eliminate reactions to secondary, probe stimuli.

The Defense Cascade: Arousal as Predator Imminence

Figure 5.12 is a diagram prompted by these considerations. Increase in judged arousal of aversive stimuli, as observed in the picture paradigm, is represented on the abscissa. This arousal parameter is seen as analogous to the dimension of predator imminence in animal behavior research. The amplitudes of various measures of orienting (and defense) are shown schematically on the ordinate. It is presumed that aversively motivated attending does not fundamentally differ from appetitive orienting at lower

The Defense Cascade

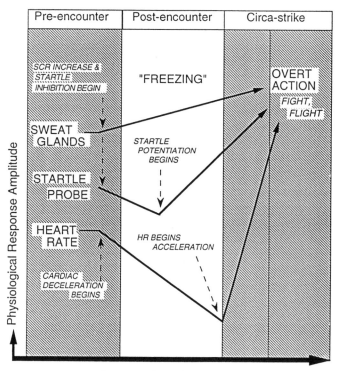

FIG. 5.12. A schematic presentation of the defense response cascade generated by increasingly arousing aversive stimuli. The arousal dimension (monotonically covarying with SCR increase) is viewed here as analogous to the dimension of predator imminence in studies of animal fear. Stimuli presented in the postencounter period occasion an initial, partial inhibition of startle probe reflexes, "freezing," immobility, "fear bradycardia," and a focused attentive set. The probability of an overt defensive action increases with predatory imminence (or aversive stimulus arousal). This motor disposition is reflected by an increase in potentiated startle to probe stimuli. Heart rate acceleration, and a general sympathetic dominance of the autonomic system are characteristic of the Circa-strike period, just prior to overt fight or flight.

levels of activation, that is, during the pre-encounter and early post-encounter periods:

1. A brief, modest, parasympathetically driven heart rate deceleration occurs in reaction to any stimulus change. This bradycardia becomes larger and more sustained as stimuli are perceived to be more arousing.

2. When stimulus arousal is low, sympathetically mediated changes in skin conductance are small and unreliable, but they increase in frequency and amplitude progressively with greater activation.
3. Regardless of the motivational system engaged, reactions to the startle probe are predominantly inhibitory when stimulus activation is not intense. This is consistent with the hypothesis of attentional resource allocation to a meaningful foreground.

Defense responding occurs late in post-encounter and in the circa-strike period. Clear evidence that the organism has changed to a defensive posture is first seen in the probe reflex response: When activation is high enough—the threatened nociception more imminent—the organism is defensively primed. The probe stimulus now acts as a trigger that releases a supranormal reflex reaction. From the perspective of predator imminence, this is a premature defense reflex. The reflex motor reaction is accompanied by heart rate acceleration (Cook & Turpin, chapter 6, this volume) that can accompany the motor reflex potentiation. The degree of potentiation increases with greater activation until the foreground stimulus itself invokes a motivationally relevant action (fight–flight). Startle potentiation occurs in the context of an increasing attentive focus and a parallel, still increasing and dominant bradycardia. Only at the highest activation level, just prior to action, does the vagus release the heart, giving way subsequently to a sympathetically driven acceleration that is the classical defense response (e.g., Vila & Fernandez, 1989).

CONCLUSIONS

In summary, the pattern of change from orienting to defense is orchestrated by increasing activation of the subcortical aversive motivation system and its efferent-specific circuitry. This is reflected cortically in a cognitive shift from a passive attentive set to the processing of action procedures. Behaviorally, this involves a progression from immobility—with increasing autonomic activation and neuromuscular tension—to a final triggering of overt reactions to threat. The initial, primarily attentive process appears to be associated with a parasympathetic emphasis in the autonomic system; as indicated by sweat gland activity, however, the sympathetic system is also engaged and ultimately dominates when action is imminent.

In the present view, the *cognitive* process in defense is less to reject the stimulus, or "shut down the analyzers," than it is a staged transition from attention to action—from sensory processes to efferent procedures that cope directly with threat stimuli. Given that aversive motivation primes defensive behavior broadly, the probe startle reflex acts as a sensitive indicator of the organism's proximity to an action outcome.

These motivational processes seem to operate in response to media, as in life. In the former context, predator imminence is clearly low, and overt defense—escape or attack—is rare and even pathological. In most individuals, nevertheless, reactions to unpleasant, frightening images (e.g., mutilated corpses, attacking animals, threatening faces) appear to engage a phylogenetically primitive survival system. Thus, despite its ecological limitations, the psychophysiological laboratory provides a virtual window into a Darwinian world of *natural selective attention,* where reactions to media illuminate the cognitive process of not only orienting, but of affective mobilization and the early stages of defense.

The neurophysiology of motivation in animals is becoming increasingly well understood. The technologies of surgical ablation, electrical stimulation, and pharmacological intervention are elucidating the circuitry involved in the orienting–defense interface. Specific neural structures have been defined, primarily subcortical, that orchestrate a sequence of responses, moving the organism from attention to action. As we have seen, picture stimuli and conditioning paradigms can evoke an analogous cascade of responses in human subjects, encouraging the inference that they depend on a parallel neurophysiology.

At this time, powerful brain imaging tools (e.g., fMRI, high-density bioelectric arrays) are increasingly available to psychophysiological researchers. These instruments are capable of high spatial resolution, great depth of view, and importantly, rapid rates of data acquisition that match those of the human experimental paradigm. We now have an exciting new psychophysiological method with which we can observe, as our experiments unfold, regional changes in bioelectric activity and vascular flow specific to neural structures deep within the human brain. Thus, we can now begin to bridge the gap of cross-species inference. Increasingly, researchers will be able to directly assess the cortical and subcortical structures—implicated by neurophysiological research with animals—that appear to actively mediate human motivation and emotional perception.

REFERENCES

Aggleton, J. P. (1992). *The amygdala: Neurobiological aspects of emotion, memory, and mental dysfunction.* New York: Wiley.

Aggleton, J. P., & Mishkin, M. (1986). The amygdala: Sensory gateway to the emotions. In R. Plutchik & H. Kellerman (Eds.), *Emotion: Theory, research and experience* (Vol. 3). New York: Academic Press.

Balaban, M. T. (1995). Affective influences on startle in five-month-old infants: Reactions to facial expressions of emotion. *Child Development, 66,* 28–36.

Berlyne, D. E. (1971). *Aesthetics and psychobiology*. New York: Appleton-Century-Crofts.

Berntson, G. G., Cacioppo, J. T., Quigley, K. S., & Fabro, V. T. (1994). Autonomic space and psychophysiological response. *Psychophysiology, 31*, 44–61.

Blanchard, R. J., & Blanchard, D. C. (1977). Aggression behavior in the rat. *Behavioral Biology, 21*, 197–224.

Blanchard, R. J., Fukunga, K. K., & Blanchard, D. C. (1976). Environmental control of defensive reactions to footshock. *Bulletin of the Psychonomic Society, 8*, 129–130.

Blaney, P. H. (1986). Affect and memory: A review. *Psychological Bulletin, 99*, 229–246.

Bower, G. H. (1981). Mood and memory. *American Psychologist, 36*, 129–148.

Boysen, S. T., & Berntson, G. G. (1989). Conspecific recognition in the chimpanzee (Pan troglodytes): Cardiac responses to significant others. *Journal of Comparative Psychology, 103*, 215–220.

Bradley, M. M., Cuthbert, B. N., & Lang, P. J. (1990). Startle reflex modification: Emotion or attention? *Psychophysiology, 27*, 513–523.

Bradley, M. M., Cuthbert, B. N., & Lang, P. J. (1991). Startle and emotion: Lateral acoustic probes and the bilateral blink. *Psychophysiology, 28*, 285–295.

Bradley, M. M., Cuthbert, B. N., & Lang, P. J. (1993). Pictures as prepulse: Attention and emotion in startle modification. *Psychophysiology, 30*, 541–545.

Bradley, M. M., Cuthbert, B. N., & Lang, P. J. (1995). Imagine that! Startle in action and perception [Abstract]. *Psychophysiology, 32*, S21.

Bradley, M. M., Cuthbert, B. N., & Lang, P. J. (1996). Lateralized startle probes in the study of emotion. *Psychophysiology, 33*, 156–161.

Bradley, M. M., Cuthbert, B. N., & Lang, P. J. (in press). Picture media and emotion: Effects of a sustained affective context. *Psychophysiology*.

Bradley, M. M., Gianaros, P., & Lang, P. J. (1995). As time goes by: Stability of affective startle modulation [Abstract]. *Psychophysiology, 32*, S21.

Bradley, M. M., Greenwald, M. K., & Hamm, A. O. (1993). Affective picture processing. In N. Birbaumer & A. Öhman (Eds.), *The structure of emotion: Psychophysiological, cognitive, and clinical aspects* (pp. 48–68). Toronto: Hogrefe & Huber.

Bradley, M. M., Greenwald, M. K., Petry, M., & Lang, P. J. (1992). Remembering pictures: Pleasure and arousal in memory. *Journal of Experimental Psychology: Learning, Memory, & Cognition, 18*, 379–390.

Bradley, M. M., & Lang, P. J. (1994). Measuring emotion: the self-assessment manikin and the semantic differential. *Journal of Behavior Therapy and Experimental Psychiatry, 25*, 49–59.

Bradley, M. M., Lang, P. J., & Cuthbert, B. N. (1991). The Gainesville murders: Imagining the worst [Abstract]. *Psychophysiology, 28*, S14.

Bradley, M. M., Lang, P. J., & Cuthbert, B. N. (1993). Emotion, novelty, and the startle reflex: Habituation in humans. *Behavioral Neuroscience, 107*, 970–980.

Bradley, M. M., Zack, J., & Lang, P. J. (1994). Cries, screams, and shouts of joy: Affective responses to environmental sounds [Abstract]. *Psychophysiology, 31*, S29.

Brown, J. S. (1961). *The motivation of behavior*. New York: McGraw-Hill.

Brown, J. S., Kalish, H. I., & Farber, I. E. (1951). Conditioned fear as revealed by magnitude of startle response to an auditory stimulus. *Journal of Experimental Psychology, 32*, 317–328.

Bullough, E. (1912). "Psychical distance" as a factor in art and an aesthetic principle. *British Journal of Psychology, 5*, 87–118.

Cacioppo, J. T., & Bernston, G. G. (1994). Relationships between attitudes and evaluative space: A critical review with emphasis on the separability of positive and negative substrates. *Psychological Bulletin, 115*, 401–423.

Cahill, L., & McGaugh, J. L. (1990). Amygdaloid complex lesions differentially affect retention of tasks using appetitive and aversive reinforcement. *Behavioral Neuroscience, 104*(4), 532–543.

Center for the Study of Emotion and Attention (CSEA-NIMH). (1995). *The international affective picture system* [Photographic slides]. Gainesville: The Center for Research in Psychophysiology, University of Florida.

Chapman, J. G., & Blumenthal, T. D. (1994). The effects of social anxiety on startle responding in college students [Abstract]. *Psychophysiology, 31*, S34.

Cuthbert, B. N., Bradley, M. M., & Lang, P. J. (1996). Probing picture perception: Activation and emotion. *Psychophysiology, 33*, 103–111.

Cuthbert, B. N., Schupp, H. T., Bradley, M. M., Birbaumer, N., & Lang, P. J. (1996). *We like to watch: Cortical potentials in emotional perception.* Manuscript submitted for publication.

Davis, M. (1989). Sensitization of the acoustic startle reflex by footshock. *Behavioral Neuroscience, 103*, 495–503.

Davis, M., Hitchcock, J., & Rosen, J. (1987). Anxiety and the amygdala: Pharmacological and anatomical analysis of the fear potentiated startle paradigm. In G. H. Bower (Ed.), *Psychology of learning and motivation* (Vol. 21, pp. 263–305). New York: Academic Press.

Depaulis, A., & Bandler, R. (1991). *The midbrain periaqueductal gray matter: Functional, anatomical, and neurochemical organization.* New York: Plenum.

DiCara, L., Braun, J. J., & Papas, B. (1970). Classical conditioning and instrumental learning of cardiac and gastrointestinal responses following the removal of neocortex in the rat. *Journal of Comparative and Physiological Psychology, 73*, 208–216.

Dickinson, A., & Dearing, M. F. (1979). Appetitive-aversive interactions and inhibitory processes. In A. Dickinson & R. A. Boakes (Eds.), *Mechanisms of learning and motivation* (pp. 203–231). Hillsdale, NJ: Lawrence Erlbaum Associates.

Drobes, D. J., Hillman, C. H., Bradley, M. M., Cuthbert, B. N., & Lang, P. J. (1995). Effects of food deprivation on affective startle modulation and eating behavior. *Psychophysiology, 32*, S28.

Everitt, B. J., & Robbins, T. W. (1992). Amygdala-ventral striated interactions and reward related processes. In J. Aggleton (Ed.), *The amygdala: Neurobiological aspects of emotion, memory, and mental dysfunction* (pp. 401–429). New York: Wiley.

Fanselow, M. S. (1994). Neural organization of the defensive behavior system responsible for fear. *Psychonomic Bulletin & Review, 1*(4), 429–438.

Fanselow, M. S., DeCola, J. P., De Oca, B. M., & Landeira-Fernandez, J. (1995). Ventral and dorsolateral regions of the midbrain periaqueductal gray (PAG) control different stages of defensive behavior: Dorsolateral PAG lesions enhance the defensive freezing produced by massed and immediate shock. *Aggressive Behavior, 21*(1), 63–77.

Fendt, M., Koch, M., & Schnitzler, H. (1994a). Amygdaloid noradrenaline is involved in the sensitization of the acoustic startle response in rats. *Pharmacology, Biochemistry, and Behavior, 48*, 307–314.

Fendt, M., Koch, M., & Schnitzler, H. (1994b). Lesions of the central gray block the sensitization of the acoustic startle response in rats. *Brain Research, 661*, 163–173.

Frijda, N. H. (1986). *The emotions.* New York: Cambridge University Press.

Graham, F. K. (1975). The more or less startling effects of weak prestimulation. *Psychophysiology, 12*, 238–248.

Graham, F. K. (1979). Distinguishing among orienting, defense, and startle reflexes. In H. D. Kimmel, E. H. van Olst, & J. F. Orlebeke (Eds.), *The orienting reflex in humans: An international conference sponsored by the Scientific Affairs Division of the North Atlantic Treaty Organization* (pp. 137–167). Hillsdale, NJ: Lawrence Erlbaum Associates.

Graham, F. K. (1992). Attention: The heartbeat, the blink, and the brain. In B. A. Campbell, H. Hayne, & R. Richardson (Eds.), *Attention and information processing in infants and adults* (pp. 3–29). Hillsdale, NJ: Lawrence Erlbaum Associates.

Graham, F. K., & Clifton, R. K. (1966). Heart rate change as a component of the orienting response. *Psychophysiology, 65*, 305–320.

Greenwald, M. K., Bradley, M. M., Cuthbert, B. N., & Lang, P. J. (1996). *Startle potentiation: Shock sensitization, affective picture modulation and aversive learning.* Manuscript submitted for publication.

Greenwald, M. K., Cook, E. W., III, & Lang, P. J. (1989). Affective judgement and psychophysiological response: Dimensional covariation in the evaluation of pictorial stimuli. *Journal of Psychophysiology, 3,* 51–64.

Grillon, C., Ameli, R., Woods, S. W., & Merikangas, K. (1991). Fear-potentiated startle in humans: Effects of anticipatory anxiety on the acoustic blink reflex. *Psychophysiology, 28,* 588–595.

Hamm, A. O., Cuthbert, B. N., Globish, J., & Vaitl, D. (in press). Startle reflex modulation and psychophysiological response patterns to affective stimulation in subjects with simple phobias and non-phobic controls. *Psychophysiology.*

Hamm, A. O., Globisch, J., Weilke, A., Wietlacke, M. (1993). Habituation and startle modulation: Persistence of fear in simple phobics [Abstract]. *Psychophysiology, 30,* S13.

Hamm, A. O., Greenwald, M. K., Bradley, M. M., & Lang, P. J. (1993). Emotional learning, hedonic change, and the startle probe. *Journal of Abnormal Psychology, 102,* 453–465.

Hamm, A. O., Stark, R., & Vaitl, D. (1990). Classical fear conditioning and the startle probe reflex [Abstract]. *Psychophysiology, 27,* S37.

Hawk, L. W., Cook, E. W., Russell, N. V., & Dillon, M. C. (1994). Do unilateral startle probes index or modulate emotion laterality effects? *Psychophysiology, 31,* S55.

Hebb, D. O. (1949). *The organization of behavior: A neuropsychological theory.* New York: Wiley.

Hess, W. R. (1957). *The functional organization of the diencephalon.* New York: Grune & Stratton.

Hull, C. L. (1943). *Principles of behavior.* New York: Appleton-Century.

Ison, J. R., & Krauter, E. E. (1975). Acoustic startle reflexes in the rat during consummatory behavior. *Journal of Comparative and Physiological Psychology, 89,* 39–49.

Iwata, J., & LeDoux, J. E. (1988). Dissociation of associative and nonassociative concomitants of classical fear conditioning in the freely behaving rat. *Behavioral Neuroscience, 102,* 66–76.

James, W. (1894). The physical basis of emotion. *Psychological Review, 1,* 516–529.

Jansen, D. M., & Frijda, N. (1994). Modulation of acoustic startle response by film-induced fear and sexual arousal. *Psychophysiology, 31,* 565–571.

Klorman, R., & Ryan, R. M. (1980). Heart rate, contingent negative variation, and evoked potentials during anticipation of affective stimulation. *Psychophysiology, 14,* 45–51.

Klorman, R., Weissberg, R., & Wiesenfeld, A. (1977). Individual differences in fear and autonomic reactions to affective stimulation. *Psychophysiology, 14,* 45–51.

Kolbert, E. (1995, August 20). Americans despair of popular culture. *The New York Times,* Sec. 2, pp. 1, 23.

Konorski, J. (1967). *Integrative activity of the brain: An interdisciplinary approach.* Chicago: University of Chicago Press.

Lacey, J. I. (1958). Psychophysiological approaches to the evaluation of psychotherapeutic process and outcome. In E. A. Rubinstein & M. B. Parloff (Eds.), *Research in psychotherapy* (Vol. 1, pp. 160–208). Washington, DC: American Psychological Association.

Lacey, J. I., & Lacey, B. C. (1970). Some autonomic-central nervous system interrelationships. In P. Black (Ed.), *Physiological correlates of emotion* (pp. 205–227). New York: Academic.

Landis, C., & Hunt, W. A. (1939). *The startle pattern.* New York: Farrar.

Lang, P. J. (1968). Fear reduction and fear behavior: Problems in treating a construct. In J. Schlien (Ed.), *Research in psychotherapy, III* (pp. 90–103). Washington, DC: American Psychological Association.

Lang, P. J. (1980). Behavioral treatment and bio-behavioral assessment: Computer applications. In J. B. Sidowski, J. H. Johnson, & T. A. Williams (Eds.), *Technology in mental health care delivery systems* (pp. 119–137). Norwood, NJ: Ablex.

Lang, P. J. (1995). The emotion probe. *American Psychologist, 50*, 372–385.

Lang, P. J., Bradley, M. M., & Cuthbert, B. N. (1990). Emotion, attention, and the startle reflex. *Psychological Review, 97*, 377–398.

Lang, P. J. Bradley, M. M., & Cuthbert, B. N. (1995). *International affective picture system (IAPS): Technical manual and affective ratings.* Gainesville, FL: The Center for Research in Psychophysiology, University of Florida.

Lang, P. J., Bradley, M. M., Drobes, D., & Cuthbert, B. N. (1995). Emotional perception: Fearful beasts, scary people, sex, sports, disgust, and disasters. *Psychophysiology, 32*, S48.

Lang, P. J., Greenwald, M. K., Bradley, M. M., & Hamm, A. O. (1993). Looking at pictures: Affective, facial, visceral, and behavioral reactions. *Psychophysiology, 30*, 261–273.

Lang, P. J., & Hnatiow, M. (1962). Stimulus repetition and the heart rate response. *Journal of Comparative and Physiological Psychology, 55*, 781–785.

LeDoux, J. E. (1990). Information flow from sensation to emotion plasticity in the neural computation of stimulus values. In M. Gabriel & J. Moore (Eds.), *Learning and computational neuroscience: Foundations of adaptive networks* (pp. 3–52). Cambridge, MA: Bradford Books/MIT Press.

Mandler, G., Mandler, J. M., Kremen, I., & Sholiton, R. (1961). The response to threat: Relations among verbal and physiological indices. *Psychological Monographs, 75*(Whole No. 513).

Masterson, F. A., & Crawford, M. (1982). The defense motivation system: A theory of avoidance behavior. *The Behavioral and Brain Sciences, 5*, 661–696.

McManis, M., & Lang, P. J. (1992). PANAS picture rating: Face, skin, heart, and blink. *Psychophysiology, 29*, S26.

Mehrabian, A., & Russell, J. A. (1974). *An approach to environmental psychology.* Cambridge, MA: MIT Press.

Miller, M. W., Levenston, G. K., Geddings, V. J., & Patrick, C. J. (1994). Affect and startle modulation during imagery of personal experiences. *Psychophysiology, 31*, S68.

Miller, N. E. (1948). Theory and experiment relating psychoanalytic displacement to stimulus–response generalization. *Journal of Abnormal and Social Psychology, 43*, 155–178.

Miller, N. E. (1951). Comments on theoretical models illustrated by the development of a theory of conflict behavior. *Journal of Personality, 20*, 82–100.

Miller, N. E. (1959). Liberalization of basic S-R concepts: Extensions to conflict behavior, motivation and social learning. In S. Koch (Ed.), *Psychology: A study of a science* (Study 1, Vol. 2). New York: McGraw-Hill.

Obrist, P. A. (1981). *Cardiovascular psychophysiology.* New York: Plenum.

Öhman, A., Esteves, F., Flykt, A., & Soares, J. J. F. (1993). Gateways to consciousness: Emotion, attention, and electrodermal activity. In J. C. Roy, W. Boucsein, D. C. Fowles, & J. H. Gruzelier (Eds.), *Progress in electrodermal research* (pp. 137–157). New York: Plenum.

Ortony, A., Clore, G. L., & Collins, A. (1988). *The cognitive structure of emotions.* Cambridge, UK: Cambridge University Press.

Osgood, C., Suci, G., & Tannenbaum, P. (1957). *The measurement of meaning.* Urbana: University of Illinois.

Patrick, C. J. (1994). Emotion and psychopathy: Startling new insights. *Psychophysiology, 31*, 319–330.

Patrick, C. J., Bradley, M. M., & Lang, P. J. (1993). Emotion in the criminal psychopath: Startle reflex modification. *Journal of Abnormal Psychology, 102*, 82–92.

Pavlov, I. P. (1927). *Conditioned reflexes.* Oxford, UK: Oxford University Press.

Polich, J. (1989). P300 from a passive auditory program. *Electroencephalography and Clinical Neurophysiology, 74*, 312–320.

Rafferty, J., & Norling, R. (1989). *Cricket Graph user's guide.* Malvern, PA: Cricket Software.

Reeves, B., & Hawkins, R. (1986). *Masscom: Modules of mass communication.* Chicago: Science Research Associates.

Ross, L. E. (1961). Conditioned fear as a function of CS–UCS and probe stimulus intervals. *Journal of Experimental Psychology, 61,* 265–273.

Roth, W. T., Dorato, K. H., & Kopell, B. S. (1984). Intensity and task effects on evoked physiological response to noise bursts. *Psychophysiology, 27*(3), 275–297.

Russell, J. (1980). A circumplex model of affect. *Journal of Personality and Social Psychology, 39,* 1161–1178.

Sanz, C., & Feeny, E. X. (1995). Coming clear. *People, 44,* 85–86.

Sapolsky, R. M. (1995). On human nature: Primate peekaboo. *The Sciences, 35,* 18.

Schlosberg, H. (1952). The description of facial expression in terms of two dimensions. *Journal of Experimental Psychology, 44,* 229–237.

Schmid, A., Koch, M., Schnitzler, H. U. (1995). Conditioned pleasure attenuates the startle response in rats. *Neurobiology of Learning and Memory, 64,* 1–3.

Schneirla, T. (1959). An evolutionary and developmental theory of biphasic processes underlying approach and withdrawal. In M. Jones (Ed.), *Nebraska Symposium on Motivation* (pp. 1–42). Lincoln: University of Nebraska Press.

Schupp, H. T., Cuthbert, B. N., Bradley, M. M., Birbaumer, N., & Lang, P. J. (in press). Probe P3 and blinks: Two measures of affective startle modulation. *Psychophysiology.*

Shaver, P., Schwartz, J., Kirson, D., & O'Connor, C. (1987). Emotion knowledge: Further exploration of a prototype approach. *Journal of Personality and Social Psychology, 52,* 1061–1086.

Simons, R. F., & Lang, P. J. (1976). Psychophysical judgement: Electrocortical and heart rate correlates of accuracy and uncertainty. *Biological Psychology, 4,* 51–64.

Sirevaag, E. J., Kramer, A. F., Coles, M. G., & Donchin, E. (1989). Resource reciprocity: An event-related potentials analysis. *Acta Psychologica, 70*(1), 77–97.

Sokolov, Y. N. (1963). *Perception and the conditioned reflex* (S. W. Waydenfeld, Trans.). New York: Macmillan. (Original work published 1958)

Spence, K. W., & Runquist, W. N. (1958). Temporal effects of conditioned fear on the eyelid reflex. *Journal of Experimental Psychology, 55,* 613–616.

Swartz, K. B., & Rosenblum, L. A. (1980). Operant responding by bonnet macaques for color videotape recordings of social stimuli. *Animal Learning and Behavior, 8,* 311–321.

Swerdlow, N. R., Caine, S. B., Braff, D. L., & Geyer, M. A. (1992). The neural substrates of sensorimotor gating of the startle reflex: A review of recent findings and their implications. *Journal of Psychopharmacology, 6,* 176–190.

Tellegen, A. (1985). Structures of mood and personality and their relevance to assessing anxiety, with an emphasis on self-report. In A. H. Tuma & J. D. Maser (Eds.), *Anxiety and the anxiety disorders* (pp. 681–706). Hillsdale, NJ: Lawrence Erlbaum Associates.

Timberlake, W. (1993). Behavior systems and reinforcement: An integrative approach. *Journal of the Experimental Analysis of Behavior, 60,* 105–128.

Trapold, M. A. (1962). The effect of incentive motivation on an unrelated reflex response. *Journal of Comparative Physiological Psychology, 55,* 1034–1039.

Ursin, H., Jellestad, F., & Cabrera, I. G. (1981). The amygdala, exploration and fear. In Y. Ben-Ari (Ed.), *The amygdaloid complex* (pp. 317–329). Amsterdam: Elsevier/North-Holland.

Vila, J., & Fernandez, M. C. (1989). The cardiac defense response in humans: Effects of predictability and adaptation period. *Journal of Psychophysiology, 3,* 245–258.

Vrana, S. R., Spence, E. L., & Lang, P. J. (1988). The startle probe response: A new measure of emotion? *Journal of Abnormal Psychology, 97,* 487–491.

Wagner, A. R. (1963). Conditioned frustration as a learned drive. *Journal of Experimental Psychology, 66,* 142–148.

Watson, D., Clark, L. A., & Tellegen, A. (1988). Development and validation of brief measures of positive and negative affect: The PANAS scales. *Journal of Personality and Social Psychology, 54,* 1063–1070.

Witvliet, C., & Vrana, S. R. (1995). Psychophysiological responses as indices of affective dimensions. *Psychophysiology, 32,* 436–443.

Wundt, W. (1896). *Gundriss der Psychologie* [Outlines of psychology]. Leipzig, Germany: Entgelmann.

6

Differentiating Orienting, Startle, and Defense Responses: The Role of Affect and Its Implications for Psychopathology

Edwin Cook III
University of Alabama at Birmingham

Graham Turpin
University of Sheffield, UK

The purpose of this chapter is to examine contemporary psychophysiological accounts of interactions between attention and affect as manifested by research on orienting and defensive reactions. The origins of the differentiation of orienting (OR), startle (SR), and defense (DR) reflexes using psychophysiological measures are briefly reviewed (Sokolov & Cacioppo, chapter 1, this volume). We argue that the majority of this early research, particularly that conducted by Graham and Sokolov, focused on the physical or sensory attributes of eliciting stimuli, together with the attentional functions of these responses. However, earlier Russian research had also stressed the motivational and functional consequences of the operation of these reflexes (e.g., Konorski, 1948; Pavlov, 1927). Accordingly, the role of affect in the elicitation of the OR, SR, and DR is a primary focus of this chapter. Finally, the implications of this research for psychopathology are examined, because many of the affective stimulus materials studied have been related to phobic anxiety. Moreover, current approaches to anxious and depressive disorders emphasize the role of cognitive factors involving attentional biases toward threat-related stimuli in the acquisition and maintenance of these conditions (Mathews & MacLeod, 1994). It is suggested, therefore, that psychophysiological methods involving OR, SR, and DR differentiation might prove highly relevant to this area of research.

MODELS OF DIFFERENTIATION FOR ORIENTING, DEFENSE, AND STARTLE RESPONSES

The classical model for OR–DR differentiation is that of Sokolov (1963; see also Sokolov & Cacioppo, chapter 1, this volume). This approach has been appraised in much detail elsewhere (Graham, 1973; Turpin, 1979, 1983, 1986) and we therefore present here only a brief summary. Sokolov suggested that the operation of the OR and DR would be easily differentiated by measuring peripheral autonomic components associated with concomitant changes in sensory thresholds. In particular, he identified changes in cutaneous blood flow within the fingers and forehead, together with electrodermal activity, as criterion measures. Both the direction of the response and its behavior following stimulus repetition were important distinguishing features. The OR was characterized by peripheral vasodilatation at the forehead and constriction at the finger, together with response habituation. The DR in contrast was said to display constriction at both peripheral sites, together with slow habituation or even response sensitization. Sokolov's scheme of response differentiation is summarized at the top of Table 6.1.

Sokolov's classification of ORs and DRs has been a major impetus to subsequent research. Psychophysiologists were particularly attracted to his proposition that different patterns of autonomic responding might reflect functionally different modes of attention or information processing. Indeed, the identification of autonomic response patterns with specific modes of attention could provide a potentially simple and powerful rationale for the inclusion of psychophysiological measures within cognitive experimental paradigms. It was hoped that such measures might yield additional information not only about the timing of cognitive events and processes, but also in relation to qualitative shifts in attention. This approach was exemplified by Graham and Clifton's classic integration of Sokolov's model with the concept of directed attention as postulated by Lacey and Lacey (1974). Essentially, heart rate deceleration was associated with information intake and orienting, whereas heart rate acceleration was linked with information rejection and defense. It is our intention, therefore, to provide a contemporary critique of these propositions relating autonomic activity to information processing, and to discuss their implications for models of dysfunctional attention and information processing.

The most frequently investigated proposition regarding OR–DR differentiation concerns stimulus specificity: whether particular stimulus attributes reliably elicit different patterns of autonomic response. Although this is the major focus of this section, it is worth emphasizing that it is not the major issue underlying Sokolov's approach. His original intention was to identify, at the periphery, centrally mediated changes in

TABLE 6.1
Summary of the Differentiation of Orienting, Startle, and Defense
Reflexes Based on the Nature of Their Autonomic Response Components

Scheme	Autonomic Response Components		
	Orienting Reflex	Defense Reflex	Startle Reflex
Sokolov (1963)	Cephalic vasodilation. Digital vasoconstriction. Electrodermal responding. Habituation.	Cephalic vasoconstriction. Digital vasoconstriction. Electrodermal responding. Nonhabituation/ sensitization.	Not specified.
Graham & Clifton (1966) Graham & Slaby (1973) Graham (1973, 1979)	Heart rate deceleration. Rapid habituation.	Heart rate acceleration, onset latency > 2 sec. Slow habituation/ sensitization.	Heart rate acceleration, onset latency < 2 sec. Rapid habituation.
Turpin & Siddle (1978, 1983) Turpin (1979, 1983)	Heart rate deceleration. Digital vasoconstriction. Cephalic vasoconstriction.	Long-latency heart rate acceleration, peak latency about 30 sec. Long-latency digital and cephalic vasoconstriction, peak latencies about 30 sec. Habituation.	Heart rate acceleration, peak latency ~ 4 sec. Digital vasoconstriction. Cephalic vasodilation. Habituation (rate dependent on intensity).

Note. From "Effects of Stimulus Intensity on Autonomic Responding: The Problem of Differentiating Orienting and Defense Reflexes," by G. Turpin, 1986, Psychophysiology, 23. Copyright © 1986 by Cambridge University Press. Reprinted with the permission of Cambridge University Press.

the efficiency of information processing. Both the OR and DR were seen as general reflexive changes in the efficiency of sensory processing and analysis, whereas autonomic measures were viewed as peripheral concomitants of central nervous system activity underlying these presumed cognitive changes. This distinction between peripheral measures and central processes is also relevant to the discussion of the "unitary" nature of the OR (cf. Turpin, 1983). It should be stressed that Sokolov did attempt to delineate these shifts in central processing using psychophysical threshold measures. In contrast, psychophysiologists have tended to merely assume functional significance and to manipulate it via stimulus variables such as intensity and duration. As Turpin (1986, 1989) suggested, without criterion measures of changes in cognitive processing, OR–DR differentiation relies on a circular definition of presumed functional significance of particular autonomic components. It is hoped that the development of psychophysiological paradigms containing performance measures such as probe startle and probe reaction time might help to clarify these issues.

A CONTEMPORARY VIEW OF GRAHAM'S MODEL
OF ATTENTION AND HEART RATE RESPONDING

The basic premise relating heart rate change to changes in the direction of attention, as argued by Graham and Clifton (1966), has developed into a robust psychophysiological theory. In this section, we merely highlight some of the stages in theory development and important sources of empirical evidence on which this theory has been established. The main framework was developed by Graham in the 1970s (e.g., Graham, 1973, 1975, 1979; Graham & Slaby, 1973). Using data from her own laboratory and elsewhere, Graham (1973, 1979) systematically reviewed the effects of varying auditory stimulus parameters such as intensity, risetime, duration, and bandwidth on autonomic responding. She concluded that heart rate responding provided a more reliable measure of OR–DR differentiation than peripheral vasomotor responses. She also introduced a third response profile, the startle reflex. Graham's scheme for differentiating OR, DR, and startle is summarized in Table 6.1. Orienting and defense are distinguished in terms of the direction of the response (OR: deceleration; DR: acceleration) and the rate of habituation (OR: fast habituation; DR: slow habituation or even sensitization). Although cardiac acceleration was also associated with startle, this acceleratory response was of shorter latency and habituated more rapidly than the accelerative component of the DR. Finally, Graham (1992; Graham, Anthony, & Zeigler, 1983) also identified a similarly rapid but brief deceleration associated with stimulus registration. This latter response might show no habituation, given repeated stimulation.

   We now review the evidence to support each of these autonomic components identified by Graham based largely on the human adult literature. We have restricted our review to adults because it is most directly comparable with subsequent research on adult clinical samples, discussed later in the chapter. However, we acknowledge that a comprehensive account of OR–DR differentiation ought to include comparative and developmental studies (see Section IV and Campbell et al., chapter 3, this volume). Similarly, due to limitations of space we have focused on more recently published research. Readers should be aware that the topic of cardiac differentiation of ORs and DRs has been a well-reviewed and, at times, controversial area (Barry, 1986; Barry & Maltzman, 1985; Turpin, 1983, 1986, 1989; but see associated invited commentaries; Simons, 1989; Vossel & Zimmer, 1989a, 1989b). We therefore only summarize some of the issues raised in these reviews.

Finally, before systematically reviewing this research, we remind the reader of two recent methodological issues that may offer some alternative explanations to those discussed within the literature. The first relates to reciprocal relationships between different autonomic innervations to the heart (Berntson, Boysen, & Cacioppo, 1992; Sokolov & Cacioppo, chapter 1, this volume) and the second to the confounding effects of motor responses (e.g., Berntson & Boysen, 1989). Both of these factors have recently made important contributions to the understanding of equivocal findings within the animal literature relating to the consistency of OR and DR cardiac responding. Accordingly, future research should apply these models more extensively to the human subject.

Cardiac Deceleration as a Component of the Orienting and Transient-Detecting Responses

The identification of heart rate deceleration with the OR was a major premise of Graham and Clifton's (1966) reformulation of Sokolov's theory of orienting and defense. Since then, Graham has refined her model to include at least two decelerative components. The first is a brief, rapid onset deceleration that is said to be elicited by brief transient stimuli and indicative of stimulus detection or registration (Graham, 1979, 1984). This is represented in the latest version of Graham's model (Fig. 6.1) as the

FILTER	LOW INTENSITY	HIGH INTENSITY
LOW-PASS	OR	DR
	HR ↓	HR ↑
LONG LATENCY	REDUCED movements	INCREASED movements
PROLONGED OUTPUT	RAPID habituation	SLOW habituation
	INPUT enhancing	INPUT reducing
HIGH-PASS	TDR	STARTLE
	HR ↓	HR ↑
SHORT LATENCY	?DIRECTED movements	FLEXOR movements
BRIEF OUTPUT	SLOW habituation	RAPID habituation
	DETECTION-GATING	INTERRUPT

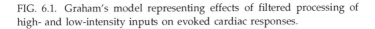

FIG. 6.1. Graham's model representing effects of filtered processing of high- and low-intensity inputs on evoked cardiac responses.

Transient-Detecting Response (TDR) and results from the active processing of the stimulus by a high-pass filter, which is sensitive to stimulus change but not steady-state stimulus characteristics. The TDR is associated with behavioral orientation (eye and head movements), particularly in neonates. Its functional significance is the detection of stimulus change, but it is not necessarily associated with stimulus identification or discrimination. Graham also argues that it is slow to habituate and may be associated with reflexive inhibition or gating of a response to a subsequent stimulus. The second component is a more sustained deceleration that is typically associated with the generalized OR and accordingly demonstrates habituation. In contrast to the TDR, this component is associated with the operation of a low-pass filter and is therefore sensitive to sustained characteristics of stimuli. It is also accompanied by reduced somatic activity and is hypothesized to be functionally related to input enhancement. Both components are elicited by stimuli of low to moderate intensity; in the case of auditory stimuli (e.g., 1 kHz tones) this is usually taken to mean between 40 and 70 dB SPL (see Turpin, 1983).

The hypothesis that cardiac deceleration is a major autonomic response component of the OR has been widely cited in the literature (cf. Berntson et al., 1992; Richards & Casey, 1992; Turpin, 1983, 1986; Turpin & Siddle, 1983). Nevertheless, this assertion has attracted some controversy due to Barry's counterargument that the cardiac component of the OR fails to habituate and merely represents stimulus registration (Barry, 1986; Barry & Maltzman, 1985). Barry's empirical studies as well as his critique of the original Graham and Clifton (1966) review have been appraised by Graham (1987), who dismisses Barry's empirical evidence as based on inappropriate experimental designs and stimuli, and insensitive autonomic response measurement. Several other authors have similarly doubted the empirical basis of Barry's position, and their critiques are published within the same volume as Barry's (1987) original review.

More recent authors have also been drawn into this debate. In a study designed to test differential predictions from Barry's and Graham's models, Vossel and Zimmer (1989a) reported failing to observe a cardiac OR in response to repeated auditory stimuli. Reliable heart rate decelerations occurred, peaking around 2 sec poststimulus. Indeed, the authors also reported significant repetition effects and linear trends, supported by response curves that indicate decrement with stimulus repetition. Finally, cardiac deceleration increased in response to a dishabituation stimulus. Despite these positive findings, Vossel and Zimmer interpreted their results as inconsistent with a habituating cardiac OR because of what they claim to be two crucial observations. First, the response decrement function for the decelerative heart rate response is not identical to the skin conductance response decline; second, the shape of the function is not a negative exponential one. The logic of Vossel and Zimmer's claim that their findings do not support Graham's position has been strongly challenged (Simons, 1989; Turpin, 1989; but see also Vossel & Zimmer's 1989b reply).

A difficulty with the Vossel and Zimmer (1989a) study was a failure to control stimulus risetime, leading to possible contamination of heart rate responses by startle (Simons, 1989; Turpin, 1989). In a subsequent study, Vossel and Zimmer (1992) examined this issue by manipulating risetime. Essentially, they attempted to replicate a study by Hatton, Berg, and Graham (1970) that is widely cited to support risetime effects on startle. However, in Vossel and Zimmer's study no effect of risetime on heart rate responding was observed, although intensity and repetition manipulations did yield the expected effects. Thus, intensity determined the direction of the initial heart rate response: deceleration to a 65 dB stimulus and acceleration to a 90 dB stimulus. Stimulus repetition led to a decrement in the size of both components, together with general changes in response topography. Vossel and Zimmer noted that these findings are "in accordance with the operational criteria as formulated for autonomic indication of the orienting response" (p. 50), suggesting that they have begun to reappraise their position on the habituation of the cardiac OR. Nevertheless, Vossel and Zimmer (1993) replicated their failure to observe a risetime effect, in the presence of reliable intensity and repetition effects, in a further study that added measurement of eyeblink. They concluded that the confounding effects of risetime on OR, SR, and DR differentiation have been overemphasized. However, their failure to observe startle responding at low stimulus intensities is inconsistent with other recent studies (Blumenthal & Goode, 1991; Schaeffer, Boucsein, & Turpin, 1991) that differ from Vossel and Zimmer's in several important ways, including stimulus duration, constant versus variable interstimulus intervals, and between-subject versus within-subject designs. Whether these factors can account adequately for the differences in risetime effects on startle will only be resolved by further research.

What should we conclude regarding Graham's scheme of OR differentiation? The identification of cardiac deceleration with the OR has been an influential and useful organizing construct in psychophysiology. Generally, the data support the habituation of decelerative responses to the repetition of stimuli of moderate intensities. Assuming that this response decrement is indicative of the development of a centrally mediated habituation state, the findings can be interpreted in support of an OR component. Additional performance data associating cardiac deceleration with enhanced attention within reaction time (Bohlin & Kjellberg, 1979) and prepulse inhibition paradigms (Graham & Hackley, 1991) also help to validate Graham's original position. Moreover, studies using complex visual stimuli (cf. Richards & Casey, 1992) suggest that cardiac deceleration (at least in infants) becomes more pronounced and sustained when the stimulus commands greater attention. In contrast, brief decelerative responses may be associated with stimulus detection or registration, as argued by both Graham and Barry.

Cardiac Acceleration as a Component of Defense and Startle Responses

Graham has identified two distinct cardiac accelerative components (Fig. 6.1). The first is identified with the DR, is elicited by high-intensity sustained stimuli, and demonstrates slow habituation. The second accelerative component, said to reflect startle, is elicited by brief high-intensity transients and shows rapid habituation. Graham (1973, 1979) previously indicated that the DR and SR can be distinguished by both the risetime of the stimulus and the temporal characteristics of the response. Startles are elicited by fast risetime stimuli and have onset latencies less than 2 sec. In contrast, DRs are characterized by more sustained aspects of the stimulus (intensity, duration, and bandwidth) and demonstrate onset latencies greater than 2 sec. Graham (1973) originally found what appeared to be a threshold independent of intensity whereby if risetime was controlled (greater than 30 msec), startle would not be elicited. Later she modified this to suggest that the stimulus had to be of sufficient strength within the first 10 msec to ensure that startle was elicited (Graham, 1980).

Evidence from human psychophysiology certainly substantiates Graham's position as regards response direction, in that more intense stimuli are associated more frequently with cardiac acceleration than deceleration (cf. Turpin, 1983, 1986; Turpin & Siddle, 1981; Vossel & Zimmer, 1992). However, the exact interpretation of these data has not been fully consistent with Graham's model of startle and defense. Turpin (1986) claimed that the distinction between short latency accelerative components of startle and defense is artificial. Instead, he argued that for simple auditory stimuli, a *single* accelerative component is elicited, peaking around 4 sec poststimulus. Response amplitude and habituation is determined by overall stimulus energy (i.e., risetime, intensity, bandwidth, and duration). Moreover, it was argued that this cardiac accelerative component is associated with the behavioral blink or startle reflex. By contrast, the DR is characterized by a longer latency response (> 30 sec) associated with sustained sympathetic activation, and is analogous to fight/flight responding in animals (Eves & Gruzelier, 1984; Fernandez & Vila, 1989; Turpin, 1986; Vila, Fernandez, & Godoy, 1992). Turpin also suggested that the long latency cardiovascular response is more compatible with Sokolov's earlier formulation of the vasomotor components of the OR and DR (Turpin, 1983, 1986).

As has already been discussed in relation to startle and the decelerative component of the OR, the effects of risetime seem to be equivocal. Studies of startle blink suggest that both risetime and intensity have important effects (Blumenthal, 1988; Blumenthal & Berg, 1986): Blink probability increases as intensity is increased and risetime decreased. However, Blumenthal failed to observe a threshold effect whereby only stimuli of a sufficient intensity elicit startle; indeed, he elicited startle responses with stimuli of quite low intensity (50 to 60 dB SPL; Blumenthal & Goode, 1991). A recent study (Schaeffer et al., 1991) supports this finding. Within this study, effects of risetime (5 vs. 200 msec) and intensity (60 vs. 100 dB) were observed on cardiac and electrodermal responding, as well as on blink and somatic activity as observed from video recordings. These data are similar to Blumenthal's in that risetime and intensity effects were demonstrated for both skin conductance and behavioral responses (eyeblink; head and body movements). The data differ from Vossel and Zimmer (1992, 1993) because a risetime main effect was observed for the initial heart rate accelerative responses (1–2 sec); greater acceleration occurred for 5 msec than for 200 msec stimuli at both intensities. There was also evidence of startle responding (measured by eyeblinks and head and body movements) occurring at the lowest stimulus intensity, particularly within the first few trials.

Included within this study was an attempt to separate the effects of transient and sustained stimulation at high intensities. Graham (1979) argued that stimulus duration might account for the fact that there have been only a few studies that have revealed an unequivocal nonhabituating accelerative DR. Studies using high-intensity auditory stimulation have tended to use brief stimuli (50 msec–1 sec). Accordingly, Schaeffer et al. (1991) also contrasted short (1 sec) and long (5 sec) presentations of the fast and slow risetime intense (100 dB) stimuli. However, no reliable effects were obtained for stimulus duration, and no evidence was obtained in support of a nonhabituating DR component in the 5 sec conditions.

We conclude, therefore, that contemporary human psychophysiological data support the linkage of cardiac acceleration with a transient detection system associated with startle blink. How this system relates to the TDR and the intensity of the stimulus is unclear. Graham has argued that physical intensity determines the response to transients: Low-intensity transients are merely detected (TDR), whereas high-intensity transients lead to startle and interrupt. However, it appears that under certain conditions low-intensity transients also elicit startle. We suggest that some of the inconsistencies surrounding Graham's model for response to transients relate to its sole reliance on physical stimulus attributes. For example, Graham hypothesizes that the boundary between the TDR and OR is not determined solely by the stimulus energy properties of the stimulus, but also by its novelty and significance. Do predictability and significance also affect the elicitation of startle? Is the difference between low-intensity transients that give rise to either a TDR or SR not due to intensity per se but to stimulus predictability and novelty? Do predictable transients give rise to the TDR, whereas unpredictable transients give rise to startle or, if they are significant and sustained, to an OR? We speculate that stimulus novelty or significance may be more important than overall intensity in determining the exact output associated with the processing of transient and sustained stimuli.

We also argue that the affective properties of a stimulus moderate responses to transient and sustained stimuli. Hence, not only high-intensity stimuli, but also those that are salient and aversive, may elicit prolonged or potentiated startle and defense. Data that support this contention come from studies of threat vocalizations in chimpanzees (Berntson & Boysen, 1989), responses to signals of punishment in humans (Balaban, Rhodes, & Neuringer, 1990), and responses of phobics to fear-relevant visual stimuli. It appears that both unpredictable/transient and affective/sustained stimuli can give rise to cardiac acceleration. The question arises, therefore, whether cardiac and other response components of startle are identical to those elicited by affective stimuli. Dimberg (1990) addressed this question by measuring both autonomic and facial electromyographic (EMG) reactions to simple auditory stimuli. He found that a high-intensity tone elicited cardiac acceleration, was rated as aversive, and elicited increased corrugator EMG activity, suggestive of a negative affective response. The facial EMG response was also of greater duration than would be expected on the basis of a pure startle response. Future research might attempt to dissociate the mechanisms underlying these short- and long-duration EMG responses. Finally, a secondary long latency fight/flight or defensive response may also be elicited by stimuli with high impact that are also highly unpredictable (cf. Turpin, 1986).

THE ROLE OF AFFECT AND EXPECTANCY

The preceding section reviewed the partial success of Graham's model, relying on sensory physiology and physical stimulus attributes, in differentiating patterns of attentional response. We now focus on data that emphasize the role of factors such as affective valence and expectancy in determining the autonomic components of these responses. Much support for this view can be found in the literature on evoked cardiac responses to pictorial stimuli, which indicates that the morphology of the response varies with affective content, is modulated by aversive conditioning, and covaries in relation to pre-existing fear. These data are first reviewed (see also Lang et al., chapter 5, this volume). We then consider recent evidence suggesting that the evoked cardiac response to startling stimuli is modified by affective context and varies with affective individual differences among subjects.

Cardiac Responses to Pictures

Early research on autonomic responses to affective pictures was directly stimulated by the publication of Graham and Clifton's (1966) review of the literature on heart rate change in orienting and defense, which integrated the Laceys' work on stimulus intake and rejection with Sokolov's research on psychophysiological manifestations of attention. Common experience of fear, as well as notions of "stimulus rejection" and "defense," suggest that viewing of aversive pictures, such as snakes, spiders, and victims of mutilating accidents or homicides, should be accompanied by cardiac acceleration, compared to neutral or pleasant control conditions. However, common experience also gives reason to doubt this view, and even predict an opposite effect. Many individuals appear to be morbidly fascinated by putatively aversive events, seeking them out in movie theaters and at accident scenes. Such naturalistic observations suggest an association between unpleasant visual stimulation and attention or orienting (i.e., cardiac deceleration). Finally, a third hypothesis suggests that stimulus salience might lead both pleasant and unpleasant scenes to evoke relative cardiac deceleration.

The most consistent experimental support has been obtained for the hypothesis that aversive pictures occasion cardiac deceleration. Early research on this topic was conducted by Hare and his collaborators. Hare, Wood, Britain, and Shadman (1971) compared responses of unselected male undergraduates to pictures of homicide victims, ordinary neutral objects, and female nudes. To assess a range of hypotheses regarding response patterning in orienting and defense, several autonomic measures were obtained in addition to heart rate. Results indicated a general pattern of cardiac deceleration to the pictures, peaking on the 8th to 10th beat after picture onset. Deceleration was clearly strongest for the homicide content. Of the remaining contents, nudes elicited somewhat greater deceleration, due perhaps, as suggested earlier, to their greater novelty and interest relative to the neutral slides. However, no support was obtained in this study for Sokolov's (1963) hypotheses regarding cephalic vasodilation and constriction as components of the OR and DR, respectively. As shown in Table 6.2, the pattern of greatest heart rate deceleration to aversive content has been replicated in numerous studies of responses to affective pictures published since Hare's initial report. It is noteworthy that the finding has been replicated not only in further studies by Hare and colleagues, but also by different investigators, in other laboratories, and across more than two decades. An example of the deceleratory cardiac

TABLE 6.2
Cardiac Deceleration to Aversive Compared
to Neutral and/or Pleasant Pictures

Study	Picture Stimuli	Sample
Hare, Wood, Britain, & Shadman (1971)	Homicides vs. everyday objects vs. female nudes	48 unselected males
Hare, Wood, Britain, & Frazelle (1971)	Homicides vs. everyday objects vs. female nudes	25 unselected males[a]
Hare (1973)	Spiders vs. common objects and landscapes	10 females selected for low spider fear
Libby, Lacey, & Lacey (1973)	Varying in attention, pleasantness, and complexity	34 unselected males
Klorman, Wiesenfeld, & Austin (1975)	Neutral vs. incongruous vs. mutilated persons	16 females selected for low mutilation fear
Klorman, Weissberg, & Wiesenfeld (1977)	Neutral vs. incongruous vs. mutilation	28 females selected for moderately low mutilation fear
Greenwald, Cook, & Lang (1989[b])	Varying in pleasantness and arousal	48 unselected males and females
Bradley, Cuthbert, & Lang (1990)	Varying in pleasantness and arousal	36 unselected subjects
Lang, Greenwald, Bradley, & Hamm (1993[b])	Varying in pleasantness and arousal	64 unselected subjects

[a]This study also included 25 unselected females who viewed the same neutral, aversive, and (notably) female nude pictures as the males. In the absence of ratings, affective characterization of this latter category is difficult, although it did evoke the greatest deceleration in female subjects.

[b]In the majority of studies the more robust deceleratory response to aversive pictures was recorded as the lowest heart rate (relative to pretrial baseline) occurring late in the picture presentation interval. However, in the Greenwald et al. (1989) and Lang et al. (1993) studies the reduction in heart rate for aversive pictures was obtained in the middle of the presentation interval, at a point where deceleration in this paradigm is frequently interrupted by modest acceleration. In these two studies then it was attenuated midinterval acceleration, rather than maximal late-interval deceleration, that distinguished cardiac responses to the aversive pictures. The studies are included here because, despite this measurement difference, they conform to the general pattern of the other studies listed in that heart rate was lower during aversive compared to neutral and pleasant picture viewing.

waveform for aversive materials, from Klorman, Weissberg, and Wiesenfeld (1977), is presented in Fig. 6.2 (left panel). Interpreted within Graham and Clifton's (1966) model, these and similar findings suggest greater attention (OR) to the aversive pictures.

Subject characteristics influence the topography of the evoked cardiac response. A point underscored by Table 6.2 is that when pictures varying in affective content are shown to unselected subjects, or to subjects selected for low fear, it is the aversive pictures that elicit the greatest cardiac

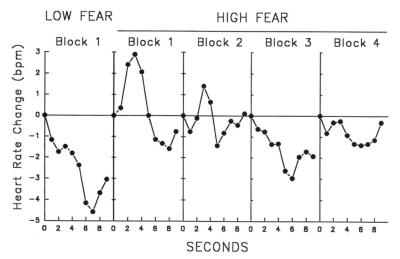

FIG. 6.2. The cardiac response to aversive pictures varies with their content as well as with subject fear. Subjects reporting moderately low mutilation fear show a deceleratory cardiac response (OR) to mutilation pictures (left panel), whereas high mutilation fear subjects respond to these pictures with cardiac acceleration (DR; second panel). With repeated exposures responses of fearful subjects are reduced (third panel), go through a deceleratory phase similar to that of low fear subjects (fourth panel, compare to first) and ultimately approach zero (last panel). From "Individual Differences in Fear and Autonomic Reactions to Affective Stimulation," by R. Klorman, R. P. Weissberg, and A. R. Wiesenfeld, 1977, *Psychophysiology, 14.* Copyright © 1977 by Cambridge University Press. Reprinted with the permission of Cambridge University Press.

deceleration. However, in some studies the opposite effect—greater acceleration, suggestive of a DR—has been obtained. As shown in Table 6.3, such a finding of greatest cardiac acceleration in response to aversive pictures appears to depend on extraordinary samples or conditions. In four of the five samples showing this effect, subjects were selected for specific fear of exactly the content depicted in the aversive slides (i.e., blood/injury, spiders, or snakes; see Fig. 6.2). In the only study that found acceleration to aversive pictures with unselected subjects (Cook, Hodes, & Lang, 1986), the acceleratory response was particularly robust when phylogenetically phobia-relevant pictures (snakes and spiders) predicted a noxious stimulus, such as electric shock.

These cardiac acceleratory findings provide a laboratory model for the racing heart experienced by phobics confronted with the object of their fear. Within Graham and Clifton's (1966) model, they suggest the formation, under specific circumstances, of a cardiac DR. In her theoretical papers, Graham (e.g., 1979) has emphasized the output-enhancing function of the

TABLE 6.3
Cardiac Acceleration to Aversive Compared
to Neutral and/or Pleasant Pictures

Study	Picture Stimuli	Sample
Hare (1973)	Spiders vs. everyday objects	10 spider-fearful females
Hare & Blevings (1975)	Spiders vs. everyday objects	9 spider-fearful females
Klorman, Weissberg, & Wiesenfeld (1977)	Neutral vs. incongruous vs. mutilation	28 females selected for high mutilation fear
Fredrikson (1981)	Phobia-relevant (snake & spider) vs. neutral (plant & mushroom) conditioned to predict a shock UCS	Snake and spider phobics
Cook, Hodes, & Lang (1986)	Phobia-relevant vs. neutral conditioned to predict a tactile UCS	110 unselected males and females

DR. Consistent with this view, Chase, Graham, and Graham (1968) demonstrated that the acceleratory response to the warning stimulus in a warned reaction time paradigm could be increased by requiring a more energetic response at S2. Thus Graham's theorizing and empirical work provides a framework within which these cardiac acceleratory responses may be interpreted. Consistent with the important role that active avoidance plays in many specific phobias, the potent combination of phobia-relevant stimuli with either pre-existing phobic fear or an especially aversive and/or relevant (e.g., phylogenetically associated or prepared; see Öhman, chapter 7, this volume) tactile UCS appears to lead subjects to develop a response-mobilizing DR.

Implications of the Aversion DR

An additional set of findings relates to individual differences in the evoked cardiac response and to the relevance of acceleration versus deceleration for other fear-related behaviors. In two studies subjects were categorized, using statistical cluster analysis, based on their cardiac response to picture stimuli that were either a priori aversive or had been made so by contingencies of aversive conditioning. Reanalyzing data from Hare, Wood, Britain, and Frazelle (1971), Hare (1972) identified subgroups of subjects who showed acceleratory, deceleratory, and moderate deceleratory responses to pictures of homicide victims, and used these groupings to predict vasomotor responses to all picture content groups. Within the response typology developed by Graham, Sokolov, and others, the extreme Accelerator and Decelerator groups might be considered to consist of subjects who developed conditioned DRs and ORs, respectively. However, the identification of these groups is not by itself a striking finding, because the statistical analysis simply divides the distribution of responses into groups. Rather, the important aspect of these data is that group membership predicted cephalic vasomotor response, proposed by Sokolov (1963) to differentiate ORs and DRs. Figure 6.3 (left panel) presents these data. Only Accelerators—showing a cardiac DR—also evinced a sharp cephalic vasoconstriction in response to the homicide slides; Decelerators and Moderate Decelerators, showing the contrasting cardiac OR, tended toward vasodilation to the homicide slides. The finding thus supports Sokolov's suggestion that cephalic vasoconstriction is a component of the DR, whereas cephalic vasodilation accompanies the OR.

As previously noted, Graham (1979) suggested that one defining characteristic of the cardiac DR is the slowness with which it habituates. Although this property has been difficult to demonstrate, a study by Hodes, Cook, and Lang (1985) obtained evidence for a related phenomenon: Conditioning of a cardiac DR predicts slowed extinction of a conditioned electrodermal response. Following Hare's lead, Hodes and colleagues used

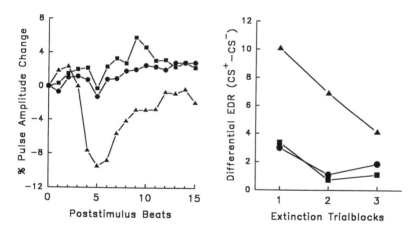

FIG. 6.3. On the left, the direction of cardiac response to an aversive slide is correlated with the vasomotor response to the slides. Accelerators (▲) showed marked vasoconstriction; Moderate Decelerators (●) and Decelerators (■) show slight vasodilation. (Adapted from "Cardiovascular Components of Orienting and Defensive Responses," by R. D. Hare, 1972, *Psychophysiology, 9.* Copyright © 1972 by Cambridge University Press. Adapted with the permission of Cambridge University Press.) The right panel illustrates the predictive value of this distinction: Accelerators continue to respond differentially during extinction following aversive classical condition, whereas Decelerators and Moderate Decelerators extinguished rapidly. (From "Individual Differences in Autonomic Response: Conditioned Association or Conditioned Fear," by R. L. Hodes, E. W. Cook III, & P. J. Lang, 1985, *Psychophysiology, 22.* Copyright © 1985 by Cambridge University Press. Reprinted with the permission of Cambridge University Press.)

cluster analysis to identify Accelerator, Moderate Decelerator, and Decelerator groups, this time on the basic of subjects' cardiac response to a CS+ picture that predicted an aversive UCS (loud noise or noise/vibrotactile compound) in a differential conditioning paradigm. Following this acquisition phase, the aversive UCS was discontinued and the CS pictures were repeatedly presented. Among Accelerators, reliable differential responding (larger skin conductance responses to CS+ compared to CS−) was observed throughout this extinction phase (see Fig. 6.3, right panel). Moreover, at the end of extinction, Accelerators rated the CS+ as more aversive than the CS−. In contrast, differential responding extinguished rapidly among Decelerators and Moderate Decelerators once the aversive UCS was discontinued, and no effects on ratings were observed. It is noteworthy that Accelerators and Decelerators conditioned equally robust differential cardiac and electrodermal responses during acquisition, so the durability of electrodermal conditioning for the Accelerator group could not be attributed to better acquisition. Rather it appears that these groups conditioned different types of responses. Hodes and colleagues interpreted the Accelerators' pattern of a conditioned cardiac DR combined with aversive ratings of CS+ and slowed electrodermal extinction as consistent with conditioned fear. In contrast, the conditioned cardiac OR among Decelerators was accompanied by rapid electrodermal extinction and no apparent affective change, suggesting that associative but not emotional learning had taken place.

In summary, the pattern of cardiac response to affective pictures is interpretable within the general framework of OR and DR theory. Most typically, picture viewing represents an attentional task that is accompanied by cardiac deceleration suggestive of the OR. In this context, conventionally unpleasant stimuli appear to command greater attention, as indexed by greater cardiac deceleration. However, when the stimuli imply personal danger, for example as the object of an individual's phobia, the context appears to shift to one of response mobilization. Cardiac deceleration gives way to an acceleratory response reminiscent of the DR elicited by an intense physical stimulus or in preparation for a energy-demanding response. Such an analysis suggests that as fear is reduced, acceleratory responses might shift to deceleration. This is in fact what was observed when mutilation phobics viewed repeated mutilation slides (Klorman et al., 1977), in a procedure similar to exposure therapy: Acceleration was robust in Blocks 1 and 2, but the pattern switched to deceleration in Block 3, and by Block 4 little response in either direction was observed (see Fig. 6.2). Finally, whereas subject fear predicts the cardiac response, it also appears possible to reverse the process and use the cardiac response to predict which subjects are more likely to manifest possible fear-related changes in other response systems (vasoconstriction, delayed extinction, and verbal report of negative affect).

Cardiac Startles: Contextual and Dispositional Influences

The findings thus point to the importance of the affective content or signal value of a picture in determining whether the cardiac response that it evokes will be deceleratory or acceleratory. Recent research on affective response to pictures has adopted an alternative strategy, using varying picture contents as setting or background stimuli against which the response to a sudden and intense stimulus—a startle probe—can be measured (see, e.g., Balaban et al., chapter 16, this volume; Lang et al., chapter 5, this volume; Vrana, Spence, & Lang, 1988). This research draws heavily on Graham's and others' work on startle modulation by selective attention (e.g., Simons & Zelson, 1985), as well as on the literature on fear-potentiated startle in rats (e.g., Davis, chapter 4, this volume; Davis, Hitchcock, & Rosen, 1991). One major focus of this research has been the covariation between startle modulation by affective state and individual differences related to psychopathology. A series of studies has demonstrated enhanced affective modulation of eyeblink startle in subjects scoring high on questionnaire measures of fearfulness, depression, anger-proneness, negative affectivity, and schizotypy (Cook, Davis, Hawk, Spence, & Gautier, 1992; Cook, Goates, Hawk, & Palmatier, 1996; Cook, Hawk, Davis, & Stevenson, 1991; Stevenson, 1994). At least some of these relationships appear to be robust, as they have been replicated in multiple laboratories using a range of methods for manipulating affect and eliciting and measuring the startle response.

In most of the affect-startle studies, eyeblink is the only component of the reflex that is measured. However, there are reasons to examine the evoked cardiac startle response as well. First, baseline muscle tension in orbicularis oculi is altered by affect (Cacioppo, Petty, Losch, & Kim, 1986), and such alterations complicate interpretation of responses evoked in the same muscle (Hawk, Stevenson, & Cook, 1992). Relatedly, replication of affect and individual difference effects with additional components of the startle reflex complex would suggest that central modulatory mechanisms, rather than specific peripheral factors, modulate startle responses. To address these issues, Cook et al. (1992) selected subjects for high and low self-reported tendencies toward phobic fear (approximately the upper and lower 40% of the distribution), using total score on the Fear Survey Schedule (Arrindell, Emmelkamp, & van der Ende, 1984). Subjects received slide trials consisting of a geometric warning slide followed by an aversive (primarily mutilation) or neutral picture. Noise probes (3 msec rise, 110 dB, 50 msec duration) were presented at various points during the trial, including during the pictures. Results for blink magnitude (see Fig. 6.4, left panel) showed an interaction effect: Only fearful subjects showed reliable potentiation of eyeblink startle in the aversive picture

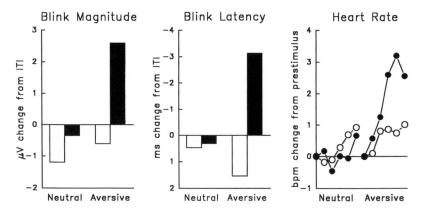

FIG. 6.4. Affective modulation of eyeblink and cardiac response to startle probes varies with dispositional tendencies toward fear. In this study (Cook et al., 1992) high and low fear subjects identified on the basis of FSS total score viewed neutral and aversive pictures. While viewing aversive pictures, high fear subjects (solid bars/circles) showed reliable potentiation of blink magnitude (left panel), reduction in blink latency (middle panel), and short-latency cardiac acceleration in response to the startle probes (right panel; each curve represents 2 sec). Low fear subjects (open bars/circles) showed little differentiation of affective contents in startle blink or heart rate.

condition; low fear subjects showed no reliable effect of picture content. Blink latency (Fig. 6.4, middle panel) showed a similar effect: Latency was reduced only for high fear subjects viewing aversive pictures. The findings for startle magnitude obtained here during picture viewing closely resemble those obtained in other studies with affective imagery (Cook et al., 1991; Stevenson, 1994).

The short-latency cardiac response to the startle probes in Cook et al. (1992) is shown in the right panel of Fig. 6.4. Paralleling the findings for blink, the sensitivity of the evoked cardiac response to picture content varied with subject fear. Among high fear subjects, probes presented during aversive pictures elicited a rapid increase in heart rate. The direction and time course of this response conforms to Graham's (1979) description of a cardiac startle. However, no such rapid cardiac acceleration was recorded following probes presented to high fear subjects during neutral pictures, nor to low fear subjects in either affective condition. Thus, like the evoked cardiac DR in aversive conditioning, the cardiac startle response in this study depended on a unique fear context, produced here by the combination of high dispositional fear and exposure to an aversive picture.

These preliminary findings encouraged a larger investigation of cardiac responses as they relate to individual differences and affective manipulations. Based on both animal and human research, Gautier and Cook (in press) reasoned that cardiac startles, cardiac defense responses, and cardiovascular mobilization in stress might have related affective influences. To assess this hypothesis, a range of cardiovascular and startle measures were obtained from a sample of high and low fear subjects (again identified by the Fear Survey Schedule) in varying affective contexts. Replicating procedures of Turpin and Siddle (1978, 1981; see also Eves & Gruzelier, 1984; Turpin, 1986), subjects initially received 110-dB noises (50 msec rise, 1 sec duration). Affective modulation of blink and heart rate responses to less intense (100 db, 50 msec, 3 msec rise) noise probes was then assessed during two blocks of affective imagery trials, in a paradigm similar to that of Cook et al. (1991). Finally, cardiovascular responses were measured during cognitively challenging mental arithmetic and Stroop tasks.

Results suggested a recurring association between fearfulness and greater cardiac acceleratory responses. The most robust finding was that high fear compared to low fear subjects showed a larger and more rapid acceleratory response to the initial intense noise. Responses to the less intense probes presented during imagery were relatively small, compared to those observed earlier in the session and in prior studies (Cook et al., 1992; Graham & Slaby, 1973). However, these cardiac responses showed a reliable biphasic pattern, consisting of brief deceleration (TDR?) followed by acceleration. The acceleratory component was generally larger for high fear than for low fear subjects, although this difference interacted in a complex manner with trial block and imagery affective content. Thus, although the findings of Gautier and Cook (in press) are generally consistent with those of Cook et al. (1992) in showing greater cardiac acceleratory responses to startle probes among high fear subjects, in this new study the effect was less context-specific. Further research is required to resolve the relative contributions of affective disposition and context to the cardiac acceleratory response to intense noises.

The desultory cardiac acceleration to startle probes observed by Gautier and Cook (in press) during imagery is consistent with other studies of the imagery startle response from our laboratory, and its interpretation relates to several issues regarding the morphology of the evoked cardiac response. A central question relates to the definition of a cardiac startle response. Blink responses to abrupt stimuli are something of a "gold standard" for startle; if the blink occurs (with appropriate short latency), startle is presumed to have occurred. What then of other aspects of the response complex? Should any reliable cardiac response to blink-eliciting stimuli be defined as cardiac startles? Or alternatively, should rapid acceleration (e.g., within 2 sec, as observed by Graham & Slaby, 1973, and Cook et al., 1992) following stimulus onset be required to designate a cardiac response as startle, recognizing that the threshold for eliciting such responses is somewhat above that for blink? If the latter approach is taken, how should we designate consistent responses to effective startle probes that include acceleratory components too slow or weak to qualify as cardiac startles?

The potentiation of cardiac acceleratory responses to intense physical stimuli among fearful subjects (Cook et al., 1992; Gautier & Cook, in press) complements the previous finding that fear is associated with an acceleratory response to affective pictures. Taken together, the two sets of findings provide construct validation for discrete acceleratory components of the cardiac response as indices of fear.

Synthesis

The evidence reviewed here has supported some general tenets of Graham's (1992) model. Response direction (acceleration vs. deceleration) is largely determined by the intensity of the eliciting stimulus. The cardiac component of the OR is viewed as a habituating decelerative response whereas the SR would appear to be a rapidly habituating accelerative response. There are also data to support the notion of a brief early decelerative response associated with stimulus detection. Aspects of the model that appear more problematic concern the nonhabituating DR and the intensity threshold for the SR. Moreover, we would argue that the model is limited by its failure to consider directly the affective properties of the stimulus. As Öhman (1987, 1993, chapter 7, this volume) argued, there are many parallels between an information processing model of the OR and a similarly founded model of emotion. Indeed, information processing models of attentional and emotional processing are being advanced by contemporary theorists (Kaspi, McNally, & Amir, 1995; Wells & Mathews, 1994).

We suggest that a similar framework—integrating attentional and affective considerations—be used to differentiate the responses that are the focus of this chapter. A starting point for such a framework is presented in Fig. 6.5. The model is essentially that proposed by Öhman (1993) to account for anxiety. However, because this model itself was based on earlier formulations of orienting, we have reintroduced processing of novel as well as threatening stimuli. Accordingly, different stimuli are perceived as novel or threatening, and such perceptions are associated with different autonomic arousal patterns, together with different behavioral consequences of either approach or withdrawal. Because we are particularly concerned with differentiating various autonomic response profiles such as ORs, SRs, and so on, we describe the operation of the model primarily with respect to its autonomic outputs. We have included

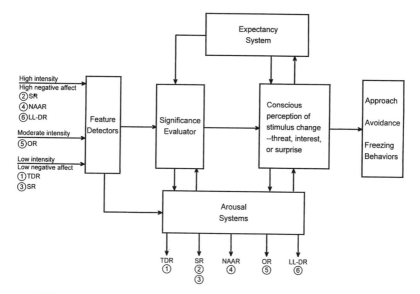

FIG. 6.5. A suggested reformulation of Öhman's (1993) model of attentional mechanisms subserving anxiety but extended to orienting (OR), startle (SR), and defensive responding (DR). In addition, the reformulated model also attempts to account for Transient Detection Responses (TDR), the Long-Latency Defense Response (LL-DR), and the Negative Affect Accelerative Response (NAAR). The numbers refer to individual responses, and the reader should consult the text for further explanation.

the traditional Graham profiles of TDR, OR, and SR, although two mechanisms leading to startle are distinguished. In addition, we include two distinct responses: the Long-Latency DR and the Negative Affect Accelerative Response. Further characteristics of these responses and the stimuli that elicit them follow:

- TDR①: This response profile is essentially that described by Graham, and demonstrates moderate or no habituation. It is elicited by moderately intense stimuli that are automatically detected but not necessarily identified.

- SR②: This response is elicited by moderate to intense stimuli with rapid risetimes that are automatically detected but not necessarily identified. It demonstrates moderate or occasionally slow habituation. In general it resembles Graham's SR, although it may not be distinguishable from Graham's DR.

- SR③: This response is elicited by stimuli that are unpredicted and result in surprise, and may be of low intensity. Due to the role of mismatch to recent stimuli in eliciting this response, habituation of SR③ is rapid.

Note that the distinction between SR② and SR③ is essentially one of processing pathways, both of which lead in parallel to the same response. Thus, stimuli that are both physically abrupt and surprising may elicit startle along both pathways. However, stimuli having only one of these characteristics may still be sufficient to produce the response.

• NAAR④: This response is elicited by affectively negative stimuli that are evaluated as significant and threatening (see, e.g., work of Klorman, Hare, and colleagues, previously described). It demonstrates habituation dependent on expectancy and significance. This response *may* be equivalent to startle but represents accelerative responses elicited by affectively negative but not necessarily physically abrupt or surprising (i.e., "startling") stimuli.

• OR⑤: This is essentially the OR of Graham's model, elicited by moderate-intensity stimuli that are significant and/or novel. Habituation depends on expectancy and task significance.

• LL-DR⑥: This is the long latency defense response described by Turpin (1983, 1986; see also Eves & Gruzelier, 1984; Vila et al., 1992). It is evoked by high-intensity affective stimuli that are unpredicted and evaluated as significant and threatening. It demonstrates moderate to rapid habituation.

Within the model, stimuli are initially processed automatically by feature detectors, which may yield either transient decelerations (TDRs) or accelerations (SR②s) based on physical stimulus characteristics. In addition, Öhman includes the possibility that biologically important stimuli elicit alarm responses (here, SR②s and possibly conditioned NAARs) via this automatic stage of processing. Such processes, operating outside of awareness, might underlie initial anxiety responses associated with phobia, panic, or posttraumatic stress disorder.

Input passed on from feature detectors is evaluated for significance related to novelty, threat, or task relevance. This selection mechanism implements operating biases or expectancies, based on representations or models in memory. Thus, prior experience influences the operation of the significance evaluator. Both matches and mismatches may be detected at this stage. Clinically relevant examples of matching would include general threat-related attentional biases demonstrated for anxiety disorder (cf. review of Mathews & MacLeod, 1994), and more specific matches, such as between a snake picture and a phobic's internal representation of snakes. Mismatches, on the other hand, result from the input of novel stimuli.

Outputs of the significance evaluator include the arousal system (specifically for SR③ to surprising stimuli, although preselection of other responses might also occur at this stage), as well as conscious perception. In general, significant stimuli are consciously perceived, and such per-

ceptions and associated controlled processing are held to play important roles in response selection for longer latency responses (OR, NAAR,
and LL-DR). Processing in awareness may modify expectancies, in turn
modifying subsequent operations of the significance evaluator. According
to Öhman, feedback from the arousal system may modulate both significance evaluation and the resulting conscious perception. Such mechanisms may moderate effects of state anxiety on performance.

As noted, output from the arousal system might depend on direct
activation or preselection via feature detectors or the significance evaluator. It might also be determined or primed by processing in awareness,
or serve to support an appropriate behavioral response to the eliciting
stimulus (e.g., approach, avoidance, or freezing). Priming of both eyeblink
and cardiac components of startle is likely to reflect operation of these
latter mechanisms, which are output- rather than input-enhancing. These
convergent processes would result in the integrated pattern of autonomic
and skeletomuscular responses currently identified as ORs, SRs, and DRs.

Our reformulation of Öhman's model emphasizes several features.
First, it provides a framework for defining attentional systems that can
be applied to a full range of inputs, not just anxiety-related stimuli.
Accordingly, stimulus significance is evaluated across a range of attributes
and will be perceived as novelty, surprise, threat, relevance, and so on.
Second, a variety of different responses are selectively manifested within
the arousal system, and may be preselected by the significance evaluator.
Öhman (1993) excluded the direct link from significance evaluation to
arousal, based on the similar effects of backward masking on conscious
perception and the skin conductance OR. However, the short latency of
startle responses to surprising stimuli suggests that at least some outputs
of the significance system need not involve conscious awareness or controlled processing. Third, different behavioral strategies will result from
stimulus appraisal and evaluation, and support for these strategies may
also influence autonomic response selection. It is hoped that this synthesis
of Graham's model of feature detection and Öhman's model of anxiety
processing might provide a basis for future experimental studies of the
interactions between physical and emotional stimulus properties to determine autonomic and behavioral outputs.

CLINICAL APPLICATIONS AND CONCLUDING
REMARKS

We have argued that a contemporary model of OR, SR, and DR differentiation would encompass both physical and affective attributes of the
stimulus. Moreover, it has been suggested that basic affective properties

of a stimulus might be detected via a subcortical preattentive mechanism (LeDoux, 1992; Öhman, 1993). If this is the case, then the use of autonomic measures of ORs, SRs, and DRs might provide a means of investigating preattentive emotional processes in people suffering with an anxiety disorder. The research previously described on responses to pictures and startle probes in fearful and phobic individuals provides preliminary support for this view. Additionally, a substantial literature (Mathews & MacLeod, 1994; Öhman, chapter 7, this volume) has developed concerning attentional biases in anxiety. Essentially, it is suggested that threat-related stimuli are attended to more readily by anxious than nonanxious subjects. Although these findings are fairly robust, they are based primarily either on reaction time to some accessory task (dot probe or Stroop) or some implicit memory measure of subsequent encoding. The level of analysis of what constitutes "attentional bias" is also somewhat limited. For example, it is not specified whether the effect is due to peripheral orientation, cortical excitation, selective engagement or disengagement, or any of the many attentional components that have been identified within the literature (cf. Posner & Petersen, 1990). We speculate, therefore, that the use of both autonomic and cortical psychophysiological measures, referenced to the typology of responses built by Graham and extended here, might help to elucidate further the nature of disordered attention in psychopathological groups.

REFERENCES

Arrindell, A., Emmelkamp, P. M. G., & van der Ende, J. (1984). Phobic dimensions: I. Reliability and generalizability across samples, gender and nations. *Advances in Behavior Research and Therapy, 6*, 207–253.

Balaban, M. T., Rhodes, D. L., & Neuringer, A. (1990). Orienting and defense responses to punishment: Effects on learning. *Biological Psychology, 20*, 203–217.

Barry, R. J. (1986). Heart rate deceleration to innocuous stimuli: An index of the orienting response or stimulus registration? *Physiological Psychology, 14*, 42–48.

Barry, R. J. (1987). Preliminary processes in orienting response elicitation. In P. K. Ackles, J. R. Jennings, & M. G. H. Coles (Eds.), *Advances in psychophysiology* (Vol. 2, pp. 131–195). Greenwich, CT: JAI Press.

Barry, R. J., & Maltzman, I. (1985). Heart rate deceleration is not an orienting reflex; heart rate acceleration is not a defensive reflex. *Pavlovian Journal of Biological Science, 20*, 15–28.

Berntson, G. G., & Boysen, S. T. (1989). Specificity of the cardiac response to conspecific vocalizations in chimpanzees. *Behavioral Neuroscience, 103*, 235–245.

Berntson, G. G., Boysen, S. T., & Cacioppo, J. T. (1992). Cardiac orienting and defensive responses: Potential origins in autonomic space. In B. A. Campbell, H. Hayne, & R. Richardson (Eds.), *Attention and information processing in infants and adults: Perspectives from human and animal research* (pp. 163–200). Hillsdale, NJ: Lawrence Erlbaum Associates.

Blumenthal, T. D. (1988). The startle response to acoustic stimuli near startle threshold: Effects of stimulus rise and fall time, duration, and intensity. *Psychophysiology, 25*, 607–611.

Blumenthal, T. D., & Berg, W. K. (1986). Stimulus rise time, intensity, and bandwidth effects on acoustic startle amplitude and probability. *Psychophysiology, 23,* 635–641.

Blumenthal, T. D., & Goode, C. T. (1991). The startle eyeblink response to low intensity acoustic stimuli. *Psychophysiology, 28,* 296–306.

Bohlin, G., & Kjellberg, A. (1979). Orienting activity in two stimulus paradigms as reflected in heart rate. In H. D. Kimmel, E. H. van Olst, & J. H. Orlebeke (Eds.), *The orienting reflex in humans* (pp. 167–197). Hillsdale, NJ: Lawrence Erlbaum Associates.

Bradley, M. M., Cuthbert, B. N., & Lang, P. J. (1990). Startle reflex modulation: Emotion or attention? *Psychophysiology, 27,* 513–522.

Cacioppo, J. T., Petty, R. E., Losch, M. E., & Kim, H. S. (1986). Electromyographic activity over facial muscle regions can differentiate the valence and intensity of affective reactions. *Journal of Personality and Social Psychology, 50,* 260–268.

Chase, W. G., Graham, F. K., & Graham, D. T. (1968). Components of HR response in anticipation of reaction time and exercise tasks. *Journal of Experimental Psychology, 76,* 642–648.

Cook, E. W., III, Davis, T. L., Hawk, L. W., Spence, E. L., & Gautier, C. H. (1992). Fearfulness and startle potentiation during aversive visual stimuli. *Psychophysiology, 29,* 633–645.

Cook, E. W., III, Goates, D. W., Hawk, L. W., & Palmatier, A. D. (1996). Specificity of startle modulation revisited: Relationships of affective and prepulse modification to fearfulness and schizotypy [Abstract]. *Psychophysiology, 33,* 533.

Cook, E. W., III, Hawk, L. W., Jr., Davis, T. L., & Stevenson, V. E. (1991). Affective individual differences and startle reflex modulation. *Journal of Abnormal Psychology, 100,* 5–13.

Cook, E. W., III, Hodes, R. L., & Lang, P. J. (1986). Preparedness and phobia: Effects of stimulus content on human visceral conditioning. *Journal of Abnormal Psychology, 95,* 195–207.

Davis, M., Hitchcock, J. M., & Rosen, J. R. (1991). Anxiety and the amygdala: Pharmacological and anatomical analysis of fear-potentiated startle. In G. H. Bower (Ed.), *The psychology of learning and motivation: Advances in research and theory* (Vol. 21, pp. 263–305). San Diego, CA: Academic.

Dimberg, U. (1990). Facial electromyographic reactions and autonomic activity to auditory stimuli. *Biological Psychology, 31,* 137–147.

Eves, F. F., & Gruzelier, J. H. (1984). Individual differences in the cardiac response to high intensity auditory stimulation. *Psychophysiology, 21,* 342–352.

Fernandez, M. C., & Vila, J. (1989). Sympathetic–parasympathetic mediation of the cardiac defense response in humans. *Biological Psychology, 28,* 123–133.

Fredrikson, M. (1981). Orienting and defensive reactions to phobias and conditioned fear stimuli in phobics and normals. *Psychophysiology, 18,* 456–465.

Gautier, C. H., & Cook, E. W., III. (in press). Relationships between startle and cardiovascular reactivity. *Psychophysiology.*

Graham, F. K. (1973). Habituation and dishabituation of responses innervated by the autonomic nervous system. In H. V. S. Peeke & M. J. Herz (Eds.), *Habituation: Behavioral studies and physiological substrates* (Vol. 1, pp. 163–218). New York: Academic.

Graham, F. K. (1975). The more or less startling effects of weak prestimulation. *Psychophysiology, 12,* 238–248.

Graham, F. K. (1979). Distinguishing among orienting, defense, and startle reflexes. In H. D. Kimmel, E. H. Van Olst, & J. F. Orlebeke (Eds.), *The orienting reflex in humans* (pp. 137–168). Hillsdale, NJ: Lawrence Erlbaum Associates.

Graham, F. K. (1980). Control of reflex blink excitability. In R. F. Thompson, L. H. Hicks, & V. B. Shvyrkov (Eds.), *Neural mechanisms of goal-directed behavior and learning* (pp. 511–519). New York: Academic.

Graham, F. K. (1984). An affair of the heart. In M. Coles, R. Jennings, & J. Stern (Eds.), *Psychophysiology: A festschrift for John and Beatrice Lacey* (pp. 171–187). New York: Van Nostrand.

Graham, F. K. (1987). Sokolov registered, model evicted. In P. K. Ackles, J. R. Jennings, & M. G. H. Coles (Eds.), *Advances in psychophysiology* (Vol. 2, pp. 211–231). Greenwich, CT: JAI Press.

Graham, F. K. (1992). The heartbeat, the blink, and the brain. In B. A. Campbell, H. Hayne, & R. Richardson (Eds.), *Attention and information processing in infants and adults: Perspectives from human and animal research* (pp. 3–29). Hillsdale, NJ: Lawrence Erlbaum Associates.

Graham, F. K., Anthony, B. J., & Zeigler, B. L. (1983). The orienting response and developmental processes. In D. Siddle (Ed.), *Orienting and habituation: Perspectives in human research* (pp. 371–430). Chichester, UK: Wiley.

Graham, F. K., & Clifton, R. K. (1966). Heart-rate change as a component of the orienting response. *Psychological Bulletin, 65*, 305–320.

Graham, F. K., & Hackley, S. A. (1991). Passive and active attention to input. In J. R. Jennings & M. G. H. Coles (Eds.), *Handbook of cognitive psychophysiology: Central and autonomic nervous system approaches* (pp. 251–356). New York: Wiley.

Graham, F. K., & Slaby, D. A. (1973). Differential heart rate changes to equally intense white noise and tone. *Psychophysiology, 10*, 347–362.

Greenwald, M. K., Cook, E. W., III, & Lang, P. J. (1989). Affective judgment and psychophysiological response: Dimensional covariation in the evaluation of visual stimuli. *Journal of Psychophysiology, 3*, 51–64.

Hare, R. D. (1972). Cardiovascular components of orienting and defensive responses. *Psychophysiology, 9*, 606–614.

Hare, R. D. (1973). Orienting and defensive responses to visual stimuli. *Psychophysiology, 10*, 453–464.

Hare, R. D., & Blevings, G. (1975). Defensive responses to phobic stimuli. *Biological Psychology, 3*, 1–13.

Hare, R., Wood, K., Britain, S., & Frazelle, J. (1971). Autonomic responses to affective visual stimulation: Sex differences. *Journal of Experimental Research in Personality, 5*, 14–22.

Hare, R., Wood, K., Britain, S., & Shadman, J. (1971). Autonomic responses to affective visual stimulation. *Psychophysiology, 7*, 408–417.

Hatton, H. M., Berg, W. K., & Graham, F. K. (1970). Effects of acoustic rise time on heart rate response. *Psychonomic Science, 19*, 101–103.

Hawk, L. W., Stevenson, V. E., & Cook, E. W., III. (1992). The effects of eyelid closure on affective imagery and eyeblink startle. *Journal of Psychophysiology, 6*, 299–310.

Hodes, R. L., Cook, E. W., III, & Lang, P. J. (1985). Individual differences in autonomic response: Conditioned association or conditioned fear? *Psychophysiology, 22*, 545–560.

Kaspi, S. P., McNally, R. J., & Amir, N. (1995). Cognitive processing of emotional information in post-traumatic stress disorder. *Cognitive Therapy and Research, 19*, 433–444.

Klorman, R., Weissberg, R. P., & Wiesenfeld, A. R. (1977). Individual differences in fear and autonomic reactions to affective stimulation. *Psychophysiology, 14*, 45–51.

Klorman, R., Wiesenfeld, A. R., & Austin, M. L. (1975). Autonomic responses to affective visual stimuli. *Psychophysiology, 12*, 553–560.

Konorski, J. (1948). *Conditioned reflexes and neuron organization*. New York: Cambridge University Press.

Lacey, J. I., & Lacey, B. (1974). On heart rate responses and behavior: A reply to Elliott. *Journal of Personality and Social Psychology, 30*, 1–18.

Lang, P. J., Greenwald, M. K., Bradley, M. M., & Hamm, A. O. (1993). Looking at pictures: Affective, facial visceral, and behavioral reactions. *Psychophysiology, 30*, 261–273.

LeDoux, J. (1992). Emotion and the amygdala. In J. P. Aggleton (Ed.), *The amygdala: Neurobiological aspects of emotion, memory, and mental dysfunction* (pp. 339–351). New York: Wiley.

Libby, W. L., Jr., Lacey, B. C., & Lacey, J. I. (1973). Pupillary and cardiac activity during visual attention. *Psychophysiology, 10,* 270–294.

Mathews, A., & MacLeod, C. (1994). Cognitive approaches to emotion and emotional disorders. *Annual Review of Psychology, 45,* 25–50.

Öhman, A. (1987). The psychophysiology of emotion: An evolutionary-cognitive perspective. In P. K. Ackles, J. R. Jennings, & M. G. H. Coles (Eds.), *Advances in psychophysiology* (Vol. 2, pp. 79–127). Greenwich, CT: JAI Press.

Öhman, A. (1993). Fear and anxiety as emotional phenomena: Clinical phenomenology, evolutionary perspectives, and information-processing mechanisms. In M. Lewis & J. M. Haviland (Eds.), *Handbook of emotions.* New York: Guilford.

Pavlov, I. P. (1927). *Conditioned reflexes* (G. V. Anrep, Ed. & Trans.). New York: Dover.

Posner, M. I., & Petersen, S. E. (1990). The attention system of the human brain. *Annual Review of Neuroscience, 13,* 25–42.

Richards, J. E., & Casey, B. J. (1992). Development of sustained visual attention in the human infant. In B. A. Campbell, H. Hayne, & R. Richardson (Eds.), *Attention and information processing in infants and adults* (pp. 30–61). Hillsdale, NJ: Lawrence Erlbaum Associates.

Schaeffer, F., Boucsein, W., & Turpin, G. (1991). The effect of physical stimulus characteristics on orienting, defense, and startle response [Abstract]. *Psychophysiology, 28,* S48.

Simons, R. F. (1989). "A rose by any other name": A comment on Vossel and Zimmer. *Journal of Psychophysiology, 3,* 125–127.

Simons, R. F., & Zelson, M. F. (1985). Engaging visual stimuli and reflex blink modification. *Psychophysiology, 22,* 44–49.

Sokolov, E. N. (1963). *Perception and the conditioned reflex.* New York: Pergamon.

Stevenson, V. E. (1994). *Affective modulation of startle in fearful and schizotypal college students.* Unpublished doctoral dissertation, University of Alabama at Birmingham.

Turpin, G. (1979). A psychobiological approach to the differentiation of orienting and defense responses. In H. D. Kimmel, E. H. van Olst, & J. F. Orlebeke (Eds.), *The orienting reflex in humans* (pp. 259–267). Hillsdale, NJ: Lawrence Erlbaum Associates.

Turpin, G. (1983). Unconditioned reflexes and the autonomic nervous system. In D. Siddle (Ed.), *Orienting and habituation: Perspectives in human research.* London: Wiley.

Turpin, G. (1986). Effects of stimulus intensity on autonomic responding: The problem of differentiating orienting and defense reflexes. *Psychophysiology, 23,* 1–14.

Turpin, G. (1989). An adequate test of the habituation of the cardiac decelerative response component of the orienting reflex: Necessary conditions and sufficient evidence: A comment on Vossel and Zimmer. *Journal of Psychophysiology, 3,* 129–140.

Turpin, G., & Siddle, D. (1978). Cardiac and forearm plethysmographic responses to high intensity auditory stimuli. *Biological Psychology, 6,* 267–281.

Turpin, G., & Siddle, D. (1981). Autonomic responses to high intensity auditory stimulation [Abstract]. *Psychophysiology, 18,* 150.

Turpin, G., & Siddle, D. (1983). Effects of stimulus intensity on cardiovascular activity [Abstract]. *Psychophysiology, 20,* 611–624.

Vila, J., Fernandez, M. C., & Godoy, J. (1992). The cardiac defense response in humans: Effects of stimulus modality and gender differences. *Journal of Psychophysiology, 6,* 140–154.

Vossel, G., & Zimmer, H. (1989a). Heart rate deceleration as an index of the orienting response? *Journal of Psychophysiology, 3,* 111–124.

Vossel, G., & Zimmer, H. (1989b). "Roses have thorns and silver fountains mud": A reply to Simons and Turpin. *Journal of Psychophysiology, 3,* 141–146.

Vossel, G., & Zimmer, H. (1992). Stimulus rise time, intensity, and the elicitation of unconditioned cardiac and electrodermal responses. *International Journal of Psychophysiology, 12,* 41–51.

Vossel, G., & Zimmer, H. (1993). On the role of stimulus rise time and intensity in eliciting startle responses. *Psychophysiology, 30,* S68.

Vrana, S. R., Spence, E. L., & Lang, P. J. (1988). The startle probe response: A new measure of emotion? *Journal of Abnormal Psychology, 97,* 487–491.

Wells, A., & Mathews, G. (1994). *Attention and emotion: A clinical perspective.* Hove, UK: Lawrence Erlbaum Associates.

7

As Fast as the Blink of an Eye: Evolutionary Preparedness for Preattentive Processing of Threat

Arne Öhman
Karolinska Institute, Stockholm

CONSCIOUS AND PREATTENTIVE INFORMATION PROCESSING

When we say that something is "as fast as the blink of an eye," we imply that it happened with a speed that goes beyond ordinary thought. Intuitive psychology is immersed in conscious awareness, and conscious mental activity is slow. Hence, it takes more than a "blink of an eye" consciously to perceive, attend, memorize, remember, think, decide, and act. But humans have evolved in a natural environment that could select for the complex behavioral control system we call consciousness only after systems able to deal with contingencies at a much more compressed time scale were already at hand. When a predator strikes, it strikes fast, and conscious deliberation before defensive action is likely to leave the genes of the prey unrepresented in the next generation. Thus, the evolution of human consciousness requires another, more basic level of mental functioning, where "the blink of an eye" provides a more convenient temporal unit of information processing. It is at this level that evolutionary facilitations and constraints on psychological events are likely to show up most clearly, uncontaminated by the culturally conditioned whims of consciousness.

This basic, very fast level of mental functioning remains inaccessible to conscious awareness, and thus it is given little room in intuitive psychology. However, whereas conscious awareness is the pivotal point of the causal nexus determining psychological events for intuitive psychologists, to their more scientifically minded colleagues it represents only one of several parallel, albeit sometimes causally important, paths in the flow of information between environment and action. Sensory events entering the nervous system produce an immediate cascade of effects, only some of which are destined to the conscious level of the psychological arena. What eventually becomes accessible to conscious awareness, therefore, is determined by a series of preconscious or preattentive processes. In contrast to the slow, effortful, serial, and voluntary information processing of consciousness, this preattentive processing is fast, parallel, and automatic. And contrary to the notion of linear processing from perception to decision to action of intuitive psychology, preattentive processing has immediate effects at the efferent level by eliciting a series of reflexes, an important example of which is the eye blink, as a component of the startle reflex. These reflexes, which have been elucidated by Graham (e.g., 1973, 1975, 1979, 1992; Graham & Hackley, 1991) and others (e.g., Hoffman, chapter 8, this volume; Lang, Bradley, & Cuthbert, 1990; Soko-lov, 1963; Sokolov & Cacioppo, chapter 1, this volume), have important effects that shape subsequent processing and determine what becomes selected for conscious processing.

Reflexes Related to Preattentive Processing

Graham (1992) distinguished between four reflexes that are elicited as a function of elementary temporal and intensity properties of the stimulation. The *startle reflex* results from high-intensity transient stimulation with a sharp onset. It involves a persistent eye blink, a widespread sudden and protective flexor movement, and a sharp heart rate increase, which like the flexor response, habituates rapidly with repeated stimulation. Startle interrupts ongoing activity and it may trigger attention. Transient stimuli of low intensity, on the other hand, elicit a *transient-detection reaction*, associated with a small, but persistent, heart rate deceleration. It indicates that a stimulus has been detected but not necessarily recognized, and it may serve to gate or attenuate subsequent high-intensity stimulation as in the reflex modulation of startle by a brief, low-intensity prepulse (e.g., Graham, 1975). The startle reflex is also modulated by the emotional and motivational context in which it is elicited (Lang et al., 1990; Lang, Bradley, & Cuthbert, chapter 5, this volume). Prolonged intense stimulation with a slow rise time elicits a Sokolovian (Sokolov, 1963) *defense reflex*, uniquely indexed by a brief heart rate acceleration peaking about 5 sec after stimulus onset, which habituates only slowly (see also Cook & Turpin, chapter 6, this volume). This reflex provides a generalized activation effect that facilitates movements, whereas the effect on sensory processing is one of dampening. The remaining reflex system, the *orienting reflex*, is the most advanced of the four in terms of the psychological and neural mechanisms that it implies. It is indexed by skin conductance responses and brief heart rate decelerations that habituate quickly with repeated stimulation. It inhibits ongoing movements and its effect on information processing is one of input enhancement (e.g., Sokolov, 1963). In previous work (Öhman, 1979, 1983, 1987, 1992) I have given it a key role in the transfer of information between preattentive and conscious levels of information processing. Thus, I assumed (Öhman, 1979) that the orienting reflex is associated with a call for conscious processing capacity when preattentive processes fail to handle a stimulus on their own, either because it is novel and thus fails to find a matching representation in memory, or because it implies consequences that cannot be dealt with at the preattentive level; that is, it has *signal value*.

Most of these reflexes are determined by simple stimulus dimensions such as sudden onset or high intensity, which are applicable across sensory modalities. Abrupt, high-intensity stimulation has been associated with danger throughout evolution, and therefore sensory systems have been tuned immediately and automatically to respond to such stimulus parameters. For example, a striking airborne predator provides abruptly expanding visual stimulation, coupled with intense noise from flapping wings, and, in the worst case, sudden, intensely painful tactile sensations. However, apart from defenses shaped by such deadly evolutionary contingencies, sensory organs typically have their maximal sensitivity at considerably less intense and more slowly starting stimulation. Therefore, one aspect of automatic defensive reflexes such as the startle and the Sokolovian defense reflex is the down-regulating of sensory intensity to prevent perceptual systems from potentially damaging overload.

For the orienting reflex, the evolutionary history is likely to be more complex and specific to a particular gene pool. Thus, even though it is generally evoked by low to moderately intense stimulation, it requires a memory or "neuronal model" (Sokolov, 1963) mismatch to be elicited. Because of its memory dependence, it may be elicited by generally significant stimuli from a biological perspective, such as approaching rather than retracting visual stimulation (Bernstein, Taylor, Austen, Nathanson, & Scarpelli, 1971), species-typical significant stimuli, such as the sound of rustling grass for rabbits (Lynn, 1966), or stimuli reflecting individual interests (Wingard & Maltzman, 1980). Thus, the orienting reflex seems to be sensitive to the meaning of the stimulus in a much more complex way than the other simple reflexes discussed by Graham (1992).

Preattentive Processing as Elucidated
by Reflex System Interactions

The reflex systems interact. Furthermore, as first described by Sokolov (1963), such interactions have important effects on stimulus processing. I have already alluded to the fact that the transient-detection reaction as elicited by a weak prepulse shortly preceding a startle probe may inhibit startle (Graham, 1975). The orienting reflex provides a particularly powerful concept in this context. For example, actively focusing attention on a particular stimulus elicits an orienting reflex as indexed by heart rate deceleration, and facilitates processing of the eliciting stimulus (see postpublication analysis of data presented in Bohlin, Graham, Silverstein, & Hackley, 1981, by Graham & Hackley, 1991, p. 292) but has no effect on startle to a following stimulus (Bohlin et al., 1981). When a signal stimulus (as a result of instruction) focused attention on the following startle probe, heart rate decelerated and startle was facilitated (Bohlin & Graham, 1977). However, when attention was focused on a stimulus presented simultaneous with the startle probe but in another modality, heart rate orienting to the preceding signal was still observed, but startle was inhibited (Silverstein, Graham, & Bohlin, 1981). Finally, when heart rate orienting was the passive result of a *novel* stimulus, responses to the novel stimulus itself were slow but startle to a following probe was facilitated regardless of the modality of the novel stimulus (Bohlin et al., 1981). These data are consistent with theoretical perspectives that give orienting a key role in the regulation of attention to novel or to expected, significant stimuli (e.g., Öhman, 1979).

The work of Graham and others (reviewed with admirable comprehensiveness by Graham & Hackley, 1991) documents a series of psychological processes that operate within the time-span of an eye-blink (see also Anthony, 1985). These processes are psychologically silent in the sense that they operate outside of conscious awareness. Thus, what eventually turns up as the conscious experience of a particular stimulation is not composed of sensory raw material, but reflects a series of automatic and obligatory processing mechanisms that operate on a vastly more extensive domain of information than the tiny fraction that eventually becomes consciously represented.

In my model of orienting (Öhman, 1979), the orienting reflex was interpreted as a "call for processing resources" in a limited-capacity processing channel that was assumed to share important features with the commonsense notion of consciousness (e.g., voluntarily controlled, selective, effort-demanding). The model gives the orienting reflex the role of a "gateway to consciousness" (Öhman, Esteves, Flykt, & Soares, 1993). Thus, preattentive processing is assumed to result in the activation of more advanced processing resources in the central channel to further analyze the stimulus and its functional ramifications. In a more recent development of this model (Öhman, 1992), I argued (on grounds detailed later in this chapter) that orienting reflexes could be elicited from stimuli after only a preattentive analysis, provided that the stimulus had been associated with aversiveness and conveyed evolutionary relevant threat, such as with pictures portraying angry faces, snakes, or spiders. For neutral or positive stimuli (pictures of happy faces, flowers, mushrooms) that had been coupled to aversiveness through Pavlovian conditioning, on the other hand, enhanced orienting reflexes (skin conductance responses) could be elicited only if central processing was allowed. Thus, from these data it appeared that some classes of stimuli conveying evolutionarily significant threat could activate responses automatically, after only a preattentive analysis. Such preattentive threat location is likely to have been critical in the evolution of predatory defense systems (e.g., Öhman, Dimberg, & Öst, 1985).

PREATTENTIVE DISCOVERY OF THREAT: EVOLUTIONARY CONSIDERATIONS

Animal evolution is predicated on the existence of perceptual systems that effectively can locate threats in the surrounding world. "False negatives" (i.e., failing to detect and respond adequately to potentially deadly stimuli) are more evolutionarily costly than "false positives" (i.e., eliciting defensive responses to an in effect harmless stimulus). Whereas the former failure is potentially lethal, a false positive response merely represents wasted energy, or, in the case of a falsely located threat, the needless experience of aversive emotion.

Effective defense must be quick, which puts a premium on early detection of threat. Furthermore, detection of threat stimuli must be independent of the momentary direction of selective attention. Coupled with the bias toward false positives, these factors mean that discovery of threat is better based on a quick, superficial analysis of stimuli anywhere in the perceptual field, than on an effortful, detailed, and complete extraction of the meaning of one particular stimulus. Thus, from the functional, evolutionary perspective, it follows that the burden for the discovery of threat should be placed on early, rapid, and parallel preattentive processing mechanisms, which define threat on the basis of relatively simple stimulus attributes.

The neural architecture of such a system was described by LeDoux (1990). He and his coworkers studied the neural control of auditorily elicited, conditioned emotional responses in the rat. This work demonstrated a direct neural link from auditory pathway nuclei in the thalamus (medial geniculate body) to the systems controlling fear in the amygdala.

This monosynaptic link was postulated to provide immediate information to the amygdala regarding gross features of emotionally relevant auditory stimuli. This information bypasses the traditionally emphasized thalamic-cortical pathway, which gives full meaning to the stimulus, and the cortical-amygdala link presumed to activate emotion. The thalamic-amygdaloid pathway was described as a "quick and dirty" transmission route that does not provide much information on stimulus details, but conveys information to the amygdala that the sensory receptor of a given modality has encountered a potentially significant stimulus. Thus, even though the activation of emotion is typically taken to require a full meaning analysis of the stimulus, what is suggested here is that emotional responses can be recruited after only minimal processing, not requiring much contact with memory (see the exchange on this issue by Zajonc, 1980, and Lazarus, 1984).

This functional and neuropsychological scenario suggests that many perceptual channels can be automatically and simultaneously monitored for potentially threatening events. When such events are located by the preattentive system, attention is drawn to the stimulus as the control for its further analysis is transferred to the controlled, conscious level of information processing (see Öhman, 1979, 1986, 1987, 1992, 1993; Öhman, Dimberg, & Esteves, 1989, for details of this argument). The transfer of control is associated with activation of physiological responses, and particularly the orienting reflex as indexed, for example, by skin conductance responses (Öhman, 1979, 1992).

This conceptualization implies that the preattentive sensory monitoring processes have a capacity to handle sensory events that clearly exceeds that of the controlled or conscious processes. Thus, automatic perceptual processes can monitor a large number of channels, only one of which can be selected for controlled processing. In other words, sensory messages have to compete for access to the strategic processing channel to be fully analyzed. Given the survival contingencies implied by potential threats in the environment, it is a natural assumption that threatening stimuli have priority to become selected for controlled processing. Thus, threat stimuli may be detected and processed by unconscious, preattentive stimulus analysis mechanisms, as they are selected for further conscious, controlled processing.

ORIENTING RESPONSES TO PREATTENTIVELY PROCESSED STIMULI

The theoretical analysis just outlined suggests that orienting reflexes under some circumstances may be initiated by preattentive processing mechanisms of which the subjects remain unaware. Empirical examination of this hypothesis requires that physiological responses that are components of the orienting reflex can be dissociated from conscious perception of the stimulus. Backward masking, that is, preventing recognition of a target stimulus by an immediately following masking stimulus, provides one method to achieve this purpose. It appears to allow quite complete analysis of the target stimulus, but prevents its conscious representation (Marcel, 1983; see also the critical discussions by Holender, 1986, and by Merikle & Reingold, 1992).

Previous work from our laboratory has explored the effect of backward masking on visual stimuli that are threat-relevant from an evolutionary perspective. Esteves and Öhman (1993) examined masking of angry and happy emotional expressions in facial stimuli by an immediately following mask portraying a neutral face. They reported that a 30 msec stimulus onset asynchrony (SOA) between the target and the mask resulted in complete masking. Thus, with these stimulus parameters, the subjects both performed and felt that they performed randomly in a forced choice recognition task, and they were only able to see one stimulus (rather than two stimuli). Similarly, Öhman and Soares (1993) reported that a 30-msec interval between target pictures, showing snakes or spiders, and masks, consisting of similar pictures lacking any central object, did not result in above chance recognition performance. Thus, by use of these temporal parameters in a backward masking design, it should be possible to provide evidence that subjects may detect threatening stimuli without being consciously aware of the stimulus to which they are responding.

These backward masking parameters were used in an experiment in which subjects selected to be highly fearful of either snakes or spiders, as well as controls fearful of neither stimulus, were exposed to pictures of snakes, spiders, flowers, and mushrooms (Öhman & Soares, 1994). By the use of backward masking, the subjects were allowed only preattentive, nonconscious access to the stimulus. The hypothesis was that fear-associated stimuli would be able to capture attention preattentively and thereby to evoke orienting skin conductance responses even when effectively masked by another stimulus.

Questionnaires measuring snake and spider fears were distributed to a large pool of university students. From 800 answered questionnaires, subjects were selected so that they were either highly snake fearful or highly spider fearful. They had to score above the 95th percentile in one of the distributions (e.g., snake fears) and below the 50th percentile in the other (e.g., spider fear). Nonfearful control subjects, on the other hand, had to score below the 50th percentile on both questionnaires. Thus, we selected three groups of 16 subjects each: snake fearful, spider fearful, and nonfearful controls.

A pilot experiment determined that fearful and nonfearful subjects did not differ in their threshold to recognize the stimuli used (Öhman & Soares, 1994). In the subsequent main experiment, all subjects were exposed to the same set of stimuli. The stimulus sequence consisted of pictures of snakes, spiders, flowers, and mushrooms, with eight exemplars in each of the categories, presented in random order. This series of pictures was presented twice. In the first presentations, the pictures were masked with a 30-msec SOA (stimulus onset asynchrony), which effectively prevented that they were consciously recognized. The procedure entailed 30-msec exposure of the target stimulus that was immediately followed by a 100-msec mask (randomly cut and reassembled pictures of snakes, flowers, etc.). The second series consisted of unmasked stimulus presentations with 130-msec exposure time. The psychophysiological dependent variables were skin conductance responses to the pictures.

The results were quite dramatic and are presented in Fig. 7.1. Regardless of masking conditions, the snake fearful subjects showed elevated skin conductance responding to snake stimuli, and the spider fearful subjects showed elevated skin conductance responding to spider pictures, whereas the control subjects did not differentiate among the four stimulus types. These results were confirmed by a highly significant interaction between groups and stimuli, with associated Tukey follow-up tests to support the elevated responding to fear stimuli in fearful subjects (see Öhman & Soares, 1994, for details). The only difference between the masked and nonmasked stimulus series pertained to overall larger responses in the former series. Because of the fixed order of presentation of the series, this effect most probably reflected overall habituation from the first to the second series. Thus it was clear that the subjects also differentiated between the feared and nonfeared stimuli when they were not able consciously to recognize them (i.e., the masked series) as when they were clearly recognizable (i.e., the nonmasked stimulus series).

These results give full support to the contention that skin conductance orienting responses can be elicited even though the stimulus has been

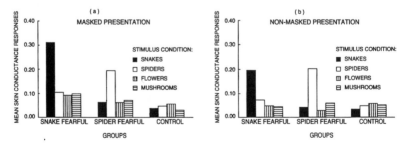

FIG. 7.1. Skin conductance responses to backwardly masked (a) and nonmasked (b) presentations of pictures of snakes, spiders, flowers, and mushrooms in snake fearful, spider fearful, and control subjects. From Öhman & Soares (1994). Copyright © 1994 by the American Psychological Association. Reprinted with permission.

processed only at a preattentive level of information processing. Indeed, it is remarkable that such clear-cut results can be generated from a stimulus that has been available to the cognitive system for such an extremely brief period of time as 30 msec. Thus, at least for the type of threatening emotionally–activating stimulation used here, preattentive processing appears sufficient to elicit physiological responses that are considered as an important component of the orienting reflex. However, as often pointed out by Graham (e.g., 1979), the skin conductance response is an ambiguous indicator of the orienting reflex because it is also related to the defense reflex. Indeed, there is good agreement that when the less ambiguous heart rate response advocated by Graham is used, the prevalent response to phobic material is a heart rate acceleration, suggesting that phobic stimuli elicit defense reflexes (e.g., Fredrikson, 1981; Hamm, Cuthbert, Globisch, & Vaitl, in press). Thus, it remains somewhat unclear whether our data demonstrate preattentively elicited orienting, defense, or both, or put in more general terms, whether the results should be attributed to attention or emotion (see the discussion in Öhman & Soares, 1994).

Similar results to those just reported (Öhman & Soares, 1994) have been reported from studies of normal subjects exposed to masked snakes or spiders (Öhman & Soares, 1993; Soares & Öhman, 1993) or masked angry faces (Esteves, Dimberg, & Öhman, 1994) after unmasked conditioning to these stimuli.

VISUAL SEARCH FOR THREATENING STIMULI

From the results reviewed so far, it appears that there are perceptual systems geared to pick up potential threat from the environment at a very early stage of information processing. These data, however, have relied on experimental paradigms where there is only one stimulus input. Thus, there is no competition for attention from different inputs, and processing is limited to the preattentive level by means of backward masking. However, in the theoretical analysis it was argued that threatening stimuli should be automatically detected independently of the current direction of attention. Thus, with multiple stimulus inputs, attention should be drawn selectively to inputs related to biologically relevant threat. This possibility has been confirmed in an independent experimental context provided by visual search studies.

Hansen and Hansen (1988) reported experiments where subjects were required to press different buttons depending on whether all pictures in a multiple stimulus display were similar or whether a deviant picture was present. The pictures consisted of faces arranged in 3×3 or 2×2 matrices. The main interest was to compare the subjects' ability to discover angry faces as deviants among happy faces, and happy faces as deviants among angry faces. The results showed that the subjects were faster to identify a deviant angry face among happy faces than vice versa. Furthermore, the time to identify deviant angry faces was independent of the size of the display (3 × 3 vs. 2 × 2 matrices), which Hansen and Hansen took to indicate a preattentive "pop-out" effect for angry, but not for happy faces. These data, then, appear to demonstrate that angry faces are special in the sense that they automatically engage attention to "pop out" from a complex stimulus array (although this conclusion recently has been retracted by the authors; see Hansen & Hansen, 1994).

We have replicated these findings with snakes and spiders as fear-relevant stimuli in my laboratory in a series of studies on normal, nonfearful subjects (Öhman, Flykt, & Esteves, unpublished data). Subjects were exposed to matrices of pictures of either snakes, spiders, flowers, or mushrooms, where in half of the cases all stimuli in the matrix were of the same category, whereas the other half had a stimulus from a deviant category. The subjects were quicker to find a deviant snake or spider among flowers and mushrooms than vice versa. This increase in speed of detection was not accompanied by more errors. Quite to the contrary, there were fewer errors in detecting fear-relevant than fear-irrelevant deviant stimuli. Response latencies were shortest for deviant snakes among background flowers and then for spiders among mushrooms. The longest latencies were found for deviant mushrooms among background snakes and flowers among spiders. This distribution of detection latencies appears to make ecological sense. Furthermore, for the typically ground-dwelling species of snakes and spiders, it turned out that latency for their discovery was shortest when they occurred at the bottom of the display. As shown in Fig. 7.2, the time to identify a deviant fear-relevant stimulus was generally longer for a large (3 × 3) than for a small (2 × 2) matrix and this effect was, as indicated by a reliable interaction between fear relevance and size of matrix, more obvious when the subject's task was to locate a fear-irrelevant than a fear-relevant target. In fact, separate tests showed a reliable size-of-matrix effect only for fear-irrelevant targets. This failure of matrix size to reliably affect the detection of deviant fear-relevant stimuli among fear-irrelevant background stimuli suggests that attention was automatically drawn to deviant snakes and spiders, whereas a more sequential search strategy was used to locate deviant flowers and mushrooms. Thus, these results indicate that fear-relevant stimuli were picked up independent of their position in the perceptual field in a process reminiscent of a "pop-out" effect of preattentive origin. Perhaps it should be explicitly noted that the inference of a preattentive origin of this effect is based on the pattern of findings, rather than on explicit control of the time allowed for processing by means of masking. As seen in Fig. 7.2, the reaction times to determine that a deviant picture was present in the display exceeded 1 sec. Thus, in

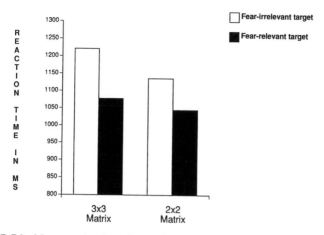

FIG. 7.2. Mean reaction times (in msec) to identify the presence of a deviant target in a matrix of pictures arranged in a 3 × 3 or a 2 × 2 pattern. The target was either a fear-relevant picture (snake or spider) occurring among fear-irrelevant (flowers or mushrooms) background pictures, or a deviant fear-irrelevant picture occurring among fear-relevant background pictures. The subjects were reliably faster in identifying fear-relevant than fear-ir-relevant targets. Furthermore, there was no significant difference between matrices of different size (3 × 3 vs. 2 × 2) for fear-relevant targets. For fear-irrelevant targets, however, it took significantly longer to identify a deviant stimulus in the large than in the small matrix.

principle, there should be ample time for controlled processes to enter the arena and affect the results. However, if this was the case, one would expect size of the display to be critical for the data.

There are at least two important differences between our experiments and their results and those of Hansen and Hansen (1988). First, in their critical experiment, they used the same angry face against a background of several identical happy faces. This method of stimulus presentation risks confounding effects that one hopes to attribute to facial expression with accidental features of the stimulus such as a particular shadow in the face (see Hansen & Hansen, 1994). Because we used categories of stimuli with several exemplars in each, this type of confounding is less likely in our study. Second, Hansen and Hansen (1988) reported that subjects were faster to decide that no deviant stimulus was present in a matrix of happy faces than in a matrix of angry faces. This result was used by Hampton, Purcell, Bersine, Hansen, and Hansen (1989) to argue that the faster discovery of deviant angry faces actually could be due to the generally faster identification of happy faces. To identify a deviant angry face, the subjects had to pass through and discard a number of background happy faces. To identify a deviant happy faces, on the other hand, they had to identify and discard a series of angry background faces.

Because they were quicker to identify happy than angry faces, the time to identify deviant angry background faces could be confounded by the generally quicker identification of the background happy faces. On the basis of such data, as well as on data indicating that the position of the deviant stimulus in the matrix was important, Hampton et al. (1989) questioned the pop-out interpretation advanced by Hansen and Hansen (1988). In our data, however, the subjects were overall faster to identify fear-relevant (snakes, spiders) than fear-irrelevant (flowers, mushrooms) background stimuli. Thus, they were quicker to decide that a deviant mushroom or flower was *not* present among snake and spider background stimuli than to decide that deviant snakes or spiders were *not* present among background flowers or mushrooms. In spite of the shorter time to identify background fear-relevant stimuli, therefore, they nevertheless were quicker to identify a deviant fear-relevant stimulus among background fear-irrelevant stimuli than vice versa. This finding, then, supports our interpretation that the subjects' attention was automatically drawn to deviant snakes and spiders.

To sum up, these results are consistent with the notion that there is a perceptual system that automatically and preattentively focuses attention on potentially threatening stimuli, where the threat has a likely origin in biological evolution.

PREATTENTIVE ASSOCIATIVE LEARNING

If biologically relevant threat stimuli can be preattentively attended, one wonders whether they can also enter into associations with other experimental events without having to reach a controlled, conscious level of processing. To formulate the question more specifically, can autonomic responses be conditioned to stimuli that are prevented from reaching awareness by means of backward masking? This appears to be a possibility that is denied by contemporary learning theory. Among learning theorists directed at both human (Dawson & Schell, 1985; Öhman, 1979, 1983) and animal (e.g., Wagner, 1976) learning, there appears to be a consensus that the forming of associations between experimental events requires the type of limited-capacity processing that is typically associated with consciousness (e.g., Posner & Boies, 1971). Thus, even though single stimuli may be encoded in memory without having to pass through consciousness, conscious representation may still be necessary if the stimulus is to be associated with some unconditioned stimulus (US).

However, there is one theoretical perspective on conditioning that at least holds the possibility open of nonconscious associative learning. Seligman (1970) developed an argument claiming that the associative apparatuses of animals are constrained by the influence of evolutionary

contingencies on their gene pools. For example, in agreement with evolutionary logic, taste is a much more effective conditioning stimulus (CS)
for malaise than for foot shock in rats, whereas the opposite relation holds
for external stimuli such as sounds or lights (Garcia & Koellig, 1966). On
the basis of such findings, Seligman (1970) proposed a concept of preparedness that reflected the ease of forming associations between events
in terms of their functional, evolutionary relatedness. This concept was
subsequently operationalized inversely in terms of the degradation of
input (e.g., number of training trials) tolerated in developing associations
between events (Seligman & Hager, 1972, p. 4): More prepared associations tolerated more input degradation (e.g., less training trials) to become
encoded in memory. Masking a CS is clearly an instance of quite extreme
degradation of the input conditions for a stimulus contingency. Thus, if
we accept Seligman's (1971) argument that potentially phobic stimuli such
as snakes, spiders, and angry faces are evolutionarily prepared to become
easily associated with aversion and fear, some conditioning could be
expected to such stimuli paired with aversion, even if they were presented
under a masking condition preventing this conscious identification.

To evaluate these hypotheses, Esteves, Dimberg, Parra, and Öhman
(1994) exposed normal subjects to pictures of angry and happy faces that
were effectively masked by a neutral face after a 30-msec SOA. Some of
the subjects had an electric shock US following the masked angry face;
other subjects had the shock following the masked happy face. Different
types of control subjects were either conditioned to pairs of angry–neutral
or happy–neutral faces at ineffective masking intervals (> 300 msec; i.e.,
allowing conscious recognition) or had random presentations of shocks
and masked faces. In a subsequent extinction session, the masks were
removed. Across two independent experiments, the results showed evidence of conditioning to effectively masked angry faces. That is to say,
skin conductance responses to angry faces were reliably larger to previously masked angry faces that had been followed by the shock US than
to previously masked happy faces not followed by shock, when the faces
were presented without masks during extinction. This effect, in fact, was
as large in groups exposed to an effective target–mask interval as in
groups exposed to a long, ineffective target–mask interval during conditioning training. Furthermore, the effect was observed with an angry but
not with a happy face CS, and no differences between angry and happy
faces were observed in groups exposed to shocks and masked pictures
in random order. Thus, these data clearly suggest that skin conductance
responses can be conditioned to nonconsciously presented CSs, provided
that they are fear-relevant, that is, convey a threat that is of some biological
relevance, exactly as could be predicted from the preparedness hypothesis
(Seligman, 1970).

These results were replicated by Öhman and Soares (1996) using snakes and spiders as fear-relevant, and flowers and mushrooms as fear-irrelevant stimuli. One group of subjects was conditioned to masked snakes or spiders with masked spiders or snakes, respectively, serving as control stimuli not associated with shock. Another group of subjects was conditioned to masked flowers or mushrooms in a similar differential conditioning paradigm. In this experiment, the effect of the conditioning contingency was not only assessed during nonmasked extinction, but also in a series of acquisition test-trials where the masked CS was presented without the shock US. Such test-trials are necessary to assess conditioning when the CS–US interval (500 msec in this case) is shorter than the latency of the response (approximately 1–2 sec in case of skin conductance responses; see Öhman, 1983, for a discussion of interpretational problems raised by this procedure). The results (see Fig. 7.3) showed clearly larger responses to the masked CS than to adjacent masked nonshocked control stimuli during the test trials, provided that the stimuli were fear-relevant. Furthermore, as in the study by Esteves et al. (1994), subjects conditioned to masked fear-relevant stimuli showed reliable differential response to conditioning and control stimuli when they were presented nonmasked during extinction. Such differential responding was not observed in subjects conditioned to fear-irrelevant stimuli.

Further experimental work by Öhman and Soares documented that subjects were unable to verbally distinguish between snakes and spiders as assessed in a concurrent forced-choice recognition test. Thus, the differential conditioning effects could not be attributed to conscious recognition of the stimuli, that is, as a result of conditioning training. However, some aspect of the CS–US contingency obviously became available to the conscious cognitive system, because a group of subjects required to rate their shock expectancy in the CS–US interval (extended to 3.5 sec) demonstrated reliably larger (albeit still low) shock expectancy to a shock-associated CS than to the control stimulus, even though they were both effectively masked. Thus, in spite of the fact that they could not consciously identify the stimuli (i.e., tell which was a snake and which was a spider) they obviously had some vague feeling of when a shock was more or less likely. This suggests that the subjects were able to use fragments of information either from the stimulus or from their own (conditioned ?) response to the stimulus to goad their shock expectancies. This latter possibility, suggesting feedback from autonomic responses as critical for the observed effect, is of course of considerable theoretical interest and clearly deserves further investigation.

However, in the present context the most important result from the masked conditioning studies is the demonstration that conditioned association can be developed to stimuli that are only preattentively processed. It should perhaps be explicitly pointed out that the associative

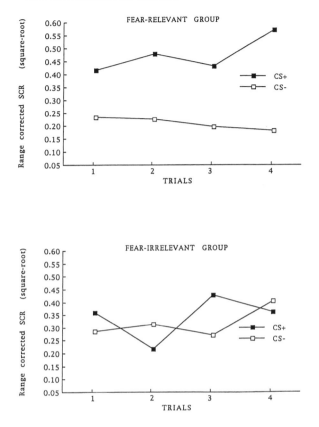

FIG. 7.3. Mean skin conductance response (SCR) to masked fear-relevant (snakes and spiders; upper panel) or masked fear-irrelevant (flowers and mushrooms; lower panel) stimuli followed (CS+) or not followed (CS-) by an electric shock unconditioned stimulus (US). The data are taken from four nonreinforced test trials interspersed among reinforced trials during an acquisition series comprising a total of 24 presentations of each of the CS+ and the CS-. The CS-US interval on reinforced trials was .5 sec.

learning we observed only was partially preattentive because the USs, of course, were consciously processed. Thus, it remains to be seen whether associations can be formed where the elements to become associated are all presented nonconsciously, as claimed, for instance, by Lewecki (1986).

CONCLUDING DISCUSSION:
THE EVOLUTIONARY PERSPECTIVE

The series of experiments described in this chapter demonstrate that preattentive processing is surprisingly advanced in the sense that it may encompass the formation of new associations between preattentively processed stimuli and aversive USs. Thus, there is more to preattentive processing than the interaction of simple reflexes. In a way this should not be surprising, because preattentive processing must be considered a key area from a functional, evolutionary perspective. For organisms to survive and breed in environments where disaster may strike fast and hard, automatic defense systems that may come into operation within the blink of an eye are a necessity. Indeed, to be faster than the blink of an eye it takes for a hidden predator to attack, it is necessary to attend to the informative features of the environment in order to be able to activate defensive action in anticipation of the attack. Thus, the capture of attention and its likely distribution across the environment is one key feature of preattentive processing that very probably is evolutionarily facilitated and constrained. From this perspective, the data on automatic orienting to threat in phobics and on visual search for deviant fear-relevant stimuli can be taken as examples of the role of preattentive processing in catching attention. The nonconscious conditioning data illustrate the investment of attentional resources in nonconscious associative learning. Thus, evolutionary preparedness appears to operate preattentively to control both the spatial extension of attention, and the encoding of particular objects or events into associative networks that include aversive unconditioned stimuli.

Consistent with the evolutionary perspective, a common theme in demonstrating the feats of preattentive processing is that the evidence of superior performance is restricted to fear-relevant stimuli conveying some degree of biologically relevant threat. Both for small animal stimuli, including snakes and spiders, as well as for angry facial stimuli, persuasive adaptive stories are readily invited (see, e.g., Öhman et al., 1985). Thus, it is tempting to frame our findings in a context of evolutionary considerations and speculations. In some respects such a perspective provides an alternative view of contemporary psychology. Not only is contemporary cognitive psychology cold in the sense that it tends to neglect motivational and emotional dynamics, but it is also, in an evolutionary perspective, unduly disinterested in content (Tooby & Cosmides, 1992). It typically assumes that lawful relationships can be formulated without considering the specifics of the elements between which the relationship is assumed to be valid. Thus, it assumes that there are general content-independent information processing systems that have been freed from evolutionary constraints to operate across widely different behavior domains. The alternative perspective, advocated by Tooby and Cosmides (1992), is that cognition is better understood in terms of a series of evolved, content-specific adaptations that have been designed by evolution to deal with the problems of a particular behavior domain. The detection of potential threat with associated defense maneuvers is a primary example of such a domain.

Thus, one would expect that there are adaptations available among cognitive systems that deal particularly with evolutionarily relevant threats.

It is a common theme across the experiments reviewed in this chapter that stimulus content counts. Whereas stimuli implying some evolutionarily relevant threat can preattentively activate skin conductance responses both in phobics and conditioned normals, automatically capture spatial attention, and preattentively enter into association with aversive USs, none of these effects were evident for fear-irrelevant stimuli.

When revising my original model of orienting (Öhman, 1979), the primary basis for the revision (Öhman, 1992) came from my program of research on preattentive processing. The evidence clearly suggested that skin conductance orienting responses to fear-relevant stimuli actually were initiated at the preattentive level, and that they, therefore, as suggested in the original model (Öhman, 1979), reflected a call for processing resources. Skin conductance responses elicited by neutral stimuli, on the other hand, appeared to be more related to the "answer to the call" than to the call itself, because they were abolished by masking. Thus, the orienting reflex to stimuli lacking evolutionary significance may be elicited only after it has been fully processed in the controlled, conscious information system, whereas orienting reflexes elicited by evolutionarily relevant stimuli may be elicited immediately after a preliminary preattentive analysis that locates stimuli by particular features that throughout evolution have been consistently associated with threat. From this conclusion, it appears that the processing of evolutionarily significant stimuli is separated from processing of neutral stimuli very early in the nervous system, to follow a separate route of its own (see Campbell, Wood, & McBride, chapter 3, this volume). This is a dramatic assumption clearly in need of much further data for its backing. After all, we have only compared a few instances of potentially threatening and neutral stimuli, and a much more comprehensive approach with regard to stimulus content is clearly called for. For example, snakes differ from flowers in many dimensions in addition to an evolutionary history of threat, and similar things can be said for angry and happy faces. To sort out these dimensions is one of the important tasks for future research.

One could argue that evolutionarily relevant behaviors would be particularly likely to be revealed by an experimental strategy focused on preattentive processes, that is, through the use of backward masking, because such behavioral tendencies would be likely to be under automatic rather than conscious control. The need for speed and automaticity in handling life-threatening situations clearly would argue in this direction. Preattentive processing may provide an arena in which it would be possible to reveal evolutionary hunches uncontaminated by conscious control. Conscious control could, in fact, hide or distort these underlying tendencies because of its sensitivity to a host of confounding factors such as hypotheses about the real purpose of the experiment, experimenter expectancies, will to please, and so on. Concentrating research efforts at the elucidation of preattentive processing thus not only would involve following the inspired path opened to psychophysiologists by Frances Graham, but it could also promise to rectify the overemphasis on controlled, conscious information processing that contemporary cognitive, social, and clinical psychology still shares with its everyday, intuitive counterpart.

ACKNOWLEDGMENTS

The research reported in this chapter was supported by grants from the Swedish Council for Research in the Humanities and Social Sciences. The author wishes to express his appreciation to Francisco Esteves, Anders Flykt, Daniel Lundqvist, Göran Semb, and Joaquim Soares for assistance at various stages in the research.

REFERENCES

Anthony, B. J. (1985). In the blink of an eye: Implications of reflex modulation for information processing. In P. K. Ackles, J. R. Jennings, & M. G. H. Coles (Eds.), *Advances in psychophysiology* (Vol. 1, pp. 167–218). Greenwich, CT: JAI Press.

Bernstein, A. S., Taylor, K., Austen, B. G., Nathanson, M., & Scarpelli, A. (1971). Orienting response and apparent movement toward or away from the observer. *Journal of Experimental Psychology, 87*, 37–45.

Bohlin, G., & Graham, F. K. (1977). Cardiac deceleration and reflex blink facilitation. *Psychophysiology, 14*, 423–430.

Bohlin, G., Graham, F. K., Silverstein, L. D., & Hackley, S. A. (1981). Cardiac orienting and startle blink modification in novel and signal situations. *Psychophysiology, 18*, 603–611.

Dawson, M. E., & Schell, A. M. (1985). Information processing and human autonomic classical conditioning. In P. K. Ackles, J. R. Jennings, & M. G. H. Coles (Eds.), *Advances in psychophysiology* (Vol. 1, pp. 89–165). Greenwich, CT: JAI Press.

Esteves, F., Dimberg, U., & Öhman, A. (1994). Automatically elicited fear: Conditioned skin conductance responses to masked facial expressions. *Cognition and Emotion, 8*, 393–413.

Esteves, F., Dimberg, U., Parra, C., & Öhman, A. (1994). Nonconscious associative learning: Pavlovian conditioning of skin conductance responses to masked fear-relevant facial stimuli. *Psychophysiology, 31*, 375–385.

Esteves, F., & Öhman, A. (1993). Masking the face: Recognition of emotional facial expressions as a function of the parameters of backward masking. *Scandinavian Journal of Psychology, 34*, 1–18.

Fredrikson, M. (1981). Orienting and defensive responses to phobic and conditioned stimuli in phobics and normals. *Psychophysiology, 18*, 456–465.

Garcia, J., & Koellig, R. A. (1966). Relation of cue to consequence in avoidance learning. *Psychonomic Science, 4*, 123–124.

Graham, F. K. (1973). Habituation and dishabituation of responses innervated by the autonomic nervous system. In H. V. S. Peeke & M. J. Herz (Eds.), *Habituation: Vol. 1. Behavioral studies and physiological substrates* (pp. 163–218). New York: Academic Press.

Graham, F. K. (1975). The more or less startling effects of weak prestimulation. *Psychophysiology, 12,* 238–248.

Graham, F. K. (1979). Distinguishing among orienting, defense, and startle reflexes. In H. D. Kimmel, E. H. van Olst, & J. F. Orlebeke (Eds.), *The orienting reflex in humans* (pp. 137–167). Hillsdale, NJ: Lawrence Erlbaum Associates.

Graham, F. K. (1992). Attention: The heartbeat, the blink, and the brain. In B. A. Campbell, H. Haynes, & R. Richardson (Eds.), *Attention and information processing in infants and adults: Perspectives from human and animal research* (pp. 3–29). Hillsdale, NJ: Lawrence Erlbaum Associates.

Graham, F. K., & Hackley, S. A. (1991). Passive and active attention to input. In J. R. Jennings & M. G. H. Coles (Eds.), *Handbook of cognitive psychophysiology* (pp. 251–356). Chichester, UK: Wiley.

Hamm, A. O., Cuthbert, B. N., Globisch, J., & Vaitl, D. (in press). Startle reflex modulation and psychophysiological response patterns to affective stimulation in subjects with specific phobias and non-phobic controls. *Psychophysiology.*

Hampton, C., Purcell, D. G., Bersine, L., Hansen, C. H., & Hansen, R. D. (1989). Probing "pop-out": Another look at the face-in-the-crowd effect. *Bulletin of the Psychonomic Society, 27,* 563–566.

Hansen, C. H., & Hansen, R. D. (1988). Finding the face in the crowd: An anger superiority effect. *Journal of Personality and Social Psychology, 54,* 917–924.

Hansen, C. H., & Hansen, R. D. (1994). Automatic emotion: Attention and facial efference. In P. M. Niedertahl & S. Kitayama (Eds.), *The heart's eye: Emotional influences in perception and attention* (pp. 217–243). San Diego, CA: Academic Press.

Holender, D. (1986). Semantic activation without conscious identification in dichotic listening, parafoveal vision, and visual masking: A survey and appraisal. *Behavioral & Brain Sciences, 9,* 1–66.

Lang, P. J., Bradley, M. M., & Cuthbert, B. N. (1990). Emotion, attention, and the startle reflex. *Psychological Review, 97,* 377–395.

Lazarus, R. S. (1984). On the primacy of cognition. *American Psychologist, 39,* 124–129.

LeDoux, J. E. (1990). Information flow from sensation to emotion: Plasticity in the neural computation of stimulus value. In M. Gabriel & J. Moore (Eds.), *Learning and computational neuroscience: Foundations of adaptive networks* (pp. 3–51). Cambridge, MA: MIT Press.

Lewecki, P. (1986). *Nonconscious social information processing.* Orlando, FL: Academic Press.

Lynn, R. (1966). *Attention, arousal, and the orientation reaction.* Oxford, UK: Pergamon.

Marcel, A. (1983). Conscious and unconscious perception: An approach to the relations between phenomenal experience and perceptual processes. *Cognitive Psychology, 15,* 238–300.

Merikle, P. M., & Reingold, E. M. (1992). Measuring unconscious perceptual processes. In R. F. Bornstein & T. S. Pittman (Eds.), *Perception without awareness: Cognitive, clinical, and social perspectives* (pp. 55–80). New York: Guilford.

Öhman, A. (1979). The orienting response, attention, and learning: An information processing perspective. In H. D. Kimmel, E. H. van Olst, & J. F. Orlebeke (Eds.), *The orienting reflex in humans* (pp. 443–471). Hillsdale, NJ: Lawrence Erlbaum Associates.

Öhman, A. (1983). The orienting response during Pavlovian conditioning. In D. A. T. Siddle (Ed.), *Orienting and habituation: Perspectives in human research* (pp. 315–369). Chichester, UK: Wiley.

Öhman, A. (1986). Face the beast and fear the face: Animal and social fears as prototypes for evolutionary analyses of emotion. *Psychophysiology, 23,* 123–145.

Öhman, A. (1987). The psychophysiology of emotion: An evolutionary-cognitive perspective. In P. K. Ackles, J. R. Jennings, & M. G. H. Coles (Eds.), *Advances in psychophysiology* (Vol. 2, pp. 79–127). Greenwich, CT: JAI Press.

Öhman, A. (1992). Orienting and attention: Preferred preattentive processing of potentially phobic stimuli. In B. A. Campbell, H. Haynes, & R. Richardson (Eds.), *Attention and information processing in infants and adults: Perspectives from human and animal research* (pp. 263–295). Hillsdale, NJ: Lawrence Erlbaum Associates.

Öhman, A. (1993). Fear and anxiety as emotional phenomena: Clinical phenomenology, evolutionary perspectives, and information processing mechanisms. In M. Lewis & J. M. Haviland (Eds.), *Handbook of emotions* (pp. 511–536). New York: Guilford.

Öhman, A., Dimberg, U., & Esteves, F. (1989). Preattentive activation of aversive emotions. In T. Archer & L.-G. Nilsson (Eds.), *Aversion, avoidance, and anxiety* (pp. 169–193). Hillsdale, NJ: Lawrence Erlbaum Associates.

Öhman, A., Dimberg, U., & Öst, L.-G. (1985). Animal and social phobias: Biological constraints on learned fear responses. In S. Reiss & R. R. Bootzin (Eds.), *Theoretical issues in behavior therapy* (pp. 123–178). New York: Academic Press.

Öhman, A., Esteves, F., Flykt, A., & Soares, J. J. F. (1993). Gateways to consciousness: Emotion, attention, and electrodermal activity. In J.-C. Roy, W. Boucsein, D. C. Fowles, & J. H. Gruzelier (Eds.), *Progress in electrodermal research* (pp. 137–157). New York: Plenum.

Öhman, A., & Soares, J. J. F. (1993). On the automatic nature of phobic fear: Conditioned electrodermal responses to masked fear-relevant stimuli. *Journal of Abnormal Psychology, 102*, 121–132.

Öhman, A., & Soares, J. J. F. (1994). "Unconscious anxiety": Phobic responses to masked stimuli. *Journal of Abnormal Psychology, 103*, 231–240.

Öhman, A., & Soares, J. (1996). *Emotional conditioning to masked stimuli: Unconsciously originated expectancies elicited by non-recognized fear-relevant stimuli.* Manuscript submitted for publication.

Posner, M. I., & Boies, S. J. (1971). Components of attention. *Psychological Review, 78*, 391–408.

Seligman, M. E. P. (1970). On the generality of the laws of learning. *Psychological Review, 77*, 406–418.

Seligman, M. E. P. (1971). Phobias and preparedness. *Behavior Therapy, 2*, 307–320.

Seligman, M. E. P., & Hager, J. E. (Eds.). (1972). *Biological boundaries of learning.* New York: Appleton-Century-Crofts.

Silverstein, L. D., Graham, F. K., & Bohlin, G. (1981). Selective attention effects on the reflex blink. *Psychophysiology, 18*, 240–247.

Soares, J. J. F., & Öhman, A. (1993). Preattentive processing, preparedness, and phobias: Effects of instruction on conditioned electrodermal responses to masked and non-masked fear-relevant stimuli. *Behaviour Research and Therapy, 31*, 87–95.

Sokolov, E. N. (1963). *Perception and the conditioned reflex.* Oxford, UK: Pergamon.

Tooby, J., & Cosmides, L. (1992). The psychological foundation of culture. In J. H. Barkow, L. Cosmides, & J. Tooby (Eds.), *The adapted mind: Evolutionary psychology and the generation of culture* (pp. 20–136). New York: Oxford University Press.

Wagner, A. R. (1976). Priming in STM: An information-processing mechanism for self-generated or retrieval-generated depression in performance. In T. J. Tighe & R. N. Leaton (Eds.), *Habituation: Perspectives from child development, animal behavior, and neurophysiology* (pp. 95–128). Hillsdale, NJ: Lawrence Erlbaum Associates.

Wingard, J. A., & Maltzman, I. (1980). Interest as a predeterminer of the GSR index of the orienting reflex. *Acta Psychologica, 46*, 153–160.

Zajonc, R. B. (1980). Feeling and thinking: Preferences need no inferences. *American Psychologist, 35*, 151–175.

III

Startle Reflex
and Electro-Cortical Studies
of Attention
and Stimulus Gating

8

Attentional Factors in the Elicitation and Modification of the Startle Reaction

Howard S. Hoffman
Bryn Mawr College

It is by now well known that when a mild sensory event, such as a weak tone or a dim light flash, precedes a startle-eliciting signal by an appropriate interval (depending on the circumstances usually between 50 and 200 msec), the amplitude of the elicited reaction can be reduced by as much as 50%. This reflex modification effect is called prepulse inhibition, and it has broad generality. Prepulse inhibition occurs in amphibians (Yerkes, 1905), birds (Stitt, Hoffman, Marsh, & Schwartz, 1976), and mammals, including man (Hoffman & Ison, 1980). It does not depend on learning. Inhibitory effects are observed the first time that a tone or light flash precedes a startle-eliciting stimulus. Nor does it require the subject's direct attention. Prepulse inhibition has been assessed while subjects were sleeping (Silverstein & Graham, 1979), while they were reading (Dykman & Ison, 1979), and while they were watching a slide show (Hoffman, Cohen, & Stitt, 1981).

This is not to say that the elicitation and/or the modification of the startle reflex is unaffected by experience (e.g., learning) or by attentional processes. On the contrary, much recent research indicates that attentional factors can substantially influence both reflex elicitation and modification (Anthony & Graham, 1985; Dawson et al., chapter 11, this volume; Hackley & Boehouwer, chapter 9, this volume). Before describing our own research on these issues, it is important to indicate that except for a number of early studies in which we measured the whole body startle reaction in rats and in pigeons, the bulk of our research employed student volunteers as subjects and focused on an early component of the startle reaction: the eyeblink. Moreover, rather than presenting a loud sound or an intense flash of light to evoke this response, the eliciting stimulus was a rather mild tap to the glabella (e.g., the flat area of skin between the eyebrows) delivered by a lightweight electromechanical system. This electromechanical system, as well as the optical system we developed to assess eyeblinks, is fully described in Marsh and Hoffman (1981) and in Marsh, Hoffman, and Stitt (1979).

It must be noted that in electing to study the eyeblink, we were following the lead of both Frances Graham and James Ison. These investigators had begun to examine prepulse inhibition in human subjects by using acoustic signals or airpuffs to elicit eyeblinks. In our own work we chose to use a tap to the glabella to elicit this reaction because we wanted our procedures to be even more unobtrusive if possible. We hoped that this would make our procedures acceptable to a wide range of subjects, and as it turned out, this was the case. In fact, we were even able to routinely use our procedures with such otherwise difficult-to-test subjects as 16-hour-old newborn infants (Anday, Cohen, & Hoffman, 1990; Anday, Cohen, Kelly, & Hoffman, 1988).

The ease and safety with which a tap to the glabella can elicit a reflex provides an easy way to demonstrate how attentional factors can modify a reflex. To do so, all one need do is try to elicit an eyeblink in oneself by tapping one's own glabella with a forefinger. If the reaction (or more likely the lack of one) is compared to the vigorous blink that occurs when a friend delivers the tap, it becomes clear that the self-presentation of a stimulus, and the attentional processes this act entails, can somehow exert powerful inhibitory control over the reaction that is elicited.

Knowledge of the response reduction engendered by self-presentation is by no means new. A number of investigators have found that if an aversive stimulus is either forewarned or self-presented, it is often reported as seeming to be weaker than when the same stimulus occurs unexpectedly (Bjorkstrand, 1973; Grings, 1960; Haggard, 1943; Maltzman & Wolff, 1970; Staub, Tursky, & Schwartz, 1971). Lykken and Tellegen (1974) proposed that with foreknowledge, subjects selectively tune the appropriate afferent system in anticipation of a stimulus; when the stimulus is aversive, the effect is to attenuate its perceived impact. Furedy and Klajner (1974), however, challenged this proposal on methodological grounds. They noted that if a stimulus is aversive, it is likely to induce increases in arousal. It is possible, they suggested, that with aversive stimuli, self-presentation and/or forewarning produce their major effects by attenuating arousal, rather than by directly influencing the afferent input from the stimulus.

In our own efforts to study the effects of self-presentation and foreknowledge (Cohen, Cranney, & Hoffman, 1983), we hoped to avoid the problem of arousal noted by Furedy and Klajner by using relatively innocuous stimuli. It seemed to us that the taps to the glabella we had been presenting to our subjects would be much less likely to induce arousal than the electrical shocks used in most prior studies. Moreover, rather than relying on reports of perceived stimulus intensity, our research would employ the objective measures of blink amplitude generated by our optical device. Clearly, this would avoid the potential problems of interpretation that can arise when subjective judgments constitute the basic datum.

Our first experiment (Cohen, Cranney, & Hoffman, 1983) was designed to assess the temporal course of the self-presentation effect. Each of a number of female student volunteers was instructed to watch a sequence of slide images and to close a handheld switch approximately 10 sec after each slide change. She was told that switch closure would sometimes initiate an eyeblink-eliciting tap to her forehead. She was also told that on some randomly selected trials, the tap would occur immediately on the switch closure whereas, on others, it would be delayed by an amount that would vary from trial to trial.

Figure 8.1 shows the mean amplitude of tap-elicited eyeblinks (averaged across subjects) at each temporal delay. The shorter the delay between switch closure and tap presentation, the smaller the elicited eyeblink. This function documents the basic self-presentation effect. In the present circumstances, the reduction in reflex amplitude engendered by self-presentation persisted for at most, only a few hundred msec. Clearly

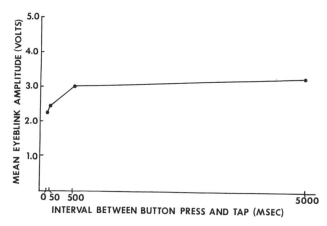

FIG. 8.1. Mean amplitude of eyeblink elicited by a self-presented tap to the glabella (the flat patch of skin between the eyebrows) as a function of the interval between the self-presentation response (pressing the button of a handheld switch) and tap delivery. From Cohen, Cranney, and Hoffman (1983). Copyright © 1983 by the Psychonomic Society. Reprinted with permission.

little or no reflex reduction occurred when the tap was delayed by as little as 500 msec.

This pattern of results can be interpreted in a number of ways. It may mean that the motor activity of switch closure (or the neural command that initiates it) generated an inhibitory process that served to reduce the amplitude of the subsequently elicited reflex, much as a prepulse serves to inhibit startle. If so, then the present findings imply that with the procedures used here this inhibitory process was quite short-lived. It persisted for less than 500 msec.

In analyzing the reflex inhibition afforded by self-presentation, Sanes (1979) concluded that this inhibition is probably initiated prior to the occurrence of the motor response. The data summarized in Fig. 8.1 are consistent with this idea. Previous studies in a number of laboratories found little, if any, inhibition when the lead interval for a prepulse was less than 10 msec. Inhibition increased as the lead interval increased, and was maximal at approximately 100 msec (Graham & Murray, 1977; Hoffman & Ison, 1980; Krauter, Leonard, & Ison, 1973). In the case of self-presentation, however, inhibition is maximal when the interval between switch closure and the tap is 0 msec and the amount of inhibition decreases (rather than increases) as the interval between switch closure and tap is increased. A reasonable way to account for this discrepancy is to assume that the inhibition afforded by self-presentation is mediated by some event that occurs just prior to switch closure. The most obvious possibility is that this event consists of the neural command that initiates the overt behavior.

Whereas the results of this experiment are consistent with the proposition that a subject's expectations may act with some aspect of the motor command system to jointly inhibit an elicited reflex, the design of the experiment does not, in fact, permit one to separate the contributions of these two factors. Our next experiment was designed to do so. In it, subjects were again required to initiate their own taps by closing a switch. Now, however, the taps were either immediate or they were delayed by 5 sec, and the probabilities of a delayed versus an immediate tap were such that subjects in one group would expect an immediate tap on most trials, whereas subjects in a second group would expect a delayed tap on most trials. With this arrangement, the effects of the differing expectations would be revealed in the comparisons between the reactions of the two groups on trials when taps were immediate as well as on trials when taps were delayed.

As in the previous experiment, subjects were run individually and were instructed to observe a sequence of slides of art objects and nature subjects. Slides were changed every 20 sec (on average) and subjects were instructed to present a tap to themselves by pressing a handheld switch approximately 10 sec after each slide change. For subjects in Group A, the probability that switch closure would produce an immediate tap was .75 and the probability of a delayed tap was .25. For subjects in Group B, these probabilities were reversed.

Figure 8.2 shows the mean amplitude (averaged across subjects within each group) of eyeblinks elicited by immediate versus delayed taps. Overall immediate taps elicited smaller blinks than when taps were delayed, and regardless of whether taps were immediate or delayed, the condition with the highest probability yielded the smallest responses.

In their overall configuration and in their details, the several features of these data point to the conclusion that the amplitude of an elicited eyeblink is reduced when the eliciting stimulus is presented at the time that the subject expects it to occur. These data also provide evidence that the effect does not depend solely on inhibitory processes that are mediated by the occurrence of the motor response (or the neural command that initiates it). To see why, compare the reactions to the immediate tap for subjects in Group A to the reactions to the immediate tap for subjects in Group B. For subjects in both groups, the same motor response preceded the immediate taps by the same interval (0 msec), yet as shown in Fig. 8.2 (and confirmed by statistical analysis), subjects in Group A exhibited reliably smaller blinks than subjects in Group B. Apparently, in Group A, for which three of four taps were immediate, subjects tended to expect

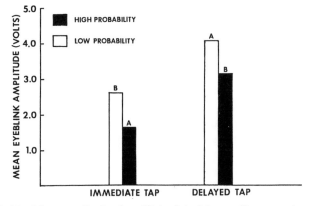

FIG. 8.2. Mean amplitude of eyeblink elicited by a self-presented tap to the glabella. For subjects in Group A (black bar in immediate tap condition, white bar in delayed tap condition), taps were delayed by 5,000 msec on one of four randomly selected trials, and taps occurred immediately on the rest of the trials. For subjects in Group B (white bar in immediate tap condition, black bar in delayed tap condition), taps occurred immediately on one of four trials, and taps were delayed by 5,000 msec on the rest. From Cohen, Cranney, and Hoffman (1983). Copyright © 1983 by the Psychonomic Society. Reprinted with permission.

an immediate tap, whereas in Group B, for which only one in four taps was immediate, subjects tended to expect that the tap would be delayed.

As also seen in Fig. 8.2, subjects in Group B gave smaller blinks to delayed taps than did subjects in Group A. This finding is consistent with the fact that for subjects in Group B, three of four taps were delayed, whereas for subjects in Group A only one in four taps was delayed. Apparently, subjects in Group B expected delayed taps, hence their reactions to them were smaller than those of subjects in Group A, who expected most taps to be immediate.

Overall, the results of this experiment imply that when exposed to events that have different probabilities, subjects exhibit appropriate expectations, and that when stimulus presentation is in accord with expectation, the amplitude of the elicited reflex is reduced. These results are also consistent with the earlier suggestion that the reflex attenuation afforded by self-presentation entails an inhibitory process that is most likely initiated by the neural command that activates the overt behavior. As seen in Fig. 8.2 and confirmed by statistical analysis, overall, responses to the immediate tap were much smaller than responses to the delayed taps, regardless of the probabilities associated with those taps.

Finally, as seen in Fig. 8.2, the effect of high versus low probability was virtually the same for immediate as for delayed tap. That is, the difference between the response amplitudes for the high and low probability conditions when taps were immediate is the same as the difference between these conditions when taps were delayed. In both cases, the expected (high probability) condition yielded the smallest reflexes. This implies that the inhibitory processes engendered by the motor (or motor command) aspects of self-presentation, and those engendered by the expectation or set that may accompany this event, make largely independent contributions to the total amount of inhibition generated. Sternberg (1969) discussed a similar finding with respect to the additive effects of expectations in reaction time experiments.

The results of the preceding experiments suggest that self-presentation of a reflex-eliciting stimulus engages two apparently independent processes, both of which serve to reduce the amplitude of the elicited reflex. One of these consists of the motor and/or the neural command component of the self-presentation act, and the other consists of the cognitive expectation (or set) that accompanies them. As noted earlier, another way to inhibit an elicited reflex is through the process of prepulse inhibition. Our next experiment (Cohen et al., 1983) was designed to determine how the reflex inhibition mediated by a prepulse might combine with the inhibition mediated by self-presentation. Student volunteers were asked to view a series of slide projected images of nature and art subjects and were informed that approximately 10 sec after each slide onset they would either be told to close a switch so as to present a tap to themselves or a tap would be presented to them by the experimenter. During the session taps occurred at intervals of approximately 20 sec and were arranged so that on 50% of the trials the tap would be self-presented and on the rest it would be presented by the experimenter. On half of the trials the tap was preceded by a 50-msec 1 kHz, 70 dB SPL tone (i.e., a prepulse). On such trials switch closure, whether by the subject or the experimenter, initiated the tone, followed 150 msec later by a tap. On the rest of the trials, switch closure also initiated a tap with a 150-msec delay, but no tone was presented.

Figure 8.3 shows the mean amplitude (averaged across subjects) of elicited eyeblinks when taps were self- versus experimenter-presented, and when taps were presented alone or were preceded by a reflex-inhibiting prepulse. As can be seen and as confirmed by the statistical analysis, the difference in amplitude between tap alone and tap-plus-tone (prepulse) conditions was essentially the same on trials when subjects presented their own taps as on trials when the experimenter presented the taps. Moreover, the difference between self-presented and experimenter-presented conditions was essentially the same on tap alone trials as on trials when the tap was preceded by a reflex inhibiting prepulse. In short, the inhibition engendered by self-presentation and the inhibition engendered by a prepulse appears to summate in a simple arithmetic fashion, implying that the two procedures make largely independent contributions to the total amount of inhibition that occurs on a given trial.

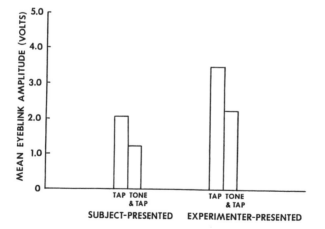

FIG. 8.3. Mean amplitude of elicited eyeblinks when taps were either self-presented or presented by the experimenter and when taps were either preceded by a reflex-inhibiting tone or occurred alone. From Cohen, Cranney, and Hoffman (1983). Copyright © 1983 by the Psychonomic Society. Reprinted with permission.

The first two of the preceding experiments assessed the inhibitory effects engendered by the motor and cognitive factors that are engaged during self-presentation of a reflex-eliciting stimulus. The third of these experiments sought to determine how these inhibitory factors might combine with the inhibitory effects generated when a prepulse leads a reflex-eliciting stimulus by an appropriate interval. Although these experiments obviously inform the interpretation of the reflex inhibition phenomenon, the experiments themselves were not designed to test any particular theoretical account. Our next experiment (Cohen et al., 1983), on the other hand, was designed to do just this. More specifically, our next experiment was arranged to provide a test of the negative perception hypothesis proposed by Lykken and Tellegen (1974). Each of a number of student volunteers was exposed to a sequence of eyeblink-eliciting taps to the glabella intermixed with an equal number of eyeblink-eliciting bursts of intense (110 dB SPL) noise. On half of the trials (randomly selected), the eyeblink eliciting event was initiated by the subject; on the rest it was initiated by the experimenter. Finally, on half of the trials (again, randomly selected), the subject was forewarned as to the type of stimulus that would be presented. On the rest of the trials, this information was withheld. We hoped that with this arrangement we would be able to determine if, as hypothesized by Lykken and Tellegen, subjects can "tune" the appropriate receptor system so as to reduce the effects of an impending reflex-eliciting stimulus.

Figure 8.4 shows the mean blink amplitude averaged across subjects for the several kinds of trials. As seen in Fig. 8.4, foreknowledge as to the type of stimulus to be presented substantially reduced the amplitude of the reflex elicited by the stimulus. In order to produce this effect, foreknowledge must have acted differentially on the stimulus input in the different modalities. Therefore the results of this experiment imply that the inhibition generated by this kind of foreknowledge acts selectively at some point on the afferent side of the reflex circuit. As such, our results support Lykken and Tellegen's (1974) negative perception hypothesis, which proposes that subjects can selectively attenuate the appropriate afferent system in anticipation of a stimulus. Finally, it is noteworthy that our results also indicate that the effects of foreknowledge were very nearly the same when trials were self-presented as when they were experimenter-presented. In doing so, this finding implies that the inhibitory effects of foreknowledge as to stimulus type are independent of the inhibition engendered by the motor and cognitive behavior entailed in the act of self-presenting the stimuli.

The experiments discussed thus far were focused on the role of attentional factors in the elicitation of a reflex. Attentional factors have also been found to play an important role in the inhibition of a reflex by a prepulse.

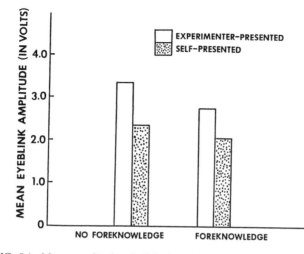

FIG. 8.4. Mean amplitude of elicited eyeblinks averaged across stimuli (tone and noise) when taps were either self-presented or presented by the experimenter under conditions in which foreknowledge about the type of eliciting stimulus was either given or withheld. From Cohen, Cranney, and Hoffman (1983). Copyright © 1983 by the Psychonomic Society. Reprinted with permission.

Ison and Ashkenazi (1980) found that the inhibitory effect of a prepulse was enhanced if its occurrence was preceded by an appropriate warning stimulus. In other experiments (Anthony & Graham, 1985; see also Dawson et al., chapter 11, this volume), it was found that if a subject's attention had previously been directed to the stimulus modality of a (to-be-presented) prepulse, the reflex inhibition engendered by that prepulse is enhanced. Our own work on this issue (DelPezzo & Hoffman, 1980) took a somewhat different tack. In it we asked if the amount of reflex inhibition engendered by a brief flash of a miniature lamp would vary as a function of the lamp's position in the subject's visual field, and if these amounts would change if subjects were forewarned as to where the flash would appear. More than a century earlier, Helmholtz (1925) had noted the "curious fact" that by mere conscious effort one can focus attention on any portion of the visual field and that the process "is entirely independent of the position and accommodation of the eyes" (p. 455). According to Helmholtz, an observer might be gazing at a fixation point while at the same time concentrating on some other part of the visual field. If, at this moment, a stimulus is presented briefly to the attended region, the observer's impression of its features will be markedly enhanced.

We wondered if a prepulse inhibition paradigm could be used to assess the attentional phenomenon that Helmholtz described. We modified a standard perimeter so as to be able to employ a brief (30 msec), small (1 cm) spot of light as a prepulse and to be able to present it at any of three visual angles (0°, 20°, or 40°; see DelPezzo & Hoffman, 1980, for a full description of the apparatus). After a subject had been fitted with a tap unit and eyeblink monitor, she was instructed to place her chin in the perimeter's chin rest and to fixate her right eye on a dim spot of light 2 inches above the 0° location. She was told that she would receive a series of taps and that on some trials, the tap would be preceded by a light flash in one or another of three positions. She was also told that she need not attend to the taps, but that she should report when and where each flash appeared. The subject then received a sequence of trials. On some trials the tap was presented alone. On other trials a reflex-inhibiting flash of light at one of the three locations was presented 150 msec prior to the tap. On half of the trials the subject was told where the light flash might appear. The information was provided in the form of an instruction: "If there is to be a visual stimulus on this trial, it will appear at location X." The information was always correct but, to achieve a balanced experimental design, the visual stimulus was only presented on some of these trials. On the remaining trials, no instructions were provided.

An infrared television system was used to continuously monitor the subject's direction of gaze. Trials were presented in random order at intervals of approximately 15 sec. On each trial the experimenter examined the TV monitor and presented a light flash plus tap or tap alone only when the direction of gaze was firmly fixed on the spot just above the foveal location.

Figure 8.5 shows the mean amplitude (across subjects) of the eyeblinks elicited by the taps on the several kinds of trials. Regardless of their position in the visual field, the light flashes produced a substantial amount of inhibition, but the flashes at the fovea had the largest inhibitory effect and those in the far periphery had the least effect. Overall, the inhibitory effects of a stimulus presented to the periphery were enhanced when the subjects anticipated its location. No such enhancement occurred when the stimulus appeared at the anticipated foveal location. We had not anticipated this latter finding, and we wondered if it meant that the inhibitory effects of stimuli presented to the fovea are unaffected by attentional factors. To examine this possibility we conducted an experiment in which subjects received a sequence of taps to the glabella while their gaze was fixed on the foveal location. Some of the taps were preceded by a reflex-inhibiting light flash at the foveal location. On half of the light flash trials, subjects were instructed to concentrate on the foveal location where their gaze was fixed. On the rest of the light flash trials, subjects were instructed to maintain their fixation on the foveal location but to ignore it and concentrate their attention on a point in the periphery, namely the 40° location.

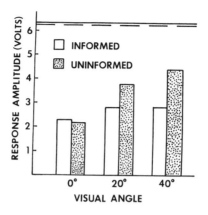

FIG. 8.5. Mean amplitude of tap-elicited eyeblinks when taps were preceded by a reflex-inhibiting light flash at various visual angles. Subjects were either informed or uninformed of where the flash might appear. Also indicated are the mean amplitudes of tap-elicited eyeblinks on control trials when subjects were informed (solid line) or uninformed (dashed line) of where a flash might appear, but the flash was withheld. From DelPezzo and Hoffman (1980). Copyright © 1980 by The American Association for the Advancement of Science. Reprinted by permission.

Figure 8.6 shows again the robust inhibitory effect of a visual stimulus presented to the fovea. It also shows that when instructed to ignore the foveal location and concentrate attention elsewhere, subjects can cooperate and that in doing so, they reduce the reflex inhibition engendered by the stimulus.

When viewed together, the data from these experiments indicate that the amount of reflex inhibition produced by a visual stimulus presented prior to a tap depends on the location of the stimulus in the visual field and on whether or not the subject is concentrating on that location. In many respects our findings are consistent with those of Posner, Snyder, Snyder, and Davidson (1980). These investigators used a reaction-time task to assess the effects of attention on the detection of signals presented to various parts of the visual field. They likened attention to a spotlight that enhances the detection of an object in its beam. Their work, like ours, reveals that attention can be directed either toward or away from the foveal location. However, whereas they studied a voluntary response, we studied an involuntary reflex and therefore we made no demand that subjects control the indicator behavior. This factor may be important in future studies of attention with subjects (such as children) who might have difficulty in meeting the demands of a voluntary task.

There is another attention-related procedure that we have recently found to produce a profound effect on the tap elicited eyeblink, namely

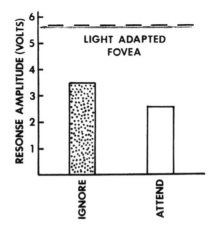

FIG. 8.6. Mean amplitude of tap-elicited eyeblinks when taps were preceded by a reflex-inhibiting flash presented to fovea. Subjects were told either to attend to or ignore this target location. On control trials, subjects were told to attend to (solid line) or to ignore (dashed line) the foveal location, but the flash was withheld. Reprinted with permission from "Attentional Factors in the Inhibition of a Reflex by a Visual Stimulus," by E. M. DelPezzo and H. S. Hoffman, 1980, *Science, 210.* Copyright © 1980 by The American Association for the Advancement of Science.

delayed auditory feedback (DAF). With DAF, subjects read aloud, or recite a memorized passage while listening to their own voices electronically delayed by about 500 msec. A number of investigators (Doehring, 1956; Hoffman, Khan, Papaconstantinou, & O'Herron, 1991; Yates, 1963) have made it clear that DAF produces a variety of physiological and behavioral effects, including an increase in pulse rate and in systolic blood pressure, an increase in vocalic intensity, and considerable vocalic confusion (i.e., slowing and slurring of speech as well as occasional stuttering). In a sense, DAF turns an otherwise articulate subject into an instant aphasic. Because it seemed reasonable to consider this to be a stressful and thus unpleasant condition, and because we knew that unpleasant conditions tended to enhance startle (Bradley, Cuthbert, & Lang, 1990; Lang, Bradley, & Cuthbert, 1990, chapter 5, this volume; Vrana, Spence, & Lang, 1988), we fully expected that if we delivered eyeblink-eliciting taps while subjects were experiencing DAF, blink amplitude would be enhanced. To our surprise, however, the effect of the DAF was quite the opposite. Under DAF, the amplitude of elicited blinks was greatly reduced.

Figure 8.7 shows the mean amplitude of eyeblinks (across subjects) as well as the means for each subject in the experiment we conducted to assess the effects of DAF on tap elicited eyeblinks. As seen in Fig. 8.7, blink amplitude was largest when subjects heard themselves reciting the assigned passage without any delay. This result makes it clear that the potential stress

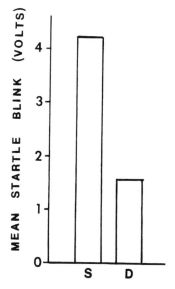

FIG. 8.7. Startle blinks elicited by a tactile stimulus while reading aloud under simultaneous (S) versus delayed (D) auditory feedback.

induced by DAF does not produce a reflex enhancement effect sufficient to overcome the reflex reductions that the procedure induces.

It seemed possible that these reductions might be a product of the rather powerful attentional demands induced by DAF. Perhaps subjects were so focused on the sounds of their own voices during DAF that they failed to attend to the tactile input produced by the taps to the glabella. Informal evidence for such modality-specific sensory gating came from several of the subjects who reported either not remembering having received taps during DAF or who thought they had received fewer and lower intensity taps during this condition. More formal evidence of this kind of modality-specific sensory gating comes from research by Anthony and Graham (1985). These investigators found attenuated responding to an acoustic startle stimulus when subjects were engaged in a visual foreground task (i.e., viewing pictures). Furthermore, they found that the amount of attenuation of the response was a function of the interest in the pictures. More interesting pictures produced more attenuation. To explain their findings, Anthony and Graham suggested that because attentional resources at a particular time are necessarily limited, any allocation of attention to a given modality should make it less available to input from some other modality.

If DAF induces excessive allocation of attentional resources to the auditory modality, then we would expect that DAF would enhance eyeblinks, rather than attenuating them, if the eyeblink-eliciting stimulus is an intense sound rather than a tap to the glabella. Figure 8.8 shows the results of the experiment we conducted to examine this possibility. As

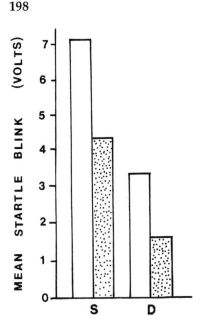

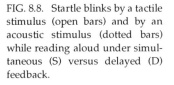

FIG. 8.8. Startle blinks by a tactile stimulus (open bars) and by an acoustic stimulus (dotted bars) while reading aloud under simultaneous (S) versus delayed (D) feedback.

before, subjects received eyeblink-eliciting stimuli while reading aloud under simultaneous or DAF. Now, however, the blink-eliciting stimulus was sometimes an intense sound and at other times it was a tap to the glabella. As seen in Fig. 8.8, the taps tended to elicit larger blinks than the acoustic stimuli, but regardless of the modality of the eyeblink-eliciting stimulus, responses were larger during simultaneous feedback than during DAF.

The configuration of these data is not what would be anticipated if DAF induces a reallocation of limited attentional resources to the auditory modality and this factor is responsible for the reduced reactions to taps. Had this been the case, it would be expected that DAF would have either enhanced the reactions to intense sounds or left them unaffected. Instead, it attenuated these reactions, and it did so to approximately the same degree as it attenuated the blinks to the taps.

It is not, at this time, possible to provide an explanation as to exactly why DAF attenuates elicited eyeblinks; that research remains to be done. In the meantime, however, there are two characteristics of the DAF effect that merit attention because they point to the kinds of experiments that are likely to cast light on the issue. As noted earlier, during DAF subjects tend to speak louder and in an abrupt and sometimes repetitive (aphasia-like) fashion. In short, DAF changes ongoing spontaneous vocal activity, and in doing so it also increases the pulselike character of the subject's acoustic environment. Either or both of these effects may be, at least in part, responsible for the attenuated eyeblinks under DAF.

Consider first the changed acoustic environment. Our initial (seren-dipitous) observation of reflex modification occurred more than 30 years ago, when we sought to elicit startle reactions in rats while they were exposed to a background of mild (70 dB SPL) pulsing noise. To our amazement, this seemingly innocuous acoustic background all but elimi-nated the rats' startle reaction to an unexpected intense, pistol-shot-like sound (Hoffman & Fleshler, 1963). Perhaps the abrupt, repetitive character of the sound of one's own speech under DAF serves as a background of pulsing noise.

The other possibility is that the enhanced spontaneous activity, under DAF, is responsible for the attenuation of startle blinks in this condition. Wecker and Ison (1986) examined the role of spontaneous activity in startle elicitation and in prepulse inhibition. Using both tone bursts and electrical shocks to elicit startle, they found substantially reduced startle responses when rats were engaged in spontaneous activity (e.g., groom-ing, turning, twisting, sniffing, or consuming) compared to when they were quiet. Furthermore, they found that the reflex inhibition, ordinarily engendered by an acoustic prepulse, was also reduced during spontane-ous activity. Wecker and Ison concluded that their findings implied some form of peripheral or sensory gating mechanism that interferes with the processing of sensory input during spontaneous activity, rather than competition within the efferent pathways. In support of this conclusion they cited Coquery (1978) who suggested that the attenuation of sensory input, marked by a pronounced reduction of cutaneous information along the lemniscal pathways during voluntary efferent programs, may protect the synchrony of motor output from interference by further sensorineural demands on the system.

As of this writing, the experiments that we hope will help clarify the roles of behavioral factors versus acoustic factors in the reflex attenuation engendered by DAF are underway. In the meantime, the studies that have been described in this chapter add to an increasing body of evidence that the overt startle reaction at a given time is influenced by a variety of cognitive and/or behavioral factors and the effects are not small. The research we have conducted focused on several of the cognitive-behav-ioral factors that seemed to us likely to modify the eyeblink elicited by a tap to the glabella. What we found can be summarized as follows:

1. The tap-elicited eyeblink is inhibited by the neural command that initiates the act of self-presenting the tap. The inhibitory effects of this factor, while quite robust, were found to be rather short lived; they persisted for something more than 100 msec but less than 500 msec.

2. The eyeblink to a self-presented tap is attenuated when the subject has anticipated the tap at the time that the tap occurs. When switch

closure can produce either an immediate or delayed tap and the probability of these two conditions is varied, eyeblinks are attenuated in the high probability condition independently of whether that condition entailed immediate or delayed taps.

3. When eyeblinks can be elicited by either a tap or a loud sound, a subject's foreknowledge as to the modality of the impending reflex-eliciting stimulus was found to attenuate the reaction. Because this kind of foreknowledge entails differential reactions to input in different modalities, it is concluded that this factor must operate at some point on the afferent side of the reflex arc.

4. A subject's direction of attention to or away from the location in the visual field of an impending reflex-inhibiting visual prepulse can influence the amount of inhibition engendered by that stimulus. Instructions to attend to its impending location enhanced the reflex inhibition engendered by a visual prepulse in the retinal periphery, whereas instructions to ignore its location reduced the inhibition engendered by a visual prepulse presented to the fovea. It was concluded that the cognitive mechanisms responsible for these effects entailed a kind of internal focusing of attention that was independent of the direction of gaze at the time. This conclusion was based on the fact that our procedures required that regardless of prepulse location and the state of a subject's foreknowledge, prepulse presentation only occurred while subject's gaze was firmly fixed on a small spot in the foveal location.

5. The nature of the activity and/or the acoustic environment at the moment a reflex-eliciting stimulus is presented can influence the amplitude of the reaction. Thus far our work indicates that both tactile and acoustic-elicited eyeblinks are attenuated if the reflex-eliciting signal is presented when subjects are attempting to read aloud while experiencing DAF.

6. In several of our studies, various pairs of these factors were tested in combination as well as individually. In each such instance, the two factors were found to make independent contributions to the reflex attenuation engendered by the pair.

CONCLUSIONS

As noted in an earlier paper (Hoffman & Ison, 1980), reflex modification procedures provide an investigator with the means to examine issues at a neural level while using purely behavioral techniques. In essence, they provide a way to carry out what seem best described as bloodless neurophysiological investigations. Based on the early work on reflex modification, it was concluded that despite its rapid onset and disruptive appearance, the startle response is not simply an overload reaction to massive sensory

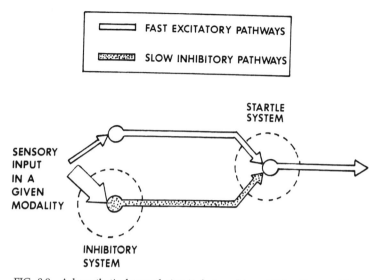

FIG. 8.9. A hypothetical neural circuit designed to exhibit reflex modification. In this circuit, sensory stimulation in a given modality activates the
startle system via two inputs, one of which impinges on an inhibitory
system. For the modality depicted in this circuit, the input to the inhibitory
system is represented as much stronger than the input to the excitatory
pathways. For a different modality, or for a different subject or species, the
relative strengths of these two inputs might be just opposite or equal. From
"Reflex Modification in the Domain of Startle: I. Some Empirical Findings
and Their Implications for How the Nervous System Processes Sensory
Input," by H. S. Hoffman and J. R. Ison, 1980, *Psychological Review, 87.*
Copyright © 1980 by The American Psychological Association. Adapted
with permission.

input. That is, it was concluded that there is a brain center where startle is
organized, and that this center is responsive to inputs of only moderate
intensity. It was also concluded that sensory signals had both excitatory and
inhibitory input into this system, but that the inhibitory input takes longer
to arrive at the system than the excitatory input.

Figure 8.9 provides a schematic representation of a neural arrangement
that exhibits these characteristics. The results of the research just summarized imply that foreknowledge as to the modality and as to the expected
time of arrival of a pending startle stimulus attenuates the response by
selectively modifying the appropriate sensory input. In short, the research
described here leads to the conclusion that foreknowledge acts on the
afferent side of the reflex arc. This conclusion seems consistent with the
finding that the reflex attenuation afforded by these two kinds of foreknowledge appears to be largely independent of the attenuation engendered by the act of self-presenting a reflex-eliciting stimulus. None of our

results, however, provide an indication of where, on the input side, the effect of foreknowledge occurs. Moreover, our results raise what at first glance seems to be a paradox. If foreknowledge acts to attenuate the reaction to a startle-eliciting signal by attenuating the signal's excitatory input to the center where startle is organized, how is it possible that foreknowledge also enhances the amount of reflex inhibition engendered by an appropriate prepulse? The paradox is resolved if we assume that in addition to acting selectively with respect to the modality of a given input, foreknowledge acts selectively with respect to where that input is directed. This could be the case if foreknowledge of the modality of a stimulus simultaneously attenuated input from that modality to excitatory pathways in the startle circuit and enhanced (or removed tonic inhibition of) input to the inhibitory center of the startle circuit in Fig. 8.9. Whether or not this is, in fact, what happens, remains to be determined. In the meantime, the issue is clearly testable, and hopefully, the information will soon be forthcoming.

ADDENDUM

Subsequent to the two experiments on DAF described here, an additional experiment on this procedure has been completed. In it we sought to determine if the pulselike character of the subject's acoustic input during DAF might be the principle cause of the reduced eyeblinks that this condition engenders. To examine this possibility, each of five student volunteers received a sequence of eyeblink eliciting taps while reading aloud with DAF and then, a short time later, received a second sequence of identical taps while listening to the recording of his or her own voice that had been obtained during the prior DAF condition.

Every one of the students exhibited much larger blink reactions in Phase 2 (when merely listening to the recording of the prior DAF reading) than in Phase 1 (when producing that recording). This result makes it clear that the acoustic input during DAF makes little, if any, contribution to the reflex suppression that the procedure engenders. By a process of elimination, we are left with the conclusion that the major contributor to reflex suppression during DAF must be the enhanced motor and/or cognitive (e.g., attentional) activity that this procedure induces.

ACKNOWLEDGMENTS

The experiments described in this chapter were supported by grants from the National Institute of Health. The studies that employed DAF were conducted by Mary K. Waibel as part of an Honors Project at Bryn Mawr College.

REFERENCES

Anday, E. K., Cohen, M. E., & Hoffman, H. S. (1990). The blink reflex: Maturation and modification in the neonate. *Developmental Medicine and Child Neurology, 32,* 142–150.

Anday, E. K., Cohen, M. E., Kelley, N. G., & Hoffman, H. S. (1988). Reflex modification audiometry: Assessment of acoustic sensory processing in the term neonate. *Pediatric Research, 23,* 257–363.

Anthony, B. J., & Graham, F. K. (1985). Blink reflex modification by selective attention: Evidence for the modulation of automatic processing. *Biological Psychology, 97,* 377–395.

Bjorkstrand, P. A. (1973). Electrodermal responses as affected by subject versus experimenter controlled noxious stimulation. *Journal of Experimental Psychology, 97,* 365–369.

Bradley, M. M., Cuthbert, B. N., & Lang, P. J. (1990). Startle reflex modification: Emotion or attention? *Psychophysiology, 27,* 513–522.

Cohen, M. E., Cranney, J., & Hoffman, H. S. (1983). Motor and cognitive factors in the modification of a reflex. *Perception & Psychophysics, 34,* 214–220.

Coquery, J. M. (1978). Selective attention as a motor program. In J. Requin (Ed.), *International symposium on attention and performance, 7* (pp. 505–515). Hillsdale, NJ: Lawrence Erlbaum Associates.

DelPezzo, E. M., & Hoffman, H. S. (1980). Attentional factors in the inhibition of a reflex by a visual stimulus. *Science, 210,* 673–674.

Doering, D. G. (1956). *Changes in psychophysiological responses produced by delayed speech feedback.* U.S. Naval School of Aviation Medicine (Research Rep., Project No. NM 001 102 502, No. 1).

Dykman, B. M., & Ison, J. R. (1979). Temporal integration of acoustic stimulation obtained in reflex inhibition in rats and humans. *Journal of Comparative & Physiological Psychology, 93,* 939–945.

Furedy, J. J., & Klajner, F. (1974). On evaluating autonomic and verbal indices of negative perception. *Psychophysiology, 11,* 121–124.

Graham, F. K., & Murray, G. M. (1977). Discordant effects of weak prestimulation on magnitude and latency of the reflex blink. *Physiological Psychology, 5,* 108–114.

Grings, W. W. (1960). Preparatory set variables related to classical conditioning of autonomic responses. *Psychological Review, 67,* 243–252.

Haggard, E. (1943). Some conditions determining adjustment during and readjustment following experimentally induced stress. *Journal of Experimental Psychology, 33,* 257–284.

Helmholtz, H. von. (1925). *Handbuch der Physiologischen Optik* [Handbook of physiology and optics] (J. P. D. Southall, Ed. & Trans.). Rochester, NY: Optical Society of America.

Hoffman, H. S., Cohen, M. E., & Stitt, C. L. (1981). Acoustic augmentation and inhibition of the human eyeblink. *Journal of Experimental Psychology: Human Perception & Performance, 7,* 1357–1362.

Hoffman, H. S., & Fleshler, M. (1963). Startle reaction: Modification by background acoustic stimulation. *Science, 141,* 928–930.

Hoffman, H. S., & Ison, J. R. (1980). Reflex modification in the domain of startle: I. Some empirical findings and their implications for how the nervous system processes sensory input. *Psychological Review, 87,* 175–189.

Hoffman, H. S., Khan, T., Papaconstantinou, V., & O'Herron, F. (1991). Cardiac reactions to two psychological stressors, acting in combination. *Perceptual and Motor Skills, 72,* 927–934.

Ison, J. R., & Ashkenazi, B. (1980). Effects of a warning stimulus on reflex elicitation and reflex inhibition. *Psychophysiology, 17*(6), 586–591.

Krauter, E. E., Leonard, D. W., & Ison J. R. (1973). Inhibition of the human eyeblink by a brief acoustic stimulus. *Journal of Comparative & Physiological Psychology, 2,* 28–37.

Lang, P. J., Bradley, M. M., & Cuthbert, B. N. (1990). Emotion, attention and the startle reflex. *Psychological Review, 97,* 377–395.

Lykken, D. T., & Tellegen, A. (1974). On the validity of the perception hypothesis. *Psychophysiology, 11,* 125–132.

Maltzman, I., & Wolff, C. (1970). Preference for immediate versus delayed noxious stimulation and concomitant GSR. *Journal of Experimental Psychology, 83,* 76–79.

Marsh, R. R., & Hoffman, H. S. (1981). Eyeblink elicitation and measurement in the human infant: A circuit modification. *Behavior Research Methods and Instrumentation, 13,* 707.

Marsh, R. R., Hoffman, H. S., & Stitt, C. L. (1979). Eyeblink elicitation and measurement in the human infant. *Behavior Research Methods and Instrumentation, 11,* 498–502.

Posner, M. I., Snyder, C. R., & Davidson, B. J. (1980). Attention and the detection of signals. *Journal of Experimental Psychology, General, 109,* 160.

Sanes, J. N. (1979). *Excitability of cutaneous eyeblink reflex in humans during organization and performance of voluntary movements.* Unpublished doctoral dissertation, University of Rochester, NY.

Silverstein, L. D., & Graham, F. K. (1979). Obicularis oculi excitability and prestimulation effects during REM and NREM sleep [Abstract]. *Psychophysiology, 16,* 177.

Staub, E., Tursky, B., & Schwartz, G. E. (1971). Self-control and predictability: Their effects on reactions to aversive stimulation. *Journal of Personality and Social Psychology, 18,* 157–162.

Sternberg, S. (1969). The discovery of processing stages: Extensions of Donder's method. *Acta Psychologica, 30,* 276–315.

Stitt, C. L., Hoffman, H. S., Marsh, R. R., & Schwartz, G. M. (1976). Modification of the pigeon's visual startle reaction by the sensory environment. *Journal of Comparative and Physiological Psychology, 90,* 601–619.

Vrana, S. R., Spence, E. L., & Lang, P. J. (1988). The startle probe response: A new measure of emotion? *Journal of Abnormal Psychology, 97,* 487–491.

Wecker, J. R., & Ison, J. R. (1986). Effects of motor activity on the elicitation and modification of the startle reflex in rats. *Animal Learning and Behavior, 14,* 287–292.

Yates, A. J. (1963). Delayed auditory feedback. *Psychological Bulletin, 60,* 213–232.

Yerkes, R. M. (1905). The sense of hearing in frogs. *Journal of Comparative Neurology & Psychology, 15,* 279–304.

9

The More or Less Startling Effects of Weak Prestimulation—Revisited: Prepulse Modulation of Multicomponent Blink Reflexes

Steven A. Hackley
University of Missouri–Columbia

A. J. W. Boelhouwer
Tilburg University

In her presidential address to the Society for Psychophysiological Research, Graham (1975) proposed a general theory of acoustic startle-blink modulation that postulated three underlying mechanisms:

1. Any onset, offset, or qualitative change in stimulation automatically engages an inhibitory mechanism that protects preattentive perceptual analyses of that stimulus from interruption by concurrent reflexive behavior.
2. Sustained prestimulation triggers an increase in immediate arousal that nonselectively facilitates motoric processes.
3. Prestimuli can also engage attentional orienting, thereby modifying sensory analyses of a subsequent reflexogenic stimulus.

The experiments on which this theory was based involved reflexive eyeblink or whole-body startle to abrupt acoustic stimuli. Acoustic blinks are unusual in that the response of the agonist orbicularis oculi muscle manifests only a single burst of electromyographic (EMG) activity. The blink in response to cutaneous stimulation of the face, by contrast, exhibits two or, in some cases, three distinct components, referred to as R1, R2, and R3. Similarly, the response of the orbicularis oculi muscle to sudden illumination involves multiple EMG bursts, of which the two referred to

as R50 and R80 are the most prominent. Because these distinct components can be modified differentially by prestimulation, they may offer
insights into the nature of reflex modulation.

In this chapter, we review some recent studies on the modulation of
multicomponent blink reflexes, as well as the underlying physiology.
Modulatory effects of simple prestimuli presented at brief lead times are
emphasized. The more complex effects produced by emotion-inducing
or attention-engaging prestimuli are reviewed in other chapters within
this volume (see Anthony, 1985, for a general review; see also Dawson,
chapter 11, this volume; Hoffman, chapter 8, this volume; Lang, Bradley,
& Cuthbert, chapter 5, this volume).

HISTORICAL BACKGROUND

Reflexology is arguably the oldest branch of experimental brain science,
with lesion studies of the underlying circuitry dating back to the middle
1700s (Whytt, 1751, cited in Fearing, 1930). One of the attractions of this
venerable field is the wealth of accumulated neurophysiological and
behavioral data on which new research can build. The eyeblink reflex is
a case in point.

The first laboratory experiment on the blink reflex was conducted by
the Viennese physiologist, Sigmund Exner (1874). In a paper published
the preceding year, Exner (1873) had coined the term *reaction time* (RT)
to describe the latency of speeded voluntary reactions, which was then
becoming a popular topic of investigation. In his 1874 article, Exner
attempted to compare voluntary RT with the latency of a reflexive response. Using a mechanical recording device, Exner measured the manual
RT to a visual stimulus, an electric spark, obtaining a mean of 113 msec.
Surprisingly, the eyeblink reflex to the same stimulus was found to have
greater latency (216 msec) and variability (range = 176–281 msec). As
Exner appears to have suspected, the latencies of these eyelid responses
were too long and variable for them to have been reflexive. Recent
mechanical recordings of the blink reflex to weak visual stimuli reveal a
two-phase response, with the initial component beginning at 50 to 70
msec and the second at 80 to 100 msec (e.g., Graham & Hackley, 1991,
Fig. 3.1; Grant, 1943, 1945). The eyelid responses recorded by Exner in
this first experiment were probably not reflexes, but rather, posttrial
spontaneous blinks (Stern, Walrath, & Goldstein, 1984) emitted after the
subject realized that the trial had finished.

In a follow-up study described in the same article, Exner tried combining the visual stimulus to one eye with an electrocutaneous stimulus
to the lid of the other eye. When the light flash was 9 cm away, the

trigeminal blink reflex had an average latency of 66 msec; at a distance of 5 cm, the latency was reduced to 57 msec. These latency values are consistent with contemporary findings for the mechanically recorded, cutaneous blink reflex (e.g., Putnam, 1975), and it seems clear that they document a cross-modal facilitation effect that varied as a function of the strength of the concurrent prepulse. (See Sherrington, 1906, p. 178, for a review of lesion studies conducted by Exner on this topic; for general historical reviews, see Fearing, 1930; Ison & Hoffman, 1983.)

PHYSIOLOGY OF THE EYEBLINK REFLEX

Reflexologists generally consider the acoustic, cutaneous, and photic eyeblink responses to constitute a family of closely related reflexes, mediated by overlapping neural circuitry. There are four lines of evidence for this. First, the adequate stimulus is apparently the same in each case, an abrupt increase in intensity (Landis & Hunt, 1939). Second, the stereotyped response is grossly similar across modalities (Landis & Hunt, 1939), notwithstanding minor kinematic differences (Manning & Evinger, 1986). Third, the three types of blink are similarly modified by a variety of experimental manipulations, including emotion (Lang, Bradley, & Cuthbert, 1990), expectancy (Zeigler, 1982), and weak prestimulation (reviewed in this chapter). Fourth, and most importantly, habituation of the blink reflex to stimuli within one modality transfers to blinks evoked by stimuli within the other two modalities (Rimpel, Geyer, & Hopf, 1982). Assuming that the site of habituation is afferent to the location within the reflex arc at which prepulse inhibition occurs (cf. Davis, Parisi, Gendelman, Tischler, & Kehne, 1982; Ison & Krauter, 1974), there must be extensive overlap in the premotor circuitry of the cutaneous, photic, and acoustic blink reflexes.

Much progress has been made toward understanding the neurophysiological basis of the blink reflex and of eyelid control in general. The account offered in this paragraph is based on recent work by Evinger and colleagues (Evinger, Manning, & Sibony, 1991; Evinger, Shaw, Peck, Manning, & Baker, 1984; Manning & Evinger, 1986). In terms of motor control, the eyeblink is an extaordinarily simple response. Palpebral movements are characterized by a single degree of freedom (the lids can only move up or down), the amount of force needed to accelerate the lids is largely independent of their initial position, and because the lid musculature has no spindles, blinks are presumably controlled under simple, open-loop mode (i.e., without proprioceptive feedback). An eyeblink begins with relaxation of the antagonistic levator palpebrae superioris muscle. The cell bodies of the neurons that innervate this muscle are located in the central caudal division of the oculomotor nucleus, with dendrites extending into the periaquaductal gray, the main premotor nucleus for levator control (Schmidtke & Büttner-Ennever, 1992). Passive tension in the ligaments of the orbicularis oculi muscle is alone sufficient to cause lid closure when the levator is relaxed. During reflexive blinking, high velocities are obtained (e.g., 3,000 degrees/sec) because this passive force is supplemented by active contraction of the orbicularis oculi muscle. This muscle is controlled by motor neurons located in the intermediate (dorsolateral) division of the facial nucleus, with reflex afference from the pontine and medullary *blink premotor nuclei of Holstege* (e.g., Holstege, Tan, van Ham, & Graveland, 1986). During lid closure, the eyeball can actually retract into the orbit as much as a centimeter, due to cocontraction of most of the extraocular muscles (Evinger et al., 1984). (Novice contact lens wearers may be interested to know that, during their first hesitant attempts at lens placement, the eye can actually withdraw from the initial contact of the approaching lens.)

Acoustic Blink Reflex

Other than the motor and immediate premotor nuclei already mentioned, little is known regarding the reflex arc for acoustic blink. Brain sections at midbulbar and intercollicular levels in rabbits have little effect, so the essential circuitry must lie within this constrained region of the brainstem (Hori, Yasuhara, Naito, & Yasuhara, 1986). The inferior colliculi and the midbrain reticular formation are apparently critical, because lesions in these areas reduce or eliminate acoustic blink (Hori et al., 1986).

For the forelimb-flexion component of acoustic startle in rats, Davis and colleagues have carefully mapped a reflex arc that includes, in the most recent version (Lee, Lopez, Meloni, & Davis, 1994), only three central synapses. The primary afferent fibers bypass the cochlear nucleus and synapse at the nucleus of the cochlear root. These cells send short axons to the adjacent nucleus reticularis pontis caudalis, which in turn transmits the signal to the relevant spinal motor neurons.

Because of the extensive parallels in findings for acoustic blink in humans and whole-body startle in rats (e.g., Braff & Geyer, 1990; Graham, 1975; Hoffman & Ison, 1980), it is tempting to assume that, except for the most efferent elements, the circuitry is the same. However, a comparison of latencies suggests that the blink reflex arc is substantially longer than the circuit for the forelimb-flexion response. The latencies of the forelimb-flexion and postauricular components of startle in rats are both around 8 msec, and both appear to be mediated by trisynaptic arcs (Cassella & Davis, 1986; Lee et al., 1994; see also Davis, chapter 4, this volume). The latency of the postauricular component in humans is similar to that observed in rats, averaging only 9 to 10 msec (e.g., Hackley, Woldorff, &

Hillyard, 1987; Sollers & Hackley, 1993), whereas the latency of the eye-blink component is typically 30 to 40 msec (e.g., Graham, 1992). The time required for conduction along the facial nerve only accounts for about 2 msec of this difference (Graham, Silverstein, & Hackley, 1979). Thus, the relatively long latency of the acoustic blink reflex makes it unlikely that this response is mediated by a pathway as short as those identified by Davis and colleagues for the forelimb-flexion and postauricular components of startle.

In addition, two dissociations between acoustic blink and the other components of startle have recently been described in the clinical neurophysiology literature. Brown and colleagues (e.g., Brown et al., 1991) reported that the early latency response recorded in the orbicularis oculi muscle to intense acoustic stimuli in patients with hereditary startle disease is normal, whereas other startle components, including the short-latency neck and jaw muscle responses, are greatly exaggerated in size. Conversely, in the mutant *quivering mouse* strain, Horner and Bock (e.g., 1985) noted that acoustic blink is normal, but that other components of acoustic startle are apparently absent.

Cutaneous Blink Reflex

Kugelberg (1952) was the first to record the cutaneous blink reflex with electromyographic methods, and he showed that differences between the consensual and direct responses are due to two distinct phases of orbicularis oculi muscle activation, termed *R1* and *R2*. The R1 component is ipsilateral to the side of stimulation in all vertebrates that have been examined. It has an onset latency in humans of 15 to 20 msec with mechanical stimulation but, if the supraorbital branch of the trigeminal nerve is directly stimulated, thereby bypassing the sensory receptors, latencies of 9 to 12 msec are observed. This short latency led Kugelberg to suggest that R1 might be proprioceptive in nature, due to a brief stretch of the underlying musculature. However, subsequent research has shown that both R1 and R2 are triggered by stimulation of cutaneous receptors (e.g., Lindquist & Martensson, 1970).

The reflex circuitry of the cutaneous blink reflex has been studied extensively (e.g., Ongerboer de Visser & Kuypers, 1978; reviewed in Holstege et al., 1986). The peripheral segment of the afferent pathway is the trigeminal nerve, as shown by the absence of R1 and R2 when transmission is blocked by local anesthesia. The necessary circuit for R1 also includes the principal trigeminal nucleus, located at the pontine level of the brainstem, a di- or trisynaptic connection to the intermediate (dorsolateral) portion of the facial nucleus located on the same side, from whence the motor fibers that innervate the orbicularis oculi muscle depart.

The late bilateral R2 component has a latency of 30 to 40 msec and a duration of 40 to 60 msec. The R2 is bilateral in humans, but ipsilateral in cats (Hiraoka & Shimamura, 1977). The afferent limb of the R2 reflex arc includes the trigeminal nerve and the spinal trigeminal nerve and nucleus. Fibers originating in that nucleus project bilaterally and multisynaptically to the intermediate portion of the facial nucleus.

A third component, R3, is variably present in some subjects at a latency of 75 to 90 msec. This EMG burst is more sensitive to anesthetic blockade than is R2, it has a higher threshold for electrical activation, and it is more highly correlated with subjective pain thresholds (Rossi, Risaliti, & Rossi, 1989). It has been reported that R2, in turn, has a higher threshold of elicitation than does R1 (Sanes, Foss, & Ison, 1982). Coupled with the fact that thick axons are more sensitive to electrical stimulation than are thin axons, these data suggest that R1, R2, and R3 are mediated by populations of receptor cells of progressively decreasing size.

Visual Blink Reflexes

There are two physiologically distinct lid-closure reactions in the visual modality, blink-to-light-flash, refered to as *photic blink*, and blink-to-threat, also known as the *Cartesian blink reflex*. The eponym alludes to the special historical significance of blink-to-threat, which was the first reflex described in the scientific literature (Descartes, 1649; reviewed in Hodge, 1890). Perceptual learning may play a role in the development of the Cartesian blink reflex because this response is absent in human newborns (reviewed in Liu & Ronthal, 1992) and in chimpanzees reared in darkness, although the same apes exhibited startle to sudden increases in illumination (Riesen, 1947).

The necessary circuitry for the Cartesian blink reflex must include regions of neocortex, because lesions of primary visual cortex, the posterior parietal lobe, or frontal eye fields can eliminate it (e.g., Liu & Ronthal, 1992). The posterior parietal lobe is considered part of the posterior attention area (Posner & Petersen, 1990), and patients with lateral neglect due to lesions in this region of the brain fail to blink in response to menacing gestures within the neglected hemispace (e.g., Liu & Ronthal, 1992). In a study of rhesus monkeys, weak electrical stimulation within a region of the posterior parietal lobe evoked blink EMG responses at an average latency of 50 msec (Shibutani, Sakata, & Hyvarinen, 1984). About half of the neurons studied in this region fired vigorously in response to the rapid movement of a 10×20 cm plate toward the face. Discharge of the representative cell discussed by Shibutani and colleagues was followed by blink EMG activity at a latency of 190 msec. Ironically, this single latency value is the only laboratory measurement of the Cartesian blink reflex that has been obtained over the past 3½ centuries since the discovery of this response.

Somewhat more quantitative research has been devoted to the photic blink reflex. Early research focused on the possibility that blink reflexes to visual stimuli could mediate alpha conditioning. This is a primitive form of Pavlovian conditioning, found even in *Aplysia*, in which the conditioned stimulus (CS) is capable of eliciting a weak version of the conditioned response (CR; termed the *alpha response*), before any training trials are given. While investigating this phenomenon, a doctoral student of Hilgard discovered that the unconditioned response to light flash has a bimodal latency distribution, with functionally dissociable peaks at 80 and 150 msec (Grant, 1943, 1945). These early, mechanically recorded data have been confirmed using EMG methods (e.g., Rushworth, 1962), but the photic blink componentry is more variable from subject to subject than is the cutaneous R1-R2-R3 complex. We refer to the two most prominent EMG components of the photic blink reflex as R50 and R80, based on the typical onset latencies observed in normal young adults.

The exact circuits underlying these components are unknown, but several lesion studies in animals and in neurological patients have shown that subcortical structures are sufficient for mediating the photic blink reflex (reviewed in Tavy, van Woerkom, Bots, & Endtz, 1984). Keane (1979), for example, described a case in which a neocortically dead patient exhibited flash-evoked blink reflexes with an EMG latency of 70 to 90 msec. The patient also blinked in response to touching of the cornea and to hand clapping, but not to visual threat.

Because no previous experiment had separately evaluated the R50 and R80 components, Hackley and Johnson (1996) used signal averaging methods to evaluate photic blink in a group of 12 patients with focalized damage to visual cortex on one side. Bright flashes of light were randomly presented at locations within the blind or spared regions of the visual field, equidistant from fixation. Figure 9.1 shows the signal averaged EMG for two representative subjects who denied awareness of blind-field flashes, as well as the grand average waveforms for the entire group. The EMG envelopes for responses to seen and unseen stimuli overlap almost perfectly. This suggests that both R50 and R80 are mediated by subcortical pathways that do not require, or benefit from, conscious visual processing.

The primary afferents for photic blink do not synapse at the lateral geniculate nucleus (Yasuhara & Naito, 1982) or at the superior colliculus (Tavy et al., 1984). Instead, the first central synapse is most likely the same as for the pupillary reflex to light, the olivary pretectal nucleus (reviewed in Tavy et al., 1984). This assumption would be consistent with tracing studies that show direct projections from the olivary pretectal nucleus to blink premotor nuclei (Holstege et al., 1986). A lesion study

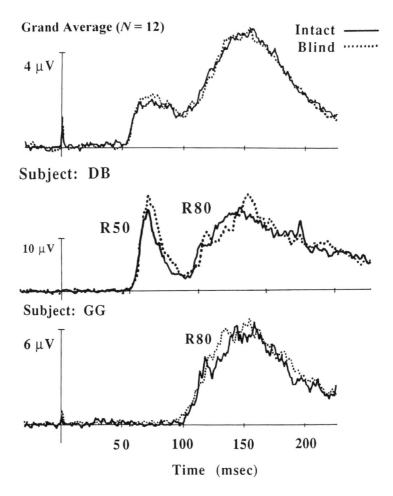

FIG. 9.1. Signal averaged electromyographic responses to flashes of light presented within the blind and intact portions of the visual field of patients with homonymous hemianopsia (Hackley & Johnson, 1996). The top panel shows the across-subjects average, and the middle and bottom panels portray photic blink reflexes for two individual subjects who denied awareness of strobe flashes within their scotomata. The absence of R50 in the waveforms for subject GG is probably unrelated to his neurological status: Nearly 15% of all normal adults we have examined fail to exhibit the early component of the photic blink reflex. Copyright 1996, The Society for Psychophysiological Research. Adapted with permission of the publisher from Hackley and Johnson (1996).

in rabbits showed that the pontomesencephalic reticular formation is essential for photic blink, and that distinct bursts of activity at 40 to 70 and 85 to 110 msec are evoked within this structure by light flashes (Yasuhara & Naito, 1982).

The importance of the photic R50 and R80, as well as the cutaneous R1, R2, and R3, for the study of sensorimotor modulation is that prestimuli can have dramatically contrasting effects on the distinct components associated with a single reflexive response. We turn now to this topic, and consider first the effects of a weak prestimulus presented at about the same time as the reflexogenic stimulus.

SHORT-INTERVAL PREPULSE FACILITATION

The distinction between blink modulation effects produced at short and intermediate lead times was first documented in Hilgard's (1933) classic study. Using a visual prestimulus followed by an acoustic reflexogenic stimulus, he reported amplitude facilitation at lead times of 25 to 50 msec, followed by inhibition at 100 to 450 msec. It appears that Hilgard implicitly attributed these effects to summation of the acoustic blink with a weak reflex and subsequent refractory period evoked by the prepulse. We discuss the inhibitory effect in later paragraphs. Regarding the facilitatory effect, there are three lines of evidence that summation is not the only mechanism involved. First, prepulse facilitation of whole-body startle and of the eyeblink reflex in particular is similar in many ways to prepulse facilitation of monosynaptic proprioceptive reflexes (e.g., Brunia & Boelhouwer, 1988). However, the mechanism underlying facilitation of the masseteric H-reflex by a weak acoustic prepulse is not summation but, rather, intracellular changes within the motor neuron produced by a neuromodulatory transmitter (norepinephrine; Stafford & Jacobs, 1990). Second, a gap in an otherwise continuous visual prestimulus has been shown to evoke prepulse facilitation of the acoustic blink (Krauter, 1987). This runs counter to the summation hypothesis if it can be assumed that a gap stimulus is nonreflexogenic. Third, the R1 component of the cutaneous blink reflex exhibits prepulse facilitation at lead times far too long to be explained by summation with a blink reflex—subliminal or otherwise—evoked by the prepulse (e.g., Ison, Sanes, Foss, & Pinckney, 1990; Sanes & Ison, 1979).

As an alternative hypothesis, Graham (1975) followed Ison, McAdam, and Hammond (1973) in suggesting that prepulse facilitation might be due to an arousal mechanism that nonspecifically primes motoric processes. Consistent with this assumption, prepulse facilitation is sensitive to the energy level of the prestimulus. Specifically, intense prepulses generate more facilitation than do weak prepulses and, at either short or long onset asynchronies, sustained prestimuli yield greater facilitation than do transient prestimuli (e.g., Graham, 1975; Weisz & Walts, 1990). Furthermore, sustained intense prestimuli are associated with heart rate acceleration, an index of arousal (Graham, 1975, 1992). More definitively, noradrenergic modulation of motoneuron excitability has now been unambiguously identified as the mechanism underlying prepulse facilitation of the jaw-jerk reflex, as previously mentioned (Stafford & Jacobs, 1990).

If the arousal hypothesis is valid in a general sense, one might expect similar facilitatory effects on voluntary and reflexive reactions. This possibility has recently been examined (Low, Larson, Burke, & Hackley, 1996). In this study, the effects of acoustic prestimulation on photic blink reflexes were compared with parallel effects on voluntary reactions to the same stimuli. Following a randomly selected warning interval of 1.5 or 4 sec, a blink-eliciting strobe flash was presented unpredictably to the right or left of fixation. The subject's task was to quickly squeeze a dynamometer grip with the hand on the same side as the flash. On 40% of the trials, a tone pip with a 40 msec rise time accompanied the light flash at an onset asynchrony of 40 msec. (In other words, the nonreflexogenic prepulse reached plateau just as the reaction stimulus was presented.) The tone pip provided no information as to which hand the subject should react with.

Figure 9.2 shows grand averages of the voluntary forearm EMG and reflexive eyelid EMG responses (top and bottom panels, respectively) on trials for which the light flash was or was not accompanied by the task-irrelevant prepulse (curves labeled *accessory* and *control*, respectively). Note facilitation of both the R50 reflex component and the voluntary choice-RT responses. The latter finding corroborates the results of many prior RT studies of intersensory facilitation (reviewed in Nickerson, 1973). Accessory stimulus effects on RT have been attributed to a phasic arousal process that speeds voluntary motor responses, but often at a cost of increased errors (e.g., Posner, 1978, chap. 5). Congruent with previous reports, a greater proportion of wrong-hand or two-handed responses was observed on accessory trials than on flash-alone control trials. A speed–accuracy trade-off such as this would appear to implicate a decision-level process, one presumably not shared with reflexes. In addition, modulation of R80 provides further evidence against a simple, unified explanation of accessory effects in terms of arousal. The R80 is presumably mediated by the same motor pathways as R50, yet it was modulated in a direction opposite to that of R50 (Fig. 9.2, bottom panel).

A mechanism in addition to the arousal process hypothesized by Ison and by Graham, such as summation of the overt reflex with a subliminal response to the prepulse, may have been involved. Under the summation hypothesis, this reciprocal pattern of modulation might have occurred

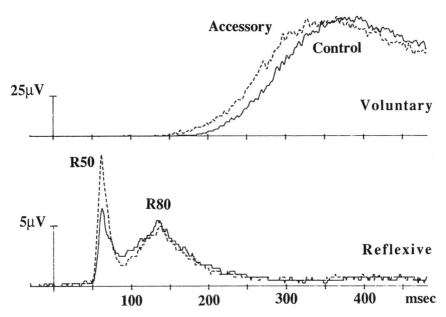

FIG. 9.2. Grand average electromyographic responses associated with voluntary manual and reflexive palpebral reactions to bright flashes of light (Low et al., 1996). The dashed line represents trials on which a task-irrelevant tone pip accompanied the visual reaction stimulus; the solid line portrays trials on which the left or right strobe stimuli were presented alone. Copyright 1996, Elsevier Press. Adapted with permission of the publisher from Low et al. (1996).

because R50 was superimposed on a subliminal blink to the acoustic prepulse, but R80 occurred during the refractory phase that followed this subliminal reflex.

A refined version of the summation hypothesis (Boelhouwer, Teurlings, & Brunia, 1991) can also account for the complex pattern of short-interval prepulse effects on the cutaneous blink reflex. In this study (see also Nakashima, Shimoyama, Yokoyama, & Takahashi, 1993), an acoustic prepulse was presented just before or after an electrical stimulus to the supraorbital branch of the trigeminal nerve. It was hypothesized that the actual moment of presentation of the prepulse in relation to the reflex-eliciting stimulus is not important. What does matter is the point in time when both the prepulse and reflexogenic volleys arrive at the facial nucleus. Assume, for instance, that when a weak acoustic prepulse with a duration of 50 msec is presented, its effects will begin at the facial nucleus about 35 msec later and last for about 50 msec (i.e., the onset and duration of the subliminal blink). The electrically elicited startle arrives at the motor neurons in two waves of excitation, one extending from 10 to 22 msec (R1), and the other from 25 to 85 msec (R2). When the prepulse and the startle stimulus are presented at the same time, the early R1 component has already "left" the facial nucleus before the prepulse volley arrives. The R1, therefore, will not be affected by the prepulse. However, because the R2 volley at 25 to 85 msec overlaps with that of the prepulse volley, 35 to 85 msec, it will show facilitation.

This summation will also be seen, although to a lesser extent, when the reflexogenic stimulus is given prior to the prepulse. For instance, the R2 component of a reflex elicited 20 msec before the prepulse will arrive at the facial nucleus about 5 msec after presentation of the acoustic prepulse and will persist until 65 msec after prepulse onset. The overlapping excitation from 35 to 65 msec implies that summation will take place, despite the fact that the reflex was elicited before presentation of the prepulse (see Fig. 9.3). Earlier researchers apparently assumed this to be impossible, and did not use negative or zero onset asynchronies. In fact, during the 1970s, modula-

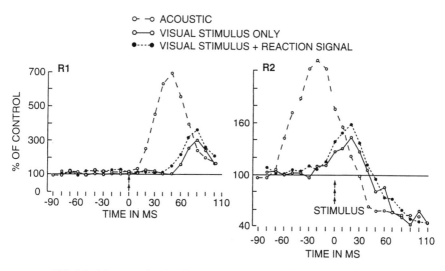

FIG. 9.3. Mean amplitude of cutaneous R1 (peak-to-peak, left panel) and ipsilateral R2 (integral, right panel) in response to an electrical stimulus presented at different points in time relative to an acoustic or visual prepulse presented at 0 msec. "Reaction Signal" refers to a condition in which the prepulse also served as a cue for a speeded voluntary response to a subsequent stimulus. Reflexes are expressed as percentages of the (baseline) reflexes elicited during the intertrial interval. Notice the similarity of the patterns portrayed in the left and right panels. The different timing of modulatory effect in relation to the prepulse is attributable to the difference in the latencies of R1 and R2, as discussed in the text (data from Boelhouwer et al., 1991, Boelhouwer et al., 1989). Copyright 1991, The Society for Psychophysiological Research. Adapted with permission of the publisher from Boelhouwer et al. (1991).

tion functions were routinely extrapolated to baseline at the origin of the X-axis (lead time = 0), on the assumption that reflex size and latency would have to equal that of the no-prepulse control condition if the prepulse were simultaneous with the reflexogenic stimulus.

A similar pattern of summation can be observed for visual prepulses as well (Boelhouwer, Frints, & Westerkamp, 1989). Because the reflexogenic volley produced by photic stimuli arrive at the facial nucleus later than that of the acoustic blink (i.e., 55 msec for photic stimuli vs. 35 msec for acoustic), it can be expected that summation effects for visual prestimuli will be delayed by 20 msec as compared with acoustic prepulses. This implies that robust facilitation should be observed at negative onset asynchronies and, as shown in Fig. 9.3, this is the case.

INTERMEDIATE INTERVALS: PREPULSE INHIBITION

At intermediate asynchronies of prepulse and reflexogenic stimuli, an inhibitory process is triggered that reduces the amplitude and, sometimes, retards the latency of startle blink. Some early investigators apparently confused prepulse inhibition with refractory effects, but the two can be distinguished by the U-shaped time course for prepulse effects (e.g., Graham, 1975; Simons & Perlstein, chapter 10, this volume), which contrasts with the exponential decline characterizing refractory effects. Also, prepulse inhibition can be evoked by stimuli near the absolute threshold of sensation (Reiter & Ison, 1977) and by offset or gap stimuli (e.g., Krauter, 1987). More importantly, prepulse inhibition can be eliminated by lesions that are extrinsic to the reflex arc itself (Leitner, Powers, & Hoffman, 1979).

Although the R2 component of the cutaneous blink reflex exhibits prepulse inhibition similar to that of acoustic blink and whole-body startle, the earlier R1 component is impervious to this effect (Sanes & Ison, 1979). On the assumption that R1 and R2 share the same peripheral afferent and efferent structures (Ongerboer de Visser & Kuypers, 1978), this implies that prepulse inhibition must modify transmission along the central, nonoverlapping portion of the R2 pathway. This conclusion is consistent with evidence from studies of whole-body startle in animals indicating an intersection of the prepulse and reflexogenic circuits in the caudal pontine reticular formation (reviewed in Swerdlow & Geyer, 1993).

A recent study has shown that subcomponents of the photic blink reflex also exhibit differential sensitivity to prepulse inhibition (Burke & Hackley, 1994). Reflexes were evoked by flashes from one of two strobe lamps, located 25° to the left and right of a fixation light. The lamps were encircled by four light-emitting diodes, which delivered prestimuli at lead times of 1,200, 600, 120, 70, 45, 20, or –50 msec. Reliable inhibition of R50 was obtained at 70 and 120 msec but, as can be seen in Fig. 9.4, the leading edge of this component was resistant to inhibition. A similar pattern has been found for the cutaneous blink. Insensitivity of the leading edge of the R2 component was first reported by Evinger and Manning (1988), and is apparent in the signal averaged data of Hackley and Graham (1987, Fig. 2), although the latter authors did not comment on this phenomenon. The resistance of the leading edge of both R2 and R50 to prepulse inhibition is important because it provides converging evidence that these EMG bursts are themselves composed of subcomponents. These are presumably mediated by parallel reflex arcs, for example, a short pathway that triggers the initial muscle activation and a longer, parallel circuit that controls the remainder of the burst. This finding is also consistent with the assumption that R2, R50, and acoustic blink are analogous responses involving a common central-efferent reflex arc.

In contrast to the pattern observed for the R50 component, the R80 was actually facilitated by the prepulse in the 120 msec condition (bottom panel of Fig. 9.4). The opposite modulation of R50 and R80 is apparently

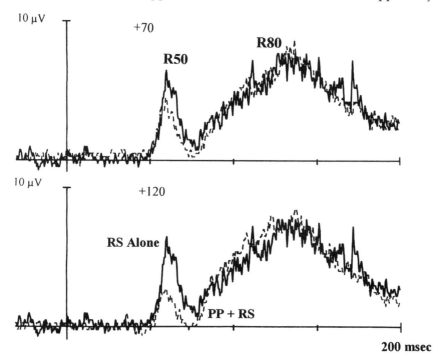

FIG. 9.4. Grand average photic blink reflexes on trials for which a weak visual prepulse preceded the reflex eliciting stimulus (dashed lines) and trials for which the reflexogenic stimulus, a strobe flash, was presented alone (Burke & Hackley, in press). In the top panel, the lead time was 70 msec, in the bottom, 120 msec.

not due to refractory effects or any reciprocal linkage between the two components. The R50 component is absent in some individuals (see Fig. 9.1), yet facilitation of R80 in the 120 msec condition was still observed by Burke and Hackley in two such cases.

Under Graham's (e.g., 1975, 1992) theory, the purpose of prepulse inhibition is to protect preattentive processing of a stimulus from disruption by reflexes such as startle during the time period required to perceptually analyze that stimulus (i.e., the prepulse). In support of this theory, it has been found that slides of interesting, biologically relevant stimuli generate longer lasting prepulse inhibition than do slides of motivationally irrelevant objects (Bradley, Cuthbert, & Lang, 1993). More direct support was obtained in a series of experiments in which subjects judged the frequency of acoustic or vibrotactile prestimuli (Norris & Blumenthal, in press). These stimuli varied randomly from trial to trial between two values (e.g., 50 or 200-Hz hand vibration) and all were of low intensity. Eyeblink responses to the subsequent intense white-noise bursts were categorized by the experimenter as to whether these reflexes were or were not inhibited by the prepulse. On trials with inhibition, perceptual judgments of prepulse frequency were more accurate than on trials without inhibition. This supports Graham's (e.g., 1975, 1992) assumption that inhibition of startle does benefit perceptual analysis of the prepulse.

How can the data shown in Fig. 9.4 and Graham's protection-of-perception hypothesis be reconciled? More specifically, why should a prepulse inhibit the brief R50 component, but not the longer duration R80 component that presumably would be the major determinant of whether lid closure during startle interrupts visual perception? According to the *startle-dazzle hypothesis* (Burke & Hackley, in press), this R50–R80 difference represents a trade-off between protecting the perceptual analysis of the prepulse from interruption by startle and prevention of retinal bleaching that would interfere with perception of subsequent stimuli. Under this hypothesis, the R50 component is assumed to be primarily a startle reflex, based on its similarities to R2 and acoustic blink. These similarities include onset latency, as well as sensitivity to habituation (Grant, 1945), prepulse inhibition (Burke & Hackley, 1994), expectancy, and cross-modal accessory stimuli (Low et al., 1996). Following Graham (e.g., 1975), we assume the function of startle is to interrupt ongoing perceptual, cognitive, and motor processes so that the organism can deal effectively with the startle-eliciting stimulus (e.g., a predator). The R80 component, along with pupil constriction, is assumed to constitute a dazzle reflex, the function of which is to minimize retinal bleaching consequent to a sudden increase in illumination.

The R50's role in determining whether the lid occludes the pupil is relatively greater for brief light flashes, because this component is insensitive to stimulus duration (Manning & Evinger, 1986). For flashes that are shorter in duration than the reflex latency, lid closure will occur too late to reduce bleaching. In this case, the startle-dazzle theory postulates that protecting the perceptual analysis of the prepulse is given precedence over protection from retinal bleaching. For longer duration increases in illumination, an evoked blink can occlude the pupil quickly enough to effectively reduce retinal bleaching. In these cases, R80 is the main determinant of reflex size and duration because the length of this component closely follows that of the eliciting stimulus (Manning & Evinger, 1986). Consequently, the theory assumes that insensitivity of R80 to prepulse inhibition is in the best interest of maximizing the intake of visual information.

LONG-INTERVAL EFFECTS

At long lead times, a prepulse can engage a variety of high- and low-level processes capable of influencing brainstem reflexes such as startle-blink. Descending pathways that are extrinsic to the essential reflex circuitry presumably mediate these effects, with modulation occuring at one or more sites along the reflex arc. Experimentally distinguishable forms of reflex modification are observed for prestimuli that, for example, induce a positive or negative emotional state (e.g., Bradley et al., 1993), cue the subject to make a voluntary eyelid movement (e.g., Boelhouwer, 1982), direct attention to the location or modality of a task stimulus (e.g., Hackley & Graham, 1983, 1987), or signal the imminent arrival of a reflexogenic stimulus (e.g., Graham, 1975).

The signaling effect is important because it links reflex modulation with the vast literature on warning and conditioned stimulus effects, including the phenomena of conditioned diminution of the unconditioned response, contingent negative variation, anticipatory autonomic responses, and foreperiod effects on reaction time. Graham (1975) was the first to point out that variations in foreperiod duration can have similar consequences for the latency of reflexive and voluntary reactions. When foreperiod varies randomly from trial to trial, the objective probability of the second stimulus increases as the foreperiod "ages," and reaction times are facilitated (e.g., Näätänen, 1970). Similarly, the latency of the startle-blink is relatively facilitated at longer foreperiods when intervals vary randomly within blocks of trials (e.g., Graham, 1975; Hackley & Graham, 1987). Graham (1975) argued that this facilitation is due to orienting triggered by uncertainty as to when the reflexogenic stimulus would occur or uncertainty as to what type of stimulus would be presented.

Congruent with this hypothesis, subsequent research has confirmed that both localized orienting (voluntary selective attention, in contemporary terminology) and generalized orienting (the automatic engagement of attention by a novel stimulus) can facilitate the latency and magnitude of the blink reflex (reviewed in Graham & Hackley, 1991). However, it has also been demonstrated that blink latency is robustly facilitated by a warning stimulus even if the subject actively ignores the reflexogenic stimulus in order to attend to a nonreflexogenic task stimulus in another modality (e.g., Silverstein, Graham, & Bohlin, 1981). Silverstein and colleagues attributed this nonselective facilitation to a generalized activation of motor systems, similar to the arousal-based mechanism hypothesized by Graham (1975) to account for short-interval prepulse facilitation.

Surprisingly, this nonselective facilitation of latency by a warning stimulus is often accompanied by a reduction in blink amplitude (e.g., Cohen, Cranney, & Hoffman, 1983; Ison et al., 1990). This finding is consistent with the observation that unconditioned reflexes decrease in amplitude during conditioning (e.g., Kimble & Ost, 1961) and with the commonsense assumption that one is more likely to be startled by an unexpected than by an expected stimulus (e.g., Sechenov, 1860/1965, p. 11).

A number of other dissociations among warning effects have been described. Consider the well established finding that when foreperiods are manipulated between rather than within blocks of trials, voluntary reactions are faster at shorter foreperiods (e.g., Woodrow, 1914). This occurs because it is easier to judge the length of short time intervals and, consequently, subjects can prepare more effectively for the reaction stimulus (e.g., Requin, Brener, & Ring, 1991). With such between-block manipulations, though, acoustic blinks are actually faster at longer foreperiods (Sollers & Hackley, 1993, 1994). Regardless of whether foreperiod durations are manipulated between or within blocks, the postauricular component of acoustic startle remains unaffected (Sollers & Hackley, 1993). To add to this complexity, R1 amplitude is facilitated by the presence of a warning stimulus, whereas R2 amplitude is inhibited (Ison et al., 1990). For the photic blink reflex, R50 shows a pattern similar to that of the acoustic blink and cutaneous R2, whereas R80 is similar to the postauricular reflex, in that it appears insensitive to foreperiod duration (Low et al., 1996; Burke & Hackley, in press). The variety of warning stimulus effects makes it clear that temporal expectancy is not a unitary phenomenon.

CONCLUSIONS

The fundamental varieties of prepulse effects described by Graham (1975) have been abundantly confirmed by subsequent research. Recent studies of the photic and cutaneous blink reflexes have shown that the distinct subcomponents in the EMG response can exhibit differential sensitivity to prestimulus effects. Systematic investigation of these differences should illuminate the nature of prestimulus effects and the reflex components themselves.

The framework for integrating reflex findings such as these within the broader scientific context has shifted over the years. Beginning with Sechenov (1860/1965) and extending through the Behaviorist era, it was widely believed that reflexes constitute the basic elements of all behavior, but subsequent empirical and theoretical advances rendered this conceptual framework untenable. Two more viable metatheories have taken its place, one that treats reflexes as probes and the other, as model systems.

The framework that considers reflexes as probes of central nervous system state or function evolved from traditional diagnostic use of reflexes within clinical neurology. Since the time of Marshal Hall's research in the early 19th century, neurologists have used reflexes to assess the integrity of discrete central and peripheral nervous system pathways. Contemporary neurology textbooks describe many such tests. For example, an absent gag reflex is said to indicate either loss of sensation via the IXth cranial nerve or loss of motor function via the Xth cranial nerve (Lindsay, Bone, & Callender, 1986, p. 18).

As Anthony (1985) pointed out, once the properties of a probe have been well characterized, the focus is no longer on the probe itself. Rather, the probe merely serves as an instrument for measuring some unknown state or condition. The difference between the thermal expansion coefficients of mercury and glass is not of interest, but the temperature of a sick baby is.

At one time, it appeared that the most probable application for reflex modulation would lie in the diagnosis of sensory disorders. The exquisite sensitivity of prepulse inhibition made this seem a promising methodology for objective psychophysical testing. However, the ability of evoked potentials to assess function at multiple points along the ascending sensory pathways, coupled with their greater applicability in infants, compensates for their lesser sensitivity, so they have instead become the method of choice.

Based on current research trends, it seems more likely that the practical applications of reflex modulation will lie in the diagnosis of psychopathologies in humans and the testing of psychopharmaceuticals in animals. The rapid progress and widespread interest in these areas is due mainly to three factors. The first is the development of key paradigms that can link reflex modulation to the study of affective disorders (Lang et al., 1990) and psychosis (Braff et al., 1978). The second is the high degree of comparability between reflex modulation findings in small, inexpensive, laboratory animals and in humans, due to conservation of the relevant circuitry throughout the course of mammalian evolution.

The third factor is the low cost of reflex modulation research. For example, the cost of equipping a state-of-the-art lab for startle-blink research is about one fourth that of setting up a lab for event-related potentials, which is the least expensive of the brain imaging technologies.

The second framework for relating reflex modulation to a broader theoretical context is known as the simple system or model system approach. According to this approach, the mechanisms underlying a complex phenonomenon can be most easily elucidated by concentrated research on the simplest system that manifests that phenomenon. Pavlovian conditioning of the nictitating-membrane blink reflex in rabbits is an example of a simple system that has revealed unprecedented insights into the mechanisms of associative learning (e.g., Thompson, 1986).

In the case of another popular model for associative learning, alpha conditioning of the gill withdrawal reflex in *Aplysia*, it has been possible to reduce behavioral phenemona to the circuit level and, from there, to a level of explanation in terms of biochemistry (Kandel & Schwartz, 1985, chap. 62). Similarly, much progress has been made in explaining the effects of emotion on the startle reflex at the level of identified neural circuits (e.g., Davis, 1986, chapter 4, this volume; Lang, 1995; Lang et al., chapter 5, this volume). These successes encourage the development of a simple systems model of attention effects using the eyeblink reflex.

ACKNOWLEDGMENTS

The authors thank Anton van Boxtel for comments on the manuscript and Bill Wolz for his translation of Exner (1874). This work was supported in part by grant R29-MH47746 from the National Instititutes of Health to the first author.

REFERENCES

Anthony, B. J. (1985). In the blink of an eye: Implications of reflex modulation for information processing. In P. K. Ackles, J. R. Jennings, & M. G. H. Coles (Eds.), *Advances in psychophysiology* (Vol. 1, pp. 167–218). Greenwich, CT: JAI Press.

Boelhouwer, A. J. W. (1982). Blink reflexes and preparation. *Biological Psychology, 14*, 277–285.

Boelhouwer, A. J. W., Frints, C. J. M., & Westerkamp, V. (1989). The effect of a visual prestimulus upon the human blink reflex [Abstract]. *Psychophysiology, 26*, S14.

Boelhouwer, A. J. W., Teurlings, R. F. M. A., & Brunia, C. H. M. (1991). The acoustic warning stimulus upon the electrically elicited blink reflex in humans. *Psychophysiology, 28*, 133–139.

Bradley, M. M., Cuthbert, B. N., & Lang, P. J. (1993). Pictures as prepulses: Attention and emotion in startle modification. *Psychophysiology, 30*, 541–545.

Braff, D., & Geyer, M. A. (1990). Sensorimotor gating and schizophrenia: Human and animal model studies. *Archives of General Psychiatry, 47,* 181–188.

Braff, D., Stone, C., Callaway, E., Geyer, M., Glick, I., & Bali, L. (1978). Prestimulus effects on human startle reflex in normals and schizophrenics. *Psychophysiology, 15,* 339–343.

Brown, P., Thompson, P. D., Rothwell, J. C., Britton, T. C., Day, B. L., & Marsden, C. D. (1991). The hyperekplexias and their relationship to the normal startle reflex. *Brain, 114,* 1903–1928.

Brunia, C. H. M., & Boelhouwer, A. J. W. (1988). Reflexes as a tool: A window in the central nervous system. *Advances in Psychophysiology, 3,* 1–67.

Burke, J., & Hackley, S. A. (1994). Prepulse modulation of early and late components of the photic blink reflex [Abstract]. *Psychophysiology, 31,* S32.

Burke, J., & Hackley, S. A. (in press). Intramodal prepulse modulation of the early and late subcomponents of the photic eyeblink reflex. *Psychophysiology.*

Cassella, J. V., & Davis, M. (1986). Neural structures mediating acoustic and tactile startle reflexes and the acoustically-elicited pinna responses in rats: Electrolytic and ibotenic acid studies. *Society for Neuroscience Abstracts, 12,* 1273.

Cohen, M. E., Cranney, J., & Hoffman, H. S. (1983). Motor and cognitive factors in the modification of a reflex. *Perception and Psychophysics, 34,* 214–220.

Davis, M. (1986). The potentiated startle as a measure of conditioned fear and its relevance to the neurobiology of anxiety. *Behavioral Neuroscience, 100,* 814–824.

Davis, M., Parisi, T., Gendelman, D. S., Tischler, M., & Kehne, J. H. (1982). Habituation and sensitization of startle reflexes elicited electrically from the brainstem. *Science, 218,* 688–690.

Evinger, C., & Manning, K. A. (1988). A model system for motor learning: Adaptive gain control of the blink reflex. *Experimental Brain Research, 70,* 527–538.

Evinger, C., Manning, K. A., & Sibony, P. A. (1991). Eyelid movements. *Investigative Ophthalmology and Visual Science, 32,* 387–400.

Evinger, C., Shaw, M. D., Peck, C. K., Manning, K. A., & Baker, R. (1984). Blinking and associated eye movements in humans, guinea pigs, and rabbits. *Journal of Neurophysiology, 52,* 323–339.

Exner, S. (1873). Experimentelle Untersuchung der einfachsten psychischen Processe: Erste Abteilung [Experimental investigation of the simplest mental process: First article]. *Pflüger's Archiv, 7,* 601–660.

Exner, S. (1874). Experimentelle Untersuchung der einfachsten psychischen Processe: Zweite Abteilung [Experimental investigation of the simplest mental process: Second article]. *Pflüger's Archiv, 8,* 526–537.

Fearing, F. (1930). *Reflex action.* Baltimore, MD: Williams & Wilkins.

Graham, F. K. (1975). The more or less startling effects of weak prestimulation. *Psychophysiology, 12,* 238–248.

Graham, F. K. (1992). Attention: The heartbeat, the blink, and the brain. In B. Campbell, H. Hayne, & R. Richardson (Eds.), *Attention and information processing in infants and adults: Perspectives from human and animal research* (pp. 3–29). Hillsdale, NJ: Lawrence Erlbaum Associates.

Graham, F. K., & Hackley, S. A. (1991). Passive and active attention to input. In J. R. Jennings & M. G. H. Coles (Eds.), *Handbook of cognitive psychophysiology* (pp. 299–356). Chichester, UK: Wiley.

Graham, F. K., Silverstein, L. D., & Hackley, S. A. (1979). [Direct stimulation of facial nerve branches innervating the fast- and slow-twitch portions of orbicularis oculi]. Unpublished data.

Grant, D. A. (1943). The pseudo-conditioned eyelid response. *Journal of Experimental Psychology, 32,* 139–149.

Grant, D. A. (1945). A sensitized eyelid reaction related to the conditioned eyelid response. *Journal of Experimental Psychology, 35,* 393–402.

Hackley, S. A., & Graham, F. K. (1983). Effects of attending selectively to the spatial position of reflex-eliciting and reflex-modulating stimuli. *Journal of Experimental Psychology: Human Perception and Performance, 13*, 411–424.

Hackley, S. A., & Graham, F. K. (1987). Effects of attending to the spatial position of reflex-eliciting and reflex-modulating stimuli. *Journal of Experimental Psychology: Human Perception and Performance, 13*, 411–424.

Hackley, S. A., & Johnson, L. N. (1996). Distinct early and late subcomponents of the photic blink reflex: Response characteristics in patients with retrogeniculate lesions. *Psychophysiology, 33*, 239–251.

Hackley, S. A., Woldorff, M., & Hillyard, S. A. (1987). Combined use of microreflexes and event-related brain potentials as measures of auditory selective attention. *Psychophysiology, 24*, 632–647.

Hilgard, E. R. (1933). Reinforcement and inhibition of eyelid reflexes. *Journal of General Psychology, 7*, 85–113.

Hiraoka, M., & Shimamura, M. (1977). Neural mechanisms of the corneal blinking reflex in cats. *Brain Research, 125*, 265–275.

Hodge, C. F. (1890). A sketch of the history of reflex action: I. Beginnings and development to the time of Charles Bell. *American Journal of Psychology, 3*, 149–167.

Hoffman, H. S., & Ison, J. R. (1980). Reflex modification in the domain of startle. I: Some empirical findings and their implications for how the nervous system processes sensory input. *Psychological Review, 87*, 175–189.

Holstege, G., Tan, J., van Ham, J. J., & Graveland, G. A. (1986). Anatomical observations on the afferent projections to the retractor bulbi motoneuronal cell group and other pathways possibly related to the blink reflex in the cat. *Brain Research, 374*, 321–334.

Hori, A., Yasuhara, A., Naito, H., & Yasuhara, M. (1986). Blink reflex elicited by auditory stimulation in the rabbit. *Journal of the Neurological Sciences, 76*, 49–59.

Horner, K. C., & Bock, G. R. (1985). Combined electrophysiological and autoradiographic delimitation of retrocochlear dysfunction in a mouse mutant. *Brain Research, 331*, 217–223.

Ison, J. R., & Hoffman, H. S. (1983). Reflex modification in the domain of startle: II. The anomalous history of a robust and ubiquitous phenomenon. *Psychological Review, 94*, 3–17.

Ison, J. R., & Krauter, E. E. (1974). Reflex-inhibiting stimuli and the refractory period of the acoustic startle reflex in the rat. *Journal of Comparative and Physiological Psychology, 86*, 420–425.

Ison, J. R., McAdam, D. W., & Hammond, G. R. (1973). Latency and amplitude changes in the acoustic startle reflex of the rat produced by variation in auditory prestimulation. *Physiology and Behavior, 10*, 1035–1039.

Ison, J. R., Sanes, J. N., Foss, J. A., & Pinckney, L. A. (1990). Facilitation and inhibition of the human startle blink reflexes by stimulus anticipation. *Behavioral Neuroscience, 104*, 418–429.

Kandel, E. R., & Schwartz, J. H. (1985). *Principles of neural science* (2nd ed.). Amsterdam: Elsevier.

Keane, J. R. (1979). Blinking to sudden illumination: A brain stem reflex present in neocortical death. *Archives of Neurology, 36*, 52–53.

Kimble, G. A., & Ost, J. W. P. (1961). A conditioned inhibitory process in eyelid conditioning. *Journal of Experimental Psychology, 61*, 150–156.

Krauter, E. E. (1987). Reflex modification of the human auditory startle blink by antecedent interruption of a visual stimulus. *Perceptual and Motor Skills, 64*, 727–738.

Kugelberg, E. (1952). Facial reflexes. *Brain, 75*, 385–396.

Landis, C., & Hunt, W. A. (1939). *The startle pattern.* New York: Farrar & Rinehart.

Lang, P. J. (1995). The emotion probe: Studies of motivation and attention. *American Psychologist, 50*, 372–385.

Lang, P. J., Bradley, M. M., & Cuthbert, B. N. (1990). Emotion, attention, and the startle reflex. *Psychological Review, 97*, 377–398.

Lee, Y., Lopez, D., Meloni, E., & Davis, M. (1994). A primary acoustic startle reflex circuit: Role of auditory root neurons and the nucleus reticularis pontis caudalis. *Society for Neuroscience Abstracts, 20*, Part 2, p. 1009.

Leitner, D. S., Powers, A. S., & Hoffman, H. S. (1979). The neural system for the inhibition of startle. *Bulletin of the Psychonomic Society, 14*, 410–412.

Lindsay, K. W., Bone, I., & Callander, R. (1986). *Neurology and neurosurgery illustrated.* London: Churchill Livingstone.

Lindquist, L., & Martensson, A. (1970). Mechanisms involved in the cat's blink reflex. *Acta Physiologica Scandinavica, 80*, 149–159.

Liu, G. T., & Ronthal, M. (1992). Reflex blink to visual threat. *Journal of Clinical Neuro-ophthalmology, 12*, 47–56.

Low, K. A., Larson, S. L., Burke, J., & Hackley, S. A. (1996). Alerting effects on choice reaction time and the photic eyeblink reflex. *Electroencephalography and Clinical Neurophysiology, 98*, 385–393.

Manning, K. A., & Evinger, C. (1986). Different forms of blinks and their two-stage control. *Experimental Brain Research, 64*, 579–588.

Näätänen, R. (1970). The diminishing time-uncertainty with the lapse of time after the warning signal in reaction-time experiments with varying fore-periods. *Acta Psychologica, 34*, 399–419.

Nakashima, K., Shimoyama, R., Yokoyama, Y., & Takahashi, K. (1993). Auditory effects on the electrically elicited blink reflex in patients with Parkinson's disease. *Electroencephalography and Clinical Neurophysiology, 89*, 108–112.

Nickerson, R. (1973). Intersensory facilitation of reaction time: Energy summation or preparation enhancement? *Psychological Review, 80*, 489–509.

Norris, C. M., & Blumenthal, T. D. (in press). A relationship between inhibition of the acoustic startle response and the protection of prepulse processing. *Psychobiology.*

Ongerboer de Visser, B. W., & Kuypers, H. G. H. M. (1978). Late blink reflex changes in medullary lesions: An electrophysiological and neuroanatomical study of Wallenburg's syndrome. *Brain, 101*, 285–294.

Posner, M. I. (1978). *Chronometric explorations of mind.* Hillsdale, NJ: Lawrence Erlbaum Associates.

Posner, M. I., & Petersen, S. E. (1990). The attention system of the human brain. *Annual Review of Neuroscience, 13*, 25–42.

Putnam, L. E. (1975). *The human startle reaction: Mechanisms of modification by background acoustic stimulation.* Unpublished doctoral dissertation, University of Wisconsin, Madison.

Reiter, L. A., & Ison, J. R. (1977). Inhibition of the human eyeblink reflex: An examination of the Wendt-Yerkes method for threshold detection. *Journal of Experimental Psychology: Human Perception and Performance, 3*, 325–336.

Requin, J., Brener, J., & Ring, C. (1991). Preparation for action. In J. R. Jennings & M. G. H. Coles (Eds.), *Handbook of cognitive psychophysiology* (pp. 357–448). Chichester, UK: Wiley.

Riesen, A. H. (1947). The development of visual perception in man and chimpanzee. *Science, 106*, 107–108.

Rimpel, J., Geyer, D., & Hopf, H. C. (1982). Changes in the blink responses to combined trigeminal, acoustic, and visual repetitive stimulation, studied in the human subject. *Electroencephalography and Clinical Neurophysiology, 54*, 552–560.

Rossi, B., Risaliti, R., & Rossi, A. (1989). The R3 component of the blink reflex in man: A reflex response induced by activation of high threshold cutaneous afferents. *Electroencephalography and Clinical Neurophysiology, 73*, 334–340.

Rushworth, G. (1962). Observations on blink reflexes. *Journal of Neurology, Neurosurgery, and Psychiatry, 25*, 93–108.

Sanes, J. N., Foss, J. A., & Ison, J. R. (1982). Conditions that affect the thresholds of the components of the eyeblink reflex in humans. *Journal of Neurology, Neurosurgery, and Psychiatry, 45*, 543–549.

Sanes, J. N., & Ison, J. R. (1979). Conditioning auditory stimuli and the cutaneous eyeblink reflex in humans: Differential effects according to oligosynaptic or polysynaptic central pathways. *Electroencephalography and Clinical Neurophysiology, 47*, 546–555.

Sechenov, I. M. (1965). *Reflexes of the brain.* Cambridge, MA: MIT Press. (Original work published 1860)

Schmidtke, K., & Büttner-Ennever, J. A. (1992). Nervous control of eyelid function: A review of clinical, experimental and pathological data. *Brain, 115*, 227–247.

Sherrington, C. (1906). *The integrative action of the nervous system.* New York: Scribner's.

Shibutani, H., Sakata, J., & Hyvarinen, J. (1984). Saccade and blinking evoked by microstimulation of the posterior parietal association cortex of the monkey. *Experimental Brain Research, 55*, 1–8.

Silverstein, L. D., Graham, F. K., & Bohlin, G. (1981). Selective attention effects on the reflex blink. *Psychophysiology, 18*, 240–247.

Sollers, J. J., & Hackley, S. A. (1993). Temporal uncertainty effects on startle-blink and the post-auricular reflex [Abstract]. *Psychophysiology, 30*, S61.

Sollers, J. J., & Hackley, S. A. (1994). Foreperiod variability effects on voluntary and reflexive reactions [Abstract]. *Psychophysiology, 31*, S92–S93.

Stafford, I. L., & Jacobs, B. L. (1990). Noradrenergic modulation of the masseteric reflex in behaving cats. II. Physiologic studies. *Journal of Neuroscience, 10*, 99–107.

Stern, J. A., Walrath, L. C., & Goldstein, R. (1984). The endogenous eyeblink. *Psychophysiology, 21*, 22–33.

Swerdlow, N. R., & Geyer, M. A. (1993). Prepulse inhibition of acoustic startle in rats after lesions of the pedunculopontine tegmental nucleus. *Behavioral Neuroscience, 107*, 104–117.

Tavy, D. L. J., van Woerkom, T. C. A. M., Bots, T. A. M., & Endtz, L. J. (1984). Persistence of the blink reflex to sudden illumination in a comatose patient: A clinical and pathologic study. *Archives of Neurology, 41*, 323–324.

Thompson, R. F. (1986). Neurobiology of learning and memory. *Science, 233*, 941–947.

Weisz, D. J., & Walts, C. (1990). Reflex facilitation of the rabbit nictitating membrane response by an auditory stimulus as a function of interstimulus interval. *Behavioral Neuroscience, 104*, 11–20.

Woodrow, H. (1914). The measurement of attention. *Psychological Monographs, 17* (76).

Yasuhara, M., & Naito, H. (1982). Potential changes and eyelid microvibration elicited by flash stimulation. *International Journal of Neuroscience, 17*, 23–31.

Zeigler, B. L. (1982). *Priming (match-mismatch) and alerting (modality) effects on reflex startle and simple reaction time.* Unpublished doctoral dissertation, University of Wisconsin, Madison.

A Tale of Two Reflexes:
An ERP Analysis of Prepulse
Inhibition and Orienting

R. F. Simons
W. M. Perlstein
University of Delaware

The general focus of the research described in this chapter is on understanding the role in higher cognitive processes played by two low-level reflexes—prepulse inhibition (PPI) and the orienting response (OR). Specifically, this research had two primary aims: to examine event-related potential (ERP) components under prepulse conditions as part of a broader effort to determine how PPI affects higher level perceptual processes, and to determine whether localized and generalized orienting are associated with attention-sensitive ERP components.

Efforts to examine the inhibition of ERP components by prestimulation have been very successful, with two initial studies finding significant prepulse inhibition beginning with the mid-latency, positive ERP component at 50 msec (P50), but no evidence of inhibition in the earlier P30 component. Because P30 and P50 are believed to reflect neural activity in two different auditory projection pathways, these effects were reproduced in a subsequent study which provided evidence that (a) prepulse inhibition present in the *nonspecific* projection system (P50) is true inhibition, and is not due to local refractory effects, and (b) the absence of prepulse inhibition characterizing P30 is a feature of other ERP components associated with the *specific* projection system. These experiments are described in the first section of the chapter.

The chapter's second section describes an independent series of studies that have utilized variations of the P300 component as a means of examining ERP characteristics associated with voluntary (active) and involuntary (passive) allocation of attention. Previous studies have agreed in finding parietal, posterior, P300s during active attention, but have been inconsistent in their findings of anterior P300s associated with passive attention, or orienting. Our own data now confirm the existence of a more anterior positive component in response to rare, nontarget events, and this component precedes, then overlaps in part, the parietal P300.

PREPULSE INHIBITION OF THE ACOUSTIC EVENT-RELATED POTENTIAL

Prepulse inhibition is a robust phenomenon, present in both human and nonhuman animals. It is elicited by any brief stimulus change (S1) that shortly precedes a reflex-eliciting stimulus (S2), and is defined as the automatic reduction of reflex size to S2 by S1. In humans, the PPI effect has been demonstrated for the startle blink, the most persistent component of startle (for reviews see Anthony, 1985; Graham, 1975; Hoffman & Ison, 1980; see also Hackley & Boelhouwer, chapter 9, this volume; Dawson, Schell, Swerdlow, & Filion, chapter 11, this volume; Hoffman, chapter 8, this volume). The effect is not due to learning (Krauter, Leonard, & Ison, 1973), frequency-dependent auditory masking (Hoffman & Searle, 1968), the protective reflex of the middle ear (Ison, Reiter, & Warren, 1979), or S1–S2 response interference or muscle refractoriness (Graham & Murray, 1977; Hammond, McAdam, & Ison, 1972).

Instead, PPI depends primarily on the transient characteristics of the prestimulus. An effective S1 can be any change in stimulation, such as an onset or offset (Lane, Ornitz, & Guthrie, 1991; Stitt, Hoffman, & Devido, 1980), a change in tone pitch (Cranney, Hoffman, & Cohen, 1984), or a brief change in the intensity of a continuous background signal (Reiter & Ison, 1977). Additionally, a change in stimulation lasting no longer than 6 msec is sufficient to produce an effect, and a 20-msec S1 produces as great an effect as an S1 sustained until S2 onset (Giardina, 1989; Graham & Murray, 1977).

Neurophysiological (Davis & File, 1984), as well as behavioral (Graham, 1980) studies indicate that PPI is a form of *active, extrinsic inhibition.* Unlike refractoriness, which is produced by mechanisms that reduce transmission efficacy of the direct pathway mediating a response, PPI is mediated via a parallel indirect midbrain path, external to but synapsing with the direct hindbrain path, which itself mediates startle.

Graham (1975) hypothesized that the mechanism underlying PPI protects preattentive stimulus processing, allowing a finer stimulus analysis to proceed with minimal interruption during the period critical for stimulus recognition. The mechanism, initiated by a rapidly conducting transient detector, attenuates the response to a shortly following intense S2, reducing the sensory impact of S2 and allowing the processing of S1 to proceed undisrupted through to recognition. "Without such a mechanism, temporally adjacent stimuli might more easily mask or merge with one another so that only a single stimulus could be perceived or two stimuli could be perceived but with altered characteristics" (Perlstein, Fiorito, Simons, & Graham, 1993, pp. 347–348).

The roughly 250 msec interval during which S1 processing moves from detection to recognition not only corresponds to the period of maximal PPI, but is also contemporaneous with the occurrence of early and mid-latency ERPs. If the mechanism underlying PPI reflects a sensory-gating or protective mechanism, then the PPI paradigm should have consequences for these exogenous ERPs *and* for the perception of both stimulus-pair members. We conducted a series of studies to explore these issues.

Ipsimodal Stimulation

Our first two studies (Perlstein et al., 1993) evaluated PPI concomitants of midline-recorded exogenous ERPs and perception using the standard intramodal PPI paradigm. 800-Hz, 40-msec duration tones of 75 dB or 110 dB were either presented alone (control) or were paired such that the low-intensity tone preceded either the high- or low-intensity tone. These stimulus configurations were tested in separate groups of subjects in which stimulus pairs were presented with stimulus onset asynchronies (SOAs) of 120 (Study 1) and 500 msec (Study 2). Stimuli were delivered at long intertrial intervals (18 to 28 sec) to allow for full recovery of ERPs between trials. Blinks were recorded from the bipolar electromyographic activity (EMG) of the orbicularis oculi; ERPs were measured from midline frontal (Fz) and vertex (Cz) sites, referred to the left mastoid. Subjects provided unspeeded, unsignaled magnitude estimates of the control stimuli and the second stimulus of each pair in the short-SOA study and of control stimuli and both pair members in the long-SOA study. Subjects' perceptual judgments were anchored to a pair of 90-dB modulus tones that were presented prior to each of four blocks of 20 trials. The magnitude estimation task not only provided data regarding perceptual effects of PPI, but also served to reduce habituation of blink.

ERPs were corrected for vertical electro-oculographic (EOG) activity using the method described by Gratton and colleagues (Gratton, Coles, & Donchin, 1983). Prior to measurement and analyses of baseline-to-peak amplitudes (mid- and longer-latency ERPs) and varimax-rotated PCA factor scores (midlatency ERPs), paired-stimulus ERPs were subtracted from ERPs evoked by the low-intensity control stimuli to remove overlap of the response to S1 from response to S2.

Averaged ERPs are presented in Fig. 10.1 and three of the main results are presented in Fig. 10.2. First, in addition to significant reductions of blink at both SOAs, stimulus pairing markedly and significantly reduced P50 and

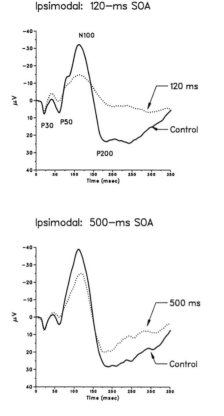

FIG. 10.1. Vertex (Cz) ERPs obtained under ipsimodal (acoustic) single- and paired-stimulus conditions when the SOA from S1 to S2 in the paired condition varied from 120 msec (top) to 500 msec (bottom).

later potentials, including N100 and P200; reductions were greater at the short than long SOA. Second, P30 was *not* affected by prestimulation at either SOA. Finally, consistent with the protection hypothesis, stimulus pairing also significantly reduced the perceived magnitude of 110-dB S2s, but magnitude estimates of the 75-dB S1s were increased relative to S1-alone levels.

These two studies demonstrate that it is possible to record mid- and longer latency ERPs within the context of a PPI paradigm, and that these ERPs are *differentially* sensitive to stimulus pairing. Furthermore, the finding that prestimulation afforded some protection to perception of the prestimulus is consistent with the protection hypothesis forwarded by Graham (1975).

Perlstein et al. (1993) suggested that prestimuli have different effects on P30 and P50 because the two potentials arise from functionally interacting thalamic-cortical pathways activated in parallel. Specifically, P30 reflects activity transmitted via the rapidly conducting lemniscal or specific path that initiates the transient-dependent PPI effect in the more

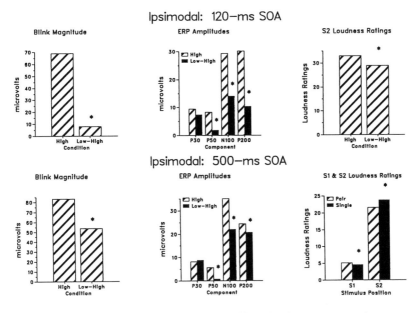

FIG. 10.2. Eyeblink, ERP, and perceptual effects (loudness estimations) as a function of ipsimodal stimulus pairing at SOAs of 120 (top) and 500 (bottom) msec.

slowly conducting, nonspecific or extralemniscal path leading to the P50 generator. This hypothesis is supported by findings of functional differences between P30 and P50 in human subjects (Buchwald, Rubinstein, Schwafel, & Strandburg, 1991) and between analogous potentials in the cat (Erwin & Buchwald, 1987). Evidence from intracranial recordings suggests that the functionally distinct P30 and P50 are generated in primary and secondary auditory cortex, respectively (e.g., Liégeois-Chauvel, Musolino, & Chauvel, 1991; Scherg & von Cramon, 1986).

Thus, existing data suggest that P30 and P50 do not depend on serial transmission via the specific projection system, but involve parallel asynchronous paths that may transmit information about transient and sustained stimulus characteristics, respectively. Furthermore, Perlstein et al. (1993) suggested that the prestimulus reductions of P50 and later potentials may be due, like blink PPI, to an active, extrinsic mechanism; that is, activity from the specific path feeds into and modulates activity in the nonspecific path. The suggestion of an extrinsic modulatory mechanism is in contrast to suggestions of others who have attributed ERP reductions in equal-intensity, paired-stimulus paradigms to passive refractory-type processes (e.g., Roemer, Shagass, & Teyler, 1984).

These first two studies, however, could not directly evaluate the hypothesis of extrinsic, rather than intrinsic, inhibition because the short

SOA elicited near-maximal PPI of the blink and ERPs. Consequently, the SOA response function for PPI of ERPs could not be distinguished from a refractory curve that also exhibits increased response size with increased SOA. Also, using ipsimodal pair members confounds refractoriness due to modality-specific effects at peripheral levels of the input path with other forms of modulation, such as PPI (Balaban, Anthony, & Graham, 1985; Rimpel, Geyer, & Hopf, 1982). Such confounding of intrinsic and extrinsic processes can be inferred from studies showing 50% greater reduction of N100 and P200 produced by ipsimodal than crossmodal pairs (e.g., Davis, Osterhammel, Wier, & Gjerdingen, 1972).

Crossmodal Stimulation

The third study in this series (Perlstein, Simons, & Graham, 1996) tested directly the hypothesis that an active form of inhibition might account for prestimulus reduction of P50 and later midline potentials. This study also evaluated the nature of the pairing effects on specific and nonspecific subcomponents of N100 described by Näätänen and Picton (1987) and whether unimpaired perception of the S1 persisted in a crossmodal paradigm.

Briefly, Näätänen and Picton (1987) described three distinct sources that contribute to the scalp-recorded N100. One source, generating *Component 3*, is modality nonspecific and can be elicited by auditory, visual, and tactile stimuli. Generator sources of this component appear to be widespread and involve a diffuse cortical system receiving projections from nonspecific thalamic nuclei via polysensory midbrain reticular formation (Velasco & Velasco, 1986; Velasco, Velasco, & Olvera, 1985) and projecting to the frontal, auditory association, and motor areas (e.g., Liégeois-Chauvel, Musolino, Badier, Marquis, & Chauvel, 1994; Giard et al., 1994).

The other two components are specific to the auditory system. *Component 1* is best recorded electrically as a frontally maximal negativity at 100 msec and, based on magnetic field (e.g., Pantev et al., 1988) and intracranial (Liégeois-Chauvel et al., 1994) recordings, reflects a source in or near the primary auditory cortex. The second specific component, *Component 2*, can be identified over temporal regions (Wolpaw & Penry, 1975) as a biphasic "T-complex" consisting of a small P105 (Ta) and larger, later negativity (Tb) ranging in latency from about 120 to 165 msec in the literature. Generators of this component have been proposed in the secondary auditory cortex based on intracranial recordings (Celesia, 1976; Liégeois-Chauvel et al., 1994) and by scalp-distribution analyses (Scherg, Vajsar, & Picton, 1989; Scherg & von Cramon, 1985).

The hypothesis of a refractory effect on ERPs was tested in two ways. First, crossmodal (tactile-acoustic) rather than ipsimodal pairs served as stimuli. Crossmodal pairs provide an unconfounded test of the refractory hypothesis because they should eliminate the modality-specific repetition or refractory effect that occurs with intramodal pairs. Second, the effects on ERPs of an SOA too short to yield significant PPI of acoustic blink were compared with the effects of a longer SOA that should yield robust blink inhibition. It is known from studies of blink PPI that prestimulation with tactile S1s at short intervals (i.e., 25 to 50 msec) may produce facilitation of the reflex elicited by an acoustic S2 (e.g., Blumenthal & Gescheider, 1987). Thus, short-SOA prestimulus effects on ERPs might differentiate between intrinsic and extrinsic mechanisms.

In this study, S1 was a weak, 10-psi air puff, psychophysically matched to a 75-dB tone, delivered to the wrist; S2 was identical in quality to the 110-dB tone used in the first study. Stimuli were delivered at SOAs of 60 and 360 msec. ERPs were recorded from midline (Fz and Cz) and lateral (F8 and T4/6) sites. Vertical and horizontal EOG and EMG from three muscles—post-auricularis, medial frontalis, and masseter—were also recorded and ERPs were corrected to remove volume-conducted activity from these sites using the multiple-pass correction program of Miller, Gratton, and Yee (1988). Puff-alone ERP waveforms were subtracted from paired-stimulus waveforms and the data were analyzed as in the first study. Subjects performed a magnitude estimation task in which they judged the magnitude of all stimuli, relative to an infrequently presented modulus.

Effects of pairing on ERPs and perception, illustrated in Fig. 10.3, replicated our previous findings of differential effects on P30 and later midline ERPs and of reduced estimates of S2s and enhanced estimates of S1s. More interesting than replicating the effects, however, was the finding that prestimulus reductions of midline P50 and N100 were significantly greater at the long than short SOA. This effect, together with the cross-modal pairing, provides strong support for the hypothesis that PPI of exogenous ERPs, like blink PPI, results from an extrinsic rather than intrinsic mechanism. Specific and nonspecific N100 components, scaled to a common amplitude (Fig. 10.4), were also differentially affected by prestimulation: The specific Component 1 showed recovery toward baseline levels at the long SOA; the nonspecific Component 3 and specific Component 2 showed parallel inhibitory effects that were greater at the long than at the short SOA.

The findings of differential pairing effects on Components 1 and 3, which parallel effects on P30 and P50, respectively, support previous work suggesting both their functional and anatomical independence. For example, the magnetically recorded N100 (N100m; Component 1) exhibits ceiling effects at higher intensities and is more dependent on stimulation rate than the electric N100/Component 3 (Hari, Kaila, Katila, Tuomisto, &

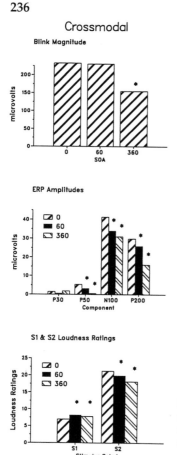

Crossmodal

Blink Magnitude

ERP Amplitudes

S1 & S2 Loudness Ratings

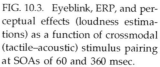

FIG. 10.3. Eyeblink, ERP, and perceptual effects (loudness estimations) as a function of crossmodal (tactile–acoustic) stimulus pairing at SOAs of 60 and 360 msec.

Varpula, 1982; Reite, Zimmerman, Edrich, & Zimmerman, 1982). Consistent with our own data, N100m is unaffected by electrical prestimulation of the median nerve at a 500-msec SOA (Huttunen, Hari, & Vanni, 1987), and is actually enhanced by pairing of moderate-intensity acoustic stimuli at SOAs from 70 to 230 msec (Loveless & Hari, 1993; Loveless, Hari, Hämäläinen, & Tiihonen, 1989). This stimulation-rate sensitivity of N100m relative to the nonspecific vertex N100, and its lack of sensitivity to attentional manipulations (Arthur, Lewis, Medvick, & Flynn, 1991), is consistent with the rapid recovery observed in the present study and with its localization to, at least, a region including the primary auditory cortex.

Prestimulus reductions of Component 2, which paralleled reductions of Component 3, indicate that the pathway generating this response must receive input from a somatosensory-processing source. Findings of attention-related enhancements of Component 2 (Hackley, Woldorff, & Hillyard, 1990; Perrault & Picton, 1984), presumably including the nonspecific

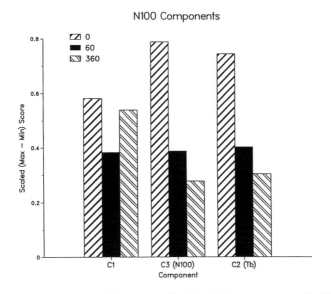

FIG. 10.4. Magnitude of the nonspecific N1 (N100) and two specific N1 components (C1 & Tb) recorded under single- and paired-stimulus conditions.

system, as attention effects are not restricted to a single modality, also suggest overlapping functional aspects of Tb and Component 3. However, Loveless and Brunia's (1990) finding that effects of increased stimulus rise-time (increased latency and decreased amplitude) were restricted to the nonspecific Component 3 indicates that Tb also exhibits functional characteristics of the specific system. Together, these data are consistent with Näätänen and Picton's (1987) suggestion that Tb receives both serial input from the primary auditory cortex and parallel input from the nonspecific thalamus; that is, the generator of Tb receives input from both specific and nonspecific projections.

Implications and Conclusions

The present research yielded four main findings regarding ERP concomitants of PPI:

1. Specific and nonspecific ERPs are consistently and differentially affected by both ipsi- and crossmodal prestimulation.
2. Prestimulus effects on midline ERPs are restricted to potentials transmitted within the nonspecific path.
3. PPI of ERPs, like blink PPI, is due to an active, extrinsic mechanism.

4. The differential effects of prestimulation on the various ERP components, together with the literature, suggest three rather than two acoustic projection systems. P30 and Component 1 of the N100 (N100m) are associated with the specific, lemniscal, system; P50 and Component 3 of the N100 (vertex N100) are associated with the nonspecific, extralemniscal, system; Component 2 of the N100 (Tb), exhibiting functional characteristics of an intermediate system, perhaps reflects processing in the "lemniscal adjunct" pathway described by Weinberger and Diamond (1987).

The perceptual effects observed in this set of experiments revealed that perception of both tactile and acoustic prestimuli was undiminished by subsequent high-intensity acoustic stimuli, and this effect has also been observed by Filion and Ciranni (1994). The dual findings of unimpaired S1 perception and reductions in S2 perceived magnitude provide preliminary support for the hypothesis that PPI reflects a protective mechanism and suggest, further, that use of the PPI paradigm to study both ERP and perceptual variables may clarify the mechanisms underlying the phenomenon as well as its adaptive function in information processing.

PASSIVE ATTENTION, ACTIVE ATTENTION, AND THE P300

The issue of whether there is a unique positive ERP component related to "novel" or "unpredictable" stimuli has been under investigation in many laboratories but still remains unresolved. This issue is important because orienting theory distinguishes between a generalized OR to passively attended novel or deviant stimuli and a localized OR to selected targets that are actively attended. If a unique ERP response, specific to low-probability stimuli, can be reliably distinguished from an ERP component to low-probability target stimuli, it would suggest that different neural mechanisms are responsible for the production of signal and nonsignal ORs and would identify the two processes much earlier in time than is possible with the slowly developing autonomic responses from which OR theory arose (Sokolov & Cacioppo, chapter 1, this volume). This issue is also of interest because it has been reported that the anterior, passively attended and posterior, actively attended P300 potentials show different developmental courses (Courchesne, 1978). The posterior P300 can be recorded from children as young as 6 years old, whereas the anterior P300 may not be present until adolescence.

Evidence for the existence of an anterior positivity, specifically related to generalized orienting, comes from two sources. The first source is a set of studies derived from procedures employed by N. K. Squires, K. C. Squires, and Hillyard (1975), in which subjects were presented with two acoustic stimuli that differed only in frequency or intensity. In separate conditions, one of the two stimuli occurred with probabilities of 0.1, 0.5, and 0.9, and the other occurred with the complementary probability. At each probability, subjects either counted tones defined as targets (either the high or low probability tone), or ignored the tones while reading a book. With event-related potentials recorded from Fz, Cz, and Pz, N. K. Squires et al. (1975) found a P300 deflection (P3b) related to both rare targets and rare nontargets, and noted another, earlier onset P300 deflection (P3a) specifically related to all low-probability stimuli (i.e., rare targets, rare nontargets, and the *ignored* rare stimuli). P3b had a parietal scalp distribution, whereas P3a, in contrast, had a more anterior distribution—centro-parietal in the rare target condition and centro-frontal in the ignore condition.

The second source of evidence suggesting that distinct P300 responses might be associated with passive and active attention derives from a series of studies by Courchesne and colleagues (e.g., Courchesne, 1978; Courchesne, Hillyard, & Galambos, 1975; Courchesne, Kilman, Galambos, & Lincoln, 1984; see also Knight, 1984). These studies employed a standard target-detection (oddball) task, but in addition to rare target (oddball) and frequent standard stimuli, a variety of unannounced complex novel stimuli were embedded within the series of standards and targets. In each of these studies, a frontal or centro-frontal positive component was observed in response to the novel stimulus (the *"novels* P3") while the parietal P300, as expected, was associated with the rare targets. It is unclear at this point whether the *novels* P3 described by Courchesne is the same potential as the P3a described by N. K. Squires et al. (1975).

The Two-Stimulus P3a Paradigm

As just described, the first and most compelling evidence for the differentiation of a small, more anterior P3 response from the much larger, later parietal P300 was provided by N. K. Squires et al. (1975) and the subsequent replication by Snyder and Hillyard (1976). Other studies, employing very similar procedures, have been less successful, however (e.g., Duncan-Johnson & Donchin, 1977; Sams, Ahlo, & Näätänen, 1984; K. C. Squires, Donchin, Herning, & McCarthy, 1977) and have called into question the existence of the P3a component or its independence from either the preceding N200 or the subsequent P300 components, both commonly associated with low-probability stimuli. Although it is frequently noted in passing that two P300 peaks are seen in ERP waveforms, they are rarely separately measured and tested statistically for differences as a function of the experimental variables (e.g., probability, electrode location, task). In fact, only N. K. Squires et al. (1975) were able to show that the two deflections were associated with different factors when the data were subjected to a Principal Components Analysis (PCA).

The present P3a study was run as an "exact" replication of N. K. Squires et al. (1975) in order to collect data relevant to three hypotheses. First, P3b and P3a would show some similar and some different effects of experimental manipulations by virtue of their association with localized and generalized orienting. Second, P3b and P3a would show different scalp distributions—the P3b characteristically parieto-central, whereas the P3a would be more anterior, either centro-parietal or centro-frontal as reported by N. K. Squires et al. (1975).

Third, explaining some of the discrepancies in the literature, the emergence and definition of P3a as a separate component in the PCA would be a function of the PCA methods employed. N. K. Squires et al. (1975) identified six components based on deflections in the ERP waveforms and measured their amplitudes with traditional "peak-picking" algorithms. These component scores were then subjected to the PCA procedure. K. C. Squires et al. (1977), on the other hand, submitted the entire ERP waveform to PCA and allowed the factor analysis to identify components and derive component scores. It would not be surprising to learn that P3a, when submitted to PCA as one of six component scores, might survive as an independent factor whereas P3a as a high-frequency portion of a complex, multicomponent waveform might not emerge as one of a small number of principal components.

In the present study (Chen, Simons, & Graham, 1994), two 70-dB pure tones with frequencies of 1000 Hz and 1500 Hz and durations of 50 msec were used as stimuli, and subjects were instructed to count "high," count "low," or ignore (read a magazine). Under each of these three instructional conditions, the probability of a "high" (1500 Hz) tone was either 0.9, 0.5, or 0.1, for a total of nine experimental conditions, each delivered twice. The order of condition presentation was fixed, but balanced across two halves of the experimental session. When high-tone probability was either 0.9 or 0.1, the condition contained 200 trials. When high-tone probability was 0.5, the number of trials was 100. In each block, all single-trial ERPs associated with the 0.1 probability tone were stored, along with the same number of trials associated with the 0.9 and the 0.5 probability tones.

Monopolar EEG was recorded from midline frontal (Fz), vertex (Cz), and parietal (Pz) electrode sites. ERP waveforms were obtained by sampling each of the EEG channels at 500 cps and then corrected for vertical eye movements and eyeblinks (Miller, Gratton, & Yee, 1988).

Grand mean ERP waveforms for the low- and high-probability tones are presented in Fig. 10.5. A computer algorithm was developed that identified and scored the amplitude of N1, P2, N2, P3a, P3b, and SW in each of the constituent ERP waveforms. These component scores and the entire 600

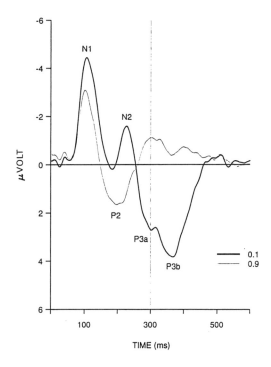

FIG. 10.5. Grand mean ERP waveform for the high (0.9)- and low (0.1)-probability stimuli across condition (attend rare, attend frequent, ignore) and electrode location (Fz, Cz, Pz). The labels identify the components that were measured as peaks. Slow Wave (SW; not indicated) was an area measure (420–520 msec) subsequent to P3b.

msec ERP waveform were then submitted to separate PCAs. A comparison of the loadings produced by submitting the individual component scores (solid lines) and the 600 msec waveform (dashed lines) is provided graphically in Fig. 10.6. The two methods of component identification yielded similar, although not identical, results. The six components identified from the peak amplitudes (as per N. K. Squires et al., 1975) are comparable to 6 of the first 10 components extracted by PCA when the entire waveform was factor analyzed (as per K. C. Squires et al., 1977). The most noteworthy discrepancy between the two solutions occurs in the P300 window. Although both PCAs contained evidence of two surface-positive components in this window, the proportion of variance attributed to each of the two factors was dependent on the PCA strategy. When submitted as one of six component scores, the P3a was the first factor identified and it accounted for 22% of the total variance. P3b emerged as Factor 5 and accounted for 13% of the variance. In the 600 msec, equal-interval, method, P3b was the first factor extracted and accounted for 43% of the variance. P3a was identified with Factor 8 and accounted for only 3% of the variance. Treating the component scores as if they were spaced at equal intervals (N. K. Squires et al., 1975), therefore, appears to overestimate the contribution of P3a to the ERP waveform and, at the same time, underestimate the contribution of P3b.

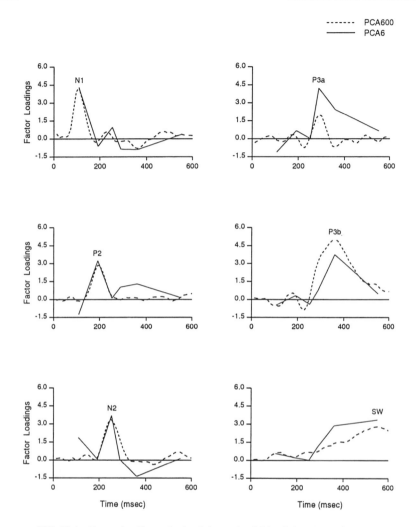

FIG. 10.6. Factor loadings obtained from the PCA of the six peak scores (PCA6) and the PCA using the entire 600 msec waveform (PCA600). The juxtaposition of the loadings was done by aligning the six discrete PCA6 loadings with the times in msec where the PCA600 factors were maximal.

These two PCA solutions were virtually identical to those described by N. K. Squires et al. (1975) and K. C. Squires et al. (1977), and the use of the two different PCA techniques can easily account for the two different conclusions reached by the authors regarding the presence and significance of the P3a. Specifically, it appears that in the equal-interval, 600 msec PCA, the P3a, a relatively high-frequency component, is generated late and accounts for little variance when forced to compete with low-frequency components, such as P3b and SW, that consist of many more data points. It would follow, then, that factor scores derived from factors that themselves account for little variance might also vary within a narrow range and show limited sensitivity to the experimental manipulations. It was this insensitivity that led K. C. Squires et al. (1977) to conclude that a positive factor observed at 250 msec (Factor 6) was *not* a P3a.

To examine this issue further, we computed an additional PCA on the 200 msec portion of the ERP waveform (220–420 msec) that contained the P300 complex. Again, both P3a and P3b emerged as independent factors, although in this case, P3a accounted for 20% of the variance—comparable to what it achieved when submitted as one of six component scores. Figure 10.7 depicts the P3a and P3b factor *scores* derived from the three PCAs as a function of electrode location and the target/nontarget status of the low-probability stimulus. The left-hand panels depict the centro-parietal scalp distribution of the early, P3a component. This topography was significantly quadratic when the P3a was a peak score submitted to PCA or when derived by PCA as a component in the narrow (220–420 msec) window. Note the lack of sensitivity in the P3a when extracted from the entire 600 msec data set in the manner of K. C. Squires et al. (1977). Although the P3b effects are less dramatic, it is nonetheless evident that underestimating the "true" variance accounted for by P3b is also reflected in the derived factor scores. P3b was consistently larger in reponse to targets, but note how the topography of P3b obtained from the peak-score factor analysis appears less well defined than it is when the P3b measure is obtained from the two equal-interval PCAs. In fact, there was not a significant difference among the three scalp sites for the P3b factor in this analysis. Interestingly, N. K. Squires et al. (1975) also reported an "equipotentiality of the P3b *factor* across the scalp" (p. 396).

We believe that the results of this study replicate both N. K. Squires et al. (1975) and K. C. Squires et al. (1977). We believe further that these data confirm the existence of an anterior P3a component that is distinct from the later, though overlapping, P3b based on the four criteria for independence discussed by Fabiani, Gratton, Karis, and Donchin (1987). In short, the two components (a) differed in morphology, (b) differed in scalp distribution, (c) were independent factors in each of three factor PCA analyses, and (d) responded differentially to the experimental manipulations.

Although this is only a first step in determining whether P3a and P3b can be associated with nonsignal and signal orienting, it is at least clear that the two ERP components are sensitive to probability. That is, both P3a and P3b were elicited by unexpected and unpredictable, low-probability events. Finding that P3b is more responsive to rare targets than to rare nontargets is compatible with P3b being associated with, or a component of, the localized OR. Finding P3a, on the other hand, sensitive only to

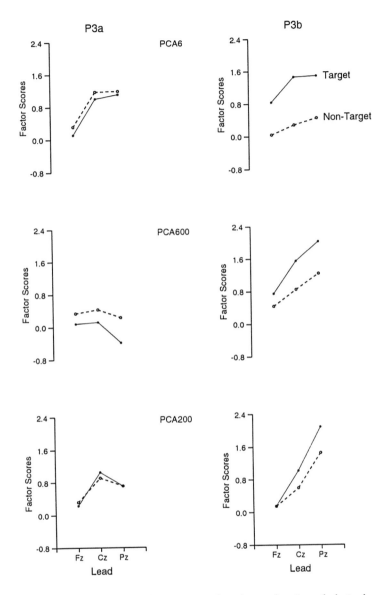

FIG. 10.7. P3a and P3b factor scores plotted as a function of electrode location and the target/nontarget manipulation when the probability of the stimulus was low (0.1). Note how, relative to the other two conditions, the PCA600 poorly represents the P3a factor and the PCA6 poorly represents the P3b factor.

stimulus probability, is compatible with an association between P3a and generalized orienting (nonselective, passive attention). This conclusion is tentative, of course, because the present study differed in many ways from those traditionally designed to measure and investigate orienting. Perhaps most importantly, it was not designed to measure habituation, a key concept in orienting theory, and a criterion for discriminating components associated with generalized versus localized ORs. Nonetheless, this successful evocation of two independent P3 components can provide a platform from which a more targeted series of studies can be initiated.

The Three-Stimulus *Novels* P3 Paradigm

In a parallel set of experiments, we have also been pursuing the anterior P300 described originally by Courchesne et al. (1975). This series of studies was designed to determine the conditions under which unattended, novel, stimuli, embedded with targets in a series of standards, would be associated with an anterior P300 response that was distinct from the posterior P300 prompted by attended targets. To examine more closely the possible association between the P300 potentials and orienting, simultaneous measurement of beat-by-beat changes in heart rate were obtained.

In our first three experiments (Simons, Balaban, Macy, & Graham, 1986; Miles, Perlstein, Simons, & Graham, 1987; Simons, Graham, Miles, & Balaban, 1996; Simons, Graham, & Rockstroh, 1996), all stimuli were simple tones, white noise bursts, light flashes, and air puffs. Novel stimuli were unannounced and of low probability. Targets were equal in probability to novels ($p = .08$), but required either overt or covert behavior from the subject when identified. For example, in one experiment, standard stimuli were a train of 1000 Hz pure tones, whereas the target was either a higher pitched (1500 Hz) pure tone or a white noise. In this case, when the high-pitched tone was the target, the white noise was novel; the high-pitched tone was novel when white noise was the target. The other two experiments were variations on this basic design across the three experiments (e.g., interstimulus intervals varied from 2 to 16 sec; target/novel distinctions were ipsi- or crossmodal, target response requirements varied). The data contained in Fig. 10.8 are representative. In short, target, novel, and even the initial six presentations of the frequently occurring standard stimulus prompted only a posterior P300 (P3b). There was no evidence at all of an anterior P300 response associated with novelty. These conclusions held whether the ERP waveform was scored by conventional "peak picking" or whether components were identified through factor analysis.

Despite this lack of sensitivity of P300, other measures consistently differentiated the targets and novels. The slow wave (SW) component

246

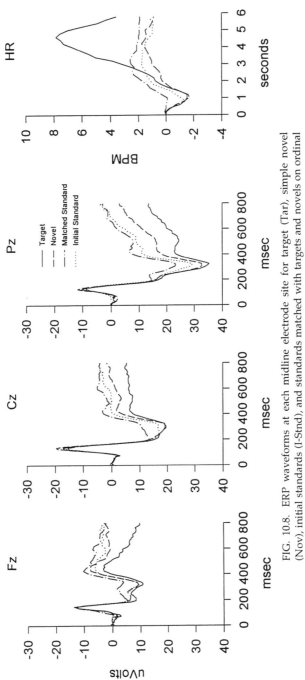

FIG. 10.8. ERP waveforms at each midline electrode site for target (Tar), simple novel (Nov), initial standards (I-Stnd), and standards matched with targets and novels on ordinal position (M-Stnd). The heart rate response to the same stimuli is presented on the right.

was significantly more positive at Pz in response to targets than it was to both novels and standards, and as illustrated in Fig. 10.8, heart rate was also sensitive to the target/novel distinction. Although the presentation of target, novel, and even initial standard stimuli was accompanied by a short-latency heart rate deceleration, the target stimulus prompted a subsequent and substantial acceleration that was not present in the cardiac response to either novels or standards. In these experiments, then, although target and novel stimuli did prompt differential HR and ERP responses, the ERP differences were subsequent to P300 and it was the target stimulus that was unique; beyond the P300 window, the ERP response to novels essentially matched the response associated with the initial and remaining high-probability standards.

Our next experiment (Miles, 1992) assessed whether the emergence of an early, anterior P300 was a function of stimulus recognizability/complexity. In the three previously described experiments, all stimuli were common, easily recognized and encoded laboratory sights and sounds. These have not been the usual stimuli employed to study the *novels* P3. Courchesne (Courchesne, 1978; Courchesne et al., 1975) and others (e.g., Friedman & Simpson, 1994; Knight, 1984; Knight, Scabini, Woods, & Clayworth, 1989) studying ERPs to "novel" stimuli have normally employed stimuli that were essentially unrecognizable, such as computer-generated sounds, synthesized dog barks, and complex color geometrical designs. In other words, novel stimuli have been both unpredictable (rare) and unrecognizable.

As an attempt to explore the issue of stimulus specificity, we obtained a copy of the Courchesne et al. (1984) stimulus set. The target stimulus in this set was the synthesized word *you* ($p = .10$), the standard was the word *me* ($p = .80$), and the novels were complex mixtures of natural sounds, mechanical noises, and digitally synthesized nonsense sounds ($p = .10$). These stimuli were presented at 75 dB, for 200 msec, to 24 undergraduate volunteers (12 female, 12 male) at SOAs of 1,900 msec. Stimuli were presented in three blocks. The first block consisted only of standards and targets. Blocks 2 and 3 contained standards, targets, and novels. In either Block 2 or Block 3, the novel stimuli varied from trial to trial; in the other block, balanced across subjects, one of the complex novels was used repetitively.

Monopolar EEG from three midline electrode sites (Fz, Cz, Pz), vertical EOG, and heart rate were recorded. The EOG-corrected (Miller et al., 1988) ERPs and the heart-rate waveforms averaged across Blocks 2 and 3 are presented in Fig. 10.9. The most striking aspect of the ERP data was the anterior negative/positive complex (N2b/P3a) that preceded and merged with the more parietal P3b. To distinguish the early and later P300s and determine the independence of the N2b and P3a portions of the waveforms,

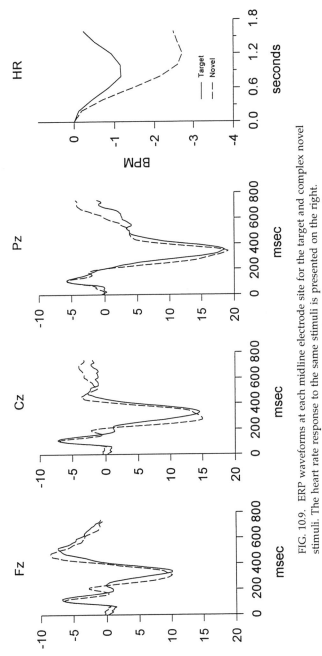

FIG. 10.9. ERP waveforms at each midline electrode site for the target and complex novel stimuli. The heart rate response to the same stimuli is presented on the right.

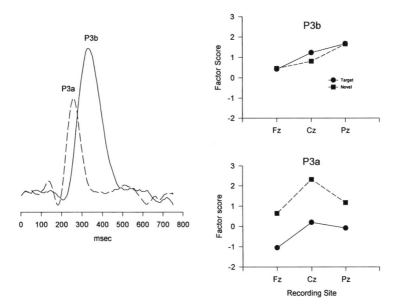

FIG. 10.10. The principal-component loadings identified as P3a and P3b (left) and their associated factor scores (right) plotted as a function of electrode for the target (solid line) and complex novel (dotted lines) stimulus.

the 750 msec ERP waveform was submitted to PCA. The factor loadings identified as the *novels* P3 and P3b are presented in the left-hand panel of Fig. 10.10 (an independent N2 component was also identified), whereas the component scores as a function of Electrode Site and Stimulus (Target/Novel) are presented on the right. The P3b factor peaked at approximately 330 msec following stimulus onset and, as expected, was largest at Pz. It was equally large in response to targets and novels. In contrast, the factor identified as the *novels* P3 peaked at approximately 250 msec. It had a centrally maximal scalp distribution and was significantly larger in response to novels than to targets. Consistent with the full-waveform PCA in our P3a study, the P3b in this study was the first factor extracted and accounted for 37% of the total variance, whereas the *novels* P3 was extracted as Factor 5 and accounted for only 5% of the variance.

Once again, both the Slow Wave and the heart rate response covaried with the target/novel manipulation. Slow Wave, most positive at Pz, was more positive in response to targets than novels. Consistent with theoretical differences between active and generalized (passive) orienting, the heart rate response to target stimuli consisted of a brief deceleration and rapid return to baseline, whereas the response to novel stimuli was a deeper and more sustained heart rate slowing.

The *novels* P3 and the P3b observed in the present study were strikingly similar to the P3a and P3b observed in the experiment previously described. Based on factor analyses of the entire ERP waveforms, P3b had a posterior scalp distibution in both studies and accounted for 43% and 37% of the total variance in the two studies, respectively. P3a and the *novels* P3 both had centro-parietal scalp distributions and accounted for 3% and 5% of the variance. Although Couchesne (1978) argued that P3a and the *novels* P3 are *not* the same component, the results of our factor analyses do not allow for such a differentiation.

The heart rate data collected in this set of experiments provide some additional support for the hypothesized relationship between the two P300s and localized versus generalized ORs. Orienting theory (see Cook & Turpin, chapter 6, this volume) would predict that novelty (generalized orienting) would be associated with heart rate deceleration whereas target detection (localized orienting) would prompt 'a more acceleratory response. This is precisely the pattern of results we observed. Heart rate acceleration occurred in response to targets and was associated with a large amplitude P3b and a more positive slow wave. A pronounced deceleratory response occurred only in conjunction with the anterior P3 and only when the stimuli were *highly* novel. Interestingly, the P3b was evident in response to the complex novels as it had been in the ERP response to the simple novels that did not give rise to an anterior P3. Table 10.1 summarizes these relationships and suggests the following scenario: All stimuli receive the same initial processing, indexed by equivalent ERP components through the N1–P2 vertex response. That is the extent of processing afforded to frequently occurring standard stimuli. Initial standard, simple novel, and target stimuli prompt a brief bradycardia and a P3b. This context updating response (Donchin, 1981) appears to be the terminus for the processing of initial standards and simple novels. Target stimuli go on to prompt SW and heart rate acceleration that in this context most likely reflect the mobilization of response processes. Complex, highly novel stimuli are associated with P3b, as were the simple novels, but, in addition, they give rise to both the *novels* P3a and heart rate deceleration. This association between the *novels* P3a and

TABLE 10.1
Type of Stimulus and the Associated
ERP and HR Response Components

Stimulus	P3a	P3b	SW	Heart Rate
Standard	No	No	No	——
Target	No	Yes	Yes	↓ ↑
Simple novel	No	Yes	No	↓
Complex novel	Yes	Yes	No	⬇

cardiac deceleration is further evidence of a link between the anterior P3 and generalized orienting, and suggests that unlike targets, which seem to prompt response processes subsequent to P3b (SW, HR accel), these complex novels give rise to sensory enhancement processes (HR decel) that facilitate further stimulus intake.

Summary

The research described in this chapter was conducted, in part, to examine the nature and information-processing effects of two reflexive mechanisms—the prepulse inhibition of startle and the nonsignal orienting response. PPI has been described as a gating mechanism that protects the processing of information in preattentive stores from interruption due to newly arriving stimuli. The work described in this chapter is consistent with this description. Lead stimuli not only inhibit the eyeblink and other indices of startle, but also impact on higher level processes as reflected in the ERPs to subsequent stimuli and their perception. The findings that these effects occur regardless of prepulse modality, that ERP components are not modulated by prestimuli prior to 50 msec, and that modulation differs among the various N100 components suggest that this gating occurs at a point somewhere beyond the convergence of somatosensory and acoustic stimulus processing. The finding that the apparent loudness of S1 is not reduced, even when followed shortly by a powerful S2, is consistent with Graham's (1975) hypothesized protective function of the PPI gate, but additional studies will be necessary to more fully understand the complex array of perceptual data we have collected to date and how these perceptual effects relate to eyeblink and ERP component modulation.

Likewise, we continue to pursue the elusive frontal P300 component. Our studies to date have confirmed the existence of an independent anterior positivity under conditions at least superficially evocative of an OR interpretation. Furthermore, the PCA results suggest that the anterior P300s obtained using the Courchesne (Courchesne et al., 1975) and N. K. Squires (Squires et al., 1975) procedures are similar if not identical. Ongoing studies have been designed to address more directly the equivalence question (P3a vs. *novels* P3) and to flesh out more completely the relationships among the P300 components and the varieties of attention/orienting with which they are associated.

ACKNOWLEDGMENTS

This research was supported by National Institute of Mental Health grant R01-MH42465 to F. K. Graham and R. F. Simons.

REFERENCES

Anthony, B. J. (1985). In the blink of an eye: Implications of reflex modification for information processing. In P. K. Ackles, J. R. Jennings, & M. G. H. Coles (Eds.), *Advances in psychophysiology* (Vol. 1, pp. 167–218). Greenwich, CT: JAI Press.

Arthur, D. L., Lewis, P. S., Medvick, P. A., & Flynn, E. R. (1991). A neuromagnetic study of selective auditory attention. *Electroencephalography and Clinical Neurophysiology, 78,* 348–360.

Balaban, M. T., Anthony, B. J., & Graham, F. K. (1985). Modality-repetition and attentional effects on reflex blinking in infants and adults. *Infant Behavior and Development, 8,* 443–457.

Blumenthal, T. D., & Gescheider, G. A. (1987). Modification of the acoustic startle reflex by a tactile prepulse: The effects of stimulus onset asynchrony and prepulse intensity. *Psychophysiology, 24,* 320–327.

Buchwald, J. S., Rubinstein, E. H., Schwafel, J., & Strandburg, R. J. (1991). Midlatency auditory evoked responses: Differential effects of a cholinergic agonist and antagonist. *Electroencephalography and Clinical Neurophysiology, 80,* 303–309.

Celesia, G. G. (1976). Organization of auditory cortical areas in man. *Brain, 99,* 403–414.

Chen, X., Simons, R. F., & Graham, F. K. (1994). P3a: Elusive or illusory [Abstract]. *Psychophysiology, 31,* S35.

Courchesne, E. (1978). Neurophysiological correlates of cognitive development: Changes in long-latency event-related potentials from childhood to adulthood. *Electroencephalography and Clinical Neurophysiology, 45,* 468–482.

Courchesne, E., Hillyard, S. A., & Galambos, R. (1975). Stimulus novelty, task relevance and the visual evoked potential in man. *Electroencephalography and Clinical Neurophysiology, 39,* 131–143.

Courchesne, E., Kilman, B. A., Galambos, R., & Lincoln, A. J. (1984). Autism: Processing of novel auditory information assessed by event-related brain potentials. *Electroencephalography and Clinical Neurophysiology, 59,* 238–248.

Cranney, J., Hoffman, H. S., & Cohen, M. E. (1984). Tonal frequency shifts and gaps in acoustic stimulation as reflex-modifying events. *Perception & Psychophysics, 35,* 167–172.

Davis, H., Osterhammel, P. A., Wier, C. C., & Gjerdingen, D. B. (1972). Slow vertex potentials: Interactions among auditory, tactile, electric, and visual stimuli. *Electroencephalography and Clinical Neurophysiology, 33,* 537–545.

Davis, M., & File, S. E. (1984). Intrinsic and extrinsic mechanisms of habituation and sensitization: Implications for the design and analysis of experiments. In H. V. S. Peek & L. Petrinovich (Eds.), *Habituation, sensitization, and behavior* (pp. 287–323). New York: Academic Press.

Donchin, E. (1981). Surprise! . . . Surprise? *Psychophysiology, 18,* 493–513.

Duncan-Johnson, C., & Donchin, E. (1977). On quantifying surprise: The variation of event-related potentials with subjective probability. *Psychophysiology, 14,* 456–467.

Erwin, R., & Buchwald, J. S. (1987). Midlatency auditory evoked responses in the human and the cat model. In R. Johnson, J. W. Rohrbaugh, & R. Parasuraman (Eds.), *Current trends in event-related potential research* (pp. 461–467). Amsterdam: Elsevier.

Fabiani, M., Gratton, G., Karis, D., & Donchin, E. (1987). Definition, identification and reliability of measurement of the P300 component of the event-related brain potential. In P. K. Ackles, J. R. Jennings, & M. G. H. Coles (Eds.), *Advances in psychophysiology* (Vol. 2, pp. 1–78). Greenwich, CT: JAI Press.

Filion, D. L., & Ciranni, M. (1994). The functional significance of prepulse inhibition: A test of the protection of processing theory. *Psychophysiology, 31,* S46.

Friedman, D., & Simpson, G. V. (1994). ERP amplitude and scalp distribution to target and novel events: Effects of temporal order in young, middle-aged and older adults. *Cognitive Brain Research, 2,* 49–63.

Giard, M. H., Perrin, F., Echallier, J. F., Thévenet, M., Froment, J. C., & Pernier, J. (1994). Dissociation of temporal and frontal components of the human auditory N1 wave: A scalp current density and dipole model analysis. *Electroencephalography and Clinical Neurophysiology, 92,* 238–252.

Giardina, B. D. (1989). *Short and long time processing in mediating prepulse inhibition of the startle blink reflex.* Unpublished doctoral dissertation, University of Delaware, Newark.

Graham, F. K. (1975). The more or less startling effects of weak prestimulation. *Psychophysiology, 12,* 238–248.

Graham, F. K. (1980). Control of reflex blink excitability. In R. F. Thompson, L. H. Hicks, & V. B. Shvyrkov (Eds.), *Neural mechanisms of goal-directed behavior and learning* (pp. 511–519). New York: Academic Press.

Graham, F. K., & Murray, G. M. (1977). Discordant effects of weak prestimulation on magnitude and latency of the blink reflex. *Physiological Psychology, 5,* 108–114.

Gratton, G., Coles, M. G. H., & Donchin, E. (1983). A new method for off-line removal of ocular artifact. *Electroencephalography and Clinical Neurophysiology, 55,* 468–484.

Hackley, S. A., Woldorff, M., & Hillyard, S. A. (1990). Cross-modal selective attention effects on retinal, myogenic, brainstem, and cerebral evoked potentials. *Psychophysiology, 27,* 195–208.

Hammond, G. R., McAdam, D. W., & Ison, J. R. (1972). Effects of prestimulation on the electromyographic response associated with the acoustic startle reaction in rats. *Physiology and Behavior, 8,* 535–537.

Hari, R., Kaila, K., Katila, T., Tuomisto, T., & Varpula, T. (1982). Interstimulus interval dependence of the auditory vertex response and its magnetic counterpart: Implications for their neural generation. *Electroencephalography and Clinical Neurophysiology, 54,* 561–569.

Hoffman, H. S., & Ison, J. R. (1980). Reflex modification in the domain of startle: I. Some empirical findings and their implications for how the nervous system processes sensory input. *Psychological Review, 87,* 175–189.

Hoffman, H. S., & Searle, J. L. (1968). Acoustic and temporal factors in the evaluation of startle. *Journal of the Acoustical Society of America, 43,* 269–282.

Huttunen, J., Hari, R., & Vanni, S. (1987). Crossmodal interaction is reflected in vertex potentials but not in evoked magnetic fields. *Acta Neurologica Scandinavica, 75,* 410–416.

Ison, J. R., Reiter, L. A., & Warren, M. (1979). Modification of the acoustic startle reflex in humans in the absence of anticipatory changes in the middle ear reflex. *Journal of Experimental Psychology: Human Perception and Performance, 5,* 639–642.

Knight, R. T. (1984). Decreased response to novel stimuli after prefrontal lesions in man. *Electroencephalography and Clinical Neurophysiology, 59,* 9–20.

Knight, R. T., Scabini, D., Woods, D. L., & Clayworth, C. C. (1989). Contributions of temporal-parietal junction to the human auditory P3. *Brain Research, 502,* 109–116.

Krauter, E. E., Leonard, D. W., & Ison, J. R. (1973). Inhibition of the human eye blink by a brief acoustic stimulus. *Journal of Comparative and Physiological Psychology, 84,* 246–251.

Lane, S. J., Ornitz, E. M., & Guthrie, D. (1991). Modulatory influence of continuous tone, tone offset, and tone onset on the human acoustic startle response. *Psychophysiology, 28,* 579–587.

Liégeois-Chauvel, C., Musolino, A., Badier, J. M., Marquis, P., & Chauvel, P. (1994). Evoked potentials recorded from the auditory cortex in man: Evaluation and topography of the middle latency components. *Electroencephalography and Clinical Neurophysiology, 92,* 204–214.

Liégeois-Chauvel, C., Musolino, A., & Chauvel, P. (1991). Localization of the primary auditory area in man. *Brain, 114,* 139–153.

Loveless, N. E., & Brunia, C. H. M. (1990). Effects of rise-time on late components of the auditory evoked potential. *Journal of Psychophysiology, 4,* 369–380.

Loveless, N. E., & Hari, R. (1993). Auditory evoked fields covary with perceptual grouping. *Biological Psychology, 35,* 1–15.

Loveless, N., Hari, R., Hämäläinen, M., & Tiihonen, J. (1989). Evoked responses of human auditory cortex may be enhanced by preceding stimuli. *Electroencephalography and Clinical Neurophysiology, 74,* 217–227.

Miles, M. A. (1992). *P300 and heart rate components in passive orienting to unrecognizable repetitive and nonrepetitive novels during a short ISI target detection task: Anhedonics and controls.* Unpublished doctoral dissertation, University of Delaware, Newark.

Miles, M. A., Perlstein, W. M., Simons, R. F., & Graham, F. K. (1987). ERP and HR components of active and passive orienting in a long-ISI paradigm: Anhedonic and normal controls [Abstract]. *Psychophysiology, 24,* 601.

Miller, G. A., Gratton, G., & Yee, C. M. (1988). Generalized implementation of an eye movement correction procedure. *Psychophysiology, 25,* 241–243.

Näätänen, R., & Picton, T. (1987). The N1 wave of the human electric and magnetic response to sound: A review and an analysis of the component structure. *Psychophysiology, 24,* 375–425.

Pantev, C., Hoke, M., Lehnertz, K., Lütkenhöner, B., Anogianakis, G., & Wittkowski, W. (1988). Tonotopic organization of the human auditory cortex revealed by transient auditory evoked magnetic fields. *Electroencephalography and Clinical Neurophysiology, 69,* 160–170.

Perlstein, W. M., Fiorito, E., Simons, R. F., & Graham, F. K. (1993). Lead stimulation effects on reflex blink, exogenous brain potentials, and loudness judgments. *Psychophysiology, 30,* 347–358.

Perlstein, W. M., Simons, R. F., & Graham, F. K. (1996). *Specific and nonspecific processing during prepulse inhibition by crossmodal stimuli.* Manuscript in preparation.

Perrault, N., & Picton, T. W. (1984). Event-related potentials recorded from the scalp and nasopharynx. I. N1 and P2. *Electroencephalography and Clinical Neurophysiology, 59,* 177–194.

Reiter, L. A., & Ison, J. R. (1977). Inhibition of the human eyeblink reflex: An evaluation of the sensitivity of the Wendt–Yerkes method for threshold detection. *Journal of Experimental Psychology: Human Perception and Performance, 3,* 325–336.

Reite, M., Zimmerman, J. T., Edrich, J., & Zimmerman, J. E. (1982). Auditory evoked magnetic fields: Response amplitude vs. stimulus intensity. *Electroencephalography and Clinical Neurophysiology, 54,* 147–152.

Rimpel, J., Geyer, D., & Hopf, H. C. (1982). Changes in the blink responses to combined trigeminal, acoustic, and visual repetitive stimulation, studied in the human subject. *Electroencephalography and Clinical Neurophysiology, 54,* 552–560.

Roemer, R. A., Shagass, C., & Teyler, T. J. (1984). Do human evoked potentials habituate? In H. V. S. Peeke & L. Petrinovich (Eds.), *Habituation, sensitization, and behavior* (pp. 325–346). New York: Academic Press.

Sams, M., Ahlo, K., & Näätänen, R. (1984). Short-term habituation and dishabituation of the mismatch negativity of the ERP. *Psychophysiology, 21,* 434–441.

Scherg, M., Vajsar, J., & Picton, T. W. (1989). A source analysis of the late human auditory evoked potentials. *Journal of Cognitive Neuroscience, 1,* 336–355.

Scherg, M., & von Cramon, D. (1985). Two bilateral sources of the late AEP as identified by a spatio-temporal dipole model. *Electroencephalography and Clinical Neurophysiology, 62,* 32–44.

Scherg, M., & von Cramon, D. (1986). Evoked dipole source potentials of the human auditory cortex. *Electroencephalography and Clinical Neurophysiology, 65,* 344–360.

Simons, R. F., Balaban, M. T., Macy, M. H., & Graham, F. K. (1986). Heart rate, blink, and ERPs to modality-defined targets and novels [Abstract]. *Psychophysiology, 24,* 461–462.

Simons, R. F., Graham, F. K., Miles, M. A., & Balaban, M. T. (1996). *Event-related potential and heart-rate change to signal and nonsignal novel stimuli at long interstimulus intervals.* Manuscript in preparation.

Simons, R. F., Graham, F. K., & Rockstroh, B. (1996). *Event-related potentials in response to target and novel stimulus events: Effects of interstimulus interval length.* Manuscript in preparation.

Snyder, E., & Hillyard, S. A. (1976). Long-latency evoked potentials to irrelevant, deviant stimuli. *Biological Psychology, 16,* 319–331.

Squires, K. C., Donchin, E., Herning, R. I., & McCarthy, G. (1977). On the influence of task relevance and stimulus probability on event-related potential components. *Electroencephalography and Clinical Neurophysiology, 42,* 1–14.

Squires, N. K., Squires, K. C., & Hillyard, S. A. (1975). Two varieties of long-latency positive waves evoked by unpredictable auditory stimuli in man. *Electroencephalography and Clinical Neurophysiology, 39,* 387–401.

Stitt, C. L., Hoffman, H. S., & DeVido, C. J. (1980). Inhibition of the human glabella reflex by antecedent acoustic stimulation. *Perception & Psychophysics, 27,* 82–88.

Velasco, M., & Velasco, F. (1986). Subcortical correlates of the somatic, auditory and visual vertex activities: II. Referential EEG responses. *Electroencephalography and Clinical Neurophysiology, 63,* 62–67.

Velasco, M., Velasco. F., & Olvera, A. (1985). Subcortical correlates of the somatic, auditory and visual vertex activities in man: I. Bipolar EEG responses and electrical stimulation. *Electroencephalography and Clinical Neurophysiology, 61,* 519–529.

Weinberger, N. M., & Diamond, D. M. (1987). Physiological plasticity in auditory cortex: Rapid induction by learning. *Progress in Neurobiology, 29,* 1–55.

Wolpaw, J. R., & Penry, J. K. (1975). A temporal component of the auditory evoked response. *Electroencephalography and Clinical Neurophysiology, 39,* 609–620.

11

Cognitive, Clinical, and Neurophysiological Implications of Startle Modification

Michael E. Dawson
University of Southern California

Anne M. Schell
Occidental College

Neal R. Swerdlow
University of California, San Diego

Diane L. Filion
Kansas University Medical Center

The past decade has witnessed a remarkable growth of interest in the psychophysiological processes underlying modification of the human startle reflex. This phenomenal growth is due in large part to the pioneering research of Graham (1975, 1979, 1980) and her coworkers, who adapted the startle modification paradigm used in animal research (see Hoffman & Ison, 1980, for a review) and applied it in a systematic program of research to the human eye-blink component of the startle reflex. The focus of the present chapter, therefore, is on human startle eye-blink modification (SEM) phenomena, although other measures of startle modification derived from animal research are cited where relevant, particularly when discussing the neurophysiology of startle modification.

SEM refers to the reliable inhibition and/or facilitation of startle reflex amplitude that occurs when innocuous, nonstartling stimuli (called *prepulses*) are presented shortly before startle-eliciting stimuli. Different SEM effects can be observed depending on the temporal "lead interval" between the onset of the prepulse and onset of the startle stimulus. When the lead interval is short (approximately in the range of 30–500 msec for auditory prepulses, and slightly longer for visual and tactile prepulses), there is reliable reduction of the startle response amplitude compared to when the reflex is elicited in the absence of the prepulse. This phenomenon is well-documented in both animals and humans and is called prepulse inhibition (PPI). In contrast, when the lead interval is long (typically greater than 1,000 msec), the amplitude of the startle reflex can be either enhanced or inhibited depending on other factors (e.g., attention to, and affective valance of, the prepulse). The latency of the startle reflex also can be modified by the presence of a prepulse, but space limitations preclude discussion of those effects in this chapter.

SEM has attracted wide research interest because it has the potential to shed light on a number of important psychological processes, such as attention and emotion. That is, the direction and amount of reflex modification can serve as involuntary, nonverbal indices of the psychological processes elicited by the prepulse (attention/inattention or positive/negative affect). Moreover, because similar paradigms can be applied to both human and animal subjects, assessment of SEM has the potential to shed light on psychological processes at very different levels of analysis. For example, similar startle modification paradigms can be used to study both the neurotransmitters involved in PPI in rats and the attentional modulation of PPI in schizophrenia patients.

The primary focus of this chapter is on the applicability of SEM to psychopathology, particularly PPI in schizophrenia. In order to meaningfully discuss the applicability of SEM to clinical science, we first briefly review the relation of SEM to cognitive science, and we close by presenting some of the implications for neuroscience.

COGNITIVE SCIENCE

Cognitive science, in its broadest sense, is a multidisciplinary effort to understand the component processes involved in how organisms process information. Most theoretical models of information processing distinguish between early automatic/preattentive processing of information and later controlled/attentional processing (e.g., Shiffrin, 1988; Shiffrin & Schneider, 1977). Automatic processing is seen as occurring quickly, independent of attention, without requiring intention, and without conscious awareness. In contrast, controlled processing occurs relatively slowly, is dependent on limited attentional resources, is under intentional control, and is associated with conscious awareness.

Graham related the short and long lead interval SEM effects to the "automatic" versus "controlled" processing distinction. The short lead interval PPI effect was hypothesized to reflect an automatic, involuntary, preattentive inhibitory process that functions to protect the initial process-

ing of the prepulse by dampening the effects of other concurrent or immediately following events, such as a startle stimulus (Graham, 1975, 1980).
Long lead interval SEM effects, in contrast, were seen as reflecting a more
controlled orienting-attentional process as well as automatic activation.

For long lead interval effects, the important role of controlled attentive
processes has been confirmed by research conducted in the nearly two
decades since the proposal of the Graham hypotheses (see reviews by
Anthony, 1985; Graham, 1992; Putnam, 1990). Generally speaking, at long
lead intervals with neutral prepulses, startle amplitude is facilitated if
attention is directed toward the modality of the startle-eliciting stimulus,
but is inhibited if attention is directed away from the modality of the startle-
eliciting stimulus. Thus, SEM at long lead intervals may be either facilitatory or inhibitory depending on the direction of attention, and therefore
may be a sensitive index of sustained modality-selective attention.

For short lead interval prepulse inhibition, two lines of research conducted since Graham's proposal have provided support for the protection-
of-processing function of PPI. One line of evidence comes from subjects'
estimates of the intensity of a startle-eliciting stimulus when it is presented
following a prepulse and in the absence of a prepulse. Cohen, Hoffman,
and Stitt (1981) and Perlstein, Fiorito, Simons, and Graham (1993) reported
that subjects judge a startling stimulus to be less intense when it is preceded
by a prepulse than when it is not, a finding consistent with the notion that
the prepulse momentarily reduces the impact of subsequent stimuli.

The second line of evidence supporting the protection-of-processing
hypothesis comes from studies that evaluate the accuracy of subjects'
perceptions of the prepulse stimulus itself. The logic underlying these
experiments is that if PPI serves to protect the perceptual processing of
the prepulse, then the presence of PPI should reduce any interfering
effects of a startle-eliciting stimulus on perception of the prepulse. In one
test of this hypothesis, Filion and Ciranni (1996) presented subjects with
four stimulus conditions: a prepulse stimulus alone, a startling stimulus
alone, the prepulse followed by the startling stimulus at a lead interval
of 120 msec, and the prepulse followed by the startling stimulus at a lead
interval of 500 msec. Subjects were asked to rate the intensity of the
prepulse under both the paired and the nonpaired conditions.

The results of this procedure revealed significant PPI of the startle eyeblink at both the 120 msec and 500 msec lead intervals, with greater PPI
at the 120 msec lead interval. In addition, the prepulse in paired conditions
was rated as significantly louder than it was in the nonpaired condition
for both lead intervals. This result indicates that in the paired conditions,
the intensity of the startling stimulus was blended with that of the low-
intensity prepulse, a phenomenon referred to as *loudness assimilation*. Of
greatest importance for the protection-of-processing hypothesis, Filion

and Ciranni observed a significant correlation between PPI magnitude and the amount of interference. For the 120 msec lead interval, subjects who exhibited the most PPI experienced the least interference from the startling stimulus, and subjects who exhibited the least PPI experienced the most interference. This finding suggests that PPI does play a role in the protection of the perceptual analysis of the prepulse, as hypothesized by Graham.

In addition to supporting the protection-of-processing hypothesis, recent research has also suggested a greater role of controlled attentional processes in PPI than originally envisioned (e.g., DelPezzo & Hoffman, 1980; Filion, Dawson, & Schell, 1993; Hackley & Graham, 1987; Hoffman, chapter 8, this volume). Filion et al. (1993), for example, used a differential tone-duration-judgment paradigm that was originally devised to study attentional processes associated with skin conductance orienting (Dawson, Filion, & Schell, 1989). College student subjects were presented an intermixed series of tones of two different pitches and were instructed to count the number of longer than usual occurrences (i.e., 7 sec rather than 5 sec) of one particular pitch and to simply ignore the other pitch. The purpose of this differential attention task was to require subjects to perform a series of different cognitive operations following the two different tones: (a) to first preattentively detect and discriminate the to-be-attended tone from the to-be-ignored tone; (b) to then allocate additional controlled processing resources necessary to confirm the identity of the tone and begin the duration-judgment task; and (c) finally, to sustain selective attention to the to-be-attended tone throughout its duration in order to determine its length and perform the required timing task.

Subjects in the Filion et al. (1993) study were instructed that a brief loud noise would be presented occasionally throughout the tone-duration-judgment task, but that the noise was unrelated to their task and could be ignored. In fact, the loud noises were used to elicit startle eye-blinks at specified lead intervals following the to-be-attended tones and the to-be-ignored tones. As summarized in the upper portion of Fig. 11.1, the noise was presented during some of the intertone intervals in order to provide a baseline measure of startle blink amplitude, and at 60, 120, 240, and 2,000 msec following both the to-be-attended and to-be-ignored tones in a semirandom unpredictable order. In effect, three short lead intervals were employed to measure the time course of PPI, and one long lead interval was used to measure sustained attention effects.

The main portion of Fig. 11.1 summarizes the SEM results of the Filion et al. (1993) study. As shown, significant PPI occurred at all three short lead intervals, with greater inhibition following the to-be-attended tone than the to-be-ignored tone at the 120 msec lead interval. Significant facilitation of startle also occurred at the 2,000 msec long lead interval, with significantly

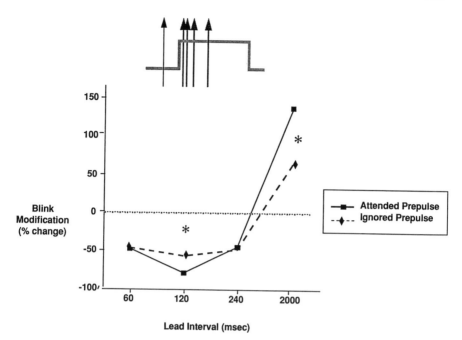

FIG. 11.1. Mean startle eyeblink modification scores as a function of prepulse type and lead interval in a group of unselected college students. (Asterisks indicate significant differences between to-be-attended and to-be-ignored prepulses.) Adapted from Filion et al. (1993).

greater facilitation following the to-be-attended tone than the to-be-ignored tone. These basic results have since been replicated and extended in five independent samples (Dawson, Hazlett, Filion, Nuechterlein, & Schell, 1993; Filion, Dawson, & Schell, 1994; Jennings, Schell, Filion, & Dawson, 1996; Schell, Dawson, Hazlett, & Filion, 1995; Seljos, Dawson, Filion, & Schell, 1994).

Conclusion

All in all, the results clearly demonstrate that both short and long lead interval SEM effects can be modulated by cognitive processes. As summarized in Fig. 11.2, four cognitively relevant processes are hypothesized to modulate startle reflexes in the tone-duration-judgment paradigm: (a) automatic stimulus detection and identification occur quickly following stimulus onset, and are hypothesized to be the dominant cognitive processes affecting PPI at the 60 msec lead interval; (b) in addition to automatic protection of processing, controlled attentional modulation of processing is engaged following automatic stimulus detection and identification, and is hypothesized to modulate PPI at the 120 msec lead interval following the

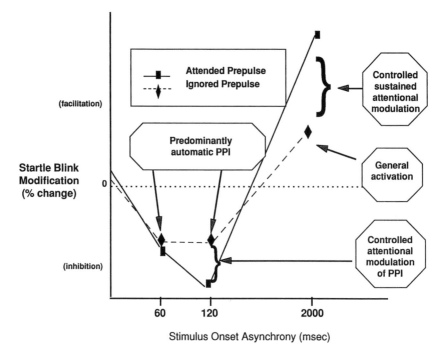

FIG. 11.2. Cognitively relevant processes hypothesized to mediate SEM at very short lead intervals (60 msec), medium short lead intervals (120 msec), and long lead intervals (2,000 msec) when tested in the tone-duration-judgment paradigm.

to-be-attended prepulse; (c) general activation and arousal are hypothesized to be present at the long lead interval; and (d) in addition to general activation, sustained modality-selective attention to the auditory modality is hypothesized to be the dominant cognitive process ongoing at the long lead interval following the to-be-attended prepulse. The long lead interval effects are entirely consistent with Graham's early hypotheses, and the short lead interval effects are consistent with and elaborate on these hypotheses. The specific time requirements associated with these processes are probably affected by both the characteristics of the task (e.g., complexity) and the characteristics of the subjects (e.g., amount of attentional resources available). However, the same processes presumably are engaged in the same order by a wide variety of tasks.

CLINICAL SCIENCE

Because the SEM paradigm, particularly PPI, potentially allows the separate measurement of both automatic and controlled processes without verbal or voluntary responses on the part of the subject, it is ideally suited for investigating cognitive dysfunctions in psychopathologies for which such dysfunctions are central. Schizophrenia is a prime example of such a psychopathology.

According to the *Diagnostic and Statistical Manual of Mental Disorders* (*DSM–IV*, American Psychiatric Association, 1994), many of the core defining symptoms of schizophrenia are cognitive (e.g., bizarre delusions) or perceptual (e.g., auditory hallucinations) in nature. In the early stages of the illness, the cognitive impairments are frequently reported as an inability to screen irrelevant stimuli and focus on relevant stimuli. For example, in a now classic series of interviews reported by McGhie and Chapman (1961), one patient reported: "If I am talking to someone they only need to cross their legs or scratch their heads and I am distracted and forget what I was saying" (p. 104). Another stated that "If there are three or four people talking at the same time I can't take it in. I would not be able to hear what they are saying properly and I would get the one mixed up with the other" (pp. 105–106).

Although there is general agreement about the presence of cognitive impairments in schizophrenia, there is considerable disagreement about the precise nature of the cognitive deficits. For example, some investigators suggest that individuals with schizophrenia suffer from primary deficits in controlled attentional processes, whereas others hypothesize that the primary cognitive deficits are in the early automatic, preattentive stages of information processing (see Dawson, Schell, Hazlett, Filion, & Nuechterlein, 1995, for elaboration). The study of short lead interval PPI may be ideally suited for distinguishing between these theoretical positions, given that it can potentially provide nonverbal separate measures of controlled and automatic processes.

In the first studies of PPI and schizophrenia (Braff, Grillon, & Geyer, 1992; Braff et al., 1978; Grillon, Ameli, Charney, Kristal, & Braff, 1992), hospitalized inpatients with schizophrenia were presented auditory prepulses followed by either auditory or tactile startling stimuli at various lead intervals in a passive attention paradigm (i.e., subjects were not explicitly instructed to attend to, or perform any task with, the stimuli). Each of these studies found significantly less PPI in patients than in normal controls across short lead intervals ranging between 30 and 120 msec, with auditory prepulses ranging in intensity from 71 to 90 dB(A), and with both auditory and tactile startling stimuli. Authors of these early studies concluded that patients with schizophrenia have poor automatic, preattentive sensorimotor gating mechanisms that can lead to sensory overload, thought disorder, and perhaps other psychotic symptoms. Moreover, the deficit in central inhibition and gating mechanisms was hypothesized to be a trait-linked permanent deficit (Braff & Geyer, 1990).

All three initial studies of PPI in schizophrenia used a passive attention paradigm. As reviewed previously, however, more recent evidence indicates that instructions to attend to the prepulses can enhance the size of the PPI effect at the 120 msec lead interval in normal subjects. If the underlying process in the tone-duration-judgment paradigm at 60 msec reflects predominately automatic processes, whereas the underlying process at 120 msec involves additional allocation of controlled processes, then this active attention PPI paradigm should be capable of shedding light on the nature of the cognitive dysfunctions in schizophrenia.

In order to test this possibility, Dawson, Hazlett, Filion, Nuechterlein, and Schell (1993) tested schizophrenia outpatients and matched normal controls with the active differential attention tone-duration-judgment paradigm. The schizophrenia subjects were outpatients at a large metropolitan hospital-based clinic and were or had been participants in a longitudinal study of the early phases of schizophrenia (Nuechterlein et al., 1992). The first psychotic episode began an average of 2.9 years before SEM testing; thus, the patients were in the relatively early phases of schizophrenia without a long history of medication and institutionalization. It is also important to note that the outpatients were relatively asymptomatic at the time of testing, as assessed by independent ratings on an expanded version of the Brief Psychiatric Rating Scale (Lukoff, Nuechterlein, & Ventura, 1986; Overall & Gorham, 1962). Therefore, any observed SEM impairments are not likely to be secondary effects of concurrent psychotic symptoms. Normal control subjects also were drawn from participants in the longitudinal research project and were matched to the outpatients on age, sex, race, and educational level.

Figure 11.3 shows the SEM results for the matched normal controls and the outpatients with schizophrenia. The normal controls show the same effects as did the college students: significantly greater PPI 120 msec following the to-be-attended prepulse, and significantly greater startle facilitation 2,000 msec following the to-be-attended prepulse, compared to the to-be-ignored prepulse. It is important to note that the control subjects in this study were not typical college students; they were demographically matched to the patients and therefore were typically males in their early 20s with a high school education, indicating that the attentional effects on SEM are replicable and generalizable beyond college student populations.

In contrast, the schizophrenia patients failed to show attentional modulation of either short lead interval PPI at 120 msec or long lead interval facilitation at 2,000 msec. However, the patients did show normal PPI at 60 and 120 msec, and normal facilitation at 2,000 msec, during the to-be-ignored prepulse. Thus, the primary conclusion suggested by these findings is that relatively asymptomatic outpatients with schizophrenia exhibit deficits in controlled attentional modulation of SEM, but not in automatic components of SEM, when tested with a paradigm requiring differential attention. This conclusion is based on our hypothesis that SEM at the very short lead interval (e.g., 60 msec) following the prepulses

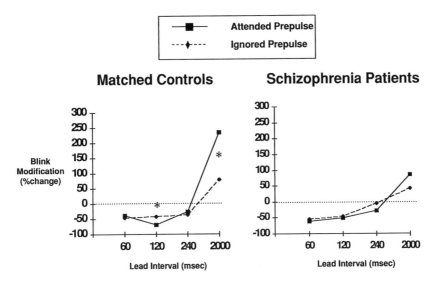

FIG. 11.3. Mean startle eyeblink modification scores as a function of prepulse type and lead interval for the demographically matched control subjects (left panel) and the schizophrenia patients (right panel). (Asterisks indicate significant differences between to-be-attended and to-be-ignored prepulses.) Adapted from Dawson et al., 1993. Copyright © 1993 by the American Psychological Association. Adapted with permission.

reflects primarily automatic information processing, whereas SEM at 120 msec and 2,000 msec following to-be-attended prepulses reflects both automatic and controlled information processing. Moreover, obtaining these findings in relatively asymptomatic schizophrenia outpatients suggests that the impairments in the "controlled" modulation of SEM are not merely secondary correlates of severe psychotic symptoms.

Dawson et al. (1993) concluded that "relatively asymptomatic outpatients are not measurably deficient in the early pre-attentive stimulus detection and evaluation process; rather, they are deficient in the allocation of controlled resources at 120 ms to evaluate the to-be-attended prepulse and in focused, sustained controlled attention at 2000 ms" (p. 639). How can this conclusion be reconciled with the findings and interpretations of the earlier studies that the schizophrenia deficit is one of the automatic preattentive sensorimotor gating mechanisms? There were important procedural and patient differences between the Dawson et al. study and the earlier studies that may account for the different conclusions. Perhaps the most important procedural difference was that Dawson et al. required active attention on the part of the subjects, whereas the earlier studies employed a passive attention paradigm. Requiring active attention may alter the underlying processes such that automatic deficits are no longer detectable; instead only controlled processing impairments are apparent. The most important difference in patient samples appears to be that the Dawson et al. outpatients were in a remitted phase of schizophrenia, whereas the inpatients in the earlier studies were more actively psychotic. It is conceivable that the apparent deficit of automatic preattentive gating in the earlier studies reflects brain processes that accompany active psychotic symptoms. Consistent with this hypothesis, reduced PPI in a passive attention startle session has been reported in psychotic patients with temporal lobe epilepsy, compared to nonpsychotic patients with temporal lobe epilepsy (Morton et al., 1994). However, active psychosis is not a necessary condition for reduced "automatic" gating in a passive startle session, because a significant reduction in passive PPI was also noted by Cadenhead, Geyer, and Braff (1993) in nonpsychotic patients with schizotypal personality disorder. Furthermore, reduced passive PPI has been noted in several other nonpsychotic clinical populations. Thus, one must conclude that there is evidence that both the automatic and controlled modulation of SEM may provide nonverbal, reflexive, state-independent markers of an underlying vulnerability to psychosis.

If impaired PPI is related to a basic vulnerability to psychosis, then it should also be present in nonclinical populations that are vulnerable but not psychotic. One putatively vulnerable "psychosis-prone" nonclinical population includes individuals who experience extreme Perceptual Aberrations and/or Magical Ideation (Chapman & Chapman, 1987; Chapman, Chapman, Kwapil, Eckblad, & Zinser, 1994). Perceptual Aberrators endorse schizophrenia-like perceptual distortions (e.g., "Occasionally, it has seemed as if my body had taken on the appearance of another person's body."). Magical Ideators endorse beliefs in forms of causation that are generally considered magical (e.g., "Sometimes people can make me aware of them just by thinking about me."). Paper-and-pencil true–false questionnaires developed for these two putative vulnerability traits are positively correlated and, following the recommendation of Chapman and Chapman (1987), investigators combine high-scoring subjects on these scales into a single group called "Per-Mag." As hypothesized, Per-Mag college students exceed normal scoring control subjects on rate of diagnosis of psychosis at a 10-year follow up (Chapman et al., 1994).

Studies of PPI with a passive attention paradigm with Per-Mag college students have produced conflicting results. Simons and Giardina (1992) found that Per-Mags exhibited less PPI than normal controls at a 120 msec lead interval, but not at 60 msec. Perlstein, Fiorito, Simons, and Graham (1989), in contrast, found impaired PPI among Per-Mag college students at a 500 msec lead interval, but not at 120 msec. Cadenhead and Braff (1992) found no differences in PPI between Per-Mags and normal controls at 30, 60, or 120 msec lead intervals, and Blumenthal and Creps

(1994) also failed to find deficiencies in PPI at either 60 or 120 msec lead intervals in Per-Mag college students. Finally, Lipp, Siddle, and Arnold (1994) failed to find differences between high- and low-scoring college students on the Perceptual Aberration Scale across a wide variety of lead intervals, including 120 msec. Thus, at best there seems to be weak and inconsistent evidence of impaired PPI in Per-Mag subjects tested with the passive attention paradigm.

In contrast to those studies that employed a passive attention paradigm, Schell et al. (1995) tested Per-Mag college students using the differential attention tone-duration-judgment paradigm described previously. As shown in Fig. 11.4, the normal controls exhibited enhanced PPI at 120 msec following the to-be-attended prepulse and enhanced SEM facilitation at 2,000 msec following the to-be-attended prepulse, consistent with earlier described normal groups. The Per-Mag subjects failed to show attentional modulation of either PPI at 120 msec or startle facilitation at 2,000 msec, similar to the schizophrenia patients. These results suggest that the impaired attentional modulation of SEM may be a vulnerability marker because it is present in individuals who are neither psychotic nor medicated, but who are hypothesized to be vulnerable to psychosis. Also

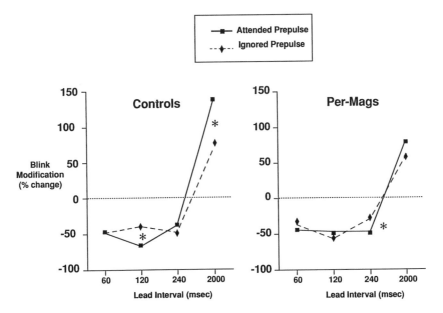

FIG. 11.4. Mean startle eyeblink modification scores as a function of prestimulus type and lead interval for normal college students (left panel) and Per-Mag college students (right panel). (Asterisks indicate significant differences between to-be-attended and to-be-ignored prepulses.) Adapted from Schell et al. (1995).

similar to findings with schizophrenia outpatients, no evidence of deficits in automatic processing was found (i.e., PPI was normal at the 60 msec lead interval). Unlike the patients, however, the Per-Mags did show attentional modulation of PPI at 240 msec, suggesting that the controlled processing effect may be slower to develop than in normal controls, rather than completely absent.

In another approach to assessing gating deficits in a nonclinical population that exhibits some cognitive features characteristic of schizophrenia, Swerdlow, Filion, Geyer, and Braff (1995) examined passive PPI in subjects recruited from the community whose profile on the Minnesota Multiphasic Personality Inventory (MMPI) is considered "psychosis-prone" based on previously published criteria (Butler, Jenkins, & Braff, 1993). Compared to controls, PPI measured at a 60 msec lead interval was significantly reduced in the MMPI-defined "psychosis prone" group. Thus, it is possible that automatic preattentive gating impairments are linked to particular traits similar to schizophrenia symptoms. The presence of schizophrenia-like traits appears to be associated with relatively reduced PPI even in nonclinical populations in the absence of psychosis or overt thought disorder.

A clinical population of patients thought to possess vulnerability factors similar to those of schizophrenia patients is that diagnosed with schizotypal personality disorder (Siever, Kalus, & Keefe, 1993). These patients manifest symptoms in the schizophrenia spectrum, but to a less severe degree than those diagnosed with schizophrenia. As noted previously, Cadenhead et al. (1993) reported abnormally reduced PPI in schizotypal patients tested with a passive paradigm. Thus, schizotypal patients exhibit impairments in passive PPI similar to those reported by Braff and his colleagues in the early studies with schizophrenia patients.

There also are several clinical populations who exhibit no overt psychotic symptoms, yet whose passive PPI is significantly reduced compared to matched controls. Reduced PPI has been reported in patients with Huntington's Disease (Swerdlow, Paulson et al., 1995), Obsessive Compulsive Disorder (Swerdlow, Benbow, Zisook, Geyer, & Braff, 1993), Temporal Lobe Epilepsy (Morton et al., 1994), Tourette Syndrome with Attention Deficit Hyperactivity Disorder (Castellanos et al., 1996), Nocturnal Enuresis (Ornitz, Hanna, & de Traversay, 1992), and in patients with Parkinson's Disease after the administration of L-DOPA (Morton et al., 1995). The clinical manifestations of these disorders include symptoms of anxiety, depression, dementia, tics, and bed wetting. Despite the common loss of "preattentive" gating capacity as measured by passive PPI, these disorders share very few clinical characteristics. Thus, clinical data do not support the linkage of reduced preattentive gating with a specific set of psychiatric symptoms.

How can we understand impaired automatic gating processes in disorders that are characterized by such a broad range of symptoms? From a phenomenological standpoint, disorders that are characterized by reduced PPI are linked by a reduced ability to inhibit or gate sensory, motor, or cognitive information. Thus, patients with schizophrenia or temporal lobe epilepsy with psychosis are unable to inhibit irrelevant or intrusive sensory and cognitive information, Huntington's Disease patients are unable to inhibit adventitious movements, patients with Obsessive Compulsive Disorder cannot suppress intrusive obsessions, patients with Tourette Syndrome cannot inhibit sensory, vocal, or motor tics, and patients with Nocturnal Enuresis cannot inhibit a motor response to visceral sensory information. (See Brunia, chapter 12, this volume, for a discussion of gating in the motor system.) From a neuroanatomical standpoint, the relative reduction in passive PPI exhibited by all of these patient groups may reflect a defect in a common automatic "gating circuitry." Defects at different levels of this gating circuitry may be responsible for the differences in the clinical presentations of these disorders, whereas the common loss of PPI among these disorders may reflect the modulation of the startle reflex by a final common output of this gating circuitry. Whether some or all of these clinical groups also would exhibit impairments in attentional modulation of prepulse inhibition, in addition to impaired passive prepulse inhibition, has not yet been tested.

Conclusion

There is evidence of impaired PPI observable in a passive attention paradigm in several populations of patients, including schizophrenia, schizotypal personality disorder, and in nonpatient populations with MMPI-defined at-risk "psychosis-prone" profiles. These results suggest that deficits in automatic preattentive gating mechanisms are related to the long-term vulnerability to schizophrenia. There also is evidence of impaired attentional modulation of PPI in an active attention paradigm in schizophrenia outpatients and in putatively at-risk Per-Mag college students. The latter results suggest that deficits in controlled attentional mechanisms also are related to the long-term vulnerability to schizophrenia.

How automatic and controlled modulation of PPI are related is an important question in need of research. No study to date has directly compared automatic PPI in a passive attention paradigm with controlled modulation of PPI in an active attention paradigm with a clinical population. Such a comparison would determine whether different subgroups exhibit deficits in automatic and controlled modulation of PPI, or whether the two types of impairments are positively correlated. It is possible that impaired preattentively mediated PPI and impaired attentively modulated

PPI have different phenomenological correlates, and reflect dysfunctions at different levels of the neurophysiological gating circuitry. We turn next to an examination of that circuitry, evidence that comes from systematic studies of the neurobiology of the startle reflex and of PPI.

NEUROSCIENCE

Figure 11.5 shows the hypothesized neurophysiological circuits of the basic acoustic startle reflex and the prepulse inhibition of startle. This figure represents a synthesis of findings by various investigators, including David Braff, Michael Davis, Mark Geyer, Michael Koch, Donald Leitner, Neal Swerdlow, and others. It is important to note that our understanding of this circuitry comes largely from studies of whole body startle with nonhuman subjects, and evidence that similar circuitry modulates startle eyeblink and PPI in humans is scarce. In fact, as noted by Hackley and Boelhouwer (chapter 9, this volume), the latency of the human startle eyeblink reflex is substantially longer than the rat forelimb-flexion reflex (approximately 40 msec vs. 8 msec), and therefore the circuit is likely to be more complicated. Nevertheless, we are able to demonstrate some cross-species similarities. For instance, reduced PPI of the human eyeblink reflex has been found in Huntington's Disease patients, and in rats with cellular lesions of the striatum that mimic to some degree the pathophysiology of Huntington's Disease. Thus, there is cross-species evidence that the striatum regulates PPI in both rats and humans. Similar cross-species conclusions can be drawn regarding brain dopamine (DA) systems. Nonetheless, particularly as it applies to pontine elements of the primary startle circuit, practically all of our understanding of the neural substrates may apply only to rats. Furthermore, because of space limitations, the model is discussed only with respect to short lead interval PPI with acoustic prepulses and startle pulses, although structures such as the amygdala are known to be involved in long lead interval effects such as fear potentiation of startle (Davis, Falls, Campeau, & Kim, 1993; see also chapter 4 by Davis in this volume).

The "primary" mammalian acoustic startle circuit, as first reported in detail by Davis, Gendelman, Tischler, and Gendelman (1982), included connections linking the auditory nerve, the ventral cochlear nucleus (VCN), an area near the ventral nucleus of the lateral lemniscus (VLL), the nucleus reticularis pontis caudalis (NRPC), and the motor neuron (see hindbrain portion of Fig. 11.5). More recent evidence, however, suggests an even simpler circuit. Specifically, it has been shown that cochlear root neurons embedded in the auditory nerve receive input from the cochlea and have direct input to the NRPC (Lee, Lopez, Meloni, & Davis, 1996;

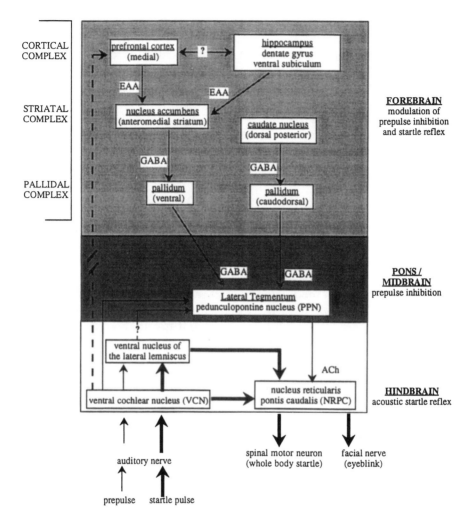

FIG. 11.5. Neural substrates regulating the elicitation and prepulse inhibition of acoustic startle in rats. This is a noninclusive schematic representation of cortical, striatal, and pallidal circuitry that regulate the pontine circuitry (the pedunculopontine tegmental nucleus) that appears to mediate prepulse inhibition, and the primary startle circuit that mediates the actual startle reflex. Neurotransmitters are indicated where known (EAA = excitatory amino acid; ACh = acetylcholine; GABA = gamma-amino-butyric acid). Other structures, pathways, and neurotransmitters that are believed to regulate prepulse inhibition are omitted from this diagram for simplicity, but are described in the text. Connections or regions that are not definite, or which are implicated as elements of the primary startle circuit in some, but not other studies, are marked by a "?." The dashed line illustrates a speculative indirect connection that may be critical for the attentional modulation of PPI. (See text for further details.)

Lingenhohl & Friauf, 1994). Thus, there is evidence that the "primary" acoustic startle circuit consists simply of the cochlear root neurons, the NRPC, and the motoneurons, although additional pathways such as those depicted in Fig. 11.5 probably exist and converge at some point with this simple pathway (Lee et al., 1996).

Because PPI in the rat is evident with lead intervals as short as 15 msec, the circuitry that mediates the inhibitory effect of the prepulse on the startle reflex cannot deviate from the primary startle circuit by more than a few neurons. One likely scenario shown in Fig. 11.5 is that the first acoustic stimulus (the "prepulse") activates the VCN and pedunculopontine nucleus (PPN). The PPN cells then send inhibitory signals to the NRPC via a cholinergic pathway (Koch, Kungel, & Herbert, 1993). The result is that the response of the NRPC to a subsequent startling stimulus is reduced. Thus, the circuitry that mediates PPI is likely very simple and is integrally related to the "primary" startle circuit.

Numerous studies have demonstrated, however, that this simple "PPI circuit" is regulated, or modulated, by higher brain circuitry that descends into the PPN. Changes in the activity of the forebrain circuitry, transmitted to the PPN, appear to "set the gain" for PPI. It is certainly possible that startle circuitry within the pons is regulated by direct, monosynaptic projections from limbic cortical regions. This mechanism is most likely applicable to the regulation of fear-potentiated startle by amygdalo-pontine projections (Davis et al., 1993), but similar circuitry may be relevant to other forms of startle plasticity, including PPI. Empirical data also clearly suggest that PPI is regulated by sequential, or segmental, connections between the cortical complex and the pontine reticular formation. As depicted in the forebrain portion of Fig. 11.5, this "indirect" forebrain regulation of PPI appears to involve, at least, cortical inputs to the striatum, striatal connections with the pallidum (globus pallidus), and pallidal inputs to the PPN.

Regulation of PPI by forebrain areas may be the mechanism by which controlled attentional modulation of PPI occurs, whereas regulation by lower subcortical structures may account for the automatic preattentive PPI effects. Two cortical regions that are known to modulate PPI in rats are the medial prefrontal cortex (MPFC; Bubser & Koch, 1994; Koch & Bubser, 1994; Swerdlow et al., 1995) and the hippocampus (Caine, Geyer, & Swerdlow, 1992; Swerdlow et al., 1995; Swerdlow, Wan, & Caine, 1993; Wan, Geyer, & Swerdlow, 1995). Dopamine activity in the MPFC appears to provide a facilitatory regulation of PPI, perhaps via secondary effects on subcortical dopamine activity (Bubser & Koch, 1994). The mechanisms by which the hippocampus regulates PPI are not fully understood, but may involve hippocampal glutamatergic efferents to the nucleus accumbens (Wan et al., 1995).

The hippocampal substrates of deficient PPI identified by this animal model may provide a functional context for interpreting reports of hippocampal dysfunction in schizophrenia based on neuropsychological (Gray, Feldon, Rawlins, Hemsley, & Smith, 1991), neuropathological (Altshuler, Conrad, Kovelman, & Scheibel, 1987), and neuroimaging studies (Suddath, Christison, Torrey, Cassanova, & Weinberger, 1990). Furthermore, the hippocampal substrate links PPI with electrophysiological measures such as P50 gating, which is believed to reflect hippocampal function and is deficient in patients with schizophrenia and asymptomatic first-degree relatives (Siegel, Waldo, Mizner, Adler, & Freedman, 1984).

Substantial evidence supports the regulation of PPI by the nucleus accumbens (NAC). This regulation includes both dopaminergic and glutamatergic substrates (Reijmers, Vanderheyden, & Peeters, 1995; Swerdlow, Geyer, Braff, & Koob, 1986; Wan et al., 1995). By one proposed mechanism, hippocampal or MPFC glutamate efferents to the NAC may regulate PPI via facilitatory effects on NAC dopaminergic transmission (Wan et al., 1995).

Both preclinical and clinical data support a role for the dorsal striatum in the regulation of PPI. In rats, when the dorsal striatum is depleted of DA, the PPI-reducing effects of the DA agonist apomorphine are magnified (Swerdlow et al., 1986). A similar phenomenon is apparently evident in patients with Parkinson's Disease, who experience a loss of DA in the dorsal striatum, and who exhibit an increased sensitivity to the PPI-disruptive effects of DA agonists (Morton et al., in press). In rats, PPI is also reduced by cell-specific lesions of the dorsal posterior caudate nucleus (Kodsi & Swerdlow, 1995). This effect may be analogous to the loss of PPI in patients with Huntington's Disease, who experience a progressive degeneration of the caudate nucleus, with earliest cell loss in dorsal posterior regions (Swerdlow, Paulsen et al., 1995).

It has been proposed that decreased PPI after NAC DA activation reflects decreased activity in GABAergic fibers projecting from the NAC to the ventral pallidum (Kodsi & Swerdlow, 1994; Swerdlow, Braff, & Geyer, 1990; Swerdlow, Caine, & Geyer, 1992). Recent studies also demonstrate a regulation of PPI by the caudal-dorsal pallidum (Kodsi & Swerdlow, 1995). Interestingly, both the ventral pallidum and the caudal-dorsal pallidum innervate the pedunculopontine nucleus (PPN).

The reduction in PPI that accompanies decreased pallidal GABA activity may reflect information translated to the primary startle circuit via pallidal efferents to the PPN (Swanson, Mogenson, Gerfen, & Robinson, 1984). Cells in the region of the PPN innervate the NRPC, and may thus provide the final linkage of the prepulse circuit with the primary startle circuit. Lesions of the PPN significantly reduce PPI in rats (Leitner, Powers, Stitt, & Hoffman, 1981; Swerdlow & Geyer, 1993). Preliminary reports suggest that there may be PPN abnormalities in some schizophrenia patients (Karson et al., 1991), indicating that dysfunction even in this most "distal" end of this neurophysiological circuit might contribute to reduced PPI in schizophrenia patients.

Conclusion

The findings reviewed in this section give support for the role of cortico-striato-pallido-pontine circuitry in modulating PPI in rats. As indicated, only limited data suggest that similar circuitry regulates PPI in humans, and perhaps even less evidence exists to suggest that rodents and humans share similar substrates for the primary startle reflex. Nevertheless, the potential utility of PPI in elaborating the functional interconnections of limbic-cortical and mesolimbic-subpallidal circuitry, and the relevance of this circuitry to the pathophysiology of psychiatric disorders (Gray et al., 1991; Swerdlow & Koob, 1987), underscores the importance of the PPI paradigm to behavioral neuroscience in general, and to the understanding of the neural basis of several forms of psychopathology.

DIRECTIONS FOR FUTURE RESEARCH

Evidence reviewed in this chapter strongly suggests that SEM generally can shed light on cognitive and physiological processes in their normal and abnormal aspects. However, more than being useful *within* the arenas of cognitive science, clinical science, and neuroscience, SEM may prove to be a powerful measure with which to integrate *across* these various domains of scientific inquiry. For example, not only may PPI distinguish automatic from controlled cognitive processes and therefore be useful within cognitive psychology, the different neurophysiological mechanisms underlying these cognitive processes also can be investigated, and the combined neurocognitive entity can be related to impairments in psychopathology. Psychophysiological approaches to psychopathology may help integrate cognitive science, clinical science, and neuroscience (Dawson, 1990), and SEM is potentially a key tool in this integrative enterprise. More speculatively, one can imagine startle modification playing a important role in the development of a new specialty called "applied cognitive neuroscience."

There is much to do before this imagined role of SEM in this imagined specialty becomes a reality. At the most basic level, research is needed to determine optimal methods of recording, scoring, and quantifying SEM, and standardization of techniques must be developed, agreed on, and adopted. At a more conceptual level, the psychophysiological significance of SEM needs to be better understood. Although much progress has been made, the field is only at the beginning of this understanding. One way to enhance that understanding is to interrelate SEM measures with other physiological, behavioral, and phenomenological measures. For example, do subjects with poor PPI show poor orienting responses to the prepulse, more distractibility, and/or less P50 ERP suppression, as suggested by contemporary sensorimotor gating hypotheses? Is the modulation of startle solely on the motor limb, as suggested by the neurophysiological model presented here, or does it also affect the afferent limb as suggested by the protection-of-processing hypothesis? How are automatic and controlled modulatory processes related to each other, and how do they interact with each other? Questions such as these need to be answered for SEM to realize its full potential to contribute to cognitive science, clinical science, and neuroscience. If future research continues to support these areas of application, we expect that the remarkable growth of interest in SEM initiated by Graham and her colleagues is only the beginning.

ACKNOWLEDGMENTS

M. Dawson, A. Schell, and D. Filion were supported by research Grant MH46433, and N. Swerdlow was supported by research Grants MH42228 and MH48381 from the National Institute of Mental Health. M. Dawson also was supported by a Research Scientist Development Award (1 KO2 MH01086) from the National Institute of Mental Health during preparation of this chapter.

The authors thank Kimberle Seljos and Sandra Navarre for their helpful comments on earlier drafts of this chapter.

REFERENCES

Altshuler, L. L., Conrad, A., Kovelman, J. A., & Scheibel, A. (1987). Hippocampal pyramidal cell orientation in schizophrenia. *Archives of General Psychiatry, 44*, 1094–1098.
American Psychiatric Association. (1994). *Diagnostic and statistical manual of mental disorders* (4th ed.). Washington, DC: Author.
Anthony, B. J. (1985). In the blink of an eye: Implications of reflex modification for information processing. In P. K. Ackles, J. R. Jennings, & M. G. H. Coles (Eds.), *Advances in psychophysiology* (Vol. 1, pp. 167–218). Greenwich, CT: JAI Press.
Blumenthal, T. D., & Creps, C. L. (1994). Normal startle responding in psychosis-prone college students. *Personality and Individual Differences, 17*, 345–355.
Braff, D. L., & Geyer, M. A. (1990). Sensorimotor gating and schizophrenia: Human and animal model studies. *Archives of General Psychiatry, 47*, 181–188.
Braff, D. L., Grillon, C., & Geyer, M. A. (1992). Gating and habituation of the startle reflex in schizophrenic patients. *Archives of General Psychiatry, 49*, 206–215.

Braff, D. L., Stone C., Callaway, E., Geyer, M., Glick, I., & Bali, L. (1978). Prestimulus effects on human startle reflex in normals and schizophrenics. *Psychophysiology, 15,* 339–343.

Bubser, M., & Koch, M. (1994). Prepulse inhibition of the acoustic startle response of rats is reduced by 6-hydroxydopamine lesions of the medial prefrontal cortex. *Psychopharmacology, 113,* 487–492.

Butler, R. W., Jenkins, M. A., & Braff, D. L. (1993). On the abnormality of normal comparison groups: The identification of psychosis-proneness and substance abuse in putative normal research subjects. *American Journal of Psychiatry, 150,* 1386–1391.

Cadenhead, K., & Braff, D. L. (1992). Which criteria select "psychosis-prone" individuals? *Biological Psychiatry, 31,* 161A–162A.

Cadenhead, K. S., Geyer, M. A., & Braff, D. L. (1993). Impaired startle prepulse inhibition and habituation in schizotypal patients. *American Journal of Psychiatry, 150,* 1862–1867.

Caine, S. B., Geyer, M. A., & Swerdlow, N. R. (1992). Hippocampal modulation of acoustic startle and prepulse inhibition in rats. *Pharmacology, Biochemistry, and Behavior, 43,* 1201–1208.

Castellanos, F. X., Fine, E. J., Kaysen, D. L., Kozuch, P. L., Hamburger, S. D., Rapoport, J. L., & Hallett, M. (1996). Sensorimotor gating in boys with Tourette's Syndrome and Attention Deficit Hyperactivity Disorder. *Biological Psychiatry, 39,* 33–41.

Chapman, L. J., & Chapman, J. P. (1987). The search for symptoms predictive of schizophrenia. *Schizophrenia Bulletin, 13,* 497–503.

Chapman, L. J., Chapman, J. P., Kwapil, T. R., Eckblad, M., & Zinser, M. C. (1994). Putatively psychosis-prone subjects 10 years later. *Journal of Abnormal Psychology, 103,* 171–183.

Cohen, L. H., Hoffman, H. S., & Stitt, C. L. (1981). Sensory magnitude estimation in the context of reflex modification. *Journal of Experimental Psychology: Human Perception and Performance, 7,* 1363–1370.

Davis, M., Falls, W. A., Campeau, S., & Kim, M. (1993). Fear-potentiated startle: A neural and pharmacological analysis. *Behavioral Brain Research, 58,* 175–198.

Davis, M., Gendelman, D., Tischler, M., & Gendelman, P. (1982). A primary acoustic startle circuit: Lesion and stimulation studies. *Journal of Neuroscience, 2,* 791–805.

Dawson, M. (1990). Psychophysiology at the interface of clinical science, cognitive science, and neuroscience. *Psychophysiology, 27,* 243–255.

Dawson, M. E., Filion, D. L., & Schell, A. M. (1989). Is elicitation of the autonomic orienting response associated with allocation of processing resources? *Psychophysiology, 26,* 560–572.

Dawson, M. E., Hazlett, E. A., Filion, D. L., Nuechterlein, K. H., & Schell, A. M. (1993). Attention and schizophrenia: Impaired modulation of the startle reflex. *Journal of Abnormal Psychology, 102,* 633–641.

Dawson, M. E., Schell, A. M., Hazlett, E. A., Filion, D. L., & Nuechterlein, K. H. (1995). Attention, startle eyeblink modification, and psychosis proneness. In A. Raine, T. Lencz, & S. A. Mednick (Eds.), *Schizotypal personality* (pp. 250–271). Cambridge, UK: Cambridge University Press.

DelPezzo, E. M., & Hoffman, H. S. (1980). Attentional factors in the inhibition of a reflex by a visual prestimulus. *Science, 210,* 673–674.

Filion, D. L., & Ciranni, M. (1996). *The functional significance of prepulse inhibition: A test of the protection of processing theory.* Manuscript in preparation.

Filion, D. L., Dawson, M. E., & Schell, A. M. (1993). Modification of the acoustic startle-reflex eyeblink: A tool for investigating early and late attentional processes. *Biological Psychology, 35,* 185–200.

Filion, D. L., Dawson, M. E., & Schell, A. M. (1994). Probing the orienting response with startle modification and secondary reaction time. *Psychophysiology, 31,* 68–78.

Graham, F. K. (1975). The more or less startling effects of weak prestimulation. *Psychophysiology, 12,* 238–248.

Graham, F. K. (1979). Distinguishing among orienting, defense, and startle reflexes. In H. D. Kimmel, E. H. van Olst, & J. F. Orlebeke (Eds.), *The orienting reflex in humans* (pp. 137–167). Hillsdale, NJ: Lawrence Erlbaum Associates.

Graham, F. K. (1980). Control of reflex blink excitability. In R. F. Thompson, L. H. Hicks, & V. B. Shryrkov (Eds.), *Neural mechanisms of goal directed behavior and learning* (pp. 511–519). New York: Academic Press.

Graham, F. K. (1992). Attention: The heartbeat, the blink, and the brain. In B. A. Campbell, H. Hayne, & R. Richardson (Eds.), *Attention and information processing in infants and adults: Perspectives from human and animal research* (pp. 3–29). Hillsdale, NJ: Lawrence Erlbaum Associates.

Gray, J. A., Feldon, J., Rawlins, J. N. P., Hemsley, D. R., & Smith, A. D. (1991). The neuropsychology of schizophrenia. *Behavioral Brain Sciences, 14*, 1–84.

Grillon, C., Ameli, R., Charney, D. S., Kristal, J., & Braff, D. L. (1992). Startle gating deficits occur across prepulse intensities in schizophrenic patients. *Biological Psychiatry, 32*, 939–943.

Hackley, S. A., & Graham, F. K. (1987). Effects of attending selectively to the spatial position of reflex-eliciting and reflex-modulating stimuli. *Journal of Experimental Psychology, 13*, 411–424.

Hoffman, H. S., & Ison, J. R. (1980). Reflex modification in the domain of startle: I. Some empirical findings and their implications for how the nervous system processes sensory input. *Psychological Review, 87*, 175–189.

Jennings, P. D., Schell, A. M., Filion, D. L., & Dawson, M. E. (1996). Tracking early and late stages of information processing: Contributions of startle blink reflex modification. *Psychophysiology, 33*, 148–155.

Karson, C. N., Garcia-Rill, E., Biedermann, J., Mrak, R. E., Husain, M. M., & Skinner, R. D. (1991). The brainstem reticular formation in schizophrenia. *Psychiatry Research, 40*, 31–48.

Koch, M., & Bubser, M. (1994). Deficient sensorimotor gating after 6-hydroxydopamine lesion of the rat medial prefrontal cortex is reversed by haloperidol. *European Journal of Neuroscience, 6*, 1837–1845.

Koch, M., Kungel, M., & Herbert, H. (1993). Cholingeric neurons in the pedunculopontine tegmental nucleus are involved in the mediation of prepulse inhibition of the acoustic startle response in the rat. *Experimental Brain Research, 97*, 71–82.

Kodsi, M., & Swerdlow, N. R. (1994). Quinolinic acid lesions of the ventral striatum reduce sensorimotor gating of acoustic startle in rats. *Brain Research, 643*, 59–65.

Kodsi, M., & Swerdlow, N. R. (1995). Prepulse inhibition in the rat is regulated by ventral and caudo-dorsal striato-pallidal circuitry. *Behavioral Neuroscience, 109*, 912–928.

Lee, Y., Lopez, D. E., Meloni, E. G., & Davis, M. (1996). A primary acoustic startle pathway: Obligatory role of cochlear root neurons and the reticularis pontis caudalis. *Journal of Neuroscience, 16*, 3775–3789.

Leitner, D. S., Powers, A. S., Stitt, C. L., & Hoffman, H. S. (1981). Midbrain reticular formation involvement in the inhibition of acoustic startle. *Physiology and Behavior, 26*, 259–268.

Lingenhohl, K., & Friauf, E. (1994). Giant neurons in the rat reticular formation: A sensorimotor interface in the elementary acoustic startle circuit? *Journal of Neuroscience, 14*, 1176–1194.

Lipp, O. V., Siddle, D. A. T., & Arnold, S. L. (1994). Psychosis proneness in a non-clinical sample: II. A multi-experimental study of "attentional malfunctioning." *Personality and Individual Differences, 17*, 405–424.

Lukoff, D., Nuechterlein, K. H., & Ventura, J. (1986). Appendix A: Manual for expanded Brief Psychiatric Rating Scale (BPRS). *Schizophrenia Bulletin, 12*, 594–602.

McGhie, A., & Chapman, J. (1961). Disorders of attention and perception in early schizophrenia. *British Journal of Medical Psychology, 34*, 102–116.

Morton, N., Chaundauri, R., Ellis, C., Gray, N. S., & Toone, B. K. (1995). The effects of apomorphine and L-dopa challenge on prepulse inhibition in patients with Parkinson's disease. *Schizophrenia Research, 15*, 181–182.

Morton, N., Gray, N. S., Mellers, J., Toone, B., Lishman, W. A., & Gray, J. A. (1994). Prepulse inhibition in temporal lobe epilepsy. *Schizophrenia Research, 11*, 191.

Nuechterlein, K. H., Dawson, M. E., Gitlin, M., Ventura, J., Goldstein, M. J., Snyder, K. S., Yee, C. M., & Mintz, J. (1992). Developmental processes in schizophrenic disorders: Longitudinal studies of vulnerability and stress. *Schizophrenia Bulletin, 18*, 387–425.

Ornitz, E. M., Hanna, G. L., & de Traversay, J. (1992). Prestimulation-induced startle modulation in attention-deficit hyperactivity disorder and nocturnal enuresis. *Psychophysiology, 29*, 437–451.

Overall, J. E., & Gorham, D. R. (1962). The Brief Psychiatric Rating Scale. *Psychological Reports, 10*, 799–812.

Perlstein, W. M., Fiorito, E., Simons, R. F., & Graham, F. K. (1989). Prestimulation effects on reflex blink and EPs in normal and schizotypal subjects. *Psychophysiology, 26*, S48.

Perlstein, W. M., Fiorito, E., Simons, R. F., & Graham, F. K. (1993). Lead stimulation effects on reflex blink, exogenous brain potentials, and loudness judgments. *Psychophysiology, 30*, 347–358.

Putnam, L. E. (1990). Great expectations: Anticipatory responses of the heart and brain. In J. W. Rohrbaugh, R. Parasuraman, & R. Johnson, Jr. (Eds.), *Event-related brain potentials: Basic issues and applications* (pp. 109–129). New York: Oxford University Press.

Reijmers, L. G., Vanderheyden, P. M., & Peeters, B. W. (1995). Changes in prepulse inhibition after local administration of NMDA receptor ligands in the core region of the rat nucleus accumbens. *European Journal of Pharmacology, 272*, 131–138.

Schell, A. M., Dawson, M. E., Hazlett, E. A., & Filion, D. L. (1995). Attentional modulation of startle in psychosis prone college students. *Psychophysiology, 32*, 266–273.

Seljos, K. A., Dawson, M. E., Filion, D. L., & Schell, A. M. (1994). Startle eyeblink modification in active and passive information processing under conditions of continuous background stimulation. *Psychophysiology, 31*, S90.

Shiffrin, R. M. (1988). Attention. In R. C. Atkinson, R. J. Herrnstein, G. Lindzey, & R. D. Luce (Eds.), *Stevens' handbook of experimental psychology* (2nd ed., Vol. 2, pp. 739–811). New York: Wiley.

Shiffrin, R. M., & Schneider, W. (1977). Controlled and automatic human information processing: II. Perceptual learning, automatic attending, and a general theory. *Psychological Review, 84*, 127–190.

Siegel, C., Waldo, M., Mizner, G., Adler, L. E., & Freedman, R. (1984). Deficits in sensory gating in schizophrenic patients and their relatives: Evidence obtained with auditory evoked responses. *Archives of General Psychiatry, 41*, 607–612.

Siever, L. J., Kalus, D. F., & Keefe, R. S. E. (1993). The boundaries of schizophrenia. *Psychiatric Clinics of North America, 16*, 217–244.

Simons, R. F., & Giardina, B. D. (1992). Reflex modification in psychosis-prone young adults. *Psychophysiology, 29*, 8–16.

Suddath, R. L., Christison, M. D., Torrey, E. F., Cassanova, M., & Weinberger, D. R. (1990). Anatomic abnormalities in the brains of monozygotic twins discordant for schizophrenia. *New England Journal of Medicine, 322*, 789–794.

Swanson, L. W., Mogenson, G. J., Gerfen, C. R., & Robinson, P. (1984). Evidence for a projection from the lateral preoptic area and substantia innominata to the mesencephalic locomotor region in the rat. *Brain Research, 295*, 161–178.

Swerdlow, N. R., Benbow, C. H., Zisook, S., Geyer, M. A., & Braff, D. L. (1993). A preliminary assessment of sensorimotor gating in patients with Obsessive Compulsive Disorder (OCD). *Biological Psychiatry, 33*, 298–301.

Swerdlow, N. R., Braff, D. L., & Geyer, M. A. (1990). GABAergic projection from nucleus accumbens to ventral pallidum mediates dopamine-induced sensorimotor gating deficits of acoustic startle in rats. *Brain Research, 532*, 146–150.

Swerdlow, N. R., Caine, B. C., & Geyer, M. A. (1992). Regionally selective effects of intracerebral dopamine infusion on sensorimotor gating of the startle reflex in rats. *Psychopharmacology, 108*, 189–195.

Swerdlow, N. R., Filion, D., Geyer, M. A., & Braff, D. L. (1995). "Normal" personality correlates of sensorimotor, cognitive and visuo-spatial gating. *Biological Psychiatry, 37*, 286–299.

Swerdlow, N. R., & Geyer, M. A. (1993). Prepulse inhibition of acoustic startle in rats after lesions of the pedunculopontine nucleus. *Behavioral Neuroscience, 107*, 104–117.

Swerdlow, N. R., Geyer, M., Braff, D., & Koob, G. F. (1986). Central dopamine hyperactivity in rats mimics abnormal acoustic startle in schizophrenics. *Biological Psychiatry, 21*, 23–33.

Swerdlow, N. R., & Koob, G. F. (1987). Dopamine, schizophrenia, mania, and depression: Toward a unified hypothesis of cortico-striato-pallido-thalamic function. *Behavioral and Brain Sciences, 10*, 197–245.

Swerdlow, N. R., Lipska, B. K., Weinberger, D. R., Braff, D. L., Jaskiw, G. E., & Geyer, M. A. (1995). Increased sensitivity to the gating-disruptive effects of apomorphine after lesions of the medial prefrontal cortex or ventral hippocampus in adult rats. *Psychopharmacology, 122*, 27–34.

Swerdlow, N. R., Paulsen, J., Braff, D. L., Butters, N., Geyer, M. A., & Swenson, M. R. (1995). Impaired prepulse inhibition of acoustic and tactile startle in patients with Huntington's Disease. *Journal of Neurology, Neurosurgery, & Psychiatry, 58*, 192–200.

Swerdlow, N. R., Wan, F. J., & Caine, S. B. (1993). Modulation of prepulse inhibition of acoustic startle through NMDA receptors in the ventral subiculum: Neurochemical and neuroanatomical substrates. *Abstract of Social Neuroscience, 19*, 144.

Wan, F. J., Geyer, M. A., & Swerdlow, N. R. (1995). Presynaptic dopamine-glutamate interactions in the nucleus accumbens regulate sensorimotor gating. *Psychopharmacology, 120*, 433–441.

12

Gating in Readiness

C. H. M. Brunia
Tilburg University

Order in our behavior is based on spatiotemporal selective processes that take place both in the input channels and in the output channels of the central nervous system. On the input side the organism is confronted with an abundance of internal and external stimuli that, without selection, would provoke behavioral chaos. Motoric behavior consists of simultaneous and successive muscle contractions in ever changing patterns, which are themselves a manifestation of selection in the output channels. Thus one of the prerequisites for normal behavior is selection. To understand behavior, we have to understand how selection takes place and where.

At the neuronal level the actual firing of a cell depends on the algebraic sum of excitatory and inhibitory influences impinging on it. If the firing threshold is reached, an action potential is produced that will contribute to similar processes at the next synapse. Excitation always takes place in a surrounding of inhibition. Inhibition is the vehicle by which selection in information processing is realized: The selected channels become or remain activated while others are shut off. These processes are ubiquitous in the central nervous system, allowing each synapse or groups of synapses within a nucleus to adapt the local response to the actual requirements of the environment. Yet there is also a particular brain structure that by its strategic position is involved in the selection of information on both the input side and the output side. This structure is the thalamic reticular nucleus (RN), a thin sheet of cells overlying the lateral side of the thalamus (see Fig. 12.1). The hypothesis put forward in this chapter is that both

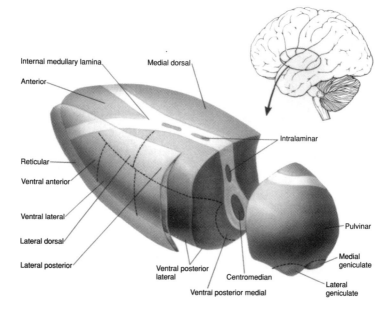

FIG. 12.1. The major nuclei of the left thalamus. The internal medullary lamina divides the thalamus into the anterior, lateral, and medial nuclei. The lateral group is divided into dorsal and ventral tiers. Each nucleus in the ventral tier relays specific sensory or motor information. The reticular nucleus (RN) caps the entire lateral aspect of the thalamus. It is the only nucleus with an inhibitory output and the only one that does not project to the cortex. Cells in the RN receive input from a particular relay nucleus and projects back to that nucleus. From Kelly (1991). Copyright © 1991 by Elsevier. Reprinted with permission.

sensoric and motoric information processing are modulated via this structure, resulting in comparable electrophysiological phenomena during expectant attention and motor preparation (see also Brunia, 1993). These phenomena are discussed after a brief description of the afferent and efferent connections of the sensoric and motoric thalamic nuclei.

INPUT TO THE SENSORY CORTEX

All somatosensory, visual, and auditory pathways are interrupted in specific thalamic relay nuclei before reaching their respective primary projection areas (see Fig. 12.2). Each of these relay nuclei receives returning afferents from the cortical area to which it sends its fibers. All leaving and returning fibers send collaterals to the RN cells *en passant*. Neurons

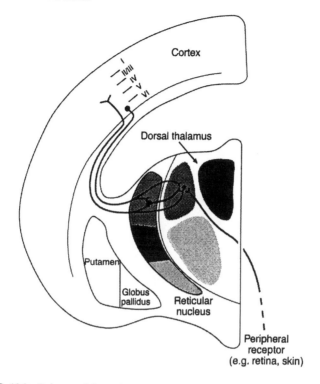

FIG. 12.2. Relay nuclei receive returning afferents from the cortical area to which it sends its fibers. All leaving and returning fibers send collaterals to a specific sector of the RN, allowing for a modulation of the local inhibitory influence the RN has on the relay nuclei. From Albin et al. (1989). Copyright © 1989 by Elsevier. Reprinted with permission.

in the RN have a local inhibitory control over the cells in the underlying relay nuclei (Scheibel & Scheibel, 1966), providing a gate for the passing information. The collaterals influence the excitability of the RN cells, and thus the status of the gates.

Primary sensory areas are connected first to unimodal association areas, then to multimodal association areas. The unimodal association areas feed back to the RN sectors belonging to the specific relay nuclei in order to gate the input of the modality in question. This might play a role in habituation by an increase in local inhibition (Watson, Valenstein, & Heilman, 1981). The multimodal sensory areas are connected to the inferior parietal lobule, a part of which is known as area PG (area 7). It has been demonstrated in monkeys that neurons in this cortical area respond upon sensory stimulation, if this stimulation is of motivational significance to the animal (Robinson, Goldberg, & Stanton, 1978). Mesulam (1981) suggested a "cortical network for directed attention" (p. 313) to extrapersonal space, in

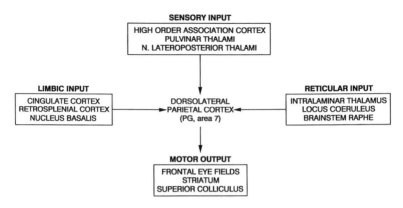

FIG. 12.3. Diagram of the major connections of area PG in the parietal cortex. From Mesulam (1981, 1983). Copyright © 1981, 1983 by Elsevier. Adapted with permission.

which at least three different brain regions take part (see Fig. 12.3). The main input to area PG stems from the multimodal sensory regions, the reticular formation, and the limbic areas. Each of these areas has a specific role in the network, the consequences of which become manifest via connections of the network to the motor system. In both the input and the output channels of this network, cortical and subcortical structures are involved. Concerning their function, Mesulam (1981, 1983) suggested the following: The posterior parietal component provides an internal sensory map of the external world, the reticular component provides the underlying level of arousal, and the limbic component in the cingulate gyrus regulates the spatial distribution of motivational valence. The frontal component of this system coordinates motor programs for exploration— that is, it translates the attention towards motivationally relevant aspects of extrapersonal space into goal-directed behavior.

INPUT TO THE MOTOR CORTEX

The motor cortex can be divided into primary motor cortex, premotor cortex, and supplementary motor cortex. Each of these subdivisions receives a separate thalamic input (Schell & Strick, 1984), which is illustrated in Fig. 12.4. The supplementary motor area gets its input from the pars oralis of the ventrolateral nucleus (VLo). The premotor cortex is innervated by the nucleus X of the ventrolateral nucleus (VLx). The primary motor cortex receives its input from the nucleus oralis of the ventroposterolateral complex (VPLo) and the nucleus caudalis of the ventrolateral complex (VLc). The different thalamic nuclei in turn receive their input

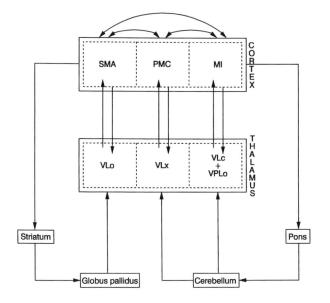

FIG. 12.4. Diagram of the major connections between cerebellum, basal ganglia, thalamus, and motor cortical areas. MI is connected via nuclei in the pons and in the cerebellum to thalamic nuclei Vlc, Vlx, and VPLo. The SMA is connected via striatum and pars interna of the globus pallidus to Vlo. The different thalamic nuclei have reciprocal connections to the different cortical motor areas, which have themselves mutual reciprocal connections. For the abbreviations see text. From Wise and Strick (1985). Copyright © 1985 by Elsevier. Adapted with permission.

from cerebellum and striatum (Wise & Strick, 1985). Efferent fibers of the cerebellum reach thalamic nuclei innervating the MI and the PMC. The striatum, functioning as the input channel of the basal ganglia, can be distinguished in the caudate nucleus and the putamen. These nuclei take part in two different thalamo-cortical loops: the complex loop and the motor loop, having different parts of the globus pallidus and substantia nigra as output channels (DeLong, Georgopoulos, & Crutcher, 1983; see Fig. 12.5). The complex loop is involved in higher order processes like the shaping of motor plans, which are supposed to be generated in the association cortex (Brooks, 1986). The motor loop, receiving place- and modality-specific somatosensory input, is involved in maintaining both the direction and force of movement.

Brooks (1986) distinguished three different functional levels: planning, programming, and execution. Planning of a movement is only possible if one is informed about the task at hand. Thus, brain structures that are involved in both programming and execution of the movement have to be activated. Motor programming asks for an adequate activation of the

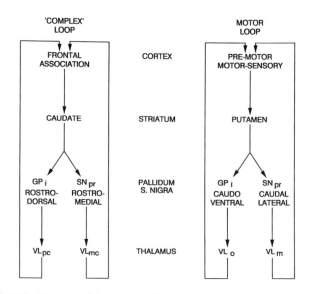

FIG. 12.5. Diagram of the "complex loop" from the association cortex and the "motor loop" from the sensory-motor cortex via basal ganglia and thalamus. From Delong et al. (1983). Copyright © 1983 by Springer-Verlag. Reprinted with permission.

premotor cortex and supplementary motor area. It implies the future execution of the movement, *given the present and to be expected circumstances*. Relevant information can be provided by the frontal and parietal association cortex and is needed for an optimal movement preparation. This information is sent to the striatum (Figs. 12.3 and 12.5), which via the pallidum reaches the thalamic motor nuclei, before arriving in the different frontal motor areas. Because all thalamocortical fibers pass the RN, we are again confronted with questions regarding its function.

Depending on their main interest, researchers describe the function of the RN either in terms of selective attention or in terms of motor preparation. The essence of the function in both cases is that of a gate via which selection is mediated.

OUTPUT FROM THE MOTOR CORTEX DEPENDS ON SENSORY AND MOTOR INPUT

From this short survey of the organization of the sensory and motor structures, it follows that the final efferent motor activity from the primary motor cortex depends on the thalamo-cortical input to different cortical motor regions. We have seen earlier that sensory information about the actual position of the body and about extrapersonal space is transmitted

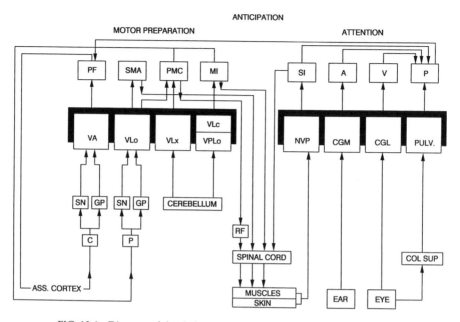

FIG. 12.6. Diagram of the thalamo-cortical connections. Sensory nuclei are depicted on the right, motor nuclei on the left. Fibers from each of the relay nuclei have to pass the RN, which has a local inhibitory control on the thalamocortical stream of information. The sensory stream of information is modulated during anticipatory attention (right). The movement-related stream of information is modulated during motor preparation (left). The RN itself is under inhibitory control of the reticular formation and under excitatory control of the frontal cortex.

to the cortex via the sensory and association nuclei of the thalamus. This information is again fed into the striatum to contribute to an adequate preparation and execution of the movement. In other words, both sensory and motor cortical areas depend heavily on thalamic input. Because sensory and motor nuclei in the thalamus are overlapped by the RN (see Fig. 12.6) and cells in different sectors of the RN exert a local inhibitory influence on different underlying relay nuclei, the RN is in a strategic position to modulate the streams of sensoric and motoric information.

THE RETICULAR NUCLEUS

Together with the intralaminar and the midline nuclei, the RN belongs to the diffuse projecting nuclei in the thalamus (for a review, see Kelly, 1991). These have a more distributed influence on other structures than the relay nuclei. Traditionally the intralaminar centromedian nucleus (Fig. 12.1) and the parafascicular nucleus have been considered a functional entity

(CMPF). Apart from its diffuse connection with cells of the RN (Mitrofanis & Guillery, 1993), the CMPF projects to the dorsolateral parietal cortex (Mesulam, Van Hoesen, Pandya, & Geschwind, 1977), the striatum (Albin, Young, & Penney, 1989) and the prefrontal cortex (Skinner & Yingling, 1977). Activated by the ascending reticular activation system (ARAS), the CMPF contributes to the creation of a state of arousal via its diffuse projection to the RN: All gates to the cortex are opened by inhibition of the inhibitory RN neurons (Yingling & Skinner, 1977).[1] Its projections to the parietal cortex and to the striatum provide an opportunity to directly influence the cortical areas involved in attention and motor preparation. Finally, the CMPF activates, via the anterior thalamic peduncle, the prefrontal cortex, while returning prefrontal fibers innervate, in turn, the RN. This mediothalamic-frontocortical system (MTFCS) as Skinner and Yingling have called it, has an excitatory influence on the RN, thereby activating the RN's inhibitory influence on the relay nuclei. Skinner and Yingling (1977) argued that "selective attention" for a preferred modality is realized via this pathway: Not activating the inhibition of RN cells in the relevant sector leaves the gate for that modality open. Skinner and Yingling concentrate on the significance of the RN for selection in the sensory domain; others underline its importance for gating in the motor domain.

Activation of relevant sectors of the RN provokes inhibitory postsynaptic potentials (IPSPs) in the ventrolateral thalamus (VL) blocking the transmission of information from the VL to the cortex (Figs. 12.1 and 12.4). Purpura, Scarff, and McMurtry (1965) found, for example, that cerebellar input to VL during these IPSPs no longer elicited the monosynaptic cortical response. Purpura (1970) suggested that this has the effect of functionally deafferenting elements of the motor cortex. The local inhibition RN is executing on underlying motor nuclei has also been described by Massion (1967), who considered the thalamic motor nuclei a gate that might be open or closed to a motor command. Investigators in neuropsychology have presented neglect patients, whose symptoms could be described in terms of akinesia as well. Thus Watson et al. (1981) presented a case of thalamic neglect as a consequence of an ischemic infarction of the right medial thalamus. They suggested that under normal circumstances the CMPF is involved in an arousal-inducing process, which permits the subject to respond to novel or important stimuli. This suggested relation to both arousal and to response intention is not surprising if one realizes that the CMPF, apart from its diffuse projection to RN, has an important input to

---

[1]There is an inconsistency here: If the CMPF as the mediator for the ARAS to the RN has an inhibitory influence on the inhibitory neurons of the RN, its innervation of the striatum should be GABAergic as well. Albin et al. (1989) argued, however, that the input to the striatum is excitatory, but the transmitter unknown (p. 368). Watson et al. (1981) underline the inhibition of the RN by the ARAS in agreement with Skinner and Yingling (1977), but seem to suppose that there is a direct connection of ascending reticular fibers and the RN.

the striatum, possibly related to motor preparation. Thus the higher motor disorder is not necessarily the consequence of the attentional deficit: Both can be the result of a lesion influencing the higher order processing in the sensory and in the motor domain simultaneously.

So far we have seen (a) that the input to the sensory and to the motor cortex has to pass the sensoric and motoric thalamic nuclei, and (b) that both types of nuclei are overlapped by the RN. Next we have seen that RN cells in sectors overlying the motoric relay nuclei exert a local inhibitory influence, comparable to the one active on sensory relay nuclei. Given this structural and functional analogy, it seems obvious that the same control systems are active on the sensory and on the motor relay nuclei. In the preceding paragraphs, two important systems have been described that take part in the control of the RN: the MTFCS and the ARAS. The first is involved in selective attention, the latter in the generation of arousal (Skinner & Yingling, 1977). *Selective attention* is the result of not activating the local inhibition of the RN on the relay nucleus in a relevant channel. *Arousal* is the result of a generalized inhibition of the multiple inhibitory RN sectors. Reasoning by analogy, this would imply for the motor system that (a) selective motoric activation goes along with a selective not activating of cells in circumscribed sectors of the RN overlying the motor nuclei, and (b) that arousal is based on a generalized inhibition of RN cells, opening all sensoric *and* motoric gates. The consequences of these considerations would be that comparable psychophysiological phenomena would be found in the research of expectant attention and motor preparation.

INDICES OF GATING

In the introduction of their seminal paper, Skinner and Yingling (1977) pointed at three different electrophysiological variables that are related to attention evoking situations: the rhythmic activity in the electroencephalo-gram (EEG), slow potentials, and faster evoked potentials (EPs). Against the backdrop of Skinner and Yingling's (1977) intracranial EEG recordings in the cat, results from surface recordings in man are described. Moreover we do not restrict ourselves to the sensory domain. Rather we point at the similarities in the control of the ascending thalamo-cortical streams of information in the sensory *and* in the motor system. First, the same variables that were used by Skinner and Yingling (1977) are discussed. Next, reflex studies are presented that are relevant not only to attention and motor preparation, but perhaps also to the domain of motivation and emotion.

Synchronous Activity

Rhythmic activity in the EEG is the consequence of the more or less simultaneous firing of large numbers of pyramidal cells in the cortex. This cortical activity is the result of subcortical input via the thalamus, which shows a similar rhythmic activity. Schlag and Villablanca (1967) produced rhythmic activity in isolated cortex by electrical low frequency stimulation of the white matter. Next, Schlag and Waszak (1970, 1971) recorded high frequency bursts of activity in RN cells during spontaneous or electrically induced synchronization. These bursts were associated with IPSPs in the underlying thalamic nuclei. Although the RN is not the only medium by which inhibition in thalamic relay nuclei is produced, it seems to be essential for the production of spontaneous rhythmic activity (Yingling & Skinner, 1977). Thalamo-cortical gates are (relatively) closed if the inhibitory RN cells discharge. This is associated with rhythmic cortical activity. When RN cells are quiet, a desynchronization of the EEG takes place, and the thalamo-cortical gates are open.

In man, the alpha rhythm is the most well known example of synchronous brain activity. This activity is not only present in the visual cortex, but also in the specific thalamic nuclei projecting to it. It reflects existence of noise in the visual system, which can be terminated by the presentation of visual information and by other alerting stimuli. Such alerting results in desynchronization: an event-related change in the pattern of cortical electrical activity caused by an inhibition of the locally inhibitory neurons. This can be the result of specific collaterals inhibiting the RN cells, or by nonspecific fibers from the ARAS inhibiting them (Lopes da Silva, Van Rotterdam, Barts, Van Heusden, & Burr, 1976). Thus event-related desynchronization (ERD) can be used as an index of a change in gating at the thalamic level. It becomes manifest if a gate is opened.

In a similar way the mu rhythm, which is present over the central somatosensory areas, can be blocked by touch stimuli applied to the hand or by reafferent somatosensory activity from a closing hand. The prevailing rhythm within the human sensorimotor cortex is the beta rhythm. Jasper and Penfield (1947) recorded this activity intracranially. They noted that the beta activity could be blocked by the initiation of voluntary movements. They further found that *preparation of a movement* also blocks the beta activity and that the blocking sometimes was restricted to the local cortical area representing the part of the limb going to be moved (Penfield & Jasper, 1956, p. 191). In other words, the preparatory processes in these cases were tuned very precisely. The subcortical input to the motor thalamus, for example, from the cerebellum, is organized in a somatotopic way. This suggests that the RN could play a role in the precise tuning of the activity allowed to pass to the cortex. Thus, ERD in surface recordings of beta activity can be used as an index for the opening of a gate.

Slow Potentials

Arduini, Mancini, and Mechelse (1957) demonstrated that a slow negative wave could be evoked by stimulation of the mesencephalic reticular formation (MRF). Caspers (1963) recorded a frontal positive wave at sleep onset, presumably associated with a decrease in MRF activity. Stimulation of the MRF and the MTFCS results in frontal slow potentials of opposite polarity. Skinner and Yingling (1977) found negative slow potentials after MRF stimulation and positive slow potentials after stimulation of the MTFCS. Simultaneous potentials of a polarity opposite to that of the frontal cortex were recorded in the RN. During positive shifts in RN, Yingling and Skinner (1977) found silence of cells in that nucleus, while during negative shifts in RN an increase in firing was recorded. Thus, no activity in RN cells goes along with frontal negativity, while discharges of RN cells are accompanied by frontal positivity. This suggests that not activating a certain sector of the RN leaves the channel open, while activating the RN closes the gates.

In man, the relevant slow potential in this context is the Contingent Negative Variation (CNV; Walter, Cooper, Aldridge, McCallum, & Winter, 1964), a slow surface-negative shift consisting of an early and a late wave. The early wave, recorded over the frontal areas, seems to reflect the processing of sensory information, that is, the information included in the warning stimulus (Loveless & Sanford, 1974). Skinner and Lindsley (1971) demonstrated that the slow potential elicited by a warning stimulus does not show up when the MTFCS is blocked. Thus it is presumable that this slow wave, which is related to the processing of sensory information, is the consequence of frontal cortical activity that can be gated by the RN.

Movement-preceding potentials can be recorded prior to a response stimulus in a warned reaction paradigm, and prior to a voluntary self-paced movement. The first is known as the late wave of the CNV, the latter as the Readiness Potential (RP; Kornhuber & Deecke, 1965). The RP can be recorded over the central cortex; the CNV has a more widespread distribution, especially into the frontal and parietal area. This difference in potential distribution is presumably related to the fact that different motor areas are involved in self-paced movements and in stimulus-evoked movements (Passingham, 1987). Moreover the preparation of the movement in a warned reaction time (RT) task is also determined by the attention to the upcoming stimulus.

The subcortical input to the motoric thalamic nuclei is a necessary prerequisite for the emergence of an RP. Evidence for this can be seen in the effects of cerebellar lesions in monkeys. Sasaki, Gemba, Hashimoto, and Mizuno (1979) were unable to record an RP from the motor cortex contralateral to the cerebellar lesion. The same holds for recordings in man (Shibasaki, Barrett, Neshige, Hirata, & Tomoda, 1986). The input from the cerebellum to the PMC and MI passes the motor nuclei in the thalamus. Thus, the RN is also in the position to modulate information transmission via the thalamus, preceding a voluntary movement (Fig. 12.6).

Evidence for the participation of subcortical areas in the CNV is provided by experiments in monkeys: Rebert (1977) recorded a contingent negativity in the mesencephalic reticular formation, while a positive shift was observed in the GABAergic caudate nucleus. We know that the reticular formation projects via the intralaminar nuclei to the RN, and that the caudate nucleus is part of the complex loop (Fig. 12.4) in which the VL and thus the RN is involved too (see Figs. 12.4 and 12.6). Thus we conclude that the RN is involved in the genesis of both movement-related potentials: the RP and the CNV late wave.

Evoked Potentials

Auditory and visual EPs have been recorded from both their specific subcortical pathways and from the primary projection areas by Skinner and Lindsley (1971). Cryogenic blockade of the MTFCS results in an enhancement of these EPs, the interpretation being that the local inhibitory neurons of the RN were not excited. The prefrontal RN connection is modality specific. This allows for a selective and modality-specific modulation of EPs (Skinner & Yingling, 1977). In contrast, electrical stimulation of the MRF provokes an enhancement of amplitudes of EPs of all modalities via a generalized aselective decrease in the tonic firing of the RN cells.

In man, EPs have been studied in a great many experiments. They are mostly used to evaluate information processing in different kinds of tasks, in which the association areas are more the locus of interest than the primary projection areas. However, afferent stimuli have to reach the primary sensory areas first before arriving in the association areas. Moreover, the thalamus is presumably passed twice: first to reach the primary areas, secondly to reach the association areas. This implies that the RN is again in the position to modulate the ongoing stream of information. Although it should be kept in mind that a direct cortico-cortical connection between primary and secondary areas exists as well (Fig. 12.6), the conclusion seems warranted that EPs from surface EEG recordings can be used to test the state of the gates. Suppose that by an experimental manipulation attention is directed to a certain modality. Then the gate in that modality is assumed to be open. If next a stimulus in that modality will be presented, a larger EP amplitude can be expected than when the intervening stimulus was of a different modality. In such a way EPs can be used to study the gating underlying selective attention in man. We see next that reflexes can be used in a similar way in the motor domain.

Reflexes

It is obvious that reflexes, in general, are mentioned in the discussion of the motor system rather than of the sensory system. Yet there is a reflex that is certainly more investigated in studies concerning attention than in those related to motor preparation, and that is the startle reflex. From the original description of the whole body startle (Landis & Hunt, 1939), it became clear that the eyeblink was the most consistent element in this behavioral defensive response. The startle reflex has afferents in three different modalities: auditory, visual, and somatosensory. This allows the study of within- and cross-modality effects of attention, which are relevant to issues discussed in this chapter (Anthony, 1985; Anthony & Graham, 1985; Putnam, 1990).

Attentional modulation of spinal reflexes is also reported. Paillard (1955), for example, found an increase in amplitude of the Achilles tendon and Hoffman reflexes 100 msec after a tone. Similar findings were reported by Davis and Beaton (1968), Beale (1971), and Rossignol and Melvill-Jones (1976). This increase in amplitude has been related to startle, although it is also present after auditory stimuli that are insufficiently intense to provoke the generalized flexor response (Rossignol, 1975). Rossignol and Melvill-Jones (1976) assume that the auditory potentiation of spinal reflexes is induced via the same pathways as the startle response itself. The cerebral cortex is not necessary for the production of a startle response, although it may have a modulatory influence (Liegeois-Chauvel, Morin, Musolino, Bancaud, & Chauvel, 1989). Brunia, Scheirs, and Haagh (1982) also found an increase in amplitude of the Achilles tendon reflex for a brief period following an acoustic warning signal (WS) that began a 4-sec RT trial. This early change did not differentiate between finger and foot responses, in contrast to changes that occurred just prior to the signal to respond. It is plausible that the early increase is not related to the kind of movement to be prepared. Rather, it reflects attentional processes to the WS (Scheirs & Brunia, 1982). The early increase in amplitude coincides with the N100 and may be related to the "nonspecific" N100 component (Brunia, Haagh, & Scheirs, 1985; Loveless & Brunia, 1990). Thus spinal reflexes, like the startle reflex, are sensitive to attentional modulation.

Based on Paillard's work, Requin, Bonnet, and Semjen (1977) and Brunia et al. (1982) used the Achilles tendon and Hoffman reflexes as a probe to study motor preparation. The latter found a differential effect preceding a plantar flexion of the foot, but not preceding a finger flexion. In contrast to what one would expect, amplitudes showed larger than baseline values if the calf muscle was not involved in the response.[2] Yet these effects were absent if no movement was prepared. Therefore a nonmotor (attentional) explanation could be rejected (Brunia, 1984; Scheirs, 1987). Rather, the anticipatory increase in excitability of spinal

---

[2]Part of the different reflex response in involved and uninvolved muscles might be caused by a peripheral phenomenon, that is, the stiffness of the involved muscle reducing the impact of the reflex eliciting stimulus (Scheirs, 1987).

motoneurons most likely reflects premovement activity parallel to the cortical preparatory activity. Taking the results of these spinal reflex studies together, we suggest that there is an essential difference between changes in reflex amplitude that occur early and late in the signaled foreperiod. The former are related to the alerting properties of the WS or the input side. The latter are related to response preparation or the output side. The changes related to the output processes could be a reflection of cortical processes, or processes that are triggered from the cortex, and that as such are an expression of the gating to the motor cortex. The same holds for the startle reflex used as a probe to investigate motor preparation at the brainstem level (Brunia & Boelhouwer, 1988).

Consistent with the original description of Landis and Hunt (1939) is the research of the startle reflex in the emotional domain. Davis (1984) published a large series of papers on fear potentiated startle in rats, in which he tried to systematically disentangle the pathways along which this response is produced. Research on the startle reflex in man has recently got a new impetus from the work of Lang and his coworkers (Lang, Bradley, & Cuthbert, 1990), who claim that the attentional effects cannot be assessed if the emotional valence of foreground and probe are ignored. This implies that modality, attention, and emotional valence determine the modulation of the startle. In the context of the unifying model of expectant attention and motor preparation presented here, it is interesting to note that limbic input to the attentional network partly passes the anterior nucleus of thalamus, which is also overlapped by the RN. A recent paper by Kultas-Ilinsky, Yi, and Ilinsky (1995) provided evidence for the existence of similar control of the RN on the anterior thalamic nucleus—an important link of subcortical limbic structures to the cingulate gyrus (Fig. 12.3). This provides a vehicle by which the RN can modulate the limbic input to the thalamus, parallel to the sensory and motor input.

EXPECTANT ATTENTION AND RESPONSE PREPARATION

Physiological changes in a state of readiness are aimed at better perception and movement execution. These changes are the result of a gating process, in which relevant channels are set or kept open, while irrelevant channels are closed. This section discusses the electrophysiological indices mentioned before, in relation to expectant attention and motor preparation.

A classic paradigm in the study of motor preparation is the warned RT task. It is known that reaction time decreases if a subject is informed by a warning stimulus about the impending presentation of an imperative stimulus (IS) upon which a quick response has to be executed. It is assumed that shortening of the RT is caused by a hypothetical process called motor preparation, which is based upon a facilitation of relevant motoric structures and an inhibition of irrelevant motoric structures. Of course, an adequate response can only be made if the IS is attended as well. This points out the weakness of this paradigm: Expectant attention and motor preparation are confounded. This confound is discussed in more detail.

During the foreperiod a number of changes in psychophysiological responses can be recorded:

1. The CNV with its early and late wave (Brunia & Vingerhoets, 1980; Rohrbaugh & Gaillard, 1983; Simons, 1988).
2. The classic triphasic pattern of changes in heart rate with an initial deceleration, an intermediate acceleration and a terminal deceleration (Lacey & Lacey, 1970, 1973; Obrist, Webb, Sutterer, & Howard, 1970).
3. The systematic changes in spinal reflex amplitudes (Brunia, 1984; Requin et al., 1977).

The early heart rate deceleration, the early increase in reflex amplitude, and the N100 following the WS are related to the alerting properties of the WS. They reflect the processing of the incoming information and might as such be related to the early negative CNV component (Brunia, Haagh, & Scheirs, 1985). The terminal changes in heart rate and the CNV late wave are undoubtedly, but not exclusively, related to motor preparation. In other words, the electrophysiological changes recorded at the onset of the foreperiod are reflecting processes different from those recorded at the end. The early changes reflect processes on the input side of the central nervous system. The late changes reflect processes on both the input side (attention to the imperative stimulus) and the output side (preparation of the response). The message of this chapter is that the thalamo-cortical stream of information during expectant attention and motor preparation is organized in a similar way (Fig. 12.6). This is discussed in light of both event-related desynchronization (ERD) and slow-potential studies. Next, it is suggested that EPs and reflexes may be used as probes to study the gating that occurs during attention and motor preparation.

Event-Related Desynchronization

Hans Berger (1929) was the first to discover that the alpha rhythm could be blocked by opening the eyes or by attentive behavior. Later, it became clear that the presentation of other stimuli was followed by a similar desynchronization. ERD takes place in parallel with the emergence of event-related brain potentials, the events being as different as the presentation of a stimulus, the execution of a motor act, or the performance of a cognitive task. Given the scope of this chapter, only the first two are discussed in more detail.

A visual ERD follows stimulus presentation and is restricted to the occipital and parietal cortex (Pfurtscheller, Steffan, & Maresch, 1988). Responses may be different for different frequencies. ERD in the upper alpha band is localized and restricted to the occipital areas, whereas ERD in the lower alpha frequencies is more widespread over the visual association areas and other extra-striate cortical areas. The authors suggest that ERD in the higher frequencies reflect stimulus-related processes, and in the lower frequencies attentional and motivational processes.

Pfurtscheller and Aranibar (1979) also investigated desynchronization of the mu rhythm over the central electrode positions (C3, C4). In essence, an effect was found similar to the blocking of the alpha rhythm. The ERD in the higher frequencies was more restricted to the central areas, and in the higher frequencies it was more generalized. An important difference with the visual ERD was the presence of mu blocking over the sensorimotor cortex preceding the voluntary movement. Blocking occurred slightly more than 1 sec prior to the movement—in other words, it occurred in the same time window in which the RP emerges over the motor cortex, contralateral to the movement side. Over the ipsilateral cortex, an ERD was present only during the last 700 msec prior to the movement (Pfurtscheller & Klimesch, 1991), suggesting a different underlying mechanism in slow potentials and ERD.

With repetitive tactile stimuli, an ERD was also found. Comparable to results in the visual modality, it was localized over C3 and C4 in the upper frequencies, and more widespread with lower frequencies. Another important observation was the fact that, contralateral to the stimulus side, the ERD preceded the stimulus presentation by some hundreds of msec. Expectancy in this case means a very localized activation of a part of the cerebral cortex. This is also reflected in the occurrence of another anticipatory slow wave, the Stimulus Preceding Negativity (SPN), that we discuss in the next paragraph. Because we know that the rhythmic cortical activity stems from thalamic input to the cortex, we suggest that ERD is a reflection of the modulation from the thalamo-cortical input to the sensory and the motor cortex by the RN (Fig. 12.6).

Slow Potentials

Usually a distinction is made between three different slow waves: the RP, the CNV, and the SPN. This distinction is only of limited importance because we know that slow waves are ubiquitous. They can be recorded in a number of tasks in which the eliciting subprocesses are not always well defined.

The RP is a slow wave that precedes self-paced voluntary movements. It emerges from the excitation of the apical dendrites of the pyramidal tract neurons in the different motor cortices of the monkey (for an overview, see Sasaki & Gemba, 1991). This is in accordance with the fact that in each of these areas, single unit activity has been recorded preceding an imminent movement (Riehle & Requin, 1989; Tanji, 1985; Tanji & Evarts, 1976; Wise & Mauritz, 1985). We have already discussed how the different motor areas are activated from different subcortical structures, the thalamus being a very crucial relay structure in a number of different thalamo-cortical circuits. The disappearance of the RP over primary motor cortex after a contralateral cerebellum destruction in both man (Shibasaki et al., 1986) and monkey (Sasaki et al., 1979) suggests that the integrity of the cerebello-thalamo-cortical pathway is a conditio-sine-qua-non for the emergence of the RP. Mutatis mutandis, one could speculate that the same holds for the input to other crucial cortical areas, the premotor, supplementary motor, and the primary somatosensory cortex. Therefore we suggest that each of the different RPs depends on an input from one of the thalamic nuclei and thus is open for modulation via the RN.

In the original description of the CNV, Walter et al. (1964) stressed expectancy as a fundamental notion to explain the meaning of the slow potential shift. They further noted that giving a response to IS was crucial, although a CNV also could be recorded during a "purely mental judgment of a time interval" (p. 382) at least in trained subjects. Thus the authors realized that learning, time estimation, and motor preparation were all important factors in the bringing about of the CNV. Loveless and Sanford (1974) were the first to note the similarity between the late wave and the RP recorded by Kornhuber and Deecke (1965) prior to a nonsignaled voluntary movement. In his later papers, Loveless (1977, 1979) became convinced that the late wave reflected motor preparation. A stronger stance was taken by Rohrbaugh and Gaillard (1983), who identified the late wave with the RP. The circumstances under which the movement is brought about are quite different, however. The presentation of an IS is a necessary condition to evoke a CNV late wave, whereas a self-paced movement is determined by available internal (i.e., proprioceptive) information. Recent studies of movement preparation (Passingham, 1987) have suggested that the cortical motor areas are different in both cases. The externally triggered movements are realized via the lateral premotor cortex and the self-paced movements via the medially localized supplementary motor area. For the slow waves it would mean that CNV late wave is brought about via the premotor, and the RP via the suppplementary motor cortex. Arguments for the latter are provided by Deecke and his coworkers (Lang et al., 1991). In summary, although both slow waves are certainly movement preceding negativities, they are not identical.

There is another problem with the warned RT paradigm, as we have indicated. Subjects are not only preparing a response, they are also attending the future arrival of the imperative stimulus. To disentangle these two processes, Damen and Brunia (1987) presented their subjects with a task which, in operant conditioning terminology, was a DRL-LH schedule (differential reinforcement of low rates of responding with a limited hold; Lacey & Lacey, 1970). Subjects had to press a button every 20 sec; a button press within 300 msec of the 20-sec target was correct. Two sec following the button press, subjects received a stimulus, providing Knowledge of Results (KR). The KR stimulus indicated whether the preceding interval was correct, too long, or too short. Thus motor preparation and expectant attention of the KR stimulus have been separated in time. In this and in a following study (Brunia & Damen, 1988), it was clearly demonstrated that the movement preceding negativity and the stimulus preceding negativity had a different potential distribution over the scalp (Brunia, 1988). As illustrated in Fig. 12.7, the RP was larger over the cortex contralateral to the finger movement; the SPN showed a right hemisphere preponderance. In a later experiment, Chwilla and Brunia (1991) compared blocks of trials in which real KR or false KR were presented. They showed that the SPN was only present preceding real KR, suggesting that the SPN was related to the anticipation of KR. Yet we realized that these results did not necessarily support our hypothesis that the CNV late wave was a combination of a RP and a SPN. After all, the KR stimulus informs the subject about what was done in the past, whereas an imperative stimulus instructs the subject what to do and exactly when to do it. Therefore, Damen and Brunia (1994) conducted an experiment that compared slow waves preceding both instructional and KR stimuli. They asked their subjects to make a voluntary button press, which 2 sec later was followed by one of three stimuli, instructing the subject to press the button again 5, 7, or 9 sec after a tone, which followed the instructional stimulus after an unpredictable interval. Two sec after the second button press, one of the three physically identical stimuli was presented, now to indicate whether this response was given in time, too late, or too early. The voluntary movement was, of course, preceded by an RP in both cases. An SPN was found prior to the KR stimulus over all electrode positions. Prior to the imperative stimulus, however, an SPN was found only over the parietal electrodes and even that was not significant. In other words, these results suggest that the contribution of an imperative stimulus to the CNV late wave might only be present over the parietal cortex, and minimal in the case of simple reaction-time instructions. It does not mean, however, that the CNV late wave and the RP are identical, both because of the functional neuroanatomical data of Passingham (1987) and the fact that the amplitude of the CNV late wave is always larger than the RP, recorded in the same session (Brunia & Vingerhoets, 1981).

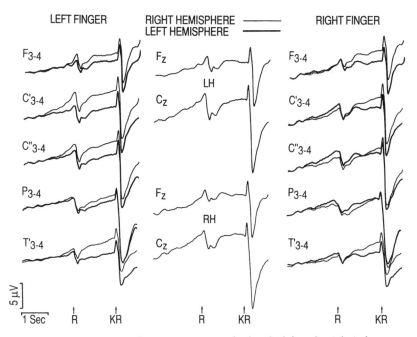

FIG. 12.7. Voluntary flexion movements of either the left or the right index finger had to be made in intervals of 20 to 22 sec in order to press a button. Two sec after each button press, a feedback stimulus was presented to give the subject knowledge of results (KR). The KR stimulus indicated whether the preceding interval was too short, correct, or too long. A RP was recorded prior to the movement, with larger amplitudes over the hemisphere contralateral to the movement side. Just prior to the presentation of the KR stimulus the SPN is larger over the right hemisphere. From Brunia (1988). Copyright © 1988 by Elsevier. Reprinted with permission.

Further arguments for the existence of a small SPN prior to (future-directed) cue stimuli can be found in recent studies of van Boxtel and Brunia (1994a, 1994b). This activity was interpreted by van Boxtel (1994) as anticipation of task-relevant sensory input. A similar indication of anticipatory tuning of a crucial brain area is the so-called Directed Attention Potential (Lang, Lang, Heise, Deecke, & Kornhuber, 1984).

These anticipatory slow potential data are in agreement with the anticipatory ERD (Pfurtscheller, Steffan, & Maresch, 1988). Both ERD and slow potentials (RP, SPN, CNV) reflect a localized increase in excitability of a cortical area, related to its impinging action at the crucial event. It is plausible that the thalamo-cortical input to the motor cortex in the case of the RP, to the primary sensory and association areas in the case of the SPN, and to sensory, motor, and association areas in the case of a CNV, is crucial for the emergence of these slow waves. The essence of this chapter is that anticipatory attention and motor preparation are based on separate thalamo-cortical streams of information that are open to modulation via the RN (Fig. 12.6).

Probing the Gates

If it is correct that both the synchronous brain activity and the slow potentials are based upon thalamo-cortical input, the state of the gates could be probed by using evoked potentials (EPs) and reflexes. This could be done in two different paradigms: A warned reaction-time task and a time estimation task.

Warned RT Task. In this task, at least two gates are open: the motor channel and the sensory channel in the modality of the imperative stimulus. EPs and startle reflexes can be recorded to study gating underlying the expectant attention to the IS. This can be done either in the modality as that of the imperative stimulus or in a different modality. The prediction is that EPs and reflexes elicited by stimuli delivered in the modality of the imperative stimulus will be increased, but unchanged or reduced when stimuli are delivered in a different modality. Response preparation can also be studied with reflexes and perhaps with the newly developed technique of transcranial magnetic stimulation. If the motor channel is open, a specific pattern of changes in reflex amplitudes will be present. If the motor channel is closed (no-response condition), no change in amplitude is found (Brunia, 1984; Brunia, Scheirs, & Haagh, 1982). It was indicated previously that in this paradigm the two crucial processes "Expectant Attention" and "Motor Preparation" are confounded. To separate both processes in time, time estimation experiments can be performed in which KR stimuli are presented following the motor response.

Time Estimation With Knowledge of Results. In this task, the subject has to press a button 3 sec after a warning stimulus, while 2 sec later a KR stimulus is presented. The idea is that the motor gate would be opened first (i.e., after warning-stimulus delivery), and would be followed, after the button press, by the opening of the sensory gate in the same modality in which the KR stimulus is anticipated. Processes associated with gate activity are reflected by the successive emergence of the RP and then the SPN. The state of the gates can be investigated by spinal reflexes, startle reflexes, and EPs. Because there is some imprecision in the timing of the movement, this particular task may be more sensitive to the expectant attention processes than it is to processes associated with motor preparation. In the interval between movement and the KR stimulus, gating underlying expectant attention can be studied by EPs and startle reflexes, with the prediction that EPs and startle reflexes will show larger amplitudes if the evoking stimuli are of the same modality as the KR stimulus. The baseline values are provided by the EPs and the startle reflexes evoked in the interval between trials. Although beyond the scope of this chapter, it should be stressed again, that the study of emotional valence can be interpreted along the same lines, as (a) the limbic structures project via the anterior nucleus of the thalamus to the cingulate gyrus, and (b) this nucleus is also influenced by the RN.

CONCLUSION

While a subject is waiting to respond, the arrival of an instruction stimulus is anticipated and the response is prepared. It has been argued here that both processes are based upon a thalamo-cortical stream of information via different thalamic nuclei. Each thalamo-cortical pathway functions as a channel which transmits specific sensoric or motoric information to the relevant cortical structures. These channels are neither completely open nor completely closed. They can be gated via a control mechanism, in which the RN plays a crucial role. This nucleus overlaps the different sensoric and motoric thalamic relay nuclei and exerts a local, topographically organized inhibitory influence upon them. The RN itself is open for a generalized inhibition from the reticular formation via the ARAS, as Skinner and Yingling (1977) demonstrated for the sensory nuclei. The claim of this chapter is that the same holds for the motoric thalamic nuclei. The generalized inhibition of the locally inhibitory RN cells results in a generalized disinhibition of the thalamic relay nuclei. This process is at the basis of an increase in the state of arousal: All gates are open, both sensoric and motoric. The RN is also open for an excitatory frontal control mechanism. In contrast to the influence from the reticular formation, this is topographically organized, allowing for a localized activation of the locally active inhibition. The consequence of activity in this system is the closing of a gate. This mechanism is responsible for selection in both the sensory and the motor domain. A gate is only open if the excitation from the frontal cortex does not arrive. Both perception and movement are possible only if the relevant gates are open. An adequate response upon a NO-GO or a STOP command could be realized via the immediate closing of the motoric gates by the frontal excitation of the local inhibitory RN activity.

ACKNOWLEDGMENTS

Thanks are due to Geert van Boxtel and others for their valuable comments on earlier versions of this chapter and to Wim Waterink for his assistance in the production of the figures.

REFERENCES

Albin, R. L., Young, A. B., & Penney, J. B. (1989). The functional anatomy of basal ganglia disorders. *Trends in the Neurosciences, 12,* 366–375.

Anthony, B. J. (1985). In the blink of an eye: Implications of reflex modification for information processing. In P. A. Ackles, J. R. Jennings, & M. G. H. Coles (Eds.), *Advances in psychophysiology* (pp. 167–218). Greenwich, CT: JAI.

Anthony, B. J., & Graham, F. K. (1985). Blink reflex modification by selective attention: Evidence for the modulation of "automatic" processing. *Biological Psychology, 21,* 43–59.

Arduini, A., Mancia, M., & Mechelse, K. (1957). Slow potential changes in the cerebral cortex by sensory and reticular stimulation. *Archives Italiens de Biologie, 95,* 127–138.

Beale, D. K. (1971). Facilitation of the knee jerk as a function of the interval between auditory and stretching stimuli. *Psychophysiology, 8,* 504–508.

Berger, H. (1929). Über das Elektrenkephalogramm des Menschen II [About the electroencephalogram in man]. *Archiv für Psychiatrie und Nervenkrankheiten, 87,* 527–570.

Brooks, V. B. (1986). *The neural basis of motor control.* New York: Oxford University Press.

Brunia, C. H. M. (1984). Selective and aselective control of spinal motor structures during preparation for a movement. In S. Kornblum & J. Requin (Eds.), *Preparatory states and processes* (pp. 285–302). Hillsdale, NJ: Lawrence Erlbaum Associates.

Brunia, C. H. M. (1988). Movement and stimulus preceding negativity. *Biological Psychology, 26,* 165–178.

Brunia, C. H. M. (1993). Waiting in readiness: Gating in attention and motor preparation. *Psychophysiology, 30,* 327–340.

Brunia, C. H. M., & Boelhouwer, A. J. W. (1988). Reflexes as a tool: A window in the central nervous system. In P. K. Ackles, J. R. Jennings, & M. G. H. Coles (Eds.), *Advances in psychophysiology* (Vol. 3, pp. 1–67). Greenwich, CT: JAI.

Brunia, C. H. M., & Damen, E. J. P. (1988). Distribution of slow potentials related to motor preparation and stimulus anticipation in a time estimation task. *Electroencephalography and Clinical Neurophysiology, 69,* 234–243.

Brunia, C. H. M., & Vingerhoets, A. J. J. M. (1980). CNV and EMG preceding a plantar flexion of the foot. *Biological Psychology, 11,* 181–191.

Brunia, C. H. M., & Vingerhoets, A. J. J. M. (1981). Opposite hemisphere differences in movement related potentials preceding foot and finger flexions. *Biological Psychology, 13,* 261–269.

Brunia, C. H. M., Haagh, S. A. V. M., & Scheirs, J. G. M. (1985). Waiting to respond: Electrophysiological measurements in man during preparation for a voluntary movement. In H. Heuer, U. Kleinbeck, & K. H. Schmidt (Eds.), *Motor behavior: Programming, control, and acquisition* (pp. 35–78). Berlin: Springer-Verlag.

Brunia, C. H. M., Scheirs, J. G. M., & Haagh, S. A. V. M. (1982). Changes of Achilles tendon reflex amplitudes during a fixed fore period of reaction time experiments. *Psychophysiology, 19,* 63–70.

Caspers, H. (1963). Relations of steady potential shifts in the cortex to the wakefullness-sleep spectrum. In M. A. B. Brazier (Ed.), *Brain function: Vol. 1. Cortical excitability and steady potentials* (pp. 117–123). Berkeley: University of California Press.

Chwilla, D. J., & Brunia, C. H. M. (1991). Event-related potentials to different feedback stimuli. *Journal of Psychophysiology, 28,* 123–132.

Damen, E. J. P., & Brunia, C. H. M. (1987). Changes in heart rate and slow potentials related to motor preparation and stimulus anticipation in a time estimation task. *Psychophysiology, 24,* 700–713.

Damen, E. J. P., & Brunia, C. H. M. (1994). Is a stimulus conveying task relevant information a sufficient condition to elicit stimulus preceding negativity? *Psychophysiology, 31,* 129–139.

Davis, C. M., & Beaton, R. D. (1968). Facilitation and adaptation of the human stretch reflex produced by auditory stimulation. *Journal of Comparative and Physiological Psychology, 66,* 483–487.

Davis, M. (1984). The mammalian startle response. In R. C. Eaton (Ed.), *Neural mechanisms of startle behavior* (pp. 287–351). New York: Plenum.

Delong, M. R., Georgopoulos, A. P., & Crutcher, M. D. (1983). Cortico-basal ganglia relations and coding of motor performance. In J. Massion, J. Paillard, W. Schultz, & M. Wiesendanger (Eds.), *Neural coding of motor performance, Experimental Brain Research,* Suppl. 7, 30–40.

Jasper, H. H., & Penfield, W. (1947). Electrocorticograms in man: Effect of the voluntary movement upon the electrical activity in the precentral gyrus. *Archiv für Psychiatrie und Zeitschrift fur Neurologie, 183,* 163–174.

Kelly, J. P. (1991). The neural basis of perception and movement. In E. R. Kandel, J. H. Schwartz, & T. M. Jessell (Eds.), *Principles of neural science* (pp. 283–295). New York: Elsevier.

Kornhuber, H. H., & Deecke, L. (1965). Hirnpotentialänderungen bei Willkürbewegungen und passiven Bewegungen des Menschen: Bereitschaftspotential und reafferente Potentiale [Changes in brain potentials by voluntary movements and passive movements in man: Readiness potentials and reafferent potentials]. *Pflügers Archiv, 284,* 1–17.

Kultas-Ilinsky, K., Yi, H., & Ilinsky, L. A. (1995). Nucleus reticularis input to the anterior thalamic nuclei in the monkey: A light and electron microscopic study. *Neuroscience Letters, 186,* 25–28.

Lacey, J. I., & Lacey, B. C. (1970). Some autonomic-central nervous system interrelationships. In P. Black (Ed.), *Physiological correlates of emotion* (pp. 205–227). New York: Academic Press.

Lacey, J. I., & Lacey, B. C. (1973). Experimental association and dissociation of phasic bradycardia and vertex-negative waves: A psychophysiological study of attention and response-intention. In W. C. McCallum & J. R. Knott (Eds.), *Event-related slow potentials of the brain: Their relations to behavior* (pp. 281–285). New York: Elsevier.

Landis, C., & Hunt, W. (1939). *The startle pattern.* New York: Farrar & Rinehart.

Lang, P. J., Bradley, M. M., & Cuthbert, B. N. (1990). Emotion, attention, and the startle reflex. *Psychological Review, 97,* 377–395.

Lang, W., Cheyne, D., Kristeva, R., Lindinger, G., & Deecke, L. (1991). Functional localization of motor processes in the human cortex. In C. H. M. Brunia, G. Mulder, & M. N. Verbaten (Eds.), *Event-related brain research (EEG Suppl. 42)* (pp. 97–115). Amsterdam: Elsevier.

Lang, W., Lang, M., Heise, B., Deecke, L., & Kornhuber, H. H. (1984). Brain potentials related to voluntary hand tracking, motivation and attention. *Human Neurobiology, 3,* 235–240.

Liegeois-Chauvel, C., Morin, C., Musolino, A., Bancaud, J., & Chauvel, P. (1989). Evidence for a contribution of the auditory cortex to audiospinal facilitation in man. *Brain, 112,* 375–391.

Lopes da Silva, F. H., Van Rotterdam, A., Barts, P., Van Heusden, E., & Burr, W. (1976). Models of neuronal populations: The basic mechanisms of rhythmicity. *Progress in Brain Research, 45,* 281–308.

Loveless, N. E. (1977). Event-related brain potentials in selective response. *Biological Psychology, 5,* 135–149.

Loveless, N. E. (1979). Event-related slow potentials of the brain as expressions of orienting function. In H. D. Kimmel, E. H. van Olst, & J. F. Orlebeke (Eds.), *The orienting reflex in humans* (pp. 77–100). Hillsdale, NJ: Lawrence Erlbaum Associates.

Loveless, N. E., & Brunia, C. H. M. (1990). Effects of rise-time on late components of the auditory evoked potential. *Journal of Psychophysiology, 4,* 369–380.

Loveless, N. E., & Sanford, A. J. (1974). Slow potential correlates of preparatory set. *Biological Psychology, 1,* 303–314.

Massion, J. (1967). The thalamus in the motor system. *Applied Neurophysiology, 39,* 222–238.

Mesulam, M. M. (1981). A cortical network for directed attention and unilateral neglect. *Annals of Neurology, 10,* 309–325.

Mesulam, M. M. (1983). The functional anatomy and hemispheric specialization for directed attention. The role of the parietal lobe and its connectivity. *Trends in the Neurosciences,* 384–387.

Mesulam, M. M., Van Hoesen, G. W., Pandya, D. N., & Geschwind, N. (1977). Limbic and sensory connections of the inferior parietal lobule (area PG) in the rhesus monkey: A study with a new method for horseradish peroxidase histochemistry. *Brain Research, 136,* 393–414.

Mitrofanis, J., & Guillery, R. W. (1993). New views of the thalamic reticular nucleus in the adult and the developing brain. *Trends in the Neurosciences, 16,* 240–245.

Obrist, P. A., Webb, R. A., Sutterer, J. R., & Howard, J. L. (1970). Cardiac deceleration and reaction time: An evaluation of two hypotheses. *Psychophysiology, 6,* 695–706.

Paillard, J. (1955). *Réflexes et Régulations d'origine proprioceptive chez l'Homme* [Reflexes and proprioceptive control]. Paris: Arnette.

Passingham, R. E. (1987). Two cortical systems for directing movement. In *Motor areas of the cerebral cortex: Ciba Foundation Symposium, 132* (pp. 151–161). Chichester, UK: Wiley.

Penfield, W., & Jasper, H. H. (1956). *Epilepsy and the functional anatomy of the human brain.* Boston: Little, Brown.

Pfurtscheller, G., & Aranibar, A. (1979). Evaluation of event-related desynchronization (ERD) preceding and following self-paced movement. *Electroencephalography and Clinical Neurophysiology, 46,* 138–146.

Pfurtscheller, G., & Klimesch, W. (1991). Event-related desynchronisation during motor behavior and visual information processing. In C. H. M. Brunia, G. Mulder, & M. N. Verbaten (Eds.), *Event-related Brain Research (EEG Suppl. 42)* (pp. 58–65). Amsterdam: Elsevier.

Pfurtscheller, G., Steffan, J., & Maresch, H. (1988). ERD mapping and functional topography: Temporal and spatial aspects. In G. Pfurtscheller & F. H. Lopes da Silva (Eds.), *Functional brain imaging* (pp. 117–130). Bern: Hans Huber Publishers.

Purpura, D. P. (1970). Operations and processes in thalamic and synaptically related neural subsystems. In F. O. Schmitt (Ed.), *The neurosciences: Second study program* (pp. 458–470). New York: The Rockefeller University Press.

Purpura, D. P., Scarff, T., & McMurtry, K. (1965). Intracellular study of internuclear inhibition in ventrolateral thalamic neurons. *Journal of Neurophysiology, 28,* 487–496.

Putnam, L. E. (1990). Great expectations: Anticipatory responses of the heart and brain. In J. W. Rohrbaugh, R. Parasuraman, & R. Johnson, Jr. (Eds.), *Event-related brain potentials: Basic issues and applications* (pp. 109–129). New York: Oxford University Press.

Rebert, C. S. (1977). Intracerebral slow potential changes in monkeys during the foreperiod of reaction time. In J. E. Desmedt (Ed.), *Attention, voluntary contraction and event-related cerebral potentials* (pp. 242–253). Basel: S. Karger.

Requin, J., Bonnet, M., & Semjen, A. (1977). Is there a specificity in the supra spinal control of motor structures during preparation? In S. Dornic (Ed.), *Attention and performance VI* (pp. 139–174). Hillsdale, NJ: Lawrence Erlbaum Associates.

Riehle, A., & Requin, J. (1989). Monkey primary motor and premotor cortex: Single-cell activity related to prior information about direction and extent of an intended movement. *Journal of Neurophysiology, 61,* 534–549.

Robinson, D. L., Goldberg, M. E., & Stanton, G. B. (1978). Parietal association cortex in the primate: Sensory mechanisms and behavioral modulations. *Journal of Neurophysiology, 41,* 910–932.

Rohrbaugh, J., & Gaillard, A. W. K. (1983). Sensory and motor aspects of the contingent negative variation. In A. W. K. Gaillard & W. Ritter (Eds.), *Tutorials in event-related potentials research: Endogenous components* (pp. 269–310). Amsterdam: North-Holland.

Rossignol, S. (1975). Startle responses recorded in the leg of man. *Electroencephalography and Clinical Neurophysiology, 39*, 389–397.

Rossignol, S., & Melvill-Jones, G. (1976). Audiospinal influence in man studied by the H-reflex and its possible role on rhythmic movements synchronized to sound. *Electroencephalography and Clinical Neurophysiology, 41*, 83–92.

Sasaki, K., & Gemba, H. (1991). Cortical potentials associated with voluntary movements in monkeys. In C. H. M. Brunia, G. Mulder, & M. N. Verbaten (Eds.), *Event-related brain research* (EEG Suppl. 42, pp. 80–96). Amsterdam: Elsevier.

Sasaki, K., Gemba, H., Hashimoto, S., & Mizuno, N. (1979). Influences of cerebellar hemispherectomy on slow potentials in the motor cortex preceding self-paced hand movements in the monkey. *Neurosciences Letters, 15*, 23–28.

Schell, G. P., & Strick, P. (1984). The origin of thalamic inputs to the arcuate premotor and supplementary motor areas. *Journal of Neurosciences, 4*, 539–560.

Scheibel, M. E., & Scheibel, A. B. (1966). The organization of the nucleus reticularis thalami: A Golgi study. *Brain Research, 1*, 43–62.

Scheirs, J. G. M. (1987). *Motor preparatory processes recording in the leg of man.* Unpublished doctoral dissertation, Tilburg University, The Netherlands.

Scheirs, J. G. M., & Brunia, C. H. M. (1982). Effects of stimulus and task factors on Achilles tendon reflexes evoked early during a preparatory period. *Physiology and Behavior, 28*, 681–685.

Schlag, J., & Villablanca, J. (1967). Cortical incremental responses to thalamic stimulation. *Brain Research, 21*, 286–288.

Schlag, J., & Waszak, M. (1970). Characteristics of unit responses in nucleus reticularis thalami. *Brain Research, 21*, 286–288.

Schlag, J., & Waszak, M. (1971). Electrophysiological properties of units of the thalamic reticular complex. *Experimental Neurology, 32*, 79–97.

Shibasaki, H., Barrett, G., Neshige, R., Hirata, I., & Tomoda, H. (1986). Volitional movement is not preceded by cortical slow negativity in cerebellar dentate lesion in man. *Brain Research, 38*, 361–365.

Simons, R. F. (1988). Event-related slow brain potentials: A perspective from ANS psychophysiology. In P. I. Ackles, J. R. Jennings & M. G. H. Coles (Eds.), *Advances in psychophysiology* (Vol. 3, pp. 223–267). Greenwich, CT: JAI.

Skinner, J. E., & Lindsley, D. B. (1971). Enhancement of visual and auditory evoked potentials during blockade of the non-specific thalamo-cortical system. *Electroencephalography and Clinical Neurophysiology, 31*, 1–6.

Skinner, J. E., & Yingling, C. D. (1977). Central gating mechanisms that regulate event-related potentials and behavior. In J. E. Desmedt (Ed.), *Attention, voluntary contraction and slow potential shifts* (pp. 30–69). Basel: Karger.

Tanji, J. (1985). Comparison of neuronal activities in the monkey supplementary and precentral motor areas. *Behavioural Brain Research, 18*, 137–142.

Tanji, J., & Evarts, E. V. (1976). Anticipatory activity of motor cortex neurons in relation to direction of an intended movement. *Journal of Neurophysiology, 39*, 1062–1068.

Van Boxtel, G. (1994). *Non-motor components of slow brain potentials.* Unpublished doctoral dissertation, Tilburg University, The Netherlands.

Van Boxtel, G., & Brunia, C. H. M. (1994a). Motor and non-motor aspects of slow brain potentials. *Biological Psychology, 38*, 35–51.

Van Boxtel, G., & Brunia, C. H. M. (1994b). Motor and non-motor components of the contingent negative variation. *International Journal of Psychophysiology, 17*, 269–279.

Walter, W. G., Cooper, R., Aldridge, V. J., McCallum, W. C., & Winter, A. L. (1964). Contingent negative variation: An electrical sign of sensorimotor association and expectancy in the human brain. *Nature, 203*, 380–384.

Watson, R. T., Valenstein, E., & Heilman, K. M. (1981). Thalamic neglect: Possible role of the medial thalamus and the nucleus reticularis in behavior. *Archives of Neurology, 38,* 501–506.

Wise, S. P., & Mauritz, K. H. (1985). Set-related neuronal activity in the premotor cortex of rhesus monkeys: Effects of changes in motor set. *Proceedings of the Royal Society, London, 223,* 331–354.

Wise, S. P., & Strick, P. (1985). Anatomical and physiological organization of the non-primary motor cortex. In E. V. Evarts, S. P. Wise, & D. Bousfield (Eds.), *The motor system in neurobiology* (pp. 315–324). Amsterdam: Elsevier.

Yingling, C. D., & Skinner, J. E. (1977). Gating of thalamic input to the cerebral cortex by nucleus reticularis thalami. In J. E. Desmedt (Ed.), *Attention, voluntary contraction and slow potential shifts* (pp. 70–96). Basel: Karger.

Magnetoencephalography in Studies of Attention

Risto Näätänen
University of Helsinki

Risto J. Ilmoniemi
Helsinki University Central Hospital

Kimmo Alho
University of Helsinki

Selective attention is, as far as perceptual processes are concerned, the ability of the brain to select a part of parallel competing sensory input for further processing or response selection and execution. Although psychological tests and psychophysical measurements have significantly contributed to our understanding of attention, the brain mechanisms responsible for attention can only be revealed by studying the brain itself. The first possibility to this end was opened by the advent of methodologies of electrical recording, which could be made either directly from the brain of experimental animals or of patients under surgery, or noninvasively with electrodes placed on the scalp. A large amount of information was obtained by means of electroencephalography (EEG) in the 1960s and has continued to accrue thereafter. More recently, attention research has been advanced by the advent of several new functional imaging techniques such as positron emission tomography (PET; ter-Pogossian, Phelps, Hoffman, & Mullani, 1975), single photon emission computed tomography (SPECT; Knoll, 1983), functional magnetic resonance imaging (fMRI; Belliveau et al., 1991), and magnetoencephalography (MEG; for reviews, see Hämäläinen, Hari, Ilmoniemi, Knuutila, & Lounasmaa, 1993; Hari, 1990; Näätänen, Ilmoniemi, & Alho, 1994). These functional imaging methods enable one to locate neural activation as well as changes in metabolism and blood flow accompanying neural activation. The EEG has been able to reveal sequences of activation with msec time resolution, but several questions have remained unanswered due to problems in separating signals arising from multiple sites simultaneously. The MEG can help solve some of these problems. It shows promise in locating brain electric sources with high spatial accuracy and good discrimination between multiple sources, thus permitting new studies aimed at identifying and quantifying brain processes underlying attention. It should be pointed out, however, that the EEG, particularly when used in combination with the MEG, remains a powerful tool for the study of cognitive brain functions.

MAGNETOENCEPHALOGRAPHY

Electric currents in the brain produce a changing magnetic field which can be detected outside the head with SQUID (Superconducting QUantum Interference Device) magnetometers. The signals measured can be used to compute the distribution of cerebral activity as a function of time. This method, called MEG, is closely related to EEG, in which the electric field pattern on the scalp is measured. The main advantages of the MEG in relation to the EEG are its superior spatial accuracy as well as ease of use, particularly when a large number of measurement channels are involved. On the other hand, the EEG complements the MEG in detecting source components not visible to the MEG. The unique combination of the characteristics of the MEG are its total noninvasiveness, simple and quick procedures, good accuracy in locating sources, and excellent resolution (msec) in time.

Neuromagnetic Fields

It is believed that the magnetic field detectable outside the head is produced by currents initiated at neural synapses and guided postsynaptically by cell structure. Magnetic field lines encircle the flow path of this primary current and extend outside the skull. Because pyramidal cells and the direction of their primary current are predominantly oriented perpendicular to the cortex. MEG is most sensitive to activity in fissural cortex where the current is oriented parallel to the nearest portion of the skull. Because the magnetic field produced by a single postsynaptic potential (PSP) is too weak to be detected outside the head, MEG reflects macroscopic coherent activity of thousands of neurons.

Central in the analysis of neuromagnetic data is the treatment of the inverse problem, that is, how the accurate determination of internal sources is based on measurements performed outside the head. The most common way to tackle this problem is to determine the single source current element (equivalent current dipole; ECD) that most completely explains the MEG pattern.

Currently, source localization data from MEG recordings are often projected onto magnetic resonance images (MRIs), which contain information about subjects' brain structure. In addition, measures of cerebral metabolism, blood volume, or blood flow obtained with PET, SPECT, and fMRI offer new possibilities for obtaining a more accurate picture of the distribution of cerebral activity than is possible with one method alone. Instead of only yielding a point of gravity of the activated area, these functional tomographic measures can determine the entire pattern of activity, although the relationship between neuronal activity and local changes in blood flow or metabolism is largely unknown.

If one can assume that the electromagnetically detected electrical activity is limited to areas defined by anatomical (MRI) or functional (fMRI, PET, SPECT) tomography, then the solution of the inverse problem can be obtained more accurately and reliably than is possible with MEG or EEG alone. For example, the combination of the fine spatial resolution of fMRI with the perfect time resolution of MEG can provide an unprecedented view to the time evolution of brain activity.

Because the MEG is insensitive to the radial component of the primary current, it is essential to also perform EEG measurements in order to get a more complete picture of cerebral electrical activity. Unfortunately, most MEG studies are still performed without EEG measurements, partly because of the additional work required in attaching the electrodes to the scalp and partly because of problems in utilizing EEG data in inverse solutions.

RESEARCH ON THE ELECTROPHYSIOLOGY OF ATTENTION

Starting in the early 1960s, research on the cerebral processes underlying human attention has been intense and has been continuously expanding, prompted by the advent and improved availability of new functional brain-imaging technologies. In the early 1960s, a large number of event-related potential (ERP) studies, then called evoked-potential (EP) studies, tried to demonstrate that attended stimuli elicit larger ERPs than unattended ones (for reviews, see Karlin, 1970; Näätänen, 1967, 1975). Several articles appeared in which it was claimed that the N1 amplitude of the auditory ERP, peaking at about 100 msec from stimulus onset, was enhanced by selective attention. Because of methodological drawbacks in many early studies, the N1 attention effect could be seriously challenged; the effect in the auditory modality was reliably demonstrated only in the 1970s (Hillyard, Hink, Schwent, & Picton, 1973). In this classic study using dichotically presented short tone pips, Hillyard et al. interpreted their enhanced N1 amplitudes in terms of a selective-attention effect on the exogenous N1 component. This particular interpretation, however, was questioned by Näätänen (1975), who proposed that despite the short onset latency of the selective effect (at 60–70 msec in most subjects), the effect might nevertheless be of endogenous rather than exogenous nature. Support was provided by Näätänen, Gaillard, and Mäntysalo (1978), who found a clearly endogenous effect of selective attention in their dichotic conditions, which they called the processing negativity (PN). These results permitted a temporally based separation of the exogenous N1 and the selective-attention effect. The PN commenced just after the N1 peak and continued for several hundreds of milliseconds. The authors further proposed that had they used interstimulus intervals (ISI) as short as those of Hillyard et al. (1973), their effect might have overlapped the N1 peak and thus enhanced its amplitude. That is, Hillyard et al.'s (1973) effect might have also been caused by the PN.

A genuine effect of attention on the exogenous N1, such as that proposed by Hillyard et al. (1973), would suggest that initial stimulus selection is based on the amplification of the exogenous neuronal activation pattern elicited by a stimulus, whereas an endogenous selective-attention effect (PN) at the N1 latency suggests that stimulus selection is based on a separate cortical attention mechanism (Näätänen, 1982, 1990, 1992). A large number of studies were conducted to decide between these two alternative interpretations. The results of these studies seem, in general, to suggest that the PN is the predominant ERP effect of selective attention in audition, but that under highly focused conditions, some exogenously elicited N1 activity to attended stimuli might also be enhanced (for reviews, see Alho, 1992; Hillyard & Picton, 1987; Näätänen, 1990, 1992; Näätänen & Alho, 1995).

Because of the problem of disentangling the attention effect from the exogenous N1, no definite answer was provided by these electrophysiological studies. It appears that in order to settle this issue, one must go to the level of generators. One should determine whether the selective-attention effect involves any of the neuronal populations generating the auditory exogenous N1, in which case one could speak of an attentional amplification of an exogenous response. Taking advantage of the ability of the MEG to locate electrical activity tangential to the surface of the head with a fairly good precision, several recent MEG studies have compared the sources of the selective-attention effect and the exogenous N1 visible to MEG recordings. These studies are reviewed later in this chapter.

In addition to these studies of brain mechanisms of selective attention (channel selection), ERP studies have also attempted to clarify attentional effects on within-channel processing, most typically, the detection of "deviant" (target) stimuli among the more frequent "standard" stimuli. The main focus of this set of studies has been to determine the extent to which the mismatch negativity (MMN), an ERP component elicited by sound change, is independent of attention as was originally claimed (Näätänen et al., 1978; Näätänen & Michie, 1979). In electrical studies trying to resolve this issue, the main impediment has been the overlap of the N2b component (Näätänen, Simpson, & Loveless, 1982; Renault & Lesevre, 1978; for a review, see Näätänen & Gaillard, 1983) in response to deviant stimuli of an attended stimulus sequence. Such an overlap makes it difficult to directly compare MMNs in attended and unattended channels (cf. Näätänen, Paavilainen, Tiitinen, Jiang, & Alho, 1993; Woldorff, Hackley, & Hillyard, 1991). The specific advantage of the MEG methodology here is that it is relatively insensitive to the N2b generator process, enabling one to compare the MMNm, the magnetic counterpart of the electric MMN (Hari et al., 1984), without N2b overlap. These studies will also be reviewed later in this chapter. An MMNm to change in tone frequency is illustrated in Fig. 13.1.

In the visual modality, the interpretation of the ERP selective-attention effects with regard to their exogenous/endogenous nature is not as problematic as in audition. Several studies (e.g., Harter, Aine, & Schroeder, 1982; Mangun & Hillyard, 1990) have convincingly established that when stimuli falling on one hemifield are attended and those on the opposite hemifield unattended (the subject fixating his or her gaze in the middle), the P1 and N1 components associated with attended stimuli are enhanced (for reviews, see Hillyard, Mangun, Woldorff, & Luck, 1995; Näätänen, 1992). These effects indeed appear to involve the exogenous components, not, however, those generated in the striate but rather those generated in the extrastriate cortex (Heinze et al., 1994).

These spatial visual-attention effects occur, however, only when the separation between the loci of origin of the attended and unattended visual stimuli in the visual field exceeds some minimum; if the two loci are too near one another, the posterior attention effect occurs in the form of a slow negative shift rather than of an enhancement of any exogenous component (Hillyard & Münte, 1984). Such visual processing negativities, called *selection negativities* by Harter and Aine (1984), also are markers of visual selective attention based on differences in any other visual attribute such as color, orientation, or size between the attended and unattended stimuli, as shown by the pioneering studies of Harter and his associates (Harter & Previc, 1978; Harter & Salmon, 1972; Harter et al., 1982; for a review, see Harter & Aine, 1984). Some recent MEG studies, reviewed later in this chapter, have also investigated visual selective-attention effects.

MEG STUDIES OF AUDITORY ATTENTION

One-Channel Conditions

The simplest paradigm used to study attention involves the presentation of a sequence of auditory stimuli, usually standards and deviants (targets), and then a comparison of effects of active (attend) and passive (ignore)

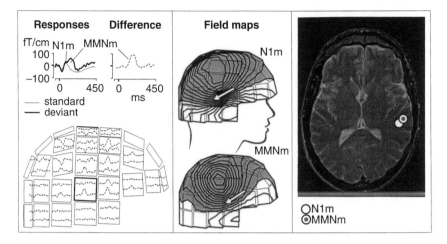

FIG. 13.1. Left Panel, Top Left: Magnetic responses recorded by one sensor over the right hemisphere to 1000-Hz standard tones (thin line) and to 1150-Hz deviant tones (thick line) occurring at a probability of 10% among standard tones delivered to the left ear of a subject concentrating on reading. Left Panel, Top Right: MMNm to deviant tones shown by a difference wave (dashed line; response to standard tones subtracted from that to deviant tones). Left Panel, Bottom: MMNm difference waves from different recording sites over the right hemisphere. Each square shows signals from two sensors of a 122-channel helmet-shaped magnetometer (Neuromag Ltd) that record orthogonal gradients of the magnetic field (Knuutila et al., 1993). Because these sensors are planar gradiometers, the recorded response is largest at the sensor above the source.

Middle Panel: Magnetic field maps for the N1m elicited by the standard tones (top) and for the MMNm elicited by the deviant tones (bottom) in the same subject. The equivalent current dipoles are indicated by white arrows. The gray area indicates magnetic flux going into the head and the white area indicates the flux coming out of the head.

Right Panel: Locations of the N1m and MMNm equivalent current dipoles in the right hemisphere indicated in the MRI of this subject's brain. Modified from Huotilainen, Ilmoniemi, Lavikainen, Tiitinen, Alho, Sinkkonen, Knuutila, and Näätänen (1993).

attention instructions. In EEG studies, the standard-stimulus response is not much affected by attention, the main effect usually being some enhancement of the N1 amplitude, probably because of increased nonspecific cortical excitability (Näätänen, 1975), and of the P2 amplitude (see Sams, Paavilainen, Alho, Reinikainen, & Näätänen, 1985). In contrast, the attention effect on the ERP elicited by the deviant (target) stimulus is quite robust, one of these being the emergence of the N2b component (Näätänen et al., 1982; Renault & Lesevre, 1978). The MMN, usually clearly visible in response to deviants in the ignore condition, is often overlapped by the N2b to an extent that makes the evaluation of the attention effect on the MMN impossible. (The MMN amplitude can, however, be separately estimated from the polarity-reversed "MMN" recordable below the Sylvian fissure; Näätänen, Jiang, Lavikainen, Reinikainen, & Paavilainen, 1993.) The N2b is followed by the positive P3a component, which tends to occur also in ignore conditions (a correlate of attention switch), as well as by slower parietal positivity, sometimes commencing even at the MMN latency, and frontal negative activity.

The principal purpose of the MEG studies comparing responses between such attend and ignore conditions has been to determine the possible attention effects on the MMNm generated in the supratemporal auditory cortex. The first two of these studies were those of Kaukoranta, Sams, Hari, Hämäläinen, and Näätänen (1989) for duration-decrement MMNm and of Lounasmaa, Hari, Joutsiniemi, and Hämäläinen (1989) for intensity-reduction MMNm. Neither study found an attention effect. Similarly, Pardo and Sams (1993) obtained no attention effect on their MMNm to the change of direction of a short frequency glide. Glide onset randomly occurred at very different frequency levels; consequently there were no constant standards. Joutsiniemi and Hari (1989), however, reported an attentional effect on an MEG response to stimulus omission in a tone sequence with constant ISIs in 6 of their 10 subjects, and this was enhanced by attention in 3 of these 6 subjects. In contrast to the MMNm with supratemporal origin, this response appeared to emerge from the posterolateral frontal cortex, possibly the frontal eye field or areas close to it. It remained unclear, however, whether the attentional enhancement observed in the 3 subjects emanated from the same locus as the omission response itself.

An attention effect on the MMNm to phonetic stimulus change was reported by Aulanko, Hari, Lounasmaa, Näätänen, and Sams (1993). These authors presented /ba/ as standard stimuli and /ga/ as deviant stimuli, or vice versa, the pitch of these phonemes randomly varying through 10 different steps. Irrespective of this irrelevant frequency variation, an MMNm was elicited by the phoneme change. This MMNm was larger in amplitude when the stimuli were attended than when they were not attended (the subject reading a book). However, in a subsequent study with phonetic stimuli (Aulanko, Ilmoniemi, & Sams, 1995), no attention effect was found.

Also, the MMNm produced by an occasional shortening of the constant ISI between consecutive stimuli (for related ERP findings, see Ford & Hillyard, 1981; Näätänen, Jiang, Lavikainen, Reinikainen, & Paavilainen, 1993; Nordby, Roth, & Pfefferbaum, 1988) might be enhanced by attention. It remained unclear, however, whether the apparent attentional enhancement involved the MMNm generator itself or whether attention caused the emergence of an overlapping component from another source.

In blind young adults, MEG evidence for neural plasticity was recently obtained by Kujala et al. (1995) in their attend condition when comparisons were made with sighted control subjects. These authors found that when the blind were instructed to detect pitch-deviant tones, the first major activation focus in the deviant-minus-standard difference maps (projected on the subject's own MRI image) occurred normally in the temporal lobe. This, however, was succeeded by an occipital activation focus not visible in the control subject data. Therefore, these results suggest that the early-blind visual cortex, in contrast to that of the sighted, participated in auditory discrimination. In the passive condition, however, the occipital cortex of the blind subjects showed no extra activity in response to the deviant tones. These results are consistent with the previous ERP recordings showing that the N2b component elicited by deviant tones in the active condition (targets) is posteriorly distributed over the scalp in early-blind adults relative to sighted adults, whereas the scalp distribution of the MMN elicited by deviant tones in a passive condition is unaffected by blindness (Kujala, Alho, Paavilainen, Summala, & Näätänen, 1992).

Multichannel Conditions

When a subject selectively attends to certain sounds that are separable from concurrent sounds on the basis of their frequency or locus of spatial origin, or both, attended sounds elicit an ERP that is negatively displaced in relation to the ERP to unattended sounds (for reviews see, e.g., Hillyard & Picton, 1987; Näätänen, 1990, 1992; Näätänen & Alho, 1995; Woods, 1990). This effect usually begins at the N1 latency and may continue for several hundreds of msec. Whereas the later portion of this attention effect is evidently caused by endogenous attention-related activity (the processing negativity; PN), there has been a long-lasting debate on the nature of the early portion of this effect at the N1 latency range.

For example, Woldorff and Hillyard (1991) proposed that the early attention effect at the N1 latency zone is caused by an enhancement of some exogenous N1 component in ERPs to attended sounds, as originally suggested by Hillyard et al. (1973). Especially the similar onset, peak, and offset latencies of the N1 and the early attention effect in dichotic conditions with very fast stimulation were regarded by Woldorff and Hillyard (1991) as strong evidence for the early attention effect being caused by an enhancement of the exogenous N1 components by strongly focused selective attention. If some exogenous N1 component was indeed enhanced by selective attention, then these results might be caused, for example, by an early cortical gating or filtering mechanism modulating the sensory input.

However, even the early attention effect might be caused by the endogenous PN overlapping with the exogenous N1 and originating from a generator source separate from that of the N1 (see Näätänen, 1975;

Näätänen et al., 1978; Näätänen & Michie, 1979). This is supported by the differences in the scalp distributions of the exogenous N1 to unattended sounds and the early attention effect, perfectly overlapping in time, even when very fast stimulation rates are used (Alho, Teder, Lavikainen & Näätänen, 1994; Näätänen, Teder, Alho, & Lavikainen, 1992; Teder, Alho, Reinikainen, & Näätänen, 1993). These studies cannot, of course, definitively rule out the possibility that there may also exist an attentional enhancement of some exogenous N1 component that contributes in some part to the early attention effect.

The PN (its earlier component) is probably generated by a cortical attentional selection process comparing each sensory input with an actively formed and maintained attentional trace, a neuronal facilitation pattern representing those features (e.g., location; Näätänen, 1982, 1990, 1992). This is supported by experimental results (e.g., Alho, Töttölä, Reinikainen, Sams, & Näätänen, 1987) showing that whereas the largest and longest duration PN is elicited by the attended sounds (perfectly matching with the attentional trace), even irrelevant sounds elicit some PN. In addition, this PN to irrelevant sounds is larger in amplitude and longer in duration the more these sounds resemble those to be attended, that is, the closer they match the attentional trace.

Several MEG studies have aimed at localizing the generator source(s) of the auditory selective-attention effect in the supratemporal auditory cortex for comparisons with the site of the N1m generator. In the dichotic selective listening experiments of Hari et al. (1989) and of Arthur, Lewis, Medvick, and Flynn (1991), ISIs were relatively long (800 msec or longer), such as those used in the ERP study of Näätänen et al. (1978), in which the long-duration PN commencing at the N1 latency was observed for the first time. Both Hari et al. (1989) and Arthur et al. (1991) found a long-duration attention effect resembling the PN of Näätänen et al. (1978), which began after the N1m peak and whose magnetic field pattern suggested a generator in the supratemporal auditory cortex. For an illustration of Hari et al.'s (1989) data, see Fig. 13.2. Hari et al., however, were not able to accurately determine the source of this magnetic counterpart of PN (PNm) due to its small size. Arthur et al. (1991), on the other hand, reported that the generator source of their PNm was, on the average, 7 mm anterior to the supratemporal N1m source. Interestingly, Hari et al. (1989) observed that in addition to the long-duration PNm elicited by attended tones, a shorter-duration PNm was elicited by the to-be-ignored tones delivered to the opposite ear (Fig. 13.2). This finding, resembling the ERP results of Alho et al. (1987), supports the theory (Näätänen, 1982) that the PN (or PNm) is generated by a cortical selection process in which sensory input is compared with an attentional trace, the PN being the longer in duration the better the stimulus matches the attentional trace.

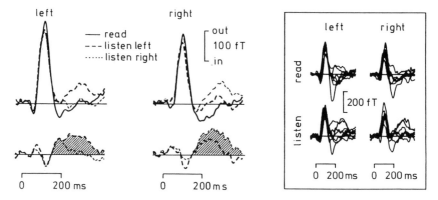

FIG. 13.2. Left: Magnetic responses (averaged across 7 subjects), recorded over the right fronto-temporal area, to the left-ear and right-ear tones when the subject was either reading or listening and silently counting the stimuli delivered to the designated ear. Below are shown the Listen-Read difference waves. The shadowed areas illustrate the magnetic counterpart of the processing negativity (PNm) which was elicited at a large amplitude by tones when they were attended (counted). A PNm, though one with a smaller amplitude and shorter duration, was elicited even by unattended tones when the tones delivered to the opposite ear were counted. Right: The individual magnetic responses of the 7 subjects. From Hari, Hämäläinen, Kaukoranta, Mäkelä, Joutsiniemi, and Tiihonen (1989). Copyright © 1989 by Springer Verlag. Reprinted with permission.

However, MEG data from auditory selective-attention experiments with very short ISIs have been regarded as indicating that enhanced activity of the supratemporal N1m source can contribute to the early attention effect. Curtis, Kaufman, and Williamson (1988; see also Kaufman & Williamson, 1987) delivered lower frequency tones (1000 and 1050 Hz) to one ear at the rate of 3 per second and higher frequency tones (3000 and 3050 Hz) to the other ear at the rate of 3.5 per second. Selective attention to tones presented to the designated ear resulted in enhancements of N1m and P2m responses. The supratemporal sources of these attentional enhancements could not be separated from the sources of N1m and P2m elicited by unattended tones. Similar results were obtained in a control condition where the two stimulus sequences were delivered to the same ear, the subject's task being to attend either to the low or high tones. However, the attention effects observed by Curtis et al. (1988) appear in many cases to be of longer duration than the exogenous N1m and P2m responses themselves, suggesting an at least partially endogenous origin.

In another short-ISI study, Arthur, Hillyard, Flynn, and Schmidt (1989) presented 1000-Hz tones to one ear and 2500-Hz tones to the other ear in random order, the ISI varying between 200 and 400 msec. Selective attention to tones delivered to a designated ear was associated with a biphasic attention effect. The source of the early portion of the attention effect at the N1m latency could not be statistically separated from the supratemporal N1m sources, although in most cases, the source of the attention effect tended to be slightly (1 cm or less) anterior to the supratemporal N1m source. The later portion (200–500 msec from stimulus onset) of the attention effect, which might correspond to the PNm discussed before, had a source that tended to be at the distance of 1.5 to 2 cm from the N1m source. In parallel ERP recordings at the midline scalp sites, both phases of the attention effect were observed as negative displacements in the response to attended tones relative to those observed in response to unattended tones.

A similar biphasic attention effect was observed by Rif, Hari, Hämäläinen, and Sams (1991), who delivered 1000-Hz tones to one ear and 3000-Hz tones to the opposite ear in random order, the subject attending either to the left- or right-ear tones. The ISI varied between 240 and 300 msec. The source of the attention effect at the N1m latency could not be statistically separated from the supratemporal N1m source, although it tended to be slightly (on the average, 4–5 mm) anterior to the N1m source. However, the later portion (peaking at around 170 msec) of the attention effect had a source which was, on the average, 9 mm anterior to the source of the early attention effect. This later attention effect, in contrast to the earlier one, was also observed when the 1000- and 3000-Hz tones were delivered to the same ear in random order with an ISI of 405 msec, the subject's task being to attend either to the low or high tones. Rif et al. (1991) suggested that their early attention effect was caused by an enhancement of the N1m to the attended tones. The authors further suggested that the later portion of the attention effect might have been caused, not by an endogenous PNm, but by an enhanced P2m to unattended tones, associated with the inhibition of their processing. However, this interpretation may be questioned because the P2m sources tended to be slightly (though not significantly) anterior and superior to the sources of the later attention effect.

As already mentioned, Arthur et al.'s (1989) and Rif et al.'s (1991) attention effect at the N1m latency tended to emanate from a source anterior to that of the N1m. Thus, these data did not strongly support the identity of the N1m as the source of the attention effect. The most convincing evidence for a genuine N1m attention effect has been provided by Woldorff et al. (1993). These authors delivered tones of 1000 and 3150 Hz to the subject's left and right ear, respectively, in random order with very short ISIs (125–325 msec), the subject attending either to the left- or right-ear tones. The tones elicited an enhanced N1m when they were attended, in relation to when they were unattended. The N1m source (calculated from responses to unattended tones) and the source of the N1m attention effect (calculated from difference waves) were found to be located in individual subject's MRIs in the supratemporal auditory cortex within a few millimeters of each other. However, as pointed out by Woldorff and Hillyard (1991), even when short ISIs are randomly varied, the overlapping time-smeared activity elicited by preceding and subsequent stimuli may distort the responses to a small but notable extent. Therefore, such overlapping activity might, to some extent, have contaminated the N1m source localization of Woldorff et al. (1993; in contrast, in difference waves obtained by subtracting responses to unattended stimuli from those to attended stimuli, the overlapping activity tends to be cancelled out, because the responses to randomly occurring attended and unattended stimuli are, on the average, similarly affected by overlapping activity). Therefore, it appears that the MEG evidence available to date for the attentional modulation of the N1m is still less than conclusive in the auditory modality.

Woldorff et al.'s (1993) N1m attention effect was preceded by an even earlier effect which also emanated from the supratemporal cortex. This effect corresponded to the early (at 20–50 msec from stimulus onset) positive displacement of the ERP to attended stimuli, in relation to that to unattended stimuli previously observed by Woldorff and Hillyard (1991).

Although the MEG is superior to the EEG in accurately localizing sources oriented tangentially to the skull, such as those in the supratemporal auditory cortex, it is insensitive, in contrast to electrical recordings, to sources oriented radially to the skull. Such sources can, for instance, be found in the auditory cortex on the lateral aspect of the temporal lobe. This may be a major disadvantage in MEG studies of auditory selective attention because ERP recordings suggest that several sources may contribute to the attention effect at the N1 latency range (Giard, Perrin, Pernier, & Peronnet, 1988; Teder, Alho, Reinikainen, & Näätänen, 1993; Woods, Alho, & Algazi, 1994). For example, in their ERP study with nose reference, Alho, Paavilainen, Reinikainen, Sams, and Näätänen (1986) observed no polarity inversion of the early attention effect at the scalp sites below the auditory cortex, whereas the N1 was inverted in polarity at these sites. This result suggests that whereas the N1 has a major source in the supratemporal auditory cortex, the attention effect at the N1 latency may get a contribution from the lateral aspect of the temporal lobe. Such an additional contribution from radially oriented sources might also explain the finding of Kuriki, Takeuchi, and Murase (1989; see also Kuriki & Takeuchi, 1991) that the attention effect at the N1 latency is more prominent in electrically than magnetically recorded brain responses.

MEG STUDIES OF VISUAL ATTENTION

The study of visual attention using the MEG or EEG is complicated by the large number and specificity of the visual areas. Although the cortical visual pathways are organized in a hierarchical manner (Van Essen & Maunsell, 1983), their activations overlap temporally. Therefore, signals seen in the MEG or EEG arise from multiple simultaneously active sources (Ahlfors, Ilmoniemi, & Hämäläinen, 1992). According to Regan (1989), "the properties of neurons in primary visual (V1) cortex seem to be unaffected by attention" (p. 236). Nonstriate visual cortex behaves differently. Moran and Desimone (1985) found that single-cell activity in area V4 and in inferotemporal cortex (IT) is strongly affected by spatially targeted attention; no such effect was found in the striate cortex.

In a representative EEG study, Luck, Heinze, Mangun, and Hillyard (1990) presented letter stimuli to both hemifields while the subject fixated on a cross and attended to one hemifield, pressing a button in response to randomly (20%) appearing target letters. When both hemifields were stimulated simultaneously, ERPs showed an enhanced positivity from about 75 to 250 msec that was largest posteriorly contralaterally to the attended hemifield. This enhancement appeared to be a modulation of the exogenous P1 component. When only one hemifield was stimulated, both P1 and N1 deflections were enhanced. On the basis of these results, the authors interpreted the P1 effect as being caused by facilitation of sensory processing for stimuli at an attended location. The effect on the N1 was conjectured to represent the orienting of attention to a task-relevant stimulus.

Although the MEG provides a powerful tool for the discrimination and localization of different evoked-response components, and the visually evoked magnetic fields have been well known and described for 20 years (Brenner, Williamson, & Kaufman, 1975; Teyler, Cuffin, & Cohen, 1975), only a few neuromagnetic visual attention experiments have been reported. Kaufman and Williamson (1987) describe an experiment in which two grating patterns, subtending 2° vertically and 3° horizontally, were presented above each other in one half of the visual field starting 0.5° to the side of the fixation point. One of the gratings was displayed for 200 msec at the rate of 3 per sec and the other one simultaneously at the rate of 2.75 per sec so that responses to the two trains could be separately averaged. One of the gratings had randomly presented spatial frequencies of 1.25 and 2.5 cycles per degree (cpd) and the other had spatial frequencies of either 3.5 or 7 cpd. The subject's task was to attend to either the lower or the higher lying grating.

It was found that the 150-msec component of the evoked magnetic field was strongly modulated by attention, so that when a particular grating site was attended, the response was enhanced relative to the response to the same stimuli when the other grating site was attended. An additional attentional effect was seen which began as early as 85 msec after stimulus onset.

Luber, Kaufman, and Williamson (1989) performed a somewhat similar study in which either 2 or 4 vertical bars were displayed for 34 ms within a $1° \times 1°$ square above the horizontal meridian either to the left or to the right of the fixation point. The stimuli were presented in random order, the 2-bar stimulus with 80% and the 4-bar stimuli with 20% probability. The subject was instructed to press a button when the 4-bar stimulus appeared in the designated attended hemifield.

In all three subjects, the magnetic fields evoked by attended and un-attended stimuli were virtually identical up to 150 to 210 msec from stimulus onset, but during the following 150 to 200 msec, the response to attended stimuli was clearly enhanced. The field pattern was markedly changed by attention at these longer latencies. It is evident from this observation that attention effects are different on different neuronal popu-lations that contribute to the visually evoked response.

Because Kaufman and Williamson (1987) reported marked attentional effects as early as 85 msec and also at 150 msec from stimulus onset, it is unclear why there were no earlier attention effects in the data of Luber at al. (1989). One possibility is that the early components of the attentional effect are oriented radially in some subjects and thus are not visible to the MEG.

In another early MEG study of visual attention, Aine et al. (1990) found enhanced MEG amplitudes but no change in location of equivalent current dipoles when subjects attended to a grating presented in the lower right quadrant instead of stimuli presented in the lower left quadrant. It there-fore appears that visual attention effects are, at least partially, modulations of exogenous responses, although probably not those generated in the striate cortex.

In their most recent study, Simpson et al. (1995) used combined MEG and EEG recordings and fMRI on the same subjects to study the effects of attention when subjects were presented with small checkerboard stimuli bilaterally. In the passive condition, fMRI indicated activity in areas V1, V2, fusiform gyrus, and other extrastriate regions. In the attend condition, the anterior cingulate, dorsolateral frontal, and inferior parietal cortices were also activated, particularly in the right hemisphere. Selective modulation of activity by the direction of attention was found in extrastriate cortex contralateral to the attended visual field. Whereas fMRI provided accurate spatial information about the attention-related activity, the combined MEG and EEG provided precise timing information, revealing effects of selective attention beginning at 90 msec from stimulus onset. In another recent study, Huotilainen et al. (1995) used a stimulus moving across the screen every 700 msec. In the passive condition, the subject fixated on a cross, ignoring the stimulus. In the active conditions, the subject was instructed to attend, in different blocks, to either the direction of movement, to stimulus color, or to the orientation of the bar stimulus. The effect of attention in fMRI was seen in extrastriate parietal, dorsal lateral, prefrontal, and anterior cingulate cortices. Temporally overlapping sources were observed in the MEG and EEG; source strengths were found to correlate with attention.

CONCLUSION

Magnetoencephalography provides a completely noninvasive tool to probe the real-time sensory and cognitive functions of the human brain, as well as their disturbances. As the previous discussion has indicated, measurements of the MMNm, the magnetic counterpart of the electrical mismatch negativity (MMN), have revealed that the processing of sensory stimulus features in audition is, at least in most conditions, independent of attention, with stimulus selection occurring beyond this phase of processing. MEG studies of auditory selective attention, however, have not been able to determine whether stimulus selection in audition is based solely on a matching type of process (comparing the current input with a neural representation of the stimulus to be attended: the attentional-trace theory) or whether in some conditions also selective modulation of the attended and unattended input channels occurs (gain theory). In the visual modality, MEG studies have confirmed that spatial selective attention does seem to be based on a gain type of selection mechanism that enhances all sensory input originating from the attended locus, at least if this locus is widely separated from that of the unattended stimuli.

In evaluating the MEG in cognitive brain research, it should be borne in mind that the MEG and EEG are the only noninvasive methodologies providing precise temporal information about the brain activation patterns studied. The MEG *locates* sources much more accurately, but this advantage of MEG over EEG applies only to the currents visible to the MEG, that is, to those that are not fully radial and not located very deep. These limitations of the MEG, however, could enable one to separately measure a single brain process rather than an amalgamate of multiple temporally overlapping processes, and then to use this process-specific information to disambiguate ERP data recorded in the same experimental situation. Therefore, the combined use of the two methodologies is strongly recommended in research aiming at an accurate description of the spatio-temporal activation patterns underlying the brain's cognitive operations (Näätänen et al., 1994).

ACKNOWLEDGMENT

This study was supported by the Academy of Finland.

REFERENCES

Ahlfors, S. P., Ilmoniemi, R. J., & Hämäläinen, M. S. (1992). Estimates of visually evoked cortical currents. *Electroencephalography and Clinical Neurophysiology, 82,* 225–236.

Aine, C., George, J., Medvick, P., Supek, S., Flynn, E., & Bodis-Wollner, I. (1989). Identification of multiple sources in transient visual evoked neuromagnetic responses. In S. J. Williamson, M. Hoke, G. Stroink, & M. Kotani (Eds.), *Advances in biomagnetism* (pp. 193–196). New York: Plenum.

Aine, C. J., George, J. S., Oakley, M. T., Medvick, P. A., & Flynn, E. R. (1990). Effects of spatial attention on visual-evoked neuromagnetic responses. In C. H. M. Brunia, A. W. K. Gaillard, & A. Kok (Eds.), *Psychophysiological brain research* (pp. 3–11). Tilburg, The Netherlands: Tilburg University Press.

Alho, K. (1992). Selective attention in auditory processing as reflected by event-related brain potentials. *Psychophysiology, 29,* 247–263.

Alho, K., Paavilainen, P., Reinikainen, K., Sams, M., & Näätänen, R. (1986). Separability of different negative components of the event-related brain potential associated with auditory stimulus processing. *Psychophysiology, 23,* 613–623.

Alho, K., Teder, W., Lavikainen, J., & Näätänen, R. (1994). Strongly focused attention and auditory event-related potentials. *Biological Psychology, 38,* 73–90.

Alho, K., Töttölä, K., Reinikainen, K., Sams, M., & Näätänen, R. (1987). Brain mechanisms of selective listening reflected by event-related potentials. *Electroencephalography and Clinical Neurophysiology, 68,* 458–470.

Arthur, D., Hillyard, S., Flynn, E., & Schmidt, A. (1989). Neural mechanisms of effects of selective auditory attention on event-related magnetic fields of the human brain. In S. J. Williamson, M. Hoke, G. Stroink, & M. Kotani (Eds.), *Advances in biomagnetism* (pp. 113–116). New York: Plenum.

Arthur, D. L., Lewis, P. S., Medvick, P. A., & Flynn, E. R. (1991). A neuromagnetic study of selective auditory attention. *Electroencephalography and Clinical Neurophysiology, 78,* 348–360.

Aulanko, R., Hari, R., Lounasmaa, O. V., Näätänen, R., & Sams, M. (1993). Phonetic invariance in the human auditory cortex. *NeuroReport, 4,* 1356–1358.

Aulanko, R., Ilmoniemi, R. J., & Sams, M. (1995). *Detection of phonetic changes in natural speech.* Manuscript submitted for publication.

Belliveau, J. W., Kennedy, D. N., McKinstry, R. C., Buchbinder, B. R., Weisskoff, R. M., Cohen, M. S., Vevea, J. M., Brady, T. J., & Rosen, B. R. (1991). Neuromagnetic evidence of spatially distributed sources underlying epileptiform spikes in the human brain. *Science, 254,* 716–719.

Brenner, D., Williamson, S. J., & Kaufman, L. (1975). Visually evoked magnetic fields of the human brain. *Science, 190,* 480–482.

Curtis, S., Kaufman, L., & Williamson, S. J. (1988). Divided attention: Selection based on location and pitch. In K. Atsumi, M. Kotani, S. Ueno, T. Katila, & S. J. Williamson (Eds.), *Biomagnetism '87* (pp. 138–141). Tokyo: Tokyo Denki University Press.

Ford, J. M., & Hillyard, S. A. (1981). Event related potentials, ERPs, to interruption of steady rhythm, *Psychophysiology, 18,* 322–330.

Giard, M.-H., Perrin, F., Pernier, J., & Peronnet, F. (1988). Several attention-related waveforms in auditory areas: A topographic study. *Electroencephalography and Clinical Neurophysiology, 69,* 371–384.

Hämäläinen, M., Hari, R., Ilmoniemi, R. J., Knuutila, J., & Lounasmaa, O. V. (1993). Magnetoencephalography—theory, instrumentation, and applications to noninvasive studies of the working human brain. *Reviews of Modern Physics, 65,* 413–497.

Hari, R. (1990). The neuromagnetic method in the study of the human auditory cortex. In F. Grandori, M. Hoke, & G. H. Romani (Eds.), *Auditory evoked magnetic fields and electric potentials* (pp. 222–282). Basel: Karger.

Hari, R., Hämäläinen, M., Ilmoniemi, R., Kaukoranta, E., Reinikainen, K., Salminen, J., Alho, K., & Sams, M. (1989). Responses of the primary auditory cortex to pitch changes in a sequence of tone pips: Neuromagnetic recordings in man. *Neuroscience Letters, 50,* 127–132.

Hari, R., Hämäläinen, M., Kaukoranta, E., Mäkelä, J., Joutsiniemi, S.-L., & Tiihonen, J. (1989). Selective listening modifies activity of the human auditory cortex. *Experimental Brain Research, 74,* 463–470.

Hari, R., Joutsiniemi, S.-L., Hämäläinen, M., & Vilkman, V. (1989). Responses of human auditory cortex to change in temporal stimulation patterns. *Neuroscience Letters, 99,* 164–168.

Harter, M. R., & Aine, C. J. (1984). Brain mechanisms of visual selective attention. In R. Parasuraman & R. Davies (Eds.), *Varieties of attention* (pp. 293–321). London: Academic Press.

Harter, M. R., Aine, C., & Schroeder, C. (1982). Hemispheric difference in the neural processing of stimulus location and type: Effects of selective attention on visual evoked potentials. *Neuropsychologia, 20,* 421–436.

Harter, M. R., & Salmon, L. E. (1972). Intra-modality selective attention and evoked cortical potentials to randomly presented patterns. *Electroencephalography and Clinical Neurophysiology, 32,* 605–613.

Harter, M. R., & Previc, F. H. (1978). Size-specific information channels and selective attention: Visual evoked potential and behavioral measures. *Electroencephalography and Clinical Neurophysiology, 45,* 628–640.

Heinze, H. J., Mangun, G. R., Burchert, W., Hinrichs, H., Scholz, M., Münte, T. F., Gös, A., Scherg, M., Johannes, S., Hundesnagen, H., Gazzaniza, M., & Hillyard, S. A. (1994). Combined spatial and temporal imaging of brain activity during visual selective attention in humans. *Nature, 372,* 543–546.

Hillyard, S. A., Hink, R. F., Schwent, V. L., & Picton, T. W. (1973). Electrical signs of selective attention in human brain. *Science, 182,* 177–180.

Hillyard, S. A., Mangun, G. R., Woldorff, M. G., & Luck, S. J. (1994). Neural systems mediating selective attention. In M. S. Gazzaniga (Ed.), *The cognitive neurosciences* (pp. 665–668). Cambridge, MA: MIT Press.

Hillyard, S. A., & Münte, T. F. (1984). Selective attention to color and location: An analysis with event-related brain potentials. *Perception and Psychophysics, 36,* 185–198.

Hillyard, S. A., & Picton, T. (1987). Electrophysiology of cognition. In F. Plum (Ed.), *Handbook of physiology, Section 1: Neurophysiology, Vol. V: Higher functions of the brain* (pp. 519–584). Baltimore: American Physiological Society.

Huotilainen, M., Ahlfors, S. P., Aronen, H. J., Dale, A. M., Foxe, J. J., Ilmoniemi, R. J., Kennedy, W. A., Korvenoja, A., Liu, A. K., Näätänen, R., Rosen, B. R., Simpson, G. V., Standertskjöld-Nordenstam, C.-G., Tootel, R. B. H., Virtanen, J., & Belliveau, J. W. (1995). Combined fMRI, EEG and MEG imaging of visual attention. *Society for Neuroscience Abstracts, 21,* p. 1760.

Huotilainen, M., Ilmoniemi, R. J., Lavikainen, J., Tiitinen, H., Alho, K., Sinkkonen, J., Khuutila, J., & Näätänen, R. (1993). Interaction between representations of different features of auditory sensory memory. *NeuroReport, 4,* 1279–1281.

Joutsiniemi, S.-L., & Hari, R. (1989). Omissions of auditory stimuli may activate frontal cortex. *European Journal of Neuroscience, 1*, 524–528.

Karlin, L. (1970). Cognition, preparation, and sensory-evoked potentials. *Psychological Bulletin, 73*, 122–136.

Kaufman, L., & Williamson, S. J. (1987). Recent developments in neuromagnetism. In C. Barber & T. Blum (Eds.), *Evoked potentials III* (pp. 100–113). Boston: Butterworths.

Kaukoranta, E., Sams, M., Hari, R., Hämäläinen, M., & Näätänen, R. (1989). Reactions of human auditory cortex to a change in tone duration. *Hearing Research, 41*, 15–22.

Knoll, G. F. (1983). Single-photon emission computed tomography. *Proceedings of the IEEE, 71*, 320–329.

Knuutila, J. E. T., Ahonen, A. I., Hämäläinen, M. S., Kajola, M. J., Laine, P. P., Lounasmaa, O. V., Parkkonen, L. T., Simola, J. T., & Tesche, C. D. (1993). A 122-channel whole cortex SQUID system for measuring the brain's magnetic fields. *IEEE Transactions on Magnetism, 29*, 3315–3320.

Kujala, T., Alho, K., Paavilainen, P., Summala, H., & Näätänen, R. (1992). Neural plasticity in processing of sound location by the early blind: An event-related potential study. *Electroencephalography and Clinical Neurophysiology, 84*, 469–472.

Kujala, T., Huotilainen, M., Sinkkonen, J., Ahonen, A. I., Alho, K., Hämäläinen, M. S., Ilmoniemi, R. J., Kajola, M., Knuuttila, J. E. T., Lavikainen, J., Salonen, O., Simola, J., Standertskjöld-Nordenstam, C.-G., Tiitinen, H., Tissari, S. O., & Näätänen, R. (1995). Visual cortex activation in blind humans during sound discrimination. *Neuroscience Letters, 183*, 143–146.

Kuriki, S., & Takeuchi, F. (1991). Neuromagnetic responses elicited by auditory stimuli in dichotic listening. *Electroencephalography and Clinical Neurophysiology, 80*, 406–411.

Kuriki, S., Takeuchi, F., & Murase, M. (1989). Event-related potentials and fields evoked by auditory stimuli: Effects of interstimulus interval and selective attention. In S. J. Williamson, M. Hoke, G. Stroink, & M. Kotani (Eds.), *Advances in biomagnetism* (pp. 109–112). New York: Plenum.

Lounasmaa, O. V., Hari, R., Joutsiniemi, S.-L., & Hämäläinen, M. (1989). Multi SQUID recordings of human cerebral magnetic fields may give information about memory processes in the human brain. *Europhysics Letters, 9*, 603–608.

Luber, B., Kaufman, L., & Williamson, S. J. (1989). Brain activity related to spatial visual attention. In S. J. Williamson, M. Hoke, G. Stroink, & M. Kotani (Eds.), *Advances in biomagnetism* (pp. 213–216). New York: Plenum.

Luck, S. J., Heinze, H. J., Mangun, G. R., & Hillyard, S. A. (1990). Visual event-related potentials index focused attention within bilateral stimulus arrays: II. Functional dissociation of P1 and N1 components. *Electroencephalography and Clinical Neurophysiology, 75*, 528–542.

Mangun, G. R., & Hillyard, S. A. (1990). Electrophysiological studies of visual selective attention in humans. In A. Scheibel & A. Wechsler (Eds.), *The neurobiological foundations of higher cognitive function* (pp. 271–294). New York: Guilford.

Moran, J., & Desimone, R. (1985). Selective attention gates visual processing in the extrastriate cortex. *Science, 229*, 782–784.

Näätänen, R. (1967). Selective attention and evoked potentials. *Annales Academiae Scientiarum Fennicae B, 151*, 1–226.

Näätänen, R. (1975). Selective attention and evoked potentials in humans—A critical review. *Biological Psychology, 2*, 237–307.

Näätänen, R. (1982). Processing negativity: An evoked-potential reflection of selective attention. *Psychological Bulletin, 92*, 605–640.

Näätänen, R. (1990). The role of attention in auditory information processing as revealed by event-related potentials and other brain measures of cognitive function. *Behavioral and Brain Sciences, 13*, 201–288.

Näätänen, R. (1992). *Attention and brain function*. Hillsdale, NJ: Lawrence Erlbaum Associates.

Näätänen, R., & Alho, K. (1995). Mismatch negativity—A unique measure of sensory processing in audition. *International Journal of Neuroscience, 80,* 317–337.

Näätänen, R., & Gaillard, A. W. K. (1983). The N2 deflection of ERP and the orienting reflex. In A. W. K. Gaillard & W. Ritter (Eds.), *EEG correlates of information processing: Theoretical issues* (pp. 119–141). Amsterdam: North Holland.

Näätänen, R., Gaillard, A. W. K., & Mäntysalo, S. (1978). Early selective attention effect on evoked potential reinterpreted. *Acta Psychologica, 42,* 313–329.

Näätänen, R., Ilmoniemi, R. J., & Alho, K. (1994). Magnetoencephalography in studies of human cognitive brain function. *Trends in Neurosciences, 17,* 389–395.

Näätänen, R., Jiang. D., Lavikainen, J., Reinikainen, K., & Paavilainen, P. (1993). Event-related potentials reveal a memory trace for temporal features. *NeuroReport, 5,* 310–312.

Näätänen, R., & Michie, P. T. (1979). Early selective attention effects on the evoked potential: A critical review and reinterpretation. *Biological Psychology, 8,* 81–136.

Näätänen, R., Paavilainen, P., Tiitinen, H., Jiang, D., & Alho, K. (1993). Attention and mismatch negativity. *Psychophysiology, 30,* 436–450.

Näätänen, R., Simpson, M., & Loveless, N. E. (1982). Stimulus deviance and evoked potentials. *Biological Psychology, 14,* 53–98.

Näätänen, R., Teder, W., Alho, K., & Lavikainen, J. (1992). Auditory attention and selective input modulation: A topographical ERP study. *NeuroReport, 3,* 493–496.

Nordby, H., Roth, W. T., & Pfefferbaum, A. (1988). Event-related potentials to time-deviant and pitch-deviant tones. *Psychophysiology, 25,* 249–261.

Pardo, P. J., & Sams, M. (1993). Human auditory cortex responses to rising versus falling glides. *Neuroscience Letters, 159,* 43–45.

Regan, D. (1989). *Human brain electrophysiology.* New York: Elsevier.

Renault, B., & Lesévre, N. (1978). Topographical study of the emitted potential obtained after the omission of an expected visual stimulus. In D. Otto (Ed.), *Multidisciplinary perspectives in event-related brain potential research, EPA 600/9-77-043* (pp. 202–208). Washington, DC: U.S. Government Printing Office.

Rif, J., Hari, R., Hämäläinen, M. S., & Sams, M. (1991). Auditory attention affects two different areas in the human supratemporal cortex. *Electroencephalography and Clinical Neurophysiology, 79,* 464–472.

Sams, M., Paavilainen, P., Alho, K., & Näätänen, R. (1985). Auditory frequency discrimination and event-related potentials. *Electroencephalography and Clinical Neurophysiology, 62,* 437–448.

Simpson, G. V., Belliveau, J. W., Ahlfors, S. P., Ilmoniemi, R. J., Baker, J. R., & Foxe, J. J. (1995, September). *Spatiotemporal mapping of human cortical areas involved in visual spatial attention.* Paper presented at the Annual Meeting of the Electroencephalographic Society, Washington, DC.

Teder, W., Alho, K., Reinikainen, K., & Näätänen, R. (1993). Interstimulus interval and the selective attention effect on auditory ERPs: N1 enhancement vs. processing negativity. *Psychophysiology, 30,* 71–81.

ter-Pogossian, M. M., Phelps, M. E., Hoffman, E. J., & Mullani, N. A. (1975). A positron emission transaxial tomograph for nuclear medicine imaging (PET). *Radiology, 114,* 89–98.

Teyler, T. J., Cuffin, B. N., & Cohen, D. (1975). The visual evoked magnetoencephalogram. *Life Sciences, 17,* 683–692.

Van Essen, D. C., & Maunsell, J. H. (1983). Hierarchical organization and functional streams in the visual cortex. *Trends in Neuroscience, 6,* 370–375.

Woldorff, M. G., Gallen, C. G., Hampson, S. A., Hillyard, S. A., Pantev, C., Sobel, D., & Bloom, F. E. (1993). Modulation of early sensory processing in human auditory cortex during auditory selective attention. *Proceedings of the National Academy of Sciences of the United States of America, 90,* 8722–8726.

Woldorff, M. G., Hackley, S. A., & Hillyard, S. A. (1991). The effects of channel-selective attention on the mismatch negativity wave elicited by deviant tones. *Psychophysiology, 28,* 30–42.

Woldorff, M. G., & Hillyard, S. A. (1991). Modulation of early auditory processing during selective listening to rapidly presented tones. *Electroencephalography and Clinical Neurophysiology, 79,* 170–191.

Woods, D. L. (1990). The physiological basis of selective attention: Implications of event-related potential studies. In J. W. Rohrbaugh, R. Parasuraman, & R. Johnson, Jr. (Eds.), *Event-related potentials: Basic issues and applications* (pp. 178–209). New York: Oxford University Press.

Woods, D. L., Alho, K., & Algazi, A. (1994). Stages of auditory feature conjunction: An event-related brain potential study. *Journal of Experimental Psychology: Human Perception and Performance, 20,* 1–14.

IV

Studies of Attention, Affect, and Action in Child Development

14

Functions of Orienting in Early Infancy

Michael I. Posner
Mary K. Rothbart
Lisa Thomas-Thrapp
University of Oregon

Study of the orienting reflex has been central to behavioral and cognitive psychology (Graham, 1979; Posner & Petersen, 1990; Sokolov, 1990). Not all sensory stimuli elicit orienting. Sokolov showed that orienting could be habituated when repetition of the stimulus showed it to be without significance to the organism; thus orienting depended not only on the stimulus itself, but also on the past history of the organism. The concept of an internal mechanism that aligns the sensory system with new input, and that has sufficient information to separate novel from repeated events, provides impetus toward developing an understanding of how expectations can guide the processing of sensory signals.

Recent studies using powerful neuroimaging methods have provided a basis for understanding the neural systems that mediate orienting to sensory events, both by behavioral adjustments and by purely covert changes within the brain (Posner & Raichle, 1994). What is most interesting about these anatomical results is that they fit rather well with results of brain lesion work and studies of normal subjects in providing a picture relating specific aspects of orienting to underlying brain systems.

Although we are still far from a complete understanding of how the brain orchestrates orienting, we have enough information to know that very specific brain areas carry out computations that, when taken together, provide amplification of the attended events. In the first section of this chapter we outline some of these computations. Next, we examine whether the development of orienting mechanisms reflects the anatomical-cognitive constraints we have reviewed. We trace two major periods related to the achievement of orienting. The first period is between 3 and 6 months of age. During this period (see also Berg & Richards, chapter 15, this volume), the infant achieves a high level of ability to shift attention to a visual stimulus and develops the capacity to anticipate its occurrence. Much of this development depends on the maturation of a brain network that includes parietal, thalamic, and midbrain mechanisms related to shifting attention to targets. This network allows infants to orient to objects, and provides a basis for distraction as a soothing method. A second important period begins later in the second year of life, and provides the child with the ability to exercise voluntary control in a more flexible fashion. The development of this system allows more complex forms of anticipation and the effective control of language and internal thought.

MECHANISMS OF ORIENTING

When people search a visual scene, they move attention from place to place. They may do so either overtly by moving their head and eyes in the direction of the stimulus, or covertly by an internal act that gives priority to a stimulus. Recent neuroimaging studies have provided clear evidence that covert shifts of attention from location to location involve areas of the parietal lobe (Corbetta, Miezen, Shulman, & Petersen, 1993).

The basic conception that has motivated this work is that these parietal cells index a shift of attention between successive locations (Mountcastle, 1978; Posner, 1988). The parietal activation can serve as a source of input to areas of the brain that process visual stimuli such as the extrastriate areas involved in processing motion, form, and color (Corbetta, Miezen, Dobmeyer, Shulman, & Petersen, 1991). Attentional areas of the parietal lobe have input to pathways that identify the visual objects. This input serves to amplify the relative contribution of stimuli occurring at the locations to which the person has been instructed to attend (Posner & Dehaene, 1994). The amplification produced by orienting of attention appears to involve a combination of boosting the signal at the attended location and inhibiting nonattended locations (Luck & Hillyard, 1994), although we are not yet sure of the details of how this is accomplished at the cellular level. Visual areas of the extrastriate cortex show the influence of orienting within the first 100 msec after input (Heinze et al., 1994), so that an attended location is relatively enhanced from this early point in processing.

When people search a visual scene, the focus of attention remains unified to one location, although it can move rapidly from place to place.

This unification of attention appears to rest on the commissures that connect the two halves of the brain (Luck, Hillyard, Mangun, & Gazzaniga, 1994). People whose commissures have been disconnected show evidence of two independent foci of attention; they appear able to search the visual scene faster when stimuli are distributed between the two fields, whereas normal subjects show no differences.

There also appears to be a basic asymmetry in the orienting mechanisms: The right parietal lobe is active irrespective of visual field; the left parietal lobe is active only when the person shifts attention within the right visual field (Corbetta et al., 1993). A second important asymmetry has also emerged. Patients with lesions of the right parietal lobe appear to have difficulty in switching from locations to move in a leftward direction, but this difficulty is no greater when the switch is within a single object or between objects (Egly, Driver, & Rafal, 1994). Patients with lesions of the left parietal lobe, however, have much greater difficulty in switching rightward when the switch involves leaving one object to go to another than when switching within a single object.

These findings provide support for previous suggestions that a network of neural areas allows orienting to the location of an attended object (Posner & Petersen, 1990). According to this view, the network is thought to involve particular anatomical areas that are both cortical (parietal lobe) and subcortical (pulvinar of the thalamus and superior colliculus). Each of these areas performs a separate computation. The parietal lobe is most associated with disengaging from a current visual location. The colliculus has been associated with shifting or moving the index of attention. The pulvinar appears to serve as an input to object recognition visual areas and is involved in the amplification of the attended input. The new results suggest that the left parietal portions of this network have a further specialization for dealing with the details of visual objects; the right parietal areas serve a more general function of attention to locations.

The localization of mental operations within the orienting network has clear implications for the development of this network. There is considerable evidence that maturation of subcortical visual areas (e.g., superior colliculus) occurs earlier than maturation of cortical areas. Thus, computations that involve subcortical systems might appear earlier in development. In addition, there are important differences in maturation of the two cerebral hemispheres (Geschwind & Galaburda, 1987), suggesting that orienting to locations may develop earlier than orienting to objects. As each of these component operations develops, one may expect to see important consequences for the naturally occurring behavior of the infant. It is also possible to distinguish between orienting to an external cue that summons attention and orienting based on a fully internal expectation. Early infancy is a time when one can study the influence of external cues with relatively little influence from high-level cognitive control. To examine these issues, we turn first to methods designed to study infant orienting to external events and later consider the role of learning and cognitive control.

DEVELOPMENT OF ORIENTING IN INFANTS

One of the important aspects of regarding attention as a neural system with its own anatomy is that one can ask quite specific questions about its development. When an anatomy of early vision was created based on the work of Hubel and Wiesel (Hubel, 1981), there was great interest in understanding how visual mechanisms developed. More recently, new knowledge concerning the anatomy of attention (Posner & Raichle, 1994) allows us to study its development. To study the development of the orienting network, we have used marker tasks (Posner & Rothbart, 1994). These are simple behavioral tasks that have been shown in adults to involve particular portions of the anatomy of the visual orienting network. These tasks generally require the infant to make an eye movement to a stimulus. By studying infants' ability to perform different marker tasks with increasing age, we try to make inferences about the development of the network.

Shifts

In our previous work we examined two marker tasks related to the orienting network (Posner & Rothbart, 1994). One required infants to disengage from a powerful attractor stimulus to move their eyes to a target. The second examined the tendency to return attention to a previously examined location. Next we briefly discuss our previous findings and then examine them in relation to new results on the mechanisms of orienting to objects and locations.

Previously we had shown that computations involving the visual orienting system underwent considerable development in the period from 3 to 6 months. For example, we showed that infants of 2 months were very poor in disengaging from a central stimulus, but by 4 to 6 months became quite fluent (Johnson, Posner, & Rothbart, 1991). Development of the "disengage" operation in our marker task appeared to fit well with the maturation of parietal areas (Chugani, Phelps, & Mazziotta, 1987) shown by brain imaging results. Moreover, the difficulty in disengaging prior to 3 to 4 months fits well with the natural phenomenon of "obligatory looking" that produces long periods of intense fixation in infants during early development (Johnson et al., 1991) that may be interpreted in connection with mother–child interaction as "love" (Fig. 14.1).

We also examined another marker task that has been called *inhibition of return*. If adults are first cued to attend to a location and then cued

FIG. 14.1. A mother and her 3-month-old engage in extended affectionate orienting that may be associated with failure to disengage.

away from that location, reaction times to targets at the previously attended location are increased in comparison to novel locations in the field. Inhibition of return works in conjunction with the saccadic system to ensure that eye movements are made more frequently to novel locations than to locations that have just been examined. Studies of patients have suggested that inhibition of return depends on midbrain structures including the superior colliculus (Rafal, Posner, Friedman, Inhoff, & Bernstein, 1988). In addition, when normal adults receive information through the temporal visual field, inhibition of return is increased over what is found for input into the nasal visual field (Rafal, Henik, & Smith, 1991). Because connections to the colliculus are more direct from the temporal visual field, this has also been treated as evidence of the collicular basis for inhibition of return.

To study the development of inhibition of return, infants of 3, 4, 6, 12, and 18 months and adults were tested (Clohessy, Posner, Rothbart, & Vecera, 1991). They faced a display of three monitors. The central monitor presented them with a powerful visual attractor that produced a strong visual fixation. The central attractor was turned off and replaced with a single visual stimulus 30° to the left or right of the central attractor. When the baby oriented to the peripheral stimulus, the central attractor was turned back on and the peripheral stimulus off. A pair of identical visual stimuli were then presented 30° to the left or right of fixation (see Fig. 14.2).

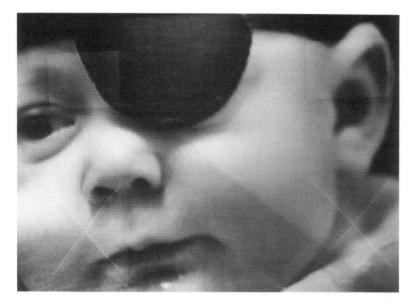

FIG. 14.2.   The inhibition of return paradigm in which infants orient to one
of two identical figures 30° from fixation. The simple X stimuli on the
computer screen are superimposed on the infant's face for easy coding of
eye movements. The patch is used to separate the temporal and nasal visual
field. The temporal visual field has dominant connections to the opposite
superior colliculus.

Evidence favoring inhibition of return would be a bias toward turning
to the side opposite the previously examined stimulus. Infants of 6, 12,
and 18 months and adults showed this bias to about the same degree.
The bias lasted for about two sec, or time for 2 to 3 eye movements.
However, there was no inhibition of return for 3- and 4-month-old infants.

In our original work we used stimuli 30° from fixation. However, as we
prepared to study orienting to objects, we wanted to present stimuli closer
to fixation (Harman, Posner, Rothbart, & Thomas-Thrapp, 1994). Thus, we
studied inhibition of return for 3-month-olds with peripheral stimuli at
both 10° and 30° from fixation. We confirmed our previous result of no
inhibition of return at 30°, but we found strong evidence of a bias not to
return to the previous location at 10°. A possible reason for this difference
arose when we examined the eye movements of these infants. Three-
month-olds did not often move directly to the target in our 30° displays.
When moving to such a target they show several head and eye fixations
that eventually reach the target location. However, for smaller movements
of 10°, where the infants moved their eyes directly to the target, inhibition
of return was observed. The reason for these surprising findings may lie in

discoveries about the conditions under which inhibition of return occurs in adults.

In adults, inhibition of return does not require an actual eye movement toward the visual event. In fact, it requires only that the person prepare an eye movement (Rafal, Calabresi, Brennan, & Scioloto, 1989). Preparing an eye movement may be seen as activating a motor program that will move the eyes from the current position to the target. The eyes normally move in a ballistic fashion to a target event once the motor program specifies the coordinates for the intended target. When adults are told where to attend by a central arrow presented at fixation, inhibition of return is not found unless they sometimes have to use the arrow as a basis for an eye movement. If they sometimes have to move their eyes to the target, inhibition of return is found, even on those targets where no eye movements actually occurred. The authors concluded that the necessary and sufficient condition to obtain inhibition of return was to program an eye movement to that location.

Recently, inhibition of return has been shown for newborn infants, presumably reflecting the midbrain mechanisms that are dominant at birth (Valenza, Simon, & Umilta, 1994). When these infants oriented directly to 30° targets, they showed clear evidence of inhibition of return. This finding, taken with our results for 10° infants, suggests that the basic computations for inhibition of return are present at birth. Their implementation will depend on whether a stimulus evokes a programmed eye movement or not. We are not sure of the factors that produce so many hypometric eye movements in infants of 3 months. However, these may relate to maturation of the cortical systems (e.g., parietal lobe, frontal eye fields) that appear to occur about this time. These data generally support the idea that the subcortical computations involved in inhibition of return are present earlier than the ability to disengage from a visual stimulus.

Locations and Objects

In adults there appear to be separate mechanisms involved in orienting to objects and to locations. Inhibition of return clearly is a kind of preference for a novel over a just-attended location. We have argued that this computation depends on midbrain structures that are strongly dominant at birth. However, preference for novel objects must depend in part on maturation of cortical systems involved in object recognition. In recent studies we have compared directly infants' novelty preference for location and for objects. In our first studies (Harman, Posner, Rothbart, & Thomas-Thrapp, 1994), we found that infants of 3 and 6 months showed much stronger novelty preferences when a novel target was shown at a novel location. When a novel object appeared at a novel location, infants showed a novelty preference on 73% of the trials at 3 months and 77% at 6 months. When location and object novelty were put in competition, 3-month-olds no longer showed an object novelty preference. By 6 months, however, infants oriented toward the novel object 63% of the time even though it occurred at a repeated location. Because object novelty seemed to be stronger at 6 months than at 3 months, we interpreted our results as indicating that object novelty develops somewhat later than preference based on location. A similar result had been found earlier when infants of 3 and 6 months were required to learn discriminative responses based on positional or stimulus identity cues (Colombo, Mitchell, Coldren, & Atwater, 1990). Three-month-olds were most likely to learn from positional cues and 6-month-olds from object cues.

Recently we have been able to extend these studies to show the relative independence of the two forms of novelty preference at 6 months. We (Thomas-Thrapp, Posner, & Rothbart, 1995) compared the same infants in single trial paradigms involving either exposure to a single object or to a single location followed by forced choice between two objects or two locations. On trials to assess novel objects, the infant was presented with a single object at fixation. After an interval they were presented with that object and a novel one, each at 10° from fixation. In the location condition, the infant's eyes were drawn to a single object and then returned to fixation. The choice trials involved identical stimuli presented either at the previous location or on the opposite side of fixation.

When infants had sufficient exposure time to the single object, they showed a preference for the novel object and for the novel location. We found the novelty preference when the infant examined the first object for 3 sec or more, but not when they oriented to it for only 1 sec. The time exposure necessary to show an object preference in our 6-month-old infants was similar to that reported for infant monkeys (Gunderson & Swartz, 1986). Location preference was established even when the orienting to the single stimulus was less than a second. Thus we were able to replicate both forms of novelty preference in these infants. Because these studies involved 33 infants, it was possible to ask if the two forms of novelty preference were correlated. The data were clear in showing that there was no significant correlation ($r = .15$). This finding is congruent with the interpretation that we are studying two independent forms of novelty preference.

In our previous work on orienting to locations, we often found a bias for turning toward the left when the infant had a choice between two lateral locations. However, these effects were not significant within any study and showed extremely high variability. In the current data, we again found that, during the novel location trials, infants were more likely to orient to their left, but the bias was not significant. Object novelty trials produced biases in the opposite direction, with infants more likely to turn to the stimulus on the right. Although these lateralized turning preferences were not strong enough to base any final interpretation, their overall direction is in accord with findings of adult studies favoring a right hemisphere bias for orienting to locations and a left hemisphere bias for orienting to objects (Egly, Driver, & Rafal, 1994).

These results support an approach to the development of orienting based on the maturation of specific brain networks. Sokolov's early work showed that the orienting reflex habituated with repeated stimulus presentations. Much of the study of infant cognitive development rests on evidence of habituation following repeated stimulation. Our studies show that evidence of habituation can occur after presentation of a single stimulus, and suggest that there may be independent forms of habituation. Inhibition of return, based on collicular computations, is present at birth, and provides an early basis for novelty preference based on visual location. Because this form of novelty preference is so closely related to eye movements, it is only exhibited when the infant is able to program movements toward objects. Although habituation based on object novelty is present to some degree even at birth, we found with our single trial procedure evidence of its development in the period between 3 and 6 months. Our data suggest that this form of novelty preference is not correlated with inhibition of return. It seems likely that it arises along with important developments in the visual pathways involved in object recognition and orienting occurring at this age. The development of a preference for novel objects has important consequences for cognition and emotion that we attempt to trace in the next section.

CONSEQUENCES OF ORIENTING

Distress

How does the ability to control attention affect the life of the infant? We have described orienting as a simple form of attention that undergoes important development during the early life of the infant. Another important aspect of early infant development is the ability to control emotional responses, in particular distress. The regulation of distress is a central concern of early infancy (see also Balaban, Snidman, & Kagan, chapter 16, this volume). In adult studies, Derryberry and Rothbart (1988) showed that self-reports of ability to focus and shift attention are inversely related to negative emotionality. We sought a model task in the infant that might allow us to study this attention–emotion relationship more directly.

Caregivers provide a hint of how attention is used to regulate the state of the infant. Earlier than 3 months, caregivers usually report themselves as using holding and rocking as the main means of quieting the infant.

However, by about 3 months, many caregivers, particularly in Western cultures, attempt to distract their infants by bringing the infants' attention to other stimuli. As infants attend, they are often quieted and their distress appears to diminish.

Systematic studies of 3- to 4- and 6-month-old infants' soothing to distractors were conducted in our laboratory (Harman, 1994; Harman, Rothbart, & Posner, in press). The infants are first distressed by over-stimulation from lights and sounds, but they then strongly orient to the interesting visual and auditory events we present (see Fig. 14.3). While they orient, the facial and vocal signs of distress disappear. However, when the orienting stops—for example, when the new object is removed after being shown for 10 sec—the distress returns to almost exactly the levels shown prior to presentation of the object. Apparently the loss of overt signs of distress is not always accompanied by a genuine loss of distress. Instead, some internal system that we have called the distress keeper appears to hold the initial level of distress, and the distress returns if the infant's orientation to the novel event is lost.

In our initial studies of the control of distress, objects were introduced for a period of 10 sec and then removed. Control experiments showed that the removal of the object did not cause distress when the infant was not

FIG. 14.3. Distress is coded from infant expression as in this figure. The distress will be absent during strong orienting and then return at full strength following the orienting.

already distressed. In subsequent efforts (Harman et al., in press), longer periods of orienting were used in order to see whether, if the distress was blocked for up to 1 min, the infant would remain soothed. In general, blocking the exhibition of distress even for a full minute did not prevent its return once orienting ended. The ability of an object to produce orienting and thus block distress also depended on its novelty. Repeating the same object tended to reduce the ability of the object to produce soothing, as one would expect if orienting tends to habituate. Also in accord with the findings discussed in the previous section, the habituation effect was stronger for infants of 6 months than for 3-month-old infants.

There appears to be a close tie between orienting mechanisms and those involved in distress. We do not yet know very much about how orienting serves to control distress, either in infancy or for adults. However, we believe there are some physiological systems that appear to relate to the interaction between attention and emotion. These systems may be of great importance in normal control of pain. One of them involves the superior colliculus. In the rat, the deeper layers of the superior colliculus contain cells that respond to pain and are in intimate contact with multimodal cells involved in orienting (McHaffie, Kao, & Stein, 1989). The close relation between pain and attention may reflect the importance of opposed approach and avoidance systems in the control of the animal's behavior.

A second system in which distress and attention are both closely coordinated lies in the anterior cingulate gyrus. The anterior cingulate has been seen as an important structure involved in voluntary attention (see anterior attention section following). A study using Positron Emission Tomography (PET) by the Montreal group (Talbot, Marrett, Evans, Meyer, Bushnell, and Duncan, 1991), attempted to determine the areas of the brain activated when a small amount of additional heat was delivered to the finger to move from the sensation of warmth to that of pain. When the heat was sufficient to produce pain, there was strong activation of the anterior cingulate. The coordinates make this area appear to be rather close to those active during higher level attention (see the section on voluntary control following). Pain has a very intrusive character, and this could be related to its close physical proximity to the anterior attention network.

Recent PET studies of depression (Drevets & Raichle, 1995) have provided another result relating affect to more general cognitive processes. Patients with depression showed a great reduction in blood flow in posterior areas of the brain, including those related to orienting to visual input. However, they showed augmented blood flow in frontal areas involved with processing the meaning of words and ideas. These frontal areas were similar to those active in normal persons when requested to think sad thoughts. Thus the inverse correlation between attention and negative affect found in normals might well reflect a part of the mechanism involved in affective disorder.

EXPECTATIONS

We began this chapter with a discussion of the importance of expectations in guiding sensory input. A task that has been widely used to explore this, the learning of expectations in adult subjects, involves pressing a key in response to a spatial target (Curran & Keele, 1993; Nissen & Bullemer, 1987). Unknown to the subject, a repeating sequence is embedded in the text. Adults exhibit having learned the skill by pressing the key more rapidly for a response in sequence than for a nonsequence light. Some normal adults, particularly when distracted, as well as amnesic patients, learn the skill normally but do not recognize that there was a sequence and cannot report anything about the correct order of events. Some lists, where each of the repeating associations are unique (e.g., 2431), can be learned easily by normal subjects, even when distracted. When subjects have learned implicitly in this way, they do not show anticipations in the form of pressing the key in advance of the stimulus light being presented. Although they are faster in responding to a light in sequence, they do not have the information to anticipate its occurrence. When an unexpected item is presented during the course of such an implicitly learned sequence, however, they are abnormally slow, as though they had somehow already oriented to the expected event and had to reorient to the new light.

The basis of sequence learning is an arbitrary association between two spatial locations. Haith, Hazan, and Goodman (1988), showed that infants' ability to learn these associations was developed at about 3.5 months. In our laboratory (Clohessy, 1994; Johnson et al., 1991) 4-month-old infants were taught such associations. If two different central attractors are presented (one of which is followed by targets on the right and the other by targets on the left), 4-month-old infants learn to move their head and eyes to the anticipated directions with increasing speed over trials and often anticipate the target. Moreover, their percentage of correct anticipations is significantly above chance. We do not find evidence of such learning in infants younger than 4 months, nor do we see any improvement in this learning ability between 4 and 10 months.

To explore the ability of infants at these ages to anticipate sequences of locations, we presented infants with a display of three monitors (Clohessy, 1994). We presented either random orderings of targets on the three monitors or a single target sequence. In the simple sequence each association was unique (e.g., 1 → 2 → 3). Under these circumstances infants showed many anticipations, and both 4- and 10-month-old infants learned the simple sequences; that is, their anticipations were correct more than would be expected by chance. One problem with sequences of this type is that each new association requires orienting to the one location that has not been examined recently. Thus, moving from 1 → 2, 2 → 3, and 3 → 1 never requires infants to return attention to the location just previously examined. A bias against returning to an already examined location could lead that infant to correctly anticipate the next location. The learning of these infants could therefore be limited to sequences that favor a bias not to return attention to a recently examined location, as is found in inhibition of return. To see if the learning was more general, Gerardi (1994) used a display with four positions arranged in a square. Target stimuli moved around the periphery of the square in either a clockwise or counterclockwise location. When infants moved from position 1 → 2, both positions 3 and 4 were novel, in the sense that they were not the immediately just attended location. We could then test if the infant could learn to anticipate the correct association even when both were two equally novel choices. Results showed that infants at 4 months could learn these associations.

It seems reasonable to suppose that our 4-month-old infants exhibited implicit learning. Although our studies of adults in this task suggest that they do better than the infants, there are striking similarities between their purely implicit learning and the infant behavior (Clohessy, 1994). It appears that the ability to learn this kind of task implicitly arises at about 3 to 4 months along with the development of cortical computations involved in orienting, and it may not show a great deal of change after that.

Haith (1980) summarized the properties of newborn infant eye movements in terms of rules that influence the direction of their looking. These rules were based on innate scan paths and salient characteristics of visual stimuli. Our research suggests these rules are supplemented by learning about where to look, and that this learning begins during the first year of life. This type of learning can tune infant orienting to important properties of their environment, including the properties of social stimuli. Many social skills appear to rest on eye contact, because we attend where important information is most likely to be gathered. Direction of gaze also reflects patterns of social dominance and submission. Even as adults we are usually unaware of these influences on our orienting behavior, but they can be brought to awareness when different rules apply, as can happen in moving to a different culture.

The kind of learning of eye position we have in mind would be different in different social contexts. In one situation, eye gaze is drawn to the eyes of another, but in another situation eye contact is no longer important.

When can infants learn to respond on the basis of context sensitive cues? The next section examines this issue.

VOLUNTARY CONTROL

So far we have been examining orienting to simple sensory events involving locations or objects. We found that infants can learn to anticipate the occurrence of such events even when they are formed into sequences that must be carried in memory. In our studies of attention in adults (Posner & Petersen, 1990), we argued that the brain mechanisms related to visual orienting constitute a special brain network involving areas of the parietal lobe, pulvinar, and colliculus. However, there is also evidence that frontal structures have input into the visual object recognition pathways during attention to visual objects (Posner & Dehaene, 1994). When we attend to the color, form, or motion of objects, there is evidence that the anterior cingulate and areas of the basal ganglia become active (Corbetta et al., 1991). The anterior cingulate is active, not only in orienting to visual objects, but in orienting to words, in creating visual images, and other high-level mental activity. We consider the development of these areas in infancy as an important means to understanding how high-level cognitions can guide the voluntary control of orienting.

Studies of adults (Curran & Keele, 1993) have distinguished between unambiguous or implicit associations, in which each stimulus always implies a single next location, and context-dependent or explicit associations, in which the nature of the association varies. These adult studies (Curran & Keele, 1993) indicated that unambiguous associations can be learned, presumably implicitly, even when attention is diverted by a secondary task, but context dependent associations cannot be learned without focal attention.

If the learning we observed in our infants depends on orienting to stimuli but not on the higher forms of attention involved in explicit learning, we reasoned that 4- and 10-month-olds should learn unambiguous associations but not ambiguous ones. The idea is that these higher forms of attention would not emerge until the second year of life. The ability to learn ambiguous associations could then serve as a marker task for the development of more complex forms of attention related to executive control by anterior structures.

In our studies of 4- and 10-month-old infants (Clohessy, 1994), we also employed a complex sequence in which one of the associations was context dependent or ambiguous whereas another association was unambiguous. In this complex sequence infants were shown a target that moved from monitor 1 to 2, and then after returning to 1 moved to 3 (i.e., 1 → 2 → 1 → 3). Thus two potentially correct associations predicted which location follows monitor 1; however, the return to monitor 1 was unambiguous because it occurred irrespective of whether the last target was 2 or 3. In our studies we found that infants of 4 and 10 months learned to correctly anticipate the unambiguous return to position 1, but showed no evidence of learning the context-dependent association (i.e., whether to go to 2 or 3 following 1).

By 18 months, infants are showing many signs of higher level attentional control. The emergence of multiple word utterances, the ability to sort and classify, and evidence of self-recognition all imply an increased capacity to understand and use relational information. For this reason we examined sequence learning in these infants. There was clear evidence that 18-month-olds learn both unambiguous and ambiguous associations. The simple sequence made up of unambiguous associations appeared to be learned within the first block of 15 trials. In contrast, 4- and 10-month-olds did not show clear evidence of learning until the second block. In the complex sequence, the return to 1 appeared to be learned more slowly by 18-month-olds than the simple sequence, but there is evidence of above chance learning of this association during the second session.

There is also clear evidence that the 18-month-olds learn the context dependent association by the second session. We have been able to replicate this finding in three different experiments. Although there was no evidence of such learning in the 4- and 10-month-olds, we cannot say for sure that the skill could not be acquired earlier than 18 months with more extensive practice. However, there is some internal evidence that the ability to learn the context was developing at about 18 months. Some infants showed by their correct anticipations that they had learned this skill very well and others showed little evidence of learning. This suggests that infants of this age are only beginning to acquire the ability to learn this skill, and that it might be worth observing how this form of learning develops in somewhat older infants.

We were also able to show some links between the learning by infants at this age and aspects of their language performance. We found a significant correlation between their laboratory performance learning the context dependent association in the complex sequence and parental reports of the number of words the infant used. Although this correlation needs to be replicated and extended, it provides support for the idea of the development of an attention system involved both in learning complex sequences and in the control of language.

The ability to learn context-dependent associations is only one sign of the development of an executive attentional system. Indeed, several very general cognitive skills, including the ability to exhibit simple grammars in multiword language (Dore, Franklin, Miller, & Ramer, 1976), the development of spontaneous alternation (Vecera, Rothbart, & Posner, 1991), and the ability to hold representations in mind while operating upon them (Meltzoff, 1990), seem to undergo important development at or near 18 months. This is also the age that self-recognition in children's operating on their own image in a mirror is first exhibited (Gallup, 1979). We believe these skills rest on the maturation of an executive attention system located in the midline of the frontal lobe and related to awareness and voluntary control (Posner & Rothbart, 1994). The evidence of a relation between context-sensitive learning and aspects of language skill present in our data also fits with this idea. In our future efforts we hope to relate the development of context-dependent associations with a number of linguistic and conceptual skills that might mark important developments in this central attention system.

The frontal mechanisms involved in higher order attention go well beyond the classical ideas of the orienting reflex. These mechanisms are more closely related to senses of selective attention popular within cognitive psychology. However, there are clear relations between these frontal networks and the networks we have discussed for visual orienting. Jackson, Marrocco, and Posner (1994) provided a specific model indicating how these midline frontal areas may work together with the parietal network in adults to produce the many complex forms of orienting we can demonstrate.

In infants we found that orienting to objects and to locations arises independently in early development. Adult studies also suggest separate mechanisms for the two forms of orienting (Egly, Driver, & Rafal, 1994). In recent work from our laboratory, a striking independence was shown in adult learning of sequences of objects and locations (Mayr, 1996). Mayr taught adult subjects two independent sequences, one involving locations and one involving object identity. Both the location and the order of the objects were repeated, but the two were uncorrelated. In this situation, Mayr showed that subjects could learn the two sequences at the same time without apparent interference between them, as long as they were learned implicitly. However, when learning was explicit there was clear evidence of interference between the learning of the two sequences. We speculate that in Mayr's study, the learning of the spatial locations involved mechanisms related to the visual orienting network we have described. This form of learning could use connections between the basal ganglia and the posterior parietal lobe. The basal ganglia are already known to be involved in the learning of procedures (Mishkin & Murray, 1994), and recent PET studies of sequences show that implicit learning activates the basal ganglia (Grafton, Hazelton & Ivry, 1995). If subsequent work supports these speculations, it seems likely that infant learning of location sequences is based on these same pathways. The clear evidence of interference between sequences when explicit learning occurs supports the idea that explicit learning is likely to involve a common attentional executive network.

The evidence for the continued presence of implicit learning of locations in adults illustrates continuity between infant and adult mechanisms. We find in studies involving sequence learning, evidence that mechanisms found in early infancy are modified and supplemented by later systems, but remain present and continue to operate in adults. We hope that a fuller picture of the emergence of these mechanisms in early life will help explicate the continuing role of attention in development.

REFERENCES

Bullemer, P., & Nissen, M. J. (1990). *Attentional orienting in the expression of procedural knowledge.* Paper presented to the Psychonomics Society, New Orleans, LA.

Chugani, H. T., Phelps, M. E., & Mazziotta, J. C. (1987). Positron emission tomography study of human brain functional development. *Annals of Neurology, 22,* 487–497.

Clohessy, A. B. (1994). Visual anticipation and sequence learning in four- and ten-month-old infants and adults. Unpublished doctoral dissertation, University of Oregon.

Clohessy, A. B., Posner, M. I., Rothbart, M. K., & Vecera, S. P. (1991). The development of inhibition of return in early infancy. *Journal of Cognitive Neuroscience, 3/4,* 345–350.

Colombo, J., Mitchell, D. W., Coldren, J. T., & Atwater, J. D. (1990). Discrimination learning during the first year: Stimulus and positional cues. *Journal of Experimental Psychology: Learning Memory and Cognition, 16*(1), 98–109.

Corbetta, M., Miezen, F. M., Dobmeyer, S., Shulman, F., & Petersen, S. E. (1991). Selective and divided attention during visual discrimination of shape, color, and speed. *Journal of Neuroscience, 11,* 1283–1302.

Corbetta, M., Miezin, F. M., Shulman, G. L., & Petersen, S. E. (1993). A PET study of visuospatial attention. *The Journal of Neuroscience, 13*(3), 1202–1226.

Curran, T., & Keele, S. W. (1993). Attentional and nonattentional forms of sequence learning. *Journal of Experimental Psychology: HLMC 19,* 189–202.

Derryberry, D., & Rothbart, M. K. (1988). Arousal, affect and attention as components of temperament. *Journal of Personality and Social Psychology, 55,* 958–966.

Dore, J., Franklin, M. M., Miller, R. T., & Ramer, A. L. H. (1976). Transitional phenomenon in early language development. *Journal of Child Language, 3,* 13–27.

Drevets, W. C., & Raichle, M. E. (1995). Positron emission tomographic imaging studies of human emotional disorders. In M. S. Gazzaniga (Ed.), *The cognitive neurosciences* (pp. 1153–1164). Cambridge, MA: MIT Press.

Egly, R., Driver, J., & Rafal, R. D. (1994). Shifting visual attention between objects and locations. *Journal of Experimental Psychology: General, 123,* 161–177.

Gallup, G. G. (1979). Self awareness in primates. *American Scientist, 67,* 417–421.

Gerardi, G. (1994). *Looking behavior as a measure of sequence learning in infancy.* Unpublished studies, University of Oregon.

Geschwind, N., & Galaburda, A. M. (1987). *Cerebral lateralization.* Cambridge, MA: MIT Press.

Grafton, S. T., Hazelton, E., & Ivry, R. (1995). Functional mapping of sequence learning in normal humans. *Journal of Cognitive Neuroscience, 7,* 497–510.

Graham, F. K. (1979). Distinguishing among orienting, defense, and startle reflexes. In H. D. Kimmel, E. H. Van Olst, & J. F. Orlebeke (Eds.), *The orienting reflex in humans*. Hillsdale, NJ: Lawrence Erlbaum Associates.

Gunderson, V. M., & Swartz, K. B. (1986). Effects of familiarization time on visual recognition memory in infant pigtailed macaques. *Developmental Psychology*, 477–480.

Haith, M. M. (1980). *Rules that babies look by: The organization of newborn visual activity*. Hillsdale, NJ: Lawrence Erlbaum Associates.

Haith, M. M., Hazan, C., & Goodman, G. S. (1988). Expectations and anticipation of dynamic visual events by 3.5 month old babies. *Child Development, 59*, 467–479.

Harman, C. (1994). *The interaction of distress and attention in early infancy*. Unpublished doctoral dissertation, University of Oregon.

Harman, C., Posner, M. I., Rothbart, M. K., & Thomas-Thrapp, L. (1994). Development of orienting to locations and objects in human infants. *Canadian Journal of Experimental Psychology, 48*(2), 301–318.

Heinze, H. J., Mangun, G. R., Burchert, W., Hinrichs, H., Scholz, M., Munte, T. F., Gos, A., Scherg, M., Johannes, S., Hundeshagen, H., Gazzaniga, M. S., & Hillyard, S. A. (1994). Combining spatial and temporal imaging of brain activity during visual selective attention in humans. *Nature, 372*, 543–546.

Hubel, D. H. (1981). *Eye, brain and vision*. New York: Scientific American Library.

Jackson, S., Marrocco, R., & Posner, M. I. (1994). Networks of anatomical areas controlling visual spatial attention. *Neural Networks, 7*, 925–944.

Johnson, M. H., Posner, M. I., & Rothbart, M. K. (1991). Components of visual orienting in early infancy: Contingency learning, anticipatory looking and disengaging. *Journal of Cognitive Neuroscience, 3/4*, 335–344.

Luck, S. J., & Hillyard, S. A. (1994). Spatial filtering during visual search: Evidence from human electrophysiology. *Journal of Experimental Psychology: HPP, 20*, 1000–1009.

Luck, S. J., Hillyard, S. A., Mangun, G. R., & Gazzaniga, M. S. (1994). Independent attention scanning in the separated hemisphere of split brain patients. *Journal of Cognitive Neuroscience, 6*, 84–91.

Mayr, U. (1996). Spatial learning and implicit sequence learning: Evidence for independent learning of spatial and nonspatial sequences. *Journal of Experimental Psychology: LMC*.

McHaffie, J. G., Kao, C.-Q., & Stein, B. E. (1989). Nioceptive neurons in the cat superior colliculus: Response properties, topography and implications. *Journal of Neurophysiology, 63*, 510–5223.

Meltzoff, A. N. (1990). Towards a developmental cognitive science. In A. Diamond (Ed.), *The development and neural bases of higher cognitive functions* (Vol. 608, pp. 1–37). New York: New York Academy of Sciences.

Mishkin, M., & Murray, E. A. (1994). Stimulus recognition. *Current Opinion in Neurobiology, 4*, 200–206.

Mountcastle, V. B. (1978). Brain systems for directed attention. *Journal Royal Society of Medicine, 71*, 14–227.

Nissen, M. J., & Bullemer, P. (1987). Attentional requirements of learning: Evidence from performance measures. *Cognitive Psychology, 19*, 1–32.

Petersen, S. E., Fox, P. T., Posner, M. I., Mintun, M., & Raichle, M. E. (1989). Positron emission tomographic studies of the processing of single words. *Journal of Cognitive Neuroscience, 1*, 153–170.

Posner, M. I. (1988). Structures and functions of selective attention. In T. Boll & B. Bryant (Eds.), *Master lectures in clinical neuropsychology and brain function: Research, measurement, and practice* (pp. 172–202). American Psychological Association.

Posner, M. I., & Dehaene, S. (1994). Attentional networks. *Trends in Neuroscience, 17*, 75–79.

Posner, M. I., & Petersen, S. E. (1990). The attention system of the human brain. *Annual Review of Neuroscience, 13*, 25–42.

Posner, M. I., & Raichle, M. E. (1994). Images of mind. *Scientific American.*

Posner, M. I., & Rothbart, M. K. (1994). Constructing neuronal theories of mind. In C. Koch & J. Davis (Eds.), *High level neuronal theories of the brain* (pp. 183–199). Cambridge, MA: MIT Press.

Rafal, R. D., Calabresi, P., Brennan, C., & Scioloto, T. (1989). Saccadic preparation inhibits reorienting to recently attended locations. *Journal of Experimental Psychology: HPP, 15,* 673–685.

Rafal, R., Henik, A., & Smith, J. (1991). Extrageniculate contributions to reflex visual orienting in normal humans: A temporal hemifield advantage. *Journal of Cognitive Neuroscience, 3/4,* 322–328.

Rafal, R. D., Posner, M. I., Friedman, J. H., Inhoff, A. W., & Bernstein, E. (1988). Orienting of visual attention in progressive supranuclear palsy. *Brain, 111,* 267–280.

Sokolov, E. N. (1990). The orienting response, and future directions of its development. *Pavlovian Journal of Biological Science, 25,* 142–150.

Talbot, J. D., Marrett, A., Evans, A. C., Meyer, E., Bushnell, M. C., & Duncan, G. H. (1991). Multiple representation of pain in the human cortex. *Science, 251,* 1355–1357.

Thomas-Thrapp, L. J., Posner, M. I., & Rothbart, M. K. (1995). *Development of orienting to objects and locations.* Poster presented to the 2nd Cognitive Neuroscience Society.

Valenza, E., Simon, F., & Umilta, C. (1994). Inhibition of return in newborn infants. *Infant Behavior and Development, 17,* 293–302.

Vecera, S. P., Rothbart, M. K., & Posner, M. I. (1991). Development of spontaneous alternation in infancy. *Journal of Cognitive Neuroscience, 3/4,* 351–354.

15

Attention Across Time in Infant Development

W. Keith Berg
University of Florida

John Richards
University of South Carolina

The process of reacting to the events transpiring in our environment is a complex one, oftentimes involving a sequence of steps. For example, the initial response to a stimulus must involve determining the type of attentive response to make: orienting versus defensive response, or selective versus nonselective attention. Once initial decisions are made, additional analyses of the stimulus events may occur, and these are influenced not only by the continuing stimulus events, but also by the outcome of previous response processing decisions. The result is that the process of reacting to events is the sequencing of a set of responses over time. A common circumstance is for later responses to be altered as a result of information gathered in the initial analysis. The evidence is growing that infants demonstrate such contingently programmed sequences of analysis, but that these behaviors undergo developmental changes in the first months of life. It is our purpose to illustrate these results, particularly as they are evidenced in the relation between cardiac activity and cognitive development.

Prior to the middle 1960s, infancy researchers employing a variety of response measures found little reason to segregate attention into components (e.g., Fantz, 1963). A careful dissection of infants' attentional capabilities into component processes was undertaken seriously by Graham and colleagues (e.g., Graham & Clifton, 1966; Graham et al., 1970). The work of Sokolov (e.g., Sokolov, 1963; Sokolov & Cacioppo, chapter 1, this volume) and of the Laceys (e.g., Lacey, Kagan, Lacey, & Moss, 1962) with adults had led Graham to conclude that physiological measures, especially heart rate, may be powerful tools in examining attention in the infant. More important, physiological measures may distinguish attentional processes such as the orienting response from other activation reactions such as defense responses (Graham & Clifton, 1966). This was critical in understanding that the developmental shift from the predominantly accelerative heart rate response of the neonate to the predominantly decelerative response of the older infant could be understood in terms of the infant's defensive and orienting reactions. This interpretation became widely accepted after a priori predictions arising from the Graham and Clifton (1966) hypotheses were empirically supported (e.g., Berg, Berg, & Graham, 1971). This finding was powerful evidence of the value of examining components of attention during the infancy period. It showed that the heart rate response was an important index of such differential stimulus processing in the infant. It provided unequivocal evidence that heart rate responses could be vital for understanding fundamental attention and cognitive mechanisms in early life.

THE SEQUENCE OF ATTENTIONAL RESPONDING: DEVELOPMENTAL CHANGES IN CARDIAC COMPONENTS

In addition to the orienting and defense response distinction, the later work from Graham's laboratory led to the notion that infants' heart rate may also index a sequence of qualitatively differing aspects of information processing that is initiated by stimulus onset and is maintained by a continuation of that ongoing event. In this section we provide an overview of the sequence of processing events suggested by the cardiac results and the indications of their developmental change. Subsequent sections detail two of the more recently investigated processing stages, sustained attention and anticipation.

The first component of the information processing sequence evident in cardiac responses is a very brief deceleration usually in response to a transient stimulus (Berg & Berg, 1987). This response was argued to represent a simple reaction to an onset of the stimulus, a response that did not involve the more elaborate evaluation of the stimulus implied by orienting. Graham (1992) developed a similar concept that she identified as a transient-detecting reaction. Depending on the stimulus intensity, this response might be expressed as a startle reflex or a nonstartle response such as the brief deceleration. Although this transient-detecting response is often considered preattentive, it involves some basic information processing and might be considered as part of an *automatic interrupt system* that at least momentarily disengages the infant from the stimuli currently undergoing processing and prepares the infant for subsequent processing (Graham, 1979, 1992; Graham, Anthony, & Ziegler, 1983). One element of this response may be to direct attentional mechanisms to the critical part of the sensory space.

Once this is accomplished by the preattentive process, the initial stimulus processing begins. The 2-month-old infant shows a large heart rate deceleration following the shift of fixation (or shift of attention) to a new stimulus, that is, the stimulus orienting response. The sequence from attention getting (i.e., transient detecting) to stimulus orienting was well laid out by Graham in her work. The cardiac result of this next step in processing was a longer lasting deceleration that either replaced or was merged with the brief deceleration indicative of transient detection. The orienting differed not only in form and duration from the automatic interrupt system, but had as its function the initial stimulus processing and, as such, could well be related to cortical functioning. Although the longer deceleration associated with orienting was difficult to elicit prior to about 2 months of age, the neonate readily elicited the brief deceleration suggestive of the interrupt response (Berg & Berg, 1987). This change from the transient to the longer decelerative response during in the first month or two of life reflects a maturational shift from the simple initial reaction to the two-step sequence of stimulus handling of interrupt followed quickly by orienting.

Models of heart rate change in infants have extended heart rate's utility as an index of attention processes even further in time. Both Porges (1976, 1980) and Richards (1988; Richards & Casey, 1992) postulated that *sustained attention* an additional process that follows orienting. Richards, among others (Ruff, 1986), hypothesized that this later attention phase is one in which the orienting to the stimulus is maintained or amplified in order to process information in the stimulus. It is during this attention phase that information acquisition occurs. Sustained attention normally incorporates two aspects of attention: intensive and selective attention. The selective nature of attention is represented by the narrowing of information processing to a single object, idea, or behavior. The intensive aspect of attention is concerned with the effects that attention engagement has on the task, leading to increased processing efficiency, shortened reaction times and so forth. Both aspects have long been recognized, being suggested even by James (1890). In a well-known quotation James indicated: "Everyone knows what attention is. It is the taking possession by the mind, in clear and vivid form, of one out of what seem several simultaneously possible objects or trains of thought . . ." (pp. 403–404). He further noted, "The immediate effects of attention are to make us: a) perceive, b) conceive, c) distinguish, d) shorten reaction time . . . better than otherwise we could . . ." (pp. 424–425).

The role of selective attention can be evidenced in different ways. In visual processing, for example, selective attention directs one's focus toward a specific location or object in the visual field. Further, selective attention inhibits one's focus toward the parts of the visual field that are not selected. A preattentive system controls this early part of this process. Cohen (1972, 1973) investigated just such a process, denoting as "attention-getting." However, this might be better labeled *receptor-getting* rather than attention-getting, because the primary function is to direct receptors in a manner to optimally sense the stimulus. Cohen (1972, 1973) also developed the notion of *attention-holding*, an aspect of selectivity that controls the duration of attention. This occurs more or less simultaneously with attention's intensive aspect. Later in this chapter we show that developmental changes in attention between 2 and 6 months of age occur primarily in this aspect of attention.

The attentional processes described thus far function to assess the eliciting stimulus, its ongoing qualities, and its immediate implications. However, past experience with the consequences of the current stimulus may allow prediction of events to follow. In this circumstance the attentional process adds a new dimension—the anticipatory response. This future-oriented system might either overlap the sustained attention to the predictive stimulus or develop out of this experience. In its most elaborate form, the anticipatory response represents some type of planning or executive control of behavior and may reflect frontal lobe activity. As such it demands the integration of several simple attention systems in order for the infant to execute specific actions (see Posner, Rothbart, & Gerardi, chapter 14, this volume). The final sections of the chapter review evidence that infants 3 months of age are just beginning to demonstrate this anticipatory behavior (Haith, Hazan, & Goodman, 1988) and it is not readily seen as part of the cardiac response until 4 months or older (Boswell, Garner, & Berg, 1994; Donohue & Berg, 1991; see also Berg & Donohue, 1992).

The picture that emerges from this brief overview is that attention, as reflected in cardiac activity, involves a distinct sequence of processing events. In its most elaborate form, a signal would initially elicit an interruption of ongoing activity, an initial determination of the basic attentional process to be engaged, and a preliminary orientation of receptors. Following this preattentive action, a more elaborate orientation process would be engaged and if the signal were found to be of sufficient interest, this process would be sustained. Provided that past experience with the signal indicates other events of importance would reliably follow, there would then be a shift to focusing on the implications of these events (anticipation), and possibly actions would then be engaged that would help plan or prepare for them. Evidence suggests that the ability to produce fully this sequence of attentional processing develops gradually over at least the first 6 months of life. This development progresses from the preattentional processes available at birth, to maturation of orienting, to expression of sustained attention and anticipation. The next sections focus on these latter two processes, which have received much less attention among investigators examining infant cognition.

SUSTAINED ATTENTION: THE SELECTIVE ASPECTS

The use of heart rate as an attention index in the early work of Graham and her colleagues was limited to the early preattentive responses and the stimulus orienting response. If stimulus presentation is sustained and the infant continues attending, the heart rate continues to be sustained below the prestimulus level. Figure 15.1 shows the responses of infants at 14, 20, and 26 weeks of age while viewing a central visual stimulus (Richards, 1985). In that study there were trials with a single stimulus (C line in Fig. 15.1) and trials with a competing visual stimulus in the periphery (S line in Fig. 15.1). The central stimulus in both trial types resulted in the typical heart rate deceleration in the first 4 to 5 sec characterizing stimulus orienting. The single stimulus trials included heart rate responses during active attention to the stimulus along with heart rate changes when the infant was no longer interested in the stimulus but would not shift fixation because there was no other stimulus to look at. In the condition with the competing stimulus, the heart rate response displayed in Fig. 15.1 includes only that period of time when the infant selected the central stimulus and did not localize the peripheral stimulus. The continued fixation on the central stimulus implies that the infant was still engaged in active information processing of the central stimulus. During that time, the heart rate response remained below the prestimulus level as long as the infant continued to look at the central stimulus, particularly for the two older age groups. This later attention phase, occurring after the first 4 to 5 sec, has been labeled *sustained attention* (Richards & Casey, 1991, 1992).

An important finding coming from that study is the developmental change implied by the response shown in Fig. 15.1. Stimulus orienting does not seem to show much change over this age range, whereas the sustained heart rate response during sustained attention increases. This suggests a major shift in attention over this age range. A major development shift emphasized in Graham's work was the change from the early heart rate response in the neonate to the stimulus orienting response in the 6- to 8-week-old infant. Given the results presented in Fig. 15.1 and subsequently verified in further research (see Richards & Casey, 1992), it

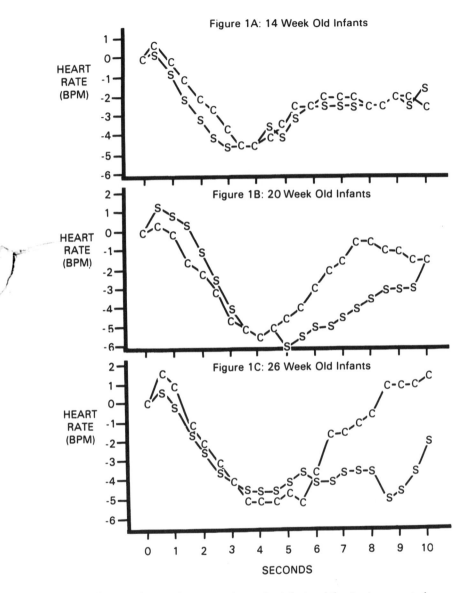

FIG. 15.1. Average heart rate change for infants while viewing a central stimulus presented alone (Infant Control, C) or viewing a central stimulus in the presence of a competing peripheral stimulus (Interrupted Stimulus, S). From Richards (1985). Reprinted with permission.

appears that after 6 to 8 weeks, the stimulus orienting attention phase shows little change. It is the sustained aspect of attention that changes over this age range.

Sustained attention's selective nature has been emphasized in a series of studies by Richards and colleagues. In these studies, infants are presented with an interesting central visual stimulus that elicits stimulus orienting and sustained attention heart rate responses. After a delay from the onset of the central stimulus, a peripheral stimulus is presented in an attempt to interrupt the infant's fixation on the central stimulus. The delay is defined by evaluating the ongoing heart rate activity and presenting the interrupting stimulus contingent on the heart rate response pattern. For example, the *sustained attention* delay is defined as when heart rate has decelerated below its prestimulus level and has sustained lowering. *Attention termination* is defined as the heart rate returning to its prestimulus level following sustained attention. This a priori selection of sustained attention and attention termination by online evaluation of the heart rate response provides experimental control over the presence or absence of attention. As a control for the simple passage of time, the delay may be defined at specific time intervals (e.g., 3, 7, 10 sec) and attention is evaluated by the ongoing heart rate response at the time of the delay.

These studies provide firm support that the period of time defined by sustained heart rate responding is selective in directing fixation. For example, in one study (Richards, 1987) the peripheral stimulus remained on until the infant looked toward it. Infants took 6.58 sec before redirecting fixation to the peripheral stimulus in the sustained attention trials and 3.29 sec in the attention termination trials. If the interrupting stimulus remained on only for a fixed duration (e.g., 2 sec), infants between 3 and 6 months localized the peripheral stimulus only 40% of the time during sustained attention to the central stimulus, more than 60% of the time during attention termination, and nearly 85% of the time when no central stimulus is present (Richards, 1995b). Sustained attention, defined by the heart rate response, focuses fixation toward the object of interest and attenuates object localization in other locations.

The *interrupted stimulus* method has revealed an interesting relation between heart rate response, behavioral response, and the need for psychophysiological methods to examine infant selective attention. In visual fixation studies a stimulus is typically presented until the infant looks away from it. The measure of attention is the duration of fixation on the stimulus. However, in many situations the infant will continue to fixate the stimulus long after attention to it has waned. Thus, the behavioral measure of attention, fixation duration, may include both attentive and inattentive periods. The heart rate responses to a single stimulus (C in Fig. 15.1) show that heart rate will return to prestimulus levels even though fixation continues, presumably indicating that the infant is no longer interested in the stimulus. The use of the competing peripheral stimulus to interrupt fixation at the time that sustained attention or attention termination is hypothesized to be occurring reveals the ease with which fixation is redirected during heart-rate-defined attention termination, and the difficulty of redirecting fixation during sustained attention. It is the combination of behavioral measures, physiological responses, and psychophysiological techniques that reveals this selective aspect of attention.

Thus, heart rate changes during fixation to continued stimuli involve both the early heart rate changes due to the *automatic interrupt* and to stimulus orienting, and a further phase of sustained lowering that has been labeled *sustained attention*. Development after 2 months of age in the heart rate response occurs primarily in this later attention phase. This later attention phase is strongly selective; that is, during visual attention, fixation is directed toward the stimulus of interest and stimuli in other parts of the visual field are not readily localized.

SUSTAINED ATTENTION: THE INTENSIVE ASPECTS

Sustained attention's intensive aspect has also been shown in infant attention. Again, sustained attention is defined by heart rate changes that occur in response to stimuli. The initial heart rate deceleration (Fig. 15.1) defines stimulus orienting, the sustained heart rate lowering (Fig. 15.1) defines sustained attention and the return of heart rate to its prestimulus level defines a period of time in which attention to the stimulus has waned even though the infant may continue to fixate on the stimulus. The models of sustained attention (e.g., Richards & Casey, 1992) posit that during this period of time, there is enhanced information processing relative to attention termination and perhaps, stimulus orienting.

Selective attention's intensive aspect has been tested in two recent studies. In one study (Richards, 1995a), it was hypothesized that infants are engaged in intensive information processing during sustained attention. Therefore, information presented during sustained attention should affect later behavior more strongly than information presented during stimulus orienting or attention termination. This was examined by eliciting heart rate changes with a Sesame Street movie, *Follow That Bird*, in infants at 14, 20, or 26 weeks of age. Scenes from this movie result in deep and sustained heart rate decelerations in young infants. The Sesame Street movie was presented until appropriate attention phases were reached. Then, a computer-generated familiarization stimulus was presented that lasted for 2.5 or 5.0 sec. The familiarization stimulus was presented either in sustained attention or attention termination. Recognition memory for the briefly presented visual stimulus was measured by testing novelty preference in a subsequent paired-comparison test phase paradigm. The paired-comparison procedure involves a presentation of a stimulus to which the infant has already been exposed and a novel stimulus previously unseen. Preference for the novel stimulus (extended looking time) in the test phase indicates that the infant recognizes the previously seen stimulus.

This study's results demonstrate sustained attention's intensive aspect. For stimuli presented during attention termination (heart rate return to prestimulus level) in the familiarization phase, the infant's preference for the novel stimulus (and presumed familiar stimulus recognition) in the subsequent test phase was at the same level as it was in the test phase of a no familiarization control trial in which the infant was exposed to neither of the paired-comparison stimuli in the familiarization phase. In contrast, for the familiarization stimulus presented during sustained attention (heart rate deceleration), infants fixated on the novel stimulus in the subsequent test phase much longer than the stimulus to which they were previously exposed and longer on the novel stimulus than during the test phase of the no familiarization control condition.

A very interesting finding in that study was that exposure for 5 sec to the familiarization stimulus during sustained attention was as effective in modifying novelty preference as was exposure for 20 sec when the attention phases were uncontrolled. There was a positive linear relation between the stimulus exposure duration during sustained attention in the familiarization phase and the subsequent recognition memory. Trials with only 1 to 2 sec of exposure time in sustained attention resulted in familiar and novel stimulus fixation durations that were not different from no-exposure control conditions. Trials with 2 to 3 sec, or 4 to 5 sec of exposure in sustained attention, resulted in novelty preference scores that were not different from those found in a 20-sec exposure trial! The typical 20-sec or 30-sec stimulus exposure given for such paired-comparison recognition-memory procedures may consist of only 5 to 10 sec of sustained attention. This study's results imply that it is stimulus exposure during sustained attention that is correlated with subsequent novelty preference, rather than the stimulus exposure per se.

A second study in which sustained attention's intensive aspect was examined was inspired by results from Anthony and Graham (1983). In their investigation, attention engagement was elicited by presenting "interesting" or "dull" visual or auditory stimuli to 16-week-old infants. The interesting stimuli were complex visual patterns or sounds that elicited heart rate deceleration. The dull stimuli were a simple light or tone and resulted in smaller heart rate deceleration than the interesting stimuli.

Following a 4-sec delay, a visual or auditory probe that was known to elicit a blink reflex was presented. The blink reflex was enhanced in magnitude when attention was the greatest (interesting vs. dull) and when the blink probe and the foreground stimulus were in the same modality (match vs. mismatch). Given that sustained attention was engaged at 4 sec, these results imply that the blink probe stimulus in the interesting, same modality condition was processed more effectively (larger blink magnitude) than during the matched, dull foreground, or the mismatched stimulus. The relative enhancement or attenuation of the blink reflex for stimuli in the matched or mismatched modalities is evidence for selective modality attention effects early in infancy.

A recent study by Richards (1994) followed up this finding with a priori definitions of sustained attention and attention termination and extended the ages that were tested from 8 to 26 weeks of age. This study used the same modality conditions as the Anthony and Graham study—a visual foreground and visual probe (match), a visual foreground and auditory probe (mismatch), an auditory foreground and visual probe (mismatch) and an auditory foreground and auditory probe (match). However, instead of presenting different stimulus types (interesting and dull), only "interesting" stimuli were used. The probe stimulus delay, rather than being defined strictly by time as in the Anthony and Graham study, was defined by the presence of heart rate deceleration (sustained attention) or the return of heart rate to its prestimulus level (attention termination). Thus, attention engagement was experimentally controlled not by different stimuli but by different attention phases to the same stimulus types.

This study's results replicate the Anthony and Graham (1983) study in several respects. For example, Fig. 15.2 shows the Anthony and Graham (1983) and the Richards (1994) results. The reflex blink occurring during the interesting foreground stimulus (Anthony & Graham) or during sustained attention (Richards; hatched bars) was significantly larger than the blink reflex occurring during the dull stimulus (Anthony & Graham) or during attention termination (Richards; solid bars). This was true only for the match conditions, whereas the opposite was true for the mismatch condition. Thus, relative to inattention or attention termination, sustained attention enhances probe stimulus processing in the same modality (selective and intensive) and attenuates processing in the different modality (selective and not intensive).

There was an extremely interesting developmental trend in the selective nature of this response. Only 16-week-old infants were tested in Anthony and Graham (1993). In Richards (1994), infants were tested at 8, 14, 20, and 26 weeks. There was no change over this age range in the absolute magnitude of the blink response to either the auditory or the visual reflex

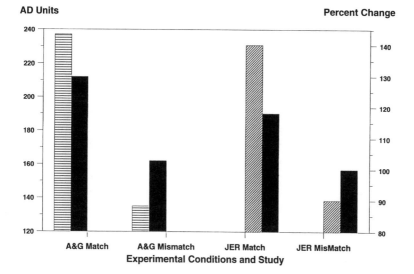

FIG. 15.2. Blink reflexes (A/D units for Anthony & Graham, Percent Change for Richards) as a function of the match between foreground modality and blink reflex stimulus modality, comparison between Anthony and Graham (1983; A&G) and Richards (1994; JER) results. The data is summed over both auditory and visual foregrounds and blink stimuli. The subjects in the Anthony and Graham study were 16 weeks. The subjects in the Richards study were 8, 14, 20, or 26 weeks. Note: Hatched bars—interesting foreground (A&G), sustained attention (JER). Solid bars—dull foreground (A&G), attention termination (JER).

probe when it was presented alone. There was a clear developmental trend in the modality selectivity over this age range. The youngest infants did not show the pattern of match–mismatch probe responses during sustained attention. The oldest infants showed the largest disparity between the match and mismatch conditions, with much larger responses during sustained attention condition relative to attention termination (e.g., the pattern shown across age groups in Fig. 15.2). The 14-week-old and 20-week-old infants showed an intermediate attention-based modality selectivity effect. Anthony and Graham's results with 16-week-olds were intermediate to the 14- and 20-week-olds in the Richards study! Developmental change in sustained attention also increases the "selective" nature of attention such that the chosen sensory modality is intensively processed. The processing of nonselected modalities is attenuated.

The attention phase in the heart rate response called *sustained attention* therefore involves intensive information processing. Recognition memory involves information extraction and inducement of a cognitive representation ("neural model"?). The finding that this occurs with ease during sustained attention, and may be primarily occurring during sustained attention, demonstrates the intensive aspect of sustained attention. Sustained attention also has a top-down influence on processing occurring in simpler response systems. The reflex blink represents both simple preattentive cognitive characteristics and is controlled by subcortical mechanisms. The reflex blink enhancement for the same modality stimulus during sustained attention implies that the intensive aspect of attention may operate by enhancing complementary sensory systems, either peripheral or subcortical in origin. At the same time, sustained attention attenuates competing attention systems, whether they are sensor redirection (shift in fixation) or automatic interrupt responses to stimuli in nonattended modalities. The enhancement of complementary systems for processing (intensive) and the attenuation of competing systems to inhibit their processing (selective) suggests that the selective and intensive aspects of attention listed by James are closely intertwined in sustained attention.

ANTICIPATION: INFANTS' ABILITY TO ATTEND TO THE FUTURE

The selective and intensive processes of sustained attention require that the infant focus on a stimulus that is ongoing or that just previously occurred. That is, they involve attention to events past or present. Attention to present events is also needed for the preattentive and orienting processes elaborated by Graham. In contrast, the focus in this final section is concerned with attention that, hypothetically at least, is focused on events yet to come—on events that the present stimulus may forecast, but that is not yet available. This looking forward to the future is the function of the attentional process of anticipation.

Despite the obvious adaptive significance of the ability to accurately anticipate, plan, and prepare for significant future events and its prominence in behavioral research with adults, there has been little systematic attention paid to its development in either empirical studies or theory. Piaget (1951, 1952) recognized the importance of the ability to anticipate significant events. He argued that this ability did not fully blossom until late in the first year of life, during Stage IV of the sensorimotor period. Although Piaget's theories and concepts have served to stimulate a very wide range of research, research on developmental changes in anticipation has only recently been evident. This is apparent in several laboratories employing a variety of paradigms and response measures (e.g., Berg & Donohue, 1992; Clohessy, Posner, & Rothbart, 1992; Haith, Hazan, & Goodman, 1988; Johnson, Posner, & Rothbart, 1991; Resnick, 1992; see also Siddle and Lipp, chapter 2, this volume).

The cardiac expressions of this process have most often been explored using the paired stimulus, or S1–S2 paradigm. This paradigm is frequently used in experimental psychology research, such as classical conditioning or foreperiod reaction time studies. It is also common in everyday life—for example, traffic lights (yellow light = S1, red light = S2) or the smell of dinner cooking prior to being served. The individual not only attends to each of the S1 stimuli themselves, but also, with repeated pairing, focuses on the upcoming S2 event *prior* to its arrival. That is, we anticipate the event. This anticipation may be highly varied, involving hypotheses as the exact nature of the S2 where this may not be certain ("What's for dinner?"), or preparing to better deal with a highly predictable, specific event when it occurs.

Research with adult subjects suggests that momentary changes in heart rate reflect this anticipatory process very effectively (see Bohlin & Kjellberg, 1979, for a review). The heart rate pattern during the interstimulus interval is basically the same for a variety of types of S1–S2 paradigms: a three component, deceleration-acceleration-deceleration pattern. The brief initial deceleration is a response to S1 onset, but often quickly habituates and therefore may not be evident when responses are shown averaged over many trials. The amplitude of the acceleration may vary from nonexistent to substantial, depending on factors such as the energy requirements of the response to occur (Chase, Graham, & Graham, 1968), stimulus significance (Coles & Duncan-Johnson, 1975), or affective valence (Lang, Ohman, & Simons, 1978), among others. The final deceleration is the most consistently reported of the components. The amplitude will vary with factors such as the salience of S2 and the motivation of the subject to respond (Bohlin & Kjellberg, 1979; Lang et al., 1978). Although there are disagreements as to the precise factors that influence the three components, there is agreement that the components are reasonably independent, being responsive to different stimulus and processing demands. Thus, the heart rate response in the paired-stimulus paradigm provides a rich source of information about anticipation.

The importance of examining the ontogeny of these anticipatory cardiac processes was illustrated in a study of neonates by Clifton (1974). In this study awake, alert neonates were trained for 20 trials. Each trial consisted of an 8-sec tone conditioned stimulus (CS) followed by a 10-sec oral presentation of a glucose unconditioned stimulus (UCS). The UCS onset began 6 sec after CS onset. The glucose and baseline tone presentation readily produced heart rate changes in initial trials. However, there was no significant heart rate response during the tone–glucose (CS–UCS) interval during conditioning trials. On the initial extinction trial substantial deceleration was produced at the point of omission of the glucose for paired but not control subjects. The finding indicated that the infants had developed an association of the two events but did not show signs of anticipation in the cardiac responses. In Clifton's terms, the neonates demonstrated a "What happened?" response, but not a "Here it comes!"

response. Forbes and Porges (1973) reported a similar finding in an aversive conditioning situation using a loud buzzer as a noxious UCS.

There have been claims of successful anticipatory heart rate conditioning in neonates but the results are quite limited (see Berg & Donohue, 1992, for review). Overall, these results and Clifton's careful study demonstrate the apparent difficulty in obtaining an anticipatory heart rate response among neonates. Failure to produce such anticipatory heart rate responding could be attributed to the response system limitations, to lower brain cardiac control mechanisms, or to the cognitive processes modulating the cardiac activity. Evidence points to the latter. Clifton's results clearly demonstrate that in a nonanticipatory condition, the omission of the UCS, the newborn is capable of producing a potent deceleratory response. This deceleration occurs even though decelerations to discrete stimuli in an unpaired-stimulus paradigm are uncommon in neonates. Further, the results point to the specific aspect of the anticipatory process that is not functioning. The inability to anticipate was not a result of an inability to time the CS–UCS interval or to a failure to associate the CS and UCS. These explanations may be rejected because the deceleration occurring on the initial extinction trial began precisely at the point in the trial where the UCS had previously been presented. Instead, the evidence strongly suggests that the lack of an anticipatory heart rate response in this study was specific to the inability to initiate the response prior to the UCS onset.

There is now evidence that anticipatory aspects of the orienting response develop within the first year of life. Donohue and Berg (1991) tested 7-month-old infants, providing a noise for an S1 and, 10 sec thereafter, an interesting, animated mechanical toy for an S2. During the first 12 trials there was no evidence of a late anticipatory deceleration (Fig. 15.3). Thereafter the infants began to demonstrate the anticipatory deceleration, thus seeming to have learned the sequence. This study also demonstrated evidence of orienting to the absence of the toy. On 3 of the 20 trials the toy was omitted and a second wave of heart rate deceleration (one in addition to the anticipatory deceleration) occurred at the point of S2 omission. Because S1 offset did not occur until well after S2 onset, neither this nor any other extant event could provide a cue to the absence of the toy. Infants begin to produce cardiac indicators of anticipation under these test circumstances between birth and 7 months.

A recently completed study has provided information on this transition (Boswell, Garner, & Berg, 1994). Infants 2, 4, and 8 months of age were presented with pairs of stimuli using timing similar to that employed in the Donohue and Berg (1991) study already described. This study differed in that the warning S1 was a bull's-eye plus a tone and the significant S2 was a 3-sec complex video image that moved in synchrony with either music

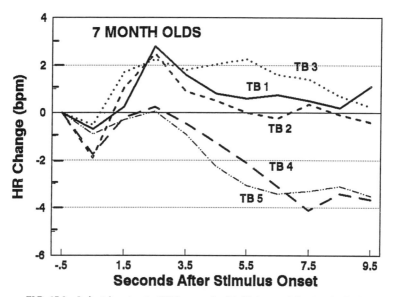

FIG. 15.3. Infant heart rate (HR) over the S1–S2 interval for Trial Blocks (TB) 1–5. (S = stimulus; ISI = interstimulus interval; TB = average of 4 trials each). From Donohue and Berg (1991). Copyright © 1991 by the American Psychological Association. Reprinted with permission.

or a woman speaking in "motherese." Subjects were divided into motorically active and quiet-alert groups based on movement late in the session. The motorically active infants had much more variable and unpredictable heart rate; the quiet-alert infant's responses will be summarized here.

The heart rate response during the S1–S2 interval for 2-month-olds (Fig. 15.4a) was an early deceleration on the initial trial block that habituated with repeated pairings. There was no sign of a late deceleration developing over trials. The first S2 omission produced deceleration virtually as large as to an S2 occurrence on the just prior trial (Fig. 15.5). The reason this response failed to occur on the second S2 omission is not certain, but may be because the trial occurred late in the session when the infant was tiring. However, in Clifton's (1974) results, the deceleratory response to UCS omission was also limited to the first extinction trial so it is possible that infants quickly habituate to the unexpected omission of S2. In this study, the deceleratory response to the first omission was significant when tested alone and did not differ significantly from the response to an actual S2 presentation. We conclude from this that at 2 months of age, as with neonates, orienting in this situation appears limited to responding to present and past events.

The responses of the 4-month-olds were very different. The response between S1 and S2 indicated clear evidence of the early deceleration

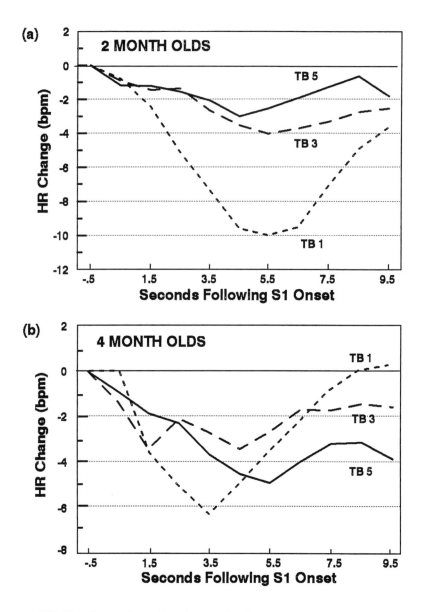

FIG. 15.4. Comparison of 2 and 4 month infant heart rate over the S1–S2 interval for TB 1–5. Only infants whose movements were below the median on TB 5 are included.

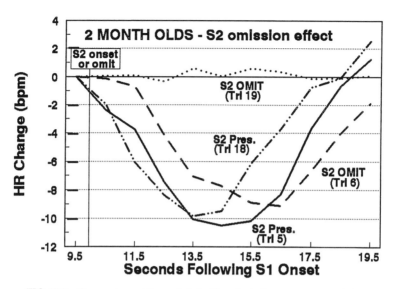

FIG. 15.5. Comparison of 2 month infant heart rate in response to omission of S2 onset (Trials 6 and 19) with HR response to presentation of S2 (Trials 5 and 18). (TRL = trial; S2 Pres. = S2 presented; S2 OMIT = S2 omitted).

habituating at the same time that the late deceleration was growing (Fig. 15.4b). The late deceleration increased almost monotonically over the five trial blocks. There was evidence of an omission response, though not as dramatic as the 2-month-old's omission response.

The 8-month-olds' response to S1 was complex and makes their data difficult to interpret. However, their responses were consistent with the results of three previous studies of this age group that demonstrated development of an anticipatory deceleration (Donohue & Berg, 1990, 1991; Donohue et al., 1992). We have found that this response is easily disrupted in 4- as well as 8-month-olds. The anticipatory responses appear to be limited to subjects who limit their movements during the stimulus period. The complex process of anticipation in the young infant may require maximal attentiveness in addition to motoric quieting.

The shift from Clifton's "What happened?" to the "Here it comes!" during the period between 2 and 4 months of life has important implications for our concepts of information processing. This review has focused on the cardiac responses of human infants, but other evidence suggests that these changes are not restricted to the autonomic nervous system. Haith and colleagues find anticipatory responding in visual fixation (rather than cardiac responses) for a variety of stimulus sequences in infants at 3 months of age (e.g., Haith et al., 1988; Lanthier, Arehart, & Haith, 1993). They report greater difficulties demonstrating this anticipatory response with 2-month-olds (Canfield & Haith, 1991). Our laboratory is currently working on additional measures of anticipation in infants including brain activity, reflex modulation, and overt behaviors. Research also shows that the development of anticipatory cardiac changes is also present in nonhuman species. Block and Montoya (1981) reported that 3-week-old kittens also fail to show classical conditioning of heart rate responses, but develop anticipatory responses by 8 weeks of age. These data suggest that the developmental change seen in anticipatory heart rate in human infants represents emergence of a basic cognitive activity during the first 4 months of life. The fact that the ability to anticipate develops sooner than what Piaget (1951, 1952) predicted is probably related to the use of measures more effective in testing very young infants and the careful attention to arousal state.

An important distinction must be made between responses occurring after an S2 event ("What happened?") and responses occurring before an S2 event ("Here it comes!"). The cognitive literature commonly assumes these responses are equivalent. For example, when following a series of similar stimuli the subject receives, without warning, a changed stimulus, the typical result is an enhanced or altered response (e.g., longer visual fixation or reaction time, or presence of a P300 component in an event related brain potential). As a class changes in these poststimulus responses are often referred to as "expectancy effects." The problem is that such terms may imply that an explicit anticipation for a particular stimulus was actively underway prior to the presentation of that stimulus. As a result, it is sometimes assumed that poststimulus and prestimulus responses are equally valid indicators of the cognitive construct of anticipation. The developmental evidence that post-S2 omission responses are present earlier than pre-S2 anticipatory responses indicates that such responses are independent processes, and thus pre- and post-S2 responses are not equally valid indicators of active, pre-S2 anticipation.

Given this, however, we are forced to provide an alternative explanation of just how an unexpected change in a previously predictable stimulus might alter a response to the changed stimulus. Sokolov's (1963) view of the neuronal model and orienting provides a reasonable answer. Sokolov proposed a neuronal comparator that takes information available from each stimulus as it is sensed and attempts to match it to the various stored "models" of previously experienced stimuli. If the new stimulus fails to match any existing model, then an orienting response is generated. But this process is not initiated until the new stimulus arrives. It does not presume nor require presence of active anticipation or prior orienting to the future event to account for this poststimulus response alteration. In this view, many of the so-called expectancy effects may rather be an indication that a mismatch to a previously stored stimulus model has occurred. Thus, the newborn infant showing a large deceleration to the omission of a learned sequence may be simply orienting to this sequence that does not match an existing model of sequences.

In contrast, the process of anticipation requires some active attentional activity that is directed toward a forewarned, upcoming event. The principal evidence thus far that such attention is directed toward an upcoming event is that the index of attention, such as heart rate deceleration, develops over trials of paired stimuli and is usually maximal just prior to the S2. Haith's work on infants' visual saccades provides evidence that the ocular muscles activated prior to the upcoming event are ones that move the eye toward the next source of visual information. The neonate may have limited orienting and neuronal comparator capability, but does not appear to have the qualitatively distinct capability to attend to future events. It is not until later that true anticipatory responding occurs.

An important question not yet addressed is how the anticipation process relates to sustained attention. The literature on sustained attention and on anticipation allows us to pose some interesting research questions. For example, does the anticipatory response develop from the sustained deceleration? That is, is the anticipatory deceleration a refinement of sustained attention when paired stimuli are presented? If so, does anticipation reflect both the selective and intensive aspects found in sustained attention? Of course, anticipation may not originate from sustained attention. Sokolov argues that conditioning can take place (signal orienting, in his terms) only when the orienting response (and presumably any sustained attention) to the CS has habituated. Putnam, Ross, and Graham (1974) reported such effects for heart rate and the conditioned blink. This would suggest that sustained attention to the S1 (or CS) is explicitly incompatible with an anticipatory response. These and related questions can and should be answered by combining the procedures outlined by Richards for identifying sustained attention, with the S1–S2 paradigm being explored by Berg and others.

SUMMARY AND CONCLUSION

In this review we have argued that presentation of a stimulus initiates a series of attentive responses that differ in function and cognitive involvement. The validity of making qualitative distinctions between them is reinforced by the developmental changes that occur in these responses. During the first half year of life, the infant is building on the basic information processes available at birth. Simple preattentive processing is present and fully functional at birth. Orienting, which supplies basic information about the stimulus, is possible at birth but not very effective for the first 6 to 8 weeks. Following thereafter are the processes that allow continued examination and exploration of the stimulus at hand and the ability to prepare for, in at least a simple way, other stimuli which may be predicted from that which is at hand. Together these allow the infant in the second half year of life to focus narrowly and intensively both on that which is present now and that which may be possible in the future. These are powerful information processing tools needed to begin to organize the complex world the young infant faces.

ACKNOWLEDGMENTS

Support for the writing of this chapter was provided in part by NIMH Grant R01-MH46568 to W.K.B., and an NICHD Grant R01-HD18942 and NIMH Research Scientist Development Award Grant K02-MH00958 to J.E.R.

REFERENCES

Anthony, B. J., & Graham, F. K. (1983). Evidence for sensory-selected set in young infants. *Science, 220,* 742–744.

Berg, K. M., Berg, W. K., & Graham, F. K. (1971). Infant heart rate response as a function of stimulus and state. *Psychophysiology, 8,* 30–44.

Berg, W. K., & Berg, K. M. (1987). Psychophysiological development in infancy: State, startle and attention. In J. Osofsky (Ed.), *Handbook of infant development* (Vol. 2, pp. 238–317). New York: Wiley.

Berg, W. K., & Donohue, R. L. (1992). Anticipatory processes in infants: Cardiac components. In B. A. Campbell, H. Hayne, & R. Richardson (Eds.), *Attention and information processing in infants and adults* (pp. 61–80). Hillsdale, NJ: Lawrence Erlbaum Associates.

Block, S. A., & Montoya, C. (1981). Reactivity to light and development of classical cardiac conditioning in the kitten. *Developmental Psychobiology, 14,* 83–92.

Bohlin, G., & Kjellberg, A. (1979). Orienting activity in two-stimulus paradigms as reflected in heart rate. In H. D. Kimmel, E. H. van Olst, & J. H. Orlebeke (Eds.), *The orienting reflex in humans.* Hillsdale, NJ: Lawrence Erlbaum Associates.

Boswell, A. E., Garner, E. E., & Berg, W. K. (1994). Changes in cardiac components of Anticipation in 2-, 4-, and 8-month-old infants [Abstract]. *Psychophysiology, 31,* S28.

Canfield, R. L., & Haith, M. M. (1991). Young infant's visual expectations for symmetric and asymmetric stimulus sequences. *Developmental Psychology, 27,* 198–208.

Chase, W. G., Graham, F. K., & Graham, D. T. (1968). Components of HR response in anticipation of reaction time and exercise tasks. *Journal of Experimental Psychology, 76,* 642–648.

Clifton, R. K. (1974). Heart rate conditioning in the newborn infant. *Journal of Experimental Child Psychology, 18,* 9–21.

Clohessy, A. B., Posner, M. I., & Rothbart, M. K. (1992, May). *Stability in anticipatory eye movement learning from four months (to adulthood?).* Paper presented at International Conference on Infant Studies, Miami, FL.

Cohen, L. B. (1972). Attention-getting and attention-holding processes of infant visual preferences. *Child Development, 43,* 869–879.

Cohen, L. B. (1973). A two-process model of infant visual attention. *Merrill-Palmer Quarterly, 19,* 157–180.

Coles, M. G. H., & Duncan-Johnson, C. C. (1975). Cardiac activity and information processing: The effects of stimulus significance and detection and response requirements. *Journal of Experimental Psychology: Human Perception and Performance, 104*, 418–428.

Donohue, R. L., & Berg, W. K. (1990). 7-month-olds display anticipatory HR decelerations in a differential conditioning paradigm [Abstract]. *Psychophysiology, 27*, S25.

Donohue, R. L., & Berg, W. K. (1991). Infant heart-rate responses to temporally predictable and unpredictable events. *Developmental Psychology, 27*, 59–66.

Donohue, R. L., Grossman, S. E., Berg, W. K., Woods, C. B., Garner, E. E., & Boswell, A. E. (1992). Anticipation in 8- and 10-month-old infants: Their heart says yes but their head says no [Abstract]. *Psychophysiology, 27*, S25.

Fantz, R. L. (1963). Visual perception from birth as shown by pattern selectivity. *Annals of the New York Academy of Sciences, 118*, 793–814.

Forbes, E. J., & Porges, S. W. (1973). Heart rate classical conditioning with a noxious stimulus in human newborns [Abstract]. *Psychophysiology, 10*, 192–193.

Graham, F. K. (1979). Distinguishing among orienting, defense, and startle reflexes. In H. D. Kimmel, E. H. van Olst, & J. F. Orlebeke (Eds.), *The orienting reflex in humans* (pp. 137–167). Hillsdale, NJ: Lawrence Erlbaum Associates.

Graham, F. K. (1992). Attention: The heartbeat, the blink, and the brain. In B. A. Campbell, H. Hayne, & R. Richardson (Eds.), *Attention and information processing in infants and adults* (pp. 3–29). Hillsdale, NJ: Lawrence Erlbaum Associates.

Graham, F. K., Anthony, B. J., & Zeigler, B. L. (1983). The orienting response and developmental processes. In D. Siddle (Ed.), *Orienting and habituation: Perspectives in human research* (pp. 371–430). Sussex, UK: Wiley.

Graham, F. K., Berg, K. M., Berg, W. K., Jackson, J. C., Hatton, H. M., & Kantowitz, S. R. (1970). Cardiac orienting response as a function of age. *Psychonomic Science, 19*, 363–365.

Graham, F. K., & Clifton, R. K. (1966). Heart rate change as a component of the orienting response. *Psychological Bulletin, 65*, 305–320.

Haith, M. M., Hazan, C., & Goodman, G. (1988). Expectation and anticipation of dynamic visual events by 3.5-month-old babies. *Child Development, 59*, 467–479.

James, W. (1890). *The principles of psychology.* New York: Henry Holt & Co.

Johnson, M. H., Posner, M. I., & Rothbart, M. K. (1991). Components of visual orienting in early infancy: Contingency learning, anticipatory looking, and disengaging. *Journal of Cognitive Neuroscience, 3*, 335–344.

Lacey, J. I., Kagan, J., Lacey, B. C., & Moss, M. A. (1962). The visceral level: Situational determinants and behavioral correlates of autonomic response patterns. In P. Knapp (Ed.), *Expression of the emotions in man* (pp. 161–196). New York: International Universities Press.

Lang, P. J., Ohman, A., & Simons, R. F. (1978). The psychophysiology of anticipation. In J. Requin (Ed.), *Attention and performance VII.* Hillsdale, NJ: Lawrence Erlbaum Associates.

Lathier, E. C., Arehart, D., & Haith, M. M. (1993, March). Infants' performance in a nonsymmetrical timing sequence in the visual expectation paradigm. Paper presented in Marshall Haith (chair), *Variations on a theme of infant visual expectations.* Poster symposium, Meeting of the Society for Research in Child Development, New Orleans, LA.

Piaget, J. (1951). *Play, dreams and imitation in childhood* (G. Gattegno & F. M. Hodgson, Trans.). New York: Norton.

Piaget, J. (1952). *The origins of intelligence in children* (M. Cook, Trans.). New York: International Universities Press.

Porges, S. W. (1976). Peripheral and neurochemical parallels of psychopathology: A psychophysiological model relating autonomic imbalance in hyperactivity, psychopathology, and autism. In H. Reese (Ed.), *Advances in child development and behavior* (Vol. 11, pp. 35–65). New York: Academic Press.

Porges, S. W. (1980). Individual differences in attention: A possible physiological substrate. In B. Keogh (Ed.), *Advances in special education* (Vol. 2, pp. 111–134). Greenwich, CT: JAI.

Putnam, L. E., Ross, L. E., & Graham, F. K. (1974). Cardiac orienting during "good" and "poor" differential eyelid conditioning. *Journal of Experimental Psychology, 102,* 563–573.

Resnick, J. S. (1992, May). *The development of visual expectations.* Presented at International Conference on Infant Studies, Miami, FL.

Richards, J. E. (1985). The development of sustained visual attention in infants from 14 to 26 weeks of age. *Psychophysiology, 22,* 409–416.

Richards, J. E. (1987). Infant visual sustained attention and respiratory sinus arrhythmia. *Child Development, 58,* 488–496.

Richards, J. E. (1988). Heart rate changes and heart rate rhythms, and infant visual sustained attention. In P. K. Ackles, J. R. Jennings, & M. G. H. Coles (Eds.), *Advances in psychophysiology* (Vol. 3, pp. 189–221). Greenwich, CT: JAI.

Richards, J. E. (1994, October). *Development of selective attention in infants from 8 to 26 weeks of age: Evidence from central-peripheral attention systems.* Paper presented at the workshop honoring Frances Graham, Society for Psychophysiological Research, Atlanta, GA.

Richards, J. E. (1995a). *Effects of attention on infants' preference for briefly exposed visual stimuli in the paired-comparison recognition-memory paradigm.* Manuscript submitted for publication.

Richards, J. E. (1995b). *Peripheral stimulus localization by infants: Age, attention and individual differences in heart rate variability.* Manuscript submitted for publication.

Richards, J. E., & Casey, B. J. (1991). Heart rate variability during attention phases in young infants. *Psychophysiology, 28,* 43–53.

Richards, J. E., & Casey, B. J. (1992). Development of sustained visual attention in the human infant. In B. A. Campbell, H. Hayne, & R. Richardson (Eds.), *Attention and information processing in infants and adults* (pp. 30–60). Hillsdale, NJ: Lawrence Erlbaum Associates.

Ruff, H. A. (1986). Components of attention during infants' manipulative exploration. *Child Development, 56,* 621–630.

Sokolov, Y. N. (1963). *Perception and the conditioned reflex.* New York: Pergamon.

16

Attention, Emotion, and Reactivity in Infancy and Early Childhood

Marie T. Balaban
John Hopkins University

Nancy Snidman
Harvard University

Jerome Kagan
Harvard University

Explorations into the orienting of attention continue to enhance our understanding of the development of sensory, perceptual, and cognitive abilities during infancy and early childhood. Although attention is often described in the cognitive terms of information processing, the connections between attention and affective/motivational processes are obvious in descriptive and theoretical accounts of early development (Berg & Sternberg, 1985; Izard & Malatesta, 1987; Piaget, 1981). Discussions of the complex relations between attention and affect are apt to proceed more quickly if we focus on the presumed phenomena rather than the words. Cognitive scientists are coming to a consensus that the abstract term *attention* involves, at a minimum, three quite different processes whose referents are (a) initial orienting following a change in the sensory field, (b) detection/selection of the event that was the source of the orienting—a more psychological phenomenon, and, finally, (c) sustained attentiveness to the event (Posner, 1995). It is reasonable to suggest that the successive and relatively seamless sequence that begins with orienting and ends with sustained attention is associated with excitability in different limbic-cortical systems (Posner, Rothbart, Gerardi, & Thomas-Thrapp, chapter 14, this volume; Robbins & Everitt, 1995; Stormack, Hugdahl, & Posner, 1994) and, therefore, with different emotions. This suggestion of connections between attention and emotion is supported, at a descriptive level, by infants' behaviors. Consider the following examples from our laboratories.

Four-month-old infants will orient to the source of the sudden onset of a taped voice of a woman speaking short sentences (Kagan, 1994). A very small proportion—less than 5%—are so startled by the unexpected increase in acoustic energy that they cry shortly after the bodily startle reaction. The majority, however, become still and quiet, suggesting that they are in a state most psychologists would call *attentiveness*. As the voice completes the first utterance—about 4 sec long—many infants begin to vocalize, suggesting that they assimilated the stimulus to their stored representation of a human voice. The babbling, occasionally accompanied by a smile, implies an affect state that is different from surprise. As the voice speaks the second sentence (the infant has been fixating the source of the sound during this period), about 20% of infants will assume a wary face and then cry. This suggests that the discrepancy represented by the sound of a human voice, without any visual support from a face or body, created an affect state that most psychologists would call fear. The unfolding of these affect states can not be conceptualized solely by variation in excitement or arousal.

Another phenomenon is demonstrated by a 9-month-old in a categorization study (Balaban & Waxman, 1996): On five consecutive trials, an experimenter holds up a toy cat and then places it on a tray in front of the infant. The exemplars differ in color and shape on each trial. Then the experimenter holds up two new objects: a pink cat and a pink bear. As the infant looks at the bear, her eyes widen, eyebrows raise, and her mouth opens with corners drawn back as she vocalizes a sound like a quick intake of breath. This facial reaction of surprise/mild fear lasts for about 2 sec (Fig. 16.1, left). As the toys are placed on the tray, she begins to reach for the cat but pauses, turns toward the bear, and touches it. A few seconds later, she looks toward the experimenter and smiles (Fig. 16.1, right). James (1890/1950) suggested that "any object may excite attention, provided it be only novel" (p. 429). In the laboratory example, not only did the novel toy elicit attention, it also evoked a sequence of affective reactions. Theoretical accounts of emotion link novelty with interest as well as with fear (Bronson, 1968; Izard, 1991; see also Colombo, 1993) and cognitive approaches suggest that an optimal level of discrepancy facilitates processing (McCall & Kagan, 1967; Piaget, 1981). Later in development, novelty and positive affective responses are assumed to play a motivational role as infants develop incentives for mastery. Like the scenario described earlier, this example highlights the dynamic combination of attention and affect in infants' reactions to events and objects.

The preceding sequences are obvious to any observer; hence, it seems reasonable to claim that states of attention and various emotions are closely linked in early development. Posner and colleagues (chapter 14, this volume) propose another such connection—between attentional orienting

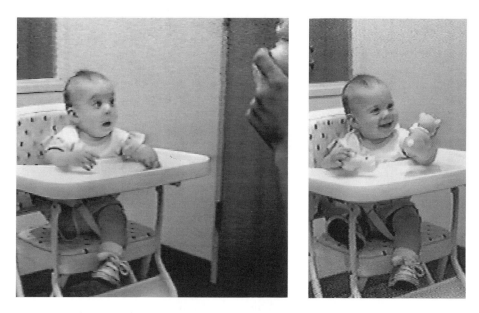

FIG. 16.1. Behavioral response of a 9-month-old infant to presentation of a toy from a novel category (bear, to the infant's left) and a toy from a familiar category (cat, to the infant's right). Her initial facial expression was accompanied by a vocalization of a quick intake of breath (left). Several seconds later, she smiles at the experimenter (right).

and the alleviation of an emotional distress state. Attentional control matures across development. For example, Gibson (1969) noted that during infancy, attention "changes from being captured to being exploratory, from being wandering and mobile to being sustained" (p. 457). These and other aspects of attentional development are described in this volume (Berg & Richards, chapter 15; Campos, Kermoian, Witherington, Chen, & Dong, chapter 17; Posner et al., chapter 14). In this chapter, we consider two specific areas of research that explore connections between attention and affect in development during infancy and early childhood. In the first part of the chapter, we summarize past research on infants' emerging appreciation of emotional signals conveyed through facial expressions, and studies of modulation of the startle reflex in infants and adults. This review provides the relevant background for the description of studies on the affective modulation of infant startle (Balaban, 1995, 1996). In the second part of the chapter, we examine the links between attention and emotion demonstrated by young children in a modified Stroop interference task (Kagan, Snidman, & Arcus, 1995) and consider individual differences in the interaction between affect and attention based on temperament and affective profiles in infancy and childhood.

ATTENDING TO EMOTION IN INFANCY

Responses to Facial Expressions of Emotion

Recent accounts of emotional development emphasize the role of emotions in regulating the relation between person and environment (Campos, Mumme, Kermoian, & Campos, 1994; Fox, 1994). In early development, the maturation of infants' abilities to regulate attentional processes has functional implications for the development of organized emotional responses. The focus in this section is on infants' attentional and affective responses to the emotional signals conveyed by facial expressions.

Neisser (1976) proposed that "babies are innately prepared to perceive smiles or frowns, soothing tones or harsh inflections, as indications of what others will do next" (p. 191). At first glance, this view seems contradicted by observations that young infants are readily engaged by faces and voices, regardless of whether those signals are positive or negative in emotional valence. For example, Darwin (1898) noted the generality of interest in facial and vocal expressions as he described his son's early development: "It is however extremely difficult to prove that our children instinctively recognize any expression. . . . When this child was about 4 months old, I made in his presence many odd noises and strange grimaces. . . . But the noises, if not too loud, as well as the grimaces, were all taken as good jokes" (p. 358). The idea that the perception of certain emotionally salient signals is biologically prepared (Izard, 1991; Öhman, chapter 7, this volume; Öhman & Dimberg, 1984) does not require that recognition of such signals, or organized responses to such signals, be present from birth. Organized emotional reactions emerge over time in human development. This developmental observation is incorporated in theories that emphasize discrete emotions (e.g., Izard, 1991) as well as theories that describe a dimensional organization of emotions (e.g., Davidson, 1992).

Infants respond to faces and voices at birth and, by 2 to 3 months of age, demonstrate marked preferences for faces or face-like stimuli (Dannemiller & Stephens, 1988; Kleiner, 1987). In a study of 2- to 8-month-old infants' responses to faces and face-like stimuli, the infants' facial expressions suggestive of the affect state *interest* were related to their visual fixation of the stimuli and to the magnitude of the cardiac deceleration evoked by the stimuli (Langsdorf, Izard, Rayais, & Hembree, 1983). Although young infants readily gaze at faces, their ability to discriminate between facial expressions and to extract affective meaning from expressions has been debated. Some studies suggest that neonates do respond to distinct facial expressions (Field et al., 1983), but others have argued that limitations on visual acuity and scanning constrain discrimination in young infants (Nelson, 1987). Infants' abilities to discriminate and categorize facial expressions become increasingly refined during the first year. The discrimination between happy and angry expressions, when based on pictures of faces posing these expressions, has sometimes been demonstrated in 7-month-old infants (Kestenbaum & Nelson, 1990; Soken & Pick, 1992), but not in younger infants. The combination of facial and vocal components of emotional expressions facilitates discrimination for 5- to 7-month-old infants (Caron, Caron, & MacLean, 1988; Walker-Andrews & Lennon, 1991).

The observation that certain facial expressions differed in their effectiveness as reinforcers for 4-month-old infants (Kaplan, Fox, & Huckeby, 1992) could indicate that infants respond affectively to facial expressions. However, the fact that infants detect a change in emotional facial expression or demonstrate a preference for a facial expression does not necessarily indicate that their responses are affectively mediated. These responses may be based on perceptual or attentional selection of particular features (Young-Browne, Rosenfeld, & Horowitz, 1977) or may result from attention to discrepancy, based on the relative unfamiliarity of the expression (Kagan, 1974).

It is important to consider what constitutes a response to the affective information conveyed via facial and/or vocal signals (Fernald, 1993; Nelson, 1987). Studies of infant behavior in response to maternal displays of affect suggest that infants as young as 3 months respond differently to affective signals (Haviland & Lelwica, 1987; Tronick, Ricks, & Cohn, 1982). For example, 10-week-old infants responded with facial expressions of joy and interest during periods when their mothers displayed joyous facial and vocal expressions, and looked away more frequently when their mothers displayed angry expressions (Haviland & Lelwica, 1987). Infants may use gaze aversion as a means of attentional regulation, in order to limit the effects of stimulation, as in the case of the posed "still-face" (Gusella, Muir, & Tronick, 1988): When parents are instructed to hold a neutral facial pose and not to respond contingently to their infant, the infants typically avert their gaze and/or become distressed. There is also some evidence for differential affective responding to vocal cues of emotion in speech. At 5 months, infants responded with positive facial affect to approving statements presented in infant-directed speech, and they responded with negative facial affect to prohibitions presented in infant-directed speech (Fernald, 1993). The onset of social referencing, later in the first year, provides a clear indication that infants use the facial expressions of others to guide their responses (Campos & Stenberg, 1981; Nelson, 1987). For example, 12-month-olds were more likely to cross over the deep side of a visual cliff if their mother posed an expression of joy or interest than if she posed fear or anger (Sorce, Emde, Campos, & Klinnert, 1985).

Modulation of the Startle Reflex

In order to investigate the processes underlying affective responses to facial expressions in young infants, we examined the affective modulation of infants' startle responses. Many aspects of startle modulation are described in other chapters of this volume. We review selected studies here in order to provide a framework for research on affective modulation of infant startle. Anthony and Graham (1982) investigated attentional allocation in 4-month-old infants during visual or auditory foreground stimuli. During the visual foregrounds (solid-color slides and slides of smiling faces), the infants' blink responses elicited by light flashes were enhanced and their blink responses elicited by sounds were reduced. During auditory foregrounds (continuous tones or musical melodies), visually elicited blinks were reduced and acoustically elicited blinks were enhanced. These effects were more pronounced during the more salient foregrounds (faces and melodies). The authors interpreted these results as consistent with the idea that infants adopted a sensory-selective attentional set (see also Richards, 1993; Berg & Richards, chapter 15, this volume). Izard and Malatesta (1987) noted that the finding that selective effects were more pronounced during the more salient, attention-engaging foregrounds (Anthony & Graham, 1982) is consistent with a connection between attentional processing and *interest* as an affect state.

A follow-up study of modality-selective processes in infants examined the effect of attention on prepulse inhibition (Balaban, Anthony, & Graham, 1985). The prepulse inhibitory effect—a reduction of startle by a transient prestimulus (Graham, 1975)—is weak and immature during infancy and early childhood (e.g., Balaban, Anthony, & Graham, 1989; Berg et al., 1985; Ornitz, Guthrie, Kaplan, Lane, & Norman, 1986). However, modality-selective attentional effects also acted to enhance the inhibitory effects of prepulses when prepulse and foreground stimuli were of the same modality (Balaban et al., 1985). Thus, the attention-engaging foreground stimulus led to preferential processing of other stimulus events in the same modality.

Initial studies of adult attention suggested that during the viewing of interesting pictures, adult subjects were less responsive to brief, startling acoustic probe stimuli than during the viewing of less interesting pictures (Anthony & Graham, 1985; Simons & Zelson, 1985). These modality-selective effects were presumed to be due either to central changes in the allocation of processing resources to input channels or to more peripheral changes in afferent pathways (Graham & Hackley, 1991). In addition to modality-selective modulation by the presence of a foreground stimulus or an instructed task, the reflex blink is also modulated by affective valence in adults (Lang, Bradley, & Cuthbert, 1990, chapter 5, this volume). Lang and colleagues demonstrated that the blink response in human adults was augmented when subjects viewed negative scenes but was reduced when subjects viewed positive scenes. They interpreted this effect within a theoretical framework emphasizing the combined dimensions of arousal (low to high) and valence (positive to negative) in both appetitive and aversive motivational sets. The modulatory influences of affective valence in humans resemble, in part, the phenomenon of fear-potentiated startle in animals (Brown, Kalish, & Farber, 1951; Davis, 1989, chapter 4, this volume).

The blink reflex does not require voluntary motor control. Blink responses to eliciting stimuli in auditory, visual, and tactile modalities can be measured in infants (see Balaban, 1996, for a review). If the neural systems mediating affective modulation of startle are functional in human infants, then the startle paradigm is a promising technique for probing responsivity to affective signals in early development. Affective startle modulation could provide evidence that extends or converges with other behavioral studies of infant emotional reactions (e.g., Fernald, 1993; Haviland & Lelwica, 1987).

Affective Startle Modulation in Infants

In order to study young infants' discrimination of emotional signals, the affective startle modulation method was adapted for infants (Balaban, 1995). The 20-week-old infants viewed a set of 24 photographic slides that included eight adults posing a neutral expression as well as exaggerated, toothy expressions of joy and anger. The experimental set-up is depicted in Fig. 16.2. During the time that the infant looked at the face (about 3 sec after their initial fixation), an acoustic probe stimulus (75 msec, 95 dB[A] white noise) was presented binaurally through headphones, and the infant's blink response to the probe stimulus was measured from the electromyographic (EMG) activity recorded from the muscle controlling the eyeblink, *m. orbicularis oculi*. The EMG signal was rectified and integrated with an 80-msec time constant. The amplitude and latency of the infants' blink responses were scored according to standard criteria for infant acoustic blink (Balaban, Losito, Simons, & Graham, 1986).

Infants' startle reactions were influenced by the affective facial expressions. The magnitude of the infants' blink responses was facilitated to the acoustic probes presented while infants viewed angry faces, relative to the acoustic probes that were presented during happy faces; the mean response during neutral faces was intermediate in size (Balaban, 1995). Startle potentiation during angry faces was highly significant in the main sample of infants and also in a small replication sample of infants who viewed only happy and angry faces (Table 16.1). Although the linear trend for the speed of the blink response, as indexed by onset latency,

FIG. 16.2. The experimental procedure for affective startle modulation in infants. The assistant monitors the headphone placement but her view of the slides is blocked by a visor. The electromyographic (EMG) activity from *m. orbicularis oculi* was computer-digitized, integrated, and scored for onset latency and peak magnitude.

was not significant ($p < .07$), the means were in the direction concordant with the magnitude results, that is, faster latencies to acoustic probes presented during the viewing of angry faces and slower latencies to probes presented during happy faces (Table 16.1).

Several rudimentary behavioral measures were coded from videotape. Although the infants appeared to be interested in the faces, they rarely showed obvious positive or negative facial expressions, such as joy or fear; this result is based on the impressions of two naive observers who rated

TABLE 16.1
Modulation of the Acoustic Blink During the Viewing of Facial Expressions

	Standardized Blink Magnitude			Blink Latency (msec)		
	Happy	*Neutral*	*Angry*	*Happy*	*Neutral*	*Angry*
Infant subjects (20 weeks, $N = 18$)	−0.20	0.04	0.24**	83.6	80.5	77.4
Infant subjects (20 weeks, $N = 7$)	−0.20		0.17*	75.4		68.2
Adult subjects ($N = 12$)						
First half of trials	0.06	0.32	0.50*	42.2	42.7	39.4*
Infant subjects (20 weeks, $N = 18$) Faces inverted	0.01	−0.07	0.04	76.7	78.3	80.2

*$p < .05$ for F_{linear} or t. **$p < .01$ for F_{linear}.

the infants' facial reactions. There were also no differences in the infants' duration of interest in the face slides, as measured by the duration of their initial glance or by their cumulative duration of visual fixation. There was, however, a marginal linear trend toward lower motor activity ratings during trials with pictures of angry expressions, relative to trials with pictures of happy expressions ($p < .06$). A reduction in motor activity during the viewing of threatening pictures fits with previous reports of freezing behavior during fear-potentiated startle in rats (Leaton & Borszcz, 1985) and with descriptions of 10-week-old infants' behavioral quieting during maternal simulations of anger (Haviland & Lelwica, 1987). Lang and colleagues (chapter 5, this volume) also link startle potentiation with immobility in their model of response to aversive external events.

A comparison study of adult subjects (Balaban, 1996) corroborated the infant findings, but only when the analysis was limited to the first half of the trials. The fact that the results were not significant over all of the trials probably indicates that the facial expressions were emotionally less salient for adults than for infants. In adult subjects' ratings of various affective pictures (Lang, Bradley, & Cuthbert, 1995), smiling, neutral, and angry faces were rated, respectively, as positive, neutral, and negative in valence; however, smiling and angry faces were rated as only modestly arousing compared to pictures with other affective contents. In analyses of adults' reactions during the initial 12 trials of the facial expressions study (Balaban, 1996), blink magnitude was significantly augmented and blink latency was significantly speeded to acoustic probes presented during the angry expressions, relative to the happy expressions (Table 16.1).

An additional control group of infants was tested with inverted, rather than upright, faces. This manipulation greatly reduces the discriminability of emotional facial expressions for adults. There was no significant difference in blink magnitude or latency to probes presented during inverted faces as a function of affective category (Table 16.1). This suggests that the differences in infants' responses to the upright faces (Balaban, 1995) stemmed from the perception of the facial expressions, rather than from arbitrary featural differences or overall slide brightness.

Although infants responded differentially in their blink reflex responses during the viewing of angry and happy faces, striking differences in the infants' behavioral responses were not apparent. Despite the 20-week-old infants' lack of behavioral avoidance of the angry faces in the upright-face studies, selective attentional influences remain a potential alternative explanation for the affective modulatory effect (Balaban, 1995). That is, if infants are more engaged by the happy expressions than by the angry expressions, they might adopt a sensory-selective set (Anthony & Graham, 1982) that would facilitate their responsiveness to other events in the visual modality while they attended to the happy facial expressions, and diminish their responsiveness to events in other modalities, such as the acoustic probe. If infants were less engaged by the angry face or were attempting to disregard the angry face, this modality-selective influence could be reduced or reversed during viewing of angry faces. In adult subjects, affective modulation occurs across modalities of startle-eliciting probe stimuli (Bradley, Cuthbert, & Lang, 1990) and across modalities of affective foreground stimuli (Bradley, Zack, & Lang, 1994), therefore modality-selective influences cannot account for affective modulation. Similar studies are needed in order to extend this claim to infants. Is there evidence that happy faces are more salient to the infants than angry faces? It is interesting to note that Nelson and colleagues (Nelson, Matheny, Sargent, Carver, & Crescione, 1993) suggested the opposite; that is, that the emotional signal conveyed via negative expressions might enable such faces to recruit attention to a greater extent than do happy expressions.

A follow-up study was conducted using a behavioral preference task and the same set of upright faces that were used in the affective startle modulation studies (Balaban, 1995). The question was whether infants would demonstrate preferences for happy, neutral, or angry faces within this stimulus set. Preferences were indexed by differences in looking time in a paired comparison task. The paired comparison task may assess preferences more sensitively than methods involving sequential stimulus presentation, thus providing a better means of ascertaining whether infants attempted to avoid the angry faces. Infants were randomly assigned to one of two slide sets. One slide set contained happy, angry, and neutral photographs of four of the adult models in the original study; the other slide set contained photographs of the other four adults. Each trial consisted of paired presentation, for 10 sec, of two pictures of the same adult model, one presented to the right side and one to the left side of a central fixation point. Side of presentation and pairing of expressions were counterbalanced across trials.

There were no significant pairwise preferences as a function of facial expression condition in a group of 26 infants who were 4 to 5 months old. The lack of any statistically significant preference can also be construed as consistent with results of previous behavioral studies that found a lack of discrimination of static happy from angry expressions prior to about 7 months of age. Caron, Caron, and MacLean (1988) suggested that this discrimination is difficult because happiness and anger are less dynamically distinct than other facial expressions, such as sadness and happiness. The averages, across all preference pairs, of looking times were 3.28 sec for happy, 3.49 sec for neutral, and 3.96 sec for angry expressions. The lack of a robust preference for happy faces and the fact that this pattern of means was in the direction of a slight preference for angry faces ($p < .10$ for the linear trend) argue against the hypothesis that infants devoted more attention to happy than to angry faces. Thus, it seems unlikely that an explanation based on modality-selective attention accounts for the affective modulation effect in infants.

Conclusions

Affective startle modulation in infants provides an interesting addition to other research on the emerging organization of processes involved in perceiving and attending to affective signals. This organization is present by at least 20 weeks for discrimination of static angry versus happy faces; it is possible that investigations using dynamic facial expressions or combined facial and vocal expressions would reveal that such events elicit affective modulation at an earlier age. What does the occurrence of affective startle modulation in infants suggest about the maturation of processes involved in the organization of emotional responses? Although the blink reflex is mediated by a brainstem circuit, there are modulatory connections from midbrain, limbic, and other cortical areas. In particular, the amygdala plays a critical role in startle potentiation and is likely to be involved in attentional regulation during an aversive stimulus or state (Davis, 1989, chapter 4, this volume; Robbins & Everitt, 1995; Stormack, Hugdahl, & Posner, 1994). As Fox (1994) emphasized, we need to revise the view that emotions act only to disrupt cognitive processes, because it is increasingly evident that emotions also organize such processes: "Emotions are not only responses to be regulated but also themselves regulators of environmental interaction" (p. 4). Despite the absence of marked functional consequences of static angry versus happy facial expressions on the infants' behavior at 20 weeks, the physiological reactivity that contributes to startle modulation may play a role in the infant's maturing regulation of attention and state.

We cannot assume that the modulatory influences of angry and happy faces on infant acoustic startle indicate the infant's awareness of the affective signal. Izard and Malatesta (1987) proposed that the "infant is innately prepared . . . to register and respond to emotion signals without cognitive appraisal" (p. 499). Aspects of processing prepared emotional signals, such as spiders or angry facial expressions, may occur without awareness (Öhman & Dimberg, 1984). Öhman and colleagues found (a) greater conditioning in adults to backward-masked angry faces than to masked happy faces and (b) evidence for implicit memory of masked angry faces, but not happy faces. In the startle modulation paradigm, the infant might respond implicitly to the affective signals in the angry or happy faces. This argument could also be relevant to the observed differences in infants' event-related potential responses to faces (e.g., Nelson et al., 1993). Thus, the fact that angry and happy faces differentially modulate infant startle indicates an affective influence, but it remains to be seen whether this influence arises at a preattentive level and/or during orienting or sustained attention. It is interesting to note that the possibility of infants responding without awareness was raised with respect to another process presumed to have limbic origins, that is, infant performance on novelty preference tasks: "it is possible that human infants are performing similar feats on the paired comparison task without the participation of higher cortical functions and, presumably, without subjective awareness. In this way, performance on the paired comparison task, although dependent on the limbic system for retention, might be classified as reflexive in the sense that it involves unconscious responses" (Overman, Bachevalier, Turner, & Peuster, 1992, p. 28).

Although infants may be actively engaged by pictures of faces, the task used in these studies is a passive viewing task. It is important to consider the potential role of emerging organized responses across development. Campos and colleagues (chapter 17, this volume) emphasize the functional role of emotions in the infant's interaction with the environment. The angry face that potentiates startle for a 5-month-old infant may convince a 1-year-old child not to cross the visual cliff. The developmental advances in cognitive competence and elaboration of emotions are accompanied by the child's increasingly adept and organized actions.

ATTENDING TO EMOTION IN CHILDHOOD

Affective Stroop Interference

From infancy through childhood, there are linkages between cognitive and emotional development (e.g., Berg & Sternberg, 1985; Harris, 1989; Kagan, 1984). Advances in language and knowledge allow the child to recognize the motivational significance of a broader range of objects and events. Investigations of the relation between attention and affect in children must take into account that (a) as children grow, the processes of attention occur more rapidly, and (b) older children do not reveal their affect states as clearly as do infants.

One method that might reveal behavioral consequences of relations between attention and affect is the Stroop interference test (Stroop, 1935). In one form of this procedure, used with adults, the subjects attend to the color of single printed words while ignoring the meaning of each word. A word can be printed in any one of several colors and the subject has to suppress reading the word and only name the color of the ink in which the word is printed. Under these conditions it is well established that words with a rich set of symbolic associations produce longer latencies than nonsense words or words with minimal associations (MacLeod, 1991).

More relevant to this chapter are the observations that clinically anxious subjects have increased color-naming latencies to threatening words (Mathews & MacLeod, 1985), people with panic disorder have slower color-naming reactions to words related to their fears (see McNally, 1994), and veterans suffering from post-traumatic stress disorder (PTSD) show longer color-naming latencies to words suggestive of war (*body bag, soldier, maim*) than to emotionally arousing words that are not linked to warfare (McNally, English, & Lipke, 1993). A version of the affective Stroop task, presented to a sample of behaviorally inhibited and uninhibited adolescent subjects (see Kagan, 1994), revealed that more of the slowest color-naming responses of inhibited adolescents occurred to threatening words (e.g., *poison, kill*) than to pleasant words (e.g., *fond, love*).

Kagan, Snidman, and Arcus (1995) modified the affective Stroop procedure for use with young children (who cannot read) by using pictures rather than words. In this study, 4½- and 5-year-old children saw pictures on a monitor; each picture was representative of either neutral, happy, or threatening symbolic content. There were nine pictures in each of the three categories. Examples including *box, cow*, and *fish* were classified as neutral; *birthday cake, puppy*, and *happy face* were classified as happy or a positive emotion; *snake, knife*, and *witch* were classified as representative of threatening or fearful content. The pictures were line drawings of individual items or figures, balanced for complexity across category (positive, neutral, and negative). Each picture was outlined in one of three different colors (blue, red, green) and the child's task was to name the color as quickly as possible. A voice-activated microphone placed on the child's throat and connected to a computer recorded the onset of the child's vocal response.

The expectation was that the symbolic meaning of the pictures with affective content would elicit a brief affective reaction, as well as cognitive associations, and delay the retrieval of the color name by several hundred msec. Faster responses were predicted to the neutral pictures because they should elicit cognitive associations without (or with reduced) interference from a brief affective reaction. It is more reasonable to posit the occurrence of affective reactions to pictures of a witch or a snake than to assume that those pictures would elicit a richer set of cognitive associations than would familiar neutral pictures such as a cow or fish.

This modified Stroop interference task was administered to two cohorts of children who are part of longitudinal samples of temperamentally inhibited and uninhibited children. First, we present results across the entire sample for each cohort; then we consider individual differences. Both cohorts came from larger samples that had been seen at 4, 14, and 21 months and either 4½ or 5 years. The larger cohort of 137 children were seen at 4½ years; the smaller cohort of 42 children were seen at 5 years of age. All children saw the pictures in the same order, and data from children with poor attentiveness or from those who named the objects, rather than colors, were eliminated. The first picture (neutral) was omitted from analyses because its novelty elicited an exceptionally long color-naming latency in most children.

The mean latency to name the color of each of the pictures for each cohort was characterized by a saw-toothed pattern of latencies over trials. Inspection of these latencies, averaged over cohorts in Fig. 16.3, reveals a noticeable divergence between neutral and affectively negative pictures during the middle and later portions of the session. For each cohort, eight of the nine pictures with the longest latencies were symbolic either of a threatening or a happy affect, thus supporting the expectation that pictures with affective content would elicit the greatest interference. By contrast, five of the nine pictures with the fastest responses belonged to the symbolically neutral category for Cohort 1, and four of the nine fastest responses belonged to the neutral category for Cohort 2. A repeated measures analysis of variance revealed a significant difference in mean latency among the three types of pictures for both cohorts (Table 16.2). The mean latency to the threat pictures was significantly longer than the latencies to the neutral and happy pictures. The latencies to the happy and neutral

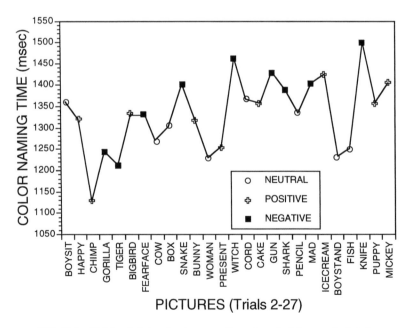

FIG. 16.3. Children's latencies to name the color of pictures selected for neutral, positive, and negative affective contents. Results are averaged across Cohorts 1 and 2. Pictures are plotted on the abscissa in trial order.

TABLE 16.2
Comparison of Mean Latencies by Picture Type
in the Stroop Interference Task for Two Cohorts
Mean Latencies (msec)

Groups	N	Threat	Positive	Neutral	F
Cohort 1	117	1,505	1,458	1,415	7.37**
Cohort 2	42	1,244	1,185	1,170	4.17*

*$p < .05$. **$p < .01$.

pictures were not significantly different from each other. Overall, the 5-year-olds (Cohort 2) had faster latencies than the 4-year-olds (Cohort 1).

These overall analyses of the two cohorts of children provide evidence for affective Stroop interference for pictures with affective content—particularly for pictures with negative or threatening content. The next sections focus on individual differences in the pattern of interference, thus the overall analysis is followed up by analyses of selected subgroups.

Reactivity, Inhibition, and Affective Stroop Interference

Over the past 15 years, Kagan, Snidman, and colleagues have studied two groups of children who exhibit stable differences in temperament: Children who are behaviorally inhibited are wary and unlikely to approach unfamiliar people or objects, whereas children who are uninhibited are likely to approach and interact with unfamiliar people and objects (Garcia-Coll, Kagan, & Reznick, 1984; Snidman, 1984). These groups of children demonstrate extremes in wariness and approach behaviors and also differ in their profiles of physiological activity (see Kagan, 1994, for a review). The behavioral and physiological differences between inhibited and uninhibited children may be linked to differences in limbic excitability, particularly in the circuits of the amygdala that are involved in the fear of novelty (Kagan, 1994). This theoretical speculation is based, in part, on empirical evidence for such individual differences in limbic excitability in timid, compared to nontimid, cats (Adamec & Stark-Adamec, 1989). In recent studies, Kagan and Snidman (e.g., 1991) have explored during infancy the early behavioral and physiological predictors of inhibited and uninhibited temperaments in children.

The cohorts of children who participated in the modified Stroop interference task had also been observed at 4 months of age when they were classified as either high or low reactive based on their motor activity and distress cries to visual, olfactory, and auditory stimuli (see Kagan, 1994; Kagan & Snidman, 1991). Briefly, each child was presented with a battery of sensory events, and the frequency of their limb movements as well as the time they spent crying were reliably coded. Infants classified as high reactive showed frequent vigorous motor activity combined with crying, whereas infants classified as low reactive showed minimal motor activity and minimal crying. The high reactive infants comprised about 20% of the original population of 400 infants in Cohort 1 and 94 infants in Cohort 2. The low reactive infants comprised approximately 40% of the original samples. These two types were the only subjects seen at 4½ or 5 years for the Stroop procedure.

As noted elsewhere (Kagan, 1994; Kagan & Snidman, 1991), high reactive infants were much more fearful when exposed to unfamiliar events and procedures at 14 and 21 months than were low reactive infants. At 14 and 21 months, children came to the laboratory and encountered a series of unfamiliar episodes that included the placing of electrodes, a blood pressure cuff, criticism from an examiner, the entrance of a stranger, a clown, and a robot. The reactions to each of these episodes were scored from videotape for the occurrence of a cry of fear. The number of episodes in which a fear reaction occurred varied across individuals; the median number was one at 14 and at 21 months.

For each cohort, the Stroop latencies for two different groups were contrasted. One group ($N = 11$ in Cohort 1 and $N = 4$ in Cohort 2) was composed of those children who had been high reactive at 4 months and, in addition, showed two or more distress fears at both 14 and 21 months. The contrasting group of 15 children (Cohort 1) and 11 children (Cohort 2) had been classified as low reactive at 4 months and showed no distress fears at both 14 and 21 months. The high reactive-fearful children in each cohort showed especially long latencies to the threat pictures. In both cohorts, two of the three longest latencies for this group occurred to threatening pictures. By contrast, low-reactive fearless children in Cohort 1 showed their three longest latencies to three happy pictures. Similarly, in Cohort 2, two of the three longest latencies were to happy pictures. The tendency for high-reactive fearful children to show longer latencies to name the color of threatening pictures is in keeping with the finding, noted earlier, that the slowest color-naming responses of inhibited adolescents tended to occur to threatening words (Kagan, 1994). These results also resemble the findings, described earlier, that threatening or fear-relevant words produced greater interference in adults with anxiety, panic, or post-traumatic stress disorders (Mathews & MacLeod, 1985; McNally, 1994; McNally et al., 1993).

Displayed Affect and Affective Stroop Interference

A third interesting result is the relation observed between early overtly displayed affect and later Stroop performance. We examined whether individual differences in children's frequency of smiling were related to their sensitivities to affective Stroop interference at a later age. Each child had been tested at 14 and 21 months by an unfamiliar woman; this test battery lasted about 1 hour. The videotapes of these sessions were rated on a 3-point scale for the frequency of smiling where a score of 1 signified minimal smiling and a score of 3 signified frequent smiling. At 4½ years of age, the videotapes of the child performing the affective Stroop task were tallied for the frequency of smiling (Kagan, 1994).

The sample of 4½-year-olds with Stroop data was divided into two contrasting groups. One group (N = 18, maximally serious) comprised those children who had the lowest rating of 1 for smiling at 14 and 21 months and who smiled less than 20 times (the median value) at 4½ years. The contrasting group of 38 children had a rating of 2 or 3 for smiling at both 14 and 21 months and smiled 20 or more times at 4½ years. It is important to note that these two groups, selected to represent affective extremes, did not overlap with the two groups considered in the previous section, who were selected for extremes on reactivity and inhibition. Only 1 of the 18 low-smiling, subdued children was high reactive and high fear, and only 8 of the 38 high-smiling children were low reactive and low fear.

The affectively subdued group had longer latencies to the happy than to the threatening pictures, whereas the high-smiling children showed the opposite pattern. The difference between the average latency to the threat pictures minus the happy pictures differentiated the two groups, $t(45)$ = 2.20, $p < .01$. (Data for 9 of the 56 children were omitted due to flawed protocols.) An additional analysis included the pictures for which there was an average increase in response latency of at least 200 msec compared with the latency to the previous picture. The affectively subdued children met that criterion for seven pictures, and three of the seven were happy pictures (*Big Bird, present,* and *cake*). The high-smiling children met that criterion only twice and none was to a happy picture.

Smiling data were not available at 14 and 21 months for Cohort 2. However, the children in Cohort 2 whose frequency of smiling during a laboratory battery at 4 months of age was above the median value ($N = 16$) had faster color-naming latencies to the happy pictures than the children whose 4-month smiling scores were below the median ($N = 26$); $t(40) = 1.87$, $p < .05$, one-tailed. This result provides converging evidence for the relation between smiling and Stroop interference observed in Cohort 1.

Conclusions

These data suggest a relation between affective phenomena and attentional processes. The fact that the results occurred for two independent cohorts tested by different examiners lends a degree of validity to this claim. The symbolic category of the picture reliably affected the profile of Stroop interference. A woman and a cow are very familiar events to

4½-year-old children, and, therefore, should have been linked to a rich set of associations. Yet the response latencies to these two pictures were relatively fast compared with the latencies to pictures of a witch, ice cream cone, and knife. Our interpretation of this result is that the latter three pictures elicited a brief affective reaction and slowed the retrieval of the color name. Overall, the children's color-naming responses were especially prolonged for the pictures with negative or threatening contents relative to pictures with neutral content. A similar phenomenon was reported by Bradley and colleagues (Bradley, Greenwald, Petry, & Lang, 1992): Reaction times of adult subjects asked to judge new from previously viewed scenes were slowed for new presentations of unpleasant pictures.

In addition, temperament and affective differences between children were related to the degree of affective Stroop interference. For the two cohorts of children, analyses of individual differences in reactivity and inhibition suggest that, compared to low-reactive fearless children, high-reactive fearful children are more likely to experience a brief affective response to the negative pictures, thus producing greater Stroop-like interference.

Perhaps the most intriguing result from the Stroop interference task is the counterintuitive, and unexpected, finding that children who were emotionally serious and smiled minimally at 14 months, 21 months, and 4½ years (for Cohort 1) and at 4 months for (Cohort 2) showed the greatest interference to pictures suggestive of a happy mood, whereas children who smiled and laughed a great deal showed the opposite pattern. These results imply that a young child's chronic mood, perhaps temperamental in origin, might influence interference in this procedure. Perhaps the emotionally subdued children found the happy pictures discrepant from their usual serious feeling state and, as a result, experienced a brief affective reaction that delayed their retrieval of the correct color name. If this interpretation has some degree of truth, it would appear that a child's chronic emotional mood can influence attentional processes.

GENERAL CONCLUSIONS

In this chapter, we considered in detail two experimental approaches that differ in methods, measures, and age of subjects but share an emphasis on probing affective processing in early development. There is more to learn about the development of both affective startle modulation and affective Stroop interference. The results obtained thus far do not specify where, in the cascade of processes from stimulus detection through sustained attention, the affective impacts occur. The time course of these affective processes is such that responses occur by at least 3 sec after picture onset for 20-week-old infants viewing angry faces, and by at least

1 to 1.5 sec after picture onset for 4½- and 5-year-old children in the Stroop task. Furthermore, in both the startle and Stroop tasks, affectively negative signals generally elicited greater reactivity or interference than positive or neutral signals. This is consistent with Öhman's (chapter 7, this volume) view that threatening events are perceptually salient and able to trigger orienting and summon further processing even when they occur outside the current attentional focus. In addition, the pattern of individual differences observed in the Stroop task suggests that temperament and/or mood might alter the specific pattern of affective influence.

Affective modulation of startle and affective Stroop interference may share some common underlying neural mechanisms. Results from behavioral and pharmacological studies in humans are consistent with empirical evidence from animals suggesting that fear potentiation of startle involves connections between the amygdala and the startle circuit (e.g., Davis, chapter 4, this volume). Similarly, the amygdala has been ascribed a role in early processing of affectively laden, threatening stimuli (e.g., Öhman, chapter 7, this volume). Furthermore, Kagan and colleagues have suggested that individual differences in reactivity may result from differences in limbic excitability; differences in activity of the amygdala circuits involved in fear of novelty provide a parsimonious explanation for the different patterns of behavioral and physiological reactions of inhibited and uninhibited children (e.g., Kagan, 1994).

These theoretical connections provide the basis for further investigations into the development of affective processing that examine how attention is engaged by threatening, aversive events versus positive events. In addition, the possibility of amygdalar contributions to startle potentiation and to affective Stroop interference suggests investigaton of the convergence between these affective processes. For example, it would be interesting to ascertain whether high reactive infants differ from low reactive infants in overall amplitude or speed of startle reactions or in the affective modulation of startle. We could also ask whether those children who showed the greatest affective Stroop interference would also show enhanced startle and/or greater startle potentiation. The link between individual differences in temperament and attentional strategies, such as heightened vigilance, could prove to be a critical factor for both startle potentiation and Stroop interference.

ACKNOWLEDGMENTS

Preparation of this chapter was supported by NIMH Grant R03-MH51131 (M.T.B.) and by grants from the John D. And Catharine T. MacArthur Foundation and the W. T. Grant Foundation (N.S. and J.K.).

REFERENCES

Adamec, R. E., & Stark-Adamec, C. (1989). Behavioral inhibition and anxiety: Dispositional, developmental, and neural aspects of the anxious personality of the domestic cat. In J. S. Reznick (Ed.), *Perspectives on behavioral inhibition* (pp. 93–124). Chicago: University of Chicago Press.

Anthony, B. J., & Graham, F. K. (1982). Evidence for sensory-selective set in young infants. *Science, 220*, 742–744.

Anthony, B. J., & Graham, F. K. (1985). Blink reflex modification by selective attention: Evidence for the modulation of "automatic" processing. *Biological Psychology, 21*, 43–59.

Balaban, M. T. (1995). Affective influences on startle in five-month-old infants: Reactions to facial expressions of emotion. *Child Development, 66*, 28–36.

Balaban, M. T. (1996). Probing basic mechanisms of sensory, attentional, and emotional development: Modulation of the infant blink response. In C. Rovee-Collier & L. P. Lipsitt (Eds.), *Advances in infancy research* (Vol. 10, pp. 219–256). Norwood, NJ: Ablex.

Balaban, M. T., Anthony, B. J., & Graham, F. K. (1985). Modality-repetition and attentional effects on reflex blinking in infants and adults. *Infant Behavior and Development, 8*, 443–457.

Balaban, M. T., Anthony, B. J., & Graham, F. K. (1989). Prestimulation effects on blink and cardiac reflexes of 15-month human infants. *Developmental Psychobiology, 22*, 115–127.

Balaban, M. T., Losito, B. D. G., Simons, R. F., & Graham, F. K. (1986). Offline latency and amplitude scoring of the human reflex eyeblink with Fortran IV [computer program abstract]. *Psychophysiology, 23*, 612.

Balaban, M. T., & Waxman, S. R. (1996). An examination of the factors underlying the facilitative effect of word phrases on object categorization in 9-month-old infants. In A. Stringfellow, D. Cahana-Amitay, E. Hughes, & A. Zukowski (Eds.), *Proceedings of the 20th annual Boston University Conference on Language Development* (Vol. 1, pp. 18–29). Somerville, MA: Cascadilla Press.

Berg, C. A., & Sternberg, R. J. (1985). Response to novelty: Continuity versus discontinuity in the developmental course of intelligence. *Advances in Child Development, 10*, 1–47.

Berg, W. K., Berg, K. M., Harbin, T. J., Davies, M. G., Blumenthal, T. D., & Avendano, A. (1985). Comparison of blink inhibition in infants, children, and young and old adults [Abstract]. *Psychophysiology, 22*, 572–573.

Bradley, M. M., Cuthbert, B. N., & Lang, P. J. (1990). Startle reflex modification: Emotion or attention? *Psychophysiology, 27*, 513–522.

Bradley, M. M., Greenwald, M., Petry, M., & Lang, P. J. (1992). Remembering pictures: Pleasure and arousal in memory. *Journal of Experimental Psychology: Learning, Memory, & Cognition, 18*, 379–390.

Bradley, M. M., Zack, J., & Lang, P. J. (1994). Cries, screams, and shouts of joy: Affective responses to environmental sounds [Abstract]. *Psychophysiology, 31*, S29.

Bronson, G. W. (1968). The fear of novelty. *Psychological Bulletin, 69*, 350–358.

Brown, J. S., Kalish, H. I., & Farber, I. E. (1951). Conditioned fear as revealed by magnitude of startle response to an auditory stimulus. *Journal of Experimental Psychology, 41*, 317–328.

Campos, J. J., Mumme, D. L., Kermoian, R., & Campos, R. G. (1994). A functionalist perspective on the nature of emotion. *Monographs of the Society for Research in Child Development, 59*, 2–3(Serial No. 240).

Campos, J. J., & Stenberg, C. R. (1981). Perception appraisal and emotion: The onset of social referencing. In M. E. Lamb & L. R. Sherrod (Eds.), *Infant social cognition: Empirical and theoretical considerations* (pp. 273–314). Hillsdale, NJ: Lawrence Erlbaum Associates.

Caron, A. J., Caron, R. F., & MacLean, D. J. (1988). Infant discrimination of naturalistic emotional expressions: The role of face and voice. *Child Development, 59*, 604–616.

Colombo, J. (1993). *Infant cognition: Predicting later intellectual functioning.* Newbury Park, CA: Sage.

Dannemiller, J. L., & Stephens, B. R. (1988). A critical test of infant preference models. *Child Development, 59,* 210–216.

Darwin, C. (1898). *The expression of the emotions in man and animals.* New York: Appleton.

Davidson, R. J. (1992). Emotion and affective style: Hemispheric substrates. *Psychological Science, 3,* 39–43.

Davis, M. (1989). The role of the amygdala and its efferent projections in fear and anxiety. In P.Tyrer (Ed.), *Psychopharmacology of anxiety* (pp. 52–79). Oxford, UK: Oxford University Press.

Fernald, A. (1993). Approval and disapproval: Infant responsiveness to vocal affect in familiar and unfamiliar languages. *Child Development, 64,* 657–674.

Field, T. M., Woodson, R. W., Cohen, D., Greenberg, R., Garcia, R., & Collins, K. (1983). Discrimination and imitation of facial expressions by term and preterm neonates. *Infant Behavior and Development, 6,* 485–489.

Fox, N. A. (1994). The development of emotion regulation: biological and behavioral considerations. *Monographs of the Society for Research in Child Development, 59,* 2–3(Serial No. 240).

Garcia-Coll, C., Kagan, J., & Reznick, J. S. (1984). Behavioral inhibition in young children. *Child Development, 55,* 1005–1019.

Gibson, E. J. (1969). *Principles of perceptual learning and development.* New York: Appleton-Century-Crofts.

Graham, F. K. (1975). The more or less startling effects of weak prestimulation. *Psychophysiology, 12,* 238–248.

Graham, F. K., & Hackley, S. A. (1991). Passive attention and generalized orienting. In J. R. Jennings & M. G. H. Coles (Eds.), *Handbook of cognitive psychophysiology: Central and autonomic nervous system approaches* (pp. 253–299). New York: Wiley.

Gusella, J. L., Muir, D., & Tronick, E. Z. (1988). The effect of manipulating maternal behavior during an interaction on three- and six-month-olds' affect and attention. *Child Development, 59,* 1111–1124.

Harris, P. L. (1989). *Children and emotion: The development of psychological understanding.* New York: Basil Blackwell.

Haviland, J. M., & Lelwica, M. (1987). The induced affect response: 10-week-old infants' responses to three emotion expressions. *Developmental Psychology, 23,* 97–104.

Izard, C. E. (1991). *The psychology of emotions.* New York: Plenum.

Izard, C. E., & Malatesta, C. Z. (1987). Perspectives on emotional development: I. Differential emotions theory of early emotional development. In J. D. Osofsky (Ed.), *Handbook of infant development* (pp. 494–554). New York: Wiley.

James, W. (1950). *Principles of psychology* (Vol. II). New York: Dover. (Original work published 1890)

Kagan, J. (1974). Discrepancy, temperament, and infant distress. In M. Lewis & L. Rosenblum (Eds.), *Origins of fear.* New York: Wiley.

Kagan, J. (1984). *The nature of the child.* New York: Basic Books.

Kagan, J. (1994). *Galen's prophecy.* New York: Basic Books.

Kagan, J., & Snidman, N. (1991). Infant predictors of inhibited and uninhibited profiles. *Psychological Science, 2,* 40–44

Kagan, J., Snidman, N., & Arcus, D. (1995). *Affective Stroop interference in children.* Unpublished raw data.

Kaplan, P. S., Fox, K. B., & Huckeby, E. R. (1992). Faces as reinforcers: Effects of pairing condition and facial expression. *Developmental Psychobiology, 25,* 299–312.

Kestenbaum, R., & Nelson, C. A. (1990). The recognition and categorization of upright and inverted emotional expressions by 7-month-old infants. *Infant Behavior and Development, 13*, 497–511.

Kleiner, K. A. (1987). Amplitude and phase spectra as indices of infants' pattern preferences. *Infant Behavior and Development, 10*, 45–55.

Lang, P. J., Bradley, M. M., & Cuthbert, B. N. (1990). Emotion, attention, and the startle reflex. *Psychological Review, 97*, 377–395.

Lang, P. J., Bradley, M. M., & Cuthbert, B. N. (1995). *International affective picture system (IAPS): Technical manual and affective ratings.* Gainesville, FL: The Center for Research in Psychophysiology, University of Florida.

Langsdorf, P., Izard, C., Rayais, M., & Hembree, E. (1983). Interest expression, visual fixation, and heart rate changes in 2- to 8-month-old infants. *Developmental Psychology, 19*, 375–386.

Leaton, R. N., & Borszcz, G. S. (1985). Potentiated startle: Its relation to freezing and shock intensity in rats. *Journal of Experimental Psychology: Animal Behavior Processes, 11*, 421–428.

MacLeod, C. M. (1991). Half a century of research on the Stroop effect: An integrative review. *Psychological Bulletin, 109*, 163–203.

Mathews, A., & MacLeod, C. (1985). Selective processing of threat cues without awareness in anxiety states. *Behaviour Research and Therapy, 21*, 233–239.

McCall, R. B., & Kagan, J. (1967). Stimulus-schema discrepancy and attention in the infant. *Journal of Experimental Child Psychology, 5*, 381–390.

McNally, R. J. (1994). *Panic disorder: A critical analysis.* New York: Guilford.

McNally, R. J., English, G. E., & Lipke, H. J. (1993). Assessment of intrusive cognition in PTSD: Use of the modified Stroop paradigm. *Journal of Traumatic Stress, 6*, 33–41.

Neisser, U. (1976). *Cognition and reality.* San Francisco: Freeman.

Nelson, C. A. (1987). The recognition of facial expressions in the first two years of life: Mechanisms of development. *Child Development, 58*, 889–909.

Nelson, C. A., Matheny, L., Sargent, P., Carver, L., & Crescione, C. (1993, March). *Neural correlates of emotions recognition in 7-month-old infants.* Paper presented at the meeting of the Society for Research in Child Development, New Orleans, LA.

Öhman, A., & Dimberg, U. (1984). An evolutionary perspective on human social behavior. In W. M. Waid (Ed.), *Sociophysiology.* New York: Springer-Verlag.

Ornitz, E. M., Guthrie, D., Kaplan, A. R., Lane, S. J., & Norman, R. J. (1986). Maturation of the startle reflex. *Psychophysiology, 23*, 624–634.

Overman, W., Bachevalier, J., Turner, M., & Peuster, A. (1992). Object recognition versus object discrimination: Comparison between human infants and infant monkeys. *Behavioral Neuroscience, 106*, 15–29.

Piaget, J. (1981). *Intelligence and affectivity: Their relationship during child development.* Palo Alto, CA: Annual Reviews.

Posner, M. I. (1995). Attention in cognitive neuroscience: An overview. In M. S. Gazzaniga (Ed.), *The cognitive neurosciences* (pp. 615–624). Cambridge, MA: MIT Press.

Richards, J. E. (1993). Infant blink reflexes as a function of visual attention status [Abstract]. *Psychophysiology, 30*, S54.

Robbins, T. W., & Everitt, B. J. (1995). Arousal systems and attention. In M. S. Gazzaniga (Ed.), *The cognitive neurosciences* (pp. 703–720). Cambridge, MA: MIT Press.

Simons, R. F., & Zelson, M. F. (1985). Engaging visual stimuli and reflex blink modification. *Psychophysiology, 22*, 44–49.

Snidman, N. (1984). *Behavioral restraint and the central nervous system.* Unpublished doctoral dissertation, University of California, Los Angeles.

Soken, N. H., & Pick, A. D. (1992). Intermodal perception of happy and angry expressive behaviors by seven-month-old infants. *Child Development, 63*, 787–795.

Sorce, J. F., Emde, R. N., Campos, J., & Klinnert, M. D. (1985). Maternal emotional signaling: Its effect on the visual cliff behavior of 1-year-olds. *Developmental Psychology, 21*, 195–200.

Stormack, K. M., Hugdahl, K., & Posner, M. I. (1994). Emotional modulation of covert spatial attention [Abstract]. *Psychophysiology, 31,* S95–96.

Stroop, J. R. (1935). Studies of interference in serial verbal reactions. *Journal of Experimental Psychology, 18,* 643–662.

Tronick, E. Z., Ricks, M., & Cohn, J. F. (1982). Maternal and infant affective exchange: Patterns of adaptation. In T. Field & A. Fogel (Eds.), *Emotion and early interaction* (pp. 83–100). Hillsdale, NJ: Lawrence Erlbaum Associates.

Walker-Andrews, A. S., & Lennon, E. (1991). Infants' discrimination of vocal expressions: Contributions of auditory and visual information. *Infant Behavior and Development, 14,* 131–142.

Young-Browne, G., Rosenfeld, H. M., & Horowitz, F. D. (1977). Infant discrimination of facial expression. *Child Development, 48,* 555–562.

17

Activity, Attention, and Developmental Transitions in Infancy

Joseph J. Campos
Rosanne Kermoian
David Witherington
Hongtu Chen
University of California at Berkeley

Qi Dong
Beijing Normal University

This chapter deals with the unexpected and surprisingly broad role of self-produced experience in generating a number of crucial developmental changes in infancy. It has several objectives: to describe important developmental transitions that occur in several psychological domains in the second half-year of life, to specify the converging research operations that are used to demonstrate that experience locomoting is a catalyst for these developmental changes, and to propose the processes through which experience facilitates these transitions. Throughout the chapter, we stress the role of attention as an important index and mediator of infant development.

In recent years developmental psychologists have shifted their focus from describing developmental transitions to explaining them. This has been a formidable task. Most explanations proposed to account for developmental transitions have been broad and general; however, as Goldman-Rakic (1994) noted, full understanding of a developmental change requires laying out the specific mechanisms by which each developmental acquisition comes about. This level of specificity has rarely been obtained. This chapter represents an attempt to be more specific in explaining aspects of a developmental transition that takes place between 6 and 9 months in human infants. It is designed to supplement prior explanations of this transition that have been dominated by nativistic or maturational views, or by accounts that make only general reference to the importance of experience.

We focus on three domains in which developmental transitions occur between 6 and 9 months of age: fear of heights, joint visual attention, and object permanence. Each of these domains has been explained as emerging through nativistic or maturational processes. We challenge the inferences about their innateness by providing several sources of evidence contrary to the nativist position. At the outset, we state two principles that guide our work on how experience plays a role in the emergence of these psychological skills.

One principle is that the acquisition of a single developmental skill (which we call a pacer) generates a family of rather different experiences (Campos, Kermoian, & Witherington, 1996). For instance, a pacer can change the social interactions of individuals, their ecology, their deployment of attention, their repertoire of problem solving behaviors, their sense of self, and their perception of the visual world. In sum, a pacer dramatically changes the relation between the person and his or her environment.

The second principle is that these different experiences affect developmental changes in a focal and domain-specific manner (Fischer & Bullock, 1981). The experiences generated by deployment of attention will not be the same as those generated by social interactions, or the self-as-agent. Because of these two principles, it follows that developmental changes can be expected to occur not at a particular age (as is usually thought), but rather (within limits) after the development of the experience-generating pacer—at whatever age that pacer begins to function. Furthermore, the several developmental changes that the pacer facilitates will not emerge in synchrony or in a rigid sequence, but rather at whatever time the specific experience generated by the pacer affects a particular psychological domain. In sum, a constellation of developmental changes can occur in apparent stage-like and synchronous fashion. Looked at within a closer time frame, the constituents of the constellation actually come about in a non-stage-like manner (Emde, Gaensbauer, & Harmon, 1976), but some elements may emerge before others in one child and the reverse in another.

FEAR OF HEIGHTS, JOINT ATTENTION, AND OBJECT PERMANENCE: THEIR ORIGINS AND SIGNIFICANCE

In this chapter, we discuss the origins and significance of fear of heights, joint attention, and object permanence. Of these, *fear of heights* is the one most widely acknowledged to be innate. It is an important phenomenon and deserves careful explanation. It is not only one of the two strongest fears manifested in infants (Scarr & Salapatek, 1970), but it is universal among terrestrial animals and is intense throughout the life span. There are good a priori reasons to consider fear of heights to be innate. Bowlby (1973) considered heights to be a natural clue to danger and avoidance of heights to have great survival value—a point also made by others such as Freedman (1974). We were thus surprised to encounter evidence suggesting that fear of heights depends on experience, and that the manner by which experience orchestrates such fear is remarkably subtle and complex. Indeed, we suggest that the threat that leads to fear of heights comes from an extraordinary perceptual discrepancy, generated from experiences locomoting, that results in vertigo.

Joint visual attention is a second phenomenon usually considered to be an innate characteristic (Trevarthen, 1988). Such attention is not as well known as fear of heights, and only recently has become a topic of intense investigation (Butterworth, 1991; Moore & Dunham, 1995). The term refers to the ability of two persons to have a common reference to a third event—an example being the mother looking at an unusual animal, and thereby drawing the infant's interest to what the mother is looking at. Through such joint attention, infants can acquire the link between words and their referents, and also catch the emotions of the other directed at the object or person that constitutes the third event. Early in life infants do not have the capability to follow another person's referential communication. In the first 6 months of life, infants are like the subject of the French proverb: When the finger points at the moon, the idiot looks at the finger (Churcher & Scaife, 1982). By the end of the first year, the infant regularly follows another person's point, or looks in the direction toward which another is looking.

The skill is deemed innate because the ability to relate two points in space separated by some distance (such as gaze and target of gaze) is believed to depend on the maturation of brain structures in the prefrontal cortex. It is also deemed innate by default: Most researchers have been at a loss to explain how any experience can bring about this developmental transformation of relating two spatially separate events (Diamond, 1990). However, in this chapter, we show that experience is critical for the development of joint visual attention, and that experience mediates such attention in at least two ways: One is based on an experientially mediated shift in the infant's ecology, whereas the second depends on experience in facilitating new, nonegocentric, spatial coding systems.

The third phenomenon typically deemed innate is what Piaget (1954) called *object permanence*, or, more precisely, the *manual search for hidden objects*. This search skill has been called one of the building blocks of representational intelligence because it presumably indexes the ability to keep in memory the identity and other properties of an object (Bloom, 1973; Goldman-Rakic, 1987). As such, it is a linchpin of both language and emotional development. The manual search for hidden objects has been deemed innate by Kagan (Kagan, Kearsley, & Zelazo, 1978) and by Diamond (1990). Kagan argued for innateness on the basis of the universal timetable of emergence of this skill. Diamond (1990) used a different source of evidence: Lesions in the dorsolateral region of the prefrontal cortex prevent monkeys from demonstrating this skill, and maturation of that region of the brain appears to be necessary for the skill to emerge. In this chapter, we present evidence that, far from being under exclusively maturational control, the manual search for hidden objects (in particular, objects hidden in one of two places) is markedly facilitated by experiential transactions.

WHAT PACES THESE DEVELOPMENTAL TRANSITIONS?

A single skill seems to be the source of the experiences that pace these developmental changes. The skill is self-produced locomotion. When infants begin to crawl,[1] they generate a number of diverse experiences. These experiences include the expansion of the infant's visual world in the third dimension, shifts in attention toward visual information about the self's location and movements in space, changes in the parent's expectations about and behavior toward the infant, new levels of intentionality and consequently a blossoming of emotionality, an increasing resistance to distraction related to the child's greater goal orientation, and shifts in spatial coding strategies. Some or all of these processes enter into the explanation of the developmental changes discussed here.

The importance of self-produced locomotion lies not so much in the act of crawling itself, but in its experiential consequences, such as the perceptual and social feedback that crawling generates. Locomotion also creates feedforward mechanisms, leading the child to postulate new goals and anticipated outcomes. Because we believe that it is not locomotion per se that is effective, but rather the experiences it generates, it follows that although locomotion may be the typical means by which the child acquires these experiences, it is not the only one. Under extraordinary circumstances, the same experiences that locomotion creates can take place for the prelocomotor infant; if so, the prelocomotor infant may show some of the developmental changes seen more frequently, more clearly, and more

[1]The terms *crawling* and *creeping* refer to somewhat different ways of prone progression. Crawling refers to forward movement dragging the belly along the floor; creeping, to prone progression on hands and knees. In this chapter, we use the terms interchangeably. However, we believe that there may be significantly different (and underinvestigated) psychological consequences of the two types of locomotion.

pervasively in the locomotor infant. If this argument is correct, then our developmental stance is quite unusual in stressing a probabilistic nature for developmental transitions (see Gottlieb, 1983, 1991, on probabilistic epigenesis; Kuo, 1976, on epigenesis in development). In short, locomotor experience is not necessary for producing developmental changes—but it is sufficient. What is both necessary and sufficient is the specific set of experiences that are typically and most effectively generated by locomotion. Hence, it is important for us to elaborate on the precise mechanisms by which locomotion typically effects developmental change. By understanding these mechansims, we can perhaps understand exceptions to the rule of locomotor experience serving to bring about developmental changes.

From Attention to Defensiveness in Reactions to Heights

The evidence for a developmental shift in fear of heights comes from work on the visual cliff (Gibson & Walk, 1960; Rader, Bausano, & Richards, 1980; Walk, 1966). The visual cliff is a large table, the surface of which is made entirely of safety glass, divided into two equal halves. One half has a checkerboard texture immediately underneath the glass, creating an impression of a solid supporting surface (called the shallow side), and the other half has a similar checkerboard surface 4 feet beneath the invisible glass surface, creating an apparent dropoff (the deep side). Early studies using a variety of terrestrial animals led to the conclusion that avoidance of heights was evident on the deep side of the cliff as soon as the animal was able to move about and could be tested on the apparatus. Support for this conclusion came from studies of neonatal monkeys (Rosenblum & Cross, 1963) and newborn ungulates (Walk, 1966) placed on a board dividing the deep and shallow sides. These precocial animals invariably moved off the board only toward the shallow side. These studies provided strong evidence in support of a nativist explanation for fear of heights.

However, work on human infants tested from 1 to 5 months of age called this conclusion into question. Prior to our research, human infants could be studied only after they could crawl, a developmental achievement that occurs at 7.1 months, on the average (Bayley, 1969). The typical manner by which infants had been tested required the mother calling to the baby to cross to her alternately over the deep or the shallow side; the dependent variable was whether or not the infant crossed to the mother differently over the two sides. Invariably, infants did not cross to the mother when called from over the deep side, but did cross the shallow. However, because infants were over 7 months, many experiences could mediate the child's differential behavior on the cliff. To confirm the hypothesis on innate wariness of heights with human infants required a method that could be used with both prelocomotor and locomotor infants.

Such a method was devised by Campos and his associates (Campos, 1976; Campos, Langer, & Krowitz, 1970). The paradigm involved placing the precrawling infant directly atop the glass surface of the deep or the shallow side, while measuring an index of fearfulness. In these early studies, the chosen index was the direction of heart rate change. The choice of heart rate change was based on an extrapolation of the Graham–Clifton hypothesis that cardiac decelerations were to be expected in states of orienting, such as to low intensity or novel stimuli, and HR accelerations were expected in states of defensiveness, such as to high-intensity stimuli or stimuli with aversive signal value (Graham & Clifton, 1966; see also Sokolov & Cacioppo, chapter 1, this volume). Campos and colleagues assumed that wariness of heights would be manifested by cardiac acceleration, even in prelocomotor human infants, a group hitherto not tested on the cliff.

We were quickly surprised by our findings. Rather than the expected cardiac accelerations on the deep side, statistically significant cardiac decelerations of 7 to 10 beats per minute (bpm) were found when infants were placed atop the deep side, and remained deceleratory for the duration of the placement atop the cliff (Campos et al., 1970). This consistently deceleratory pattern was found in infants at 1, 2, 4, and 5 months of age; by our interpretation of the meaning of the direction of heart rate changes, we concluded that in the first 6 months of life, infants showed no wariness of heights. Only when infants were 9 months of age (i.e., 2 months after the expected age of crawling onset) did they show statistically significant cardiac accelerations when placed on the deep side (Schwartz, Campos, & Baisel, 1973). These accelerations were on the order of 5 to 7 bpm and were significantly different from both base levels of heart rate, and from the heart rate (HR) decelerations obtained by 5-month-olds. At no age did HR depart significantly from base levels when infants were placed atop the shallow side. Clearly, an unexpected developmental shift was found between 5 and 9 months of age. This shift involved a change from cardiac deceleratory orienting responses to acceleratory defensive ones when the infant was exposed to the apparent dropoff.

Subsequent studies were designed to determine the role of crawling experience in accounting for the onset of wariness of heights. Our attention was drawn to the possible role of self-produced locomotion by the work of Held and Hein (1963; Hein, 1972). In their research, dark-reared kittens divided into an experimental group given self-produced locomotor experience and a yoked control group given passive locomotion in the same environment—a flat but lighted and visually patterned surface that permitted circular locomotion—differed dramatically in visual cliff performance. Held and Hein found that the experimental animals subsequently avoided descending onto the deep side of the cliff, whereas their dark-reared control littermates did not avoid the deep side, despite having the same amount of visual experience as the actively moving animals. Extrapolation of Held and Hein's findings to human infants suggested that prelocomotor infants should behave like the passively moved yoked control kittens, and locomotor infants should behave like the active, self-moving experimental kittens.

A number of converging research operations are required to test the hypothesis that crawling experience accounts for the developmental shift in HR on the deep side of the cliff between 5 and 9 months of age. We developed three such converging operations designed to separate the role of locomotor experience from that of age. The first strategy was the use of an age-held-constant design, wherein infants of the same age were blocked according to whether they had a given amount of locomotor experience (usually about 6 weeks), or whether they were prelocomotor. We expected the locomotor infants to show significant cardiac accelerations, but that prelocomotors would not. In these studies, HR change was measured not during the direct placement of the infant atop the glass surface of the cliff, as in earlier research, but rather during the lowering of the infant from a distance of 3 feet above the deep side or the shallow side—that is, before the infants made contact with the solid glass surface of the cliff table.

Because differences in the performance of locomotor and prelocomotor infants in the age-held-constant design can be due to a third factor that influences both age of onset of locomotion and visual cliff performance, we devised two quasi-experimental methods to assess the role of locomotor experience as an antecedent of the shift on the visual cliff. One such paradigm is analogous to the enrichment paradigm used in developmental psychobiology, in which animals are provided with experiences before they ordinarily would attain them in order to test for a facilitation or early induction of the skill in question. We implemented the enrichment approach by studying two groups of prelocomotor infants who were at the same age, one which had experience with forward movement through their use of walker devices, and the other which had no such experience. We assumed that the walker experience would be functionally similar to crawling experience, and hence, that prelocomotor-walker infants would show cardiac accelerations when lowered onto the deep side of the cliff, whereas prelocomotor controls of the same age would not.

The other quasi-experimental method was modeled after the developmental psychobiologist's deprivation design, in which animals that would ordinarily have had experiences are prevented from such by keeping them from obtaining the necessary stimulation. Our attempt at mimicking a deprivation paradigm involves studying infants who are delayed in the acquisition of locomotion for orthopedic or neurological factors. The design involves longitudinal study of such infants with a locomotor delay

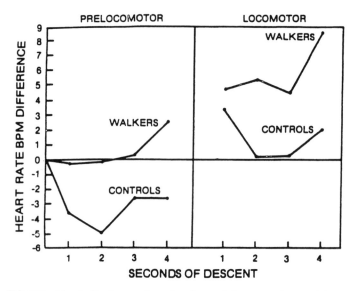

FIG. 17.1.   Heart rate changes from baseline as infants were lowered 3 feet in 3 sec toward either the deep or the shallow side of the visual cliff. One group was prelocomotor, the second is prelocomotor with walker experience, the third group had been crawling for 5 days and had 40 hours of experience moving in a walker, and the fourth group had been locomoting for 5 days, but had no walker experience.

to determine whether they are also delayed in visual cliff performance (or other psychological skills) for the duration of their locomotor delay. In addition, this design permits assessment of the emergence of cardiac accelerations on the deep side (or the onset of other psychological skills) following the delayed onset of locomotion.

Results were strikingly consistent, with infants (all approximately 7.5 months old) in every group that had locomotor experience—even the prelocomotor walker babies—showing statistically significant cardiac accelerations of 3 to 7 bpm on being lowered to the deep side, and no infant showing significant departures from base levels on the shallow side at any age or in any group (see Fig. 17.1). In our locomotor deprivation condition, one infant was selected for testing because he had an orthopedic cast that impeded locomotion, but was otherwise normal in Bayley Developmental Quotient (DQ = 126). He was tested longitudinally from 6 to 10 months of age, and showed no differential cardiac responses on the two sides of the cliff until he had 6 weeks of locomotor experience (i.e., at 10 months—2½ months after normally developing subjects). It is thus clear that locomotor experience is an antecedent of the origins of wariness of heights. (See Campos, Bertenthal, & Kermoian, 1992, for additional details of these studies.)

Explaining the Origins of Fear of Heights

What is the process by which locomotor experience gives rise to the emergence of wariness of heights? We (e.g., Bertenthal & Campos, 1990) have hypothesized an explanation based on three assumptions: One is Gibson's (1979) hypothesis of visual proprioception, which we explain shortly. The second is the prediction that detection of aspects of visual proprioception depends on self-produced locomotor experience. The third is that visual and vestibular proprioception are discrepant from one another when a person encounters a dropoff. The wariness comes from that discrepancy, and self-produced locomotion is implicated both in the differentiation of the visual stimuli that create visual proprioception, as well as in the expectation that visual and vestibular sources of information will provide the same information. Next, we elaborate on these points, and describe two experiments that constitute a test of this line of reasoning.

Our hypothesis starts with the notion of visual proprioception. Visual proprioception, as coined by Gibson (1979), refers to the sense of self-movement derivable not from traditional sources like the vestibular apparatus or the muscles and joints, but from information contained in the optical flow patterns that accompany movement through space. It is well established that visual proprioception is a primary source of information about self-motion in adults. When stationary observers are placed in a "moving room," a small enclosure in which both walls and ceiling can be moved around the enclosed subject, they report sensations of self-motion and show particular patterns of postural sway in response to the movement of the room (Stoffregen, 1985). (See Fig. 17.2.)

What is remarkable about this visually induced illusion of movement and consequent postural adjustment is that the illusion occurs despite vestibular and kinesthetic information that the observer is stationary: Vision overrides bodily information about self-movement (Lishman & Lee, 1973). Furthermore, infants as young as 7 months show comparable patterns of postural sway in response to a room moved around them (Bertenthal & Bai, 1989; postural sway is measured by sensors located on a force plate underneath an infant seat and sensitive to left–right and front–back motion). This demonstrates that 7-month-olds can coordinate visual and vestibular input, because postural compensations are enacted via the vestibular system (Dichgans & Brandt, 1978). However, 7-month-old infants only show postural compensations under conditions when there is optic flow in both the peripheral and central visual fields. Most movement of infants in large-scale space involves only peripheral optic flow, coming typically from texture in the terrain. Central optic flow is usually minimal because of the distance of the children from walls and large surfaces ahead of them. Seven-month-olds are not sensitive to pe-

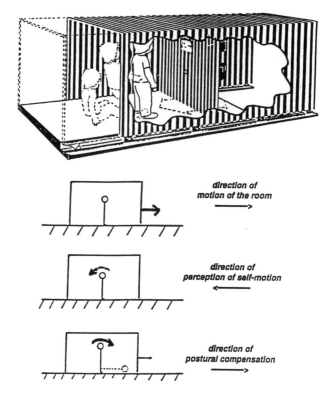

FIG. 17.2. The moving room apparatus consists of an enclosure that
permits the side walls and ceiling to be moved while the front wall remains
stationary, or the entire room to move, or only the front wall. It induces a
powerful illusion of self-movement. When the side walls of the room move,
the infant perceives herself to be moving in the direction opposite to the
movement of the walls, and makes postural compensations in the same
direction as the room, so as to maintain apparent vertical position. Older
infants capable of standing show postural compensation by falling down
in the direction of room movement; younger infants show postural
compensation within a seat placed atop appropriate sensors.

ripheral optic flow alone (Bertenthal & Bai, 1989; Higgins, Campos, &
Kermoian, in press).

This unresponsiveness to optic flow is corrected by 9 months of age,
when 9-month-olds, but not 7-month-olds, attend to optic flow presented
only to the visual periphery, even when no optic flow is present in the
central visual field (Bertenthal & Bai, 1989; Higgins et al., in press). Visual
proprioception undergoes a transition, then, between 7 and 9 months,
during which infants begin to attend to and utilize more spatially delimited portions of the visual field to specify their self-motion (in particular,
lamellar or parallel patterns of optic flow in the visual periphery).

Our research suggests that locomotor experience accounts for this transition. Both infants with hands-and-knees creeping experience and prelocomotor infants with walker experience posturally compensate to peripheral optic flow as contrasted with prelocomotor infants who only exhibit postural sway to optic flow from both the central and peripheral visual fields. More specifically, infants with crawling experience show a statistically significant cross-correlation (on the order of .63) between direction and speed of movement of the side walls of the moving room, on the one hand, and direction and magnitude of postural compensation on the other hand. Prelocomotor infants with walker experience also show a significant cross-correlation of .56, but prelocomotor infants show no significant cross-correlation (around .25; Higgins et al., in press). In short, infants become responsive to peripheral optic flow patterns relevant to visual proprioception after having locomotor experience, either from crawling or by walker devices.

The link between locomotor experience and responsiveness to optic flow patterns that underlies this transition has been forecast by others besides ourselves. As a number of authors have hypothesized (e.g., Bertenthal & Bai, 1989; Dichgans & Brandt, 1978), the process of locomotion affords infants the opportunity to simultaneously attend to their own motion through space and to the layout of their environment. In fact, to avoid collisions, infants must constantly monitor their motion in the midst of changes in their surroundings. Thus, infants who locomote should rely on more spatially delimited portions of their visual field to register self-motion. Furthermore, locomoting infants' attentional focus coincides with their direction of motion, thereby generating consistent and specific patterns of optic flow especially in the peripheral visual field. In sum, infants who can locomote necessarily orient their eyes and nose straight ahead, thereby permitting them to be exposed to peripheral optic flow specifying movement forward or backward; infants with no locomotor experience may not be exposed in that manner to optic flow because when they are moved passively, peripheral optic flow is not reliably correlated with direction of movement.

We have hypothesized that, because infants with locomotor experience direct increasing attention to the visual periphery, they will establish a strong correlation between specific patterns of peripheral optic flow specifying self-movement, and specific patterns of vestibular input also specifying self-movement (Bertenthal & Campos, 1990). The repeated pairing of visual and vestibular inputs for self-motion will prompt an expectancy for specific patterns of correlated input. When infants with this expectancy for correlated visual–vestibular input approach an edge or dropoff, they will experience a decoupling or discrepancy between the input sources. The vestibular feedback generated through their forward motion will remain the same with approach to the edge, but the available visual textures for detecting self-motion will be vastly reduced, because instead of visual texture being adjacent to the child, it is now several feet away with nothing in between. Therefore, the infants' vestibular feedback will fail to correspond to their visual feedback, and their expectation of correlated input will be violated.

A violation of expectancy in itself is not sufficient to account for the generation of fear (Sroufe, Waters, & Matas, 1974). We contend that the discrepancy between visual and vestibular input becomes affectogenic in large part through the hedonic qualities of vestibular feedback, which can produce either distress or pleasure depending on context. Vestibular feedback, coupled with the reduction of visual support for self-motion, suggests a threat of instability for the infant and, in the context of a violated expectation, will give rise, we hypothesize, to wariness of heights.

Recently, we have gathered support for this hypothesis. By looking at infants' responses in both the moving room and on the visual cliff, we have assessed the degree to which infants' sensitivity to peripheral optic flow maps onto their avoidance of heights. In a sample of infants with locomotor experience, we have found, in fact, a statistically significant and robust correlation (preliminary analyses of which estimate it at .63) between infants' postural sway in the moving room and their avoidance of the deep side of the visual cliff (Witherington, Campos, & Kermoian, 1995). In other words, the infants who respond with appropriate postural shifts in conjunction with peripheral visual stimulation are the ones who show hesitation to cross the deep side of the cliff. Our findings lend support, then, to the role of visual–vestibular decoupling in the emergence of wariness of heights.

THE DEVELOPMENT OF JOINT ATTENTION

Sometime during the second half of the first year of life, human infants begin to show a tendency to follow the direction of referential gestures (e.g., gaze or pointing of the hand) of another. Such an ability to coordinate one's visual attention to external objects with the attention of another is called *joint attention*. Researchers believe that joint attention serves several important functions in infant development. For example, Bruner (1983) believes that joint attention provides the basis of shared experience necessary for the acquisition of language. Joint attention is also considered a basic form of prelinguistic communication about objects of interest or desire (Butterworth, 1991). It is also a form of social referencing whereby emotional information about an event can be conveyed from adult to infant (Campos & Stenberg, 1981). Recently, some authors have proposed that joint attention indicates a rudimentary social understanding of the mental life (e.g., attentional state) of others (Baldwin, 1993; Tomasello, 1995).

In the last 20 years, research on joint attention in infancy has basically been devoted to examining infants' performance in following referential gestures of another under different conditions. Scaife and Bruner (1975), who first established the paradigm for testing infants' joint attention, found that by 11 to 14 months of age, almost all infants tested demonstrated head turning in the appropriate direction on at least one of two trials.

Butterworth and his colleagues (Butterworth & Grover, 1988) documented a developmental progression of joint attention between 6 and 18 months. Although the conclusions of this line of research are compromised by the lack of controls for pseudo-following of another's gestures, Butterworth reported that at 6 months of age infants reliably turn their heads to the correct side of the room for targets within their own visual field. At 12 months of age, infants follow the direction of gestures and pinpoint the location of targets with geometric precision. At 18 months of age, infants can precisely search for targets, even if the target is out of their visual field (i.e., behind them).

In one of our studies on joint attention, we examined infants' responses to two major referential gestures—gaze (head-eye orienting), and gaze and pointing (head–eye orienting with hand pointing)—while keeping other relevant factors constant across all four tested age groups (i.e., 6, 8, 10, and 12 months; Chen, Kermoian, & Campos, 1991). The setting for this study was a curtained room in which there were four objects placed on one wall of the room (to the infant's right), and four on the other side (to the infant's left).

We found a dramatic improvement in following both gaze and pointing gestures between 6 and 8 months of age. Six-month-old infants primarily stared at the experimenter when the experimenter displayed a referential gesture. By contrast, 8-month-old infants looked away from the experimenter and also looked in the general direction of the gesture rather than to the opposite, nonreferenced side of the room (see Fig. 17.3). From 8 to 12 months of age, infants showed an increasing trend in following the general direction of referential gestures of another and looked to the correct side of the room, but still did not look to the specific target of the referential gesture. Similar results were obtained when hand pointing was added to the gaze gesture. In sum, there is a developmental shift between 6 and 8 months in following referential gestures, just as there is on the visual cliff and the moving room.

The dramatic improvement of joint attention between 6 and 8 months, as shown in our studies, might be brought about by experiences associated

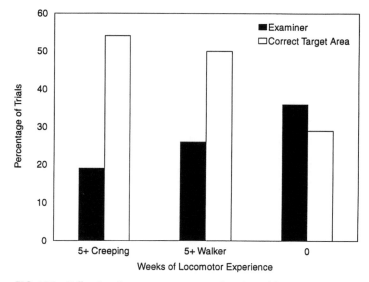

FIG. 17.3. Following the gaze gesture as a function of locomotor experience.

with self-produced locomotion. Several converging lines of research demonstrated that with the onset of crawling, the whole ecological relation between infant and environment undergoes a set of extraordinary changes (Campos, Kermoian, & Zumbahlen, 1992). We hypothesized that at least two aspects of these changes may contribute to the development of infant joint attention. First, locomotor experience facilitates the infant's cognitive capacity of relating two spatially separated objects or events (Bertenthal & Campos, 1990; Diamond, 1990; Kermoian & Campos, 1988). Put another way, infants in the first 6 months of life relate objects only to the position of their body, not to one another (Piaget, 1954); by the end of the first year of life, they can relate two objects to one another by using stable spatial landmarks. Prior studies by our group have shown that the ability to relate objects to stable landmarks follows the acquisition of self-produced locomotion (Bertenthal, Campos, & Barrett, 1984). As an instance of relating two points separated in space (one being the finger, the other the target of the gesture), following the point or gaze of another may also be a consequence of locomotor experience.

Furthermore, when an infant begins to locomote there are major changes in social interaction between the parent and the infant (Campos, Kermoian, & Zumbahlen, 1992). The onset of locomotion thus creates the opportunities for new chances for frequent exchanges of emotional information across distal space between an infant and a caretaker, which consequently familiarizes infants with nonverbal signals, including referential gestures of a caretaker. We therefore predicted that infants who have had experience with self-produced locomotion would display higher levels of performance on joint attention than infants of the same age who do not have locomotor experience.

To examine whether locomotor experience is related to improved joint attention, we conducted a study of infants' response to the gaze gesture of another as a function of locomotor history (Kermoian, Campos, & Chen, 1992). We compared the responses of prelocomotor infants to the responses of infants who had been locomoting on hands and knees 1 to 4 weeks, and infants who had been locomoting 5 or more weeks. In addition, to rule out the possibility that improved performance in locomoting infants was due to the maturation of creeping, we included two groups of infants who were prelocomotor, but who had been moving with the aid of a walker for different lengths of time (1–4 weeks vs. 5 or more weeks).

We found a strong link between locomotor experience and the likelihood that infants would shift their attention away from the person generating a referential gesture, a necessary first step in achieving joint attention. Specifically, the longer infants had been locomoting, the more likely they were to look away from the experimenter. Moreover, prelocomotor infants who were moving with the aid of a walker did not significantly differ from locomotor infants, suggesting that performance was not merely due to the maturation of creeping. On trials in which infants looked away from the experimenter, locomotor infants were more likely to use the gaze gesture as a cue to look in a specific direction than were prelocomotors. The longer infants had been locomoting, either on hands or knees or with the aid of a walker, the more likely they were to look in the general direction of the gesture. In addition, they looked significantly more in the general direction of the target than to the other nonreferenced areas of the room. Prelocomotor infants, in contrast, were as likely to look to the correct target area as to nonreferenced locations. Taken together, the findings on looking to the experimenter and looking in the general direction of the referent suggest that locomotor experience facilitates joint attention.

STUDY OF INFANTS WITH LOCOMOTOR DELAYS

Locomotor experience is an antecedent of improved performance in joint attention. Other evidence supporting this notion comes from a longitudinal study conducted in our laboratory, using seven infants 8 to 13 months of age at the beginning of the study. These infants were delayed 1 to 6 months in the onset of locomotion due to spina bifida with lesion level at L4–5 or below (Telzrow, 1990). We tested these infants monthly on their response to the point/gaze gesture using a setting similar to that used in the age and locomotor studies of pointing and gaze previously described. We coded the data monthly, but analyzed the data from 2 months prior to and 2 months following locomotor onset. If locomotor experience facilitates following the point/gaze gesture of another, as suggested by the results of the locomotor study, then we would expect that these locomotor-delayed infants would show deficits in performance for the period of the delay, and a spurt in performance following the delayed onset of locomotion.

Preliminary results supported the hypothesis (Telzrow, 1990). When we compared infants' responses during the assessments taken 2 months prior to, and 2 months following, locomotor onset, we observed a striking shift away from focusing on the examiner's face or finger during the point/gaze gesture. Looking at the experimenter occurred nearly 90% of the time prior to locomotion, but only 30% of the time after the acquisition of locomotion—an acquisition that was delayed by nearly 4 months. In addition, looking in the general direction of the gesture increased from less than 5% to about 30% of the trials. The pattern of these findings was consistent when we examined the data from individual subjects. Six of the seven infants we tested began to look less at the experimenter and more in the general direction of the gesture within 2 months after the onset of locomotion, regardless of the age when locomotion began.

OBJECT PERMANENCE

Another dramatic improvement in infants' ability during the second half of the first year of life is object permanence—the manual search for hidden objects after a period of delay. It indicates the infant's growing ability to use familiar means to attain new ends, and subsequently, to call on new means to reach a goal. It also indexes the infant's use of spatial coding strategies, which, at first, involve locating the position of objects by reference to the child's body, and later, by reference to stable spatial landmarks.

The manual search for hidden objects emerges between 7 and 9 months of age (Bremner, 1994; Bremner & Bryant, 1977; Harris, 1975, 1983, 1989; Piaget, 1954). Prior to 7 months of age, infants are rarely successful in searching for a hidden object. Infants at this age also make a striking error in manual search: After having successfully found an object in one location, they continue to search for the object in the same location despite their observing its being hidden in a second location. This is called the A-not-B error, an error that stops occurring by 9 months, so long as the period between hiding and finding is sufficiently brief (on the order of a few seconds). In sum, by 9 months of age, infants appear able to code the location of an object independently of where they had succeeded in searching for it earlier, an ability that may index a shift in spatial localization abilities, and hence, in spatial coding strategies.

Why and how does this development in searching for an object hidden in one of two locations happen during the second half of the first year of life? What is the process by which such a developmental shift can be explained? Many researchers have speculated that this developmental shift is functionally related to the new demands placed on the infants following the onset of locomotion (Bertenthal, Campos, & Barrett, 1984; Bremner, 1994; Goldfield & Dickerson, 1981).

Many studies have demonstrated the link between locomotor experience and infants' performance on the object permanence task (Bai & Bertenthal, 1992; Campos & Bertenthal, 1990; Horobin & Acredelo, 1986; Kermoian & Campos, 1988; Telzrow, Campos, Shepard, Bertenthal, & Atwater, 1987). On a series of tasks corresponding to an object performance scale reported in Kagan, Kearsley, and Zelazo (1978), locomotor infants and prelocomotor infants who used walkers were found to pass more of the testing items than did prelocomotor infants (Kermoian & Campos, 1988). In particular, infants with the greatest amount of locomotor experience (i.e., 9 weeks) passed the A-not-B task, whereas prelocomotor infants were not able to pass a task involving even a single visible displacement. (See Fig. 17.4.)

The link between locomotion and the improvement on the object permanence task may be accounted for by several interrelated processes.

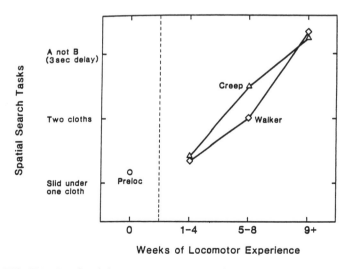

FIG. 17.4. Results of object permanence (manual search for hidden objects) as a function of locomotor experience.

Earlier, we mentioned a series of studies that has shown the importance of the dorsolateral region of the prefrontal cortex as an important neurophysiological mediator of two-position search performance following delays. Although the emergence of the organization of the prefrontal cortex has traditionally been relegated to endogenous maturational factors, recent work suggests that frontal lobe functioning may be reorganized following experience crawling. Bell and Fox (in press), in a longitudinal study, showed that both successful performance and frontal lobe functioning changed after their human infant subjects had locomotor experience. The findings by Bell and Fox thus suggest that the subjects' active movements in the environment may facilitate or induce the functioning of cortical structures, thereby reversing the typical order of interpreting brain–behavior relations.

Locomotion, such as crawling, also induces changes in the relation of the infant to the environment. Prior to locomotion, infants typically remain in the same location for extended periods of time. Infants accordingly develop a body-centered coding scheme, that is, they code the location of objects in front of them to their left or to their right. Such a body-centered coding scheme is generally successful so long as the child is stationary. Once an infant begins to crawl, the probability that an object's position relative to the infant will persist for any extended period of time becomes quite low. As a consequence, to replace the increasingly inadequate egocentric frame of reference, infants must develop new strategies of using a stable landmark for localizing the object. At first, infants use a more complex body-centered coding strategy to locate objects after self- or object-displacement. This more complex strategy involves infants learning that one simple way to localize objects is to update the effects of one's movements by "keeping an eye" on a target object— visually tracking it during either their own movement or during the displacement of the object. During the hiding phase of the object permanence task, infants looked where the object was hidden and this tendency was greater the longer they had been locomoting. The infants' visual experience tended to mediate correct performance on the object permanence task, and in turn the deployment of visual attention seemed to be a function of locomotor experience (Horobin & Acredolo, 1986). Eventually, this more complex egocentric spatial coding strategy is replaced by the ability to locate an object by reference to stable but spatially distant landmarks, such as a door, picture, or staircase.

Further evidence supporting the effect of locomotion on infants' response to changes of relation with the environment was provided by Bai and Bertenthal (1992). In their study, prelocomotor and locomotor infants were tested using a search test in which either infants were rotated around a table containing the hiding wells, or the table itself was rotated in front of the stationary infant. The results of the study revealed that locomotor status was related to search performance following a displacement of the infant, but not following a displacement of the container. This study supports the notion that the experiences produced by self-produced loco-motion have very specific consequences on the cognitive organization of the child.

With experiences of locomoting, the infant learns that certain changes in spatial orientation are contingent on his or her own movement (e.g., in self-displacement situations), whereas the visual changes produced by other agents (e.g., in table-displacement situations) are not generally contingent on the movements of the infant. As a consequence, locomotor infants are better prepared to anticipate and adequately respond to changes of spatial orientation following self-displacement than are prelocomotor infants. This result also suggests that the effect of locomotor experience on infants' search performance is quite specific and is consistent with a context-specific view of development (e.g., Thelen, 1989).

SUMMARY

The evidence is steadily accumulating that experiences generated by locomotion bring about dramatic improvements in several important aspects of psychological development, such as onset of wariness of heights, joint attention, and object permanence (manual search) skills. Our research not only demonstrates the link between locomotor experience and infants' performance on the tasks described, it also suggests that locomotor experience may facilitate different aspects of development through different processes. For instance, as we have seen, the developmental shift toward fear of heights comes about from visual–vestibular decoupling; joint attention comes from a number of social, ecological, and cognitive changes related to an emerging ability to relate two objects separate in space and time; object permanence is related to still other experiential processes including shifts in spatial coding strategy, changes in deployment of attention, and greater attentiveness to self and object motion.

A set of more intriguing questions now arises to explain precisely how these interrelated processes organize experiences into each important task performance. These processes, which we have assumed, discussed, or partially examined in this chapter, involve reorganization of attention, memory, intention, and social communication following self-produced locomotion. We believe that three principles should be considered for future research to address more precisely issues of process. First, we need more research programs that not only can manipulate process variables and measure their contribution to task performance, but also deal with functional changes of the relation between organism and environment. The visual–vestibular coupling process as discussed in this chapter is an attempt at such an effort. Second, the interrelation between function and structure—specifically, the relation between activity-generated experience, changes of cerebral functioning following the experience, and changes in measures of psychological processes just described—will continue to benefit our understanding of the role that experiences play in development. Finally, while tackling effects of experience on human development, we must recognize that development typically proceeds through hierarchical organization of component processes or skills. Self-produced locomotion may catalyze hierarchical development, but we must specify what other skills besides the experiences generated by locomotion must be in place for the induction or facilitation of developmental transitions. If these ancillary skills are not in place, the effects of locomotor experience will be constrained, and the scope of our explanation involving locomotor experience will be limited.

ACKNOWLEDGMENTS

Preparation of this chapter was conducted while the first and fifth authors were Fellows at the Center for Advanced Study in the Behavioral Sciences, where their fellowships were funded by grants from the National Science Foundation, the John D. and Catherine T. MacArthur Foundation, and the Johann Jacobs Foundation. Data collection and analyses were supported by NIH Grant HD-25066, and grants from the Oregon Medical Research Foundation, and the John D. and Catherine T. MacArthur Foundation. We thank Dr. Rosemary Campos for her helpful comments and editorial assistance on this chapter.

REFERENCES

Bai, D. L., & Bertenthal, B. I. (1992). Locomotor status and the development of spatial search skills. *Child Development*, *63*, 215–226.
Baldwin, D. A. (1993). Infants' ability to consult the speaker for clues to word reference. *Journal of Child Language*, *20*, 395–418.
Bayley, N. (1969). *Bayley scales of infant development*. New York: Psychological Corporation.
Bell, M., & Fox, N. (in press). Crawling experience is related to changes in cortical organization during infancy: Evidence from EEG coherence. *Developmental Psychobiology*.
Bertenthal, B. I., & Bai, D. L. (1989). Infants' sensitivity to optical flow for controlling posture. *Developmental Psychology*, *25*, 936–945.
Bertenthal, B. I., & Campos, J. J. (1990). A systems approach to the organizing effects of self-produced locomotion during infancy. *Advances in Infancy Research*, *6*, 1–60.
Bertenthal, B. I., Campos, J. J., & Barrett, K. C. (1984). Self-produced locomotion: An organizer of emotional, cognitive, and social development in infancy. In R. N. Emde & R. J. Harmon (Eds.), *Continuities and discontinuities in development*. New York: Plenum.

Bloom, L. (1973). *One word at a time: The use of single word utterances before syntax*. The Hague: Mouton.

Bowlby, J. (1973). *Attachment and loss: Vol. 2. Separation*. New York: Basic Books.

Bremner, J. G. (1994). *Infancy*. Oxford, UK: Basil Blackwell.

Bremner, J. G., & Bryant, P. E. (1977). Place versus response as the basis of spatial errors made by young infants. *Journal of Experimental Child Psychology, 23*, 162–171.

Bruner, J. (1983). *Child's talk: Learning to use language*. New York: Norton.

Butterworth, G. E. (1991). The ontogeny and phylogeny of joint visual attention. In A. Whiten (Ed.), *Natural theories of mind: Evolution, development, and simulation of everyday mind-reading* (pp. 223–232). Oxford, UK: Basil Blackwell.

Butterworth, G. E., & Grover, L. (1988). The origins of referential communication in human infancy. In L. Weiskrantz (Ed.), *Thought without language* (pp. 5–25). Oxford, UK: Oxford University Press.

Campos, J. J. (1976). Heart rate: A sensitive tool for the study of emotional development. In L. P. Lipsitt (Ed.), *Developmental psychobiology: The significance of infancy*. Hillsdale, NJ: Lawrence Erlbaum Associates.

Campos, J., & Bertenthal, B. (1990). Locomotion and psychological development in infancy. In F. Morrison, K. Lord, & D. Keating (Eds.), *Applied developmental psychology*. Vol. 3. *Psychological development in infancy* (pp. 229–258). New York: Academic Press.

Campos, J. J., Bertenthal, B. I., & Kermoian, R. (1992). Early experience and emotional development: The emergence of wariness of heights. *Psychological Science, 3*, 61–64.

Campos, J., Kermoian, R., & Witherington, D. (1996). An epigenetic perspective on emotional development. In R. Kavanaugh, B. Zimmerberg, & S. Fein (Eds.), *Emotion: Interdisciplinary perspectives* (pp. 119–138). Hillsdale, NJ: Lawrence Erlbaum Associates.

Campos, J. J., Kermoian, R., & Zumbahlen, M. R. (1992). Socioemotional transformations in the family system following infant crawling onset. In N. Eisenberg & R. A. Fabes (Eds.), *Emotion and its regulation in early development* (New Directions for Child Development, No. 55). San Francisco: Jossey-Bass.

Campos, J. J., Langer, A., & Krowitz, A. (1970). Cardiac responses on the visual cliff in prelocomotor human infants. *Science, 170*, 196–197.

Campos, J. J., & Stenberg, C. R. (1981). Perception, appraisal, and emotion: The onset of social referencing. In M. E. Lamb & L. R. Sherrod (Eds.), *Infant social cognition: Empirical and theoretical considerations* (pp. 273–314). Hillsdale, NJ: Lawrence Erlbaum Associates.

Chen, H., Kermoian, R., & Campos, J. J. (1991, April). *Development of following referential gestures during the second half of the first year of life*. Paper presented at the meeting of the Society for Research in Child Development, Seattle, WA.

Churcher, J., & Scaife, M. (1982). How infants see the point. In G. Butterworth & P. Light (Eds.), *Social cognition: Studies of the development of understanding* (pp. 110–136). Chicago: University of Chicago Press.

Diamond, A. (Ed.). (1990). *The development and neural bases of higher cognitive functions*. Annals of the New York Academy of Sciences, *608*.

Dichgans, J., & Brandt, T. (1978). Visual-vestibular interaction: Effects on self-motion and postural control. In R. Held, H. Leibowitz, & H. Teuber (Eds.), *Handbook of sensory physiology* (Vol. 8, pp. 755–804). Heidelberg: Springer-Verlag.

Emde, R. N., Gaensbauer, T. J., & Harmon, R. J. (1976). Emotional expression in infancy: A biobehavioral study. *Psychological issues* (Vol. 10, No. 37). New York: International Universities Press.

Fischer, K., & Bullock, D. (1981). Patterns of data: Sequence, synchrony, and constraint in cognitive development. In K. Fischer (Ed.), *New directions in child development* (Vol. 12, pp. 1–20). San Francisco: Jossey-Bass.

Freedman, D. (1974). *Human infancy: An evolutionary perspective*. Hillsdale, NJ: Lawrence Erlbaum Associates.

Gibson, E. J., & Walk, R. (1960). The "visual cliff." *Scientific American*, *202*, 64–71.

Gibson, J. J. (1979). *The ecological approach to visual perception*. Boston, MA: Houghton-Mifflin.

Goldfield, E. C., & Dickerson, D. J. (1981). Keeping track of locations during movements in 8- to 10-month-old infants. *Journal of Experimental Child Psychology*, *32*, 48–64.

Goldman-Rakic, P. (1987). Circuitry of primate prefrontal cortex and regulation of behavior by representational memory. *Handbook of Physiology*, *5*, 373–417.

Goldman-Rakic, P. S. (1994). Foreword. In G. Dawson & K. W. Fischer (Eds.), *Human behavior and the developing brain*. New York: Guilford.

Gottlieb, G. (1983). The psychobiological approach to developmental issues. In P. Mussen (Series Ed.) & M. Haith & J. Campos (Eds.), *Handbook of child psychology: Vol. II. Infancy and developmental psychobiology* (4th ed.; pp. 1–26). New York: Wiley.

Gottlieb, G. (1991). Experiential canalization of behavioral development: Theory. *Developmental Psychology*, *27*, 4–13.

Graham, F. K., & Clifton, R. K. (1966). Heart rate change as a component of the orienting response. *Psychological Bulletin*, *65*, 305–320.

Harris, P. L. (1975). Development of search and object permanence during infancy. *Psychological Bulletin*, *82*, 332–344.

Harris, P. L. (1983). Infant cognition. In P. H. Mussen (Series Ed.) & M. M. Haith & J. J. Campos (Vol. Eds.), *Handbook of child psychology: Vol. 2. Infancy and developmental psychobiology* (pp. 689–782). New York: Wiley.

Harris, P. L. (1989). Object permanence in infancy. In A. Slater & G. Bremner (Eds.), *Infant development* (pp. 103–121). Hillsdale, NJ: Lawrence Erlbaum Associates.

Hein, A. (1972). Acquiring components of visually guided behavior. In A. Pick (Ed.), *Minnesota Symposia on Child Psychology* (Vol. 6). Minneapolis: University of Minnesota Press.

Held, R., & Hein, A. (1963). Movement-produced stimulation in the development of visually-guided behavior. *Journal of Comparative and Physiological Psychology*, *56*, 872–876.

Higgins, C. I., Campos, J. J., & Kermoian, R. (in press). Effect of self-produced locomotion on infant postural compensation to optic flow. *Developmental Psychology*.

Horobin, K., & Acredolo, L. (1986). The role of attentiveness, mobility history, and separation of hiding sites on Stage IV search behavior. *Journal of Experimental Child Psychology*, *41*, 114–127.

Kagan, J., Kearsley, R., & Zelazo, P. R. (1978). *Infancy: Its place in human development*. Cambridge, MA: Harvard University Press.

Kermoian, R., & Campos, J. J. (1988). Locomotor experience: A facilitator of spatial cognitive development. *Child Development*, *59*, 908–917.

Kermoian, R., Campos, J. J., & Chen, H. (1992, May). *Self-produced locomotion facilitates development of referential gestural communication*. Paper presented at the meeting of the International Conference on Infant Studies, Miami, FL.

Kuo, Z. Y. (1976). *The dynamics of behavior development: An epigenetic view*. New York: Plenum.

Lishman, J. R., & Lee, D. N. (1973). The autonomy of visual kinaesthesis. *Perception*, *2*, 287–294.

Moore, C., & Dunhan, P. (1995). *Joint attention: Its origins and role in development*. Hillsdale, NJ: Lawrence Erlbaum Associates.

Piaget, J. (1954). *The construction of reality in the child*. New York: Basic Books.

Rader, N., Bausano, M., & Richards, J. E. (1980). On the nature of the visual-cliff-avoidance response in human infants. *Child Development*, *51*, 61–68.

Rosenblum, L., & Cross, H. (1963). Performance of neonatal monkeys in the visual cliff situation. *American Journal of Psychology*, *76*, 318–320.

Scaife, M., & Bruner, J. S. (1975). The capacity for joint visual attention in the infant. *Nature*, *253*, 265–266.

Scarr, S., & Salapatek, P. (1970). Patterns of fear development during infancy. *Merrill-Palmer Quarterly, 16*, 53–90.

Schwartz, A. N., Campos, J. J., & Baisel, E. J. (1973). The visual cliff: Cardiac and behavioral responses on the deep and shallow sides at five and nine months of age. *Journal of Experimental Child Psychology, 15*, 86–99.

Sroufe, L. A., Waters, E., & Matas, L. (1974). Contextual determinants of infant affective response. In M. Lewis & L. Rosenblum (Eds.), *The origins of fear*. New York: Wiley.

Stoffregen, T. (1985). Flow structure versus retinal location in the optical control of stance. *Journal of Experimental Psychology: Human Perception and Performance, 11*, 554–565.

Telzrow, R. (1990, February). *Studies of the link between locomotor delay and psychological development in infants with spina bifida*. Invited presentation at the International Seating Conference, Vancouver, BC, Canada.

Telzrow, R. W., Campos, J. J., Shepherd, A., Bertenthal, B. I., & Atwater, S. (1987). Spatial understanding in infants with motor handicaps. In K. M. Jaffe (Ed.), *Childhood powered mobility: Developmental, technical and clinical perspectives*. Seattle: RESNA.

Thelen, E. (1989). The (re)discovery of motor development: Learning new things from an old field. *Developmental Psychology, 25*, 946–949.

Tomasello, M. (1995). Joint attention as social cognition. In C. Moore & P. J. Dunham (Eds.), *Joint attention: Its origins and role in development* (pp. 103–132). Hillsdale, NJ: Lawrence Erlbaum Associates.

Trevarthen, C. (1988). Universal cooperative motives: How infants begin to know the language and culture of their parents. In G. Jahoda & I. Lewis (Eds.), *Acquiring culture: Cross cultural studies in child development* (pp. 37–90). London: Croom Helm.

Walk, R. D. (1966). The development of depth perception in animals and human infants. *Monographs of the Society for Research in Child Development, 31*(Whole No. 5).

Witherington, D., Campos, J. J., & Kermoian, R. (1995, March). *What makes babies become afraid of heights?* Poster presented at the Society for Research in Child Development, Indianapolis, IN.

Afterword: Pre-Attentive Processing and Passive and Active Attention

Frances K. Graham
University of Delaware

Reviewers of edited volumes often point out the need for comparison and integration of findings of individual chapters. This chapter is intended to supply that need. It illustrates how a biocognitive approach contributes to understanding information processing, specifically, to understanding the processing of sensory input. Such topics as motor processing and clinical populations are discussed only as they relate to the main focus. The chapter covers four systems hypothesized to affect information processing: (a) a high-pass filtering system operating preattentively, (b) an arousal orienting system (OR) responsive to novel change and operating automatically, (c) an arousal defense system (DR) sensitive to aversive stimulation that also operates automatically, and (d) a system that selects task-relevant stimuli and requires voluntary control. I consider for each system scalp-recorded, event-related potentials (ERPs) from the brain and autonomic nervous system (ANS) components, effects on reflex probes, and associated behaviors—detection, recognition, and identification/selection. There has been important biocognitive research on memory, but too little is included in this volume to allow more than cursory mention.

PREATTENTIVE PROCESSING OF TRANSIENTS

By definition, preattentive processing does not require attention, although it may be affected by attentional sets that alter processing elements in advance of a stimulus. Its characteristics have been described as early

417

occurring, automatic, involuntary, unconscious, parallel, and effortless: A stimulus may be detected and simple physical features such as intensity, pitch, or form processed, but spatial relations among features are not identified and the stimulus is not recognized as an object (Treisman & Gelade, 1980). Responses that are elicitable during both sleep and waking states can be considered preattentive and, by this criterion, include early ERP peaks, a transient-detecting response (TDR) of brief heart rate deceleration, and the startle blink. They presumably arise from processing by neural elements with high-pass filtering characteristics capable of preserving rapid *transient* changes to onsets and offsets of sufficiently long-lasting stimuli, even when the change is nearly instantaneous.

Three functions of preattentive processing are initiating sensory processing, interrupting current processing, and initiating a protective gating mechanism.

Initiating Sensory Processing

Research on ERPs suggests a period of preattentive processing in the lower brainstem, lasting for at least 10 msec, and perhaps ending when processing begins in secondary sensory or association cortices—at about 200 msec for the auditory system. The series of positive (P) and negative (N) potentials that lie between these regions are elicited automatically at varying latencies depending on modality (see reviews by Graham & Hackley, 1991, p. 271ff; Näätänen, 1992, pp. 254ff). Näätänen suggested that, within this region, auditory transients may trigger attention if a momentary threshold is exceeded by either the auditory-specific N100 Component 1 or the nonspecific N100 Component 3, or by a potential between 150 and 200 msec—the mismatch negativity (MMN)—elicited when a sound deviates in any physical characteristic from a memory model of recent stimulation. MMN's sensitivity to deviance approximates that of perceptual measures. Although MMN is preserved for only about 10 sec and lacks the multimodal and expectancy modeling characteristics of Sokolov's neuronal model, it verifies that the brain responds to mismatch.

Näätänen, Ilmoniemi, and Alho (chapter 13, this volume) discuss localizing brain sources by means of the magnetoencephalogram (MEG) and functional magnetic resonance imaging (fMRI). These methods show that MMN and the specific N100 have different sources in or near primary cortex. The methods are also capable of identifying, within an individual subject, discrete sources responsive to duration, intensity, and pitch (Näätänen, 1992, Fig. 5.10). Similarly, the methods have been used to localize preattentive visual processing to the primary striate areas. Thus, activity tracked by ERPs from the receptor to cortical sensory areas indicate in real time when various potentials are activated, and the imaging techniques add more precise localization information.

Evidence for preferential treatment of fear-relevant stimuli has been obtained by Ohman (chapter 7, this volume). In a series of studies, he employed backward masking to limit stimuli to preattentive analysis. With a 100 msec mask after 30 msec exposures of fear-relevant or neutral pictures, forced choice recognition is at chance levels. However, hypothesizing that danger signals may be adapted by evolution to capture attention, he tested several situations in which capture occurred: (a) Subjects, selected for pre-existing fear of snakes or spiders, responded to masked pictures of the specifically feared object with skin conductance responses, a response that indicates an OR or DR. (b) Even in unselected subjects, masked fear but not masked neutral stimuli could be differentially conditioned to shock. (c) Unselected subjects also showed *popout* responses to fear-relevant but not to fear-irrelevant pictures. That is, a single snake or spider among flower or mushroom distractors was identified rapidly, independent of the number of distracting stimuli, suggesting that the pictures were processed in parallel. Further, there were fewer errors than in the slower, serial search for a single flower or mushroom among snake or spider distractors. A recent study by Theeuwes (1995) shows that popout also occurs for luminance changes, which are processed by high-pass filtering, but not for color changes, which receive only low-pass filtering. Several other studies have demonstrated that abrupt stimulus onsets or offsets can draw attention to a stimulus (e.g., Juola, Koshino, & Warner, 1995; Todd & Van Gelder, 1979).

Interrupting Current Processing

Abrupt, large transients capable of eliciting startle may interrupt ongoing processing. Landis and Hunt (1939) described a primary startle flexor reaction that includes blink, and secondary reactions that are situation specific and include withdrawal and other protective responses. Davis (chapter 4, this volume) is developing a model circuit in rats that, considered together with the human work on startle probes, will hopefully be as successful in explaining information processing as has Kandel's work on the gill withdrawal reflex (Kandel, Schwartz, & Jessel, 1991). He has identified a direct, entirely subcortical path for acoustic startle that includes only three synapses—from auditory nerve to cochlear root neurons, to nucleus reticularis pontis caudalis, and to either the spinal motor neuron (whole body startle, hindlimb EMG) or the facial motor nucleus (pinna and blink reflexes). Ongoing research suggests that neural transmission is mediated by glutamate at all three synapses, but the central and spinal motor sites each have two types of receptor that are sensitive to different chemicals and preferentially eliminate an early 8 msec or later 15 msec peak in the hindlimb EMG. Such an organization would allow for flexibility in connections modulating startle. Swerdlow (in Dawson, Schell, Swerdlow, & Filion, chapter 11, this volume) has integrated research from his and other laboratories to show the forebrain circuitry and transmitters that modulate startle.

Hackley and Boelhouwer (chapter 9, this volume) note that the circuit underlying the acoustic startle blink in humans—with a single EMG component at 30 to 40 msec—is longer and probably has more synapses than the primary circuit described by Davis. The human cutaneous and visual startle blinks have three and two components, respectively. However, Hackley and Boelhouwer neatly simplify the situation by identifying which components show the same functional effects across modalities. They conclude that the single component of the acoustic blink is analogous to the second cutaneous component and to the first visual component. For all three modalities, the analogous components peak between about 30 to 60 msec. They presumably share a common neural substrate in their central, premotor circuitry. For the photic visual blink, at least, both components appear to be mediated entirely by subcortical paths: Patients with unilateral hemispheric lesions, who could not see flash stimuli delivered to the damaged hemisphere, nonetheless had reflexes identical to those elicited by stimuli to the undamaged hemisphere. Of particular interest for research on aversive stimulation, Hackley and Boelhouwer also describe a physiologically distinct lid-closure, the *Cartesian blink reflex* in response to threat.

Finally, the nonspecific N100 has not only been associated with attention-triggering, but also with a startle-interrupt function (Näätänen, 1992) based, in large part, on demonstrations that N100 and blink change similarly as a function of stimulus repetition, rise time, and duration (Putnam & Roth, 1990).

Initiating a Protective Gating Mechanism

A low-intensity transient onset, offset, or other change that does not itself elicit startle, nonetheless reduces the startle elicited by a subsequent high-intensity transient occurring within about 15 to 1000 msec. This prepulse inhibition (PPI) is a robust, reflexive response that has been found in amphibians, birds, and mammals, including sleeping humans. Although Hoffman (chapter 8, this volume) only briefly refers to his series of pioneering studies on rats and pigeons begun in the mid-1960s, those studies were the major impetus to 2 decades of still continuing research on PPI in humans. The importance of PPI for information processing is its possible function as a sensory gate to protect processing of a weak prepulse.

Consistent with the protection hypothesis, prepulses are judged louder when paired with a startling sound at intervals yielding PPI than when they occur singly. The finding holds for both ipsi- and cross-modal pairing (Simons & Perlstein, chapter 10, this volume). Dawson et al. (chapter 11, this volume) also found that greater accuracy in judging loudness of acoustic prepulses was correlated with greater PPI, and Hackley and Boelhouwer (chapter 9, this volume) cited Norris and Blumenthal's (in press) findings of greater discrimination accuracy for both auditory and vibrotactile prestimuli on trials yielding PPI than on trials without PPI. Evidence for greater accuracy in judging prestimuli is clearly compatible with a protective function for PPI. However, Perlstein, Fiorito, Simons, and Graham (1993) also obtained a context effect with paired stimuli—compared to single stimuli, not only were weak prestimuli judged louder but loud, blink-eliciting sounds were judged softer. Existence of a context effect, in which judgments of weak and strong stimuli shift toward one another, has also been observed in a variety of perceptual paradigms and is not imposed at a response selection stage. Thus, it is unclear whether "protection" of a prestimulus is an independent mechanism or a by-product of a more general context effect.

Gating implies a mechanism other than, or in addition to, refractoriness in the direct sensory path. Two findings exclude refractoriness as the sole mechanism: (a) A refractory process exhibits maximal reduction immediately after stimulus delivery and then declines exponentially, but PPI is a U-shaped function that does not reach maximum for about 100 msec, and (b) prepulses and startle stimuli in different modalities do not share a common sensory path but, nonetheless, produce PPI. There is also anatomical evidence that PPI involves a path extrinsic to the direct reflex path. Research from Hoffman's laboratory (e.g., Leitner, Powers, Stitt, & Hoffman, 1981) demonstrated, for rat startle, that PPI depended on a more rostral subcortical path extending through lateral tegmentum. Further, PPI cannot be due to the prepulse capturing attention because the effect is robust during sleep (Silverstein, Graham, & Calloway, 1980).

Simons and Perlstein (chapter 10, this volume) found that the same conditions producing blink PPI also affected simultaneously recorded midline ERP potentials, even after correction for muscle contaminating activity: The early N19 and P30 potentials were unaffected by a prepulse, but P50 and later potentials were reduced. These initial findings with paired auditory stimuli were replicated with tactile–auditory pairs and with ERPs recorded from both midline leads and from lateral leads over auditory cortex. Prepulses again reduced midline P50 but not P30 and, in addition, did not affect potentials from auditory cortex before Component 2 of the N100 (Tb) which arises in secondary auditory cortex. The authors inferred from cat studies and human intracranial recordings (Liegeois-Chauvel, Musolino, Badier, Marquis, & Chauvel, 1994) that the unmodulated early information was transmitted by the direct, specific-system projection to primary auditory cortex, and that the later PPI effect on midline potentials was transmitted through the nonspecific projection system.

Despite the fact that PPI is a reflex, it is late in maturing, apparently because high-pass filtering is relatively immature in early development. Although the TDR and blink occur in newborns, stimuli must be longer (350 msec) and more intense than in adults to elicit any response (see review in Graham, Anthony, & Zeigler, 1983, pp. 389ff). Newborns do show PPI when intervals between paired stimuli are very long (Hoffman, Cohen, & Anday, 1987; Hoffman, chapter 8, this volume) but, at the short intervals yielding robust PPI in adults, PPI is weak in 2- to 4-month-old infants and no PPI is evident between 7 and 30 months (Berg et al., 1985). Balaban, Snidman, and Kagan (chapter 16, this volume) reported only facilitatory effects at 15 months.

Summary

Preattentive sensory processing is initiated by the high-pass filtering of stimuli and is reflected in a series of ERP peaks for about 200 msec. Attention may be triggered earlier by detection of a mismatch or, still earlier, by N100 components exceeding threshold because a transient is intense and elicits a startle–interrupt or because arousal, reflected in increased skin conductance and popout detection, is elicited by stimuli associated with danger. Low-intensity transients also initiate the protective PPI that reduces startle and ERPs, beginning with P50, to any shortly following high-intensity transient. PPI is late in developing, presumably because the immature nervous system is relatively unresponsive to low-intensity, rapid transients.

PASSIVE ATTENTION: GENERALIZED ORIENTING

Näätänen's theory (1992) suggests that the three routes by which preattentive processing of transients might trigger attention automatically lead to a momentary conscious awareness of a stimulus, to the interruption of ongoing processing, or to a generalized orienting response (OR). The onsets of longer duration, sustained stimuli also activate high-pass filters and might, therefore, trigger attention as well or, if stimulus duration is long enough and intense enough, activate a defense response (DR).

Sokolov (1963; Sokolov & Cacioppo, chapter 1, this volume) describe ORs and DRs as generalized systems that respond nonselectively to stimuli in any modality. The OR is viewed as an information filter or regulator: Past stimuli are represented in a neuronal model, and when incoming stimuli mismatch the model, physiological changes result in an

OR that enhances stimulus perception. An important characteristic of the OR is its rapid habituation as information in the stimulus is extracted. ORs to simple stimuli may habituate after one or two brief exposures whereas ORs to complex stimuli, containing more information, habituate more slowly. Berlyne (1969), who pointed out that an unexpected stimulus is surprising and thus involves arousal, demonstrated differential habituation with visual patterns that subjects had rated for complexity, interest, and pleasingness. Habituation is also delayed by any departure from the standard paradigm of repeating a single stimulus at a fixed interval; that is, varying the interstimulus interval or interspersing different stimuli increases uncertainty.

The following paragraphs discuss four issues: brain systems and ERPs, OR components, reflex probing of orienting, and comparator and non-comparator theories of orienting.

Brain Arousal and Attention Systems

Brain Arousal Systems. The brainstem reticular activating system has long been identified as a major arousal system with ascending projections facilitating sensory processing and descending paths facilitating motor activity (Moruzzi & Magoun, 1949). Sokolov (1963) identified the system as underlying the DR and, together with cortical structures amplifying or habituating stimulus effects, as underlying the OR. The thalamus was identified as necessary for the fine tuning associated with ORs. Sokolov's later neurophysiological research (1975) suggested hippocampus as an intermediary between cortical analyzers and the brainstem activating system.

Other research, discussed in this volume, has added new findings but the basic outline proposed by Sokolov is still current. Papez (1937) suggested that a limbic system consisting of hypothalamus, cingulate gyrus, and hippocampus was the anatomical substrate for emotions (e.g., Kandel et al., 1991). Later, the subcortical amygdala was incorporated into the system. LeDoux (1989) described the amygdala as the key structure in computing preattentively the affective significance of both appetitive and aversive stimuli, although Lang, Bradley, and Cuthbert (chapter 5, this volume) suggest its relevance may be greater for negative affect. The amygdala not only has reciprocal connections with hippocampus but also with sensory cortical areas, and it projects to a number of subcortical motor and ANS nuclei, including a direct connection with the startle center (Rosen, Hitchcock, Sananes, Miserendino, & Davis, 1991; see also Davis, chapter 4, this volume). Amygdala also has a monosynaptic input from thalamus.

The thalamus is a necessary relay for sensory information to cortex. Brunia (chapter 12, this volume) calls attention to the classic papers of

Yingling and Skinner (1976) and Skinner and Yingling (1977) in demonstrating that the reticular nucleus of thalamus serves to gate sensory information. The nucleus is admirably positioned for this role because it receives inputs from cerebral cortex and brainstem as well as all other thalamic nuclei, but its sole output is either to inhibit or not inhibit selected modality-specific thalamic nuclei. It is the only thalamic nucleus that does not project to cortex and the only thalamic nucleus with an inhibitory output. Yingling and Skinner suggest that activation by the mesencephalic reticular system could override the selective inhibition and underlie the arousal that initiates orienting. Brunia hypothesizes that the thalamic reticular nucleus may also gate voluntary motor processing.

Brain Attention Systems. Posner (1995; Posner, Rothbart, Gerardi, & Thomas-Thrapp, chapter 14, this volume) describe three attention networks—a posterior parietal system that locates stimuli in space, a norepinephrine alerting system in right frontal cortex that enhances the speed of response but does not affect the buildup of information, and a dopaminergic, anterior frontal system that locates objects or targets and serves as an executive. Each is also associated with specific subcortical structures. The major evidence for these systems is derived from neuroimaging studies of human subjects during the execution of various attentional tasks.

ERP Indices of Automatic Processing. Following the period of preattentive processing indexed by ERPs, rare stimuli may elicit P300s, labeled in latency order as P3a and P3b, that are followed by a positive slow wave or, if stimuli are sustained for several seconds, by a negative slow wave that is centrally maximal with auditory stimuli and has a more posterior maximum with visual stimuli (see review by Graham & Hackley, 1991, pp. 286ff). The centro-parietal P3b has been associated with the localized OR (see section entitled Active Selective Attention; Localized Orienting) but, when elicited by high-intensity stimuli in the absence of an instructed task, shows functional characteristics of a DR (Putnam & Roth, 1990).

   The earlier, more anterior P3a, and a presumably independent *novels*-P3 (Courchesne, Hillyard, & Galambos, 1975), may reflect generalized ORs, but the literature is inconsistent. Simons and Perlstein (chapter 10, this volume) report a series of studies to determine conditions under which these ERPs can be identified. One apparently necessary condition is a relatively short interstimulus interval (ISI). A second requirement for identifying P3a as a distinct factor in Principal Components Analysis is to avoid the method's inherent bias against high-frequency components. Chen (1995) accomplished this by using a single measure of each ERP, its peak, or by using a narrow window so that P3a was not swamped by the low-frequency P3b and slow wave. Simons and Perlstein also described a study (Miles, 1993) using the "unrecognizable" sounds yielding a *novels*-P3 in Courchesne, Kilman, Galambos, and Lincoln (1984). The finding of an anterior positive ERP was confirmed, and its status as an OR was supported by an accompanying, large heart rate deceleration. However, because the factors associated with *novels*-P3 and P3a were very similar in time spanned and in their scalp distribution, Simons and Perlstein questioned the assumption (Courchesne et al., 1975) that the two components are independent of one another.

Components of Generalized Orienting

The OR and DR consist of response systems, with some components common to both systems—for example, skin conductance increase and peripheral vasoconstriction—and some distinguishing between them, such as the direction of cephalic vasomotor change. However, Sokolov and Cacioppo (chapter 1, this volume) note that "the phasic heart rate response to stimuli has proven to be a more reliable and discriminating index of ORs and DRs in the Western literature" (p. 4). Simons and Perlstein (this volume, Fig. 10.9) report unusually large heart rate decelerations, associated with the OR to "unrecognizable" novel sounds. Their figure illustrates changes averaged for both single, repeated novels and multiple never-repeated novels. Responses to the latter were larger and showed a precipitous fall of nearly 4 bpm within 1 sec that was sustained for the 2-sec length of the ISI. Lang et al. (this volume, Fig. 5.11, lower panel) found that never-repeated aversive slides also showed decreases of nearly 4 bpm in 5 sec.

The principal criteria identifying a generalized OR component are its rapid habituation, its recovery with a stimulus change and, following recovery, dishabituation of response to the original stimulus. Skin conductance increase and heart rate deceleration to simple neutral stimuli have generally satisfied these criteria in adult humans (see Siddle, 1983, and Cook and Turpin, chapter 6, this volume).

Orienting also occurs in the young infant but not reliably before 2 to 3 months of age, whether measured by visual fixation (Posner et al., chapter 14, this volume) or by long heart rate decelerations (Berg & Richards, chapter 15, this volume). Although newborns may show precocious behavior that disappears before reappearing in its final form, so do animals released by decerebration from descending influences. Rapid heart rate habituation appears by 3 to 4 months and, at about the same time, the infant develops sustained decelerations to long-duration stimuli. If a distractor is presented during the sustained deceleration, the infant is slower to redirect fixation but, compared to presentation during "attention termination" when heart rate is returning to baseline, more often recognizes the distractor on a subsequent recognition test. By 7 months, infant heart rate also decelerates in anticipation of, and to omission of, a second stimulus that regularly follows the first (Berg & Richards).

Prior to 3 to 4 months, Posner et al. (chapter 14, this volume) also found poor ability to disengage fixation of a central attractor or to show "inhibition of return," that is, to favor a novel location. Consistent with Posner's theory that attending to locations and to objects are separable processes, preferences for novel objects seemed to be stronger at 6 than at 3 months and were uncorrelated with preferences for novel locations.

Reflex Probing of Orienting

Three types of reflex blink modulation, demonstrable in rats, have also been demonstrated in human subjects: short-interval latency facilitation, PPI, and long-interval latency and magnitude facilitation by sustained stimuli (Graham, 1975). In addition, human subjects show an effect not seen in rats: If transient prestimuli are followed at long but varying intervals, not only is blink facilitated but heart rate decelerations and the contingent negative slow wave variation (CNV) occur during the unpredictable interval. I have suggested that the long-interval effects of sustained stimuli involve the classical activating system and reflect a DR, but that temporal uncertainty leads to an OR. The OR is slow to habituate if there is no repetition in the pattern of ISI assignments and the temporal uncertainty is, therefore, difficult to resolve (Graham, 1992).

The sustained-stimulus facilitation effect can even be seen in lesser inhibition during the period of prepulse inhibition and, as Putnam (1976) found, does not reach a peak until about 4 sec. She also found that the effect acts cross-modally and, in keeping with arousal theory, shows a curvilinear change as intensity increases to about 65 dB and then declines with higher intensities. Like PPI, the effect occurs in a variety of species (Hoffman & Ison, 1980). Unlike PPI, it tends to be more pronounced in the young infant than in the adult (Balaban et al., chapter 16, this volume; Berg & Richards, chapter 15, this volume).

Hoffman (chapter 8, this volume) has demonstrated that the reflex facilitation due to uncertainty can be manipulated by various methods that have independent effects according to additive factors logic. One method required the subject, rather than the experimenter, to initiate specified trials. Blinks were larger with experimenter than with subject initiation (Hoffman, Fig. 8.3 & Fig. 8.4), when onset of the blink-eliciting stimulus was delayed rather than immediate (Hoffman, Fig. 8.2), when the eliciting stimulus had a lower probability of occurring at a particular time (Hoffman, Fig. 8.2), and when subjects were not informed of whether the blink-eliciting stimulus would be a tap or noise (Hoffman, Fig. 8.4).

Another study showed that the effect of experimenter- versus subject-initiation of the trial was also independent of the amount of PPI induced by equally probable trials with and without a prepulse.

Boelhouwer, Teurlings, and Brunia (1991; Hackley & Boelhouwer, chapter 9, this volume) pointed out that early facilitation of reflex magnitude as well as latency may occur with short intervals between a prepulse and startle pulse and varies as a function of modality of the two stimuli. It is, therefore, necessary to take into account the time at which the stimuli, whether same or different in modality, activate the final common path from the facial nucleus. They give a compelling example of how summation can lead to facilitating effects even when the startle stimulus precedes the prepulse.

Other studies, discussed in the following sections, have probed the processing of affective stimuli and of attentional instructions, but only one study (Bohlin, Graham, Silverstein, & Hackley, 1981) has used reflex probes to show that orienting elicited by novel stimuli has nonselective enhancing effects. The study found that rare auditory or visual stimuli, interspersed among frequent tactile stimuli, elicited prolonged heart rate decelerations and facilitated auditory blinks elicited during the decelerations. Facilitation was nonselective; that is, independent of the modality of the novel stimuli.

Comparator and Noncomparator Theories of Orienting

Interest in theoretical implications of generalized orienting has focused on whether findings require a comparator, associative model that extrapolates anticipated events or can be explained by a noncomparator, nonassociative model based on spatial/temporal contiguity of specific stimulus traces and on nonspecific sensitization by high-intensity stimuli (e.g., Groves & Thompson, 1970). A volume edited by Siddle (1983) thoroughly reviewed the implications of 20 years of OR research following the English translation of Sokolov (1963). Siddle and Lipp (chapter 2, this volume) continue the quest with a discussion of recent findings that are difficult to explain by a noncomparator theory.

Response to *stimulus omission* would seem to imply comparison with something anticipated but, as Siddle and Lipp (chapter 2, this volume) note, the omission effect has been "fragile" when omission occurs after regular presentations of a single, simple stimulus. More recent studies, using a 2-element compound, show a robust recovery when the second element is omitted and selective dishabituation to the second but not to the first element, when the compound is re-presented. It has been argued that if the compound were encoded as a whole, a comparison operation need not be assumed. It is likely that the compound was indeed encoded, but there is evidence that the separate elements were also encoded because, on initial habituation trials, skin conductance was elicited by each of the 4-sec elements. Further, the fact that dishabituation was selective implies that it was not due to a generalized arousal but to the violation of a specific expectation.

The development of *expectancies* during habituation could explain both the omission findings and another phenomenon incompatible with a noncomparator theory; namely, greater response to a modality change than to the same stimulus when it is first presented. By having subjects rate their certainty that Element 2 of a compound stimulus would occur, Siddle and Lipp (chapter 2, this volume) demonstrated that subject expectancies do change. Consistent with skin conductance changes, certainty increased to about 90% during habituation but fell to about 15% after an omission trial. Another study found a von Restorff-like effect of a single exposure to one modality before habituation to a second modality; that is, it eliminated the above-initial-level response to a modality change (Siddle, Lipp, & Dall, 1994).

Summary

Novel stimuli activate a generalized orienting or attentional arousal system with a specific ERP component, P3a, and rapidly habituating ANS components, including skin conductance increase and heart rate deceleration. In theory, orienting facilitates the extraction of information, and reflexes elicited 2 sec after a novel stimulus do show nonspecific facilitation. Orienting is also elicited when conditions produce uncertainty or mismatch a neuronal model of past stimulation and is, therefore, difficult to explain by a noncomparator, nonassociative theory. In contrast, sustained stimuli delivered predictably at long ISIs do not elicit orienting and do facilitate blinks, presumably reflecting a defensive arousal system, the DR. Unlike PPI, orienting and blink facilitation are robust by 3 to 4 months of life.

GENERALIZED DEFENSE RESPONSE AND AFFECT

Sokolov's second generalized system, the DR, is described by Sokolov and Cacioppo (chapter 1, this volume) as denoting "threatening, noxious, or intense stimulation" and as serving a protective function complementary to the OR; that is, "fostering retreat from the provocative stimulus and a blunting of sensation" (p. 3). Unlike the OR, it is slowly habituating or nonhabituating and appears to be closely allied with the aversive motivation system discussed by Lang et al. (chapter 5, this volume). Lang et al. emphasize action dispositions rather than stimulus rejection, but

Sokolov (1963) also described the DR as having both a passive form of immobilization and an active form "directed to the removal of or escape from the destructive agent" (p. 14).

Although Lang et al. have not been primarily concerned with ORs and DRs, they have shown that affective pictures, each exposed for 6 sec, do elicit ORs. With 6 different slides interspersed between 12 repetitions of the slide set, habituation of skin conductance responses and heart rate deceleration occurred in four trials and recovered to the first novel slide. Re-presentation of the original slides did not produce dishabituation, but this phenomenon has generally been difficult to demonstrate and might be more so with use of 6 different slides.

This section reviews affect and arousal, affect and valence, development and affective response, reflex probing of affective stimulus processing, and bradycardia evolution and resolution.

Affect and Arousal

Normative ratings of arousal, valence, and other dimensions are available for some 500 pictures that are used by Lang et al. (chapter 5, this volume). The studies typically present sets of 12 to 18 different slides of each valence—aversive, appetitive, and neutral—and intersperse slides from each set. Some studies follow picture exposure with rating tasks, a second free-viewing condition, imaging, or recall. Because aversive and appetitive sets include slides covering the full range of an 8-point arousal scale, but neutral slides do not exceed the scale's midpoint, any comparison of affective sets with the neutral valence set necessarily confounds valence and arousal.

ERPs to slide onsets include the exogenous preattentive potentials, followed by P3b and a positive slow wave peaking at about 2 sec and then diminishing slowly. Cuthbert et al. (1995) found that P3b amplitude was greater for the high arousal affective slides and smaller for the low arousal neutral slides, consistent with intensity effects (Roth, Dorato, & Kopell, 1984) and a DR (Putnam & Roth, 1990). As noted in the previous section, the slow wave to sustained stimuli is normally negative to stimuli that do not elicit a P3. However, at least for brief stimuli that do elicit P3, some subsequent centro-parietal, slow positive activity is also found and is greater with high intensity stimuli (Roth et al., 1984).

Skin conductance responses increase with arousal but do not distinguish between aversive and appetitive slides (Lang et al., chapter 5, this volume) or between ORs and DRs (Sokolov, 1963).

Memory is also a function of arousal. High arousal slides were recalled more often than low arousal slides on immediate and delayed (1 year) free recall and, in a second experiment, speeded choice recognition of seen versus new slides. Valence had an effect only in slowing recognition of new aversive slides more than new appetitive slides (Bradley, Greenwald, Petry, & Lang, 1992; Lang et al., this volume).

Affect and Valence

Not surprisingly, given that heart rate distinguishes ORs and DRs, it shows high loadings on a valence factor and very small negative loadings on an arousal factor identified by Principal Component Analyses (Lang et al., this volume; Table 5.1).

In a review of the literature employing aversive slides, Cook and Turpin (chapter 6, this volume) found nine studies in which unselected subjects, or subjects low in a specific fear, showed greater decelerative heart rate changes to aversive than to neutral and/or pleasant pictures. The findings were interpreted as indicating more attention to aversive pictures. In contrast, heart rate accelerated to aversive slides in four studies of phobic subjects shown slides of their feared objects or, in a fifth study of unselected subjects, when phylogenetically phobic material (snakes, spiders) predicted shock. Thus, aversive slides elicit heart rate acceleration, compatible with a DR, when slide content is relevant to individual-subject fears and, otherwise, appear to command more attention than pleasant slides. Further, Cook and Turpin cited research showing that cardiac acceleration to the CS+ during differential conditioning to shock predicted slower extinction and, in another study, acceleration to homicide slides predicted cephalic vasoconstriction, a DR component identified by Sokolov (1963).

Lang et al. (chapter 5, this volume) report similar effects in a recent study by Hamm, Cuthbert, Globisch, and Vaitl (in press) that confirms heart rate acceleration in animal-phobics shown phobia relevant slides and, compared to control subjects, a relatively greater heart rate increase in mutilation phobics shown phobia relevant slides. Also compatible with occurrence of a DR, free-viewing times were shorter in animal phobics viewing phobia relevant slides.

Generally, the cardiac response to nonstartling, long duration stimuli is triphasic—with an initial decelerative TDR, an acceleration peaking around 4 sec, and a deceleration or return to base level (Graham, 1979; Lang et al., chapter 5, this volume). Turpin (1986; Cook & Turpin, chapter 6, this volume) interpreted an additional large, long-latency (35 sec) acceleration as a fight/flight response. Because it was present only on Trial 1, it can be equated with Sokolov's DR only if it is a tonic change invisible to the recording system. Turpin described short-latency (4-sec) peak accelerations as startle responses; I classify them as DRs because they are relatively persistent with nonstartling, slowly rising stimuli and differ from a rapidly habituating acceleration at 2 sec when stimuli have very rapid onsets (Graham, 1979).

Development and Affective Response

Responsiveness to affective stimuli is present early in life. Balaban et al. (chapter 16, this volume) review evidence for response to human faces and voices at birth and a marked preference for faces or facelike stimuli by 2 to 3 months of age. Some studies have exploited the infant's facial expressiveness to argue that discrimination, revealed in fixation or cardiac deceleration, is based on affective content and not solely on attention to particular features. Posner et al. (chapter 14, this volume) emphasize the inverse relation between attention and negative emotion: In adult studies, Rothbart and Derryberry (1981) found that self-reports of ability to focus and shift attention were inversely related to negative emotionality. They note a similar effect in 3- to 4-month-old infants capable of orienting; that is, interesting, novel stimuli that elicit attention block distress produced by overstimulation, although distress returns when the novel object is removed. Younger infants require physical comforting to relieve distress.

A dramatic age change in affective response was shown by Campos (1976; Campos, Kermoian, Witherington, Chen, & Dong, chapter 17, this volume) using the Gibson visual cliff. Prior work suggested an innate fear of heights because animal and human infants always moved across the shallow rather than the deep side of the cliff. To adapt the test for prelocomotor infants, Campos measured heart rate when infants were placed on the deep or shallow sides. At no age from 1 to 5 months or at 9 months did heart rate change with placement on the shallow side. In contrast, infants placed on the deep side showed large decelerations through 5 months of age but, at 9 months, shifted to the expected accelerations. This shift from OR to DR is discussed in the last section.

Reflex Probing of Affective Stimulus Processing

Facilitating effects on blink elicited several seconds after onset of a sustained neutral prestimulus were noted in the previous section. Anthony and Graham (1983, 1985) also probed, in infants and adults, the processing of "interesting" versus "dull" sustained prestimuli. Smiling-face slides or folk tunes elicited larger heart rate deceleration than equal-intensity blank slides or pure tones. Further, same-modality probing of interesting slides and tones elicited larger, shorter latency blinks than same-modality probing of dull prestimuli. In contrast, blinks to different-modality probes were smaller and slower than to same-modality probes, and relatively more so for interesting prestimuli. Thus, sensory-central processing of probes appears to be delayed and briefer if attention is already engaged by an interesting slide or tone in a different modality but less so if the slide or tone is less engaging. Had the prestimulus effect been due to priming of the motor limb of the reflex, effects would have been nonselective. It is not assumed that probe stimuli compete with prestimuli for limited resources; rather, it is assumed that modulations are by-products of whether or not probes occur in a modality channel that is already activated and of how capacity is allocated to interesting and dull prestimuli in that channel.

Lang et al. (chapter 5, this volume) have also probed affective-slide processing with startle stimuli. They typically find that, beyond the PPI period, blinks are larger to aversive than to neutral slides and smallest to appetitive slides. This ordering held for both auditory and visual blinks (Bradley, Cuthbert, & Lang, 1990) and for phobic and control subjects (Hamm et al., in press) even though skin conductance was greater and viewing time longer for unpleasant and pleasant compared to neutral slides. Interestingly, slides probed between 2 and 5 sec had an effect on P3b opposite to the effect of slide onset on P3b: Arousing slides were associated with larger P3bs at slide onset, but smaller P3bs when probed later (Schupp, Cuthbert, Bradley, Birbaumer, & Lang, in press). Schupp et al. interpreted smaller P3bs to probes during arousing slides as evidence that those slides required greater attentional resources for their processing, leaving fewer resources available to process the probe stimulus.

Lang (1995) felt that the same-valence ordering of auditory and visual probes (Bradley et al., 1990) "disconfirmed" the modality-selective hypothesis but, because the hypothesis requires an interaction between at least two probe and two prestimulus modalities, and Bradley et al. did not vary prestimulus modality, they could not test the hypothesis. It should be noted that their finding of blink differences associated with valence is due entirely to slides in the upper quarter of the rating scale (see Lang et al., this volume, Fig. 5.9); judged by normative ratings for happy faces, the Anthony and Graham slides are below the middle of Lang et al.'s arousal scale, at least for adults. Balaban (1995; Balaban et al., chapter 16, this volume) used auditory probes during happy, neutral, and angry faces and found the Lang et al. ordering in 5-month-old infants. The author noted that the study could not distinguish between competing hypotheses.

Berg and Richards (chapter 15, this volume, Fig. 15.2) also studied infants and, in a clever design for measuring attention engaging effects, replicated the modality-selective effect. The design was counterbalanced, with both auditory and visual prestimuli and auditory and visual probes. Instead of engaging attention with more or less interesting prestimuli, they introduced probes either when prestimuli were eliciting sustained attention (heart rate deceleration) or when attention was terminating (heart rate accelerating toward baseline). Same-modality probing during sustained attention elicited larger blinks than same-modality probing when attention was terminating, and blinks to different-modality probes were smaller and relatively more so when delivered during sustained attention. Like Anthony and Graham (1983), the findings suggest reduced sensory-central processing of probes when attention is strongly engaged by a different-modality prestimulus but less reduction if the prestimulus is dull or attention to it is terminating. The effects were not present in 8-week-old infants but were present by 14 weeks and through 26 weeks.

Modality-selective effects need not be incompatible with affective modulation. Anthony and Graham tested for a selective attention effect acting on sensory input, and Bradley et al. (1990) found a nonselective effect—negative slides enhanced visual and acoustic blinks and positive slides reduced visual and acoustic blinks—consistent with a response synergism between blink and emotion. In theory, both selective sensory and nonselective motor effects are possible and could be tested in a single design (Graham, 1992).

Bradycardia: Evolution and Resolution

It is an important question whether bradycardia elicited by phobia relevant pictures reflects a DR or, like the response to novel stimuli, reflects increased attention to sensory input. The research and ideas discussed in this section do not resolve the issue but, from an evolutionary-comparative perspective on the one hand, and a mathematical modeling approach on the other hand, reach a consensus that resolution requires looking beyond peripheral components of ORs and DRs to the mechanisms that activate them.

Evolutionary Analysis. Campbell, Wood, and McBride (chapter 3, this volume), comparing species from different vertebrate classes, point out that parasympathetic central neurons connect to the heart in lampreys, one of the most primitive families of fish still living, but central sympathetic fibers do not connect to the heart before amphibians—millions of years later. It is known that both amphibians and the still later reptiles show cardiac responses to prey and predators, but little research has been conducted with "neutral" stimuli. In studies of two reptilian species, Campbell et al. could not demonstrate any cardiac response to stimuli that included 80 dB pulsating noise, 130 dB startle pulses, and three odors—amyl acetate, crickets (prey), and fox urine (predator). These stimuli elicit large, prolonged decelerations in the mammal (rats). Further, other rat experiments have shown that rapidly habituating bradycardia to a wide variety of visual, auditory, and olfactory stimuli is almost exclusively produced via vagal inhibition—vagotomy and cholinergic blockade eliminated the bradycardia without affecting behavioral orienting (e.g., Haroutunian & Campbell, 1981).

Campbell et al. (this volume) suggest that bradycardia during diving to escape a predator might have evolved because it prolongs submersion and that it, in turn, might have generalized to nondiving species whenever immobility served as an antipredator strategy. They note (p. 59) that if fear-induced decreases in heart rate during immobility "also facilitated tracking a predator and judging its intentions" (reducing self-generated noise improves detection of faint sounds?), those species might be expected also to display orienting to novel, neutral stimuli. They suggest that fear bradycardia may be distinguished from the bradycardia of orienting by its greater magnitude, slower habituation, greater responsiveness to high than to low to moderate stimulus intensity, and by the context in which it is elicited.

Both the absence of orienting to neutral stimuli in reptiles and the freezing response to prey and predator are compatible with Porges (1995), who inferred from evolutionary changes that reptiles, the first to have two separate vagal nuclei in the medulla, the nucleus ambiguous (NA) and the dorsal motor nucleus (DMNX), are affected by DMNX during challenges but, having low metabolic demands, do not employ the NA as a vagal brake during periods without challenge. In contrast, the high metabolic needs of mammals are seen as requiring a vagal brake under normal conditions. However, Campbell et al. note that the wide variability in size of the two nuclei suggests that species-specific environmental challenges had more influence in determining their relative importance than their order of appearance during evolution.

Autonomic Space. The concept of a bivariate autonomic space is discussed in Sokolov and Cacioppo (chapter 1, this volume) and in a series of articles by Cacioppo, Berntson, and collaborators. The bivariate surface, bounded by sympathetic and parasympathetic axes, reflects their uncoupled, reciprocal, or coactivated effects on heart rate and is specified by a formal mathematical model. Quigley and Berntson (1990) found, with autonomic blockade in adult rats, that both bradycardia elicited by 55 dB tones and tachycardia elicited by 75 dB tones resulted from coactivation of the two ANS branches. Kurtz and Campbell (1994) delivered more intense, 80 and 100 dB white noise and found that ANS control changed with development and that phasic response shifts were opposite to known ontogenetic shifts in tonic control. Using autonomic blockade and applying the Berntson, Cacioppo, and Quigley (1994) method of testing for bias, Kurtz and Campbell also found that noise stimuli elicited bradycardia in preweanling rats due to parasympathetic activation, tachycardia in peri-adolescents due to parasympathetic withdrawal, and tachycardia in adult rats due to reciprocal parasympathetic withdrawal and sympathetic activation. The boundary between ORs and

DRs in the human adult (Sokolov, 1963) lies near or between 75 dB tones (coactivating effects) and 80 to 100 dB noise (reciprocal effects).

The bivariate space model may also be useful in conceptualizing how positive and negative evaluative processes combine or act independently to affect behavior and physiology. Cacioppo and Berntson (1994), in proposing such an approach, note that it is more in line with Lang's separation of appetitive and aversive emotions than is the traditional bipolar scaling.

Spectral Analysis. Noninvasive measures may also distinguish between contributions of the two ANS systems. One simple measure is the difference in response onset latency—absence of heart rate change in the first second following stimulation is consistent with sympathetic action. Other measures include respiratory sinus arrhythmia as an index of parasympathetic activity, and length of the pre-ejection period as an index of sympathetic action. Low frequency cardiac variability in the spectral analysis of heart period variability has been proposed as another index of sympathetic action. However, in a study employing single and double blockade, spectral analysis confirmed association of the high frequency peak with respiratory sinus arrhythmia but found that low frequency and very low frequency peaks reflected parasympathetic as well as sympathetic contributions. Sokolov and Cacioppo (chapter 1, this volume) suggest that the three peaks might be more useful as indicants, respectively, of respiratory, vascular, and metabolic (humoral) mechanisms. Evidence of humoral effects was described in Cacioppo (1994). Further, factor analysis of heart rate variability in low and high anxious groups, studied in Sokolov's laboratory, identified three orthogonal factors whose loadings were the same under rest and mental arithmetic conditions. The task difference mainly affected the high frequency respiratory peak, but it was the low and very low frequency components during rest that distinguished between the presumably more stable, tonic differences in trait anxiety.

Summary

Intense noxious stimuli activate a generalized defensive arousal system reflected in slowly habituating P3b and increased skin conductance and heart rate. In theory, the DR reduces stimulus effects and energizes responses. Picture representations of aversive stimuli also elicit DRs when content is relevant to subject phobias. In nonphobic subjects, both highly arousing aversive and appetitive stimuli elicit heart rate deceleration, but probe blinks suggest DRs during aversive and ORs during appetitive pictures, a differentiation that is present by 5 months of age. In both infants and adults, blink probing of low-arousal pictures and sounds shows modality-selective enhancement to attention engaging stimuli. Although parasympathetic connections to the heart developed earlier than sympathetic during evolution, bradycardia to neutral stimuli is not present until mammals. A model of autonomic space that represents the various ways in which the two systems combine or act via respiratory, vascular, or humoral mechanisms may prove useful in distinguishing the mechanisms underlying ORs and DRs.

ACTIVE SELECTIVE ATTENTION: LOCALIZED ORIENTING

Active attention has been described as controlled processing, voluntary, conscious, serial, effortful, and dependent on limited resources or capacity. Occurrence of a generalized OR or any switch to attention implies that controlled processing is in effect, however briefly. The previous two sections considered passive attention situations in which any instructions were nonselective; the present section reviews studies in which subjects were instructed to associate selected stimuli with some task. Sokolov (1963) referred to the ANS responses elicited under such instructions as localized ORs that, unlike the generalized OR, do not habituate until the stimulus-response relation has been acquired.

The following paragraphs discuss effects of selection under four headings: ERP and ANS response, probing selective attention effects, probing sensory and motor processing, and development of controlled processing.

ERP and ANS Indices of Selective Attention

The nature and timing of selective attentional effects on ERPs is discussed by Näätänen (1992; Näätänen et al., chapter 13, this volume). Two main types of effect have been identified: (a) An endogenous trace, the slow "processing negativity" (PN), is a representation of the selected (target) stimulus, built up and maintained by rehearsal, with which input is matched; (b) a sensory gain process selectively enhances or inhibits exogenous, preattentive components. The earliest demonstrations of a selective attention effect appeared to show selective facilitation of the auditory N100, but Näätänen (1992) argued that most voluntary attentional effects in the auditory system include the endogenous PN and, in the visual system, the similar "selection negativities" described by Harter and Aine (1984). However, selection of the location of a stimulus in visual space appears to occur earlier through a gain mechanism, consistent with the special status of location as the major function of Posner's posterior attention network (chapter 14, this volume). Näätänen et al. review recent studies using MEG and fMRI to determine more accurately whether or not generators of endogenous and exogenous attention effects differ. In general, these studies confirm both the importance of endogenous effects and the existence of a special gain mechanism for visual location. The ERP findings also support Öhman's (1979) extension of OR theory in which he hypothesized a match mechanism to account for the processing of significant selected stimuli in active attention tasks.

A P300 or P3b centroparietal potential, peaking between about 300 to 450 msec, provides the clearest evidence of controlled sensory processing when stimuli are rare targets: Its peak amplitude may reflect resource allocation and the updating of expectancies, its latency indexes the time of completing stimulus evaluation, and neither latency nor amplitude reflects response planning (Donchin, 1981). P3b is normally followed by a positive slow wave. Brunia (chapter 12, this volume) discusses studies in which the slow CNV develops in anticipation of a second stimulus providing information or a respond signal: If a response is to be made, there is also a slow negative readiness potential whose scalp distribution is lateralized if the response is lateralized.

Simons and Perlstein (chapter 10, this volume) describe two long-ISI studies in which six targets and six unannounced nontargets, presented among 60 standards, elicited equal P3b and no P3a, suggesting that passive orienting and active attention command equal resources when there are only a few widely spaced stimuli. Although P3b did not distinguish between novels and targets, the following slow positive wave and heart rate acceleration were greater for targets. Accelerations in this case were not due to a DR or to sustained stimulation (stimuli lasted 50 or 75 msec) but could be associated either with internal manipulations, such as a memory comparison, or with response preparation.

As discussed in the second section, Simons and Perlstein did find a P3a when short ISIs (1.1 sec) were employed, even when rare targets and nontargets were simple tones differing only in pitch. With tone probabilities of .1, .5, or .9 and with target status counterbalanced across blocks within subjects, the P3a associated with generalized orienting was non-selectively present to both rare targets and nontargets but, presumably due to the time pressure and the need to maintain a count of targets, P3b was selectively larger to rare targets than rare nontargets.

Probing Selective Attention Effects

Several chapters in this volume report effects of attention or cognitive manipulations on blink or the automatic modulations of blink. The studies have either used tasks that require information to be extracted from the blink-eliciting stimulus or the prepulse in a prepulse-elicitor pair, or the studies have provided or withheld information making when, where, or what stimulus will occur more or less predictable.

Hoffman (chapter 8, this volume) describes a study in which subjects maintained fixation at the fovea (0°) and received no prepulse or a flash at 0°, 20°, or 40°. Foreknowledge of flash location produced greater PPI to a subsequent blink-eliciting tap. Hoffman commented that the finding is something of a paradox in light of his studies of expectancy effects, reviewed in the second section, which showed that knowledge concerning a prepulse led to lesser PPI. However, the fixation study had cued trials, delivering location information, and required subjects to report when and where a flash occurred. Thus, knowledge of location permitted advance shifting of covert attention to the specified location while still maintaining foveal fixation. This should improve stimulus reception; more important, the need to obtain information from the prepulse in order to comply with instructions should yield more processing of the stimulus. More elaborately processed prepulses, like more intense prepulses, should yield the obtained finding of more PPI.

Studies from other laboratories confirm that if a subject has to extract information from a reflex-eliciting target, target processing is enhanced (Bohlin & Graham, 1977; Bohlin, Graham, Silverstein, & Hackley, 1981, Exp. 1; Hackley & Graham, 1983, Exp. 1; Hackley & Graham, 1987, Exp. 1). For example, instructing subjects to discriminate between equally unpredictable targets and nontargets and to judge the duration of a reflex-eliciting target, had effects opposite to those of valid foreknowledge in the absence of a task; that is, judging duration of a blink-eliciting stimulus shortened blink latency and, less often, increased blink magnitude. Similarly, judging duration of a prepulse increased its PPI effect (Hackley & Graham, 1987, Exp. 2). These effects must have been mediated in the sensory-central path rather than the motor path because blinks to nontarget stimuli were unaffected. Had attention affected the motor path, it would necessarily have affected reflexes elicited by both attended and unattended stimuli (for reviews, see Graham & Hackley, 1991; Hackley & Graham, 1987).

Blink magnitude is decreased, however, when attention is directed away from the reflex-eliciting stimulus to a simultaneous weak stimulus whose duration is judged (Hackley & Graham, 1983, Exp. 1; Silverstein, Graham, & Bohlin, 1981, Exp. 2). The Silverstein et al. effects could have been due to greater timing uncertainty on unwarned trials rather than inhibition of response to reflex stimuli that competed with a nonreflex target stimulus. However, when the reflex stimulus was itself the focus of attention, as in the similar Bohlin and Graham (1977) studies, response was greater on warned trials.

The changes in reflex response to attended stimuli just discussed were presumably due to the need to extract information from the stimuli; that is, to discriminate targets and judge duration. In contrast when all blink-eliciting stimuli, either warned or unwarned, need only to be detected as signals for a simple key press, reaction time (RT) is faster and blinks smaller and faster with warning (Brown, 1975). The shorter RT with warning is a well-known effect of reducing time uncertainty. That this explanation also applies to blinks was shown by comparison with a second experiment, identical except that there was no task. The task effect was statistically significant and was due to the absence of blink habituation on unwarned trials.

In contrast, an uninformative accessory stimulus appears to influence a later stage in choice RT preparation—either a decision (Posner, 1995) or motor (Sanders, 1979) stage. Hackley and Boulhouwer (chapter 9, this volume) discuss a study in which an uninformative weak tone sometimes accompanied a blink-eliciting flash to the right or left that identified the side on which a voluntary choice reaction should occur. The accessory stimulus enhanced the visual R50 blink component but not R80, and it also speeded RT but at an accuracy cost. Hackley and Boelhouwer note that such a speed/accuracy trade-off implicates a decision level process influenced by immediate alerting; that is, alerting speeds the decision so that it occurs when stimulus processing is incomplete and, therefore, likely to yield an inaccurate decision. Presumably, no decision process is involved in activating blink: Further, blink latency and magnitude were uncorrelated with RT and, unlike the voluntary response, blink did not interact with foreperiod length. Thus, the accessory facilitating effects on blink and RT must either involve different mechanisms or, more parsimoniously, affect only motor processing of blink but both decision and motor processing of voluntary responses.

Hoffman (chapter 8, this volume) has described a situation—delayed auditory feedback—which is known to have dramatic effects on physiology and behavior, turning "an otherwise articulate subject into an instant aphasic" (p. 196). Assuming that this unpleasant condition would enhance startle, he found, instead, that blinks were greatly reduced. The probable explanation is the pulsating character of the feedback. Hoffman and Fleshler (1963) found a similar effect in rats—mild pulsing noise nearly eliminated startle to intense, shotlike, sounds. It was this serendipitous finding that instigated the research on PPI.

Probing Sensory and Motor Processing

Dawson et al. (chapter 11, this volume) have traced the time course of processing sustained (5/7 sec) stimuli in a 2-decision task that requires discriminating targets from nontargets and maintaining a count of long-duration targets. In a series of studies, target–nontarget differences have been varied from none (single stimulus), to easily discriminable (modality or predictable location), to less discriminable (pitch or unpredictable location). Under all conditions, targets elicited greater skin conductance responses that habituated slowly. In two pitch-difference studies, blink-reflex probing with white noise bursts during targets also showed enhanced and persistent PPI to early probes and enhanced slowly habituating startle to targets probed late (2 sec). Thus, attending to targets enhanced both the PPI that presumably protects sensory processing and the late facilitation presumably associated with localized orienting.

Most of the studies also measured voluntary RT to visual probes delivered between 50 and 600 msec of stimulus onset. With single targets or easily discriminated targets and nontargets, RTs during the first half of trials were slower to probed targets at 150 msec, whereas RTs during nontargets did not differ from ISI values. This pattern could be explained by assuming that once targets are identified, controlled processing is devoted to the timing task while identified nontargets need not be processed further and, therefore, do not interfere with responding to probes. However, when the target–nontarget difference was harder to distinguish, the effect was reversed and it is not self-evident how slower RTs to probed nontargets can be explained.

Various interpretations are possible (see Kramer & Spinks, 1991). Filion, Dawson, and Schell (1994) suggested that because "attention is engaged tonically on the attended [task-relevant] channel," physically similar nontargets are "preattentively identified as a possible target" and require an attention switch to the task-irrelevant channel, making resources temporarily unavailable for the probe RT task (p. 76). I assume that "channel" refers to an internal representation or memory. This is a viable hypothesis, but is difficult to reconcile with differences in the time course of RTs; that is, with small target–nontarget differences, RTs during nontargets were maximally slowed to a 50 msec probe but slowing during targets did not peak until 150 msec (Filion, Dawson, & Schell, 1991). Such early effects suggest that onsets of both stimuli trigger controlled processing. Further, only reactions probed during the target stimulus were significantly correlated with skin conductance (Filion et al., 1994), suggesting that the target was judged to be significant but the nontarget was not. According to Näätänen (1992), targets would be matched to the endogenous PN maintained by rehearsal, but an automatic MMN to nontargets might not occur because of the long ISI and the equiprobability of targets and nontargets. Other questions relevant to interpreting the findings are whether targets or nontargets are ever misidentified, how costs of identifying stimuli compare with costs of monitoring stimulus duration, and whether larger pitch separations would yield the target-slowing RT effects seen with modality and predictable location differences.

Motor preparation is frequently probed with monosynaptic reflexes, particularly the T-reflex elicited by tapping the Achilles tendon. Brunia (1993; chapter 12, this volume) reviews studies in which the muscle involved in a lateralized leg movement and the uninvolved contralateral muscle were probed throughout a 4 sec interval between a warning signal (WS) and a ready signal (RS). Both muscles show a brief early period of facilitation between 100 to 300 msec (note that the monosynaptic reflex does not show PPI). Brunia suggests that the early response reflects "alerting" and processing of input information. Only if a response is required is there evidence of motor preparation during the second half of the period when the uninvolved muscle shows some facilitation, whereas absence of any increase in the agonist suggests presynaptic inhibition of the motoneuron pool. As Brunia notes, CNV and heart rate changes suggest that there is also anticipation of a stimulus input (i.e., the RS). In this volume, he addresses the question of how to disentangle sensory and motor preparation. One approach has been to separate CNV from the lateralized readiness potential. He also proposes that, like Lacey and Lacey (1973), they can be disentangled by probing with ERPs and reflexes during two types of task: time estimation and warned reaction time.

Development of Controlled Processing

Head-turning towards and fixation of a stimulus have been commonly employed to indicate attention in infants. Although Sokolov (1963) excluded receptor-aligning movements as components of generalizing orienting, Pavlov (1928) and Posner et al. (chapter 14, this volume) do include such activity. In a review of infant studies, Graham et al. (1983) noted that stimulus-directed eye movements appear to be reflexive nonhabituating responses during the first two months of life but, beyond that period, may be accompanied by heart rate decelerations and may show rapid habituation and dishabituation. Balaban et al. (chapter 16, this volume) also note that it is debatable whether eye fixations reflect an automatically elicited component of generalized orienting or reflect conscious recognition. In either case, the measure has proven useful in demonstrating competencies in infants too young to respond to verbal task instructions. Berg and Richards (chapter 15, this volume) argued from the fact that 14- to 26-week-old infants fixated the novel of a pair of stimuli, that the nonnovel stimulus was "recognized," perhaps by means of implicit learning. Balaban et al. used the paired preference method to test affective response to the same faces employed in her reflex probe study (see third section) and found no significant differences in viewing time.

Posner et al. (chapter 14, this volume) describe head turning and eye movement responses that suggest implicit learning of simple fixed sequences as early as 4 months of life. For example, infants learned to anticipate target movement, either clockwise or counterclockwise, through four positions arranged in a square. Performance did not improve between 4 and 10 months, and infants at these ages could not learn a more complex, ambiguous sequence dependent on "context"—that is, go from position 1 to 3 if prior move was from 2 to 1 but go from 1 to 2 if prior move was from 3 to 1. By 18 months, the task was learned but only after two sessions. Even in adults, learning of context dependent associations requires focal attention which, Posner et al. suggest, depends on control by a frontal executive system related to awareness and volition. The earlier development of preference for novel locations and, later, for novel objects, presumably reflects sequential maturation at subcortical and, then, at cortical levels of the posterior attention network (see second section); the subsequent context learning requires that the posterior network be connected to the frontal executive network.

Campos et al. (chapter 17, this volume) demonstrate how self-produced locomotion leads to changed perceptions of the environment which, in turn, influence abilities believed to be innate that normally appear between 6 and 9 months of life: (a) fear of heights; (b) joint attention (to an object pointed to by another person); (c) object permanence. As noted in the previous section, infants placed on the deep side of the visual cliff did not show fear of heights at 5 months but did at 9 months. Citing the classical Held and Hein (1963) study of kittens with active versus passive locomotor experience, Campos et al. suggest that the acquisition of crawling between 5 and 9 months provides experience of discrepant visual–vestibular input at drop-offs. The perceptual hypothesis was confirmed by a positive relationship between infants' behavior on the cliff and in a "moving room" enclosure (Campos et al., Fig. 17.2). They also directly tested the locomotion hypothesis by comparing same-age infants with and without locomotor experience, same-age prelocomotor infants given or not given experience with a walker, and infants with and without delayed locomotion due to orthopedic factors. Similar logic and tests were applied to explain how locomotor experience, by providing stable landmarks such as the walls of a room instead of the infant's own body, could yield knowledge of the relation between spatially separated objects and lead an infant to follow the gesture or gaze of another or to separate a hidden object from the object or location in which it was hidden.

In a long-term follow-up of infants, Kagan and Snidman (1991; Balaban et al., chapter 16, this volume) have traced emotional development. The work discussed here relates characteristics identified during testing at 4, 14, and 21 months of age to performance on a modified Stroop task at 4.5 years ($N = 137$) or, in a cross-validation sample ($N = 42$), at 5 years. The modified Stroop, instead of using names of colors printed in color, uses emotional words or, in the child version, emotional pictures framed in color. Unlike the original, in which latency slowing is due to response interference when the word color name differs from the color in which it is printed (Duncan-Johnson & Kopell, 1981), slowing in the modified version is presumably due to greater sensory processing of words or pictures with more associations.

In both cohorts, color-naming latencies were significantly longer with threat pictures and did not differ between neutral and happy pictures. Stroop performance could also be related to whether infants had been consistently identified as high or low fearful at 4, 14, and 21 months: The high-fear group ($N = 15$) had longer latencies to threat pictures and the low-fear group ($N = 26$) to happy pictures. In addition, performance varied as a function of whether infants tested at 14 and 21 months were unsmiling or smiling: The serious group ($N = 18$) had slowed response to happy pictures and the smiling group ($N = 26$) to threat pictures. If effects with the modified Stroop are more closely related to attention than to response interference, they are in line with the adult evidence discussed in the previous section. As a general conclusion from the studies of Balaban et al. (chapter 16, this volume), it appears that even young infants are responsive to affective pictures and show the same relative ordering as do adults. Further, behaviors at the affective extremes in early infancy, judged by a variety of measures, appear to have some long-term stability.

Summary

Selective attention directed to target stimuli by instructions is reflected in endogenous slow waves or increased gain of specific peaks and, for equally rare targets and nontargets, in a larger P3b to targets. Selective attention can also enhance blink reflexes and PPI to targets that differ from nontargets in location or modality, and thus reflect processing in the sensory-central limb of the reflex. Blink probing of a pitch discrimination shows similar effects, but effects of early RT probes may reverse as a function of target–nontarget discriminability. Sensory processing can also be separated from motor processing by employing lateralized tasks and recording CNV and lateralized readiness potentials. Developmental studies suggest that locomotor experience explains some affective and perceptual development, but the late-developing ability to learn complex sequences probably requires maturation of a frontal executive system. Fearfulness identified in early infancy may also show affective persistence at 21 months and 5 years.

WHAT DO WE KNOW? WHERE DO WE GO?

Previous sections have integrated findings drawn from individual chapters. This section highlights findings that have implications for, or extend, existing theories of information processing. I also consider directions for future research. In general, biocognitive research appears to fit less well with the discrete-stage theories that have dominated information processing theory in the past, but see Sternberg (1984) in defense of the adaptability of stage theory. The biocognitive approach appears more compatible with newer theories assuming parallel, distributed processing and continuous outputs of partially analyzed information that excite both lower and higher level processors (e.g., Ericksen & Schultz, 1979; Rumelhart, McClelland, & The PDP Research Group, 1986).

Preattentive processing is recognized in cognitive theory as a necessary but rather uninteresting stage in which bits and pieces of information are extracted. However, an impressive number of new features have emerged from the research presented in this volume. The significance of *high-pass filtering* has been relatively unappreciated in cognitive theory generally, although it has a long history beginning in neurophysiology with recognition of functional differences associated with cell size. It has been suggested that neuronal size may constitute "one of the few general rules of organization" (Luscher, Ruenzel, Fetz, & Henneman, 1979, p. 1161). It can be observed in all sensory modalities, as well as in the motor system, and has been associated with masking differences (Breitmeyer & Ganz, 1976) and detection versus discrimination (MacMillan, 1973), to mention only two examples. A recent edited volume, *Temporal Information Processing in the Nervous System* (Tallal, Galaburda, Llinas, & von Euler, 1993), implicates difficulties in processing brief, rapid inputs as a cause of dysphasia and dyslexia. It would be interesting to test such patients for deficient PPI.

The brilliant ERP work of Näätänen hardly needs comment. Not only does his finding of a *mismatch mechanism* support Sokolov's neuronal model theory but, in demonstrating a cortical comparison process that is automatic, he frees theory from the suspicion of inserting an homunculus. The ability of ERPs to reflect preattentive processing of *PPI*, and to separate sensory and nonspecific system transmission of information, is further evidence that ERP methodology is as important for understanding process as it is for identifying brain activity in real time. Used with cognitive paradigms, ERPs provide a powerful means of exploring information processing. This volume should encourage psychophysiologists, who already have the necessary equipment and technical skill, to add it to their armamentarium. The *short-circuited response to masked threat stimuli*, demonstrated by Öhman with a variety of methods, is an exciting finding and should also encourage other laboratories to replicate and explore its implications. If the effects are robust enough, the phenomenon could be studied with ERPs. Would an auditory analogue work and, if so, would it show effects opposite to those of PPI—for example, would the nonspecific P50 be enhanced rather than reduced? It is also possible that there would be differences in processing in the color and form areas of extrastriate visual cortex as color, unlike form, is associated with the small cells active in low-pass filtering. Abrupt luminance change shows popout whereas abrupt color change does not (Theeuwes, 1995). PPI should also be absent with color prestimuli. Öhman (personal communication, July 20, 1995) suggests that the masked threat stimuli should be tested for implicit memory effects, that is, for evidence of priming despite inability to recognize. In brief, there are a host of interesting phenomena to be investigated using the measures of preattentive processing that have been identified and the variety of differentiating cognitive tasks that are available.

Despite the durability of Sokolov's theory of *orienting* and the worldwide recognition that it has received in many disciplines, it has played only a small role in cognitive research, primarily with respect to memory. New findings discussed in this volume include the verification of a specific ERP component reflecting novelty, the onset of orienting with the maturation of cortical connections, and the subsequent development of sustained attention and of the phenomenon of "inhibition of return" which ensures priority to novel stimuli. The developmental work and Campbell's tracing of evolutionary origins—especially of the earlier development of parasympathetic than of what is commonly viewed as the more primitive, sympathetic system—provide a broader perspective on orienting as an adaptation important for survival. To detect change is to acquire information, and that should be a useful adaption whether for locating food or dealing with danger.

Reflex probing has also added to an understanding of orienting in showing that it arises in anticipation, not only of a stimulus relevant to some task (a localized OR), but also to resolve uncertainty about when, what, or where a stimulus will occur. Hoffman has shown that various methods of manipulating uncertainty all lead to blink facilitation. Finally, Siddle has advanced what appear to be definitive arguments that orienting cannot be explained by a noncomparator, nonassociative model but requires a comparator, associative model that extrapolates anticipated events. A major problem for future research on orienting is to measure its effects on information processing. Sokolov (1963) briefly reported experiments showing that stimuli delivered following an OR-eliciting stimulus had lowered thresholds. There have been no attempts to replicate this finding other than the Bohlin et al. (1981) study showing that reflex blink was nonselectively facilitated following a novel stimulus. If orienting enhances information processing, what processes under what conditions are enhanced? Is detection enhanced, as the threshold lowering would suggest? What about recognition? Is the attentional spotlight broader—are, for example, visual stimuli in the periphery enhanced? Presumably, reaction time should not be speeded but accuracy should be greater. In brief, although a great deal has been learned about the physiological changes in response to a novel stimulus, very little has been learned about information processing. The developmental work is an exception, in particular, the finding that more is learned about a stimulus delivered during a state of sustained attention indexed by heart rate deceleration (Berg & Richards, chapter 15, this volume).

Sokolov hypothesized a second generalized arousal system, the *defense* response associated with protective actions and the reduction of stimulation. Important new findings have emerged from the Lang Laboratory studies of affective pictures that may facilitate the study of this system. Although rated arousal level of pictures is the main determinant of increases in skin conductance and the ERP late positive complex, the ratings do not distinguish between arousal associated with action dispositions (DRs) and with attention (ORs). However, at very high-arousal levels, appetitive and aversive pictures yield heart rate, reflex blink, and free-viewing-time changes consistent, respectively, with ORs and DRs. Because all of the effects, at least for blink, are due to the upper quarter of the arousal scale, it would be helpful if the effects of these high-arousal stimuli were shown separately. The differentiation must be much diluted when 75% of the trials are nondifferentiating.

These findings will certainly be an impetus to research in many areas, including information processing, and they add a whole new dimension to the study of Sokolov's two arousal systems. It would be a major advantage to be able to substitute symbolically aversive for high-intensity stimulation but, to coordinate the research based on long-duration (6 sec) affective slides with the generally brief neutral-valence stimuli eliciting ORs and DRs, a study is needed that would psychophysically match the effects of intensity and affective stimuli. The complexity of slides also needs to be equated, as Berlyne's pioneering work (e.g., Berlyne, Craw, Salapatek, & Lewis, 1963) demonstrated. The critical problem is to determine the type of arousal that is being measured. Because interest and arousal ratings are highly correlated, the main determinant might be attention. Again, research is needed that employs only high-arousal, valence-discriminating pictures equated for complexity and that records heart rate, blink, and ERPs. The question of determining the type of arousal also arises in connection with the memory study showing better recall of more arousing pictures but no valence difference. Whether heart rate would be useful here is debatable, as retrieving from memory is itself capable of accelerating heart rate.

An important contribution to the problem of interpreting heart rate findings derives from the concept of autonomic space discussed by Sokolov and Cacioppo (chapter 1, this volume). Future research might profit from testing the methods they propose to distinguish between the contributions of sympathetic and parasympathetic nervous systems. Because the two systems may work jointly or in opposition to varying degrees, the same absolute change in heart rate can arise from different constituent patterns. This approach might be particularly valuable in separating fear and OR bradycardia or perhaps in showing that fear bradycardia reflects a strong attentive stance rather than a disposition to action.

Selective attention is the area least explored by psychophysiologists but is the most important for understanding behavioral effects of information processing. A particularly interesting finding is Näätänen's discovery of *processing negativity*, interpreted as representing a trace of the target stimulus to which input is matched, as Öhman's theory had hypothesized. The trace mechanism operates with both auditory and visual stimuli but, in addition, visual location appears to use a special gain mechanism, again consistent with theories that location is analyzed by a distinct attention network. Use of ERPs might be helpful in explaining why reaction time differs when probes are delivered during targets and nontargets in the studies of Dawson et al. (chapter 11, this volume) and, in particular, the apparently earlier, more resource-consuming processing of nontargets. The reaction time literature has found that "same" judgments are generally faster, but that "different" judgments may be faster when stimuli are very discriminable. These behavioral studies differ in numerous respects from the Dawson et al. studies, but reconciling findings from the two approaches could inform theories in both cognition and psychophysiology.

The original studies showing very early selective attention effects on blink were able to separate sensory from motor effects because targets and nontargets were delivered unpredictably to different locations or modalities so that, had the effect of instructions modified response preparation, targets and nontargets having the same final motor path would not have been distinguishable. However, the recent studies using only a single type of blink-reflex to probe long-duration targets and nontargets, and no invalid trials, cannot separate sensory attention from response processing effects. Brunia's chapter discusses how anticipatory slow waves can distinguish between anticipating a sensory input and preparing a lateralized motor response. The Dawson et al. paradigm might also be adapted to use this procedure, as well as measuring the early ERPs to determine whether or when they show the processing negativities representing targets and/or the automatic mismatch negativity.

The question of sensory versus motor effects might also be approached in another manner. A major tenet of Sokolov's theory is that the OR and DR have opposed effects on stimulus processing but, as with tests for sensory-enhancing effects of orienting, research is conspicuous by its absence. At least one method would seem well-suited to providing evidence—namely, what are the speed/accuracy trade-off functions for OR-eliciting and DR-eliciting stimuli?

The developmental research provides still another approach to distinguishing separable processes, their relations to one another, and their effects on perception and cognition. One strength of developmental studies is that the general ventral-rostral and posterior-anterior axes along which maturation proceeds allows a glimpse of how subcortical portions of hypothesized networks function (see Posner et al., chapter 14, this volume).

In conclusion, biocognitive research extends information processing theory along two main lines. First, it shows that information processing is not only carried out pre-attentively and under controlled attention, but also that one or the other of two arousal systems may be activated under special conditions—the occurrence of a novel, unexpected stimulus or of an aversive stimulus. Second, it suggests that the filtering properties of the nervous system determine major pathways along which parallel processing occurs.

REFERENCES

Anthony, B. J., & Graham, F. K. (1983). Evidence for sensory-selective set in young infants. *Science, 220,* 742–744.

Anthony, B. J., & Graham, F. K. (1985). Blink reflex modification by selective attention: Evidence for the modulation of "automatic" processing. *Biological Psychology, 20,* 43–59.

Balaban, M. T. (1995). Affective influences on startle in five-month-old infants: Reactions to facial expressions of emotion. *Child Development, 66,* 28–36.

Berg, W. K., Berg, K. M., Harbin, T. J., Davies, M. G., Blumenthal, T. D., & Avendano, A. (1985). Comparisons of blink inhibition in infants, children, and young and old adults [Abstract]. *Psychophysiology, 22,* 572–573.

Berlyne, D. E. (1969). The development of the concept of attention in psychology. In C. R. Evans & T. B. Mulholland (Eds.), *Attention in neurophysiology* (pp. 1–20). Hillsdale, NJ: Lawrence Erlbaum Associates.

Berlyne, D. E., Craw, M. A., Salapatek, P. H., & Lewis, J. L. (1963). Novelty, complexity, incongruity, extrinsic motivation, and the GSR. *Journal of Experimental Psychology, 66,* 560–567.

Berntson, G. G., Cacioppo, J. T., & Quigley, K. S. (1994). Autonomic cardiac control: I. Estimation and validation from pharmacological blockades. *Psychophysiology, 31,* 572–585.

Boelhouwer, A. J. W., Teurlings, R. J. M. A., & Brunia, C. H. M. (1991). The effect of an acoustic warning stimulus upon the electrically elicited blink reflex in humans. *Psychophysiology, 28,* 133–139.

Bohlin, G., & Graham, F. K. (1977). Cardiac deceleration and reflex blink facilitation. *Psychophysiology, 14,* 423–430.

Bohlin, G., Graham, F. K., Silverstein, L. D., & Hackley, S. A. (1981). Cardiac orienting and startle blink modification in novel and signal situations. *Psychophysiology, 18,* 603–611.

Bradley, M. N., Cuthbert, B. N., & Lang, P. J. (1990). Startle reflex modification: Emotion or attention? *Psychophysiology, 27,* 513–523.

Bradley, M. M., Greenwald, M. K., Petry, M. C., & Lang, P. J. (1992). Remembering pictures: Pleasure and arousal in memory. *Journal of Experimental Psychology, 18,* 379–390.

Breitmeyer, B. G., & Ganz, L. (1976). Implications of sustained and transient channels for theories of visual pattern masking, saccadic suppression, and information processing. *Psychological Review, 83,* 1–36.

Brown, J. W. (1975). *Contingent negative variation and cardiac orienting preceding startle modification.* Unpublished doctoral dissertation, University of Wisconsin, Madison.

Brunia, C. H. M. (1993). Waiting in readiness: Gating in attention and motor preparation. *Psychophysiology, 30,* 327–340.

Cacioppo, J. T. (1994). Social neuroscience: Autonomic, neuroendocrine, and immune response to stress. *Psychophysiology, 31,* 44–61.

Cacioppo, J. T., & Berntson, G. G. (1994). Relationship between attitudes and evaluative space: A critical review, with emphasis on the separability of positive and negative substrates. *Psychological Bulletin, 115,* 401–423.

Campos, J. J. (1976). Heart rate: A sensitive tool for the study of emotional development. In L. P. Lipsitt (Ed.), *Developmental psychobiology: The significance of infancy.* Hillsdale, NJ: Lawrence Erlbaum Associates.

Chen, X. (1995). *P3a: A component in the late positive complex?* Unpublished master's thesis, University of Delaware, Newark.

Courchesne, E., Hillyard, S. A., & Galambos, R. (1975). Stimulus novelty, task relevance, and the visual evoked potential in man. *Electroencephalography & Clinical Neurophysiology, 39,* 131–143.

Courchesne, E., Kilman, B. A., Galambos, R., & Lincoln, A. J. (1984). Autism: Processing of novel auditory information assessed by event-related brain potentials. *Electroencephalography & Clinical Neurophysiology, 59,* 238–248.

Cuthbert, B., Schupp, H., McManis, M., Hillman, C., Bradley, M., & Lang, P. (1995). Cortical slow waves: Emotional perception and processing [Abstract]. *Psychophysiology, 32*(Supp. 1), S26.

Donchin, E. (1981). Surprise! . . . Surprise? *Psychophysiology, 18,* 493–513.

Duncan-Johnson, C. C., & Kopell, B. S. (1981). The Stroop effect: Brain potentials localize the source of interference. *Science, 214,* 938–940.

Eriksen, C. W., & Schultz, D. W. (1979). Information processing in visual search: A continuous flow conception and experimental results. *Perception and Psychophysics, 25,* 249–263.

Filion, D. L., Dawson, M. E., & Schell, A. M. (1991). The relationship between skin conductance orienting and the allocation of processing resources. *Psychophysiology, 28,* 410–424.

Filion, D. L., Dawson, M. E., & Schell, A. M. (1994). Probing the orienting response with startle modification and secondary reaction time. *Psychophysiology, 31,* 68–78.

Graham, F. K. (1975). The more or less startling effects of weak prestimulation. *Psychophysiology, 12,* 238–248.

Graham, F. K. (1979). Distinguishing among orienting, defense, and startle reflexes. In H. D. Kimmel, E. H. van Olst, & J. F. Orlebeke (Eds.), *The orienting reflex in humans* (pp. 137–167). Hillsdale, NJ: Lawrence Erlbaum Associates.

Graham, F. K. (1992). Attention: The heartbeat, the blink, and the brain. In B. A. Campbell, H. Hayne, & R. Richardson (Eds.), *Attention and information processing in infants and adults: Perspectives and human and animal research* (pp. 3–29). Hillsdale, NJ: Lawrence Erlbaum Associates.

Graham, F. K., Anthony, B. J., & Zeigler, B. L. (1983). The orienting response and developmental processes. In D. A. T. Siddle (Ed.), *Orienting and habituation: Perspectives in human research* (pp. 371–430). Sussex, UK: Wiley.

Graham, F. K., & Hackley, S. A. (1991). Passive and active attention to input. In J. R. Jennings & M. G. H. Coles (Eds.), *Handbook of cognitive psychophysiology* (pp. 251–356). New York: Wiley.

Groves, P. M., & Thompson, R. F. (1970). Habituation: A dual-process theory. *Psychological Review, 77,* 419–450.

Hackley, S. A., & Graham, F. K. (1983). Early selective attention effects on cutaneous and acoustic blink reflexes. *Physiological Psychology, 11,* 235–242.

Hackley, S. A., & Graham, F. K. (1987). Effects of attending selectively to the spatial position of reflex-eliciting and reflex-modulating stimuli. *Journal of Experimental Psychology: Human Perception and Performance, 13,* 411–424.

Hamm, A. O., Cuthbert, B. N., Globisch, J., & Vaitl, D. (in press). Fear and the startle reflex: Blink modulation and visceral response patterns in animal and mutilation fearful subjects. *Psychophysiology.*

Haroutunian, V., & Campbell, B. A. (1981). Development and habituation of the heart rate orienting response to auditory and visual stimuli in the rat. *Journal of Comparative and Physiological Psychology, 95,* 166–174.

Harter, M. R., & Aine, C. J. (1984). Brain mechanisms of visual selective attention. In R. Parasuraman & R. Davies (Eds.), *Varieties of attention* (pp. 293–321). London: Academic Press.

Held, R., & Hein, A. (1963). Movement-produced stimulation in the development of visually-guided behavior. *Journal of Comparative and Physiological Psychology, 56,* 872–876.

Hoffman, H. S., Cohen, M. E., & Anday, E. K. (1987). Inhibition of the eyeblink reflex in the human infant. *Developmental Psychobiology, 20,* 277–283.

Hoffman, H. S., & Fleshler, M. (1963). Startle reaction: Modification by background stimulation. *Science, 141,* 928–930.

Hoffman, H. S., & Ison, J. R. (1980). Reflex modification in the domain of startle: I. Some empirical findings and their implication for how the nervous system processes sensory input. *Psychological Review, 87,* 175–189.

Juola, J. F., Koshino, H., & Warner, B. (1995). Tradeoffs between attentional effects of spatial cues and abrupt onsets. *Perception & Psychophysics, 57,* 333–342.

Kagan, J., & Snidman, N. (1991). Infant predictors of inhibited and uninhibited profiles. *Psychological Science, 2,* 40–44.

Kandel, E. R., Schwartz, J. H., & Jessell, T. M. (1991). *Principles of neural science* (3rd ed.). New York: Elsevier.

Kramer, A., & Spinks, J. (1991). Capacity views of human information processing. In J. R. Jennings & M. G. H. Coles (Eds.), *Handbook of cognitive psychophysiology* (pp. 179–249). New York: Wiley.

Kurtz, M. W., & Campbell, B. A. (1994). Paradoxical autonomic responses to aversive stimuli in the developing rat. *Behavioral Neuroscience, 108,* 962–971.

Lacey, J. I., & Lacey, B. C. (1973). Some autonomic-central nervous system interrelationships. In P. Black (Ed.), *Physiological correlates of emotion* (pp. 205–227). New York: Academic Press.

Landis, C., & Hunt, W. A. (1939). *The startle pattern.* New York: Farrar & Rinehart.

Lang, P. J. (1995). The emotion probe. *American Psychologist, 50,* 372–385.

LeDoux, J. E. (1989). Cognitive-emotional interactions in the brain. *Cognition & Emotion, 3,* 267–289.

Leitner, D. S., Powers, A. S., Stitt, C. L., & Hoffman, H. S. (1981). Midbrain reticular formation involvement in the inhibition of acoustic startle. *Physiology & Behavior, 26,* 259–268.

Liegeois-Chauvel, C., Musolino, A., Badier, J. M., Marquis, P., & Chauvel, P. (1994). Evoked potentials recorded from the auditory cortex in man: Evaluation and topography of the middle latency components. *Electroencephalography & Clinical Neurophysiology, 92,* 204–214.

Lüscher, H.-R., Ruenzel, P., Fetz, E., & Henneman, E. (1979). Postsynaptic population potentials recorded from ventral roots perfused with isotonic sucrose: Connections of groups Ia and II spindle afferent fibers with large populations of motoneurons. *Journal of Neurophysiology, 42,* 1146–1164.

MacMillan, N. A. (1973). Detection and recognition of intensity changes in tone and noise: The detection-recognition disparity. *Perception and Psychophysics, 13,* 65–75.

Miles, M. A. (1993). *P300 and heart rate components in passive orienting to unrecognizable repetitive and nonrepetitive novels during a short-ISI target detection task: Anhedonics and controls.* Unpublished doctoral dissertation, University of Delaware, Newark.

Moruzzi, G., & Magoun, H. W. (1949). Brain stem reticular formation and activation of the EEG. *Electroencephalography & Clinical Neurophysiology, 1,* 455–473.

Näätänen, R. (1992). *Attention and brain function.* Hillsdale, NJ: Lawrence Erlbaum Associates.

Norris, C. M., & Blumenthal, T. D. (in press). A relationship between inhibition of the acoustic startle response and the protection of prepulse processing. *Psychobiology.*

Öhman, A. (1979). The orienting response, attention, and learning: An information processing perspective. In H. D. Kimmel, E. H. van Olst, & J. F. Orlebeke (Eds.), *The orienting reflex in humans* (pp. 443–472). Hillsdale, NJ: Lawrence Erlbaum Associates.

Papez, J. W. (1937). A proposed mechanism of emotion. *Archives of Neurology & Psychiatry, 38,* 725–743.

Pavlov, I. P. (1928). *Lectures on conditioned reflexes* (W. H. Gantt, Trans.). New York: International.

Perlstein, W. M., Fiorito, E., Simons, R. F., & Graham, F. K. (1993). Lead stimulation effects on reflex blink, exogenous brain potentials, and loudness judgements. *Psychophysiology, 30,* 347–358.

Porges, S. W. (1995). Orienting in a defensive world: Mammalian modifications of our evolutionary heritage, a polyvagal theory. *Psychophysiology, 32,* 301–318.

Posner, M. I. (1995). Attention in cognitive neuroscience: An overview. In M. S. Gazzaniga (Ed.), *The cognitive neurosciences* (pp. 615–624). Cambridge, MA: MIT Press.

Putnam, L. E. (1976). The human startle reaction: Mechanisms of modification by background acoustic stimulation (Doctoral dissertation, University of Wisconsin-Madison, 1975). *Dissertations Abstracts International, 36,* 6419B.

Putnam, L. E., & Roth, W. T. (1990). Effects of stimulus repetition, duration and rise time on startle blink and automatically elicited P300. *Psychophysiology, 27,* 275–297.

Quigley, K. S., & Berntson, G. G. (1990). Autonomic origins of cardiac responses to nonsignal stimuli in the rat. *Behavioral Neuroscience, 104,* 751–762.

Rosen, J. B., Hitchcock, J. M., Sananes, C. B., Miserendino, M. J. D., & Davis, M. (1991). A direct projection from the central nucleus of the amygdala to the acoustic startle pathway: anterograde and retrograde tracing studies. *Behavioral Neuroscience, 105,* 817–825.

Roth, W. T., Dorato, K. H., & Kopell, B. S. (1984). Intensity and task effects on evoked physiological responses to noise bursts. *Psychophysiology, 21,* 466–481.

Rothbart, M. K., & Derryberry, D. (1981). Theoretical issues in temperament. In M. Lewis & L. Taft (Eds.), *Developmental disabilities: Theory, assessment and intervention* (pp. 383–400). New York: Spectrum.

Rumelhart, D. E., McClelland, J. L., & The PDP Research Group. (1986). *Parallel distributed processing: Explorations in the microstructure of cognition* (Vol. 1). Cambridge, MA: MIT Press.

Sanders, A. F. (1979). Some effects of instructed muscle tension on choice reaction time and movement. In R. S. Nickerson (Ed.), *Attention and performance VIII* (pp. 59–74). Hillsdale, NJ: Lawrence Erlbaum Associates.

Schupp, H. T., Cuthbert, B. N., Bradley, M. M., Birbaumer, N., & Lang, P. J. (in press). Probe P3 and blinks: Two measures of affective startle modulation. *Psychophysiology.*

Siddle, D. A. T. (Ed.). (1983). *Orienting and habituation: Perspectives in human research.* New York: Wiley.

Siddle, D. A. T., Lipp, O. V., & Dall, P. J. (1994). Effects of stimulus preexposure and intermodality change on electrodermal orienting. *Psychophysiology, 31,* 421–426.

Silverstein, L. D., Graham, F. K., & Bohlin, G. (1981). Selective attention effects on the reflex blink. *Psychophysiology, 18,* 240–247.

Silverstein, L. D., Graham, F. K., & Calloway, J. M. (1980). Preconditioning and excitability of the human orbicularis oculi reflex as a function of state. *Electroencephalography & Clinical Neurophysiology, 48,* 406–417.

Skinner, J. E., & Yingling, C. D. (1977). Central gating mechanisms that regulate event-related potentials and behavior. In J. E. Desmedt (Ed.), *Attention, voluntary contraction, and event-related cerebral potentials. Progress in clinical neurophysiology* (Vol. 1, pp. 30–69). Basel, Switzerland: Karger.

Sokolov, E. N. (1963). *Perception and the conditioned reflex.* New York: Macmillan.

Sokolov, E. N. (1975). The neuronal mechanisms of the orienting reflex. In E. N. Sokolov & O. S. Vinogradova (Eds.), *Neuronal mechanisms of the orienting reflex* (pp. 217–235). Hillsdale, NJ: Lawrence Erlbaum Associates.

Sternberg, S. (1984). Stage models of mental processing and the additive-factor method. *Behavioral and Brain Sciences, 7,* 82–84.

Tallal, P., Galaburda, A. M., Llinas, R. R., & von Euler, C. (1993). Temporal information processing in the nervous system: Special reference to dyslexia and dysphasia. *Annals of the New York Academy of Sciences, 682.*

Theeuwes, J. (1995). Abrupt luminance change pops out; abrupt color change does not. *Perception & Psychophysics, 57,* 637–644.

Todd, J. T., & Van Gelder, P. (1979). Implications of a transient-sustained dichotomy for the measurement of human performance. *Journal of Experimental Psychology: Human Perception and Performance, 5,* 625–638.

Treisman, A. M., & Gelade, G. (1980). A feature-integration theory of attention. *Cognitive Psychology, 12,* 97–136.

Turpin, G. (1986). Effects of stimulus intensity on autonomic responding: The problem of differentiating orienting and defense reflexes. *Psychophysiology, 23,* 1–14.

Yingling, C. D., & Skinner, J. E. (1976). Selective regulation of thalamic sensory relay nuclei by nucleus reticularis thalami. *Electroencephalography & Clinical Neurophysiology, 41,* 476–482.

Author Index

A

Acredolo, L., 409, 410, *414*
Adamec, R. E., 383, *388*
Adams, D. B., 61, *64*
Adler, L. E., 273, *278*
Aggleton, J. P., 108, 112, *129*
Ahlfors, S., 319, *322, 323, 325*
Aine, C., 311, 320, *322, 323*
Aine, C. J., 436, *450*
Albin, R. L., 283, 288, *302*
Aldridge, V. J., 291, 297, *305*
Algazi, A., 318, *326*
Alho, K., 239, *254*, 307, 310, 311, 312, 314,
      315, 318, *322, 323, 324, 325, 326,*
      418, 436, 437
Allison, R. D., 49, 51, 53, 54, 56, 61, *66*
Altshuler, L. L., 273, *275*
Ameli, R., 112, *132*, 263, *277*
American Psychiatric Association, 262, *275*
Amir, N., 156, *162*
Anday, E. K., 186, *203*, 422, *450*
Anogianakis, G., 234, *254*
Anthony, B. J., 23, *39*, 48, *65*, 140, *162*, 168,
      182, 185, 193, 197, *203*, 206, 222,
      223, 230, 234, *252*, 259, *275*, 293,
      302, 349, 355, 356, 357, *366, 367,*
      374, 377, *388*, 422, 431, 432, 433,
      441, *448, 449*
Aranibar, A., 296, *304*
Arcus, D., 371, 381, *389*
Arduini, A., 290, *302*
Arehart, D., 363, *367*
Arnold, S. L., 259, 267, *277*

Arrindell, A., 153, *160*
Arthur, D. L., 236, *252*, 315, 316, 317, *322*
Askenazi, B., 193, *203*
Atwater, J. D., 334, *343*, 409, *415*
Aulanko, R., 313, *322*
Austen, B. G., 167, *182*
Austin, M., 49, 56, *65*
Austin, M. L., 148, *162*
Avendano, A., *388*, 422, *448*
Axelsson, M., 47, *64*

B

Baccelli, G., 61, *64*
Bachevalier, J., 380, *390*
Badier, J. M., 234, *253*, 421, *450*
Bagiella, E., 13, *22*
Baker, R., 207, *224*
Bai, D. L., 401, 402, 403, 409, 410, *412*
Baisel, E. J., 398, *415*
Balaban, M. T., 113, 129, 146, *160*, 234, 245,
      252, 254, 255, 278, 370, 371, 374,
      375, 377, *388*, 422, 431, 432, 441,
      442, 443, *448*
Baldwin, D. A., 405, *412*
Bali, L., 222, *224*, 263, *276*
Bancaud, J., 293, *303*
Bandler, R., 108, *131*
Barrett, G., 291, 297, *305*
Barrett, K., 406, 409, *412*
Barry, R. J., 140, 142, *160*
Barts, P., 290, *303*
Bausano, M., 397, *414*
Bayley, N., 397, *412*

453

Beale, D. K., 293, *302*
Beaton, R. D., 293, *303*
Beers, J. R., 27, *38*
Belkin, D. A., 51, 53, 55, 57, 58, 59, *64*
Bell, M., 410, *412*
Belliveau, J. W., 307, *322, 323, 325*
Benbow, C. H., 268, *278*
Bennett, J. A., 47, *64*
Berg, C. A., 369, 380, *388*
Berg, K. M., 61,*65, 92*, 347, 348, 349, 358, *366, 367, 388*, 422, *448*
Berg, W. K., 61, *65*, 143, *145, 161, 162*, 347, 348, 349, 350, 360, 361, 363, *366, 367*, 374, *388*, 422, 425, 426, 432, 441, 446, *448*
Berger, H., 295, *302*
Berger, T. W., 25, *40*
Berlyne, D. E., 98, *130*, 423, 446, *448*
Berman, P. W., xi
Bernstein, A. S., 23, *38, 167, 182*
Bernstein, E., 331, *345*
Berntson, G. G., 5, 6, 7, 8, 10, 11, 12, 14, 15, 17, *20, 21*, 56, 57, *64*, 98, 101, 123, 124, *130*, 141, 142, 146, *160*, 434, 435, *448, 449, 451*
Berry, S. D., 25, *40*
Bersine, L., 176, *183*
Bert, P., 55, *64*
Bertenthal, B. I., 400, 401, 402, 403, 406, 409, 410, *412, 413, 415*
Biedermann, J., 274, *277*
Binkley, P., 5, 11, 12, 14, 15, 17, *20, 21*
Birbaumer, N., 105, 116, 121, 122, *131, 134*, 432, *451*
Bjorkstrand, P. A., 186, *203*
Blanchard, D. C., 119, 120, *130*
Blanchard, R. J., 119, 120, *130*
Blaney, P. H., 110, *130*
Blevings, G., 150, *162*
Blix, A. S., 56, 59, 60, 61, *64*
Block, S. A., 364, *366*
Bloom, L., 395, *412*
Blumenthal, T. D., 121, *130*, 143, 145, *160, 161*, 219, *226*, 235, *252*, 267, *275, 388*, 421, 422, *448, 451*
Bock, G. R., 209, *225*
Boelhouer, A. J. W., 115, 205, *213*, 215, 216, 217, 220, *223, 224*, 230, 294, *302*, 420, 421, 427, 439, *448*
Bohlin, G., 143, *161*, 168, *182, 184*, 221, *227*, 230, 359, *366*, 427, 438, 445, *448, 451*
Boies, S. J., 176, *184*
Bond, N. W., 25, 26, 27, 29, *38, 40*
Bone, I., 222, *226*
Bonnet, M., 293, 295, *304*

Booth, M. L., 25, 26, 29, *40*
Borszcz, G. S., 377, *390*
Bots, T. A. M., 211, *227*
Boucsein, W., 143, 145, *163*
Boudoulas, H., 11, *20*
Bower, G. H., 110, *130*
Bowlby, J., 395, *413*
Boxwell, A. E., 350, 360, 363, *366, 367*
Boysen, S., 5, 8, 10, *20*
Boysen, S. T., 98, *130*, 141, 142, 146, *160*
Bradley, M. M., 102, 103, 104, 105, 106, 107, 110, 112, 113, 114, 115, 116, 117, 118, 121, 122, 124, 125, *130, 131, 132, 133, 134*, 148, *161, 162*, 166, *183*, 196, *203, 204*, 206, 207, 219, 220, 222, 223, *223, 226*, 294, *303*, 374, 377, 378, 386, *388, 390*, 423, 425, 428, 429, 430, 431, 432, 433, 446, *448, 449, 451*
Braff, D. L., 118, *134*, 208, 222, *224*, 263, 266, 268, 272, 273, *275, 276, 277, 278, 279*
Brandt, T., 401, 403, *413*
Braun, J. J., 108, *131*
Breitmeter, B. G., 444, *448*
Bremner, J. G., 408, 409, *413*
Brener, J., 221, *226*
Brennan, C., 333, *345*
Brenner, D., 319, *322*
Britain, S., 147, 148, 150, *162*
Britton, T. C., 209, *224*
Bronson, G. W., 370, *388*
Brooks, V. B., 285, *302*
Brown, J. S., 111, 117, *130*, 375, *388*
Brown, J. W., 439, *449*
Brown, P., 209, *224*
Bruner, J. S., 404, 405, *413, 414*
Brunia, C. H. M., 213, 215, 216, *223, 224*, 237, 253, 281, 282, 293, 294, 295, 298, 299, 300, *302, 303*, 423, 424, 427, 437, 441, 447, *448, 449*
Bubser, M., 272, *276, 277*
Buchwald, J. S., 233, *252*
Bullemer, P., 338, *343, 344*
Bullock, D., 394, *413*
Bullough, E., 98, *130*
Burchert, W., *323, 344*
Burger, J., 59, *64*
Burke, J., 214, 215, 217, 218, 219, 221, *224, 226*
Burnstock, G., 41, 43, *64*
Burr, W., 290, *303*
Bushnell, H. C., 4, *21*
Bushnell, M. C., 337, *345*
Butler, P. J., 47, 55, 56, *64, 66*
Butler, R. W., 268, *276*
Butters, N., 268, 272, 273, *279*

Butterworth, G. E., 395, 404, 405, *413*
Buttner-Ennever, J. A., 208, *227*

C

Cabrera, I. G., 108, *134*
Cacioppo, J. T., xxi, 5, 6, 7, 8, 9, 10, 11, 12, 14,
    15, 16, 17, *20, 21,* 56, 57, *64,* 101,
    119, 123, 124, *130,* 141, 142, 153,
    160, 161, 347, 398, 422, 425, 428,
    434, 435, 446, *448, 449*
Cadenhead, K., 266, 268, *276*
Cahill, L., 108, *130*
Caine, S. B., 118, *134,* 272, 273, *276, 279*
Calabresi, P., 333, *345*
Callander, R., 222, *226*
Callaway, E., 222, *224,* 263, *276*
Calloway, J. M., 421, *451*
Campbell, B. A., 4, 10, 11, 12, 19, *21,* 48, 49,
    50, 51, 54, 61, *65, 66,* 119, 124, 433,
    434, 445, *450*
Campeau, S., 270, 272, *276*
Campos, J. J., 372, 373, *388, 390,* 394, 398,
    400, 401, 402, 403, 404, 405, 406,
    407, 409, *412, 413, 414, 415,* 431,
    442, *449*
Campos, R. G., 372, *388*
Canfield, R. L., 364, *366*
Cannon, W. B., 52, *64*
Carew, T. J., 24, *38*
Caron, A. J., 373, 378, *388*
Caron, R. F., 373, 378, *388*
Carver, L., 378, *390*
Casey, B. J., 142, 144, *163,* 349, 351, 354, *368*
Caspers, 290, *302*
Cassanova, M., 273, *278*
Cassella, J. V., 208, *224*
Castellanos, F. X., 268, *276*
Caudill, W., 335, *343*
Causby, L. A., 61, *64*
Celesia, G. G., 234 *252*
Chapman, J., 263, *277*
Chapman, J. G., 121, *131*
Chapman, J. P., 266, *276*
Chapman, L. J., 266, *276*
Charney, D. S., 263, *277*
Chase, W. G., 150, *161,* 359, *366*
Chaudhuri, K. R., 268, 273, *278*
Chauvel, P., 233, 234, *253, 278, 293, 303,* 421,
    450
Chen, H., 405, 407, *413, 414,* 431, 442
Chen, X., 240, *252,* 424, 442
Cheyne, D., 297, *303*
Christison, M. D., 273, *278*
Chugani, H. T., 330, *343*
Churcher, J., 395, *413*

Chwilla, D. J., 298, *302*
Ciranni, M., 238, *252,* 259, *276*
Clark, L. A., 114, *135*
Clayworth, C. C., 247 *253*
Clifton, R. K., xix, 3, 4, 19, *21,* 49, 53, *65,* 119,
    124, *131,* 139, 140, 142, *162,* 347,
    359, 361, *366, 367,* 398, *414*
Clohessy, A. B., 331, 338, 339, 340, *343,* 358,
    366
Clore, G. L., 100, *133*
Coghill, R., 4, *21*
Cohen, D., 319, *389*
Cohen, D. H., 47, 60, *64, 66*
Cohen, L. B., 350, *366*
Cohen, L. H., 259, *276*
Cohen, M. E., *185, 186, 187, 189, 190, 191,
    192, 193, 203,* 221, *224,* 230 *252,*
    422, *450*
Cohn, J. F., 373, *391*
Coldren, J. T., 334, *343*
Coles, M. G. H., 116, *134,* 231, *253,* 359, *367*
Collins, A., 100, *133*
Collins, K., *389*
Colombo, J., 334, *343,* 370, *389*
Conrad, A., 273, *275*
Cook, E. W., III, 114, 121, 124, 128, *132,* 148,
    149, 150, 151, 153, 154, 155, 156,
    161, 162, 250, 425, 430
Cooper, R., 291, 297, *305*
Cooper, W. E., 49, *64*
Coquery, J. M., 199, *203*
Corbetta, M., 328, 329, 340, *343*
Cosmides, L., 180, *184*
Courchesne, E., 239, 245, 247, 250, 251, *252,*
    424, 425, *449*
Courtice, G., 59, *64*
Cowey, A., 4, *21*
Cranney, J., 186, 187, 189, 190, 191, 192, 193,
    203, 221, *224,* 230, *252*
Craw, M. A., 446, *448*
Crawford, M., 120, 126, *133*
Creps, C. L., 267, *275*
Crescione, C., 378, *390*
Cross, H., 397, *414*
Crowder, W. E., 49, 51, 53, 54, 56, 61, *66*
Crutcher, M. D., 285, 286, *303*
Cuffin, B. N., 319, *325*
Curran, T., 338, 340, *343*
Curtis, S., 316, *322*
Cuthbert, B. N., 102, 103, 104, 105, 106, 107,
    110, 112, 113, 114, 115, 116, 117,
    118, 121, 122, 124, 125, *130, 131,
    132, 133, 134,* 148, *161,* 166, 173,
    183, 196, *203, 204,* 206, 207, 219,
    220, 222, *223, 226,* 294, *303,* 374,
    377, 378, *388, 390*

D

Dall, P. J., 33, *40*, 428, *451*
Damen, E. J. P., 298, *302*
Danilova, N. N., 17, 18, *21*
Dannemiller, J. L., 372, *389*
Darwin, C., 372, *389*
Davidson, B. J., 195, *204*
Davidson, R. J., 372, *389*
Davies, M. G., *388*, 422, *448*
Davis, C. M., 293, *303*
Davis, H., 234, *252*
Davis, M., *92*, 109, 111, 120, *131*, 153, *161*,
        207, 208, 223, *224*, *226*, 230, *252*,
        270, 272, *276*, *277*, 294, *303*, 375,
        379, *389*, 419, 420, 423, *451*
Davis, T. L., 114, 121, 124, 128, *131*, 153, 154,
        156, *161*
Davison, W., 47, *64*
Dawson, M. E., 23, 27, *38*, 115, 118, 176, *182*,
        230, 260, 261, 263, 264, 265, 267,
        274, *276*, *277*, *278*, 420, 421, 439,
        440, 447, *449*
Day, B. L., 209, *224*
De Carvalho, M. C., 52, 54, 57, 61, 62, *66*
De Oca, B. M., 108, 109, 120, *131*
Dearing, M. F., 100, *131*
DeCola, J. P., 108, 109, 120, *131*
Deecke, L., 291, 297, 299, *303*
Dehaene, S., 328, 340, *344*
DeLong, M. R., 285, 286, *303*
DelPezzo, E. M., *193, 194, 195, 196, 203*, 260,
        276
Depaulis, A., 108, *131*
Derryberry, D., 335, *345*, 431, *451*
Desimone, R., 319, *324*
DeTraversay, J., 268, *278*
DeVido, C. J., 230, *255*
Diamond, A., 395, 396, 406, *413*
Diamond, D. M., 238, *255*
DiCara, L., 108, *131*
Dichgans, J., 401, 403, *413*
Dickerson, D. J., 409, *414*
Dickinson, A., 100, *131*
Dillon, M. C., 114, *132*
Dimberg, U., 146, *161*, 169, 170, 173, 177, *182*,
        184, 372, 379, *390*
Dobmeyer, S., 328, *343*
Doering, D. G., 196, *203*
Donchin, E., 116, *134*, 220, 222, 223, *226*, 231,
        239, 240, 241, 242, 243, *250*, *252*,
        253, 255, 294, 303, 374, 377, 378,
        388, 390, 437, *449*
Dong, Q., 431, 442
Donohue, R. L., 350, 358, 360, 361, 363, *366*,
        367

Dorato, K. H., 116, *134*, 429, *451*
Dore, J., 341, *343*
Drevets, W. C., 337, *343*
Driver, J., 329, 335, 343, *344*
Drobes, D. J., 117, 118, *131*, *133*
Drummond, P. C., 57, *64*
Duncan, G. H., 4, *21*, 337, *345*
Duncan-Johnson, C. C., 239, *252*, 359, *367*,
        443, *449*
Dunham, P., 395, *414*
Dykman, B. M., 185, *203*

E

Echallier, J. F., 234, *253*
Eckblad, M., 266, *276*
Edrich, J., 236, *254*
Egly, R., 329, 335, 343, *344*
Ellis, C., 268, 273, *278*
Emde, R. N., 373, *390*, 394, *413*
Emmelkamp, P. M. G., 153, *160*
Endtz, L. J., 211, *227*
English, G. E., 381, *390*
Eriksen, C. W., 444, *449*
Erwin, R., 233, *252*
Espmark, Y., 55, 61, *64*
Esteves, F., 126, *133*, 168, 170, 171, 173, 174,
        177, *182, 184*
Evans, A., 4, *21*
Evans, A. C., 337, *345*
Evans, D. H., 41, *64*
Evarts, E. V., 297, *305*
Everitt, B. J., 108, *131*, 369, 379, *390*
Eves, F. F., 144, 155, 158, *161*
Evinger, C., 207, 208, 218, 220, *224*, *226*
Exner, S., 206, 223, *224*

F

Fabiani, M., 243, *252*
Fabro, V. T., 7, 9, *20*, 124, *130*
Falck, B., 45, *64*
Falls, W. A., 270, 272, *276*
Fanselow, M. S., 108, 109, 120, 126, *131*
Fantz, R. L., 347, *367*
Farber, I. E., 111, *130*, 375, *388*
Farrell, A. P., 47, *64*
Fearing, F., 206, 207, *224*
Feeny, E. X., 99, *134*
Feldon, J., 273, 274, *277*
Fendt, M., 111, 120, *131*
Fernald, A., 373, 375, *389*
Fernandez, 128, *134*
Fernandez, M. C., 144, 158, *161*, *163*
Fetz, E., 444, *450*

Field, T. M., 372, *389*
Fieldstone, A., 5, 12, 14, 15, 17, *20, 21*
File, S. E., 230, *252*
Filion, D. L., 115, 118, 230, 238, *252*, 259, 260, 261, 263, 264, 265, 267, 268, *276, 277, 278, 279,* 420, 421, 439, 440, 447, *449*
Fine, E. J., 268, *276*
Fiorito, E., 231, 232, 233, *254*, 259, 266, *276, 278,* 421, *451*
Fischer, K., 394, *413*
Fishkin, P. E., 13, *22*
Fleshler, M., 199, *203*, 439, *450*
Flykt, A., 126, *133*, 168, 174, *184*
Flynn, E. R., 236, *252*, 315, 316, *322*
Forbes, E. J., 360, *367*
Ford, J.M., 313, *322*
Forester, W. F., 11, *21*
Forster, M. E., 47, *64*
Foss, J. A., 210, 213, 221, *225, 227*
Fox, K. B., 373, *389*
Fox, N. A., 372, 379, *389*, 410, *412*
Fox, P. T., *344*
Franklin, C. E., 58, *67*
Franklin, M. M., 341, *343*
Frazelle, J., 148, 150, *162*
Fredrikson, M., 150, *161*, 173, *182*
Freedman, D., 395, *413*
Freedman, R., 273, *278*
Friauf, E., 272, *277*
Friedman, D., 247, *252*
Friedman, J. H., 331, *345*
Frijda, N. H., 99, 113, *131, 132*
Frints, C. J. M., 216, 217, *223*
Froment, J. C., 234, *253*
Frost, L., 335, *343*
Frysinger, R. C., 48, *65*
Fukunga, K. K., 120, *130*
Furedy, J. J., 28, *39, 203,* 186, 187

G

Gabrielsen, G. W., 56, 59, 60, 61, *64*
Gaddy, J. R., 48, *66*
Gaensbauer, T. J., 394, *413*
Gaillard, A. W. K., 295, 297, *304,* 310, 311, *325*
Galaburda, A. M., 329, *343*, 444, *452*
Galambos, R., 239, *252*, 424, 425, *449*
Gallagher, M., 48, *65*
Gallup, G. G., *343, 344*
Gans, C., 53, 55, 61, *64*
Ganz, L., 444, *448*
Garcia, J., 177, *182*
Garcia, R., *389*

Garcia-Coll, C., 383, *389*
Garcia–Rill, E., 274, *277*
Garner, E. E., 350, 360, 363, *366, 367*
Gatchel, R. J., 34, *39*
Gaunt, A. S., 53, 55, 61, *64*
Gautier, C. H., 114, 121, 124, 128, *131*, 153, 154, 155, 156, *161*
Gazzaniga, M. S., 329, *344*
Geddings, V. J., 121, *133*
Gelade, G., 418, *452*
Gemba, H., 291, 297, *305*
Gendelman, D., 270, *276*
Gendelman, D. S., 207, *224*
Gendelman, P., 270, *276*
Genofre, G. C., 56, *66*
Gentile, C. G., 61, *64*
Georgopoulos, A. P., 285, 286, *303*
Gerardi, G., 338, 339, *343, 344,* 350, 424, 425, 426, 431, 436, 441, 442, *448*
Gerfen, C. R., 273, *278*
Gescheider, G. A., 235, *252*
Geschwind, N., 288, *304*, 329, *343*
Geyer, D., 207, 227, 234, *254, 279*
Geyer, M. A., 118, *134*, 208, 217, 222, *224,* 227, 263, 266, 268, 272, 273, *275, 276, 278*
Gianaros, P., 114, *130*
Giard, M. H., 234, *253*, 318, *323*
Giardina, B. D., 230, *253*, 266, *278*
Gibson, E. J., 371, *389*, 397, *414*
Gibson, J. J., 401, *414*
Gitlin, M., 23, *38*, 264, *278*
Gjedde, A., 4, *21*
Gjerdingen, D. B., 234, *252*
Glick, I., 222, *224*, 263, *276*
Globisch, J., 106, 114, 124, 125, *132*, 173, *183*, 430, 432, *450*
Goates, D. W., 153, *161*
Gochfeld, M., 59, *64*
Godoy, J., 144, 158, *163*
Goff, D. M., 60, *64*
Goldberg, M. E., 283, *304*
Goldfield, E. C., 409, *414*
Goldman-Rakic, P. S., 393, 395, *414*
Goldstein, M. J., 264, *278*
Goldstein, R., 206, *224*
Goode, C. T., 143, 145, *161*
Goodman, G. S., 338, *344,* 350, 358, 363,*367*
Gorham, D. R., 264, *278*
Gorman, J. M. 13, *22*
Gos, A., *344*
Gottlieb, G., 397, *414*
Grafton, S. T., 342, *343*
Graham, D. T., 150, *161*, 359, *366*
Graham, F. K., ix, x, xi, xii, xiii, xiv, xx, 3, 4, 19, *21,* 23, 24, 28, 31, 34, 37, *38, 39,*

48, 49, 50, 53, 60, 61, 62, *65, 67,* 98,
   111, 115, 118, 119,121, 124, 126,
   131, 138, 139, 140, 141, 142, 143,
   144, 145, 147, 148, 149, 150, 151,
   155, *161, 162,* 166, 167, 168, 173,
   183, 185, 188, 193, 197, *203, 204,*
   205, 206, 208, 209, 213, 214, 217,
   218, 219, 220, 221, *224, 225, 227,*
   230, 231, 232, 233, 240, 245, 251,
   252, 253, 254, 255, 257, 258, 259,
   260, 266, *276, 277, 278,* 293, *302,*
   327, *344,* 348, 349, 355, 356, 357,
   359, 365, *366, 367, 368,* 398, *414*
Grant, D. A., 206, 211, 219, *224*
Gratton, G., 231, 235, 240, 243, *252, 253, 254*
Graveland, G. A., 208, 209, 211, *225*
Gray, J. A., 25, *39,* 266, 273, 274, *277, 278*
Gray, N. S., 266, 268, 273, *278*
Greenberg, R., *389*
Greenwald, M. K., 103, 104, 106, 107, 112,
   130, 132, 133, 148, *162,* 386, *388,*
   430, *448*
Grigg, G. C., 58, *67*
Grillon, C., 112, *132,* 263, *275, 277*
Grings, W. W., 186, *203*
Grossman, P., 12, *21*
Grossman, S. E., 363, *367*
Grover, L., 405, *413*
Groves, P. M., 23, 24, 34, 36, *39,* 427, *449*
Gruzelier, J. H., 144, 155, 158, *161*
Guillery, R. W., 288, *304*
Gulyas, B., 4, *21*
Gunderson, V. M., 334, *344*
Gusella, J. L., 373, *389*
Guthrie, D., 230, *253,* 374, *390*

H

Haagh, S. A. V. M., 293, 295, 300, *302*
Habib, R., 4, *22*
Hackley, S. A., 23, *39,* 115, 143, *162,* 166, 168,
   183, 205, 206, 208, 209, 211, 212,
   214, 215, 216, 217, 218, 219, 220,
   221, *224, 225, 226, 227,* 230, 236,
   253, 260, *277,* 311, *326,* 374, *389,*
   418, 420, 421, 422, 427, 438, 439,
   441, 445, *448, 449, 450*
Hager, J. E., 177, *184*
Haggard, E., 186, *203*
Haith, M. M., 338, 339, *344,* 350, 358, 363,
   364, *366, 367*
Hall, G., 23, *39*
Hallett, M., 268, *276*
Hämäläinen, M., 236, *254,* 307, 313, 316, 317,
   319, *322, 323, 324, 325*
Hamburger, S. D., 268, *276*

Hamm, A. O., 103, 104, 106, 107, 112, 113,
   114, 124, 125, *130, 132, 133,* 148,
   162, 173, *183,* 430, 432, *450*
Hammond, G. R., 213, *225,* 230, *253*
Hampton, C., 176, *183*
Hanna, G. L., 268, *278*
Hansen, C. H., 173, 174, 175, 176, *183*
Hansen, R. D., 173, 174, 175, 176, *183*
Harbin, T. J., *388,* 422, *448*
Hare, R. D., 147, 148, 150, 151, *162*
Hari, R., 235, 236, *253, 254,* 307, 311, 313, 315,
   316, 317, *322, 323, 324, 325*
Harley, J. P., 30, *39*
Harman, C., 332, 333, 337, *344*
Harmon, R. J., 394, *413*
Haroutunian, V., 48, 49, *65,* 433, *450*
Harris, P. L., 380, *389,* 408, *414*
Harris, W. S., 11, *21*
Harrison, R. J., 56, *65*
Harter, M. R., 311, *323,* 436, *450*
Haselton, J. R., 48, *65*
Hashimoto, S., 291, 297, *305*
Hatton, H. M., 61, *65,* 143, *162,* 347, *367*
Haviland, J. M., 373, 375, 377, *389*
Hawk, L. W., 114, 121, 124, 128, *132,* 153, 154,
   155, 156, *161, 162*
Hawkins, R., 98, *134*
Hayne, H., 48, *65*
Hazan, C., 338, *344,* 350, 358, 363, *367*
Hazelton, E., 342, *343*
Hazlett, E. A., 261, 263, 264, 265, 267, *276*
Hebb, D. O., 99, *132, 278*
Heilman, K. M., 283, 288, *306*
Hein, A., 398, *414,* 442, *450*
Heinze, H. J., 311, 319, *323, 324,* 328, *344*
Heise, B., 299, *303*
Held, R., 398, *414,* 442, *450*
Helmholz, H. von., 193, *203*
Hembree, E., 372, *390*
Hemsley, D. R., 273, 274, *277*
Henik, A., 331, *345*
Henneman, E., 444, *450*
Herbert, H., 272, *277*
Herning, R. I., 239, 240, 241, 242, 243, *255*
Heron, P. A., 25, 30, *40*
Hess, M., 54, 61, *66*
Hess, W. R., 100, *132*
Heywood, C., 4, *21*
Higgins, C. I., 402, 403, *414*
Hilgard, E. R., 213, *225*
Hillman, C. H., 117, 118, *131,* 429, *449*
Hillyard, S. A., 209, *225,* 236, 239, 240, 241,
   242, *252, 253, 255,* 309, 310, 311,
   314, 316, 318, 319, *322, 323, 324,*
   325, 326, 328, 329, *344,* 424, 425,
   449

Hink, R. F., 309, *323*
Hiraoka, M., 210, *225*
Hirata, I., 291, 297, *305*
Hirschhorn, T., 26, 36, *40*
Hitchcock, J., 111, *131*
Hitchcock, J. M., 153, *161*, 423, *451*
Hnatiow, M., 124, *133*
Hodes, R. L., 149–152, *161*, *162*
Hodge, C. F., 210, *225*
Hofer, M. A., 55, *65*
Hoffman, E. J., 307, *325*
Hoffman, H. S., 118, 121, 185, 186, 187, 188,
    189, 190, 191, 192, 193, 194, 195,
    196, 199, 200, 201, *203*, *204*,
    206–208, 217, 221, *224*, *225*, 230,
    252, *253*, *255*, 257, 259, 260, 273,
    276, *277*, 420, 421, 422, 426, 438,
    439, 445, *450*
Hoke, M., 234, *254*
Holender, D., 171, *183*
Holmgren, S., 41, 43, 45, 47, *66*
Holstege, G., 208, 209, 211, *225*
Hopf, H. C., 207, *226*, 234, *254*
Hori, A., 208, *225*
Horner, K. C., 209, *225*
Horobin, K., 409, 410, *414*
Horowitz, F. D., 373, *391*
Houck, R. L., 28, *39*
Houle, S., 4, *22*
Howard, J. L., 295, *304*
Hubel, D. H., 330, *344*
Huckeby, E. R., 373, *389*
Hugdahl, K., 369, 379, *391*
Hull, 116, *132*
Hunt, P. S., 50, 54, *65*
Hunt, W., 293, 294, *303*
Hunt, W. A., 111, *132*, 207, *225*, 419, *450*
Huotilainen, M., 312, 321, *323, 324*
Husain, M. M., 274, *277*
Huttunen, J., 236, *253*
Huxley, F. M., 56, *65*
Hyvarinen, J., 210, *227*

I

Ilinsky, L. A., 294, *303*
Ilmoniemi, R. J., 307, 312, 313, 319, *322, 323,
    325,* 418, 436, 437
Inhoff, A. W., 331, *345*
Ison, J. R., 117, *132*, 185, 188, 193, 199, 200,
    201, *203*, *204*, 207, 208, 210, 213,
    217, 221, *225*, *226*, *227*, 230, *253*,
    254, 257, *277*, 426, *450*
Ivry, R., 342, *343*

Iwata, J., *132*
Izard, C. E., 369, 370, 372, 374, 379, *389, 390*

J

Jackson, J., 61, *65*
Jackson, J. C., 347, *367*
Jackson, J. E., 56, *66*
Jackson, S., 342, *344*
Jacobs, B. L., 213, 214, *227*
Jacobsen, N. K., 55, *65*
James, W., 99, *132*, 349, *367*, 370, *389*
Jansen, D. M., 113, *132*
Jarrel, T. W., 61, *64*
Jaskiw, G. E., 272, 273, *279*
Jasper, H. H., 290, *303*, *304*
Jellestad, F., 108, *134*
Jenkins, M. A., 268, *276*
Jennings, P. D., 261, *277*
Jessel, T. M., 419, 423, *450*
Jiang, D., 311, 313, *325*
Johannes, S., *344*
Johnson, C., 55, *67*
Johnson, L. N., 211, 214, *225*
Johnson, M. H., 330, 338, *344*, 358, *367*
Jones, D. R., 55, 56, 57, *64*
Jordan, D., 47, *65*
Jordan, J., 30, 31, 32, *40*
Joutsiniemi, S. L., 313, 316, *323, 324*
Juola, J. F., 419, *450*

K

Kagan, J., 3, 19, *21,* 347, *367*, 370, 371, 373,
    380, 381, 383, 384, 385, 387, *389,
    390,* 396, 409, *414,* 422, 431, 432,
    441, 442, 443, *450*
Kaila, K., 235, *253*
Kalish, H. I., 111, *130*, 375, *388*
Kalus, D. F., 268, *278*
Kandel, E. R., 223, *225*, 419, 423, *450*
Kantowitz, S., 61, *65*, 347, *367*
Kao, C.-Q., 337, *344*
Kaplan, A. R., 374, *390*
Kaplan, P. S., 373, *389*
Kapp, B. S., 48, *65*
Kapur, S., 4, *22*
Karemaker, J. K., 12, *21*
Karis, D., 243, *252*
Karlin, L., 309, *324*
Karson, C. N., 274, *277*
Kaspi, S. P., 156, *162*
Katila, T., 235, *253*

Kaufman, L., 316, 319, 320, *324*
Kaukoranta, E., 313, 316, *323, 324*
Kaysen, D. L., 268, *276*
Keane, J. R., 211, *225*
Kearsley, R., 396, 409, *414*
Keefe, R. S. E., 268, *278*
Keele, S. W., 338, 340, *343*
Kehne, J. H., 207, *224*
Kelley, N. G., 186, *203*
Kelly, A., 27, *38*
Kelly, J. P., 282, 287, *303*
Kermoian, R., 372, *388*, 394, 400, 402, 403,
    404, 405, 406, 407, 409, *413, 414,*
    415, 431, 442
Kerr, B., 27, *39*
Kestenbaum, R., 373, *390*
Khan, T., 196, *203*
Kidd, C., 47, *64*
Kilman, B. A., 239, *252,* 424, 425, *449*
Kim, H. S., 153, *161*
Kim, M., 270, 272, *276*
Kimble, G. A., 221, *225*
Kirson, D., 100, *134*
Kjellberg, A., 143, *161,* 359, *367*
Klajner, F., 186, 187, *203*
Kleiner, K. A., 372, *390*
Klimesch, W., 296, *304*
Klinnert, M. D., 373, *390*
Klorman, R., 124, *132,* 148, 149, 150, 152, *162*
Knight, R. T., 239, 247, *253*
Knoll, G. F., 307, *324*
Knuutila, J., 307, 312, *323, 324*
Koch, M., 111, 117, 120, *131, 134,* 272, *276, 277*
Kodsi, M., 273, *277*
Koellig, R. A., 177, *182*
Kolbert, E., 99, *132*
Konorski, J., 100, 110, *132,* 137, *162*
Koob, G. F., 273, 274, *279*
Kopell, B. S., 116, *134,* 429, 443, *449, 451*
Kornhuber, H. H., 291, 297, 299, *303*
Koshino, H., 419, *450*
Kovelman, J. A., 273, *275*
Kozuch, P. L., 268, *276*
Kramer, A., 440, *450*
Kramer, A. F., 116, *134*
Krauter, E. E., 117, *132,* 188, *203,* 207, 213,
    217, *225,* 230, *253*
Kremen, I., 101, *133*
Kristal, J., 263, *277*
Kristeva, R., 297, *303*
Krowitz, A., 398, *413*
Kugelberg, E., 209, *225*
Kujala, T., 313, 314, *324*
Kultas-Ilinsky, K., 294, *303*
Kungel, M., 272, *277*
Kuo, Z. Y., 397, *414*

Kuriki, S., 318, *324*
Kurtz, M. W., 434, *450*
Kuypers, H. G. H. M., 209, 217, *226*
Kwapil, T. R., 266, *276*

L

Lacey, B. C., xx, 3, 19, *21,* 49, *65,* 101, 119,
    132, 138, 148, *162, 163,* 295, 298,
    303, 359, *367,* 441, *450*
Lacey, J. I., xx, 3, 19, *21,* 49, *65,* 101, 119, 125,
    132, 138, 148, *162, 163,* 295, 298,
    303, 359, *367,* 441, *450*
Laitano, S. Y., 56, *66*
Laming, P. R., 49, 56, *65*
Landeira-Fernandez, J., 108, 109, 120, *131*
Landis, C., 111, *132,* 207, *225,* 293, 294, *303,*
    419, *450*
Lane, S. J., 230, *253,* 374, *390*
Lang, M., 299, *303*
Lang, P. J., 100, 101, 102, 103, 104, 105, 106,
    107, 110, 113, 114, 115, 116, 117,
    118 121, 122, 124, 125, *130, 131,*
    132, 133, 134, 148, 149, 150, 151,
    153, *161, 162, 164,* 166, *183,* 196,
    203, 204, 206, 207, 219, 220, 222,
    223, 225, 226, 294, *303,* 359, *367,*
    374, 377, 378, 386, *388, 390*
Lang, W., 297, 298, *303*
Langer, A., 398, *413*
Langsdorf, P., 372, *390*
Langvatin, R., 55, 61, *64*
Larson, S. L., 214, 215, 219, 221, *226*
Latbier, B. C., 363, *367*
Latif, A. B., 47, *64*
Lavikainen, J., 312, 313, 315, *322, 325*
Lazarus, R. S., 170, *183*
Leaton, R. N., 377, *390*
LeDoux, J. E., 108, 109, *132, 133,* 160, *162,*
    169, *183,* 423, *450*
Lee, D. N., 401, *414*
Lee, Y., 208, *226,* 270, *277*
Lehnertz, K., 234, *254*
Leigh, P. N., 268, 273, *278*
Leighton, R. F., 11, *21*
Leitner, D. S., 217, *226,* 273, *277,* 421, *450*
Lelwica, M., 373, 375, 377, *389*
Lennon, E., 373, *391*
Leonard, D. W., 188, *203,* 230, *253*
Leong, S. K., 47, *65*
Lesérve, N., 311, 312, *325*
Levenston, G. K., 115, 121, *133*
Lewicki, P., 179, *183*
Lewis, J. L., 446, *448*
Lewis, P. S., 236, *252,* 315, *322*
Lewis, R. P., 11, *21*

Libby, W. L., 148, *163*
Liegeois-Chauvel, C., 233, 234, *253*, 293, *303*, 421, *450*
Lillo, R. S., 56, 57, 58, *65*
Lincoln, A. J., 239, *252*, 424, 425, *449*
Lindinger, G., 297, *303*
Lindquist, L., 209, *226*
Lindsay, K. W., 222, *226*
Lindsley, D. B., 291, 292, *305*
Lingenholh, K., 272, *277*
Lipke, H. J., 381, *390*
Lipp, O. V., 33, *40*, 267, *277,* 358, 427, 428, *451*
Lipska, B. K., 272, 273, *279*
Lishman, J. R., 401, *414*
Lishman, W. A., 266, 268, *278*
Liu, G. T., 210, *226*
Llinas, R. R., 444, *452*
Lojewski, D., 34, *39*
Lombruso, U., 56, *66*
Lopes da Silva, F. H., 290, *303*
Lopez, D., 208, *226*
Lopez, D. E., 270, 272, *277*
Losch, M. E., 153, *161*
Losito, B. D. G., 375, *388*
Lounasmaa, O. V., 307, 313, *322, 323, 324*
Loveless, N. E., 236, 237, *253, 254*, 291, 297, *303*, 311, *325*
Low, K. A., 214, 215, 219, 221, *226*
Luber, B., 320, *324*
Luck, S. J., 311, 319, *323, 324,* 328, 329, *344*
Lukoff, D., 264, *277*
Lukomskaya, N. J., 45, *66*
Luscher, H.-R., 444, *450*
Lutkenhoner, B., 234, *254*
Lykken, D. T., 186, 192, *204*
Lynn, R., 167, *183*

M

Mackintosh, N. J., 37, *38, 39*
MacLean, D. J., 373, 378, *388*
MacLeod, C., 137, 158, *160, 163*, 381, 384, *390*
MacLeod, C. M., 380, *390*
MacMillan, N. A., 444, *450*
MacWilliam, P. N., 47, *64*
Macy, M. H., 245, *254*
Magliero, A., 34, *39*
Magoun, H. W., 423, *451*
Mäkelä, J., 316, *323*
Malatesta, C. Z., 369, 374, 379, *389*
Maltzman, I., 140, 142, *160*, 167, *184*, 186, *204*
Mancia, G., 61, *64*
Mancia, M., 290, *302*
Mandler, G., 101, *133*

Mandler, J. M., 101, *133*
Mangun, G. R., 311, 319, *323, 324*, 329, *344*
Manning, K. A., 207, 218, 220, *224, 226*
Mäntysalo, S., 310, *325*
Marcel, A., 171, *183*
Maresh, H., 296, 299, *304*
Markowitsch, H. J., 4, *22*
Marquis, P., 234, *253*, 421, *450*
Marrett, A., 337, *345*
Marrocco, R., 342, *344*
Marsden, C. D., 209, *224*
Marsh, R. R., 185, 186, *204*
Martensson, A., 209, *226*
Massion, J., 288, *303*
Masterson, F. A., 120, 126, *133*
Matas, L., 404, *415*
Matheny, L., 378, *390*
Mathews, A., 137, 158, *160, 163*, 381, 384, *390*
Mathews, G., 156, *164*
Maunsell, J. H., 319, *325*
Mauritz, K. H., 297, *306*
Mayr, U., 342, *344*
Mazziotta, J. C., 330, *343*
McAdam, D. W., 213, *225*, 230, *253*
McBride, T., 433, 434
McCabe, P. M., 61, *64*
McCall, R. B., 370, *390*
McCallum, W. C., 291, 297, *305*
McCarthy, G., 239, 240, 241, 242, 243, *255*
McClelland, J. L., 444, *451*
McGaugh, J. L., 108, *130*
McGhie, A., 263, *277*
McHaffie, J. G., 337, *344*
McManis, M., 114, *133*, 429, *449*
McMurtry, K., 288, *304*
McNally, R. J., 156, *162*, 381, 384, *390*
Mechelse, K., 290, *302*
Mecklenburg, C. V., 45, *64*
Medvick, P. A., 236, *252*, 315, *322*
Mefferd, R. B., Jr., 28, *39*
Mehrabian, A., 101, 102, *133*
Mellers, J., 266, 268, *278*
Meloni, E., 208, *226*
Meloni, E. G., 270, 272, *277*
Meltzoff, A. N., 342, *344*
Melvill-Jones, G., 293, *305*
Merikangas, 112, *132*
Merikle, P. M., 171, *183*
Mesulam, M. M., 283, 284, 288, *304*
Meyer, E., 4, *21,* 337, *345*
Michelson, M. J., 45, *66*
Michie, P. T., 310, 315, *325*
Miezen, F. M., 328, *343*
Miles, M. A., 245, 247, *254, 255*, 425, *450*
Miller, G. A., 235, 240, 247, *254*
Miller, M. W., 121, *133*

Miller, N. E., 123, *133*
Miller, R. T., 341, *343*
Mintun, M., *344*
Mintz, J., 264, *278*
Miserendino, M. J. D., 423, *451*
Mishkin, M., 108, *129*, 342, *344*
Mitchell, D. W., 334, *343*
Mitrofanis, J., 288, *304*
Mizner, G., 273, *278*
Mizuno, N., 291, 297, *305*
Moberly, W. R., 59, *66*
Mogenson, G. J., 273, *278*
Montoya, C., 364, *366*
Moore, C., 395, *414*
Moran, J., 319, *324*
Morin, C., 293, *303*
Morris, J. L., 43, *66*
Morrison, P., 61, *66*
Morton, N., 266, 273, *278*
Moruzzi, G., 423, *451*
Moss, H. A., 3, 19, *21*
Moss, M. A., 347, *367*
Mountcastle, V. B., 328, *344*
Mrak, R. E., 274, *277*
Muir, D., 373, *389*
Mullani, M.A., 307, *325*
Mumme, D. L., 372, *388*
Münte, T. F., 311, *323*
Murase, M., 318, *324*
Murdaugh, H. V., 56, *66*
Murray, E. A., 342, *344*
Murray, G. M., 188, *203*, 230, *253*
Musolino, A., 233, 234, *253*, 293, *303*, 421, *450*
Myers, M. M., 13, *22*
Myhrberg, H., 45, *64*

N

Näätänen, R., 220, *226*, 234, 237, *254*, 307, 309, 310, 311, 312, 313, 314, 315, 318, 321, *322, 323, 324,* 418, 420, 422, 436, 437, 440, 444, 447, *451*
Naito, H., 208, 211, *227*
Nakashima, K., 215, *226*
Nathanson, M., 167, *182*
Neisser, U., 372, *390*
Nelson, C. A., 373, 378, 379, *390*
Neshige, R., 291, 297, *305*
Neuringer, A., 146, *160*
Nickerson, R., 214, *226*
Niewenhuys, R., 45, 46, *66*
Nikundlwe, A. M., 46, *66*
Nilsson, S., 41, 42, 43, 45, 47, *66*
Nissen, M. J., 338, *343, 344*
Nordby, H., 313, *325*
Norling, R., 122, *133*

Norman, R. J., 374, *390*
Norris, C. M., 219, *226*, 421, *451*
Nuechterlein, K. H., 23, *38,* 261, 263, 264, 265, *276, 277, 278*

O

O'Connor, C., 100, *134*
Obrist, P. A., 120, *133*, 295, *304*
O'Gorman, J. G., 24, 25, *39*
O'Herron, F., 196, *203*
Öhman, A., 23, 31, *39*, 116, 126, *133*, 156, 157, 159, *160, 163,* 167, 168, 169, 170, 171, 172, 173, 174, 176, 178, 180, 181, *182, 183, 184,* 359, *367,* 372, 379, *390,* 419, 437, 444, 445, 447, *451*
Olvera, 234, *255*
Ongerboer de Visser, B. W., 209, 217, *226*
Ornitz, E. M., 230, *253,* 268, *278, 374, *390*
Ortony, A., 100, *133*
Osgood, C., 100, *133*
Ost, J. W. P., 221, *225*
Öst, L.-G., 169, *184*
Osterhammel, P. A., 234, *252*
Overall, J. E., 264, *278*
Overman, W., 380, *390*

P

Paavilainen, P., 311, 312, 313, 314, *322, 325*
Packer, J. J., 25, 26, 27, 29, *38, 40*
Paillard, J., 293, *304*
Palmatier, A. D., 153, *161*
Pandya, D. N., 288, *304*
Pantev, C., 234, *254*
Papaconstantinou, V., 196, *203*
Papas, B., 108, *131*
Papez, J. W., 423, *451*
Pardo, P. J., 313, *325*
Parisi, T., 207, *224*
Parra, C., 177, 178, *182*
Passingham, 291, 297, 298, *304*
Patrick, C. J., 115, 121, *133*
Paulsen, J., 268, 272, 273, *279*
Pavlov, I. P., xix, 1, *21,* 23, *39,* 41, 98, *133,* 137, *163,* 441, *451*
PDP Research Group, 444, *451*
Pearce, J. M., 23, *39*
Peck, C. K., 207, *224*
Peeters, B. W., 273, *278*
Penfield, W., 290, *303, 304*
Penney, J. B., 288, *302*
Penry, J. K., 234, *255*

Perlstein, W. M., 115, 124, 231, 232, 245, *254,* 259, 266, *278,* 421, 424, 425, 437, *451*
Pernier, J., 234, *253,* 318, *323*
Peronnet, F., 318, *323*
Perrault, N., 236, *254*
Perrin, F., 234, *253,* 318, *323*
Persson, H., 45, *64*
Petersen, S. E., 160, *163,* 210, *226,* 327, 328, 329, 340, *344, 345*
Petry, M., 106, *130,* 386, *388*
Petry, M. C., 430, *448*
Petty, R. E., 153, *161*
Peuster, A., 380, *390*
Pfefferbaum, A., 313, *325*
Pfurtscheller, G., 296, 299, *304*
Phelps, M. E., 307, *325,* 330, *343*
Piaget, J., 358, 364, *367,* 369, 370, *390,* 395, 406, 408, *414*
Pick, A. D., 373, *390*
Picton, T. W., 234, 236, 237, *254,* 309, 310, 314, *323*
Pinckney, L. A., 213, 221, *225*
Polich, J., 116, *133*
Popplewell, D. A., 4, *21*
Porges, S. W., 349, 360, *367, 368,* 434, *451*
Posner, M. I., 160, *163,* 176, *184,* 195, *204,* 210, 214, *226,* 327, 328, 329, 330, 332, 334, 336, 338, 340, 341, *343, 344,* 350, 358, *366, 367,* 369, 379, *390, 391,* 424, 425, 426, 431, 436, 439, 441, 442, *448, 451*
Powers, A. S., 217, *226,* 273, *277,* 421, *450*
Previc, F. H., 311, *323*
Purcell, D. G., 176, *183*
Purpura, D. P., 288, *304*
Putnam, L. E., 207, *226,* 259, *278,* 293, *304,* 365, *368,* 420, 424, 426, 429, *451*

Q

Quigley, K. S., 5, 6, 7, 8, 10, 11, 12, 14, 15, 17, *20, 21,* 56, 57, *64,* 124, *130,* 434, *448, 451*

R

Rader, N., 397, *414*
Rafal, R. D., 329, 330, 331, 333, 335, 338, 343, *344, 345*
Rafferty, J., 122, *133*
Raichle, M. E., 327, 337, *343, 344*
Ramer, A. L. H., 341, *343*
Ranson, R. N., 47, *66*
Rapoport, J. L., 268, *276*

Rawlins, J. N. P., 273, 274, *277*
Rayais, M., 372, *390*
Rebert, C. S., 291, *304*
Reeves, B., 98, *134*
Regan, D., 319, *325*
Reijmers, L. G., 273, *278*
Reingold, E. M., 171, *183*
Reinikainen, K., 312, 313, 315, 318, *322, 323, 325*
Reite, M., 236, *254*
Reiter, L. A., 217, *226,* 230, *253, 254*
Renault, B., 311, 312, *325*
Requin, J., 221, *226,* 293, 295, 297, *304*
Reznick, J. S., 358, *368,* 383, *389*
Rhodes, D. L., 146, *160*
Richards, J., 425, 426, 432, 441, 446, *448*
Richards, J. E., 142, 144, *163,* 349, 351, 352, 353, 354, 356, *368,* 374, *390,* 397, *414*
Richardson, R., 4, 10, 11, 12, 19, *21,* 48, 50, 51, 61, *65, 66*
Ricks, M., 373, *391*
Riehle, A., 297, *304*
Riesen, A. H., 210, *226*
Rif, J., 317, *325*
Rimpel, J., 207, *226,* 234, *254*
Rinaldi, P. C., 25, *40*
Ring, C., 221, *226*
Risaliti, R., 210, *226*
Robbins, T. W., 108, *131,* 369, 379, *390*
Robinson, D. L., 283, *304*
Robinson, P., 273, *278*
Rockstroh, B., 245, *255*
Roemer, R. A., 233, *254*
Rohrbaugh, J., 295, 297, *304*
Roland, P. E., 4, *21*
Ronthal, M., 210, *226*
Rosen, J., 111, *131*
Rosen, J. B., 423, *451*
Rosen, J. R., 153, *161*
Rosenblum, L., 397, *414*
Rosenblum, L. A., 98, *134*
Rosenfeld, H. M., 373, *391*
Rosenmann M., 61, *66*
Ross, L. E., 111, *134,* 365, *368*
Rossi, A., 210, *226*
Rossi, B., 210, *226*
Rossignol, S., 293, *305*
Roth, W. T., 116, *134,* 313, *325,* 429, *451*
Rothbart, M. K., 330, 332, 334, 336, 338, 341, *343, 344, 345,* 350, 358, *366, 367,* 424, 425, 426, 431, 436, 441, 442, *448, 451*
Rothwell, J. C., 209, *224*
Rubenstein, E. H., 233, *252*
Ruenzel, P., 444, *450*

Ruff, H. A., 349, *368*
Rumelhart, D. E., 444, *451*
Rundman, 338, *343*
Runquist, W. N., 111, *134*
Rushworth, G., 211, *226*
Russell, J. A., 101, 102, *133*, *134*
Russell, N. V., 114, *132*
Rust, J., 34, *39*
Ryan, R. M., 124, *132*

S

Saiers, J. A., 4, 10, 11, 12, 19, *21, 50, 66*
Sakata, J., 210, *227*
Salapatek, P. H., 394, *415, 446, 448*
Salmon, L. E., 311, *323*
Sams, M., 239, *254*, 312, 313, 315, 317, 318, *322, 323, 324, 325*
Sananes, C. A., 48, *66*
Sananes, C. B., 423, *451*
Sanders, A. F., 439, *451*
Sanes, J. N., 188, *204*, 210, 213, 217, 221, *225, 227*
Sanford, A. J., 291, 293, 297, *303*
Santos, E. A., 56, *66*
Sanz, C., 99, *134*
Sapolsky, R. M., 98, *134*
Sargent, P., 369, 379, *390*
Sasaki, K., 291, 297, *305*
Scabini, D., 247, *253*
Scaife, M., 395, 405, *413, 414*
Scarff, T., 288, *304*
Scarpelli, A., 167, *182*
Scarr, S., 394, *415*
Schaeffer, F., 143, 145, *163*
Scheibel, A. B., 283, *305*
Scheibel, M. E., 283, *305*
Scheilbel, A., 273, *275*
Scheirs, J. G. M., 293, 295, 300, *302, 305*
Schell, A. M., 23, 27, *38*, 115, 118, 176, *182*, 230, 260, 261, 263, 264, 265, 267, *276, 277, 278*, 420, 421, 439, 440, 447, *449*
Schell, G. P., 284, *305*
Scherg, M., 233, 234, *254*
Schlag, J., 290, *305*
Schlosberg, H., 101, *134*
Schmid, A., 117, *134*
Schmidt, A., 316, *322*
Schmidtke, K., 208, *227*
Schneider, W., 258, *278*
Schneiderman, N., 61, *64*
Schneirla, T., 100, *134*
Schnitzler, H. U., 111, 117, 120, *131, 134*

Schoenfeld, C. D., 11, *21*
Scholz, M., *344*
Schroeder, C., 311, *323*
Schultz, D. W., 444, *449*
Schupp, H. T., 105, 116, 121, 122, *131, 134*, 429, 432, *449*
Schwaber, J. S., 47, *66*
Schwafel, J., 233, *252*
Schwartz, A. N., 398, *415*
Schwartz, G. E., *204*, 186
Schwartz, G.M., *204*, 185
Schwartz, J., 100, *134*
Schwartz, J. H., 223, *227*
Schwartz, J. L., 419, 423, *450*
Schwent, V. L., 309, *323*
Scioloto, T., 333, *345*
Searle, J. L., 230, *253*
Sechenov, I. M., 221, 222, *227*
Seligman, M. E. P., 176, 177, *184*
Seljos, K. A., 261, *278*
Semjen, A., 293, 295, *304*
Shadman, J., 147, 148, *162*
Shagass, C., 233, *254*
Shapiro, P. A., 13, *22*
Shaver, P., 100, *134*
Shaw, M. D., 207, *224*
Shepherd, A., 409, *415*
Sherrington, C., 207, *227*
Shibasaki, H., 291, 297, *305*
Shibutani, H., 210, *227*
Shiffrin, R. M., 258, *278*
Shimamura, M., 210, *225*
Shimoyama, R., 215, *226*
Sholiton, R., 101, *133*
Shulman, F., 328, *343*
Siboney, P. A., 207, *224*
Siddle, D. A. T., 23, 24, 25, 26, 27, 28, 29, 30, 31, 32, 33, 34, 36, *38, 39, 40*, 139, 142, 144, 155, *162, 163*, 267, *277*, 358, 425, 427, 428, 445, *451*
Siegel, C., 273, *278*
Siegel, M. A., 10, 19, *21*, 48, *66*
Siever, L. J., 268, *278*
Silverstein, L. D., 168, *182, 184*, 185, *204*, 209, 221, *224, 227*, 421, 427, 438, 445, *448, 451*
Simon, F., 333, *345*
Simons, R. F., 115, 124, *134*, 140, 143, 153, *163*, 231, 232, 233, 234, 240, 245, 251, *252, 254, 255*, 259, 266, *278*, 295, *305*, 359, *367*, 374, 375, *388, 390*, 421, 424, 425, 437, *451*
Simpson, G. V., 247, *252*, 320, *323, 325*
Simpson, M., 311, *325*
Sinkkonen, J., 312, *324*
Sirevaag, E. J., 116, *134*

Skinner, J. E., 288, 289, 290, 291, 292, 301, 305, 306, 424, 452
Skinner, R. D., 274, 277
Slaby, D. A., 139, 140, 155, 162
Sloan, R. P., 13, 22
Smith, A. D., 273, 274, 277
Smith, E. N., 49, 51, 52, 53, 54, 55, 56, 57, 61, 62, 64, 66, 67
Smith, J., 331, 345
Snidman, N., 371, 381, 383, 384, 389, 390, 422, 431, 432, 441, 442, 443, 450
Snyder, C. R., 195, 204
Snyder, E., 239, 255
Snyder, K. S., 264, 278
Soares, J. J. F., 126, 133, 168, 170, 172, 173, 178, 184
Soken, N. H., 373, 390
Sokolov, E. N., xix, xx, xxi, 2, 3, 4, 5, 17, 19, 22, 23, 24, 25, 28, 40, 53, 57, 67, 98, 119, 123, 124, 134, 138, 139, 150, 151, 162, 163, 166, 167, 168, 184, 238, 327, 345, 347, 364, 368, 398, 418, 422, 423, 425, 427, 428, 429, 430, 434, 435, 436, 441, 444, 445, 446, 447, 452
Sollers, J. J., 209, 221, 227
Sorce, J. F., 373, 390
Spence, E. L., 111, 113, 114, 121, 124, 128, 134, 153, 154, 155, 156, 161, 164, 196, 204
Spinks, J., 23, 25, 34, 40, 440, 450
Spyer, K. M., 47, 65
Squires, K. C., 238, 239, 240, 241, 242, 243, 251, 255
Squires, N. K., 238 239 240 241 242 243 255
Sroufe, L. A., 404, 415
Stafford, I., 213, 214, 227
Stanton, G. B., 283, 304
Stark, 113, 132
Stark-Adamec, C., 383, 388
Staub, E., 186, 204
Steffan, J., 296, 299, 304
Stein, B. E., 337, 344
Stenberg, C. R., 373, 388, 404, 413
Stephens, B. R., 372, 389
Stephenson, D., 25, 34, 40
Stern, J. A., 206, 227
Sternberg, R. J., 369, 380, 388
Sternberg, S., 190, 204, 444, 452
Stevenson, V. E., 153, 154, 155, 161, 162, 163
Stitt, C. L., 185, 186, 203, 204, 259, 273, 276
Stone, C., 222, 224, 263, 276, 277
Stormack, K. M., 369, 379, 391
Strandburg, R. J., 233, 252
Strick, P., 284, 285, 305, 306
Stroffregen, T., 401, 415

Stroop, J. R., 380, 391
Suci, G., 100, 133
Suddath, R. L., 273, 278
Summala, H., 314, 324
Sutterer, J. R., 295, 304
Swanson, L. W., 273, 278
Swartz, K. B., 98, 134, 334, 344
Swenson, M. R., 268, 272, 273, 274, 279
Swerdlow, N. R., 115, 118, 134, 217, 227, 230, 268, 272, 273, 274, 276, 277, 278, 279, 420, 421, 439, 447

T

Takahashi, K., 215, 226
Takeuchi, F., 318, 324
Talbot, J. D., 4, 21, 337, 345
Tallal, P., 444, 452
Tan, J., 208, 209, 211, 225
Tanji, J., 297, 305
Tannenbaum, P., 100, 133
Tassinary, L. G., 7, 21
Tavy, D. L. J., 211, 227
Tay, S. W., 47, 65
Taylor E. W., 46, 47, 66, 67
Taylor, K., 167, 182
Teder, W., 315, 318, 322, 325
Teich, A., 61, 64
Tellegen, A., 101, 114, 134, 135, 186, 192, 204
Telzrow, R. W., 408, 409, 415
ter-Pogossian, M. M., 307, 325
Teurlings, R. F. M. A., 215, 216, 223, 427, 448
Teyler, T. J., 233, 254, 319, 325
Theeuwes, J., 419, 445, 452
Thelen, E., 411, 415
Thevenet, M., 234, 253
Thomas-Thrapp, L., 332, 334, 344, 345, 424, 425, 426, 431, 436, 441, 442, 448
Thompson, P. D., 209, 224
Thompson, R. F., 23, 24, 25, 34, 36, 39, 40, 223, 227
Tiihonen, J., 236, 254, 316, 323
Tiitinen, H., 311, 312, 325
Timberlake, W., 126, 134
Tischler, M., 207, 224, 270, 276
Tobey, E. W., 54, 57, 67
Todd, J. T., 419, 452
Tomasello, M., 405, 415
Tomlinson, J. D. W., 56, 65
Tomodo, H., 291, 297, 305
Tooby, J., 180, 184
Toone, B. K., 266, 268, 273, 278
Torrey, E. F., 273, 278
Töttölä, K., 315, 322

Trapold, M. A., 117, *134*
Treisman, A. M., 418, *452*
Trevarthen, C., 395, *415*
Tronick, E. Z., 373, *389, 391*
Tulving, E., 4, *22*
Tuomisto, T., 235, *253*
Turner, M., 380, *390*
Turpin, G., 4, *22,* 121, 124, 128, 138, 139, 140, 142, 143, 144, 145, 146, 155, 158, *163,* 250, 425, 430, *452*
Tursky, B., 186, *204*

U

Uchino, B. N., 5, 12, 14, 15, 17, *20, 21*
Umilta, C., 333, *345*
Ursin, H., 56, 59, 60, 61, *64,* 108, *134*

V

Vaitkyavicus, G. G., 5, *22*
Vaitl, D., 106, 113, 114, 124, 125, *132,* 173, *183,* 430, 432, *450*
Vajsar, J., 234, *254*
Valenstein, E., 283, 288, *306*
Valenza, E., 333, *345*
Van Boxtel, G., 299, *305*
van der Ende, J., 153, *160*
Vanderheyden, P. M., 273, *278*
Van Essen, D. C., 319, *325*
Van Gelder, P., 419, *452*
van Ham, J. J., 208, 209, 211, *225*
Van Heusden, E., 290, *303*
Van Hoesen, G. W., 288, *304*
Vanni, S., 236, *253*
Van Rotterdam, A., 290, *303*
van Woerkom, T. C. A. M., 211, *227*
Varpula, T., 236, *253*
Vecera, S. P., 331, 341, *343, 345*
Velasco, F., 234, *255*
Velasco, M., 234, *255*
Ventura, J., 23, *38,* 264, *277, 278*
Vila, J., 128, *134,* 144, 158, *161, 163*
Villablanca, J., 290, *305*
Vingerhoets, A. J. J. M., 295, 298, *302*
von Cramon, D., 233, 234, *254*
von Euler, C., 444, *452*
Vossel, G., 140, 142, 143, 144, 145, *163, 164*
Vrana, S. R., 113, 121, *134, 135,* 153, *164,* 196, *204*

W

Wagner, A. R., 23, 29, 31, *38, 40,* 117, *135,* 176, *184*
Waldo, M., 273, *278*
Walk, R. D., 397, *414, 415*

Walker-Andrews, A. S., 373, *391*
Walrath, L. C., 206, *227*
Walter, W. G., 291, 297, *305*
Walts, C., 214, *227*
Wan, F. J., 272, 273, *279*
Wang, P., 50, *66*
Warner, B., 419, *450*
Warren, M., 230, *253*
Waszak, M., 290, *305*
Waters, E., 404, *415*
Watson, D., 114, *135*
Watson, R. T., 283, 288, *306*
Waxman, S. R., 370, *388*
Webb, R. A., 295, *304*
Wecker, J. R., *204,* 199
Weilke, A., 114, *132*
Weinberger, D. R., 273, *278*
Weinberger, N. M., 238, *255, 278, 279*
Weisbard, C., 61, *67*
Weissberg, R., 124, *132*
Weissberg, R. P., 148, 149, 150, 152, *162*
Weissler, A. M., 11, *21*
Weisz, D. J., 214, *227*
Wells, A., 156, *164*
Westerkamp, V., 216, 217, *223*
Wever, E. G., 52, *67*
Wieling, W., 12, *21*
Wier, C. C., 234, *252*
Wiesenfeld, A. R., 124, *132,* 148, 149, 150, 152, *162*
Wietlacke, M., 114, *132*
Williamson, S. J., 316, 319, 320, *322, 324*
Wingard, J. A., 167, *184*
Winter, A. L., 291, 297, *305*
Wise, S. P., 285, 297, *306*
Witherington, D., 394, 404, *413, 415,* 431, 442
Withington-Wray, D. J., 47, *65*
Wittkowski, W., 234, *254*
Witvliet, 121, *135*
Woldorff, M., 208, *225,* 236, *253*
Woldorff, M. G., 311, 314, 317, 318, *323, 325, 326*
Wolff, C., 186, *204*
Wolpaw, J. R., 234, *255*
Wong, W. C., 47, *65*
Wood, K., 147, 148, 150, *162*
Wood, L. M., 47, *65*
Wood, T., 433, 434
Woodrow, H., 221, *227*
Woodruff, R. A., 55, 61, *67,* 363, *367*
Woods, C. B., 112, *132*
Woods, D. L., 247, *253,* 314, 318, *326*
Woodson, R. W., *389*
Worth, D. J., 55, *67*
Wright, J. C., 58, *67*
Wundt, W., 100, *135*

Y

Yasuhara, A., 208, 211, 213, *225*
Yasuhara, M., 208, *225, 227*
Yates, A. J., 196, *204*
Yee, C. M., 235, 240, *254*, 264
Yerkes, R. M., 185, *204*
Yi, H., 294, *303*
Yingling, C. D., 288, 289, 290, 291, 292, 301, *305, 306*, 424, *452*
Yokoyama, Y., 215, *226*
Young, A. B., 288, *302*
Young-Browne, G., 373, *391*

Z

Zack, J., 102, 114, *130*, 378, *388*
Zajonc, R. B., 170, *184*
Zanchetti, A., 61, *64*
Zeigler, B. L., 23, *39*, 48, *65,* 140, *162*, 207, 227, 349, *367,* 422, 441, *449*
Zelazo, P. R., 396, 409, *414*
Zelson, M. F., 153, *163*, 374, *390*
Zimmer, H., 140, 142, 143, 144, 145, *163, 164*
Zimmerman, J. E., 236, *254*
Zinser, M. C., 266, *276*
Zumbahlen, M. R., 406, *413*

Subject Index

A

Accessory stimulus effect, 214
Acoustic startle pathway
    cAMP, 85
    cochlear root neurons, 70–74, 83
    CRH, 85
    EMG, 69, 76–78, *see also* Blink reflex, Electromyogram, Facial EMG
    facial motor nucleus, 72
    Forskolin-DHA, 85
    glutamate-NMDA receptors, 70, 74–77
    glutamate-non-NMDA receptors, 70, 74–77
    neurotransmitters, 74–78
    nucleus reticularis pontis caudalis, 69–76, 78, 83, 85, 86
    Pinna reflex, 72
    reticulospinal neurons, 76–78, 85
    spinal motoneurons, 69, 71, 76
    substance P, 85
    ventral cochlear nucleus, 69, 72
    ventral nucleus of the lateral lemniscus, 70, 72
Action dispositions,
    emotions as, 99–100
Adaptation, 181
Adrenals
    evolution of, 44–45, 146–160, 207, 220, 222, 423, 428–436
Affect
Affective modulation, 114
Alerting, 424, 439, 441

Amphibian
    autonomic nervous system, 41, 44–48
    diving bradycardia, 58
    fear bradycardia, 58
    heartrate, 44–48
    orienting responses, 48
    vagal tone, 47–48
Amygdala, 108, 110, 113, 169, 170, 369, 383, 387, *see also* Brain arousal systems
Amygdala, lesions of, 117, *see also* Conditioned inhibition; Fear-potentiated startle; Sensitization
Angry face, 173–178, 180
ANS, *see* Autonomic nervous system
Anterior cingulate, 337, 340
Anticipation, 328, 338–340, 350, 358–365
    S1-S2 paradigm, 358
    S2 omission response, 3, 61
Anxiety disorder, 121, 158, 160
Appetetive motivational system, 98, 107, 110, 116, 117
Appetetive stimuli, 100, 117
Approach and avoidance, 101, 123, 337
ARAS, 289–290
Areas,
    association, 283
    input to, 282–284, 286–287
    primary sensory, 283
Arousal, 98, 101, 105, 114, 205, 213, 214, 417, 422–424, 428, 429–430, *see also* Brain arousal systems
    and reflex modulation, 114–116
Arousal system, 158, 159

Ascending Reticular Activation System, *see* ARAS
Associative learning, 126
  nonconscious, 177
  preattentive, 176–179
Associative theory, *see* Comparator theory
Attention, 78–79, 81–8298, 118, 119, 120, 121, 138– 140, 143–148, 152–160, 168, 173, 176, 180, 181, 283, 289, 294–300, *see also* Orienting
  and action, 120–121
  and affect, 336–338, 369, 371, 374, 379–380, 385–387
  alertness, *see* Arousal
  apomorphine, 81, 82
  and arousal, interest, 105–107
  attention-getting, 349, 350
  attention-holding, 350
  attention termination, 353
  automatic interrupt system, 348, 349, 354
  and brain mechanisms, 328–331, 333–334, 337–338, 340–343
  developmental changes, 330–343
  directed attention, 283
  disengaging, 329, 330
  expectant attention, 294–300
  intensive aspects, 349, 354–358
  laterality, 329
  to locations, 328–329, 333–335, 340, 342–343
  match/mismatch, 356
  modality-selective, 374, 377–378
  and motivation, 118–120
  network for, 283
  to objects, 328–329, 333–335, 342
  orienting, 205, 220, 219, 220
  posterior attention area, 210
  pre-attentive processing, 350
  prepulse inhibition as measure, 78–82
  prior footshock stress, 81–82
  selective aspects, 349, 351–354
  selective attention, 289, 342, 350
  sensory gating, 78–79
  shifts, 328–329
  sustained attention, 349–358, 365
  unilateral neglect, 210
  voluntary, 328, 340–343
Attention, active, *see* Selective attention
Attention capture, *see* Preattentive processing
Attention, passive, *see* Generalized orienting response
Attention systems, 424, 436–437, 443, 447
Attention trigger, *see* Generalized orienting response; Preattentive processing
Automatic information processing, 168, 258, 417

Autonomic activity
  autonomic blockades, 8–11, 14–17
  autonomic space, 5–9, 14, 446, *see also* Generalized defense response
Autonomic nervous system (ANS), 423, 434–435, 436, *see also* Evolution
Aversive/defensive motivational system, 98, 100, 101, 107, 120
Aversive stimuli, 448, *see also* Generalized defense response
Avoidance, 101, 123

B

Backward masking, 173
Basal ganglia, 285–287, 343
Behavioral inhibition, 381, 383–384, 386–387
Behaviorism, 222
Blindness, 313–314
Blindsight, 211
Blink reflex, 113, 121, 375–377, 419–422, 426–427, 446, *see also* Startle
  acoustic blink reflex, 205, 208, 209, 213, 220, 221
  Cartesian blink reflex, 210, 211
  components, 420
  conditioned blink, *see* Classical conditioning
  corneal blink reflex, 211
  cutaneous blink reflex, 205, 207, 209, 210, 214–218, 221
  eyeblink modification, *see* Prepulse inhibition and Prepulse facilitation
  facilitation, 422, 426–427
  history, 206, 207, 222
  modality effects, 420–421, 427
  motor control, 207, 208
  nictitating membrane reflex, 223
  photic blink reflex, *see* Blink reflex, visual blink reflex
  prepulse inhibition, 420–422, 426
  trigeminal blink reflex, *see* Blink reflex, cutaneous blink reflex
  visual blink reflex, 206, 210–220
Blink response, *see* Blink reflex, Startle
Blood pressure, 109
Bradycardia, *see* Diving bradycardia, Fear bradycardia,
  orienting bradycardia, 119
Brain arousal systems, 423–424
  amygdala, 423
  limbic system, 423
  reticular activating system, 423
Brain attention systems, 424, 436–437, 442
Brain development, 329–330, 333–335, 337, 341–343

C

Capacity allocation, *see* Resource allocation
Cardiac acceleration, 138–141, 143–150,
        152–156
Cardiac deceleration, 138–144, 147–150,
        152–156
Cardiac response, 1, 3–5, 7–10, 12–13, 16–20,
        see also Heart rate
    heart rate variability, 14, 17–20
    noninvasive indices, 17–Oct
    psychometrics, 10, 12–14
Cardiac startle, 144–146, 153–155
Cerebral commissures, 329
Children, 380–387
    individual differences, 383–387
    smiling and reactivity, 384–386
Choice viewing behavior, 106
Classical conditioning, 211, 213
Cluster analysis, 150, 152
CNV, *see* Potentials, Slow waves
Coma, 211
Comparator theory, 445, *see also* Generalized
        orienting response
Conditioned emotional response, 169
Conditioned inhibition, 88–91
    amygdala lesions, 89–91
Conditioned stimulus, 177
Conditioning, 113, 150–152, 158, 173, 178,
        359, *see also* Classical conditioning
    contingency, 178
    masked, 177
    nonconscious, 180
    paradigm, 178
    test trials, 178
Conscious
    awareness, 165, 166, 168
    processes, 170
    processing, 167
    recognition, 178
Consciousness, 165, 168, 177
Context effect, 421
Contingent negative variation (CNV), *see* Slow
        waves
Controlled information processing, 258
Controlled processing, 170, *see* Resource; Selec-
        tive attention
Cortex, 418, 423–424
    input to, 282–287
    motor cortex, 284–286
    output from, 286–287
    sensory cortex, 282–284
Cortical slow waves, 105, 107, 122, *see also*
        Slow waves

D

Defense, 121–123
Defense behavior target specific, 126
Defense cascade, 125–128
    circa-strike, 126
    post-encounter, 126
    pre-encounter, 126
Defense reflex, 111, 117, 118, 125, 126, 128,
        166, 173
Defense response (DR), 1–5, 8–12, 17, 19–20,
        137–159, 337, 348, 419, 422–424,
        see also Defense reflex; Generalized
        defense response
Defensive non-opiate analgesia, 126
Defensive systems, 108–110
Depression, 338
Desynchronization
    event-related, *see* ERD
Detection versus discrimination, recognition, or
        identification, 417, 438–440,
        443–445, 447
Development, 445–446, 446
    of affective response, 431–433, 442–443
    of blink facilitation, 426, 428
    of fear of heights, 431
    of generalized orienting, 425–426
    of prepulse inhibition, 422, 428
Dishabituation, 24, 34, 37, 38, 425, 427–428,
        429, 441
    and effects of omission, 26
    and intermodality change, 34
    and secondary task performance, 28
    and theories of habituation, 34, 38
Diving bradycardia, 55–58
    autonomic control of, 57
    evolution of, 58–59
    forced versus voluntary, 56–58
    relation to fear bradycardia, 58–59
Dorsal central gray, 120
Dorsal motor nucleus, 46, 47
DR, *see* Affect, Generalized defense response

E

EEG, 289–292, 295–301
Electrodermal response, 138, 145, 151, 152
Electroencephalogram, *see* EEG
Electromyogram (EMG), *see* Blink reflex; Fa-
        cial EMG; Orbicularis oculi muscle
EMG, *see* Electromyogram
Emotion, *see* Affect
    as action dispositions, 99–100
    circuit, 423

developmental changes, 335–338, 372–373, 379–380
dimensional theories, 372
discrete theories, 372
Emotional context, 101
Emotional perception, 99, 121
Emotional states, 99
Equivalent current dipole, 308
ERD, 295–296
ERP, *see* Event-related potentials
Event-related potentials, 222, 223, 418, 420–421, 424, 429
attention, novelty and, 238–251
auditory projection and midlatency ERP, 232–233
N100, *see* N1/N100
P300, *see* P300/P3
prepulse inhibition of, 231–238
principal components analysis and, 241–245, 249–250
varieties of, 234–234
Evolution, 169, 176, 419, 433–434, 445
adrenal glands, 44
autonomic nervous system, 41–48
cardiac vagal tone, 47–48
diving bradycardia, 58–59
fear bradycardia, 52–59
neural control of the heart, 42–48
orienting bradycardia, 48–52, 58–60
Evolutionary constraints, 165, 180
Evolutionary perspective, 171, 179–182
Expectancy, 28, 36, 146, 157–159, 428
and amount of habituation training, 33
and effects of stimulus omission, 28, 29
and intermodality change, 30
measurement of, 29
Expectancy effects, *see* Anticipation
Extinction, 87–88
Glutamate-NMDA receptors, 87
Eye movements, 331–333, 335

F

Facial EMG, 103
Facial nucleus, 208–210, 215, 216
Facial stimuli, 171
Fear, 107, 109, 370, 384
fear-irrelevant stimulus, 178
fear-relevant stimuli, 178, 180, 419, 430–431, 434, 442
Fear bradycardia, 124
autonomic control of, 52–54, 57
discovery of, 53
evolution of, 52–59
orienting bradycardia, 60–62
Fear conditioning, 108

Fear potentiated startle
amygdala lesions, 83–84, 86–87, 89–91, 375
central gray lesions, 84
Glutamate-NMDA receptors, 84
Glutamate-non-NMDA receptors, 84
lateral geniculate, 83
perirhinal cortex, 83, 86
visual cortices, 86
Fear startle circuit, 111
Fearfulness, 149, 150, 153–156
Fearful subjects, *see* Phobic subjects
Filter/filtering, 418–419, 422, 444–445, 448
Fish
autonomic nervous system, 42–47
evolution of, 41–47
Fixation, visual, 425, 431
fMRI, *see* Magnetic resonance imaging, functional
Food deprivation, 117, *see also* Hunger
Freezing, 108, 113, 119–120, 159
Frontal cortex, *see* Attention systems
Future-oriented behavior, *see* Anticipation

G

Gag reflex, 222
Gating, 289, 420, 421, 424
indices of, 289–294
Gaze direction, 340
Generalized defense response (DR), 428–436, 446
affect and arousal, 429–430
affective valence, 429, 430–433
autonomic space, 434–435
characteristics of, 428
development, 431, 432–433
ERP indices of, 429
and evolution, 433–434
of fear bradycardia and orienting, 434
modality-selective vs. valence effects, 431–433
rating scales, 429
reflex probing of, 431–433
sensory vs. motor synergism effects, 432–433
spectral analysis, 435
Generalized drive, 116
Generalized orienting response (OR), 422–428, 445
attention trigger, 422
brain systems, 423–424
components of, 425–426
development, 425–426
dishabituation, 425
ERP indices, 424–425
habituation, 423, 425, 427–428

modality effects, 427
reflex probing of, 426–427
sensory effects, 423
stimulus omission, 427–428
theories of, 422–423, 427–428
Gill withdrawal reflex, 223

H

Habituation, 23, 138–145, 156–158, 207, 423,
    425, 427–428, 429–430, 435, 436,
    441
comparator theories, 24, 37
context specificity of, 38
noncomparator theories, 24, 37
and priming, 29, 38
and stimulus preexposure, 33
theories of, 24, 29, 33
Happy face, 173–176, 178
Heart rate, 103, 107, 109, 124–126, 128,
    348–365, 418, 425–428, 429–436,
    437, 441, 446–447, see also Cardiac
    response
acceleration, 126, 166, 173
and arousal, 124–126
deceleration, 126, 166, 168
Heights, fear of, 394, 397, 398, 401–404, 411
crawling, 398, 403
experience, 395
Gibson's hypothesis, 401
innate, 394, 395, 397
kitten studies, 398
moving room, 401, 403, 404
universal, 394, 395
vestibular feedback, 403
vestibular proprioception, 401, 403, 411, 412
visual feedback, 404
visual proprioception, 401, 403, 405, 411,
    412
H reflex, 213, 214
Hidden objects, manual search for, see Object
    permanence
High density bioelectric arrays, 129
Highlights and prospects, 443–448
Hippocampus, 423, 433–436
Hunger, 117, see Food deprivation

I

Individual differences, 147–156
Infant, see Development
anticipation, 328, 338–340
attention shifts, 330–333
caregiving, 335
distraction, 328

distress, 335–338
expectation, see Anticipation
eye movements, 331–333, 335, 339
habituation, 334–335, 336
inhibition of return, 330–333, 334
language, 341–342
learning, 338–341
novelty, 333–335
orienting, 328, 330–343
self-recognition, 341–342
social stimuli, 340
state regulation, 335, 370–380, 383–384
mastery motivation, 370
motor quieting, 377
novelty, 370
prepulse inhibition, 374
prelocomotor infant, 396, 397, 399, 400,
    403, 407, 409, 410
response to discrepancy, 370
response to facial expressions, 372–373,
    375–380
response to vocal expressions, 373
response with or without awareness,
    379–380
social referencing, 373
startle modulation, 374–377, 379–380,
    386–387
"still-face," 373
visual cliff, 373, 380
Inferior colliculus, 208
Information processing, 97, 348–349, 351
Information regulator, see Generalized orienting
    response
Inhibition, prepulse, see Prepulse inhibition
Inhibition of return, 330–333, 426, 445
Interest, 370, 372, see Ratings
Intermodality change, 30
and amount of habituation training, 33
and dishabituation, 34
and response recovery, 30, 31
and stimulus preexposure, 33
International Affective Picture System, 102, 113
Interrupt, see Preattentive processing; N1; Star-
    tle
Interrupted stimulus technique, 353
Inverse problem, 308–309

J

Joint visual attention, 394, 395, 404–408, 411
experience, 395
gaze, 395, 404–408
innate, 395
pointing, 404, 405, 406, 408
referential gestures, 404–407
social referencing, 404

K

Knowledge of results, 289–301

L

Language, 328, 341
Lateral hypothalamus, 108
Laterality, 329
Learning, 210, 211, 223, *see also* Classical conditioning
    context-dependent associations, 340–342
    implicit, 339, 342–343
    sequence learning, 338, 343
Levator palpebrae muscle, 207, 208
Limbic system, *see* Amygdala
Limited-capacity processing, 168, 177
Localized orienting, *see* Selective attention
Locomotion, self-produced, 396, 397, 399, 406–412
    cognitive capacity, 408
    crawl, 396, 406, 410–412
    experience, 399–401, 403, 409, 412
    feedforward mechanisms, 396
Locomotor handicap, 399, 400, 407, 408
Long-latency defense response, 157
Loudness judgments, 421

M

Magnetic resonance imaging, 308–309
    functional (fMRI), 129, 418
Magnetoencephalogram (MEG), 308–309, 418
    superconducting quantum interference, 308
Masking, backward, 419, 444–445
Masseteric reflex, 213
MEG, *see* Magnetoencephalogram
Memory, 429–430
Mismatch negativity (MMN), 310–311, 312–313, 418
MMN, *see* Mismatch negativity
Modality effects, 423–424, 427–428
Monkey, 210
Motivation, 97, 99, 118–121
Motivational priming, 110–116
Motor processing, 439–441

N

N1/N100, 418, 420–421
Negative affect acceleratory response, 157

Neuronal Model, 167, 364, 418, 422
Nonassociative, noncomparator theory, 445, *see* Generalized orienting response
Novel
    location, 426, 442
    stimulus, 425, 427–429, 431, 437, 445, 448
Novelty, 146, 147, 156–159, 333–335, 370
Nucleus ambiguous, 46–47
Nucleus reticularis pontis caudalis, 208

O

Object permanence, 394, 395, 408–411
    A-not-B error, 408, 409
    dorsolateral region, 410
    innate, 395, 396
    prefrontal cortex, 395, 396, 410
    spatial coding strategies, 408, 409
Object recognition, 329, 335, 340
Oddball paradigm, 97
Optic flow, 401–404
    central visual field, 401–403
    peripheral visual field, 401–403
OR, *see* Orienting response
Orbicularis oculi muscle, 205, 207, 208
Orienting, 23, 121–124, *see also* Attention
    and defense, 121–124
    effects of stimulus omission, 25–27, 36, 37
    expectancy, 28
    heart rate and, 247, 250, 251
    infants, 327–300
    intermodality change, 30
    P300 and, 238–251
    reflex, 167–171, 173, 181
    response recovery, 25, 26, 30, 31
    secondary task performance, 28
    stimulus change, 24
Orienting response, 1–5, 8–12, 17, 19–20, 137–152, 156–160, 348–349, 351–352, *see also* Generalized orienting response
Orienting Response Bradycardia
    autonomic control of, 56
    distinguishing from fear bradycardia, 60–62
    evolution of, 41–42, 48–52, 59–60
    stimuli eliciting, 48–52

P

P300/P3 potentials
    novels P3, 425
    P3a, 424, 428, 437
    P3b, 424, 427, 432, 443

Pacer, 394
Pain, 337
PANAS, 114
Parasympathetic nervous system, 433–436, 445–447
Parietal lobe, 210, 328–329, 333, 340, 342
Periaqueductal gray area, 108
Periaqueductal gray nucleus, 208
Phobia, 149–153, 158, 160, *see also* Fear
Phobic subjects, 124, 430, 432
Phonetic processing, 313
Picture processing, 98–106, 147–154, 158
Pinna flexion reflex, *see* Postauricular reflex
Pop-out effect, 174, 419, 422, 445
Positron emission tomography, 337–338, 343
Postauricular reflex, 208, 209, 221
Posterior parietal cortex, *see* Attention systems
Potentials
    CNV, 291, 292, 296–299
    RP, 291, 292, 297–299
    slow, 290–292, 296–300
    SPN, 298, 299
PPI, *see* Prepulse inhibition
Preattentive analysis, 169, 170
Preattentive processing, 116–118, 166–170, 173, 180, 181, 417–422, 441, 444–445
    attention trigger, 418–419
    characteristics, 417–418
    detection vs. object recognition, 418–419
    high-pass filtering, 419
    initiating interrupt, 419–420
    initiating protective gating, 420–422
    initiating sensory processing, 418–419
    localizing cortical sources, 418
Predator imminence, 126, *see also* Defense cascade
Preparedness, 177, 180
Prepulse facilitation, 205, 207, 213–217, 220, 221
Prepulse inhibition, 118, 205, 207, 216–220, 222, 230–238, 258–260, 420–422
    attention and, 192
    description of, 230
    determinants of, 230
    effects on ERP components, 231–238
    effects on information processing, 230–231
    effects on perception, 232, 235, 238
    probability of prepulse and, 189–190
    self-presentation of prepulse, 186–192
Priming, 110–111
    refractoriness and, 230, 234–237
Probe, *see* Reaction time; Reflex probe; Selective attention
Processing capacity, 167

Processing negativity (PN), 310, 314–317, *see also* Slow waves
Processing resources, 168
Projection systems
    nonspecific extrinsic path, 421–422
    specific, direct path, 421
Propranolol, 47
Psychopathology, 115
Psychophysics, 222
Pulvinar, 329, 340
Pupil, 211, 219, 220

Q

Quivering mouse mutants, 209

R

Ratings, 102
    arousal, 429, 432, 446
    certainty/expectancy of future stimulus, 197, 429
    complexity, 423, 446
    interest, 423, 431, 446
    pleasingness, 423
    valence, 429–430
Reaction time, 206, 214–216, 220, 221, 445, 447, *see also* Selective attention
Readiness potential, *see* Slow waves
Recognition, 418, 426, 441, 445
Reflex modulation, 114
Reflex probe, 426–427, 431–433, 439–441, 443, 445, 447
Refractoriness, 421
Refractory period, 213, 217
Reptile
    autonomic nervous system, 41, 44–48
    cardiac response to neutral stimuli, 48–52
    cardiac response to threatening stimuli, 52–56
    diving bradycardia, 58
    evolution of, 41–44
    fear bradycardia, 52–58
    heart, 44–48
    vagal tone, 47–48
Resource allocation, 105, 432, 436, 439, *see also* Selective attention
Reticular formation, 213, *see also* Nucleus reticularis pontis caudalis
Retina, 220
RP, *see* Potentials

S

Secondary task performance, 27
    and effects of stimulus omission, 27, 28
    and intermodality change, 31, 32, 33

and probe reaction time, 27
and processing resources, 28
Selective attention, 436–443, 447
  affective, 442–443
  ANS indices, 436–437
  attending, 441
  characteristics of, 436
  development, 441–443
  electrophysiology of, 309–311
  ERP indices, 436–437
  exogeneous vs. endogeneous effects on,
    309–321
  of expectancy effects, 438
  matching mechanism, 436–437
  MEG studies of, 311–321
  monosynaptic T-reflex probing of motor
    preparation, 441
  N1 effect of, 309–310, 314–316
  preference for novelty, 441–442
  processing negativity and, 310
  P3b amplitude and resource allocation, 437
  P3b latency and stimulus evaluation time,
    437
  role of self-produced motion in perception,
    442
  of sensory vs. motor effects, 438
  slow habituation, 436, 439
  speed/accuracy tradeoff, 439
  to target detection and discrimination,
    438–440, 443

  T-reflex probing of motor preparation,
    309–321, 441
  in visual modality, 311, 319–321
  warning stimulus effects, 438–439
Self-Assessment-Manikin (SAM), 102
Semantic differential, 100
Sensitization, 84
  amygdala lesions, 80
Sensorimotor gating, 263
Sensory vs. response processing, 447, see also
    Selective attention
Signal stimulus, 168, 347–348, 351–366
Signal value, 167
Skin conductance, 25, 105, 107, 121–122, 128,
    171–173, 178, 181, 419, 425, 428,
    429, 446
  and dishabituation, 26, 35
  and effects of stimulus omission, 25–27
  and intermodality change, 30–33
Slow waves, 424, 447
  contingent negative variation (CNV), 426,
    437, 441, 443
  late positive slow wave, 429, 443, 446
  negative sustained potential, 429
  processing negativity (PN), 436, 447

readiness potential, 437, 443
Snake, 171, 174, 177, 178, 180
  fearful, 171–172
Society for Psychophysiological Research, 205
Spider, 171, 174, 177, 178, 180
  fearful, 171, 172
Spina bifida, 407
Split-brain patients, 329
SPN, see Potentials
Startle, 116–117, 137–140, 143–146, 153– 160,
    168, 348, 356, 418–421, 423, 430,
    see Acoustic startle pathway; Blink
    reflex; Fear potentiated startle
  inhibition, 114
  potentiation, 111, 114, 126
  probe reflex, 99, 111, 113–115, 117–118,
    122, 128, 166, 168
Startle Eyeblink Modification (SEM)
  attention, 260–262
  definition, 257–258
  drug effects, 219, 213
  forebrain modulation, 420
  hereditary startle disease, 209
  neural substrates, 270–274
  psychosis-prone subjects, 266–268
  schizophrenia, 262–266
  schizotypal personality disorder, 268
  startle-dazzle reflex, 219, 220
  subcortical circuit, 419–420
Startle modulation, see also Infant
  affective modulation, 374, 377, 386–387
  delayed auditory feedback, 196–199, 202
  negative perception hypothesis, 192
Stimulus arousal, 124–126
Stimulus intensity, 102
Stimulus omission, see Generalized orienting re-
    sponse
Stimulus-onset asynchrony, 171
Stimulus risetime, 140, 143–145
Stress, 121
Stroop task, modified, 371, 380–387
Superior colliculus, 329, 331, 337, 340
Surprise, 370
Sympathetic nervous system, 433–436, 445–447

T

TDR, see Transient detection response
Temperament, 371, 381, 383–387
Thalamus, 169
Transient detection response (TDR), 126, 141,
    142, 145, 146, 155, 157, 166, 168,
    348, 418–420, 422, 430
T-reflex probing of motor preparation, 441
Trigeminal blink reflex, see Blink reflex
Trigeminal nucleus, 209

U

Uncertainty, 426–427, 445
Unconditioned stimulus, 177

V

Vagal tone, 47–48
Valence, 98–103, *see* Ratings
Vasoconstriction, 139, 151, 152
Vasodilation, 139, 147, 151
Vasomotor response, 425, 430
Ventral central gray, 119
Ventral periaqueductal gray, 120

Verbal semantic differential, 102
Viewing time, 430, 432, 441, 446
Vision, 330
Visual cliff, 373, 380, 397–400, 404, 405, 431, 442
    Bayley developmental quotient, 440
    cardiac acceleration, 398–400
    cardiac deceleration, 398
    crawling, 399
    Graham-Clifton hypothesis, 398
    heart rate, 398, 399
    precrawling infant, 397–398
Visual cortex, 211
Visual search, 328